Global Power Shift

Ample empirical evidence points to recent power shifts in multiple areas of international relations taking place between industrialized countries and emerging powers, as well as between states and non-state actors. However, there is a dearth of theoretical interpretation and synthesis of these findings, and a growing need for coherent approaches to understand and measure the transformation. The central issues to be addressed include theoretical questions and empirical puzzles: How can studies of global power shift and the rise of 'emerging powers' benefit from existing theories, and which alternative aspects and theoretical approaches might be suitable? How can the meanings, perceptions, dynamics, and consequences of global power shift be determined and assessed? This edited series will include highly innovative research on these topics. It aims to bring together scholars from all major world regions as well as different disciplines, including political science, economics and human geography. The overall aim is to discuss and possibly blend their different approaches and provide new frameworks for understanding global affairs and the governance of global power shifts.

More information about this series at http://www.springer.com/series/10201

Hendrik W. Ohnesorge

Soft Power

The Forces of Attraction
in International Relations

 Springer

Hendrik W. Ohnesorge
Center for Global Studies
University of Bonn
Bonn, Germany

ISSN 2198-7343   ISSN 2198-7351   (electronic)
Global Power Shift
ISBN 978-3-030-29921-7   ISBN 978-3-030-29922-4   (eBook)
https://doi.org/10.1007/978-3-030-29922-4

This Springer imprint is published by the registered company Springer Nature Switzerland AG.
The registered company address is: Gewerbestrasse 11, 6330 Cham, Switzerland

"What I call Attraction may be perform'd by impulse, or by some other means unknown to me. I use that Word here to signify only in general any Force by which Bodies tend towards one another, whatsoever be the Cause."

—*Sir Isaac Newton,*
Opticks: Or, A Treatise of the Reflections, Refractions, Inflections, and Colours of Light,
The Second Edition, with Additions (London: W. and J. Innys, 1718), Query 31, p. 351.

Preface: Lessons from the Fence

It is a remarkable historical coincidence that both the years of Samuel Langhorne Clemens' birth and death—1835 and 1910—saw the appearance of Halley's Comet in the night sky.[1] Today, Clemens, who himself had predicted this curious happenstance in his later life, is more commonly known by his pen name Mark Twain and his claim to fame is less based on an astronomical peculiarity but rather on his quips and aphorisms, his essays and travel descriptions, his poems and plays, as well as his short stories and novels. In fact, Twain's immense prolificacy, originality, and lasting impact earned him the epitaph "father of American literature."[2]

Among Mark Twain's works, *Adventures of Huckleberry Finn* (1884) and *The Adventures of Tom Sawyer* (1876) arguably take pride of place. While the former has been a frequent contestant for the myth-enshrouded Great American Novel,[3] the latter, according to Lee Clark Mitchell, even "lays claim to being America's most popular novel."[4] In it, Twain tells his readers about the gests and follies of the eponymous hero growing up in the 1830s or 1840s along the Mississippi River in the small (and fictional) town of St. Petersburg. The author takes us into the rural world of Missouri, a world filled with deep-rooted superstition and imperturbable piety, boyhood friendships and adolescent love, kindhearted ladies, and reckless villains. In the words of Mark Twain himself, as set down in the novel's preface, the author's intention was not merely to present a children's book but also "to try to pleasantly

---

[1]Ron Power, *Mark Twain: A Life* (New York, N.Y.: Free Press, 2005), p. 9.

[2]Quoted in Allen P. Mendenhall, *Literature and Liberty: Essays in Libertarian Literary Criticism* (Lanham, Md.: Lexington Books, 2014), p. 114.

[3]Lawrence Buell, *The Dream of the Great American Novel* (Cambridge, Mass.: Harvard University Press, 2014), p. 258.

[4]Lee Clark Mitchell, "Introduction," in Mark Twain, *The Adventures of Tom Sawyer*, Edited with an Introduction and Notes by Lee Clark Mitchell (Oxford: Oxford University Press, 1993), p. x.

remind adults of what they once were themselves, and of how they felt and thought and talked, and what queer enterprises they sometimes engaged in."[5] Arguably, the most famous among these "queer enterprises" is Tom Sawyer's handling of the task to whitewash a fence.

Caught by his aunt Polly while climbing in through the window late one night with his clothes torn and tattered after scrambling with a newcomer to the town of St. Petersburg, Tom is condemned to "captivity at hard labor" the following Saturday. Tom's task, set by the loving yet hopelessly overburdened Polly as punishment for this most recent misconduct, is to whitewash "[t]hirty yards of board fence nine feet high." On a fair Saturday morning, when "all the summer world was bright and fresh, and brimming with life" and other children are out playing and enjoying themselves, Tom "surveyed the fence, and all gladness left him and a deep melancholy settled down upon his spirit. Life to him seemed hollow, and existence but a burden." After a few spiritless strokes of his brush, Tom sits down in despair as a slave called Jim comes by, charged with fetching water, a task which "had always been hateful work in Tom's eyes." Yet considering his present situation, Tom is eager to swap chores with Jim, who, however, steadfastly declines. Even as Tom offers to pay him with an exceptionally beautiful marble (a treasured possession for a boy in those days for sure!), he cannot be easily convinced. While Jim eventually begins to waver, Aunt Polly puts a halt to further negotiations and Tom reluctantly returns to the tedious task imposed upon him. However, "Tom's energy did not last" very long and he soon begins to count his meager worldly belongings which are "not half enough to buy so much as half an hour of pure freedom." Thus discouraged, Tom "gave up the idea of trying to buy the boys." Yet, as Mark Twain goes on, "[a]t this dark and hopeless moment an inspiration burst upon him! Nothing less than a great, magnificent inspiration."

With this "inspiration" in mind, Tom takes a different approach to his plight and subsequently, the first boy to come along—a boy by the name of Ben Rogers—finds Tom deeply bound up in his work. Tom, pretending to not even perceive the boy's presence, "surveyed his last touch with the eye of an artist; then he gave his brush another gentle sweep and surveyed the result, as before." Expectedly, Ben commences to mock Tom for having to work while he is about to go swimming on this beautiful summer's day. Tom, however, nonchalantly disregards such mockery and pretends to immensely enjoy his task, asking the perplexed Ben, "'What do you call work? [...] Does a boy get a chance to whitewash a fence every day?'" These questions "put the thing in a new light" for Ben and as Tom continues to vigorously paint the fence, Ben ultimately takes the bait. "'Say, Tom,'" he begs, "'let *me* whitewash a little.'" Tom, however, does not give up his brush that easily, arguing that "'I reckon there ain't one boy in a thousand, maybe two thousand, that can do it the way it's got to be done'" and even telling Ben—untruthfully of course—that both

---

[5]Mark Twain, *The Adventures of Tom Sawyer* (Hartford, Conn.: The American Publishing Company, 1876), p. ix. As far as not indicated otherwise, all quotations in the following paragraph are taken from this, the first edition of *The Adventures of Tom Sawyer*, pp. 25–32.

his half-brother Sid and Jim had been refused before for that very reason. Now it is for Ben, meanwhile irretrievably ensnared, to offer Tom compensation in the form of an apple in order to be allowed to whitewash a small portion of the fence in return. Tom, "with reluctance in his face, but alacrity in his heart," finally yields to Ben's proposition. Consequently, while Ben "worked and sweated in the sun, the retired artist sat on a barrel in the shade close by, dangled his legs, munched his apple, and planned the slaughter of more innocents." Further "innocents" are not long in coming and finally, "when the middle of the afternoon came, from being a poor poverty-stricken boy in the morning, Tom was literally rolling in wealth." What is more, "[h]e had had a nice, good, idle time all the while—plenty of company—and the fence had three coats of whitewash on it!"

While arguably in itself among the finest episodes in American literature, masterfully combining literary elegance and down-to-earth wit, which place does Tom Sawyer's "queer enterprise" of whitewashing a fence have in a study on soft power in international relations?

To answer this question, we shall briefly recall what has happened more soberly than with direct recourse to Twain's unrivaled pen: Tom Sawyer is faced with the unpleasant and wearisome chore of whitewashing a vast fence. Recognizing that to accomplish his task would take a considerable amount of time and effort, and perhaps is even beyond Tom's capability altogether, he seeks the help of others. Considering the circumstances outlined above, getting others to help him in his troublesome task seems hopeless if not impossible from the outset. Having to choose between a day of carefree fishing and swimming on the one hand and the tedious whitewashing of a fence in the blazing sun on the other hand, chances seem to be very slim at best to convince others to lend a helping hand. Nevertheless, Tom—in different ways—tries to acquire assistance: At first, he seeks to exchange chores in order to take up a less gruesome task. Next, he contemplates to buy others' help with his meager belongings. Recognizing the futility of both these endeavors, however, Tom sets out to win over the boys' support in yet another way. Pretending to greatly enjoy the demanding task and even simulating reluctance in relinquishing it, Tom effectively changes the preferences of the boys to help him—without recourse to brute force or monetary inducements but solely by *attracting* the boys to the task he is instructed to perform.

On that score, Mark Twain's famous fence episode offers an excellent (if literary) example to illustrate a core concept in human interactions in general as well as international relations in particular: the concept of power. Succinctly defined as the ability to get somebody to do something they would not otherwise do, power can be found in various guises.[6] Among these, to be elaborated in greater detail below, is the variety of soft power, which shall gain center stage in the work in hand and at whose very core lies the notion of "getting others to want the outcomes you want."[7]

---

[6]For definitions and different varieties of power, see Chap. 2.

[7]Joseph S. Nye, Jr., *Soft Power: The Means to Success in World Politics* (New York, N.Y.: PublicAffairs, 2004), p. 5.

It is in this vein that soft power—resting upon attraction and persuasion—complements hard power—resting upon (physical) coercion and/or (economic) inducement—and thus accounts for the classic (if somewhat simplistic) dichotomy in our understanding of power in international relations today.[8]

With these cursory insights regarding the concept of power in mind, we can now return to the episode outlined above: Which possibilities does Tom Sawyer have at his disposal to influence others in order to get them to do his bidding? Which course of action might he take to get the outcome he wants, which in this case is a whitewashed fence, preferably without much toil on his own part? One conceivable option is to resort to physical force. Tom might use hard power to coerce others and thus force them to whitewash the fence for him. As depicted in an earlier chapter of Mark Twain's novel, Tom by no means is averse to physical confrontation. In fact, his very wrangling with another boy got him into the position to whitewash the fence in the first place. However, Tom is not even contemplating to physically force or intimidate others to get the outcome he wants in this particular instance and apparently recognizes that the endeavor to coerce others to whitewash the fence for him is futile. Power, as we shall see in greater detail below, depends on context, and in the present context, the exercise of physical power does not present itself as very promising.

This option being off the table, Tom might attempt to economically or financially induce others in order to get his preferred outcome, thus resorting to the second component of hard power. In fact, he actually does. As briefly illustrated above, Tom first tries to swap chores with Jim and offers—in a more prosaic than belletristic phrasing—a non-monetary exchange. Jim, however, declines this proposition. In his desperation, Tom goes one step further and offers a marble for his help, which in the rural Missouri of those days is as close to pecuniary resources as a poor boy could possibly get.[9] As this attempt likewise fails due to the disruptive intervention of his aunt, Tom counts his modest belongings and recognizes his lack of sufficient funds to buy others' help. As a consequence, economic or financial instruments, just as physical coercion, likewise forsake Tom in order to get the outcome he wants in this particular instance.

Being thus denied the hard power options of either coercive threats or economic inducements, Tom, in his moment of "magnificent inspiration," in Twain's words, bethinks of his true capital: his personal, non-physical, and non-financial powers of attraction and persuasion. Instead of forcing or buying others, he sets out to get the other boys—to paraphrase Joseph S. Nye's key definition of soft power—to want the outcome he wants with recourse to the only means at his disposal in this particular context. Tom thus effectively changes the values of the boys who henceforth no longer want to wander the streets pretending to be a Mississippi steamer or go

---

[8]This simplified dichotomy is frequently complemented by a third variety, i.e., structural power, to be elaborated upon below; see Chap. 2.

[9]To be sure, in the further course of the novel, Tom wins a fortune in a series of further "queer enterprises."

swimming in a nearby waterhole, but now rather wish to whitewash a board fence instead. In short: Tom applies soft power.

How does Tom succeed? He makes a wearisome task look attractive and leads by example in order to do so. He *pretends* to greatly enjoy his task and even refuses to give up the brush at first. Tom thus wields what might more precisely be called *delusive* soft power: getting others to do something one does *not* want to do oneself, but rather convincing others of the desirability of the task and then generously standing back. Tom, with his deceptive behavior, therefore, might admittedly be reproached with foul play as he brazenly exploits the boys' credulity. In fact, this reproach goes along perfectly with the observation that soft power, although conversely alleged by some commentators and critics, is by no means a mere normative concept but is explicitly impartial—being available for noble and selfish or downright bad purposes alike (as we shall also see in more detail later).

In any case, Tom's success at the end of his scheme is obvious and presents itself to be manifold: Not only is the fence whitewashed three times over and Tom's main goal thus more than achieved, Tom also enjoys a restful day and is later even rewarded with an apple by his aunt for his miraculous feat. Furthermore, Tom rakes in—besides the apple supplied by Ben Rogers in exchange for the first few strokes referred to above—a kite, a dead rat, a dozen marbles, and countless further goods certainly treasured by the other boys who gave them away. After this "substantial change which had taken place in his worldly circumstances," as Mark Twain puts it, Tom is able to re-trade his new-found wealth for more desirable objects with other boys later on in the novel.

Summarizing, the whitewashing of the fence and Tom Sawyer's scheme to get others to want what he wants (or in this case more precisely: to get others to want what he does *not* want to do) offers an excellent example of the successful application of soft power.[10] It depicts a situation in which an actor achieves his desired outcome while other forms of power prove unavailable or ineffective to him under the given circumstances. Attractive soft power, although perhaps less tangible and measurable (for it cannot be as easily "counted" as can apples, marbles, or dead rats), it turns out, can at times be even more resourceful than other varieties of power. Mark Twain himself elaborated on the immense powers of attraction when he argued that on this bright summer's day in St. Petersburg, Tom Sawyer "had discovered a great law of human action,"

> If he [Tom] had been a great and wise philosopher, like the writer of this book, he would now have comprehended that Work consists of whatever a body is *obliged* to do, and that Play consists of whatever a body in not obliged to do. And this would help him to understand why constructing artificial flowers or performing on a treadmill is work, while rolling ten-pins or climbing Mont Blanc is only amusement.

---

[10]With the reference to the attraction emanating mainly from a particular individual rather than other resources frequently attributed to soft power, the episode also foreshadows the introduction of a hitherto neglected source of soft power within the proposed taxonomy; see below, Sect. 3.1.4.

While the fence episode is, of course, fictional (even though Mark Twain states to have included autobiographical and personally experienced elements in his novel), most of us have experienced comparable situations in our daily lives. The attractive powers of activities, objects, ideas, or even individuals thus often rest upon the ability of somebody attracting us to them by praising them, by leading by example, or simply by possessing them and perhaps withholding them from us. Toys, for example, not uncommonly build their attraction upon the very fact that they are possessed by siblings or other children and—just as often—lose their value when others have lost their interest in them. In this understanding, soft or attractive power might indeed be understood—in Twain's words—"a great law of human action."

It shall be the objective of the work in hand to offer new insights into this "great law" by, first, introducing a comprehensive and sophisticated taxonomy of soft power and, second, by providing a methodological roadmap for its empirical study in international relations.

References

Buell, Lawrence. *The Dream of the Great American Novel*. Cambridge, Mass.: Harvard University Press, 2014.

Power, Ron. *Mark Twain: A Life*. New York, N.Y.: Free Press, 2005.

Mendenhall, Allen P. *Literature and Liberty: Essays in Libertarian Literary Criticism*. Lanham, Md.: Lexington Books, 2014.

Mitchell, Lee Clark. "Introduction." In Mark Twain, *The Adventures of Tom Sawyer*. Edited with an Introduction and Notes by Lee Clark Mitchell, pp. vii–xxxiv. Oxford: Oxford University Press, 1993.

Nye, Joseph S., Jr. *Soft Power: The Means to Success in World Politics*. New York, N.Y.: PublicAffairs, 2004.

Twain, Mark. *The Adventures of Tom Sawyer*. Hartford, Conn.: The American Publishing Company, 1876.

Acknowledgments

Like a tree, a book grows little by little over the course of several years. As it steadily takes root and develops ever-denser foliage, it is likely to branch out in various, sometimes even unforeseen directions. During this process of growth, I have profited profoundly from many different people who time and again offered climbing support and shared their advice for pruning.

Among these, I want to first and foremost express my deep gratitude to Professor Dr. Xuewu Gu, Chair in International Relations and Director of the Center for Global Studies (CGS) at the University of Bonn. Professor Gu superbly guided me through the process of researching and writing this book, which is based on a doctoral dissertation submitted to the University of Bonn in early 2019, with his encouragement, council, and assistance. Anyone having a doctoral advisor and academic mentor with so deep a knowledge and so obvious a passion for his discipline can count themselves lucky, indeed. Special thanks is due also to my second examiner Professor Dr. Tilman Mayer as well as to Professor Dr. Ludger Kühnhardt and Professor Dr. Jörg Blasius, who kindly agreed to serve as chairman and fourth member of the board of examiners, respectively.

My colleagues at the CGS, especially Dr. Enrico Fels, Dr. Ying Huang, Professor Dr. Maximilian Mayer, Dr. Andrej Pustovitovskij, Christiane Heidbrink, Philip Nock, Pavlina Schmitz, and Marion Romagna, have been a great and constant source of encouragement and inspiration over the years. Furthermore, I have profited immensely from the countless debates with my students, in class and on numerous other occasions. The wonderful time I have had the privilege of spending at the University of Bonn, as a learner and as a teacher, has been made highly rewarding by the conversations and discussions I have shared with all of them.

Exceeding this immediate work environment, I am much obliged for the helpful comments and valuable suggestions I have time and again received while presenting parts of this work at various academic conferences. Additionally, in the summer and fall of 2017, I had the good fortune to spend time at the University of California, Berkeley, on a scholarship by the German Academic Exchange Service (DAAD), for which I am deeply thankful. UC Berkeley provides a highly stimulating environment and its picturesque campus overlooking San Francisco Bay, with its Beaux-Arts buildings, its rolling lawns, and its groves of eucalyptus trees growing alongside Strawberry Creek, comes as close to a *locus amoenus* as one could possibly hope for.

My most profound thanks is due to Milena Niesen for her superb and indefatigable assistance with the manuscript and especially the index. Many thanks also to Dr. Johannes Glaeser from the Springer publishing company.

The years I have spent researching and writing the book in hand have been enriched immeasurably, both personally and professionally, by my friends who have offered their support and the occasional—and much needed—pat on the back.

Finally, I am forever grateful to my family—my parents Martina and Dr. Willi Ohnesorge, my sister Friederike Ohnesorge, and my grandparents—for their unconditional encouragement and unwavering support in more ways than I will even try to put into words. It is to them that I dedicate this book.

Bonn, Germany
Summer 2019

Contents

List of Abbreviations

AAUP	American Association of University Professors
CDU	Christian Democratic Party of Germany
CHA	Comparative Historical Analysis
CNN	Cable News Network
CSIS	Center for Strategic and International Studies
EU	European Union
IBE	Inference to the Best Explanation
ICC	International Criminal Court
IR	International Relations
IVLP	International Visitor Leadership Program
MNC	Multinational Cooperation
NATO	North Atlantic Treaty Organization
NGO	Nongovernmental Organization
PD	Public Diplomacy
PRC	People's Republic of China
SCO	Shanghai Cooperation Organization
SPD	Social Democratic Party of Germany
UK	United Kingdom (of Great Britain and Northern Ireland)
U.N./UN	United Nations (Organization)
UNGA	United Nations General Assembly
USIA	United States Information Agency
U.S./US	United States (of America)
USNS	United States Navy Ship
USS	United States Ship
U.S.S.R.	Union of Soviet Socialist Republics

List of Figures

List of Tables

Chapter 1
Introduction: In the Midst of Global Power Shifts

The book in hand seeks to elucidate and elaborate on the concept of soft power in international relations. Hence, it addresses the forces of attraction in world politics—forces that have been a mainspring in political and indeed all social interactions from the first. In the recent past, however, these forces have experienced ever-increasing importance. As shall be demonstrated, this fact renders a through scientific engagement with the issue crucial for our understanding of international relations today.

In fact, *any* scientific research starts with a question to be answered, a hypothesis to be tested, a phenomenon to be explained, or a puzzle to be solved. Still, there are certain requirements regarding the object of investigation that have to be met in order to render the research particularly worthwhile. First, it has been noted—rather obviously—that a research question should be both simple in its formulation and allowing the possibility of yielding negative results.[1] The possibility of fallacy, consequently, has been rightly identified as an integral part of any scientific endeavor.[2] With respect to the work in hand, this means that we may very well come to the conclusion that a substantiated operationalization of soft power (at least as approached here) could not be achieved. Second, research questions in the social sciences ought to be of relevance.[3] In this regard, a social or academic relevance can be distinguished.[4] Matthias Lehnert, Bernhard Miller, and Arndt Wonka agree on

---

[1]Bob Hancké, "The Challenge of Research Design," in *Theory and Methods in Political Science*, eds. David Marsh and Gerry Stoker (Basingstoke: Palgrave Macmillan, 2010), p. 236.

[2]Friedrich Dürrenmatt, "Kunst und Wissenschaft," in *Versuche/Kants Hoffnung: Essays und Reden* (Zürich: Diogenes, 1998), p. 75.

[3]Thomas Geschwend and Frank Schimmelfennig, "Introduction: Designing Research in Political Science – A Dialogue between Theory and Data," in *Research Design in Political Science: How to Practice What They Preach*, eds. Thomas Geschwend and Frank Schimmelfennig (Basingstoke: Palgrave Macmillan, 2011), p. 3.

[4]Gary King, Robert O. Keohane, and Sidney Verba, *Designing Social Inquiry: Scientific Inference in Qualitative Research* (Princeton, N.J.: Princeton University Press, 1994), pp. 15–19; Geschwend and Schimmelfennig, "Introduction," p. 3.

© Springer Nature Switzerland AG 2020
H. W. Ohnesorge, *Soft Power*, Global Power Shift,
https://doi.org/10.1007/978-3-030-29922-4_1

these two crucial dimensions: whereas research that is academically relevant seeks to
improve a theory or concept, socially relevant research offers new approaches for the
understanding of certain political or social issues for policy-makers and the public
alike.[5] Of course, both dimensions are by no means mutually exclusive.[6] Connected
with the required relevance, research ideally should be topical, that is, addressing an
issue of relevance for the present.

The work in hand meets these standards and arguably ranks exceedingly high in
both regards. In particular, it is the phenomenon of shifting power configurations
observable in international relations today that lends academic, political, and social
relevance as well as a particular topicality to the study. These power shifts, according
to Joseph Nye, can be perceived in two different yet interdependent dimensions: "a
power transition among states and a power diffusion away from all states to nonstate
actors."[7]

1.1 Power Transition in International Relations

Beginning with the former, power transition, identified by Joseph Nye as constituting the first of the major power shifts in the twenty-first century, concerns the
shifting distribution of power among different nation-states.[8] This process, as well
as its recognition, is, of course, nothing distinctly new: the ancient Greeks and
Romans envisioned different ages (i.e., Iron, Heroic, Bronze, Silver, and Golden
Age), which were thought to be constantly recurrent and they had no illusions as to
the perpetuity of human affairs and social institutions[9]; Herodotus, to offer just one
example in this vein, hence opened his *Histories* with the exposition,

> I shall go forward with my history, describing equally the greater and the lesser cities. For the
> cities which were formerly great, have most of them become insignificant; and such as are at
> present powerful, were weak in the olden time. I shall therefore discourse equally of both,
> convinced that human happiness never continues long in one stay;[10]

---

[5]Matthias Lehnert, Bernhard Miller, and Arndt Wonka, "Increasing the Relevance of Research
Questions: Considerations on Theoretical and Social Relecance in Social Science," in *Research
Design in Political Science: How to Practice What They Preach*, eds. Thomas Geschwend and
Frank Schimmelfennig (Basingstoke: Palgrave Macmillan, 2011), pp. 23–27.

[6]Lehnert, Miller, and Wonka, "Increasing the Relevance of Research Questions," p. 28.

[7]Joseph S. Nye, Jr., *The Future of Power* (New York, N.Y.: PublicAffairs, 2011), p. xv.

[8]Nye, *The Future of Power*, pp. 153–204.

[9]The most famous expression of this view can arguably be found in Ovid's *Metamorphoses* (I,
89–150), a passage which opens with famed line, "Aurea prima sata est" (Ov. Met. I, 89); Ovid
(P. Ovidius Naso), *Matamorphosen/Metamorphoseon Libri* (München: Artemis & Winkler,
1992), p. 10.

[10]Herodotus, *The History*, Translated from the Ancient Greece by George Rawlinson, Volume I
(New York, N.Y.: The Tandy-Thomas Company, 1909), p. 31 (Hdt. I, 5).

Church Father Augustine of Hippo famously declared in the early fifth century, against the immediate backdrop of the Sack of Rome by the Visigoths in 410, that every secular state (*civitas terrena*), however powerful, is but ephemeral and only the City of Good (*civitas dei*) will prove eternal[11]; one millennium later, Florentine Renaissance scholar and historian Francesco Guicciardini remarked, confining himself to this world alone, "All cities, states and governments are mortal, since either by nature or accident everything in this world must some time have an end."[12]

In the light of such notions, recurrent changes in the power positions among nations and states may, in fact, be considered, to paraphrase Heraclitus, the single greatest constant in world history: Ancient China, Egypt, the Greek poleis, Rome, the Byzantine Empire, the Italian Renaissance principalities, the overseas empires of Portugal or Spain, the nations conducting the Concert of Europe in the nineteenth and twentieth century, all saw their rise and fall. As Henry Kissinger has aptly written in this regard, "The history of most civilizations is a tale of the rise and fall of empires."[13] Historian Norman Davies, in his magnificent *Vanished Kingdoms: The Rise and Fall of States and Nations*, agreed emphatically,

> [S]tudents of history need to be constantly reminded of the transience of power, for transience is one of the fundamental characteristics of both the human condition and of the political order. Sooner or later, all things come to an end. Sooner or later, the centre cannot hold. All states and nations, however great, bloom for a season and are replaced.[14]

Politicians frequently subscribe to this observation of power shifts among nations as well. British Prime Minister Tony Blair, for example, reminded his audience in a 2003 address before the United States Congress, "As Britain knows, all predominant power seems for a time invincible, but in fact, it is transient."[15] Actually, it was with respect to Britain that Rudyard Kipling had warned an empire on the very apogee of its power on the occasion of the Diamond Jubilee of Queen Victoria in 1897,

> Far-called our navies melt away—
>   On dune and headland sinks the fire—
> Lo, all our pomp of yesterday
> Is one with Nineveh and Tyre!
> Judge of the Nations, spare us yet,
> Lest we forget—lest we forget![16]

---

[11]Peter Heather, *The Fall of the Roman Empire: A New History* (London: Pan Books, 2006), pp. 228–232.

[12]Quoted in Vincent Cronin, *The Florentine Renaissance* (London: Pimlico, 1992), p. 300.

[13]Henry Kissinger, *World Order: Reflections on the Character of Nations and the Course of History* (London: Allen Lane, 2014), p. 11.

[14]Norman Davies, *Vanished Kingdoms: The Rise and Fall of States and Nations* (New York, N.Y.: Viking, 2011), p. 5.

[15]Tony Blair, "Address by the Right Honorable Tony Blair, Prime Minister of the United Kingdom of Great Britain and Northern Ireland," Washington, D.C., July 13, 2003, in *Congressional Record: Proceedings and Debates of the 108th Congress, First Session, Vol. 149 – Part 14, July 17, 2003 to July 25, 2003* (Washington, D.C.: United States Government Printing Office, 2003), p. 18598.

[16]Rudyard Kipling, "Recessional," *The Times*, July 17, 1897, p. 13.

As the course of further events has shown, Kipling's fears, voiced even before the turn of the twentieth century, were not unfounded. In our days, the "Rise of China" (which more accurately should be termed "Return of China" or "Reemergence of China"[17]) and a presumed coincidental decline in the global position of the United States of America are especially high on the agenda with respect to power transitions. In recent years, observers thus identified a global power shift in the direction of the Middle Kingdom as well as other emerging countries (frequently subsumed under the acronym BRICS[18]) with regard to the hard power factors of military expenditures and capabilities as well as economic strength and technological innovation.[19] Fareed Zakaria accordingly identified what he has called "the Rise of the Rest" as the defining characteristic of the most recent among the "three tectonic power shifts over the last 500 years."[20] Christopher Layne pointed out in the same vein in 2010,

> Even before the current financial and economic meltdown, the dramatic ongoing shift in the distribution of global economic—and ultimately geopolitical—power from the Euro-Atlantic world to Asia was prompting calls that international institutions reflect the diminishing clout of the 'West'—especially the USA.[21]

As a result of these developments, discussions about the United States decline have flared up again in recent years, albeit—as shall be argued below at greater length—they have accompanied the United States virtually since its foundation and can be detected even prior to that. However, in recent years "declinism" gained considerable momentum. With Stephen G. Brooks and William C. Wohlforth, "The narrative regarding the US international position has clearly shifted: pundits, scholars, and policymakers frequently and prominently argue that the United States

---

[17]Henry Kissinger, *On China* (London: Allen Lane, 2011), p. 514. See also Nye, *The Future of Power*, p. 179 and Gordon H. Chang, *Fateful Ties: A History of America's Preoccupation with China* (Cambridge, Mass.: Harvard University Press, 2015), p. 9.

[18]The BRICS states include Brazil, Russia, India, the People's Republic China, and South Africa. The term (first styled as BRIC and soon to be augmented by the addition of South Africa) was coined in 2001, see Jim O'Neill, "Building Better Global Economic BRICs," *Global Economics Paper No: 66*, Goldman Sachs, November 30, 2001, online at: http://www.goldmansachs.com/our-thinking/archive/archive-pdfs/build-better-brics.pdf (accessed September 4, 2017).

[19]James F. Hodge, Jr., "A Global Power Shift in the Making," *Foreign Affairs*, Vol. 83, No. 4 (July/August 2004), pp. 2–7.

[20]Fareed Zakaria, "The Future of American Power: How America Can Survive the Rise of the Rest," *Foreign Affairs*, Vol. 87, No. 3 (May/June 2008), p. 42; the previous two shifts having been the rise of the Western world from the beginning of Early Modern Age until Enlightenment and the rise of the United States in the late 19th century; see also Fareed Zakaria, *The Post-American World: And the Rise of the Rest* (London: Penguin Books, 2009).

[21]Christopher Layne, "The Unbearable Lightness of Soft Power," in *Soft Power and US Foreign Policy: Theoretical, Historical and Contemporary Perspectives*, eds. Inderjeet Parmar and Michael Cox (Abingdon: Routledge, 2010), p. 72.

has tumbled from its previous global position and that a fundamental, system-altering power shift is underway."[22]

In this context, power shifts have not only been detected in the realm of hard power alone. In fact, the realm of military power has been considered to be the one dimension in which power has *not* been shifting away from US preeminence.[23] By contrast, the dimension of soft power has been identified as witnessing fundamental power shifts today in particular. Joseph Nye has hence pointed out,

> [S]oft power is not static. Resources change with the changing context. They have varied in the past and will continue to do so in the future. Historical trends from the Cold War era may not prove reliable guides when forecasting the ebb and flow of American soft power in the war on terrorism.[24]

Other commentators agree that equal to hard power, soft power may also be subjected to change and competition between nation-states.[25] For instance, the "Rise of China" has not only been touching upon the dimensions of hard power but has crucially included the dimension of soft power as well.[26] At the same time, others have hinted at the declining US soft power.[27] Kostas Ifantis, for example, pointed out in 2011 that "foreign perceptions of the United States have declined considerably in the past few years as a result of various unpopular international American actions."[28] Joseph Nye, drawing on the results of a 2007 Congressional Smart Power Commission (cochaired by Richard Armitage and Nye himself), agreed, "We concluded that America's image and influence had declined in recent years and that the United States had to move from exporting fear to inspiring optimism and hope."[29] After the most recent change of government in Washington, the issue of (declining) US soft power returned to the very top of the agenda once more. Eliot A. Cohen, for example, has recently detected a "rot that is visible in America's standing and ability to influence global affairs."[30] The fact that soft power has for long been a prominent and important part in US foreign policy renders this perceived decline particularly significant.[31]

---

[22]Stephen G. Brooks and William C. Wohlforth, *America Abroad: The United States' Global Role in the 21st Century* (New York, N.Y.: Oxford University Press, 2016), p. 3.

[23]Zakaria, "The Future of American Power," p. 43.

[24]Joseph S. Nye, Jr., *Soft Power: The Means to Success in World Politics* (New York: PublicAffairs, 2004), p. 68.

[25]R. S. Zaharna, *The Cultural Awakening in Public Diplomacy, CPD Perspectives on Public Diplomacy, Paper 4, 2012* (Los Angeles, Cal.: Figueroa Press, 2012), p. 42.

[26]Richard Falk, *Power Shift: On the New Global Order* (London: Zed Books, 2016), p. 13.

[27]Layne, "The Unbearable Lightness of Soft Power," p. 66.

[28]Kostas Ifantis, "Soft Power: Overcoming the Limits of a Concept," in *Routledge Handbook of Diplomacy and Statecraft*, ed. B. J. C. McKercher (Abingdon: Routledge, 2011), p. 444.

[29]Joseph S. Nye, Jr., "The War on Soft Power," *Foreign Policy*, April 12, 2011, online at: http://foreignpolicy.com/2011/04/12/the-war-on-soft-power/ (accessed September 4, 2017).

[30]Eliot A. Cohen, "Is Trump Ending the American Era?," *The Atlantic* (October 2017), p. 71.

[31]Matthew Fraser, *Weapons of Mass Distraction: Soft Power and American Empire* (New York, N. Y.: St. Martin's Press, 2003), p. 9.

1.2   Power Diffusion and the Growing Importance of Soft Power

Turning to the second power shift identified, it has become a much discussed theme that a diffusion of power has been taking place, resulting in a declining importance of nation-states as the traditional actors in international relations.[32] The entry of various other actors onto the international scene, including international organizations, terrorist networks, large enterprises, and even individuals, underlines this observation, which has become common since the accelerated advent of globalization in the early 1990s. Werner Weidenfeld hence pointed out in 1996,

> The East-West conflict is no longer one of the main strategic determinants of world politics—and the dominating significance of security policy has also waned. The number of actors on the international political stage is growing, and with it the scope for different patterns of cooperation and conflict is also increasing. This development means that the power structures of old are having to be increasingly relativized. Although the USA has remained the only 'superpower,' it is finding it increasingly difficult to bring its weight to bear, because military and political domination is no longer as crucial as it once was when it comes to solving the conflicts of the day (civil wars, economic crisis, nuclear proliferation).[33]

After the turn of the century, Niall Ferguson has likewise argued that "[t]he paradox of globalization is that as the world becomes more integrated, so power becomes more diffuse."[34] For Joseph Nye, five major trends contribute to the global diffusion of power: "economic interdependence, transnational actors, nationalism in weak states, the spread of technology, and changing political issues."[35] Not all these trends identified by Nye need to be considered in detail at this point. (Some of them shall be picked up again below when discussing the origins of soft power.) What is important, however, is the changed setting in which international politics is being made today. In an age of globalization, nation-states today are more economically interdependent than ever before, as events like the most recent global financial and economic crises have so dramatically demonstrated. Additionally, the (realist) view of the state as the foremost, and indeed only relevant, actor on the international stage is being heavily contested. Large multinational corporations or even private foundations, for example, frequently have larger revenues than a great number of nation-states. As a consequence of these developments, Joseph Nye has fittingly noted, "States will remain the dominant actor on the world stage, but they will find the stage

---

[32]Nye, *The Future of Power*, pp. 113–151.

[33]Werner Weidenfeld, *America and Europe: Is the Break Inevitable?* (Gütersloh: Bertelsmann Foundation Publishers, 1996), pp. 19–20.

[34]Niall Ferguson, *Colossus: The Price of America's Empire* (New York, N.Y.: Penguin Press, 2004), p. 298.

[35]Joseph S. Nye, Jr., *Bound to Lead: The Changing Nature of American Power* (New York: Basic Books, 1990), p. 182.

far more crowded and difficult to control."[36] And Laura Roselle, Alister Miskimmon, and Ben O'Loughlin have elaborated in this regard, "States, non-state actors, great powers, normal powers, rogue states, terrorists, NGOs (Non-Governmental Organizations), and MNCs (multinational corporations) are all actors associated with the international system today."[37]

Consequently, along with an ever increasing dispersion of power between a growing number of actors comes a shift in the importance among the different varieties of power. While Edward Bulwer-Lytton famously claimed in his play *Richelieu* as early as 1839, "The pen is mightier than the sword,"[38] today's new and more sophisticated technologies of information and communication make his observation more topical than ever. Claudia Auer, Alice Srugies, and Martin Löffelholz have, thus, appropriately argued that the parameters of interaction and communication in international relations have changed over the last few decades.[39] Accordingly, in the words of John Arquilla and David Ronfeldt, the decisive question of the twenty-first century may no longer be about "whose military or economy wins," but rather "about whose story wins."[40] Joseph Nye, echoing these very words, likewise noted that "in the information age, success is not merely the result of whose army wins, but also whose story wins."[41]

Nye has also elaborated on the consequence of such developments,

> Some observers have argued that the sources of power are, in general, moving away from the emphasis on military force and conquest that marked earlier eras. In assessing international power today, factors such as technology, education, and economic growth are becoming more important, whereas geography, population, and raw materials are becoming less important.[42]

---

[36]Nye, *The Future of Power*, p. 114.

[37]Laura Roselle, Alister Miskimmon, and Ben O'Loughlin, "Strategic Narrative: A New Means to Understand Soft Power," *Media, War & Conflict*, Vol. 7, No. 1 (2014), p. 75.

[38]Edward Bulwer-Lytton, *Richelieu; Or, The Conspiracy: A Play, in Five Acts* (London: Saunders and Otley, 1839), p. 39.

[39]Claudia Auer, Alice Srugies, and Martin Löffelholz, "Schlüsselbegriffe der internationalen Diskussion: Public Diplomacy und Soft Power," in *Kultur und Außenpolitik: Handbuch für Wissenschaft und Praxis*, ed. Kurt-Jürgen Maaß (Baden Baden: Nomos Verlagsgesellschaft, 2015), p. 39.

[40]John Arquilla and David Ronfeldt, *The Emergence of Noopolitik: Toward an American Information Strategy* (Santa Monica, Cal.: RAND Corporation, 1999), p. 53.

[41]Joseph S. Nye, Jr., "The Future of Soft Power in US Foreign Policy," in *Soft Power and US Foreign Policy: Theoretical, Historical and Contemporary Perspectives*, eds. Inderjeet Parmar and Michael Cox (Abingdon: Routledge, 2010), p. 8.

[42]Joseph S. Nye, Jr., "The Changing Nature of World Power," *Political Science Quarterly*, Vol. 105, No. 2 (Summer 1990), p. 179.

In line with this argumentation, it has frequently been pointed out that "military force's utility is declining"[43] and that a "declining leverage of hard power"[44] in international affairs can be detected. Different rationales account for this development. First, political issues such as ecological threats, global health issues, or transnational and cyber terrorism escape the boundaries of nation-states and their traditional spheres of influence and do not easily lend themselves to the instruments of hard power, particularly military force.[45] Kostas Ifantis in this regard fittingly remarked, "Hard power is of little use with a range of today's security challenges: nuclear proliferation, jihadism, collapsed states, refugees, piracy, suicide bombers, and 'black swan' (high-impact, difficult to foresee, and usually outside customary expectations) events."[46] Consequently, power has increasingly been losing its dependence on stipulated territorial boundaries.[47] Secondly, with rising interdependence among nation-states, the costs of applying military force have increased dramatically. As Nye aptly pointed out, "In earlier periods, the costs of coercion were relatively low. Force was acceptable and economies less interdependent."[48] Today, global interdependence has increased dramatically. Ali S. Wyne, with respect to the application of hard power, thus, noted that "the world's interconnectivity ensures that the use of conventional power is mutually inimical."[49] This view, of course, also gave rise to the International Relations theory of interdependence first formulated by Robert O. Keohane and Joseph S. Nye in 1977.[50] While hence already observable for decades, these developments gathered pace dramatically after the end of the Cold War. Recently, Richard Falk has accordingly elaborated on this issue,

> I wish to critique the old geopolitics which is based on the primacy of hard power, essentially conceived as military power and its accompanying diplomatic clout, as the essential agent of historical change in the affairs of sovereign states. It seems appropriate at this stage of history to contrast this old geopolitics with an emerging but yet not emergent new geopolitics that relies on soft power and grasps the limits of the role of force in achieving the goals of peoples and the objectives of national governments and international institutions.[51]

---

[43] Ali S. Wyne, "Public Opinion and Power," in *Routledge Handbook of Public Diplomacy*, eds. Nancy Snow and Philip M. Taylor (New York, N.Y.: Routledge, 2009), p. 43.

[44] Falk, *Power Shift*, p. 15.

[45] Nye, *The Future of Power*, p. 231.

[46] Ifantis, "Soft Power," p. 444.

[47] Byung-Chul Han, *Was ist Macht?* (Stuttgart: Reclam, 2005), pp. 120–121.

[48] Nye, *Bound to Lead*, p. 190

[49] Wyne, "Public Opinion and Power," p. 42.

[50] Robert O. Keohane and Joseph S. Nye, Jr., *Power and Interdependence: World Politics in Transition* (Boston, Mass.: Little Brown and Company, 1977).

[51] Falk, *Power Shift*, p. 10.

In fact, commentators have in recent times increasingly agreed to such assessments.[52] Eytan Gilboa, for example, has in the same vein noted, "Favorable image and reputation around the world, achieved through attraction and persuasion, have become more important than territory, access, and raw materials, traditionally acquired through military and economic measures."[53]

As a consequence of these trends, the currency of soft power in world politics has been gaining in importance and is likely to become even more crucial for years to come. Actually, particularly since the end of the Cold War, countless observers have explicitly pointed to the growing importance of soft power and its fundamental resources, including culture, in international affairs. Of course, Nye himself had led the way in this regard in his 1990 *Bound to Lead*, which introduced the very concept of soft power (at least under this designation) in the first place.[54] However, Nye's was hardly a lone voice in the wilderness. Benjamin R. Barber, for example, has argued as early as 1992 in a much-noted article,

[C]ulture has become more potent than armaments. What is the power of the Pentagon compared with Disneyland? Can the Sixth Fleet keep up with CNN? McDonald's in Moscow and Coke in China will do more to create a global culture than military colonization ever could. It is less the goods than the brand names that do the work, for they convey life-style images that alter perception and challenge behavior. They make up the seductive software of McWorld's common (at times much too common) soul.[55]

In the twenty-first century, voices on that score, if anything, grew even louder. Giulio M. Gallarotti thus pointed out, while underlining the fact that soft power has continuously been a major component of national power in the past, that recent developments have rendered it all the more important today.[56] In fact, the list of authors subscribing to the increased importance of soft power today could be expanded considerably.[57]

Going yet one step further, Simon Anholt even claimed that the variety of soft power constitutes the most important variety of power in the world today.[58] While

---

[52]See, for example, Xuewu Gu, "Ist Globalität gestaltbar?," in *Bonner Enzyklopädie der Globalität*, eds. Ludger Kühnhardt and Tilman Mayer (Wiesbaden: Springer Fachmedien, 2017), p. 1537.

[53]Eytan Gilboa, "Searching for a Theory of Public Diplomacy," *The ANNALS of the American Academy of Political and Social Sciences*, Vol. 616, Public Diplomacy in a Changing World, No. 1 (March 2008), p. 56; see also p. 60.

[54]Nye, *Bound to Lead*, p. 33 & p. 188.

[55]Benjamin R. Barber, "McWorld vs. Jihad," *The Atlantic Monthly* (March 1992), online at: http://www.theatlantic.com/magazine/archive/1992/03/jihad-vs-mcworld/303882/ (accessed September 4, 2017).

[56]Giulio M. Gallarotti, *Cosmopolitan Power in International Relations: A Synthesis of Realism, Neoliberalism, and Constructivism* (Cambridge: Cambridge University Press, 2010), pp. 38–42.

[57]See, for example, Jan Melissen, "The New Public Diplomacy: Between Theory and Practice," in *The New Public Diplomacy: Soft Power in International Relations*, ed. Jan Melissen (Basingstoke: Palgrave Macmillan, 2005), p. 4 and David Ronfeldt and John Arquilla, "Noopolitik: A New Paradigm for Public Diplomacy," in *Routledge Handbook of Public Diplomacy*, eds. Nancy Snow and Philip M. Taylor (New York, N.Y.: Routledge, 2009), p. 353.

[58]Simon Anholt, "Soft Power," *Internationale Politik* (January/February 2014), p. 49.

the work in hand subscribes to observations of a growing importance of soft power in international politics, Anholt's assumption, arguably, goes too far. Hard power, that is, military might and economic prowess, of course, remains vitally important in international affairs. Countless empirical events in the recent past all around the world, from Crimea to Syria to North Korea, underline this point. At the same time, power—across all its varieties—is no zero-sum game and the increasing importance of one variety does not necessarily result in the decrease of others *in all instances*. However, as Tom Sawyer's fence episode referred to above has demonstrated (and as shall be elaborated upon at greater length in the following), power is always dependent on context—and in recent decades, this context of international relations has shifted considerably, rendering soft power more important than ever before. As Joseph Nye aptly put it, "Winning hearts and minds has always been important, but it is even more so in a global information age."[59] Today, in a nutshell, "[s]oft power is more relevant than ever."[60] This development points at the great topicality of the central concept of the work in hand. At the same time, it emphasizes the need to elaborate a more detailed conceptual framework for the understanding and study of soft power.

Hand in hand with this perceived increase in the *importance* of soft power in international relations also went an ever-greater *interest* in the concept of soft power itself, both in the more theoretically oriented academic world and in the practical political arena. With particular respect to the United States, Christopher Layne, though a fierce critic of the concept of soft power itself, has accordingly admitted, "Soft power and its associated concepts have resonated both with those who make American foreign policy policies [sic!] and those who write about it."[61] Others have shared this view,

> Given the ubiquity of the term 'soft power' it is clear that the concept represents, without doubt, one of the key elements of international relations. The strength of the concept lies in the fact that it allows theorists and practitioners to think about power in more complex and dynamic ways—at least in ways more complex than some Realist [sic!] assertions of hard power.[62]

Detecting a regional focal point in the concept's triumphal march, Michael Mandelbaum has recently pointed out,

> The concept came to have a considerable appeal because it promised influence without exertion. It appealed in particular to the Western Europeans, who had ceased to field formidable military forces but believed—not without reasons—that the peaceful,

---

[59]Nye, *Soft Power*, p. 1.

[60]Joseph S. Nye, Jr., "Responding to My Critics and Concluding Thoughts," in *Soft Power and US Foreign Policy: Theoretical, Historical and Contemporary Perspectives*, eds. Inderjeet Parmar and Michael Cox (Abingdon: Routledge, 2010), p. 226.

[61]Layne, "The Unbearable Lightness of Soft Power," p. 58.

[62]Gitika Commuri, "'Are You Pondering What I am Pondering?' Understanding the Conditions Under Which States Gain and Loose Soft Power," in *Power in the 21st Century: International Security and International Political Economy in a Changing World*, eds. Enrico Fels, Jan-Frederik Kremer, and Katharina Kronenberg (Berlin: Springer-Verlag, 2012), p. 43.

prosperous, cooperative community they had built since World War II inspired others to emulate them.[63]

In line with these sentiments, Su Changhe has even asserted, "In contemporary diplomacy and international relations, there is probably no concept more widely accepted among policy-makers and students of international relations than that of soft power."[64] Actually, a simple Google search seems to substantiate these widely shared estimations, as the phrase "soft power" yields 4,730,000 results with the search engine in general, 187,000 with Google Books, 149,000 with Google News, and 104,000 with Google Scholar.[65]

Concurrently, not only has much ink been spilled on the issue but also various countries around the world have sought to add the arrow of soft power to their quiver of statecraft. Matthew Fraser has in this context fittingly observed, "No empire— Greek, Roman, French, Ottoman, British—has been indifferent to the effects of its soft power resources."[66] In our present information age, however, a wide range of countries as well as other actors in international relations have dramatically increased their quest for soft power on an hitherto unprecedented scale.[67]

Finally, on a more personal note, it has fittingly been pointed out that a strong individual interest in and identification with a given topic is required on the part of any researcher.[68] This requirement becomes all the more important when pursuing an extensive research project conducted over the course of several years. With the present study and its focus on the concept of soft power, which is decidedly interdisciplinary and which touches upon a plethora of different literatures, this requirement is met with flying colors. The study of power in general, and soft power in particular, this "great law of human action," thus proves to be a highly rewarding endeavor and the desire to shed some new light on so old a phenomenon is intellectually stimulating, indeed.

Given the concurrency of the factors, especially the two different yet highly interdependent power shifts outlined above and not least the growing interest in the concept of soft power itself, it seems utterly timely to offer ways to empirically analyze the workings of soft power in international relations by providing a sound conceptual basis and rigorous methodological approaches.

---

[63]Michael Mandelbaum, *Mission Failure: America and the World in the Post-Cold War Era* (New York, N.Y.: Oxford University Press, 2016), p. 375.

[64]Su Changhe, "Soft Power," in *The Oxford Handbook of Modern Diplomacy*, eds. Andrew F. Cooper, Jorge Heine, and Ramesh Thakur (Oxford: Oxford University Press, 2013), p. 544.

[65]Searches were conducted by the author on April 17, 2019.

[66]Fraser, *Weapons of Mass Distraction*, p. 13.

[67]Janice Bially Mattern, "Why 'Soft Power' Isn't So Soft: Representational Force and the Socio-linguistic Construction of Attraction in World Politics," *Millennium: Journal of International Studies*, Vol. 33, No. 3 (2005), p. 589; Su, "Soft Power," pp. 547–548 & p. 554.

[68]Hancké, "The Challenge of Research Design," pp. 232–233.

1.3   Composition of the Work in Hand

The work in hand is divided into three parts: The first of which—this chapter and Chap. 2—have commenced with the introduction of the central topic of research and a discussion of the topicality and relevance of the present study. Subsequently, the state of research on (soft) power in international relations is presented and the research gap to be addressed is identified (this chapter). Furthermore, the pivotal phenomenon of power in international relations is discussed, including its different manifestations as well as key characteristics. At this point, the concept of soft power is presented in detail, tracing its origins, addressing its workings and placement in International Relations theory, as well as elaborating upon its reception and critique directed at the concept (Chap. 2).

Proceeding from these foundations—and especially with an eye on the research gap as well as the points of criticism identified—the second part (Chaps. 3 and 4) can be regarded the very centerpiece of the work in hand as it provides an innovative theoretical-conceptual elaboration as well as a methodological roadmap for the study of soft power in international relations. To that purpose, a new paradigm of soft power is put forth, building on existing works but at the same time substantially expanding and elaborating on the concept by integrating further and thus far neglected components (Chap. 3). Most pivotally, a comprehensive taxonomy of soft power is presented, which allows for holistic, structured, and comparative empirical application. The centerpiece of this chapter, and in a way the whole work, can hence be found in Fig. 3.1, depicting the introduced taxonomy of soft power, which is subsequently elaborated upon in greater detail along the lines of its four subunits. In this context (and summarized in Table 3.2), respective indicators for empirical analysis are deduced and discussed, thus, for the first time providing a rigorous operationalization of a hitherto too fragmented and vague concept. An excursus to the soft power on the Roman Empire rejoins the four subunits and illustrates their coherent workings with reference to a select historical example. Subsequently, a methodological roadmap for resilient empirical studies of soft power in international relations is developed (Chap. 4). Within this context, different research methods are discussed and the method of comparative-historical analysis (CHA), innovatively complemented by the technique of structured, focused comparison, is identified as an eminently applicable approach (Sect. 4.2.3). Finally, suitable timeframes (Sect. 4.3), actors (Sect. 4.4), as well as data sources to draw upon for substantiated empirical studies are set out (Sect. 4.5). The third part, ultimately, discusses lessons learned by the work in hand as well as more general future prospects (Chap. 5). To that end, both the newly introduced taxonomy of soft power and the methodological roadmap developed are critically evaluated (Sect. 5.1). Additionally, an outlook on the future significance of soft power in international relations as well as prospective research questions offering promising starting points for future research are discussed (Sect. 5.2).

1.4 Literature Discussion and Research Gap

Weighing in on the scholarly discussion whether Greek philosophy was an actual contrivance of Greek philosophers devised in ancient Greece or whether it was a mere "import" from other countries and cultures, Friedrich Nietzsche remarked in his classic (and unfinished) *Philosophy in the Tragic Age of the Greeks*, "The very reason they got so far is that they knew how to pick up the spear and throw it onward from the point where others had left it. Their skill in the art of fruitful learning was admirable."[69]

In fact, all scholarly endeavors, be they in Greek philosophy during classical times or in International Relations today, build on existing work by those who went before. At the same time, however, genuine research seeks to address hitherto unanswered questions or elucidate yet unexplained phenomena and in doing so endeavors to increase our understanding of the world around us. (It may be argued that in *this* respect the classical Greek philosophers excelled, indeed.) In order to identify this added value, it is necessary to place one's research within the landscape of existing literature regarding its main subjects.[70] The following chapter, therefore, first discusses literature existent and drawn upon in the work in hand. Subsequently, the particular research gap to be addressed is identified.

1.4.1 State of Research

It should be noted at the outset that the study at hand, by addressing its central research question, draws on a vast and highly interdisciplinary body of literature. The focal phenomenon of (soft) power, thus, has been subject to extensive research and writing dating back millennia, but nonetheless still remains highly contentious to this very day.[71] Accordingly, literature to be drawn upon in an attempt to define or differentiate power in its different manifestations spans a wide period of time, ranging from ancient classics to the latest publications on the issue. As English poet and classicist Robert Graves, putting the words into the mouth of Gaius Asinius Pollio, Roman statesman and man of letters of the late republic and early empire as well as founder of Rome's first public library,[72] has cautioned us, "Books when they grow out of date only serve as wrappings for fish."[73] On the subject of (soft) power,

---

[69]Friedrich Nietzsche, *Philosophy in the Tragic Age of the Greeks*. Translated, with an Introduction by Marianne Cowan (Washington, D.C.: Regnery Publishing, 1962), p. 30.

[70]Alexander L. George and Andrew Bennett, *Case Studies and Theory Development in the Social Sciences* (Cambridge, Mass.: MIT Press, 2005), p. 70.

[71]See below, Sect. 2.1.

[72]Edith Hall, "Adventures in Ancient Greek and Roman Libraries," in *The Meaning of the Library: A Cultural History*, ed. Alice Crawford (Princeton, N.J.: Princeton University Press, 2015), p. 24.

[73]Robert Graves, *I, Claudius* (London: Collectors Library, 2013), p. 169.

as it turns out, some classical works are by no means outdated. Rather, they have
retained a surprisingly fresh odor and still provide some highly expressive insights.
A closer look at them, therefore, can help us considerably in our understanding of so
fundamental and controversial a phenomenon today.

With respect to the concept at the very core of the work in hand, it has been noted
that "soft power touches on multiple literatures about international relations
(IR) theory and foreign policy decision making."[74] At it, the fundamental theoretical
writings on the subject of soft power are still largely dominated by the works of
Joseph Nye, the eponym and propagator of the concept of soft power.[75] Kostas
Ifantis has hence fittingly pointed out in 2011, "Nye's works on the soft power have
achieved great authoritative stature, with a visible impact on American foreign
policy as well as on that of other countries. His terminology and concepts are
indispensable for analysis of and discourse about this subject."[76]

Nye first laid out the concept of soft power in his 1990 monograph *Bound to
Lead: The Changing Nature of American Power*[77] as well as two contemporaneous
articles.[78] However, it was, in particular, his 2004 study *Soft Power: The Means to
Success in World Politics*,[79] which elaborated on the concept (while drawing on the
fundamentals of his earlier works) and introduced it to a wider public. Underlining
this work's centrality, Nye himself has stated that "it was not until 2004 that I
focused a book on soft power as such"[80] and Geraldo Zahran and Leonardo Ramos
fittingly noted that "Nye's 2004-book *Soft Power* is entirely devoted to the theoretical development of the concept and its implications."[81] A 2011 addition, entitled
The Future of Power,[82] included some updates and extensions, but nevertheless did
not substantially supersede Nye's previous monograph on soft power. Besides, Nye
has widely published on the concept of soft power in a plethora of articles frequently
appearing in the discipline's leading journals. Taken together, Nye's works on the
subject of soft power, with his 2004 monograph leading the way, shall serve as the
main theoretical-conceptual reference points for the work in hand.

---

[74]Layne, "The Unbearable Lightness of Soft Power," p. 53.

[75]See below, Sect. 2.5.1.

[76]Ifantis, "Soft Power," p. 441.

[77]Joseph S. Nye, Jr., *Bound to Lead: The Changing Nature of American Power* (New York: Basic
Books, 1990).

[78]Joseph S. Nye, Jr., "The Changing Nature of World Power," *Political Science Quarterly*, Vol.
105, No. 2 (Summer 1990), pp. 177–192; Joseph S. Nye, Jr. "Soft Power," *Foreign Policy*,
No. 80 (Autumn 1990), pp. 153–171.

[79]Joseph S. Nye, Jr., *Soft Power: The Means to Success in World Politics* (New York, N.Y.:
PublicAffairs, 2004).

[80]Nye, "Responding to My Critics and Concluding Thoughts," p. 216.

[81]Geraldo Zahran and Leonardo Ramos, "From Hegemony to Soft Power: Implications of a
Conceptual Change," in *Soft Power and US Foreign Policy: Theoretical, Historical and Contemporary Perspectives*, eds. Inderjeet Parmar and Michael Cox (Abingdon: Routledge, 2010), p. 16.

[82]Joseph S. Nye, Jr., *The Future of Power* (New York, N.Y.: PublicAffairs, 2011).

Nevertheless, in the wake of Joseph Nye's own writings and particularly following the growing popularity of the concept after the publication of *Soft Power* in 2004, a considerable number of scholars have provided elaborations of the concept. While particulars of these writings and their respective contributions to the concept of soft power—some of them attempts to operationalize it, others efforts to elucidate particular components—shall be elaborated below at corresponding places, significant writings include, in chronological order, works by Janice Bially Mattern,[83] Geun Lee,[84] Todd Hall,[85] Geraldo Zahran and Leonardo Ramos,[86] Su Changhe,[87] Jean-Marc F. Blanchard and Fujia Lu,[88] Benjamin E. Goldsmith and Yusaku Horiuchi,[89] Laura Roselle, Alister Miskimmon, and Ben O'Loughlin,[90] Ty Solomon,[91] Artem Patalakh,[92] as well as Peter Baumann and Gisela Cramer.[93] Besides these journal articles, contributing valuable refinements of the concept, various edited volumes on the issue of soft power have been published, frequently seeking to combine theoretical-conceptual elaborations and empirical analyses.[94]

---

[83]Janice Bially Mattern, "Why 'Soft Power' Isn't So Soft: Representational Force and the Sociolinguistic Construction of Attraction in World Politics," *Millennium: Journal of International Studies*, Vol. 33, No. 3 (2005), pp. 583–612.

[84]Geun Lee, "A Theory of Soft Power and Korea's Soft Power Strategy," *The Korean Journal of Defense Analysis*, Vol. 21, No. 2 (June 2009), pp. 205–218.

[85]Todd Hall, "An Unclear Attraction: A Critical Examination of Soft Power as an Analytical Category," *The Chinese Journal of International Politics*, Vol. 3, No. 2 (2010), pp. 189–211.

[86]Geraldo Zahran and Leonardo Ramos, "From Hegemony to Soft Power: Implications of a Conceptual Change," in *Soft Power and US Foreign Policy: Theoretical, Historical and Contemporary Perspectives*, eds. Inderjeet Parmar and Michael Cox (Abingdon: Routledge, 2010), pp. 12–31.

[87]Su Changhe, "Soft Power," in *The Oxford Handbook of Modern Diplomacy*, eds. Andrew F. Cooper, Jorge Heine, and Ramesh Thakur (Oxford: Oxford University Press, 2013), pp. 544–558.

[88]Jean-Marc F. Blanchard and Fujia Lu, "Thinking Hard about Soft Power: A Review and Critique of the Literature on China and Soft Power," *Asian Perspective*, Vol. 36, No. 4 (2012), pp. 565–589.

[89]Benjamin E. Goldsmith and Yusaku Horiuchi, "In Search of Soft Power: Does Foreign Public Opinion Matter for US Foreign Policy?," *World Politics*, Vol. 64, No. 3 (July 2012), pp. 555–585.

[90]Laura Roselle, Alister Miskimmon, and Ben O'Loughlin, "Strategic Narrative: A New Means to Understand Soft Power," *Media, War & Conflict*, Vol. 7, No. 1 (2014), pp. 70–84.

[91]Ty Solomon, "The Affective Underpinnings of Soft Power," *European Journal of International Relations*, Vol. 20, No. 3 (2014), pp. 720–741.

[92]Artem Patalakh, "Assessment of Soft Power Strategies: Towards an Aggregative Analytical Model for Country-Focused Case Study Research," *Croatian International Relations Review*, Vol. 22, No. 76 (2016), pp. 85–112.

[93]Peter Baumann and Gisela Cramer, "Power, Soft or Deep? An Attempt at Constructive Criticism," *Las Torres de Lucca: International Journal of Political Philosophy*, No. 10 (January-June 2017), pp. 177–214.

[94]See for example Watanabe Yasushi and David L. McConnell, eds., *Soft Power Superpowers: Cultural and National Assets of Japan and the United States* (Armonk, N.Y.: M.E. Sharpe, 2008); Inderjeet Parmar and Michael Cox, eds. *Soft Power and US Foreign Policy: Theoretical, Historical and Contemporary Perspectives* (Abingdon: Routledge, 2010); and Naren Chitty, Li Ji, Gary

Regarding methodological approaches to the empirical study of soft power in international relations, provided by the work in hand subsequent to the introduction of a comprehensive taxonomy of soft power, pivotal literature on the method of comparative-historical analysis, subsequently to be identified as particularly suited for the study of soft power, includes the two edited volumes by James Mahoney and Dietrich Rueschemeyer (2003)[95] as well as James Mahoney and Kathleen Thelen (2015)[96] and the essential 2013 monograph on the issue by Matthew Lange.[97]

1.4.2 Research Gap

Despite the vast amount of literature dealing with the phenomenon of soft power, two distinct research gaps can be identified in particular. Contributing to the edited volume *Soft Power and US Foreign Policy: Theoretical, Historical and Contemporary Perspectives*, Joseph Nye himself has thus urged, "We need more studies like the chapters in this book that explore both the nature of the concept, as well as empirical studies of policy examples and limitations."[98] In fact, the work in hand addresses both interconnected deficits identified by Nye: in addressing the former by providing a theoretical-conceptual elaboration of the concept with the introduction of a comprehensive taxonomy of soft power, it not least provides a remedy for the latter by offering the groundwork for future empirical studies. In this sense, the following research question can be established as fundamental for the work in hand:

Q_0
What is soft power and how does it take effect in international relations?

In order to address this overarching question properly, two more precise research questions can be deduced:

D. Rawnsley, and Craig Hayden, eds., *The Routledge Handbook of Soft Power* (Abingdon: Routledge, 2017).

[95] James Mahoney and Dietrich Rueschemeyer, eds., *Comparative Historical Analysis in the Social Sciences* (Cambridge: Cambridge University Press, 2003). The volume's first chapter contributed by the editors is particularly vital; James Mahoney and Dietrich Rueschemeyer, "Comparative Historical Analysis: Achievements and Agendas," in *Comparative Historical Analysis in the Social Sciences*, eds. James Mahoney and Dietrich Rueschemeyer (Cambridge: Cambridge University Press, 2003), pp. 3–38.

[96] James Mahoney and Kathleen Thelen, eds., *Advances in Comparative-Historical Analysis* (Cambridge: Cambridge University Press, 2015). Once more, see especially the volume's first chapter contributed by the editors; Kathleen Thelen and James Mahoney, "Comparative-Historical Analysis in Contemporary Political Science," in *Advances in Comparative-Historical Analysis*, eds. James Mahoney and Kathleen Thelen (Cambridge: Cambridge University Press, 2015), pp. 3–36.

[97] Matthew Lange, *Comparative-Historical Methods* (Los Angeles, Cal.: SAGE Publications, 2013).

[98] Nye, "Responding to My Critics and Concluding Thoughts," p. 226.

Q₁

How can the concept of soft power be operationalized and made more resilient?

Q₂

How can the impact of soft power in international relations be empirically studied?

First and foremost, therefore, the present work seeks to contribute to the sharpening of the concept of soft power itself. While having gained considerable currency in academia, the media, and the political arena alike, the concept still is insufficiently elaborated in a number of its key components and hence is in dire need for amendments and improvements. It is in this very vein that Giulio M. Gallarotti has noted in 2015,

> The concept of soft power and the corollary concept of smart power (i.e., the use of both hard and soft power to attain foreign policy objectives) have generated significant attention in scholarly, policy and popular discourses on power. Both President Barack Obama, and Hillary Clinton in her confirmation hearing as Secretary of State explicitly used the term in talking about an optimal US foreign policy. The scholarly attention to the concepts has risen conterminously. Yet with all this scholarly attention, the concepts have evolved little theoretically, and their historical applications have been limited and far from rigorously executed.[99]

Accordingly, the concept has drawn substantial criticism and many commentators have identified inherent weaknesses.[100] Geraldo Zahran and Leonardo Ramos, for example, have pointed out, "Unfortunately, the definition of soft power given by Nye lacks rigour; its use is problematic and uncertain, making a strict definition of the concept hard to obtain."[101] Other critical voices have likewise "argued that soft power is a confusing concept or that it suffers from many theoretical deficiencies"[102] and, with Christopher Layne, that it is "marred by some important weaknesses."[103] In particular, it has been noted that the concept of soft power lacks applicability and operationalization.[104] Jean-Marc F. Blanchard and Fujia Lu, in their literature review and critique on the issue, accordingly noted, "A deficiency in the literature is the operationalization of soft power."[105] Perhaps Craig Hayden summed up this aspect best—while rightly recognizing it as an eminently promising starting point for further research, "Soft power's conceptual ambiguity is an invitation for the concept to be appropriated and resituated in localised discourses of international strategy."[106]

---

[99]Giulio M. Gallarotti, "Smart Power: Definitions, Importance, and Effectiveness," *Journal of Strategic Studies*, Vol. 38, No. 3 (2015), pp. 245–246.

[100]See below, Sect. 2.5.4.

[101]Zahran and Ramos, "From Hegemony to Soft Power," p. 16.

[102]Gilboa, "Searching for a Theory of Public Diplomacy," p. 62.

[103]Layne, "The Unbearable Lightness of Soft Power," p. 52.

[104]Auer, Srugies, and Löffelholz, "Schlüsselbegriffe der internationalen Diskussion," p. 41.

[105]Blanchard and Lu, "Thinking Hard about Soft Power," p. 570. For further points of criticism directed at the concept see especially, Sect. 2.5.4.

[106]Craig Hayden, "Scope, Mechanism, and Outcome: Arguing Soft Power in the Context of Public Diplomacy," *Journal of International Relations and Development*, Vol. 20, No. 2 (2017), p. 349.

The work in hand pays tribute to this fundamental deficit and seeks to offer a new taxonomy of soft power. By deconstructing the overarching and rather undifferentiated concept of soft power into qualitatively different aspects (the so-called subunits), a more sophisticated and applicable understanding of soft power shall be presented. The taxonomy, to be developed in the following in greater detail, thus, distinguishes between the four subunits of soft power (1) resources, (2) instruments, (3) reception, and (4) outcomes, each of which containing distinct components by itself.[107] In doing so, the taxonomy explicitly draws on the works of Joseph Nye and adopts major components of his (as well as others') elaborations on the concept of soft power. At the same time, however, it offers major clarifications and additions. For example, in the taxonomy's first subunit, that is, resources, the variety of personalities is introduced as a fourth major soft power resource and, correspondingly, the second subunit includes the soft power instrument of personal diplomacy. Taken as a whole, the proposed taxonomy addresses the identified major deficiency in the literature on soft power by offering a comprehensive understanding and operationalization of soft power. At it, the taxonomy lends itself to varying empirical applications (e.g., different actors or time frames), thus, making future studies of soft power more structured and comparable. Bearing in mind Johann Wolfgang von Goethe's time-honored dictum, "Dear friend, all theory is grey,/ And green life's golden tree,"[108] the study at hand time and again seeks to elucidate the introduced taxonomy with a wide range of empirical examples.

Additionally, the present study charters the way toward a substantiated empirical analysis of the workings of soft power in international relations not only by introducing a theoretical-conceptual elaboration but also by providing resilient methodological approaches. Navigating both the Scylla of selectiveness and the Charybdis of generalization, the work in hand thus argues that any substantiated empirical study should be (1) comprehensive in its analysis by drawing on the entire taxonomy of soft power presented (as opposed to addressing just selected aspects as is frequently done in literature); (2) focused on a distinct soft power relationship between two (or more) selected actors; (3) comparative in its nature in order to allow for the detection of possible soft power shifts (between actors or over a given period of time); and (4) spanning an extended and carefully selected period of time allowing for resilient results (rather than picking just one individual point in time). Taken together, these methodological approaches, to be addressed and justified in greater detail below, not least pay tribute to major conceptual requirements set by the very nature of soft power itself.

Todd Hall, very much in line with Nye's demand quoted at the very outset of this paragraph, has pointed out in 2010, "The concept of soft power, given its adaptations by both practitioners and students of international relations, has so far led a dual

---

[107]See below, Chap. 3.

[108]Johann Wolfgang von Goethe, *Faust: A Dramatic Poem*, Translated into English Verse by Theodore Martin (Edinburgh: William Blackwood & Sons, 1871), p. 92. (Act II, Scene I – Faust's Study).

existence as a category of practice and a category of analysis."[109] The present study, by providing both a theoretical-conceptual elaboration as well as a methodological roadmap for a substantiated empirical analysis of the workings of soft power in international relations, seeks to bridge this divide.

Bearing in mind the long traditions as well as persistent controversies regarding the study of power, Joseph Nye has aptly cautioned, "There are no final answers about power."[110] While mindful of this insight, the work in handsets out to at least address some persisting questions and by introducing a comprehensive taxonomy of soft power it endeavors to provide some new perspectives. Far from claiming to provide "final answers," it thus seeks to contribute to our understanding of one of the fundamental phenomena in the international relations and, indeed, the *conditio humana*.

References

Anholt, Simon. "Soft Power." *Internationale Politik* (January/February 2014), pp. 48–53.

Arquilla, John and David Ronfeldt. *The Emergence of Noopolitik: Toward an American Information Strategy*. Santa Monica, Cal.: RAND Corporation, 1999.

Arquilla, John and David Ronfeldt. "Noopolitik: A New Paradigm for Public Diplomacy." In *Routledge Handbook of Public Diplomacy*, edited by Nancy Snow and Philip M. Taylor, pp. 352–365. New York, N.Y.: Routledge, 2009.

Auer, Claudia, Alice Srugies, and Martin Löffelholz. "Schlüsselbegriffe der internationalen Diskussion: Public Diplomacy und Soft Power." In *Kultur und Außenpolitik: Handbuch für Wissenschaft und Praxis*, edited by Kurt-Jürgen Maaß, pp. 39–54. Baden Baden: Nomos Verlagsgesellschaft, 2015.

Barber, Benjamin R. "McWorld vs. Jihad." *The Atlantic Monthly* (March 1992). Online at: http://www.theatlantic.com/magazine/archive/1992/03/jihad-vs-mcworld/303882/ (accessed September 4, 2017).

Baumann, Peter and Gisela Cramer. "Power, Soft or Deep? An Attempt at Constructive Criticism." *Las Torres de Lucca: International Journal of Political Philosophy*, No. 10 (January–June 2017), pp. 177–214.

Blair, Tony. "Address by the Right Honorable Tony Blair, Prime Minister of the United Kingdom of Great Britain and Northern Ireland." Washington, D.C., July 13, 2003. In *Congressional Record: Proceedings and Debates of the 108th Congress, First Session, Vol. 149 – Part 14, July 17, 2003 to July 25 2003*, pp. 18596–18598. Washington, D.C.: United States Government Printing Office, 2003.

Blanchard Jean-Marc F. and Fujia Lu. "Thinking Hard about Soft Power: A Review and Critique of the Literature on China and Soft Power." *Asian Perspective* Vol. 36, No. 4 (2012), pp. 565–589.

Brooks, Stephen G. and William C. Wohlforth. *America Abroad: The United States' Global Role in the 21st Century*. New York, N.Y.: Oxford University Press, 2016.

Bulwer-Lytton, Edward. *Richelieu; Or, The Conspiracy: A Play, in Five Acts*. London: Saunders and Otley, 1839.

Chang, Gordon H. *Fateful Ties: A History of America's Preoccupation with China*. Cambridge, Mass.: Harvard University Press, 2015.

---

[109] Hall, "An Unclear Attraction," p. 195.

[110] Nye, "Responding to My Critics and Concluding Thoughts" p. 226.

Chitty, Naren, Li Ji, Gary D. Rawnsley, and Craig Hayden, eds. *The Routledge Handbook of Soft Power*. Abingdon: Routledge, 2017.

Cohen, Eliot A. "Is Trump Ending the American Era?." *The Atlantic* (October 2017), pp. 69–73.

Commuri, Gitika. "'Are You Pondering What I am Pondering?' Understanding the Conditions Under Which States Gain and Loose Soft Power." In *Power in the 21st Century: International Security and International Political Economy in a Changing World*, edited by Enrico Fels, Jan-Frederik Kremer, and Katharina Kronenberg, pp. 43–57. Berlin: Springer-Verlag, 2012.

Cronin, Vincent. *The Florentine Renaissance*. London: Pimlico, 1992.

Davies, Norman. *Vanished Kingdoms: The Rise and Fall of States and Nations*. New York, N.Y.: Viking, 2011.

Dürrenmatt, Friedrich. "Kunst und Wissenschaft." In *Versuche/Kants Hoffnung: Essays und Reden*, pp. 72–97. Zürich: Diogenes, 1998.

Falk, Richard. *Power Shift: On the New Global Order*. London: Zed Books, 2016.

Ferguson, Niall. *Colossus: The Price of America's Empire*. New York, N.Y.: Penguin Press, 2004.

Fraser, Matthew. *Weapons of Mass Distraction: Soft Power and American Empire*. New York, N. Y.: St. Martin's Press, 2003.

Gallarotti, Giulio M. *Cosmopolitan Power in International Relations: A Synthesis of Realism, Neoliberalism, and Constructivism*. Cambridge: Cambridge University Press, 2010.

Gallarotti, Giulio M. "Smart Power: Definitions, Importance, and Effectiveness." *Journal of Strategic Studies*, Vol. 38, No. 3 (2015), pp. 245-281.

George, Alexander L. and Andrew Bennett. *Case Studies and Theory Development in the Social Sciences*. Cambridge, Mass.: MIT Press, 2005.

Geschwend, Thomas and Frank Schimmelfennig. "Introduction: Designing Research in Political Science – A Dialogue between Theory and Data." In *Research Design in Political Science: How to Practice What They Preach*, edited by Thomas Geschwend and Frank Schimmelfennig, pp. 1–18. Basingstoke: Palgrave Macmillan, 2011.

Gilboa, Eytan. "Searching for a Theory of Public Diplomacy." *The Annals of the American Academy of Political and Social Science*, Vol. 616, Public Diplomacy in a Changing World (March 2008), pp. 55–77.

Goethe, Johann Wolfgang von. *Faust: A Dramatic Poem*. Translated into English Verse by Theodore Martin. Edinburgh: William Blackwood & Sons, 1871.

Goldsmith, Benjamin E. and Yusaku Horiuchi. "In Search of Soft Power: Does Foreign Public Opinion Matter for US Foreign Policy?." *World Politics*, Vol. 64, No. 3 (July 2012), pp. 555–585.

Graves, Robert. *I, Claudius*. London: Collector's Library, 2013.

Gu, Xuewu. "Ist Globalität gestaltbar?." In *Bonner Enzyklopädie der Globalität*, edited by Ludger Kühnhardt and Tilman Mayer, pp. 1527–1541. Wiesbaden: Springer Fachmedien, 2017.

Hall, Edith. "Adventures in Ancient Greek and Roman Libraries." In *The Meaning of the Library: A Cultural History*, edited by Alice Crawford, pp. 1–30. Princeton, N.J.: Princeton University Press, 2015.

Hall, Todd. "An Unclear Attraction: A Critical Examination of Soft Power as an Analytical Category." *The Chinese Journal of International Politics*, Vol. 3, No. 2 (2010), pp. 189–211.

Han, Byung-Chul. *Was ist Macht?*. Stuttgart: Reclam, 2005.

Hancké, Bob. "The Challenge of Research Design." In *Theory and Methods in Political Science*, edited by David Marsh and Gerry Stoker, pp. 232–248. Basingstoke: Palgrave Macmillan, 2010.

Hayden, Craig. "Scope, Mechanism, and Outcome: Arguing Soft Power in the Context of Public Diplomacy." *Journal of International Relations and Development*, Vol. 20, No. 2 (2017), pp. 331–357.

Heather, Peter. *The Fall of the Roman Empire: A New History*. London: Pan Books, 2006.

Herodotus. *The History*. Translated from the Ancient Greece by George Rawlinson, Volume I. New York, N.Y.: The Tandy-Thomas Company, 1909 (Hdt.).

Hodge, James F., Jr. "A Global Power Shift in the Making." *Foreign Affairs*, Vol. 83, No. 4 (July/August 2004), pp. 2–7.

Ifantis, Kostas. "Soft Power: Overcoming the Limits of a Concept." In *Routledge Handbook of Diplomacy and Statecraft*, edited by B. J. C. McKercher, pp. 441–452. Abingdon: Routledge, 2011.

Keohane, Robert O. and Joseph S. Nye, Jr. *Power and Independence: World Politics in Transition*. Boston, Mass.: Little Brown and Company, 1977.

King, Gary, Robert O. Keohane, and Sidney Verba. *Designing Social Inquiry: Scientific Inference in Qualitative Research*. Princeton, N.J.: Princeton University Press, 1994.

Kipling, Rudyard. "Recessional." *The Times*, July 17, 1897, p. 13.

Kissinger, Henry. *On China*. London: Allen Lane, 2011.

Kissinger, Henry. *World Order: Reflections on the Character of Nations and the Course of History*. London: Allen Lane, 2014.

Lange, Matthew. *Comparative-Historical Methods*. Los Angeles, Cal.: SAGE Publications, 2013.

Layne, Christopher. "The Unbearable Lightness of Soft Power." In *Soft Power and US Foreign Policy: Theoretical, Historical and Contemporary Perspectives*, edited by Inderjeet Parmar and Michael Cox, pp. 51–82. Abingdon: Routledge, 2010.

Lee, Geun. "A Theory of Soft Power and Korea's Soft Power Strategy." *The Korean Journal of Defense Analysis*, Vol. 21, No. 2 (June 2009), pp. 205–218.

Lehnert, Matthias, Bernhard Miller, and Arndt Wonka. "Increasing the Relevance of Research Questions: Considerations on Theoretical and Social Relevance in Social Science." In *Research Design in Political Science: How to Practice What They Preach*, edited by Thomas Geschwend and Frank Schimmelfennig, pp. 21–38. Basingstoke: Palgrave Macmillan, 2011.

Mahoney, James and Dietrich Rueschemeyer. "Comparative Historical Analysis: Achievements and Agendas." In *Comparative Historical Analysis in the Social Sciences*, edited by James Mahoney and Dietrich Rueschemeyer, pp. 3–38. Cambridge: Cambridge University Press, 2003.

Mahoney, James and Dietrich Rueschemeyer, eds. *Comparative Historical Analysis in the Social Sciences*. Cambridge: Cambridge University Press, 2003.

Mahoney, James and Kathleen Thelen, eds. *Advances in Comparative-Historical Analysis*. Cambridge: Cambridge University Press, 2015.

Mandelbaum, Michael. *Mission Failure: America and the World in the Post-Cold War Era*. New York, N.Y.: Oxford University Press, 2016.

Mattern, Janice Bially. "Why 'Soft Power' Isn't So Soft: Representational Force and the Sociolinguistic Construction of Attraction in World Politics." *Millennium: Journal of International Studies*, Vol. 33, No. 3 (2005), pp. 583–612.

Melissen, Jan. "The New Public Diplomacy: Between Theory and Practice." In *The New Public Diplomacy: Soft Power in International Relations*, edited by Jan Melissen, pp. 3–27. Basingstoke: Palgrave Macmillan, 2005.

Nietzsche, Friedrich. *Philosophy in the Tragic Age of the Greeks*. Translated, with an Introduction by Marianne Cowan. Washington, D.C.: Regnery Publishing, 1962.

Nye, Joseph S., Jr. *Bound to Lead: The Changing Nature of American Power*. New York: Basic Books, 1990.

Nye, Joseph S., Jr. "The Changing Nature of World Power." *Political Science Quarterly*, Vol. 105, No. 2 (Summer 1990), pp. 177–192.

Nye, Joseph S., Jr. "Soft Power." *Foreign Policy*, No. 80 (Autumn 1990), pp. 153–171.

Nye, Joseph S., Jr. *Soft Power: The Means to Success in World Politics*. New York, N.Y.: PublicAffairs, 2004.

Nye, Joseph S., Jr. "The Future of Soft Power in US Foreign Policy." In *Soft Power and US Foreign Policy: Theoretical, Historical and Contemporary Perspectives*, edited by Inderjeet Parmar and Michael Cox, pp. 4–11. Abingdon: Routledge, 2010.

Nye, Joseph S., Jr. "Responding to My Critics and Concluding Thoughts." In *Soft Power and US Foreign Policy: Theoretical, Historical and Contemporary Perspectives*, edited by Inderjeet Parmar and Michael Cox, pp. 215–227. Abingdon: Routledge, 2010.

Nye, Joseph S., Jr. *The Future of Power*. New York, N.Y.: PublicAffairs, 2011.

Nye, Joseph S., Jr. "The War on Soft Power." *Foreign Policy*, April 12, 2011. Online at: http://foreignpolicy.com/2011/04/12/the-war-on-soft-power/ (accessed September 4, 2017).

O'Neill, Jim. "Building Better Global Economic BRICs." *Global Economics Paper No: 66*, Goldman Sachs, November 30, 2001. Online at: http://www.goldmansachs.com/our-thinking/archive/archive-pdfs/build-better-brics.pdf (accessed September 4, 2017).

Ovid (P. Ovidius Naso). *Metamorphosen: Metamorphoseon Libri*. Translated and Edited by Erich Rösch, with an Introduction by Niklas Holzberg. München: Artemis & Winkler 1992 (Ov. Met.).

Parmar, Inderjeet and Michael Cox, eds. *Soft Power and US Foreign Policy: Theoretical, Historical and Contemporary Perspectives*. Abingdon: Routledge, 2010.

Patalakh, Artem. "Assessment of Soft Power Strategies: Towards an Aggregative Analytical Model for Country-Focused Case Study Research." *Croatian International Relations Review*, Vol. 22, No. 76 (2016), pp. 85–112.

Roselle, Laura, Alister Miskimmon, and Ben O'Loughlin. "Strategic Narrative: A New Means to Understand Soft Power." *Media, War & Conflict*, Vol. 7, No. 1 (2014), pp. 70–84.

Solomon, Ty. "The Affective Underpinnings of Soft Power." *European Journal of International Relations*, Vol. 20, No. 3 (2014), pp. 720–741.

Su Changhe. "Soft Power." In *The Oxford Handbook of Modern Diplomacy*, edited by Andrew F. Cooper, Jorge Heine, and Ramesh Thakur, pp. 544–558. Oxford: Oxford University Press, 2013.

Thelen, Kathleen and James Mahoney. "Comparative-Historical Analysis in Contemporary Political Science." In *Advances in Comparative-Historical Analysis*, edited by James Mahoney and Kathleen Thelen, pp. 3–36. Cambridge: Cambridge University Press, 2015.

Weidenfeld, Werner. *America and Europe: Is the Break Inevitable?*. Gütersloh: Bertelsmann Foundation Publishers, 1996.

Wyne, Ali S. "Public Opinion and Power." In *Routledge Handbook of Public Diplomacy*, edited by Nancy Snow and Philip M. Taylor, pp. 39–49. New York, N.Y.: Routledge, 2009.

Yasushi, Watanabe and David L. McConnell, eds. *Soft Power Superpowers: Cultural and National Assets of Japan and the United States* (Armonk, N.Y.: M.E. Sharpe, 2008).

Zaharna, R. S. *The Cultural Awakening in Public Diplomacy, CPD Perspectives on Public Diplomacy, Paper 4, 2012*. Los Angeles, Cal.: Figueroa Press, 2012.

Zahran, Geraldo and Leonardo Ramos. "From Hegemony to Soft Power: Implications of a Conceptual Change." In *Soft Power and US Foreign Policy: Theoretical, Historical and Contemporary Perspectives*, edited by Inderjeet Parmar and Michael Cox, pp. 12–31. Abingdon: Routledge, 2010.

Zakaria, Fareed. "The Future of American Power: How America Can Survive the Rise of the Rest." *Foreign Affairs*, Vol. 87, No. 3 (May/June 2008), pp. 18–43.

Zakaria, Fareed. *The Post-American World: And the Rise of the Rest*. London: Penguin Books, 2009.

Chapter 2
Power in International Relations: Understandings and Varieties

"Power," Joseph Nye aptly noted, "is like the weather. Everyone depends on it and talks about it, but few understand it."[1] In line with this assessment, power today unquestionably constitutes one of the most central concepts within the social sciences in general and International Relations in particular.[2] Just like the weather, to stick with Nye's comparison, it seems to have an immense influence on virtually all aspects of human life. In fact, ever since people started to philosophize about the world around them, their self, and the society in which they are set, power has been at the very core of this reasoning. In recent years, particularly after the incisive events of September 11, 2001, however, the discourse on power in International Relations theory gained even greater importance and reappeared at the very top of the agenda.[3] In the twenty-first century, which according to legions of observers has already been experiencing shifts in the distribution and characteristics of power in

---

[1]Joseph S. Nye, Jr., *Soft Power: The Means to Success in World Politics* (New York, N.Y.: PublicAffairs, 2004), p. 1.

[2]For the centrality of power in the social sciences and particularly International Relations see, for example, David A. Baldwin, "Power and International Relations," in *Handbook of International Relations*, eds. Walter Carlsnaes, Thomas Risse, and Beth A. Simmons (Los Angeles, Cal.: SAGE Publications, 2013), pp. 273–274 & p. 280; Mark Haugaard and Stewart R. Clegg, "Introduction: Why Power is the Central Concept of the Social Sciences," in *The SAGE Handbook of Power*, eds. Stewart R. Clegg and Mark Haugaard (London: SAGE Publications, 2009), p. 1; Joshua S. Goldstein and Jon C. Pevehouse, *International Relations* (New York, N.Y.: Pearson Longman, 2014), p. 45; Juliet Kaarbo and James Lee Ray, *Global Politics* (Boston, Mass.: Wadsworth, 2011), p. 98; Enrico Fels, "Power Shift? Power in International Relations and the Allegiance of Middle Powers," in *Power in the 21st Century: International Security and International Political Economy in a Changing World*, eds. Enrico Fels, Jan-Frederik Kremer, and Katharina Kronenberg (Berlin: Springer-Verlag, 2012), p. 5; and Geraldo Zahran and Leonardo Ramos, "From Hegemony to Soft Power: Implications of a Conceptual Change," in *Soft Power and US Foreign Policy: Theoretical, Historical and Contemporary Perspectives*, eds. Inderjeet Parmar and Michael Cox (Abingdon: Routledge, 2010), p. 16.

[3]Michael Barnett and Raymond Duvall, "Power in International Politics," *International Organization*, Vol. 59, No. 1 (Winter 2005), p. 39.

© Springer Nature Switzerland AG 2020
H. W. Ohnesorge, *Soft Power*, Global Power Shift,
https://doi.org/10.1007/978-3-030-29922-4_2

the international system, as argued above, questions concerning the varieties and mechanisms of power are, therefore, more topical than ever.[4] Accordingly, underlining its centrality, power has in the recent past variably been described as constituting "the true reserve currency in international affairs,"[5] "the currency of world politics,"[6] or "the platinum coin of the international realm."[7] Significantly, despite fundamental differences in various other regards, this estimate of the centrality of power is shared across different theoretical schools in International Relations.[8]

At the same time, power remains a topic of extensive academic debate including various, sometimes even contradictory, definitions and conceptions.[9] As a result, the phenomenon of power still is not satisfactory, and much less conclusively, elucidated in its highly complex mechanisms and processes. It is in this very vein, offering yet another comparison from the world of nature, that Paul Pierson has aptly pointed out, "Power is like an iceberg; at any moment in time most of it lies below the waterline."[10] Consequently, the phenomenon of power shall be discussed in greater detail in the following, in this way facilitating to cast a searching glance below the waterline.

2.1 Definitional Approximations

For that purpose, it is particularly important to first of all present a working definition of power, not least since its very understanding may shape the academic and political discourse about it.[11] As argued, up until today power in international relations

---

[4]William Inboden, "What is Power? And How Much of It Does America Have?," *The American Interest*, Vol. 5, No. 2 (November/December 2009), p. 15.

[5]Daniel W. Drezner, "Does Obama Have a Grand Strategy? Why We Need Doctrines in Uncertain Times," *Foreign Affairs*, Vol. 58, No. 4 (July/August 2011), p. 59.

[6]Janice Bially Mattern, "Why 'Soft Power' Isn't So Soft: Representational Force and the Sociolinguistic Construction of Attraction in World Politics," *Millennium: Journal of International Studies*, Vol. 33, No. 3 (2005), p. 587.

[7]Leslie H. Gelb, *Power Rules: How Common Sense Can Rescue American Foreign Policy* (New York, N.Y.: HarperCollins, 2009), p. 26.

[8]See, for example, Alexander Wendt, *Social Theory of International Politics* (Cambridge: Cambridge University Press, 1999), pp. 96–97 and Stefano Guzzini, *Power, Realism and Constructivism* (Abingdon: Routledge, 2013), p. 47.

[9]R. S. Zaharna, *The Cultural Awakening in Public Diplomacy, CPD Perspectives on Public Diplomacy, Paper 4, 2012* (Los Angeles, Cal.: Figueroa Press, 2012), p. 42.

[10]Paul Pierson, "Power and Path Dependence," in *Advances in Comparative-Historical Analysis*, eds. James Mahoney and Kathleen Thelen (Cambridge: Cambridge University Press, 2015), p. 124.

[11]Stefano Guzzini, "The Concept of Power: A Constructivist Analysis," *Millennium: Journal of International Studies*, Vol. 33, No. 3 (2005), p. 508.

constitutes one of the most debated and contested concepts.[12] Steven Lukes, one of the foremost scholars on the issue, even noted that "the concept of power is troublesomely controversial"[13] and elsewhere he held that "disputes over how to define and recognize power are endless."[14] Xuewu Gu likewise pointed out that "[t]he study of 'power' is probably among the most arduous tasks in the realm of International Relations."[15] Byung-Chul Han, to provide a final example of this widely shared perception, attested a theoretical confusion and even chaos regarding the concept of power.[16] Consequently, while over the centuries many thinkers and writers have offered various definitions of and approaches to the five-letter word, building on their respective predecessors, rejecting some aspects and adopting others, there is still no general agreement of what power is and how it works.[17] In the following, definitions and concepts that are fundamental for our understanding of power today shall be presented without making any claims to completeness but rather by including those definitions, which have been of particular prominence and lasting influence on the field.[18]

Seeking a first approximation, one might start by consulting the dictionary. The *Oxford Dictionary of English*, for example, defines power (among other things) as "the ability or capacity to direct or influence the behaviour of others or the course of events."[19] Such a general definition, though valuable, can, of course, only serve as a starting point for anyone doing research on the phenomenon of power in the social sciences. A glance at some classical political writers and philosophers offers more instructive hints in this regard, yet. Thus, in Greek philosophical tradition the topic of power became a prominent subject of reasoning and writing: fifth century BC

---

[12]Kenneth N. Waltz, "Reflections on Theory of International Politics: A Response to My Critics," in *Neorealism and its Critics*, ed. Robert O. Keohane (New York, N.Y.: Columbia University Press, 1986), p. 333; Barnett and Duvall, "Power in International Politics," p. 66.

[13]Steven Lukes, "Power and the Battle for the Hearts and Minds," *Millennium: Journal of International Studies*, Vol. 33, No. 3 (2005), p. 484.

[14]Steven Lukes, "Power," in *The Oxford Companion to International Relations*, ed. Joel Krieger, Volume 2 (Oxford: Oxford University Press, 2014), p. 197.

[15]Xuewu Gu, "Global Power Shift: Soft, Hard and Structural Power," in *Die Gestaltung der Globalität: Annährungen an Begriff, Deutung und Methodik*, eds. Ludger Kühnhardt and Tilman Mayer (Bonn: Zentrum für Europäische Integrationsforschung, Discussion Paper C198, 2010), p. 53.

[16]Byung-Chul Han, *Was ist Macht?* (Stuttgart: Reclam, 2005), p. 7.

[17]Baldwin, "Power and International Relations," p. 273 & p. 281.

[18]Anthologies compiling approaches on power in international relations from different theoretical perspectives are numerous, e.g., Richard J. Stoll and Michael D. Ward, eds., *Power in World Politics* (Boulder, Colo.: Lynne Rienner Publishers, 1989); Mark Haugaard, *Power: A Reader* (Manchester: Manchester University Press, 2002); Felix Berenskoetter and M. J. Williams, eds., *Power in World Politics* (New York, N.Y.: Routledge, 2007); Stewart R. Clegg and Mark Haugaard, eds., *The SAGE Handbook of Power* (London: SAGE Publications, 2009); Keith Dowding, ed., *Encyclopedia of Power* (Thousand Oaks, Cal.: SAGE Publications, 2011).

[19]*Oxford Dictionary of English*, ed. Angus Stevenson (Oxford: Oxford University Press, 2010), p. 1393.

sophists such as Polus or Callicles reflected about the issue of power as did Thucydides, Socrates, Aristotle, and—perhaps most prominently—Plato. In the Roman Republic of the first century BC, the orator, philosopher, and politician M. Tullius Cicero famously distinguished, building on older Roman traditions, between different varieties of power (to be elaborated upon below), a distinction, which became vital in the Principate and was later adopted by the Roman Catholic Church and the Holy See.[20] Turning from these early thinkers and writers on the issue of power to classic political philosophers of the modern era, Thomas Hobbes, counted among the intellectual progenitors of classical realism,[21] defined power as an actor's "present means, to obtain some future apparent Good" and famously claimed, "Reputation of power, is Power."[22] John Locke, often called the father of liberalism, recognized the relational character of power and presented a twofold definition of power as being "able to make, or able to receive, any change."[23] In the *Federalist Papers*, that great compendium to the U.S. Constitution published in 1787/1788 in New York newspapers, Alexander Hamilton who as one of the U.S. Founding Fathers had profoundly been influenced by Locke's philosophy, rhetorically asked, "What is a power but the ability or faculty of doing a thing?"[24] Moving on from these seventeenth- and eighteenth-century classics and considering more recent writers on the issue, power was defined by British philosopher Bertrand Russell in his eponymous work, quite simply, "as the production of intended outcomes."[25] Writing a decade after Russell, the father of classical realism in International Relations, Hans J. Morgenthau, provided another definition in his meanwhile classical *Politics Among Nations*, first published in 1948. According to Morgenthau, power—in his view, both the ultimate end and means of international politics—can be defined as "man's control over the minds and action of other men."[26] From a neorealist perspective, in the words of its premier proponent Kenneth N. Waltz, power is understood as "the capacity to produce an intended effect."[27]

---

[20]Wilfried Nippel, "The Roman Notion of *Auctoritas*," in *The Concept of Authority: A Multidisciplinary Approach, From Epistemology to the Social Sciences*, eds. Pasquale Pasquino and Pamela Harris (Rome: Fondazione Adriano Olivetti, 2007), pp. 13–34. See below, Sect. 2.5.1.2.

[21]Xuewu Gu, *Theorien der Internationalen Beziehungen: Einführung* (Berlin: Walter de Gruyter, 2018), p. 59.

[22]Thomas Hobbes, *Leviathan*, With an Essay by the Late W. G. Pogson Smith (Oxford: Clarendon Press, 1909), p. 66.

[23]John Locke, "An Essay Concerning Human Understanding," in *Great Books of the Western World*, ed. Robert Maynard Hutchins, Volume 35 (Chicago, Ill.: Encyclopædia Britannica, 1952), p. 178.

[24]Alexander Hamilton, "Federalist No. 33," in *The Federalist Papers*, ed. Clinton Rossiter (New York, N.Y.: Signet Classic, 2003), p. 198.

[25]Bertrand Russell, *Power: A New Social Analysis* (London: George Allen and Unwin, 1938), p. 35.

[26]Hans J. Morgenthau, *Politics Among Nations: The Struggle for Power and Peace* (New York, N. Y.: McGraw-Hill, 2006), p. 30.

[27]Kenneth N. Waltz, *Man, the State and War: A Theoretical Analysis* (New York, N.Y.: Columbia University Press, 1959), p. 205.

German sociologist Max Weber offered yet another—and perhaps even the most frequently cited—definition of power. In one of the last century's most fundamental writings on sociology and political science, Weber hence famously presented a more detailed definition of power as a relationship and argued that power is "the probability that one actor within a social relationship will be in a position to carry out his own will despite resistance, regardless of the basis on which that probability rests."[28] Xuewu Gu has rightly observed the importance in Weber's choice of words and pointed to the significance of "probability" rather than "capability" as an indicator of the contextuality of power.[29] Like the phenomenon of contextuality, the augmentation "regardless of the basis on which that probability rests" of Weber's definition shall be picked up again in the course of this chapter.[30]

Building on this definition and emphasizing the understanding of power as a relationship, Robert A. Dahl devised the seemingly simple formula, "A has power over B to the extent that A can get B to do something that B would not otherwise do."[31] Central to this definition, which some consider among the best attempts to define power up to this day and which shall be at the core of the work in hand, is that power results in the *changed* behavior on the part of B.[32] Joseph Nye offered two further definitions of power (which in itself may be regarded as additional evidence for the intricacy of defining power, if any was needed) as "the ability to achieve one's purposes or goals"[33] and, more recently, "the ability to influence the behavior of others to get the outcomes one wants."[34] With these definitions—bringing the examples referred to above full circle—Nye subscribed to "an agent-focused definition of power that was quite close to the common usage implied by the dictionary."[35]

As has already been mentioned, the above discussion of definitional approximations is by no means intended to be exhaustive. However, it offers a sufficient basis for further examination of different concepts of power. Additionally, the very variety of definitions and understandings not least hints at the fact that power in international relations still is a highly contested and extensively discussed phenomenon today.

---

[28]Max Weber, *The Theory of Social and Economic Organization*, Translated by A. M. Henderson and Talcott Parsons, Edited with an Introduction by Talcott Parsons (New York, N.Y.: Free Press, 1947), p. 152.

[29]Xuewu Gu, "Strukturelle Macht: Eine dritte Machtquelle?," *Österreichische Zeitschrift für Politikwissenschaft*, Vol. 41, No. 3 (2012), p. 266.

[30]See below, Sect. 2.2.

[31]Robert A. Dahl, "The Concept of Power," *Behavioral Science*, Vol. 2, No. 3 (1957), pp. 202–203.

[32]Gelb, *Power Rules*, p. 32. See also Ernest J. Wilson III, "Hard Power, Soft Power, Smart Power," *The Annals of the American Academy of Political and Social Sciences*, Vol. 616, Public Diplomacy in a Changing World (March 2008), p. 114.

[33]Joseph S. Nye, Jr., *Bound to Lead: The Changing Nature of American Power* (New York: Basic Books, 1990), pp. 25–26.

[34]Nye, *Soft Power*, p. 2.

[35]Joseph S. Nye, Jr., "Notes for a Soft-Power Research Agenda," in *Power in World Politics*, eds. Felix Berenskoetter and M. J. Williams (New York, N.Y.: Routledge, 2008), p. 163.

However, while various concepts of and approaches to power exist, this juxtaposition of varying understandings of power should not necessarily result in a competition between the concepts, rather they should be considered interconnected and complementary. Only by accepting "power's polymorphous character,"[36] a deeper understanding of international politics can, thus, be reached.

2.2 Varieties of Power

"Power," as Joseph Nye has fittingly argued, "comes in many guises."[37] In fact, already the classical definition of power by Max Weber referred to above—"the probability that one actor within a social relationship will be in a position to carry out his own will despite resistance, regardless of the basis on which that probability rests"[38]—indicates different varieties—or "bases"—of power. It is in this vein that Bertrand Russell, for example, argued that "power has many forms, such as wealth, armaments, civil authority, influence on opinion."[39] Russell, thus, offered an early attempt to classify power into different categories. Accordingly, he distinguished between "direct physical power," "rewards and punishments as inducements," and "influence on opinion," the latter of which including the "opportunity for creating desired habits in others."[40] Similarly, Joseph Nye, who propagated the idea of soft power some 60 years after Russell's writings, argued that "there are several ways to affect the behavior of others. You can coerce them with threats; you can induce them with payments; or you can attract and co-pot them to want what you want."[41] This triad of coercion and inducement on the one hand and attraction on the other hand has led to the meanwhile classic—if somewhat simplifying—dichotomy of hard and soft power.[42] Along these lines, we shall in the following first briefly deal with the power of coercion and inducement, frequently subsumed under the term hard power, while subsequently special emphasis shall be put on the variety of soft power, the concept of power at the very core of the work in hand.

---

[36]Barnett and Duvall, "Power in International Politics," p. 40 & p. 44. See also Wilson, "Hard Power, Soft Power, Smart Power," p. 37.

[37]Joseph S. Nye, Jr., "Soft Power and Higher Education," *Forum Futures 2005*, EDUCAUSE, January 1, 2005, online at: https://net.educause.edu/ir/library/pdf/ffp0502s.pdf (accessed February 19, 2015).

[38]Weber, The Theory of Social and Economic Organization, p. 152.

[39]Russell, *Power*, pp. 10–11.

[40]Russell, *Power*, pp. 35–36.

[41]Nye, *Soft Power*, p. 2.

[42]However, as we shall see later, the distinction between the two is not always as clear-cut in the field as it may appear on paper and with the introduction of structural power, a third dimension has been put forward. Additionally, there are further criteria along whose lines different varieties of power may be distinguished (e.g., relational and resource-based understandings of power). For a recent discussion on the dichotomy of power, see Xuewu Gu, "Strukturelle Macht," pp. 259–276.

   Traditionally, the mark of great power has been its ability to prevail in the armed confrontation with reliance on its military and economic capabilities.[43] Joseph Nye referred to these two sources of hard power as "sticks" and "carrots."[44] In the words of Founding Father and fourth U.S. President James Madison this dyad of power is epitomized by "the sword" and "the purse."[45] The significance of and interplay between a nation's military might (or "sword") and its economic strength (or "purse"), can perhaps best be illustrated by considering them to constitute the two faces of a coin: applying terms of numismatics, they constitute the obverse and reverse of what may be called the hard power coin.

   In terms of this image, on the obverse (also known as heads) of the hard power coin, the recourse to coercion, intimidation, and threats is embossed, that is, the coercive "sticks." In international relations, this form of power is generally associated with a nation's military forces and capabilities. It is in this vein that John J. Mearsheimer argued that "a state's actual power is embedded mainly in its army and the air and naval forces that directly support it."[46] Ranging from the active use of military force to intimidation through threats and deterrence, the head side of the hard power coin itself offers different scales of power application and allows for distinctions between offensive and defensive power.[47] While classical realists throughout the ages—such as Thucydides, Thomas Hobbes or, more recently, Hans Morgenthau—consider human nature as the primary source for the perpetual application of force and the continual strife for (ever greater) power in international relations,[48] more structurally minded realists like Kenneth N. Waltz, John J. Mearsheimer, and Stephen M. Walt ascribe formative importance to the structure of the international system characterized as a "self-help system."[49]

   On the reverse of the hard power coin (also known as tails), to return to the image introduced above, a nation's economic prowess is imprinted, that is, the inducing "carrots." Again, instruments vary greatly between different scales of inducement, ranging from payments to economic sanctions. Sometimes measures like economic sanctions mark the first stage in a conflict between nations and are followed by military actions; sometimes sanctions and military actions go hand in hand (think of

---

[43]Paul Kennedy, *The Rise and Fall of the Great Powers* (New York, N.Y.: Vintage Books, 1987), p. xv. See also A. J. P. Taylor, *The Struggle for Mastery in Europe, 1848–1918* (Oxford: Oxford University Press, 1954), p. xxix.

[44]Nye, *Soft Power*, p. 5.

[45]James Madison, "Helvidius Number I," in *The Pacificus-Helvidius Debates of 1793-1794: Toward the Completion of the American Founding, Alexander Hamilton and James Madison*, Edited and with an Introduction by Morton J. Frisch (Indianapolis, Ind.: Liberty Fund, 2007), p. 62.

[46]John J. Mearsheimer, "Anarchy and the Struggle for Power," in *Essential Readings in World Politics*, eds. Karen Mingst and Jack Snyder (New York, N.Y.: W. W. Norton and Company, 2008), p. 68.

[47]Jamie Gaskarth, *British Foreign Policy: Crises, Conflicts and Future Challenges* (Cambridge: Polity Press, 2013), p. 120.

[48]Morgenthau, *Politics Among Nations*, p. 4.

[49]See, for example, Waltz, *Man, the State and War*, pp. 159–223.

the Continental System imposed by Napoleon against the British in the early nineteenth century or the sanctions imposed by the United Nations Security Council against Iraq after its invasion of Kuwait in 1990). At it, both military and economic strengths are almost inextricably linked, as economic prowess frequently translates into military capabilities. For example, during World War II, as Paul Kennedy matter-of-factly put it, U. S. shipyards were "launching vessels faster than the [enemy] U-boats could sink them."[50] Consequently, Kennedy argued, in that particular conflict, "the countries with the deepest purse had prevailed in the end."[51] However, as we have already seen above, the deepest purse—or even the biggest gun—may not be enough to succeed in world politics today.

Summarizing, power, particularly in the sense of military and economic hard power, is frequently understood in terms of available resources,[52] which commonly "include population, territory, natural resources, economic size, military forces, and political stability, among others."[53] David A. Baldwin defined power resources like these as the "raw materials out of which power relationships are formed."[54] Many writers, particularly from the neorealist school of International Relations, ascribe predominant importance to these categories of power in order to successfully compete in the eternal chess game of international relations.[55] It is true, of course, that power may be a product of visible, countable resources such as money or arms.[56] However, equating the power of a nation merely with its underlying resources alone—including its size or wealth—falls utterly short of reality.[57] This phenomenon, sometimes termed "vehicle fallacy,"[58] raises a couple of problems, which shall be addressed in the following.

---

[50]Kennedy, *The Rise and Fall of the Great Powers*, p. 353.

[51]Kennedy, *The Rise and Fall of the Great Powers*, p. 356.

[52]Baldwin, "Power and International Relations," p. 279.

[53]Nye, *Bound to Lead*, p. 26. See also Su Changhe, "Soft Power," in *The Oxford Handbook of Modern Diplomacy*, eds. Andrew F. Cooper, Jorge Heine, and Ramesh Thakur (Oxford: Oxford University Press, 2013), p. 551.

[54]Baldwin, "Power and International Relations," p. 277.

[55]Gu, *Theorien der Internationalen Beziehungen*, p. 84.

[56]Timo Kivimäki, "'Reason' and 'Power' in Territorial Disputes: The South China Sea," *Asian Journal of Social Science*, Vol. 30, No. 3 (2002), p. 526.

[57]A. F. K. Organski, *World Politics* (New York, N.Y.: Alfred Knopf, 1958), pp. 103–104.

[58]Peter Morriss, *Power: A Philosophical Analysis* (Manchester: Manchester University Press, 2002), p. 18. See also Edward Lock, "Soft Power and Strategy: Developing a 'Strategic' Concept of Power," in *Soft Power and US Foreign Policy: Theoretical, Historical and Contemporary Perspectives*, eds. Inderjeet Parmar and Michael Cox (Abingdon: Routledge, 2010), pp. 45–46.

2.3   The Relative and Contextual Nature of Power

With these intricacies in mind, some essential observations on the nature of power shall be discussed. First, as already indicated by the definitions presented above, power relies on social *relationships*.[59] Influential writers such as Paul Kennedy have hence rightly argued that "power is a relative thing."[60] In fact, classical realist Hans Morgenthau has similarly pointed at the relative nature of power.[61] It is in the same vein that A. F. K. Organski argued that power always requires a relationship between at least two actors and that, furthermore, each and every relationship involves the aspect of power.[62] This observation holds true especially with respect to soft power, insofar as its success or failure depends not only on the actor wielding it but also on the one at its receiving end. "Soft power," Joseph Nye aptly reminded us, "is a dance that requires partners."[63]

Along with the understanding of power as a relationship comes the possibility of asymmetries in the distribution of power between the actors involved. This distribution of power may take different forms under different circumstances and may change from time to time. Thus, power always has to be considered within the *context* in which the power relationships are set.[64] In this very sense, Leslie Gelb pointed out that power is not only "relational" but also "situational" insofar "it depends on the exact circumstances once the pulling and tugging begin."[65] Nye likewise argued,

> Statements about power always depend upon a specified or implied context. Your boss may have great power over you in the workplace, but none in your home. Athletic skills may make a student powerful on the playground, but not in the classroom. And athletic ability in pole vaulting does not mean athletic power in the shot put.[66]

Consequently, it does not suffice to suggest that any state may get the outcomes it wants merely because it has copious resources at its disposal. Particularly when seeking to assess possible shifts in the distribution of power between different actors or across time, the mere reference to power resources—albeit temptingly tangible

---

[59]Han, *Was ist Macht?*, p. 34. See also James MacGregor Burns, *Leadership* (New York, N.Y.: HarperCollins, 2010), p. 11 and David A. Baldwin, "Interdependence and Power: A Conceptual Analysis," *International Organization*, Vol. 34, No. 4 (Autumn 1980), p. 496.

[60]Kennedy, *The Rise and Fall of the Great Powers*, p. 17.

[61]Morgenthau, *Politics Among Nations*, pp. 166–168.

[62]Organski, *World Politics*, pp. 96–98.

[63]Nye, *The Future of Power*, p. 84.

[64]Nye, *Soft Power*, pp. 2–4; see also Nye, *Bound to Lead*, p. 27.

[65]Gelb, *Power Rules*, p. 34.

[66]Joseph S. Nye, Jr., "Responding to My Critics and Concluding Thoughts," in *Soft Power and US Foreign Policy: Theoretical, Historical and Contemporary Perspectives*, eds. Inderjeet Parmar and Michael Cox (Abingdon: Routledge, 2010), p. 220. See also Joseph S. Nye, Jr. "Hard, Soft, and Smart Power," in *The Oxford Handbook of Modern Diplomacy*, eds. Andrew F. Cooper, Jorge Heine, and Ramesh Thakur (Oxford: Oxford University Press, 2013), p. 561.

and measurable—is defective.[67] Rather, the respective context in which respective actors and their relationship are set has to be considered in order to reach substantiated estimations.[68] David A. Baldwin, drawing on his understanding of power resources as the "raw materials" of power relationships, likewise emphasized the importance of context and reminded us that "[t]he accuracy of one's estimate of whether an architect has adequate raw materials to complete his or her project is likely to improve if one first ascertains whether the architect plans to build a birdhouse or a cathedral."[69] To illustrate the point, consider a game of skat. Holding four jacks and a couple of aces may be of great advantage when playing grand, when playing null or ramsch they are more than useless and holding them in such situations is even likely to cause you losing the particular round. (To be sure, some rule variations allow players to declare a grand solo in a round of ramsch—rendering jacks and aces powerful one more in this changed context.) In another—more American—card game analogy, Joseph Nye argued accordingly, "As a first step in any card game, it helps to start by figuring out who is holding the high cards and how many chips they have. Equally important, however, is that policy-makers have the contextual intelligence to understand what game they are playing."[70]

Furthermore, although proverbially the ends may justify the means, the means do not always guarantee the desired ends. Thus—connected with the relational and contextual observations stated above and underlining once more the inadequacy to focus on the sources of power alone—the question of power conversion arises, thus, the phenomenon that resources do not equal outcomes.[71] Power, therefore, cannot always easily be translated into influence due to its relational and highly contextual character.[72] Or, as Steven Lukes put it, "having the means of power is not the same as being powerful."[73] Examples in the history of international politics are numerous: Consider, for instance, the Roman legions in the Germanic woods of which classical authors like Tacitus, Suetonius, or Cassius Dio tell. Even though superiorly trained and equipped, P. Quinctilius Varus' forces, generally considered invincible at the time, suffered a bitter defeat in AD 9 when confronted with the guerilla-like tactics of the Germanic tribes in the Battle of the Teutoburg Forest, a defeat which according to prevailing historical opinion (and despite later campaigns in Germania Magna)

---

[67]Nye, "Responding to My Critics and Concluding Thoughts," p. 221.

[68]Verena Andrei and Volker Rittberger, "Macht, Interessen und Normen: Auswärtige Kulturpolitik und Außenpolitiktheorien illustriert am Beispiel der deutschen auswärtigen Sprachpolitik," in *Kultur und Außenpolitik: Handbuch für Wissenschaft und Praxis*, ed. Kurt-Jürgen Maaß (Baden Baden: Nomos Verlagsgesellschaft, 2015), p. 15.

[69]Baldwin, "Power and International Relations," p. 277.

[70]Nye, "Hard, Soft, and Smart Power," p. 560.

[71]Nye, *Bound to Lead*, p. 27.

[72]Richard Ned Lebow, *A Cultural Theory of International Relations* (Cambridge: Cambridge University Press, 2008), p. 551.

[73]Lukes, "Power and the Battle for the Hearts and Minds," p. 478.

put a halt to permanent Roman expansion beyond the Rhine ad infinitum.[74] Fourteen centuries later, the French knights at Agincourt were likewise far superior in terms of numbers and armaments to the English forces under Henry V, Shakespeare's famed "band of brothers," but likewise they could not convert their overwhelming power resources under the given circumstances and consequently suffered one of the decisive defeats in the Hundred Years' War.[75] Turning to more recent times, during the Vietnam War the United States was, in a way not incomparable to these earlier instances mentioned, unable to achieve its desired outcomes of containing a Communist North Vietnam and preserving a non-Communist South Vietnam despite the overwhelming prevalence in hard power resources. "Tanks," as Joseph Nye has aptly noted in this regard, "are not a great military power resource in swamps or jungles."[76]

The point being made by way of these examples is that a mere focus on resources alone tells us little about an actor's actual power due to the intricacies of relationality, contextuality, and power conversion. Therefore, even though "defining power in terms of resources is a shortcut that policy-makers find useful,"[77] it is necessary to not only focus on the underlying power resources but also on the instruments of wielding power as well as their success or failure in respective relationships and particular circumstances.[78]

2.4 Measuring Power

Along with the desire to define power comes the equally great desire to quantify, measure, and thus compare the power between different actors (or of one actor across time) in order to assess their status in world politics, their prospects for prevailing in conflict, as well as the existence of possible shifts in the global distribution of power. In his *Reflections on the Causes of the Rise and Fall of the Roman Empire* (1734), to offer a classic example of such a quantification, Montesquieu claimed in his attempt

---

[74]Adrian Murdoch, *Rome's Greatest Defeat: Massacre in the Teutoburg Forest* (Stroud: The History Press, 2008), pp. 5 6. See also Peter S. Wells, *The Barbarians Speak: How the Conquered Peoples Shaped Roman Europe* (Princeton, N.J.: Princeton University Press, 1999), pp. 91–92 and Peter S. Wells, *The Battle That Stopped Rome: Emperor Augustus, Arminius, and the Slaughter of the Legions in the Teutoburg Forest* (New York, N.Y.: Norton & Company, 2003), pp. 208–209.

[75]For a fascinating study of the 1415 Battle of Agincourt, see Anne Curry, *The Battle of Agincourt: Sources & Interpretations* (Woodbridge: The Boydell Press, 2000); for estimates of respective troop strengths, see Anne Curry, *Henry V: Playboy Prince to Warrior King* (London: Penguin Books, 2018), p. 66.

[76]Nye, *Soft Power*, p. 12.

[77]Nye, "Hard, Soft, and Smart Power," p. 560.

[78]These insights shall explicitly be taken into account with the subsequent introduction of the soft power taxonomy.

to assess the power of both Rome and Athens when the former was on the rise while the latter was in decline,

> We find that the number of citizens grown up to manhood, made at Rome a fourth part of its inhabitants, and at Athens a little less than the twentieth: the strength of Rome therefore, to that of Athens, was at these different times almost as four to twenty, that is, it was five times larger.[79]

With respect to the two Mediterranean powers of classical antiquity, Montesquieu, hence offered a tangible calculation of their respective power. However, regarding the possibility of measuring and relating power in social relationships, Bertrand Russell noted that although "it is easy to say, roughly, that A has more power than B, if A achieves many intended effects and B only a few," a precise measurement of power is almost impossible.[80] Similar observations can be found with A. F. K. Organski who pointed out that while "[e]verybody knows that the United States is powerful and that Luxembourg is not," it is much harder to define what it is that makes nations powerful.[81] Addressing the longings for definition and measurement, Joseph Nye not only compared power to the weather, as we have seen, but also to love. "Power," he thus argued, "is also like love, easier to experience than to define or measure, but no less real for that."[82]

Deficiencies in this regard, it may be argued, still persist today—though not for the lack of trying. Deriving from the desire to quantify and compare power, much like the search for a Theory of Everything, which for long has been the philosophers' stone in physics,[83] the formulation of a comprehensive computational model for calculating power has in fact been a constant object of academic and governmental research in International Relations. The Chinese government, for example, has recently charged as much as five different research institutes to compile power indices, a hint not only toward the great topicality but also toward the difficulties accompanying such attempts.[84] In this everlasting quest for finding a comprehensive formula to compute (and at times even forecast) power, countless efforts have been made over the course of the centuries. For instance, as early as 1741 Johann Peter Süßmilch tried his hand at devising a mathematical formula for calculating national power.[85] Generally, such attempts take into consideration influencing variables like the size of population and territory as well as military and economic strength, with

---

[79]Montesquieu, *Reflections on the Causes of the Rise and Fall of the Roman Empire* (London: Geo. B. Whittaker, 1825), p. 17.

[80]Russell, *Power*, p. 35.

[81]Organski, *World Politics*, p. 94.

[82]Nye, *Soft Power*, p. 1.

[83]The term "Theory of Everything" was coined by John Ellis in 1986; John Ellis, "The Superstring: Theory of Everything, or of Nothing?," *Nature*, Vol. 323, No. 6089 (1986), pp. 595–598.

[84]Mark Leonard, *What Does China Think?* (New York, N.Y.: PublicAffairs, 2008), pp. 83–85.

[85]Johann Peter Süßmilch, *Die göttliche Ordnung in den Veränderungen des menschlichen Geschlechts, aus der Geburt, dem Tode und der Fortpflanzung desselben erwiesen* (Göttingen: Jürgen Chrom Verlag, 1988).

their respective definitions and weighting frequently diverging. Literature today is therefore ripe with a huge variety of elaborate computational models allowing for an empirical calculation of national power.[86] The ongoing topicality of such attempts is demonstrated, for example, by the work of Enrico Fels who recently presented a sophisticated composite indicator to calculate and compare the power of nation-states and applied it to the Asia-Pacific in order to examine possible power shifts within this region.[87]

William Inboden, who himself proposed a comprehensive metric of (national) power, held that despite an observed elusiveness of power, measurement attempts and the introduction of power indices are worthwhile endeavors, even though indicators may sometimes be at odds with each other.[88] Others, however, have loudly voiced their doubts as to the value and significance of comprehensive power metrics.[89] Therefore, in view of such criticism and bearing in mind the relationality and contextuality of power elaborated upon above, the possibility of finding a grand and magic formula for the calculation of power in international relations may very well be a wild-goose chase—just like some skeptics contend with regard to the Theory of Everything.[90]

A major issue in such endeavors seeking to assess the aggregate power of an actor and to collate its power to other actors in the international system is the fact that analysts frequently resort to the "counting" of underlying power resources. Different problems present themselves when following this road: To begin with, the question arises, which indicators to include in the formula in the first place. Commonly, it encompasses factors such as military capabilities and budgets, economic indicators,

---

[86]See, for example, Ferdinand Friedensburg, *Die mineralischen Bodenschätze als weltpolitische und militärische Machtfaktoren* (Stuttgart: Ferdinand Enke Verlag, 1936); F. Clifford German, "A Tentative Evaluation of World Power," *Journal of Conflict Resolution*, Vol. 4, No. 1 (1960), pp. 138–144; Wilhelm Fucks, *Formeln zur Macht: Prognosen über Völker, Wirtschaft, Potentiale* (Stuttgart: Deutsche Verlags-Anstalt, 1965); Norman Z. Alcock and Alan G. Newcombe, "The Perception of National Power," *Journal of Conflict Resolution*, Vol. 14, No. 3 (September 1970), pp. 335–343; J. David Singer and Melvin Small, *The Wages of War, 1816-1965: A Statistical Handbook* (New York, N.Y. John Wiley, 1972); Jacek Kugler and William Domke, "Comparing the Strength of Nations," *Comparative Political Studies*, Vol. 19, No. 1 (April 1986), p. 39–69; Ray S. Cline, *The Power of Nations in the 1990s: A Strategic Assessment* (Lanham, Md.: University Press of America, 1994); Arvind Virmani, "VIP²: A Simple Measure of a Nation's (Natural) Global Power," *Indian Council for Research on International Economic Relations*, July 2005, online at: http://www.icrier.org/pdf/VIPP4.pdf (accessed July 24, 2014).

[87]Enrico Fels, *Shifting Power in Asia-Pacific? The Rise of China, Sino-US Competition and Regional Middle Power Allegiance* (Cham: Springer International Publishing, 2017).

[88]Inboden, "What is Power?," p. 16 & p. 27.

[89]Inboden, "What is Power?," p. 19 & p. 16.

[90]For example, Stephen Hawking initially subscribed to the possibility of finding "an ultimate theory" but later changed his mind; Stephen Hawking, "Gödel and the End of Physics," University of Cambridge Department of Applied Mathematics and Theoretical Physics, July 20, 2002, online at: http://www.damtp.cam.ac.uk/events/strings02/dirac/hawking/ (accessed June 17, 2014).

size of population and territory, or the level of political stability.[91] At the same time, the influence of such factors arguably varies over time and within different contexts. In today's world, for example, it is hardly sufficient, as Montesquieu has done with respect to ancient Athens and Rome nigh on three centuries ago, to compare (male) citizens eligible for military service in order to provide an assessment of national power. Likewise, while analysts as well as statesmen have long since agreed on the pivotal role economic and financial resources play in the power position of a state (in the eighteenth century, Prussian King Frederick the Great, for example, repeatedly referred to finances as the "nerve" of any state[92]), a variety of other resources has to be taken into consideration as well. Finally, while with regard to hard power such resources can be considered fairly tangible, they tend to be "characteristically intangible"[93] when it comes to the realm of soft power, as we shall see in greater detail below.

Mindful of the widely shared criticism toward resource-based understandings of power referred to above, power in international relations frequently tends to be, in the words of Joseph Nye, "reduced to measurable, tangible resources. It was something that could be dropped on your foot or on cities, rather than something that might change your mind about wanting to drop anything in the first place."[94] In this sense, and in line with the above discussion, the fixation on resource-based understandings alone can only result in a decidedly incomplete picture when assessing an actor's power in international affairs.[95] This observation becomes even more glaring when considering the realm of soft power in particular—a variety of power which presents itself especially intangible and elusive. After these general deliberations on the nature of power, we shall now turn to that, in Nye's words, "something that might change your mind wanting to drop anything in the first place" in greater detail.

---

[91]Carl von Clausewitz, for example, denominated territorial size and population as the sources of all (military) power; Carl von Clausewitz, *On War*, Translated by Colonel J. J. Graham. New and Revised Edition with Introduction and Notes by Colonel F. N. Maude, Volume 1 (London: Kegan Paul, Trench, Trubner & Co., 1918), p. 9.

[92]See, for example, Friedrich der Große, "Fürstenspiegel, oder Unterweisung des Königs für den jungen Herzog Karl Eugen von Württemberg," in *Ausgewählte Schriften*, ed. Ulrike-Christine Sander (Frankfurt am Main: Fischer, 2011), p. 48 and Friedrich der Große, "Abriß der preußischen Regierung und der Grundsätze, auf denen sie beruht, nebst einigen politischen Betrachtungen," in *Ausgewählte Schriften*, ed. Ulrike-Christine Sander (Frankfurt am Main: Fischer, 2011), p. 73.

[93]Zahran and Ramos, "From Hegemony to Soft Power," p. 17.

[94]Joseph S. Nye, Jr., "Foreword," in *Soft Power Superpowers: Cultural and National Assets of Japan and the United States*, eds. Watanabe Yasushi and David L. McConnell (Armonk, N.Y.: M.E. Sharpe, 2008), p. xiii.

[95]Organski, *World Politics*, pp. 103–104.

2.5   The Notion of Soft Power

As has been argued above, power in international relations is frequently (and somewhat oversimplifyingly) understood as forming a dichotomy of hard and soft power. Recourse to hard power, comprising the highly interdependent dimensions of military and economic power can be considered "the directive or commanding method of exercising power."[96] However, as Niall Ferguson argued with reference to the U.S. Dollar and the U.S. Army Special Forces Command, in the twenty-first century "wielding true global power takes more than just greenbacks and green berets."[97] James Madison's "purse" and "sword" cited above, it may be argued, may therefore be no longer enough to tell the whole tale of power in the twenty-first century.

In line with such deliberations, Joseph Nye claimed in his 1990 *Bound to Lead: The Changing Nature of American Power* that besides "classic" hard power resources "there is also an indirect way to exercise power. A country may achieve the outcomes it prefers in world politics because other countries want to follow it or have agreed to a system that produces such effects."[98] While the forms of power elaborated upon above primarily rest on the ability of one actor to economically induce or militarily coerce others, "[t]his aspect of power—that is, getting others to want what you want—might be called indirect or co-optive power behavior."[99] This definition of co-optive power presented in 1990, resting on attraction rather than coercion, constitutes the integral part of the notion of soft power to this day.[100]

In the wake of these deliberations, different authors have tried their hands at providing a simple formula illustrating the fundamental contrast between hard and soft power Geraldo Zahran and Leonardo Ramos thus noted, "Command power is the ability to change what others do, while co-optive power is the ability to shape what others want;"[101] Matthew Fraser argued, "Hard power threatens; soft power seduces. Hard power dissuades; soft power persuades,"[102] and Joseph Nye, more pointedly still, recently declared, "Hard power is push; soft power is pull."[103] In the

---

[96]Nye, *Bound to Lead*, p. 31.

[97]Niall Ferguson, "Think Again: Power," *Foreign Policy*, No. 134 (January/February 2003), p. 18.

[98]Nye, *Bound to Lead*, p. 31. In his later writings, Joseph Nye generally omitted the second part of the formulation ("or have agreed to a system that produces such effects"), a formulation which is reminiscent of the concept of structural power put forth by Susan Strange, as shall be discussed below.

[99]Nye, *Bound to Lead*, p. 31.

[100]First predominantly labeled "co-optive power," the term "soft power" stuck in public, political, and academic debate. While in *Bound to Lead* no index entry exists for "soft power," the publication of an eponymous article in *Foreign Policy* in the autumn of 1990 heralded the ultimate triumph of the term.

[101]Zahran and Ramos, "From Hegemony to Soft Power," p. 17.

[102]Matthew Fraser, *Weapons of Mass Distraction: Soft Power and American Empire* (New York, N.Y.: St. Martin's Press, 2003), p. 10.

[103]Nye, "Hard, Soft, and Smart Power," p. 565.

following, we shall take a closer look at the origins and key characteristics of this idea of a seductive or attractive variety of power.

2.5.1 Origins

Ever since its introduction to the public, political, and academic debate almost three decades ago, the concept of soft power has enjoyed great and constantly growing popularity.[104] As already mentioned above, it has been extensively referred to in academic writings, newspaper articles, and political speeches alike. In order to draw a comprehensive picture of the notion of soft power, it is necessary to first provide an overview of its origins and development.[105] It is in this vein that Robert W. Cox reminded us, "Theory is always *for* someone and *for* some purpose. All theories have a perspective. Perspectives derive from a position in time and space, specifically social and political time and space."[106] Illustrating origins as well as lines of traditions with respect to the concept of soft power shall accordingly be at the center of the following subchapter.

2.5.1.1 A New Concept

It was the widespread debate on American declinism that crucially provided the background against which Joseph Nye introduced the concept of soft power.[107] In a 2014 article, he thus noted, "I first coined the term 'soft power' in my 1990 book *Bound to Lead*, which challenged the then-conventional view of the decline of US power."[108] Accordingly, Nye opened his *Bound to Lead* with the simple

---

[104]Zahran and Ramos, "From Hegemony to Soft Power," pp. 12–13.

[105]For a brief "historiography" of the concept, see Zahran and Ramos, "From Hegemony to Soft Power," pp. 12–16.

[106]Robert W. Cox, "Social Forces, States and World Orders: Beyond International Relations Theory," *Millennium: Journal of International Studies*, Vol. 10, No. 2 (1981), p. 128; Cox' emphasis.

[107]Joseph S. Nye, Jr., "Soft Power: The Origins and Political Progress of a Concept," *Palgrave Communications*, Vol. 3 (February 21, 2017), online at: https://www.nature.com/articles/palcomms20178 (accessed August 14, 2017), p. 2; Nye, "Notes for a Soft-Power Research Agenda," p. 162. See also Zahran and Ramos, "From Hegemony to Soft Power," p. 13; Lock, "Soft Power and Strategy," p. 32; and Christopher Layne, "The Unbearable Lightness of Soft Power," in *Soft Power and US Foreign Policy: Theoretical, Historical and Contemporary Perspectives*, eds. Inderjeet Parmar and Michael Cox (Abingdon: Routledge, 2010), p.

[108]Joseph S. Nye, Jr., "The Information Revolution and Power," *Current History*, Vol. 133, No. 759 (2014), p. 20. For an almost word-for-word quotation, see also Joseph S. Nye, Jr., "China's Soft Power Strategy," in *Bridging the Trust Divide: Cultural Diplomacy and Fostering Understanding Between China and the West*, eds. Helmut K. Anheier and Bernhard Lorentz (Essen: Stiftung Mercator, 2012), p. 30.

observation, "Americans are worried about national decline."[109] At it, "American decline" combines the two (interdependent) aspects of a relative, exterior decline vis-à-vis other nations contesting American preponderance and absolute, domestic decline encompassing internal national decay.[110]

Despite the new urgency attested to the discourse at the time, debates on U.S. national decline are nothing distinctly new. Fareed Zakaria, for example, opined in 2008 that "[t]he United States has a history of worrying that it is losing its edge"[111] and Josef Joffe, writing 1 year later, remarked, "Every ten years, it is decline time in the United States."[112] Zakaria and Joffe, with respect to their observations of a recurring fear of a decline in U.S. history, are in good company. None other than Charles Dickens, thus, famously penned in his *The Life and Adventures of Martin Chuzzlewit* as early as 1844, "Martin knew nothing about America, or he would have known perfectly well that if its individual citizens, to a man, are to be believed, it always *is* depressed, and always *is* stagnated, and always *is* at an alarming crisis, and never was otherwise."[113] Taking into consideration more recent times than the pre-Civil War United States Dickens spoke of, American declinism was fueled time and again in the twentieth century: the Sputnik shock in 1957, the oil and economic crises in the early 1970s, and the budget deficits of the 1980s being the most popular examples.[114] In the late 1970s—a decade which saw the United States defeat in Vietnam and the resignation of President Richard Nixon in the aftermath of the Watergate Scandal—and early 1980s, declinism again reemerged on top of the agenda as other nations seemed to contest U.S. preeminence, especially in the economic arena, with Japan and the Federal Republic of Germany leading the way.[115] At that time, U.S. political decision-makers addressed the currents of declinism forthright,. Jimmy Carter hence argued in his remarks accepting the nomination as Democratic Party's presidential nominee in the 1976 election, "I have never had more faith in America than I do today. We

---

[109]Nye, *Bound to Lead*, p. ix.

[110]Joseph S. Nye, Jr., *Is the American Century Over?* (Cambridge: Polity Press, 2015), p. 20.

[111]Fareed Zakaria, "The Future of American Power: How America Can Survive the Rise of the Rest," *Foreign Affairs*, Vol. 87, No. 3 (May/June 2008), p. 40.

[112]Josef Joffe, "The Default Power: The False Prophecy of America's Decline," *Foreign Affairs*, Vol. 88, No. 5 (September/October 2009), p. 21.

[113]Charles Dickens, *The Life and Adventures of Martin Chuzzlewit* (London: Chapman and Hall, 1844), p. 203; Dickens' emphasis.

[114]Joseph S. Nye, Jr., "The Future of American Power: Dominance and Decline in Perspective," *Foreign Affairs*, Vol. 89, No. 6 (November/December 2010), p. 3. See also Samuel P. Huntington, "The United States: Decline or Renewal?," *Adelphi Papers*, Vol. 29, No. 235 (1989), pp. 63–80 and Zakaria, "The Future of American Power," p. 40.

[115]Not for no reason did Country Music singer-songwriter Merle Haggard's 1982 release "Are the Good Times Really Over (I Wish a Buck Was Still Silver)" about the pre-Vietnam War and pre-Watergate United States become a hit both in the United States and Canada and—having the finger on the pulse—was rewarded Academy of Country Music Song of the Year for 1982; Paul Kingsbury, Michael McCall, and John W. Rumble, eds., *The Encyclopedia of Country Music* (New York, N.Y.: Oxford University Press, 2012), p. 616.

have an America that, in Bob Dylan's phrase, is busy being born, not busy dying."[116] Despite these reaffirmations of unbridled U.S. prowess to be heard from politicians, a large amount of literature has been published on the topic of U.S. decline since the mid-1970s.[117] Jimmy Carter himself, speaking 3 years to the day after accepting the Democratic nomination, attested to the perception that the United States was lacking confidence in facing the future in what was to become known as "The Malaise Speech," "The erosion of our confidence in the future is threatening to destroy the social and the political fabric of America."[118] A decade later, it was most notably Paul Kennedy's *The Rise and Fall of the Great Powers* that propelled the discussions on declinism once more.[119] (Interestingly, Kennedy's highly-influential work gained particular prominence with various future members of the George W. Bush administration.[120])

Against this very backdrop of declinism, Nye examined the changing nature of power in the international system and the position of the United States within this system. He concluded that despite growing interdependence and transnational challenges, "[t]he United States is likely to remain the leading power,"[121] notwithstanding the fact that its position is less dominant as the century draws to its end than it had been after World War II.[122] His main argument for the enduringly predominant position in the world, however, was not merely the dominance in "traditional resources," but rather the United States' "ideological appeal," which—in contrast to that of contending powers like Japan—proved far more extensive.[123] Taking into account only "traditional" understandings of power hence would be insufficient when assessing the position of the United States at the end of the Cold War and only by incorporating the dimension subsequently labeled as "soft power" the

---

[116]Jimmy Carter, "Our Nation's Past and Future: Address Accepting the Presidential Nomination at the Democratic National Convention in New York City," New York, N.Y., July 15, 1976, online at: http://www.presidency.ucsb.edu/ws/?pid=25953 (accessed September 5, 2017).

[117]Terry Boswell and Albert Bergesen, "American Prospects in a Period of Hegemonic Decline and Economic Crisis," in *America's Changing Role in the World System*, eds. Terry Boswell and Albert Bergesen (New York, N.Y.: Praeger, 1987), p. 3.

[118]Jimmy Carter, "Energy and National Goals: Address to the Nation," Washington, D.C., July 15, 1979, in *Public Papers of the Presidents of the United States: Jimmy Carter, 1979, Book II – June 23 to December 31, 1979* (Washington, D.C.: United States Government Printing Office, 1980), p. 1237.

[119]James T. Patterson, *Restless Giant: The United States from Watergate to Bush v. Gore* (New York, N.Y.: Oxford University Press, 2005), p. 202. See also Stephan G. Bierling, "Das Ende des langen Booms? Die amerikanische Wirtschaft unter Bill Clinton und George W. Bush," in *Die Clinton-Präsidentschaft: Ein Rückblick*, eds. Stephan G. Bierling and Reinhard C. Meier-Walser (München: Hanns-Seidel-Stiftung, 2001), p. 27 and James Mann, *Rise of the Vulcans: The History of Bush's War Cabinet* (New York, N.Y.: Viking, 2004), pp. 160–164.

[120]Mann, *Rise of the Vulcans*, p. 160.

[121]Nye, *Bound to Lead*, p. 22.

[122]Joseph S. Nye, Jr. "Soft Power," *Foreign Policy*, No. 80 (Autumn 1990), p. 153.

[123]Nye, "Soft Power," p. 155.

picture would become complete.[124] While himself recognizing the concept's deep historical roots (which shall be elaborated upon below), Nye on that note thus "found that something was still missing"[125] and he declared, "Throughout the centuries, statesmen and other observers have mistakenly perceived the metric of power."[126]

At least in part, as Christopher Layne has argued, the introduction of the concept of soft power grew out of "fears that the USA was losing its lead in hard power."[127] In an early reference to the concept of soft power, Gregory F. Treverton, therefore, pointed out in 1992,

> And it is also true that the United States has attributes of soft power—the appeal of its culture, for instance, or the spread of multinational corporations that are less and less national but still probably 'American' in a pinch. It is not, however, very reassuring to notice these have been discovered or rediscovered now that measures of harder power are less in America's favor.[128]

In Joseph Nye's analysis, as presented at the time, the abundance of soft power, thus, constituted a crucial factor for the United States to continually occupy a dominant position in the world. Especially with regard to this particular dimension of power, Nye detected a major and decisive difference to other great powers that over the centuries had been in comparably hegemonic positions as the United States since the end of World War II and which had been confronted with national decline as well.[129] In the words of Nye, "As the nature of power in world politics continues to change, the United States will be as well placed as any other nation in terms of the new, intangible sources of power."[130] In the twenty-first century, when the talk on American declinism has reemerged on the very top of the agenda with virtually unparalleled ferocity, the concept of soft power arguably gained new topicality for this very reason.[131]

---

[124]Lock, "Soft Power and Strategy," p. 32.

[125]Nye, "Foreword," p. ix.

[126]Nye, *Bound to Lead*, p. 7.

[127]Layne, "The Unbearable Lightness of Soft Power," p. 52.

[128]Gregory F. Treverton, *America, Germany, and the Future of Europe* (Princeton, N.J.: Princeton University Press, 1992), p. 208.

[129]Nye, *Bound to Lead*, pp. 37–48.

[130]Nye, *Bound to Lead*, p. 199.

[131]For recent discussions on the topic of American decline see Aaron L. Friedberg, "Same Old Song: What the Declinists (and Triumphalists) Miss," *The American Interest*, Vol. 5, No. 2 (November/December 2009), pp. 28–35; Robert Kagan, "Not Fade Away," *The New Republic*, January 11, 2012, online at: http://www.newrepublic.com/article/politics/magazine/99521/america-world-power-declinism (accessed February 10, 2015); Tom Donilon, "We're No. 1 (and We're Going to Stay That Way)," *Foreign Policy*, July 3, 2014, online at: http://foreignpolicy.com/2014/07/03/were-no-1-and-were-going-to-stay-that-way/ (accessed February 10, 2015); Hal Brands, "The Era of American Primacy is Far from Over," *The National Interest*, August 24, 2016, online at: http://nationalinterest.org/blog/the-skeptics/the-era-american-primacy-far-over-17465 (accessed August 25, 2016). Expressively, in July/August 2014 *Foreign Policy* dedicated a whole issue to the topic of American decline that included Elbridge Colby and Paul Lettow, "Have We Hit Peak

Besides the background of American declinism, various concurrent and intertwined developments have contributed to the triumphal march of the concept of soft power at that particular point in time: economic liberalization, growing global democratization, globalization, the dawn of the information age, and new challenges to established International Relations theories arguably rank most prominently among these.

Thus, with the demise of the Soviet Union, capitalism proved to be victorious over the command economy.[132] Ronald Reagan in this regard famously argued in 1994—as he had predicted in a 1982 speech in the House of Commons[133]—"that communism was destined for the ash-heap of history."[134] Such sentiments, however, were hardly restricted to triumphal political speeches alone. Concurrently, Francis Fukuyama thus famously declared "the end of history" in the face of a seemingly irresistible triumph of Western liberalism and democracy.[135] With this highly influential claim, Fukuyama self-admittedly became, "more than most people, [...] associated with the idea that history's arrow points to democracy."[136] At it, the global rise in democracies—what Samuel P. Huntington called the "third wave of democratization"[137]—seems an expressive indicator in this regard, indeed. John Arquilla and David Ronfeldt accordingly noted, "The end of the Cold War inspired the conviction that liberal democratic societies with strong market systems and civil societies were best, having won the evolutionary competition."[138] In fact, despite tendencies in democratization already observable in the 1970s and 1980s in

---

America? The Sources of U.S. Power and the Path to National Renaissance," *Foreign Policy*, No. 207 (July/August 2014), pp. 54–63.

[132]Andreas Rödder, *21.0: Eine kurze Geschichte der Gegenwart* (München: C. H. Beck, 2015), p. 41.

[133]For Reagan's 1982 speech and detailed study on its significance, see Robert C. Rowland and John M. Jones, *Reagan at Westminster: Foreshadowing the End of the Cold War* (College Station, Tex.: Texas A&M University Press, 2010).

[134]Ronald Reagan, "Remarks on the Occasion of 83rd Birthday Gala," Simi Valley, Cal., February 3, 1994, online at: http://www.americanrhetoric.com/speeches/ronaldreagan83rdbirthday.htm (accessed November 16, 2015).

[135]Francis Fukuyama, "The End of History," *The National Interest*, No. 16 (Summer 1989), pp. 3–18. It is an interesting observation that Fukuyama's widely-noticed article had been published *before* the Berlin Wall came down. Three years later, Fukuyama elaborated his historico-philosophical view in Francis Fukuyama, *The End of History and the Last Man* (New York, N. Y.: Simon & Schuster, 1992).

[136]Francis Fukuyama, "The Neoconservative Moment," *The National Interest*, No. 76 (Summer 2004), p. 60.

[137]Samuel P. Huntington, "Democracy's Third Wave," *Journal of Democracy*, Vol. 2, No. 2 (Spring 1991), pp. 12–34 and Samuel P. Huntington, *The Third Wave: Democratization in the Late Twentieth Century* (Norman, Okla.: University of Oklahoma Press, 1991).

[138]John Arquilla and David Ronfeldt, *The Emergence of Noopolitik: Toward an American Information Strategy* (Santa Monica, Cal.: RAND Corporation, 1999), p. 23.

Southern Europe and Latin America,[139] the number of democracies rose notably from 69 in 1988/1989 to 99 in 1992 according to the annual Freedom House Reports.[140]

Concurrently, another phenomenon gathered pace dramatically in the early 1990s: globalization.[141] In the eyes of Hans-Peter Schwarz, therefore, "[a]lmost simultaneously with the political upheaval [of 1989–1991], a radical globalization of capital markets occurred in the late 1980s-early 1990s."[142] Admittedly, the process designated "globalization" has a long tradition and dates back even centuries, as Tilman Mayer and others have recognized.[143] The term "globalization" itself, however, is much more recent and has been introduced to a wider public by Theodore Levitt in a 1983 *Harvard Business Review* article[144] and in the following "has successfully passed into common currency."[145] In the 1990s, the concept, thus, spread widely[146] and, as Ludger Kühnhardt has aptly noted, even "became *the* buzzword for diagnosing the era at the end of the twentieth century."[147] While the archive of *The New York Times* lists its first entry of "globalization" as early as

---

[139]Andreas Wirsching, *Der Preis der Freiheit: Geschichte Europas in unserer Zeit* (München: C. H. Beck, 2012), p. 28.

[140]Freedom House, "Freedom in the World: Electoral Democracies," online at: https:// freedomhouse.org/sites/default/files/Electoral%20Democracy%20Numbers,%20FIW%201989-2013.pdf (accessed August 15, 2018).

[141]Joseph Duffey, "How Globalization Became U.S. Public Diplomacy at the End of the Cold War," in *Routledge Handbook of Public Diplomacy*, eds. Nancy Snow and Philip M. Taylor (New York, N.Y.: Routledge, 2009), p. 331.

[142]Hans-Peter Schwarz, "America, Germany, and the Atlantic Community after the Cold War," in *The United States and Germany in the Era of the Cold War, 1945-1990: A Handbook, Volume II: 1968-1990*, ed. Detlef Junker, associated editors Philipp Gassert, Wilfried Mausbach, and David B. Morris (Cambridge: Cambridge University Press, 2004), p. 547.

[143]Tilman Mayer, Robert Meyer, Lazaros Miliopoulos, H. Peter Ohly, and Erich Weede, "Globalisierung im Fokus von Politik, Wirtschaft, Gesellschaft: Einführende Betrachtungen," in *Globalisierung im Fokus von Politik, Wirtschaft, Gesellschaft: Eine Bestandsaufnahme*, eds. Tilman Mayer, Robert Meyer, Lazaros Miliopoulos, H. Peter Ohly, and Erich Weede (Wiesbaden: Verlag für Sozialwissenschaften, 2011), pp. 9–13. See also Rödder, *21.0*, pp. 42–44.

[144]Theodore Levitt, "The Globalization of Markets," *Harvard Business Review*, May 1983, online at: https://hbr.org/1983/05/the-globalization-of-markets (accessed September 28, 2015).

[145]Stanley J. Paliwoda and Stephanie Slater, "Globalisation Through the Kaleidoscope," *International Marketing Review*, Vol. 26, No. 4/5 (2009), p. 374. See also Xuewu Gu, "Ist Globalität gestaltbar?," in *Bonner Enzyklopädie der Globalität*, eds. Ludger Kühnhardt and Tilman Mayer (Wiesbaden: Springer Fachmedien, 2017), pp. 1528–1529.

[146]Joseph Duffey, "How Globalization Became U.S. Public Diplomacy at the End of the Cold War," in *Routledge Handbook of Public Diplomacy*, eds. Nancy Snow and Philip M. Taylor (New York, N.Y.: Routledge, 2009), p. 331.

[147]Ludger Kühnhardt, "Globality: Concept and Impact," in *The Bonn Handbook of Globality, Volume 1*, eds. Ludger Kühnhardt and Tilman Mayer (Cham: Springer International Publishing, 2019), p. 21. For a similar view, see Konrad H. Jarausch, "Intellectual Dissonance: German-American (Mis-)Understandings in the 1990s," in *The German-American Encounter: Conflict and Cooperation between Two Cultures, 1800-2000*, eds. Frank Trommler and Elliott Shore (New York, N.Y.: Berghahn Books, 2001), p. 224.

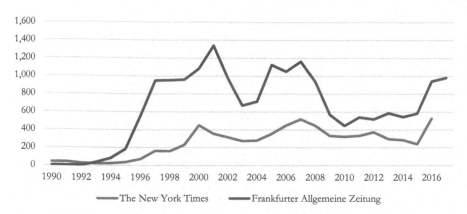

Fig. 2.1 Occurrence of the terms "globalization" and "Globalisierung" in *The New York Times* and *Frankfurter Allgemeine Zeitung*, 1990–2017 [Own illustration based on data retrieved from *The New York Times Article Archive*, online at: http://www.nytimes.com/ref/membercenter/nytarchive. html and the *Frankfurter Allgemeine Archiv*, online at: https://fazarchiv.faz.net (both accessed August 2, 2018)]

December 31, 1974, the number of usages grew dramatically in the years after the end of the Cold War, indeed, as shown in Fig. 2.1. In Germany, "Globalisierung" made its first appearance in the *Frankfurter Allgemeine Zeitung* in 1993, with numbers growing significantly in subsequent years.[148] On the other side of the Atlantic, the trend took place with some delay, yet comparable in its characteristics.

A further contributing factor has been the rapid development in information and communication technology setting in at around the same time. In the wake of these technological developments, as Ludger Kühnhardt recognized in 1996, the world thus turned into "a global village," despite that fact that profound cultural, societal, and political differences remained.[149] A crucial milestone in this development, the first website was thus launched on August 6, 1991, by Tim Berners-Lee, a British physicist then at the European Organization for Nuclear Research (more commonly known today as Conseil Européen pour la Recherche Nucléaire, or CERN). Subsequently, the number of websites grew from a modest 10 in 1992 to almost 1.8 billion in 2017, while the number of internet users concurrently rose from 14 million in 1993 to about 3.2 billion in 2015.[150] As shall be argued below at greater length, this development, depicted in Fig. 2.2, can be regarded as highly consequential for

---

[148]Rüdiger Robert, "Globalisierung als Herausforderung für das politische System," in *Bundesrepublik Deutschland: Politisches System und Globalisierung, Eine Einführung*, ed. Rüdiger Robert (Münster: Waxmann, 2007), p. 28.

[149]Ludger Kühnhardt, *Von der ewigen Suche nach Frieden: Immanuel Kants Vision und Europas Wirklichkeit* (Bonn: Bouvier Verlag, 1996), p. 2.

[150]Internet Live Stats, "Total Number of Websites," online at: http://www.internetlivestats.com/total-number-of-websites/ (accessed August 2, 2018). See also Joseph S. Nye, Jr., *The Future of Power* (New York, N.Y.: PublicAffairs, 2011), pp. 114–115.

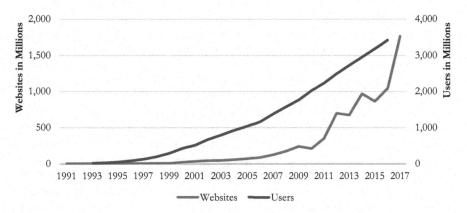

Fig. 2.2 Internet statistics: global websites and users, 1991–2017 [Own illustration based on data retrieved from Internet Live Stats, "Trends & More (Statistics)," online at: http://www.internetlivestats.com/statistics/ (accessed August 2, 2018)]

politics in general and the wielding of soft power through public diplomacy and other instruments in particular.

Additionally, for International Relations as an academic discipline, the end of the Cold War led to widespread challenges (which subsequently have produced counterarguments) of hitherto seemingly irrevocable paradigms, particularly neorealist/ structural realists' perspectives and triggered a rise in constructivist views.[151] Along with the emergence of constructivism (formulated in particular by Alexander Wendt[152]), came a growing emphasis, in political science as well as international historiography, on "the role of ideas, culture, domestic politics, statesmanship, and

---

[151]Colin Elman and Miriam Fendius Elman, "Negotiating International History and Politics," in *Bridges and Boundaries: Historians, Political Scientists, and the Study of International Politics*, eds. Colin Elman and Miriam Fendius Elman (Cambridge, Mass.: The MIT Press, 2001), p. 34. See also Stephen G. Brooks and William C. Wohlforth, "Power, Globalization, and the End of the Cold War: Reevaluating a Landmark Case for Ideas," *International Security*, Vol. 25, No. 3 (Winter 2000/2001), pp. 5–53. For a discussion of international relations theory, particularly (neo-)realism and the end of the Cold War, see, for example, Richard Ned Lebow, "The Long Peace, the End of the Cold War, and the Failure of Realism," *International Organization*, Vol. 48, No. 2 (Spring 1994), pp. 249–277; Paul W. Schroeder, "Historical Reality vs. Neorealist Theory," *International Security*, Vol. 19, No. 1 (Summer 1994), pp. 108–148; William C. Wohlforth, "Realism and the End of the Cold War," *International Security*, Vol. 19, No. 3 (Winter 1994/1995), pp. 91–129; Richard Ned Lebow and Thomas Risse-Kappen, eds. *International Relations Theory and the End of the Cold War* (New York, N.Y.: Columbia University Press, 1995); Jeffrey W. Legro and Andrew Moravcsik, "Is Anybody Still a Realist?." *International Security*, Vol. 24, No. 2 (Fall 1999), pp. 5–55; and, providing a counter-perspective, Kenneth N. Waltz, "Structural Realism after the End of the Cold War," *International Security*, Vol. 25, No. 1 (Summer 2000), pp. 5–41.

[152]Alexander Wendt, "Anarchy is What States Make of It: The Social Construction of Power Politics," *International Organization*, Vol. 46, No. 2 (Spring 1992), pp. 391–425.

the possibility of change."[153] Nye's introduction of the concept of soft power, therefore, ignited a public, political, and academic debate that grew to no small amount out of perceived shortcomings in the explanatory power and thoroughness of then predominant International Relations theories in general and concepts of power in particular. In the wake of the bipolarity of the Cold War era, Nye, thus, argued that he "who focuses only on the balance of hard power will miss the power of transnational ideas."[154] When with the end of the Cold War the structures that for more than four decades had dominated world politics crumbled and some of the prevailing International Relations theories were being contested, Nye—and others—recognized the need for a more nuanced assessment of politics and power in the changing international setting, taking into consideration, but far exceeding, conventional perspectives.[155] This perceived inability to characterize (the United States) power satisfactorily after the watershed events of 1989/1990 hence motivated Nye to put forth a novel reading on power.[156] Consequently, the two central questions asked in *Bound to Lead* are (1) "How is power changing in modern international politics?"[157] and (2) "How should we measure power in a changing world?"[158]

Summarizing, the introduction of the concept of soft power by Joseph Nye in 1990 took place against the immediate backdrop of the prevalent debate on American decline. At a time of fundamental shifts in the conduct and configuration of international relations at the end of bipolarity, it certainly struck a nerve. Not for no reasons, therefore, did the concept gain considerable currency in the political discourse as well as in the media in the years that followed its introduction, as exemplarily depicted in Fig. 2.3.

2.5.1.2 An Old Habit

As the above discussion has shown, Joseph Nye, beginning with *Bound to Lead* and two contemporaneous journal articles, undoubtedly set into motion the academic, political, and public debate on soft power continuing in much vigor until this very day and subsequently formatively developed and elaborated the concept. However, though hitherto apparently unnoticed in the extensive body of literature on the topic, earlier mentions of the very term "soft power" itself can be found.[159]

---

[153]Elman and Elman, "Negotiating International History and Politics," pp. 32–33. See also Brooks and Wohlforth, "Power, Globalization, and the End of the Cold War," p. 5.

[154]Nye, "Soft Power," p. 170.

[155]Nye, *Bound to Lead*, p. 20.

[156]Zahran and Ramos, "From Hegemony to Soft Power," p. 13.

[157]Nye, *Bound to Lead*, p. ix.

[158]Nye, *Bound to Lead*, p. 7.

[159]Admittedly, Giles Scott-Smith argued that "[t]he genealogy of the term 'soft power' stretches back several decades," but still he does not expand on any details; Giles Scott-Smith, "Soft Power in an Era of US Decline," in *Soft Power and US Foreign Policy: Theoretical, Historical and*

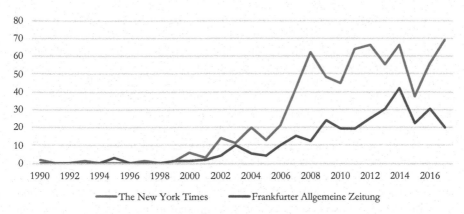

Fig. 2.3 Occurrence of the term "soft power" in *The New York Times* and *Frankfurter Allgemeine Zeitung*, 1990–2017 (Own illustration based on data retrieved from *The New York Times Article Archive* and the *Frankfurter Allgemeine Archiv*)

Thus, in a 1971 *New York Times* article, Robert E. Meagher—arguably already contrasting the term with hard power—declared, "Our ears are more diligently attuned to the wailing of bomb sirens than to the *soft power* of the bridegroom's invitations."[160] More prominent perhaps and even more in tune to Nye's later application of the term is sociologist Robert Nisbet's reference to "the softening of power" in his 1975 *Twilight of Authority*.[161] In it, Nisbet stated, "The greatest power, as major political theorists from Plato to Rousseau have declared, is that which shapes not merely individual conduct but also the mind behind that conduct" and he goes on that increasingly today and through different means "mind and spirit are invaded and thus affected by power, in however *soft* a form."[162] In a contemporary review of Nisbet's book, again published in *The New York Times*, famed writer and critic Anatole Broyard argued that in this very sense the soft form of power may be regarded as "the miracle drug in politics."[163] Already in a 1969 article published in *The Public Interest* and likewise entitled "The Twilight of Authority," Nisbet had referred to the authority vested in culture (including language, science, and the arts) and values (including justice, liberty, and equity).[164] Interestingly, these assumptions are highly reminiscent of Joseph Nye's later writings on soft power—particularly, the established triad of its resources—as we shall see in more detail below.

Contemporary Perspectives, eds. Inderjeet Parmar and Michael Cox (Abingdon: Routledge, 2010), p. 166.

[160]Robert E. Meagher, "A Man Is Defined by His Longings," *The New York Times*, October 12, 1971, p. L43; emphasis added.

[161]Robert Nisbet, *Twilight of Authority* (New York, N.Y.: Oxford University Press, 1975), p. 223.

[162]Nisbet, *Twilight of Authority*, pp. 226–227; emphasis added.

[163]Anatole Broyard, "Book of The Times: Human vs. Humanitarian," *The New York Times*, December 22, 1975, p. L27.

[164]Robert Nisbet, "The Twilight of Authority," *The Public Interest*, Vol. 15 (Spring 1969), p. 5.

Turning from the roots of the term "soft power" itself to its underlying substance, it may, in fact, be pointedly argued, with Nancy Snow, that "[s]oft power is a new concept for an old habit."[165] Su Changhe likewise pointed out, "As a form of cultural power, of course, soft power existed long before it was put forward as a concept within the framework of International Relations."[166] In the same vein, John Krige highlighted "the fact that soft forms of power have long been the subject of intellectual analysis."[167] In fact, Joseph Nye himself admitted, "Though the concept of soft power is recent, the behavior it denotes is as old as human history."[168] And elsewhere, he recently noted, "I thought of soft power as an analytic concept to fill a deficiency in the way analysts thought about power, but it gradually took on political resonance. In some ways the underlying thought is not new and similar concepts can be traced back to ancient philosophers."[169] Indeed, political and International Relations theory have known some of the fundamental elements that constitute the concept of soft power long before Nye popularized the term in 1990. Thus, while having become as much as a vogue word in our age, soft power can look back on a long history.[170]

The realization that one can get the outcomes one wants not only by coercion but by attraction too—and at times perhaps easier or even exclusively this way—accordingly has a millennia-old tradition and can be found, for example, in Chinese political and philosophical thought.[171] The underlying principles of soft power, thus, can be traced back to the writings of some of the most influential Chinese thinkers: Kostas Ifantis, for example, claimed that "[s]oft power has a Chinese pedigree in the form of the seventh-century thinker Lao-Tzu;"[172] Sun Tzu famously held, "To subdue the enemy without fighting is the acme of skill;"[173] and Xuewu Gu aptly

---

[165]Nancy Snow, "Rethinking Public Diplomacy," in *Routledge Handbook of Public Diplomacy*, eds. Nancy Snow and Philip M. Taylor (New York, N.Y.: Routledge, 2009), p. 4. See also Kostas Ifantis, "Soft Power: Overcoming the Limits of a Concept," in *Routledge Handbook of Diplomacy and Statecraft*, ed. B. J. C. McKercher (Abingdon: Routledge, 2011), p. 449.

[166]Su, "Soft Power," p. 544.

[167]John Krige, "Technological Leadership and American Soft Power," in *Soft Power and US Foreign Policy: Theoretical, Historical and Contemporary Perspectives*, eds. Inderjeet Parmar and Michael Cox (Abingdon: Routledge, 2010), p. 123.

[168]Nye, "Foreword," p. ix. See also Nye, "Hard, Soft, and Smart Power," p. 566.

[169]Nye, "Soft Power: The Origins and Political Progress of a Concept," p. 2.

[170]Simon Anholt, "Soft Power," *Internationale Politik* (January/February 2014), p. 49.

[171]Jean-Marc F. Blanchard and Fujia Lu, "Thinking Hard about Soft Power: A Review and Critique of the Literature on China and Soft Power," *Asian Perspective*, Vol. 36, No. 4 (2012), p. 567; Su, "Soft Power," p. 545.

[172]Ifantis, "Soft Power," p. 446.

[173]Quoted in Mark Kilbane, "Military Psychological Operations as Public Diplomacy," in *Routledge Handbook of Public Diplomacy*, eds. Nancy Snow and Philip M. Taylor (New York, N.Y.: Routledge, 2009), p. 187.

emphasized the significance of the powers of attraction (as opposed to coercion) in Confucian philosophy.[174]

In the Western philosophical tradition, M. Tullius Cicero, as already briefly argued above, famously distinguished between *potestas* on the one hand and *auctoritas* on the other hand in his *De Legibus*[175] and *De Re Publica*.[176] *Potestas* translates, among other meanings, into "power," "rule," "force," and—interestingly enough when bearing in mind Weber's definition of power presented above— "chance" and essentially refers to the legally held coercive power of Roman magistrates. By contrast, *auctoritas* translates, again among other meanings, into "power," "(legal) title," "decree," or "right to sanction," and refers rather to the prestige, dignity, or reputation of an individual or group of individuals (such as the Roman Senate).[177] As Richard Heinze, who has traced the roots and elaborated on the substance of *auctoritas*, has shown almost a century ago, the latter variety crucially rested on prestige and reputation and therefore is in fact highly evocative of the workings of soft power.[178] Interestingly, Heinze repeatedly stressed the importance of individuals and their respective personalities for the wielding of this particular form of power[179]—an aspect to be elaborated upon below at greater lengths. At the same time, the differentiation was by no means purely academic but rather played an exceedingly important role in Roman political thought and was referred to by different writers in antiquity, the most famous—and arguably most consequential—reference being made by none other than Augustus.[180] In his famous *Res Gestae*, brought down to us through inscriptions found in different parts of the Roman world, the first Roman Emperor, thus, argued that it was not in *potestas* but only in *auctoritas* that he exceeded his contemporaries upon his accession to absolute rule.[181] Consequently, a distinction between different varieties of

---

[174]Xuewu Gu, *Die Große Mauer in den Köpfen: China, der Westen und die Suche nach Verständigung* (Hamburg: Edition Körber-Stiftung, 2014), p. 38.

[175]M. Tullius Cicero, *Über die Gesetze: De Legibus/Stoische Paradoxien: Paradoxa Stoicum*, Edited, Translated, and Annotated by Rainer Nickel (München: Artemis & Winkler, 1994), p. 176–177 (Cic. Leg. III, 28).

[176]M. Tullius Cicero, *Der Staat: De Re Publica*, Edited and Translated by Rainer Nickel (Mannheim: Artemis & Winkler, 2010), pp. 198–207 (Cic. Rep. II, 55-61).

[177]Christoph R. Hatscher, *Charisma und Res Publica: Max Webers Herrschaftssoziologie und die Römische Republik* (Franz Steiner Verlag: Stuttgart, 2000), pp. 70–72; Nippel, "The Roman Notion of *Auctoritas*," pp. 18–24; Richard Heinze, "Auctoritas," *Hermes*, Vol. 60 (1925), p. 354. For the two varieties, see also Dietmar Hübner, "Der Ort der Macht: *Potestas* und *auctoritas* als Deutungslinien für Markt und Medien," *Deutsche Zeitschrift für Philosophie*, Vol. 58, No. 3 (2010), pp. 395–415.

[178]Heinze, "Auctoritas," p. 354.

[179]Heinze, "Auctoritas," pp. 354–356 & p. 362 & p. 366. See also Nippel, "The Roman Notion of *Auctoritas*," pp. 22–23.

[180]Heinze, "Auctoritas," p. 348; Nippel, "The Roman Notion of *Auctoritas*," pp. 27–31.

[181]Augustus, *Meine Taten: Res Gestae Divi Augusti*, Edited by Ekkehard Weber (München: Heimeran Verlag, 1975), pp. 40–43 (Aug. RG 34).

power—already foreshadowing today's dichotomy of hard and soft power—can already be found in antiquity.

In more recent times, the classification of power proposed by Bertrand Russell into the triad of "direct physical power," "rewards and punishments as inducements," and "influence on opinion," the latter of which including the "opportunity for creating desired habits in others,"[182] is likewise highly reminiscent of the concept of soft power and, in fact, its very definition as "getting others to want what you want." Similarly, traditional realist E. H. Carr, in his 1939 *Twenty Years' Crisis*, included "power over opinion" as a third category of power in international relations, alongside military and economic power.[183] Hans Morgenthau equally argued,

> The power of a nation, then, depends not only upon the skill of its diplomacy and the strength of its armed forces but also upon the *attractiveness* for other nations of its political philosophy, political institutions, and political policies.[184]

Other thinkers who have dealt with the idea of power being exercised without recourse to threats or inducements are numerous and include such "heavyweights" as Antonio Gramsci (hegemony), Pierre Bourdieu (symbolic power), Michel Foucault (disciplinary power), or Jürgen Habermas (communicative power).[185] Despite this long and illustrious genealogy, however, it were in particular Joseph Nye's writings on the subject (not least since his formulation and subsequent elaborations of the soft power concept are regularly accompanied by action orientations designed to provide political decision-makers with a set of tools to enhance national soft power) which, in the words of Janice Bially Mattern, "captured imaginations."[186]

In the final analysis, therefore, Joseph Nye may have popularized the concept of soft power, the underlying notion itself, however, is far older.[187] With recourse to a crucial distinction in innovation theory frequently attributed to Joseph Schumpeter, Nye may thus have been responsible for the concept's "diffusion," albeit not for its "invention."[188] In fact, the force now commonly entitled soft power, the workings of which shall be elaborated upon in the following in greater detail, has always played a prominent role in human and international relations.

---

[182]Russell, *Power*, pp. 35–36.

[183]Gu, "Strukturelle Macht," p. 260. See Edward H. Carr, *The Twenty Years' Crisis: 1919-1939, An Introduction to the Theory of International Relations*, Reissued with a New Introduction and Additional Material by Michael Cox (Basingstoke: Palgrave, 2001), pp. 120–134.

[184]Morgenthau, *Politics Among Nations*, p. 162; emphasis added.

[185]Mattern, "Why 'Soft Power' Isn't So Soft," p. 588. Geun Lee, "A Theory of Soft Power and Korea's Soft Power Strategy," *The Korean Journal of Defense Analysis*, Vol. 21, No. 2 (June 2009), p. 206 and Peter Baumann and Gisela Cramer, "Power, Soft or Deep? An Attempt at Constructive Criticism," *Las Torres de Lucca: International Journal of Political Philosophy*, No. 10 (January-June 2017), p. 179.

[186]Mattern, "Why 'Soft Power' Isn't So Soft," p. 588.

[187]Baldwin, "Power and International Relations," p. 289.

[188]See, for example, Thomas S. Robertson, "The Process of Innovation and the Diffusion of Innovation," *Journal of Marketing*, Vol. 31, No. 1 (January 1967), pp. 14–19.

2.5.2   Workings

As already mentioned above, Joseph Nye first defined the essence of his concept of soft power in 1990 as "getting others to want what you want."[189] In his essential 2004 monograph *Soft Power: The Means to Success in World Politics*, he took on his prior definition of soft power almost verbatim as "getting others to want the outcomes you want."[190] Soft power, thus, refers to "the ability to get what you want through attraction rather than coercion or payments."[191] Nye in this vein elaborated, "If I am persuaded to go along with your purpose, without any explicit threat or exchange taking place—in short, if my behavior is determined by an observable but intangible attraction—soft power is at work."[192] "Simply put," Nye concluded, "in behavioral terms soft power is attractive power."[193] On that account, attraction constitutes one of the most fundamental aspects in the soft power discourse.[194]

Besides identifying soft power as a variety of power in its own right, Nye not least attested to its efficaciousness.[195] Thus, it is not necessarily the case that soft power is inferior to hard power in its ability to achieve desired outcomes. On the contrary, there even are instances in which actors do not get anywhere with recourse to hard power—and only by applying soft power they are able to reach their goals.[196] In fact, attracting or convincing people by the power of ideas may hence even be more potent, particularly in the long run, since in such cases power does not take effect from *without* but rather from *within* as one actor adopts the desired outcomes of another actor as his own.[197] As Xenophon, not only a writer on tactics and warfare but a general himself, knew nigh 25 centuries ago, "He who conquers by force may fancy that he can continue to do so, but the only conquests that last are when men willingly submit to those who are better than themselves. The only way really to conquer a country is through generosity."[198] In this context, one is also reminded of Napoleon's famous dictum, set down in 1808, that of the two great powers in the world—the sword and the spirit—the sword will in the long run always come out on the short end.[199] It is in this very vein that Michel Foucault cited eighteenth century French writer Joseph Michel Antoine Servan, "A stupid despot may constrain his slaves with iron chains; but a true politician binds them even more strongly by the

---

[189]Nye, *Bound to Lead*, p. 31.

[190]Nye, *Soft Power*, p. 5.

[191]Nye, *Soft Power*, p. x.

[192]Nye, *Soft Power*, p. 7.

[193]Nye, *Soft Power*, p. 6.

[194]The significance of attraction in world politics shall be elaborated upon below, see Sect. 3.3.

[195]Nye, *Soft Power*, p. x.

[196]Think, for example, the Tom Sawyer episode referred to in the preface of the work in hand.

[197]Han, *Was ist Macht?*, p. 34 & p. 69.

[198]Quoted in Edith Hamilton, *The Greek Way* (London: W. W. Norton & Company, 1993), p. 162.

[199]Vincent Cronin, *Napoleon: Eine Biographie* (Hamburg: Classen Verlag, 1973), p. 261.

chain of their own ideas."[200] Servan's compatriot Jean-Jacques Rousseau, to offer another example, likewise argued in his *Economie Politique* that "the most absolute authority is that which penetrates into a man's inmost being, and concerns itself no less with his will than with his actions."[201] In view of such sentiments, it may with good reason be argued that soft power—taking effect by the inside ways of attraction and persuasion—can be far more potent and sustainable than the outside forces of hard power ever could.

2.5.2.1 The Power Spectrum

Despite the seemingly clear-cut differences between hard and soft power in theory, it may in practice at times be hard to discern which variety of power—hard or soft—is at work at a given moment. Thus, while soft and hard power may be regarded as seemingly contradictory at first sight, they "are related because they are both aspects of the ability to achieve one's purpose by affecting the behavior of others" and therefore a "distinction between them is one of degree."[202] Zachary Keck has accordingly argued that "as in most things in life, the distinction between soft and hard power is not so clean cut as comparing apples with oranges."[203] This observation in part relativizes the classical dichotomy of power introduced above. Bertrand Russell, having put forth the distinction between "direct physical power," "rewards and punishments as inducements," and "influence on opinion,"[204] mentioned above, thus, likewise recognized that the distinctions between the three varieties are not always "very clear cut."[205]

In this context, Nye has noted, "Hard power and soft power sometimes reinforce and sometimes interfere with each other."[206] In fact, as shall be discussed later in more detail, some critics of Nye's concept argue that soft power is merely existent and relevant where hard power has paved the way: Elliot A. Cohen, thus, argued that "American military power underwrote a world where people can even talk about soft power, and some people dwell on that term as if that underwriting by hard power does not and never did exist."[207] It is in the same vein that Peter van Ham observed,

---

[200]Quoted in Michel Foucault, *Discipline and Punish: The Birth of Prison* (New York, N.Y.: Vintage Books, 1977), pp. 102–103.

[201]Quoted in Patrick Riley, "The General Will Before Rousseau," in *Jean-Jacques Rousseau: Critical Assessment of Leading Political Philosophers, Volume III: Political Principles and Institutions*, ed. John T. Scott (Abingdon: Routledge, 2006), p. 152.

[202]Nye, *Soft Power*, p. 7.

[203]Zachary Keck, "The Hard Side of Soft Power," *The Diplomat*, July 24, 2013, online at: http://thediplomat.com/2013/07/the-hard-side-of-soft-power/ (accessed June 1, 2016).

[204]Russell, *Power*, pp. 35–36.

[205]Russell, *Power*, p. 37.

[206]Nye, *Soft Power*, p. 25.

[207]Eliot A. Cohen, "Presidents and Their Generals: A Conversation with Eliot Cohen," *The American Interest*, Vol. 6, No. 1 (Autumn 2010), p. 14.

"Without hard power, attractiveness turns into shadow-boxing, and at worst, political bimboism."[208] Janice Bially Mattern likewise pointed out that "soft power is rather ironically rooted in hard power."[209] Of particular importance in this regard, of course, is the availability of resources required to wield soft power in the first place; or, as Cynthia P. Schneider put it, "Soft power requires hard dollars."[210]

However, reproaches according to which soft power hinges on—or even requires—hard power, fall decidedly short. While recognizing the interconnectedness of hard and soft power, Robert O. Keohane and Joseph Nye, thus, rejected such views when they argued, "The soft power of the Vatican did not wane because the size of the papal states diminished."[211] In fact, the attractive power wielded by Tom Sawyer, it may be argued, did not require any hard power at all. Still, mindful of the occasional haziness in the separation of hard and soft power, Nye argued that power may be thought of as creating a spectrum of different power behaviors: According to Nye, this spectrum ranges from "command," that is, "the ability to change what others do," resting on coercion and inducement on the hard power end, to "co-option," that is, "the ability to shape what others want," resting on agenda setting and attraction on the soft power end of the spectrum.[212] "In this sense," Geraldo Zahran and Leonardo Ramos aptly observed, "soft power is the opposite of hard power, the ability to make others do what you want."[213] However, as illustrated by the fluent passage between the different behaviors, borders sometimes are blurred (relativizing the dichotomy of power referred to above). Thus, hard and soft power are frequently interlocked in practice and many instances come to mind in which a clear distinction or attribution is not possible.[214] Some observers even detected a trend of soft power being increasingly associated with "traditional bastions of hard power."[215]

---

[208]Peter van Ham, "Power, Public Diplomacy, and the *Pax Americana*," in *The New Public Diplomacy: Soft Power in International Relations*, ed. Jan Melissen (Basingstoke: Palgrave Macmillan, 2005), p. 52.

[209]Janice Bially Mattern, "Why 'Soft Power' Isn't So Soft: Representational Force and Attraction in World Politics," in *Power in World Politics*, eds. Felix Berenskoetter and M.J. Williams (New York, N.Y.: Routledge, 2008), p. 100. See also Ifantis, "Soft Power," p. 443. This observation is somewhat reminiscent of the proverb "When you've got 'em by the balls, their hearts and minds will follow." The proverb has its origins in the Vietnam War era and rose to prominence by being on display on a plaque in the McLean, Virginia, home of Charles Colson, advisor to President Richard M. Nixon during the Watergate scandal; Charles C. Doyle, Wolfgang Mieder, and Fred Shapiro, *The Dictionary of Modern Proverbs* (New Haven, Conn.: Yale University Press, 2012), p. 12.

[210]Cynthia P. Schneider, "Culture Communicates: US Diplomacy at Work," in *The New Public Diplomacy: Soft Power in International Relations*, ed. Jan Melissen (Basingstoke: Palgrave Macmillan, 2005), p. 163.

[211]Robert O. Keohane and Joseph S. Nye, Jr., "Power and Interdependence in the Information Age," *Foreign Affairs*, Vol. 77, No. 5 (September/October 1998), p. 86.

[212]Nye, *Soft Power*, pp. 7–8; Nye, *The Future of Power*, p. 21.

[213]Zahran and Ramos, "From Hegemony to Soft Power," p. 13.

[214]Ifantis, "Soft Power," p. 443.

[215]Laura Roselle, Alister Miskimmon, and Ben O'Loughlin, "Strategic Narrative: A New Means to Understand Soft Power," *Media, War & Conflict*, Vol. 7, No. 1 (2014), p. 73.

Accordingly, Nye argued that military prowess (obviously attributable to hard power) culminating in "myths of invincibility" may at times result in growing attraction (quintessential soft power).[216] Gitika Commuri agreed on this point of soft power being potentially created by hard power resources,[217] and Walter Russell Mead, in a comparable sense, introduced the concept of "sticky power" to account for the attraction created by a successful economy.[218] This argument being made by different scholars is not merely a theoretical one. Rather, the fact that the tangibles of hard power and the intangibles of soft power at times go hand in hand has been recognized in practice as well. Consider, for example, the words of (then) Lieutenant General George S. Patton, commander of the Seventh United States Army during the invasion of Sicily in July and August 1943. In General Order Number 18, dated August 22, 1943, "Old Blood and Guts" reminded his victorious troops of their great achievements during this particular operation,

> As a result of this combined effort [of ground, naval, and air forces], you have killed or captured 113,350 enemy troops. You have destroyed 265 of his tanks, 2324 vehicles, and 1162 large guns, and in addition, have collected a mass of military booty running into hundreds of tons.
>
> But your victory has significance above and beyond this *physical* aspect—you have destroyed the *prestige* of the enemy.[219]

In some cases, therefore, instruments at first sight distinctly classed as hard power instruments may themselves be wielded for soft power purposes as well, as Joshua Kurlantzick emphasized with recourse to the humanitarian aid provided by U.S. aircraft carrier USS *Lincoln* and hospital ship USNS *Mercy* in Indonesia after the 2004 tsunami.[220] Other scholars have added to this point and examined, for example, the role of technology and innovation for U.S. soft power.[221]

Furthermore, the presentation of strength through military parades offers yet another example. On the one hand, such parades are meticulously planned stagings of one's hard, military power. On the other hand, through the presentation of disciplined and illustrious troops wearing a dress uniform, soft, and attractive

---

[216]Nye, *Soft Power*, p. 7.

[217]Gitika Commuri, "'Are You Pondering What I am Pondering?' Understanding the Conditions Under Which States Gain and Loose Soft Power," in *Power in the 21st Century: International Security and International Political Economy in a Changing World*, eds. Enrico Fels, Jan-Frederik Kremer, and Katharina Kronenberg (Berlin: Springer-Verlag, 2012), pp. 46–48.

[218]Walter Russell Mead, "America's Sticky Power," *Foreign Policy*, No. 141 (March/April 2004), pp. 46–53.

[219]George S. Patton, *War as I Knew It* (Boston, Mass.: Houghton Mifflin Company, 1995), p. 64; emphasis added.

[220]Joshua Kurlantzick, *Charm Offensive: How China's Soft Power is Transforming the World* (New Haven, Conn.: Yale University Press, 2007), pp. 227–228. See also Nye, "The War on Soft Power" and Nye, "Hard, Soft, and Smart Power," p. 564.

[221]Krige "Technological Leadership and American Soft Power," pp. 121–136.

power may be created as well.[222] Additionally, the participation in United Nations peacekeeping missions, though at first sight to be attributed to the realm of hard power, can likewise be considered an effort to display the taking up of international responsibility and, thus, contribute to the enhancement of national soft power.[223] As Peter van Ham has recognized, "[I] t is important to recognize that the use of coercion and force, even through military intervention, may pay off in soft power by increasing a country's credibility and reputation."[224] The same, however, may just as well be true in the other direction (i.e., decreasing soft power through "unwise" or excessive application of hard power).[225] It is in this vein that Ali S. Wyne argued that spending extensively on hard power may "bread fear of, not respect for, American power."[226] Simon Anholt, once more underlining this identified interconnectedness, even asserted that "no country can effectively conduct a military offensive and a charm-offensive at the very same time.[227] This view, however, may be considered too broad-brush, bearing in mind the high contextuality of soft power depending on respective perceptions.[228] Conducting a "just war" (what qualifies as such may very well be subject to extensive debate and in fact the eyes of the beholder) by means of hard power, for example, could very well contribute to a simultaneous increase in soft power.

2.5.2.2   Smart Power

It is not least this perceived difficulty in separating hard and soft power, which has led to further attempts in classification and denomination of different varieties of power. As one observer has therefore argued, "'Soft versus hard power' is a false

---

[222]Think, for example, of the military parade on Beijing's Tiananmen Square on the occasion of the 60th anniversary of the founding of the People's Republic of China in 2008, which included, among others, a march-past of a company of female militia wearing bright pink uniforms. The instance was brought to the appreciative author's attention through Dr. Bernd Jakob of the *Bundesakademie für Sicherheitspolitik*.

[223]Blanchard and Lu, "Thinking Hard about Soft Power," p. 568.

[224]van Ham, "Power, Public Diplomacy, and the *Pax Americana*," p. 53.

[225]For example, Western military interventions have played into the hands of both Beijing and Moscow in their quest to get political support from regional governments in Central Asia via the Shanghai Cooperation Organization (SCO). SCO member states thus seek to maintain autocratic regimes in fear of Western hard power usage that led to regime changes in other regions, which in consequence decreased Western political attractiveness and influence in Central Asia quite considerably; Enrico Fels, "Beyond Military Interventions? The Shanghai Cooperation Organisation and its Quest for *cuius regio, eius dicio*," in *Military Interventions: Considerations from Philosophy and Political Science*, eds. Christian Neuhäuser and Christoph Schuck (Baden-Baden: Nomos, 2017), pp. 182–183.

[226]Ali S. Wyne, "Public Opinion and Power," in *Routledge Handbook of Public Diplomacy*, eds. Nancy Snow and Philip M. Taylor (New York, N.Y.: Routledge, 2009), p. 42.

[227]van Ham, "Power, Public Diplomacy, and the *Pax Americana*," p. 63.

[228]See below, Sect. 3.3.

dichotomy."[229] Sharing this verdict, Markos Kounalakis and Andras Simonyi proposed a division into soft-soft, soft-hard, hard-hard, and hard-soft power[230] and Walter Russell Mead distinguished between the four types of "sharp," "sticky," "sweet," and "hegemonic power."[231] Attempts like these, undertaken to add theoretical clarity and selectivity to the varieties of power, are manifold—and frequently they achieve the exact opposite of what was intended by them. A particularly famous and influential addition to the dichotomy of power is the introduction of the concept of smart power.[232] According to Nye, the introduction of the term has been a proposition to address misconceptions regarding soft power and its mechanisms.[233] Laid out in detail in *The Future of Power*,[234] the concept can be seen as representing a combination of hard and soft power resources and instruments into a successful policy, viz. "the combination of hard power of coercion and payment with the soft power of persuasion and attraction."[235] Christopher Layne hence formulated the simple equation "hard power plus soft power = smart power."[236] Accordingly, it can be defined as "the capacity of an actor to combine elements of hard power and soft power in ways that are mutually reinforcing such that the actor's purposes are advanced effectively and efficiently."[237] With respect to the significance of smart power, Nye argued that while hard and soft power forms two distinct varieties of power, "they work best when they reinforce each other."[238] Consequently, Nye called present and future (Washington, D.C.) policy-makers to pursue "an integrated grand strategy that combines hard military power with soft attractive power."[239] In this sense, an example of the successful application of smart power frequently put

---

[229]Ifantis, "Soft Power," p. 443.

[230]Markos Kounalakis and Andras Simonyi, *The Hard Truth about Soft Power, CPD Perspectives on Public Diplomacy, Paper 5, 2011* (Los Angeles, Cal.: Figueroa Press, 2011).

[231]Walter Russell Mead, *Power, Terror, Peace, and War: America's Grand Strategy in a World at Risk* (New York, N.Y.: Alfred A. Knopf, 2004), pp. 21–55.

[232]The origin of the term of smart power (a somewhat "generous" amalgamation of soft and hard power) is contested. Both Joseph S. Nye and Suzanne Nossel, then-U.S. Deputy Ambassador to the United Nations, claim to have introduced the term. Nye himself thanks Fen Hampson for the term and also recognizes Nossel's use, of which he claims to have learned only after having used it himself; Nye, *The Future of Power*, p. 244, fn. 55. See also Suzanne Nossel, "Smart Power," *Foreign Affairs*, Vol. 83, No. 2 (March/April 2004), pp. 131–142.

[233]Nye, *The Future of Power*, p. 22. See also Nye, "Responding to My Critics and Concluding Thoughts," p. 224.

[234]Nye, *The Future of Power*, pp. 207–234.

[235]Nye, *The Future of Power*, p. xii. See also Nye, *The Future of Power*, p. 23 & p. 234; Nye, *Soft Power*, p. 32 & p. 147; and Joseph S. Nye, Jr., "Get Smart: Combining Hard and Soft Power," *Foreign Affairs*, Vol. 88, No. 4 (July/August 2009), pp. 160–163.

[236]Layne, "The Unbearable Lightness of Soft Power," p. 67.

[237]Wilson, "Hard Power, Soft Power, Smart Power," p. 115.

[238]Joseph S. Nye, Jr., "The Power We Must Not Squander," *The New York Times*, January 3, 2000, online at: http://www.nytimes.com/2000/01/03/opinion/the-power-we-must-not-squander.html (accessed October 10, 2015).

[239]Nye, "The Future of Soft Power in US Foreign Policy," p. 7.

forth is the overall U.S. strategy during the Cold War, which combined the use of "hard power to contain Soviet aggression, while soft power was used to undermine the beliefs and faith in the communist system: this was smart power."[240]

Like the concept of soft power, smart power has received broad reception in academia. Giulio M. Gallarotti, for example, took the notion of smart power as a basis to develop his theory of "cosmopolitical power."[241] However, the meaning of the term is frequently still not conclusively made clear.[242] Additionally, it regularly has become more of a political and normative term than a theoretical and descriptive notion, particularly in the United States. Nye consequently noted, "Unlike soft power, it is an evaluative concept as well as a descriptive concept. Soft power can be good or bad from a normative perspective, depending on how it is used. Smart power has the evaluation built into the definition."[243] Elsewhere, Nye recently noted explicitly, "The term 'smart power' (the successful combination of hard and soft power resources into effective strategy) was clearly prescriptive rather than just analytical."[244] Smart power, consequently, features a normativity that soft power is explicitly lacking.[245]

Apparently, the proposition to combine hard and soft power and, thus, complement "the ying and yang of foreign policy,"[246] as Ernest J. Wilson III put it, has not fallen on deaf ears. Thus, the Center for Strategic and International Studies (CSIS) has initiated a "Smart Power Commission," co-chaired by Richard L. Armitage and Joseph Nye, which presented a comprehensive report encompassing policy recommendations regarding U.S. foreign policy in the twenty-first century.[247] Meanwhile, the term has also become a regular in Washington political parlance and commentaries.[248] Notably, its usage by top-level political decision-makers such as Hillary Clinton, who frequently applied the term in her speeches and writings, has earned the term particular prominence.[249] Still, as with soft power itself (and as already argued

---

[240]Zahran and Ramos, "From Hegemony to Soft Power," p. 25.

[241]Giulio M. Gallarotti, Cosmopolitan Power in International Relations: A Synthesis of Realism, Neoliberalism, and Constructivism (Cambridge: Cambridge University Press, 2010), p. 1.

[242]Eytan Gilboa, "Searching for a Theory of Public Diplomacy," The ANNALS of the American Academy of Political and Social Sciences, Vol. 616, Public Diplomacy in a Changing World, No. 1 (March 2008), p. 62

[243]Nye, "Responding to My Critics and Concluding Thoughts," pp. 224–225.

[244]Nye, "Soft Power: The Origins and Political Progress of a Concept," p. 2.

[245]Nye, "Hard, Soft, and Smart Power," p. 565. For the non-normative nature of soft power see below, Sect. 2.5.3.2.

[246]Wilson, "Hard Power, Soft Power, Smart Power," p. 37.

[247]Center for Strategic and International Studies, CSIS Commission on Smart Power: A Smarter, More Secure America (Washington, D.C.: The CSIS Press, 2007).

[248]See, for example, Christian Whiton, Smart Power: Between Diplomacy and War (Washington, D.C.: Potomac Books, 2013).

[249]Keck, "The Hard Side of Soft Power." See, for example, Hillary Rodham Clinton, "Confirmation Hearing," Washington, D.C., January 13, 2009, online at http://www.cfr.org/elections/transcript-hillary-clintons-confirmation-hearing/p18225 (accessed February 12, 2015); Hillary Rodham

above), the concept has drawn considerable criticism. Richard Haas accordingly warned in early 2017,

> The problem is that smart power is not that smart. It does not tell you how to mix various forms of power (be it military, diplomatic, economic, or whatever) in order to achieve a desired outcome. It is akin to a recipe that lists the ingredients without telling you how many cups or teaspoons. Try baking a cake that way.[250]

In the final analysis, despite contrary allegations,[251] Nye emphasized that smart power "is certainly not simply 'soft power 2.0.'"[252] Especially due to its prescriptive directionality, as opposed to the distinctly analytical nature of soft power, it shall not be elaborated upon further at this point.[253]

2.5.3 Soft Power and International Relations Theory

Anyone doing research in the social sciences and particularly in International Relations has from the outset to ponder and articulate his or her ontological position since it shapes the very orientation and approach to the subject.[254] Realist-, liberal-, or constructivist-minded scholars, for example, start from different premises, lay different foci in their analyses, and consequently more often than not reach different conclusions. With regard to the phenomenon of power itself, Joseph Nye has on that

---

Clinton, "Leading Through Civilian Power," Foreign Affairs, Vol. 89, No. 6 (November/December 2010), p. 13; Hillary Rodham Clinton, "American Global Leadership: Remarks at the Center for American Progress," Washington, D.C., October 12, 2011, online at: http://www.state.gov/secre tary/20092013clinton/rm/2011/10/175340.htm (accessed February 12, 2015); and Hillary Rodham Clinton, Hard Choices (New York, N.Y.: Simon & Schuster, 2014), p. 33. Some, like Senator Jim Webb (D.-Va., 2007-2013), however saw the insistence on the term of smart power with mixed feelings. With reference to Clinton's repeated usage of the term during her confirmation hearings, Webb thus argued, "I guess the phrase of the week is 'smart power.'" And he continued, "I've been doing this a long time, in and out of government. People come up with different phrases;" quoted in Eric Etheridge, "How 'Soft Power' Got 'Smart,'" The New York Times, January 14, 2009, online at: http://opinionator.blogs.nytimes.com/2009/01/14/how-soft-power-got-smart/ (accessed August 12, 2016).

[250]Richard N. Haass, "13 International Relations Buzzwords That Need to Get Taken to the Woodshed," Foreign Policy, February 3, 2017, online at: http://foreignpolicy.com/2017/02/03/ 13-international-relations-buzzwords-that-need-to-get-taken-to-the-woodshed/ (accessed March 26, 2017).

[251]Layne, "The Unbearable Lightness of Soft Power," p. 58 & p. 67.

[252]Nye, "Responding to My Critics and Concluding Thoughts," p. 225.

[253]For a particularly elaborate take on smart power, see Giulio M. Gallarotti, "Smart Power: Definitions, Importance, and Effectiveness," Journal of Strategic Studies, Vol. 38, No. 3 (2015), pp. 245–281.

[254]Paul Furlong and David Marsh, "A Skin Not a Sweater: Ontology and Epistemology in Political Science," in Theory and Methods in Political Science, eds. David Marsh and Gerry Stoker (Basingstoke: Palgrave Macmillan, 2010), p. 184. See below for a more detailed discussion of different ontological and epistemological positions, Sect. 4.1.

score argued, "People's choice of definition of power reflects their interests and values."[255] In this sense, to quote British scholar and novelist C. S. Lewis, "what you see and hear depends a good deal on where you are standing: it also depends on what sort of person you are."[256] As shall be discussed in the following with regard to soft power, however, a definite localization of the concept within the International Relations theoretical landscape is hardly possible—nor particularly reasonable.

2.5.3.1 Placement in International Relations Theory

According to some observers, the concept of soft power belongs to the liberal camp in IR theory and from a realist perspective on world politics ruled by hard power, some argue that it plays little to no role.[257] Christopher Layne thus opined that soft power "is a quintessential liberal perspective" and "on close examination, soft power is just a pithy term for multilateralism, institutionalism, the democratic peace theory and the role of norms in international politics. In other words, it is liberal institutionalism."[258] Layne accordingly claimed, "Soft power is nothing more than a catchy term for a bundle of liberal internationalist policies that have driven US foreign policy since World War II, and which are rooted in the Wilsonian tradition."[259] Besides aligning soft power to a particular school in International Relations, others have argued with regards to U.S. domestic politics that soft power in the United States is generally favored by Democrats whereas Republicans favor hard power.[260] Nye, however, has explicitly rejected such pigeonholing. As early as 1988, that is, before formulating the concept of soft power itself, he asserted,

> The time has come to transcend the classical dialectic between Realist and Liberal theories of international politics. Each has something to contribute to a research program that increases our understanding of international behavior. Perhaps work in the 1990s will be able to synthesize rather than repeat the dialectic of the 1970s and 1980s.[261]

With regard to the concept of soft power, it seems, Nye has followed his own advice. Accordingly, he argued that a distinction between the two major schools in IR—liberal and realist—is pointless if not impossible when it comes to a classification of soft power into the established compartments of IR.[262] Confronted with the accusation of being relevant only when subscribing to a liberal tradition in IR theory,

---

[255]Nye, "Hard, Soft, and Smart Power," p. 559.

[256]C. S. Lewis, *The Chronicles of Narnia: Book 1, The Magician's Nephew* (New York, N.Y.: HarperTrophy, 1994), p. 148.

[257]For (realist) criticism, see below, Sect. 2.5.4.

[258]Layne, "The Unbearable Lightness of Soft Power," p. 62 & p. 71.

[259]Layne, "The Unbearable Lightness of Soft Power," p. 73.

[260]Gelb, *Power Rules*, p. 68.

[261]Joseph S. Nye, "Neorealism and Neoliberalism," *World Politics*, Vol. 40, No. 2 (January 1988), p. 251.

[262]Nye, "Hard, Soft, and Smart Power," p. 567.

and contrary to reproaches by Christopher Layne and others, Nye pointed out instead, "There is no contradiction between realism and soft power. Soft power is not a form of idealism or liberalism. It is simply a form of power—one way of getting desired outcomes."[263] In the same vein, Nye argued that even though some observers try to distinguish between hard and soft power as belonging to the realist and liberal camp in IR theory, respectively, "the shoe does not fit."[264]

In so far as soft power is a variety of power which can contribute to the enforcement of one's (national) interest just as much as hard power can, the concept undoubtedly bears some deep realist features, indeed. Observations already laid out above—E. H. Carr as well as "arch-Realist Hans Morgenthau"[265] having respectively identified "power over opinion"[266] and "attractiveness for other nations"[267] as decisive elements in (national) power—impressively underline this assessment. George Kennan, to add another illustrious name generally attributed to the realist camp in IR, also recognized the political power of culture and cultural contacts as well as exchanges between nations, aspects usually regarded as key elements of soft power.[268] The detection of realist aspects in the ontology of soft power is shared by many observers[269]—some of which include fierce critics of the concept of soft power.[270] In fact, as has been argued above, the significance of opinion and attractiveness ascribed to the concept of power by E. H. Carr and Hans Morgenthau indicates that classical realists have been keenly aware of the influence of ideas and did not exclusively focus on what today is commonly labeled as hard power. Addressing both the insight that notions of soft power can be found in the writings of (classical) realists and the observation that criticism of soft power today frequently is harshest from the realist camp in IR, Nye has therefore fittingly argued, "Many classical realists of the past understood the role of soft power better than some of their modern followers."[271]

Still, it may be argued that the concept of soft power also shares some basic assumptions of interdependence theory, including the influence of other actors besides the nation-state and the pivotal role of international exchange, interaction, and communication.[272] And indeed, this theoretical approach, developed by Joseph

---

[263]Nye, "Foreword," p. xiii.

[264]Nye, "Notes for a Soft-Power Research Agenda," p. 170. See also Nye, "Soft Power," p. 170 and Nye, *Bound to Lead*, p. 195.

[265]Giles Scott-Smith, "Exchange Programs and Public Diplomacy," in *Routledge Handbook of Public Diplomacy*, eds. Nancy Snow and Philip M. Taylor (New York, N.Y.: Routledge, 2009), p. 55.

[266]Carr, The Twenty Years' Crisis, pp. 120–134.

[267]Morgenthau, *Politics Among Nations*, p. 162.

[268]Nye, *Soft Power*, p. 45.

[269]See, for example, Andrei and Rittberger, "Macht, Interessen und Normen," p. 25.

[270]Gelb, *Power Rules*, p. 69.

[271]Nye, "Hard, Soft, and Smart Power," p. 563.

[272]Joseph S. Nye, Jr. and Robert O. Keohane, "Transnational Relations and World Politics: An Introduction," *International Organization*, Vol. 25, No. 3 (Summer 1971), pp. 329–349. See also

Nye and Robert Keohane in the 1970s and highly influential to this day, is commonly assigned to the liberal-institutional school in IR theory.[273] However, interdependence theory itself shares basic assumptions of realist ontology such as the existence of global anarchy in which international relations are set.[274] In fact, this synthesis of interdependence and anarchy has caused, according to Xuewu Gu, great confusion.[275] Andrew Moravcsik accordingly held that liberal institutionalism should more adequately be labeled "modified structural realism."[276] Therefore, even if the concept of soft power is reminiscent of assumptions of interdependence theory, it does not per se indicate a "liberal character" of the concept.

Finally, some particular features of the concept of soft power not least share fundamental constructivist assumptions regarding the importance of values, norms, and ideas in international relations.[277] In line with these reflections on the placement of soft power in International Relations theory, and especially in view of the partly harsh criticism often directed toward soft power from the realist camp, Joseph Nye himself fittingly noted that soft power "fits with realist, liberalist or constructivist perspectives. Since it is a form of power, only a truncated and impoverished version of realism would ignore soft power. Traditional realists did not."[278]

2.5.3.2 The Non-normative Nature of Soft Power

Along with the question regarding the positioning of soft power in International Relations theory comes the reproach, already briefly referred to above, of soft power being a mere normative rather than a descriptive category. David Shambaugh thus argued that soft power is "highly normative in nature."[279] Bially Mattern equally

---

Robert O. Keohane and Joseph S. Nye, Jr., "Power and Interdependence," *Survival*, Vol. 15, No. 4 (1973), pp. 158–165; Robert O. Keohane and Joseph S. Nye, Jr., *Power and Interdependence: World Politics in Transition* (Boston, Mass.: Little Brown and Company, 1977); Robert O. Keohane and Joseph S. Nye, Jr., "Power and Interdependence Revisited," *International Organization*, Vol. 41, No. 4 (Autumn 1987), pp. 725–753; Robert O. Keohane and Joseph S. Nye, Jr., "Power and Interdependence in the Information Age," *Foreign Affairs*, Vol. 77, No. 5 (September/October 1998), pp. 81–94; and the most recent edition of Robert O. Keohane and Joseph S. Nye, Jr., *Power and Interdependence: World Politics in Transition* (Boston, Mass.: Longman, 2012).

[273]Gu, *Theorien der Internationalen Beziehungen*, pp. 151–163.

[274]Robert O. Keohane, *After Hegemony: Cooperation and Discord in World Political Economy* (Princeton, N.J.: Princeton University Press, 1984).

[275]Gu, *Theorien der Internationalen Beziehungen*, pp. 153–154.

[276]Andrew Moravcsik, "Taking Preferences Seriously: A Liberal Theory of International Politics," *International Organization*, Vol. 51, No. 4 (Autumn 1997), p. 537.

[277]Lee, "A Theory of Soft Power and Korea's Soft Power Strategy," pp. 206–207.

[278]Nye, "Responding to My Critics and Concluding Thoughts," p. 219.

[279]David Shambaugh, *China Goes Global: The Partial Power* (New York: Oxford University Press, 2013), p. 209. In the subsequent paragraph, Shambaugh focuses merely on the passive approach of soft power and the "appeal by example" in an oversimplifying understanding of soft power.

pointed out that soft power frequently has been "embraced by ethically minded scholars and policy-makers."[280] Others argued that the concept of soft power implies "that there is some kind of good power out there."[281] As already observed by Carl Schmitt, however, any form of power is normatively indifferent—neither good nor bad but rather subject to the acts and choices of man.[282] Soft power, being a variety of power just like any other, shares this characteristic.

Hence, from the perspective of the author, normative understandings of soft power are profoundly mistaken.[283] Nancy Snow has thus rightly observed, "[S]oft power is not the same as little old ladies sipping tea; it is often used in conjunction with more forceful and threatening forms of compliance and persuasion."[284] In fact, the often ruthless game of power politics is by no means restricted to the realm of hard power alone, but may very well be practiced by means of soft power as well.[285] Accordingly, an ever-increasing competition within the realm of soft power between different international actors can be observed in the recent past.[286] Finally, soft power has not least been understood, for example, by cultural critic Edward Said, as "another form of cultural hegemony" and its wielding, therefore, as "actually motivated by the particular desire for cultural hegemony."[287]

Such observations indicate that soft power can indeed have "*a very hard edge*."[288] It is in the same vein that John Arquilla and David Ronfeldt have argued that "soft power is not simply about beckoning in a nice way. It can be wielded in a tough, heavy, even dark manner too, for example, through messages to warn, embarrass, denounce, shun, or repel a target actor."[289] Nye equally rejects the normative nature of soft power and argued that soft power constitutes "a descriptive rather than a normative concept. Like any form of power, it can be wielded for good and bad purposes."[290] It is in this sense that Kurt-Jürgen Maaß, to offer an empirical example, emphasized that German foreign cultural policy, encompassing many key

---

[280]Mattern, "Why 'Soft Power' Isn't So Soft: Representational Force and Attraction in World Politics," p. 117.

[281]Zahran and Ramos, "From Hegemony to Soft Power," p. 28.

[282]Andreas Anter, *Theorien der Macht: Zur Einführung* (Hamburg: Junius, 2012), p. 48.

[283]However, such mistaken observations can be regarded as further evidence that the concept of soft power is still characterized by great ambiguity and deserves clarification and elaboration.

[284]Snow, "Rethinking Public Diplomacy," p. 3.

[285]Andrei and Rittberger, "Macht, Interessen und Normen," p. 25.

[286]See below, Sect. 5.2.

[287]Su, "Soft Power," p. 547.

[288]Anthony Pratkanis, "Public Diplomacy in International Conflicts: A Social Influence Analysis," in *The New Public Diplomacy: Soft Power in International Relations*, ed. Jan Melissen (Basingstoke: Palgrave Macmillan, 2005), p. 111; Pratkanis' emphasis.

[289]David Ronfeldt and John Arquilla, "Noopolitik: A New Paradigm for Public Diplomacy," in *Routledge Handbook of Public Diplomacy*, eds. Nancy Snow and Philip M. Taylor (New York, N. Y.: Routledge, 2009), p. 361.

[290]Nye, *The Future of Power*, p. 81. See also Nye, "Foreword," p. xii; Nye, "Notes for a Soft-Power Research Agenda," p. 162; and Nye, "Responding to My Critics and Concluding Thoughts," p. 225.

features of soft power, has to be considered just another instrument of German foreign policy.[291] Former German Chancellor Willy Brandt (SPD), thus, famously denoted this variety of foreign policy as the third column (Dritte Säule) of German foreign policy, standing alongside classic diplomacy and foreign trade policy as a means to further national interests.[292]

Joseph Nye himself offered further empirical evidence the non-normative nature of soft power when arguing that "Hitler, Stalin, and Mao all possessed a great deal of soft power in the eyes of their acolytes, but that did not make it good. It is not necessarily better to twist minds than to twist arms."[293] Additionally, in a 2009 interview with *Der Spiegel*, Nye has in this same vein emphasized the soft power exerted by Osama bin Laden, "Sure, he has a lot of soft power. He proved this when he brought down the Twin Towers. Bin Laden did not hold a gun to the heads of the people who flew the planes. He did not pay them either. They did it because they were attracted by his convictions."[294] Arquilla and Ronfeldt, on that same score, fittingly noted that "soft power does not necessarily favor good guys."[295] Christopher Walker, to offer a further example in this vein, has lately elaborated on the (recently increasing) soft power of authoritarian governments.[296]

Despite these pieces of evidence for the non-normative nature of soft power, Nye admitted that there might be a "normative preference for greater use of soft power" and claimed that it might at times be advisable to try to use soft power before resorting to hard power measures, for, as he has rightly pointed out, "[M]inds can change over time while the dead cannot be revived."[297] Or, as British Prime Minister Harold Macmillan craftily put it during a state visit to Australia in 1958 in words frequently—and falsely—attributed to Winston Churchill, "Jaw, jaw is better than war, war."[298] In fact, this view that diplomacy should take precedence before

---

[291]Kurt-Jürgen Maaß, "Vielfältige Umsetzungen – Ziele und Instrumente der Auswärtigen Kulturpolitik," in *Kultur und Außenpolitik: Handbuch für Wissenschaft und Praxis*, ed. Kurt-Jürgen Maaß (Baden Baden: Nomos Verlagsgesellschaft, 2015), p. 47.

[292]Steffen R. Kathe, *Kulturpolitik um jeden Preis: Die Geschichte des Goethe-Instituts von 1951 bis 1990* (München: Martin Meidenbauer, 2005), p. 251.

[293]Nye, *The Future of Power*, p. 81. See also Nye, "Notes for a Soft-Power Research Agenda," p. 169.

[294]Joseph S. Nye, Jr., "Harvard Professor Joseph Nye on Hard and Soft Power: 'It Is Pointless to Talk to Al-Qaida,'" Interview conducted by Gabor Steingart and Gregor Peter Schmitz, *Der Spiegel*, 34/2009, August 17, 2009, online at: http://www.spiegel.de/international/world/harvard-professor-joseph-nye-on-hard-and-soft-power-it-is-pointless-to-talk-to-al-qaida-a-643189-2.html (accessed July 17, 2018).

[295]Ronfeldt and Arquilla, "Noopolitik," p. 361.

[296]Christopher Walker, "The Hijacking of 'Soft Power,'" *Journal of Democracy*, Vol. 27, No. 1 (January 2016), pp. 49–63.

[297]Nye, "Notes for a Soft-Power Research Agenda," p. 170.

[298]International Churchill Society, "Quotes Falsely Attributed to Winston Churchill: Jaw-Jaw," online at: https://www.winstonchurchill.org/resources/quotes/quotes-falsely-attributed (accessed September 9, 2017).

resorting to military means may have become increasingly popular today.[299] While sharing this view, Nye engaged in a number of counterfactuals and asked if Martin Luther King and Mahatma Gandhi were more successful because they had chosen a soft power strategy while "Yassir Arafat's choice of the gun" has until today not yielded success with regard to the outcomes intended, that is, the creation of a Palestinian state.[300] Such questions cannot, of course, be conclusively answered. However, they provided interesting starting points for further research.

In the final analysis, while normative-minded scholars and practitioners may be inclined to argue in favor of taking soft power measures before resorting to hard power, soft power in itself is not normative in nature. Rather, it simply depicts a form of power, which, just like hard power, can be wielded with both noble and reprehensible intentions. Still, Ernest J. Wilson III certainly has a point when he noted, "Soft power advocates need to be more convincing that their particular strengths can advance the national well-being, and be much more Machiavellian about how to do so."[301] A major step in this direction is the formulation of a more sophisticated theoretical-conceptual framework, while another step is the accumulation of tangible empirical evidence regarding its efficacy. Both steps shall be addressed in the further course of this study.

2.5.4   Reception and Critique

As has been argued, soft power has become a much noticed and attended topic of academic research and political debate and—in the eyes of some—has even become as much as a panacea for all the ailments of the world.[302] Consequently, the man who propagated the term of soft power (albeit, as we have seen, he did not "invent" it), Joseph Nye has become one of the most influential and prolific scholars in International Relations. For example, *Foreign Policy* listed Nye as number 64 on its "Top Global Thinkers" list in 2011, "[f]or seeing the future of power."[303] When four out of ten foreign-policy professionals who had been asked to recommend books on foreign affairs in the presidential election year of 2012 included works of Joseph Nye, Daniel W. Drezner argued that apparently "[a]ll roads to understanding American foreign policy run through Joe Nye."[304] Comparable results as to the influence

---

[299]Frederick W. Kagan, "Power and Persuasion," *The Wilson Quarterly*, Vol. 29, No. 3 (Summer 2005), p. 57.

[300]Nye, "Notes for a Soft-Power Research Agenda," p. 170.

[301]Wilson, "Hard Power, Soft Power, Smart Power," p. 122.

[302]Mattern, "Why 'Soft Power' Isn't So Soft," p. 584.

[303]Foreign Policy Staff, "The FP Top 100 Global Thinkers," *Foreign Policy*, November 28, 2011, online at: http://foreignpolicy.com/2011/11/28/the-fp-top-100-global-thinkers-3/ (accessed February 10, 2015).

[304]Daniel W. Drezner, "Get Smart: How to Cram for 2012," *Foreign Policy*, No. 187 (July/August 2011), p. 32.

of Joseph Nye can be found in surveys conducted by *Foreign Policy* among practitioners and scholars in foreign affairs and international relations alike. Policy makers, thus, named Joseph Nye as having the greatest influence on U.S. foreign policy in a 2012 survey (45%), thus beating Samuel P. Huntington (39%) and Henry Kissinger (34%) to second and third place. In the same survey, 8% of those scholars polled named Nye as doing the most interesting work, making him the runner-up (behind Martha Finnemore scoring 10%).[305] A 2014 *Foreign Policy* survey confirmed those findings: according to policy-makers, Nye still ranked on the top spot (45%), while scholars placed him on rank six (19%).[306]

However, while soft power is meanwhile firmly fixed in the vocabulary of practitioners and scholars of international relations alike and Nye's consequently has become a highly influential voice, criticism and caveats of "that elusive concept,"[307] as William Inboden once called soft power, is also abundant. Edward Lock hence aptly argued, "If the value of a concept were to be measured by the breadth and frequency of its use, Nye's notion of soft power could only be considered a success. However, while popular usage of the term has bloomed, this concept has also drawn a significant volume of criticism."[308] Thus, while soft power today has become an integral component of the international relations discourse, many—theoretical as well as methodological—challenges remain in understanding and explaining its mechanisms.[309] Consequently, "there has been a call for greater clarity regarding the concept"[310]—as Joseph Nye himself acknowledged.[311] Some of these challenges and points of criticism shall be addressed in the following, not least since they can be considered valuable starting points for putting forth a new conceptual paradigm of soft power as well as a methodological roadmap for its empirical analysis in international relations.

Leslie Gelb, giving expression to the doubts of many a critic, argued that "soft power is foreplay, not the real thing. It's very important, but it isn't power."[312] Similar assessments can be found in the works of other critics as well.[313] "Power," according to Gelb, "entails pushing people around."[314] He thus concluded, applying the very metaphor Joseph Nye used to describe the two varieties of hard power

---

[305]Paul C. Avey, Michael C. Desch, James D. Long, Daniel Maliniak, Susan Peterson, and Michael J. Tierney, "The FP Survey: Who Inhabits the Ivory Tower?," *Foreign Policy*, No. 191 (January/February 2012), p. 92.

[306]Foreign Policy Staff, "Does the Academy Matter?," *Foreign Policy*, No. 205 (March/April 2014), p. 64.

[307]Inboden, "What is Power?," p. 17.

[308]Lock, "Soft Power and Strategy," p. 32.

[309]Roselle, Miskimmon, and O'Loughlin, "Strategic Narrative," p. 74.

[310]Lock, "Soft Power and Strategy," p. 32.

[311]Nye, "Notes for a Soft-Power Research Agenda," pp. 163–164.

[312]Gelb, *Power Rules*, p. 219.

[313]Gilboa, "Searching for a Theory of Public Diplomacy," p. 62.

[314]Gelb, *Power Rules*, p. 224.

introduced above, that ultimately "only strong carrots and sticks"[315] are capable of inducing a certain action. With these objections, Gelb voiced some of the most fundamental points of criticism directed toward the concept of soft power: namely that soft power does not constitute a valid variety of power in itself; it may be suited to prepare the road for "real" power and facilitate its application at times but as an independent source of power it can be neglected. (Bearing in mind reproaches like these, one recollects the famous quip by Frederick the Great, "Diplomacy without arms is like music without instruments."[316]) Niall Ferguson perhaps expressed this view most vividly when he argued that "the trouble with soft power is that it's, well, soft"[317]—and elsewhere he opined, "Soft power is merely the velvet glove concealing an iron hand."[318] In response to these points of criticism, as already noted above, it may be argued that soft power can at times be considered to be a force even *more* potent than hard power. However, recalling Nye's argument that power has frequently been understood as "something that could be dropped on your foot or on cities, rather than something that might change your mind about wanting to drop anything in the first place,"[319] soft power can at times be considered a precursor to the application of hard power in chronological terms, indeed. Power, in its frequent resource-based, hard power understanding, thus is sometimes thought of as coming into play only in times of conflict and crisis. Soft power, however, can occasionally set in prior to the application of hard power, creating a favorable environment preventing conflicts and making its use unnecessary. In this sense, the wielding of soft power may have greater leverage than any hard power coercion ever could have. It is in this vein that Steven Lukas has emphasized "the crucial point that the most effective and insidious use of power is to prevent such conflict from arising in the first place."[320] Or, as Jim Garrison put it, "Brute force does not make friends and cannot change a person's mind."[321]

A further point of criticism refers to the role of attraction in the concept of soft power. The significance of attraction is shared by most scholars who have dealt with the concept of soft power, including Joseph Nye himself.[322] Nye, thus, compared the role of attraction to that of the "invisible hand" ruling the market as put forth by Adam Smith in the late eighteenth century.[323] Bially Mattern, however, argued

---

[315]Gelb, *Power Rules*, p. 234.

[316]Quoted in Gaskarth, *British Foreign Policy*, p. 122. For a slightly different version of the same quote, see Gelb, *Power Rules*, p. 7.

[317]Ferguson, "Think Again: Power," p. 21.

[318]Niall Ferguson, *Colossus: The Price of America's Empire* (New York, N.Y.: Penguin Press, 2004), p. 20.

[319]Nye, "Foreword," p. xiii.

[320]Steven Lukes, *Power: A Radical View* (Basingstoke: Palgrave Macmillan, 2005), p. 27.

[321]Jim Garrison, *America's Empire: Global Leader or Rogue Power* (San Francisco, Cal.: Berrett-Koehler Publishers, 2004), p. 21.

[322]Joseph S. Nye, Jr., "The Decline of America's Soft Power: Why Washington Should Worry," *Foreign Affairs*, Vol. 83, No. 3 (May/June 2004), p. 20.

[323]Nye, *Soft Power*, p. 7.

that—though subscribing to its decisive role—the mechanisms of attraction have not been made sufficiently clear in Nye's writings.[324] Accordingly, Ty Solomon attested "a curious omission for Nye and others who have elaborated upon soft power."[325] Todd Hall shared these observations and discussed the concept of attraction, which he identified as "problematic" at best in its value as an analytical category and central plank in the soft power concept.[326] Nye agreed on these points of criticism and consequently called the mechanisms of attraction within the soft power concept "ripe for further research."[327]

Additionally, some critics argue, the concept of soft power is too heavily tailor-made for the United States of America—and thus lacking generalizability.[328] Christopher Layne accordingly pointed out that "Nye, of course, focused on the sources of *American* soft power."[329] Consequently, Geun Lee has argued that soft power is "reflecting American hegemonic position and interests, and cannot be mechanically copied by lesser powers."[330] As has been mentioned above, the concept has indeed been introduced against the immediate backdrop of the discourse on American decline at the end of the Cold War.[331] However, Nye explicitly argued that he does not regard soft power as an exclusively *American* phenomenon. On the contrary, he claimed that soft power, as one particular form of power, is available to other countries as well and is not even restricted to nation-states alone but can likewise be exercised by other actors in international relations[332]—and even beyond. Nye thus recently noted, "[T]hough I developed the term soft power in the context of my work on American power, it is not restricted to international behaviour or to the United States."[333] Nancy Snow agreed on this point, arguing, "The United States holds no patent on soft power."[334] Empirical data prove this assessment, as we observe that countless governments around the world have over the last years sought to devise soft power strategies drawing on their respective soft power resources and instruments. For example, the Japanese Foreign Ministry issued a statement declaring its intention to draw explicitly on soft power resources "in order to raise the

---

[324]Mattern, "Why 'Soft Power' Isn't So Soft," p. 591.

[325]Ty Solomon, "The Affective Underpinnings of Soft Power," *European Journal of International Relations*, Vol. 20, No. 3 (2014), p. 723.

[326]Todd Hall, "An Unclear Attraction: A Critical Examination of Soft Power as an Analytical Category," *The Chinese Journal of International Politics*, Vol. 3, No. 2 (2010), p. 211.

[327]Nye, "Notes for a Soft-Power Research Agenda," p. 164. The issue of attraction in world politics shall be picked below in detail, see Sect. 3.3.

[328]Simona Vasilevskyte, "Discussing Soft Power Theory After Nye: The Case of Geun Lee's Theoretical Approach," *Regional Studies*, No. 7 (2013), p. 150.

[329]Layne, "The Unbearable Lightness of Soft Power," p. 53; Layne's emphasis.

[330]Lee, "A Theory of Soft Power and Korea's Soft Power Strategy," p. 206.

[331]Nye, "Foreword," p. ix. See above, Sect. 2.5.1.

[332]Nye, "Foreword," p. ix.

[333]Nye, "Soft Power: The Origins and Political Progress of a Concept," p. 2.

[334]Snow, "Rethinking Public Diplomacy," p. 4.

position of Japan in the world."[335] Daya Thussu accordingly argued that in the wake of current power shifts and rising developing countries, especially China and India, new actors have already appeared on the global soft power scene, whose—long ranging—influence and success in this regard remains to be seen in years ahead.[336] Additionally, as countless historical references indicate—some of which dating back to times long before the United States had even been founded and to be elaborated upon below—soft power can indeed be regarded as an universal concept, both with regard to times and places of its application in the long annals of human history.

Perhaps the gravest point of criticism shared by many observers, however, is that of an inherent vagueness and even crudeness of the concept of soft power, something that has already been addressed above as marking the very starting point for the work in hand and something that shall be picked up below in greater detail in connection with the introduction of the proposed soft power taxonomy. Comments in that direction can frequently be found: Eytan Gilboa, for example, in general attests "many theoretical deficiencies" to the concept.[337] John Arquilla and David Ronfeldt likewise subscribe to a growing importance or even primacy of soft power, albeit recognizing the need for further elaboration and clarification of the concept.[338] Recently, Peter Baumann and Gisela Cramer have perhaps found the harshest words of criticism in this regard,

> Nye's attempt to give a conceptually mature and empirically solid account of soft power fails. His general conceptual explanations of soft power are too vague while his descriptions of specific phenomena are not recognizable as cases of soft power and sometimes not even as cases of power in general.[339]

What is more, Nicholas J. Cull even argued that "[s]oft power is increasingly seen as a dated concept" which has given way to the term of "smart power."[340] The author of this work, however, does not share this estimate—not least since smart power (as argued above) should be considered a normative, political rather than an empirical, analytical concept. However, the criticism aptly points toward a widely shared assessment of the still deficiently defined and operationalized character of soft power and its components. Soft power has thus been attested to be a "rather amorphous concept."[341] Or, as Benjamin E. Goldsmith and Yusaku Horiuchi have aptly noted

---

[335]Quoted in Hall, "An Unclear Attraction," p. 190.

[336]Daya Thussu, *De-Americanizing Soft Power Discourse?, CPD Perspectives on Public Diplomacy, Paper 2, 2014* (Los Angeles, Cal.: Figueroa Press, 2014), pp. 17–21.

[337]Gilboa, "Searching for a Theory of Public Diplomacy," p. 62.

[338]Ronfeldt and Arquilla, "Noopolitik," pp. 359–361.

[339]Baumann and Cramer, "Power, Soft or Deep?," p. 199.

[340]Nicholas J. Cull, *Public Diplomacy: Lessons from the Past, CPD Perspectives on Public Diplomacy* (Los Angeles, Cal.: Figueroa Press, 2011), p. 15.

[341]Thussu, *De-Americanizing Soft Power Discourse?*, p. 5.

on that score, "In short, it is not readily apparent how the theory [of soft power] might be tested."[342]

In this regard, the wide application and enormous popularity of the concept can be regarded as both a blessing and a curse. On the one hand, the extensive discourse on the concept of soft power has led to a certain degree of clarification of some of its basic mechanisms. On the other hand, the concept has frequently been broadened to the point that it incorporates anything other than the application of military force.[343] Thus, as has been demonstrated above with regard to the alleged normativity of soft power, erroneous or at least oversimplifying understandings of soft power have been put forth. According to some observers, for example, economic sanctions, as well as trade and other economic tools, have been considered as constituting soft power instruments.[344] Leslie Gelb, to offer a further example, even argued,

> Soft power now seems to mean almost everything. It includes military prowess (presumably demonstrated by military action) and all kinds of economic transactions involving the giving or withholding of money for coercive purposes, as well as the old standbys—leadership, persuasion, values, and respect for international institutions and law.[345]

The term "soft power," therefore, has been applied in various understandings, some of which have taken forms beyond recognition compared to the concept's original understanding.[346] Joseph Nye himself recently elaborated—somewhat nostalgically—on this point,

> With time, I have come to realize that concepts such as soft power are like children. As an academic or a public intellectual, you can love and discipline them when they are young, but as they grow they wander off and make new company, both good and bad. There is not much you can do about it, even if you were present at the creation.[347]

Some of such readings of soft power (including Gelb's) are, in the words of Joseph Nye, "simply wrong."[348] David A. Baldwin, thus, likewise noted that "Nye's discussion of soft power stimulated and clarified the thoughts of policy makers and scholars alike—even those who misunderstood or disagree with his views."[349]

---

[342]Benjamin E. Goldsmith and Yusaku Horiuchi, "In Search of Soft Power: Does Foreign Public Opinion Matter for US Foreign Policy?," *World Politics*, Vol. 64, No. 3 (July 2012), p. 558.

[343]Nye, "Foreword," p. ix.

[344]Peter Brooks, "Iran: Our Military Options," *The Heritage Foundation*, January 23, 2006, online at: at: http://www.heritage.org/research/commentary/2006/01/iran-our-military-options (accessed February 13, 2015); Robert Kagan, "Power and Weakness," *Policy Review*, No. 113 (June/July 2002), p. 13.

[345]Gelb, *Power Rules*, p. 69.

[346]Joseph S. Nye, Jr., "Think Again: Soft Power," *Foreign Policy*, February 23, 2006, online at: http://foreignpolicy.com/2006/02/23/think-again-soft-power/ (accessed February 13, 2015); Nye, "Notes for a Soft-Power Research Agenda," p. 162; Zahran and Ramos, "From Hegemony to Soft Power," p. 14.

[347]Nye, "Soft Power: The Origins and Political Progress of a Concept," p. 3.

[348]Nye, "Responding to My Critics and Concluding Thoughts," p. 219.

[349]Quoted in Nye, "Soft Power: The Origins and Political Progress of a Concept," p. 3.

In any event, the wide use of the term in academic publications as well as in the media and not least by political decision-makers has therefore led to an understanding that has been "widely diffused."[350] Consequently, Todd Hall argued, the concept "has so far led a dual existence as a category of practice and a category of analysis."[351] One reason for this observation may be the absence of a differentiated theoretical framework underlying the concept of soft power as put forth by Nye.[352] Geraldo Zahran and Leonardo Ramos accordingly pointed out that Nye's conceptual assumptions and even his very definitions of soft power "are not free of contradictions among them."[353] Christopher Layne likewise observed that soft power "is marred by some important weaknesses" and noted that "Nye's definition of the term is maddeningly inconsistent."[354] In the same vein, Till Geiger pointed out that "soft power is protean and arguably imprecise."[355] Consequently, Layne maintained, "As a concept, soft power is beguiling but as a theoretical construct it is not robust."[356]

A further—and connected—point of criticism frequently put forth is the inherent intangibility of soft power and its underlying resources and mechanisms. For example, it is much easier to count or collate hard power resources such as military assets (e.g., aircraft carriers, intercontinental missiles, or tanks) or economic indicators and figures (e.g., national gross domestic product, foreign direct investments, or monetary reserves) than doing likewise with the intangibles of culture or values. Recognizing this very aspect, but still subscribing to the significance of soft power in international relations, Rajen Harshe has thus fittingly noted, "Soft power is not tangible, but it certainly is not a mirage."[357] In fact, different scholars, including Joseph Nye himself, have frequently shared this assessment.[358]

Additionally, and again related to the identified intangibility, the long and intertwined causal chains which exist between cultural attraction and visible political outcomes have been subject to fierce criticism. As has been argued above, soft power tends to have long-term effects rather than yielding quick results. This observation, which has not least been recognized by Nye,[359] further complicates empirical research regarding the mechanisms of soft power and decidedly hampers the task to identify coherencies between soft power resources or instruments and (political)

---

[350]Zahran and Ramos, "From Hegemony to Soft Power," p. 14.

[351]Hall, "An Unclear Attraction," p. 195.

[352]Lee, "A Theory of Soft Power and Korea's Soft Power Strategy," p. 207.

[353]Zahran and Ramos, "From Hegemony to Soft Power," p. 16.

[354]Layne, "The Unbearable Lightness of Soft Power," pp. 53–54.

[355]Till Geiger, "*The Power Game*, Soft Power and the International Historian," in *Soft Power and US Foreign Policy: Theoretical, Historical and Contemporary Perspectives*, eds. Inderjeet Parmar and Michael Cox (Abingdon: Routledge, 2010), p. 86.

[356]Layne, "The Unbearable Lightness of Soft Power," p. 71. This line of criticism is frequently shared and has in particular led to the introduction of the soft power subunits by the work in hand.

[357]Rajen Harshe, "Culture, Identity and International Relations," *Economic and Political Weekly*, Vol. 41, No. 37 (September 16-22, 2006), p. 3948.

[358]Nye, *Soft Power*, p. 6; Zahran and Ramos, "From Hegemony to Soft Power," p. 17.

[359]Nye, *Soft Power*, p. 99.

outcomes—particularly when compared to the wielding of hard power. Fred I. Greenstein confronted with a comparable argument regarding the allegedly somewhat murky connection of individual decision-makers' personalities and their political conduct, however, argued—with reference to Abraham Kaplan[360]—that such a line of argument "has no more merit than that of a drunkard who lost his keys in a dark alley and searched for them under a street lamp, declaring, 'It's lighter here.'"[361] Accordingly, the fact that a causal chain may be excruciatingly long or tortuous is no reason not to at least *try* to decipher it—quite the contrary.

In sum, the points of criticism directed toward the concept of soft power, even though some of which stem from a somewhat simplified or even downright false understanding of soft power, can be regarded as valuable starting points for further research. Theoretical clarification, operationalization, methodological accessibility, and not least empirical examinations are thus necessary indeed to develop a more feasible and resilient understanding of soft power. In today's world, characterized by the real-time exchange of ideas and information, by globalization, and by a plethora of challenges beyond the means of traditional power politics, this exercise becomes particularly important. Therefore, in the final analysis, the conceptual and methodological intricacies regarding an examination of the workings of soft power should all the more prompt any researcher to commit time and thought to this dimension of power—an undertaking on which the work in hand embarks in its subsequent chapters.

2.6 Interim Conclusion I: The Phenomenon of Power

Before turning to this very undertaking, a concise roundup regarding the phenomenon of power in international relations, as elaborated upon to this point, seems expedient: (1) As agreed upon by authors hailing from the most diverse camps in International Relations theory, power can be regarded as *the* quintessential phenomenon in international affairs—and indeed all social relations. (2) Equally undisputed, power still constitutes one of the most heavily contested concepts in the social sciences. (3) Beyond that, however, differences in opinion abound, as already apparent by the plethora of different definitions and understandings of power, the most fundamental and influential of which having been referred to above. (4) What is generally agreed upon again, however, is that different varieties of power can be identified. In fact, this insight can draw upon a long tradition, dating back as far as

---

[360] Abraham Kaplan, *The Conduct of Inquiry: Methodology for Behavioral Sciences* (San Francisco, Cal.: Chandler Publishing Company, 1964), p. 11 & pp. 16–17.

[361] Fred I. Greenstein, "The Impact of Personality on the End of the Cold War: A Counterfactual Analysis," *Political Psychology*, Vol. 19, No. 1 (March 1998), p. 14. For a similar comparison, see Dietrich Rueschemeyer, "Can One or a Few Cases Yield Theoretical Gains?," in *Comparative Historical Analysis in the Social Sciences*, eds. James Mahoney and Dietrich Rueschemeyer (Cambridge: Cambridge University Press, 2003), p. 327.

ancient philosophy and the earliest writers on the subject. (5) Power is best understood as a social *relationship*. While power resources, such as armaments, wealth, or culture, are crucially important, of course, they merely provide the feedstock of power. Only by taking into account respective relationships and contexts, issues of power conversion (i.e., the translation of such resources into changed behavior and desired outcomes) can adequately be addressed and the picture of power become complete. (6) While an age-old endeavor, there still is no single, magic formula for measuring (or even predicting) power in international relations. In fact, due to their frequently displayed resource-based understandings of power, such attempts regularly fall short. (7) In what to some extent at least presents a simplification of a multifaced and multi-faceted phenomenon, a dichotomy between hard and soft power can be established, capturing two fundamentally different varieties of power. While the former rests upon the forces of (military or physical) coercion and (economic or financial) inducements, the latter rests upon the forces of attraction and persuasion. (8) Although introduced to the international relations discourse by Joseph Nye after the end of the Cold War, soft power can look back on a millennia-old tradition, as the identification of references to the concept's key mechanisms throughout the centuries has shown. (9) Distinctly non-normative in its nature, soft power can be wielded, like any form of power, for "good" and "bad" purposes alike. (10) At the same time, and arguably for that very reason, it eludes an explicit classification within the International Relations theoretical landscape. (11) The concept of soft power has started a triumphal march after its introduction and meanwhile has become a ubiquitous topic in the public, political, and academic debate alike. (12) However, and arguably not least due to its immense prevalence and extensive discussion, the concept of soft power is still plagued by a high degree of vagueness and imprecision, calling for a thorough (re-)examination. This very objective shall be at the center of the following chapters: First, the concept shall be made more robust by providing a conceptual-theoretical elaboration and differentiation by means of the introduction of a comprehensive soft power taxonomy. Secondly, promising approaches toward its empirical examination shall be presented by offering a detailed methodological roadmap for the study of soft power in international relations.

References

Alcock, Norman Z. and Alan G. Newcombe. "The Perception of National Power." *Journal of Conflict Resolution*, Vol. 14, No. 3 (September 1970), pp. 335–343.
Andrei, Verena and Volker Rittberger. "Macht, Interessen und Normen: Auswärtige Kulturpolitik und Außenpolitiktheorien illustriert am Beispiel der deutschen auswärtigen Sprachpolitik." In *Kultur und Außenpolitik: Handbuch für Wissenschaft und Praxis*, edited by Kurt-Jürgen Maaß, pp. 13–38. Baden Baden: Nomos Verlagsgesellschaft, 2015.
Anholt, Simon. "Soft Power." *Internationale Politik* (January/February 2014), pp. 48–53.
Anter, Andreas. *Theorien der Macht: Zur Einführung.* Hamburg: Junius, 2012.
Arquilla, John and David Ronfeldt. *The Emergence of Noopolitik: Toward an American Information Strategy.* Santa Monica, Cal.: RAND Corporation, 1999.

Arquilla, John and David Ronfeldt. "Noopolitik: A New Paradigm for Public Diplomacy." In *Routledge Handbook of Public Diplomacy*, edited by Nancy Snow and Philip M. Taylor, pp. 352–365. New York, N.Y.: Routledge, 2009.

Augustus. *Meine Taten: Res Gestae Divi Augusti.* Edited by Ekkehard Weber. München: Heimeran Verlag, 1975 (Aug. RG).

Avey, Paul C., Michael C. Desch, James D. Long, Daniel Maliniak, Susan Peterson, and Michael J. Tierney. "The FP Survey: Who Inhabits the Ivory Tower?" *Foreign Policy*, No. 191 (January/February 2012), pp. 90–93.

Baldwin, David A. "Interdependence and Power: A Conceptual Analysis." *International Organization*, Vol. 34, No. 4 (Autumn 1980), pp. 471–506.

Baldwin, David A. "Power and International Relations." In *Handbook of International Relations*, edited by Walter Carlsnaes, Thomas Risse, and Beth A. Simmons, pp. 273–297. Los Angeles: SAGE Publications, 2013.

Barnett, Michael and Raymond Duvall. "Power in International Politics." *International Organization*, Vol. 59, No. 1 (Winter 2005), pp. 39–75.

Baumann, Peter and Gisela Cramer. "Power, Soft or Deep? An Attempt at Constructive Criticism." *Las Torres de Lucca: International Journal of Political Philosophy*, No. 10 (January-June 2017), pp. 177–214.

Berenskoetter, Felix and M. J. Williams, eds. *Power in World Politics.* New York, N.Y.: Routledge, 2008.

Bierling, Stephan G. "Das Ende des langen Booms? Die amerikanische Wirtschaft unter Bill Clinton und George W. Bush." In *Die Clinton-Präsidentschaft: Ein Rückblick*, edited by Stephan G. Bierling and Reinhard C. Meier-Walser, pp. 27–34. München: Hanns-Seidel-Stiftung, 2001.

Blanchard Jean-Marc F. and Fujia Lu. "Thinking Hard about Soft Power: A Review and Critique of the Literature on China and Soft Power." *Asian Perspective* Vol. 36, No. 4 (2012), pp. 565–589.

Boswell, Terry and Albert Bergesen. "American Prospects in a Period of Hegemonic Decline and Economic Crisis." In *America's Changing Role in the World System*, edited by Terry Boswell and Albert Bergesen, pp. 3–13. New York, N.Y.: Praeger, 1987.

Brands, Hal. "The Era of American Primacy is Far from Over." *The National Interest*, August 24, 2016. Online at: http://nationalinterest.org/blog/the-skeptics/the-era-american-primacy-far-over-17465 (accessed August 25, 2016).

Brooks, Peter. "Iran: Our Military Options." *The Heritage Foundation*, January 23, 2006. Online at: http://www.heritage.org/research/commentary/2006/01/iran-our-military-options (accessed February 13, 2015).

Brooks, Stephen G. and William C. Wohlforth. "Power, Globalization, and the End of the Cold War: Reevaluating a Landmark Case for Ideas." *International Security*, Vol. 25, No. 3 (Winter 2000/2001), pp. 5–53.

Broyard, Anatole. "Book of The Times: Human vs. Humanitarian." *The New York Times*, December 22, 1975, p. L27.

Burns, James MacGregor. *Leadership.* New York, N.Y.: HarperCollins, 2010.

Carr, Edward H. *The Twenty Years' Crisis: 1919-1939, An Introduction to the Theory of International Relations.* Reissued with a New Introduction and Additional Material by Michael Cox. Basingstoke: Palgrave, 2001.

Carter, Jimmy. "Our Nation's Past and Future: Address Accepting the Presidential Nomination at the Democratic National Convention in New York City." New York, N.Y., July 15, 1976. Online at: http://www.presidency.ucsb.edu/ws/?pid=25953 (accessed September 5, 2017).

Carter, Jimmy. "Energy and National Goals: Address to the Nation." Washington, D.C., July 15, 1979. In *Public Papers of the Presidents of the United States: Jimmy Carter, 1979, Book II – June 23 to December 31, 1979*, pp. 1235–1241. Washington, D.C.: United States Government Printing Office, 1980.

Center for Strategic and International Studies. *CSIS Commission on Smart Power: A Smarter, More Secure America.* Washington, D.C.: The CSIS Press, 2007.

Cicero, M. Tullius. *Über die Gesetze: De Legibus/Stoische Paradoxien: Paradoxa Stoicum*. Edited, Translated, and Annotated by Rainer Nickel. München: Artemis & Winkler, 1994 (Cic. Leg./ Cic. Parad.).

Cicero, M. Tullius. *Der Staat: De Re Publica*. Edited and Translated by Rainer Nickel. Mannheim: Artemis & Winkler, 2010 (Cic. Rep.).

Clausewitz, Carl von. *On War*. Translated by Colonel J. J. Graham. New and Revised Edition with Introduction and Notes by Colonel F. N. Maude, Volume 1. London: Kegan Paul, Trench, Trubner & Co., 1918.

Clegg, Stewart R. and Mark Haugaard, eds. *The SAGE Handbook of Power*. London: SAGE Publications, 2009.

Cline, Ray S. *The Power of Nations in the 1990s: A Strategic Assessment*. Lanham, Md.: University Press of America, 1994.

Clinton, Hillary Rodham. "Confirmation Hearing." Washington, D.C., January 13, 2009. Online at: http://www.cfr.org/elections/transcript-hillary-clintons-confirmation-hearing/p18225 (accessed February 12, 2015).

Clinton, Hillary Rodham. "Leading Through Civilian Power: Redefining American Diplomacy and Development." *Foreign Affairs*, Vol. 89, No. 6 (November/December 2010), pp. 13–24.

Clinton, Hillary Rodham. "American Global Leadership: Remarks at the Center for American Progress." Washington, D.C., October 12, 2011. Online at: http://www.state.gov/secretary/ 20092013clinton/rm/2011/10/175340.htm (accessed February 12, 2015).

Clinton, Hillary Rodham. *Hard Choices*. New York, N.Y.: Simon & Schuster, 2014.

Cohen, Eliot A. "Presidents and Their Generals: A Conversation with Eliot Cohen." *The American Interest*, Vol. 6, No. 1 (Autumn 2010), pp. 6–14.

Colby, Elbridge and Paul Lettow. "Have We Hit Peak America? The Sources of U.S. Power and the Path to National Renaissance." *Foreign Policy*, No. 207 (July/August 2014), pp. 54–63.

Commuri, Gitika. "'Are You Pondering What I am Pondering?' Understanding the Conditions Under Which States Gain and Loose Soft Power." In *Power in the 21st Century: International Security and International Political Economy in a Changing World*, edited by Enrico Fels, Jan-Frederik Kremer, and Katharina Kronenberg, pp. 43–57. Berlin: Springer-Verlag, 2012.

Cox, Robert W. "Social Forces, States and World Orders: Beyond International Relations Theory." *Millennium: Journal of International Studies*, Vol. 10, No. 2 (1981), pp. 126–155.

Cronin, Vincent. *Napoleon: Eine Biographie*. Hamburg: Classen Verlag, 1973.

Cull, Nicholas J. *Public Diplomacy: Lessons from the Past, CPD Perspectives on Public Diplomacy*. Los Angeles, Cal.: Figueroa Press, 2011.

Curry, Anne. *The Battle of Agincourt: Sources & Interpretations*. Woodbridge: The Boydell Press, 2000.

Curry, Anne. *Henry V: Playboy Prince to Warrior King*. London: Penguin Books, 2018.

Dahl, Robert A. "The Concept of Power." *Behavioral Science*, Vol. 2, No. 3 (1957), pp. 201–215.

Dickens, Charles. *The Life and Adventures of Martin Chuzzlewit*. London: Chapman and Hall, 1844.

Donilon, Tom. "We're No. 1 (and We're Going to Stay That Way)." *Foreign Policy*, July 3, 2014. Online at: http://foreignpolicy.com/2014/07/03/were-no-1-and-were-going-to-stay-that-way/ (accessed February 10, 2015).

Dowding, Keith, ed. *Encyclopedia of Power*. Thousand Oaks, Cal.: SAGE Publications, 2011.

Doyle, Charles C., Wolfgang Mieder, and Fred Shapiro. *The Dictionary of Modern Proverbs*. New Haven, Conn.: Yale University Press, 2012.

Drezner, Daniel W. "Does Obama Have a Grand Strategy? Why We Need Doctrines in Uncertain Times." *Foreign Affairs*, Vol. 58, No. 4 (July/August 2011), pp. 57–68.

Drezner, Daniel W. "Get Smart: How to Cram for 2012." *Foreign Policy*, No. 187 (July/August 2011), p. 32.

Duffey, Joseph. "How Globalization Became U.S. Public Diplomacy at the End of the Cold War." In *Routledge Handbook of Public Diplomacy*, edited by Nancy Snow and Philip M. Taylor, pp. 325-334. New York, N.Y.: Routledge, 2009.

Ellis, John. "The Superstring: Theory of Everything, or of Nothing?." *Nature*, Vol. 323, No. 6089 (1986), pp. 595–598.

Elman, Colin and Miriam Fendius Elman. "Negotiating International History and Politics." In *Bridges and Boundaries: Historians, Political Scientists, and the Study of International Relations*, edited by Colin Elman and Miriam Fendius Elman, pp. 1–36. Cambridge, Mass.: MIT Press, 2001.

Etheridge, Eric. "How 'Soft Power' Got 'Smart.'" *The New York Times*, January 14, 2009. Online at: http://opinionator.blogs.nytimes.com/2009/01/14/how-soft-power-got-smart/ (accessed August 12, 2016).

Fels, Enrico. "Power Shift? Power in International Relations and the Allegiance of Middle Powers." In *Power in the 21st Century: International Security and International Political Economy in a Changing World*, edited by Enrico Fels, Jan-Frederik Kremer, and Katharina Kronenberg, pp. 3–28. Berlin: Springer-Verlag, 2012.

Fels, Fels. "Dancing with the Dragon: Indonesia and Its Relations to a Rising China." In *Indonesia's Search for Democracy: Political, Economic, and Social Developments*, edited by Matthias Heise and Kathrin Rucktäschel, pp. 163–190. Baden-Baden: Nomos, 2013.

Fels, Enrico. "Beyond Military Interventions? The Shanghai Cooperation Organisation and its Quest for *cuius regio, eius dicio.*" In *Military Interventions: Considerations from Philosophy and Political Science*, edited by Christian Neuhäuser and Christoph Schuck, pp. 149–191. Baden-Baden: Nomos, 2017.

Fels, Enrico. *Shifting Power in Asia-Pacific? The Rise of China, Sino-US Competition and Regional Middle Power Allegiance*. Cham: Springer International, 2017.

Ferguson, Niall. "Think Again: Power." *Foreign Policy*, No. 134 (January/February 2003), pp. 18–22 & 24.

Ferguson, Niall. *Colossus: The Price of America's Empire*. New York, N.Y.: Penguin Press, 2004.

Foreign Policy Staff. "The FP Top 100 Global Thinkers." *Foreign Policy*, November 28, 2011. Online at: http://foreignpolicy.com/2011/11/28/the-fp-top-100-global-thinkers-3/ (accessed February 10, 2015).

Foreign Policy Staff. "Does the Academy Matter?." *Foreign Policy*, No. 205 (March/April 2014), pp. 60–69.

Foucault, Michel. *Discipline and Punish: The Birth of Prison*. Translated by Alan Sheridan. New York, N.Y.: Vintage Books, 1977.

Frankfurter Allgemeine Archiv. Online at: https://fazarchiv.faz.net (accessed August 2, 2018).

Fraser, Matthew. *Weapons of Mass Distraction: Soft Power and American Empire*. New York, N.Y.: St. Martin's Press, 2003.

Freedom House. "Freedom in the World: Electoral Democracies." Online at: https://freedomhouse.org/sites/default/files/Electoral%20Democracy%20Numbers,%20FIW%201989-2013.pdf (accessed August 15, 2018).

Friedberg, Aaron L. "Same Old Song: What the Declinists (and Triumphalists) Miss." *The American Interest*, Vol. 5, No. 2 (November/December 2009), pp. 28–35.

Friedensburg, Ferdinand. *Die mineralischen Bodenschätze als weltpolitische und militärische Machtfaktoren*. Stuttgart: Ferdinand Enke Verlag, 1936.

Friedrich der Große. "Abriß der preußischen Regierung und der Grundsätze, auf denen sie beruht, nebst einigen politischen Betrachtungen." In *Ausgewählte Schriften*, edited by Ulrike-Christine Sander, pp. 73–82. Frankfurt am Main: Fischer, 2011.

Friedrich der Große. "Fürstenspiegel, oder Unterweisung des Königs für den jungen Herzog Karl Eugen von Württemberg." In *Ausgewählte Schriften*, edited by Ulrike-Christine Sander, pp. 47–51. Frankfurt am Main: Fischer, 2011.

Fucks, Wilhelm. *Formeln zur Macht: Prognosen über Völker, Wirtschaft, Potentiale*. Stuttgart: Deutsche Verlags-Anstalt, 1965.

Fukuyama, Francis. "The End of History." *National Interest*, No. 16 (Summer 1989), pp. 3–18.

Fukuyama, Francis. *The End of History and the Last Man*. New York, N.Y.: Simon & Schuster, 1992.

Fukuyama, Francis. "The Neoconservative Moment." *The National Interest*, No. 76 (Summer 2004), pp. 57–68.

Furlong, Paul and David Marsh. "A Skin Not a Sweater: Ontology and Epistemology in Political Science." In *Theory and Methods in Political Science*, edited by David Marsh and Gerry Stoker, pp. 184–211. Basingstoke: Palgrave Macmillan, 2010.

Gallarotti, Giulio M. *Cosmopolitan Power in International Relations: A Synthesis of Realism, Neoliberalism, and Constructivism*. Cambridge: Cambridge University Press, 2010.

Gallarotti, Giulio M. "Smart Power: Definitions, Importance, and Effectiveness." *Journal of Strategic Studies*, Vol. 38, No. 3 (2015), pp. 245–281.

Garrison, Jim. *America's Empire: Global Leader or Rogue Power*. San Francisco, Cal.: Berrett-Koehler Publishers, 2004.

Gaskarth, Jamie. *British Foreign Policy: Crises, Conflicts and Future Challenges*. Cambridge: Polity Press, 2013.

Geiger, Till. "*The Power Game*, Soft Power and the International Historian." In *Soft Power and US Foreign Policy: Theoretical, Historical and Contemporary Perspectives*, edited by Inderjeet Parmar and Michael Cox, pp. 83–107. Abingdon: Routledge, 2010.

Gelb, Leslie H. *Power Rules: How Common Sense Can Rescue American Foreign Policy*. New York, N.Y.: HarperCollins, 2009.

German, F. Clifford. "A Tentative Evaluation of World Power." *Journal of Conflict Resolution*, Vol. 4, No. 1 (1960), pp. 138–144.

Gilboa, Eytan. "Searching for a Theory of Public Diplomacy." *The Annals of the American Academy of Political and Social Science*, Vol. 616, Public Diplomacy in a Changing World (March 2008), pp. 55–77.

Goldsmith, Benjamin E. and Yusaku Horiuchi. "In Search of Soft Power: Does Foreign Public Opinion Matter for US Foreign Policy?." *World Politics*, Vol. 64, No. 3 (July 2012), pp. 555–585.

Goldstein, Joshua S. and Jon C. Pevehouse. *International Relations*. New York, N.Y.: Pearson Longman, 2014.

Greenstein, Fred I. "The Impact of Personality on the End of the Cold War: A Counterfactual Analysis." *Political Psychology*, Vol. 19, No. 1 (March 1998), pp. 1–16.

Gu, Xuewu. "Global Power Shift: Soft, Hard and Structural Power." In *Die Gestaltung der Globalität: Annährungen an Begriff, Deutung und Methodik*, edited by Ludger Kühnhardt and Tilman Mayer, pp. 53-60. Bonn: Zentrum für Europäische Integrationsforschung, Discussion Paper C198, 2010.

Gu, Xuewu. "Strukturelle Macht: Eine dritte Machtquelle?" *Österreichische Zeitschrift für Politikwissenschaft*, Vol. 41, No. 3 (2012), pp. 259–276.

Gu, Xuewu. *Die Große Mauer in den Köpfen: China, der Westen und die Suche nach Verständigung*. Hamburg: Edition Körber-Stiftung, 2014.

Gu, Xuewu. "Ist Globalität gestaltbar?." In *Bonner Enzyklopädie der Globalität*, edited by Ludger Kühnhardt and Tilman Mayer, pp. 1527–1541. Wiesbaden: Springer Fachmedien, 2017.

Gu, Xuewu. *Theorien der Internationalen Beziehungen: Einführung*. Berlin: Walter de Gruyter 2018.

Guzzini, Stefano. "The Concept of Power: A Constructivist Analysis." *Millennium: Journal of International Studies*, Vol. 33, No. 3 (2005), pp. 495–521.

Guzzini, Stefano. *Power, Realism and Constructivism*. Abingdon: Routledge, 2013.

Haass, Richard N. "13 International Relations Buzzwords That Need to Get Taken to the Woodshed." *Foreign Policy*, February 3, 2017. Online at: http://foreignpolicy.com/2017/02/03/13-international-relations-buzzwords-that-need-to-get-taken-to-the-woodshed/ (accessed March 26, 2017).

Hall, Todd. "An Unclear Attraction: A Critical Examination of Soft Power as an Analytical Category." *The Chinese Journal of International Politics*, Vol. 3, No. 2 (2010), pp. 189–211.

Hamilton, Alexander. "Federalist No. 33." In *The Federalist Papers*, edited by Clinton Rossiter, pp. 197–201. New York, N.Y.: Signet Classic, 2003.

Hamilton, Edith. *The Greek Way*. London: W. W. Norton & Company, 1993.

Han, Byung-Chul. *Was ist Macht?* Stuttgart: Reclam, 2005.

Harshe, Rajen. "Culture, Identity and International Relations." *Economic and Political Weekly*, Vol. 41, No. 37 (September 16-22, 2006), pp. 3945 & 3947–3951.

Hatscher, Christoph R. *Charisma und Res Publica: Max Webers Herrschaftssoziologie und die Römische Republik*. Stuttgart: Franz Steiner Verlag, 2000.

Haugaard, Mark. *Power: A Reader*. Manchester: Manchester University Press, 2002.

Haugaard, Mark and Stewart R. Clegg. "Introduction: Why Power is the Central Concept of the Social Sciences." In *The SAGE Handbook of Power*, edited by Stewart R. Clegg and Mark Haugaard, pp. 1–24. London: SAGE Publications, 2009.

Hawking, Stephen W. "Gödel and the End of Physics." University of Cambridge Department of Applied Mathematics and Theoretical Physics, July 20, 2002. Online at: http://www.damtp.cam. ac.uk/events/strings02/dirac/hawking/ (accessed June 17, 2014).

Heinze, Richard. "Auctoritas." *Hermes*, Vol. 60 (1925), pp. 348–366.

Hobbes, Thomas. *Leviathan*. With an Essay by the Late W. G. Pogson Smith. Oxford: Clarendon Press, 1909.

Hübner, Dietmar. "Der Ort der Macht: *Potestas* und *auctoritas* als Deutungslinien für Markt und Medien." *Deutsche Zeitschrift für Philosophie*, Vol. 58, No. 3 (2010), pp. 395–415.

Huntington, Samuel P. "The United States: Decline or Renewal?." *Adelphi Papers*, Vol. 29, No. 235 (1989), pp. 63–80.

Huntington, Samuel P. "Democracy's Third Wave." Journal of Democracy, Vol. 2, No. 2 (Spring 1991), pp. 12–34.

Huntington, Samuel P. *The Third Wave: Democratization in the Late Twentieth Century*. Norman, Okla.: University of Oklahoma Press, 1991.

Ifantis, Kostas. "Soft Power: Overcoming the Limits of a Concept." In *Routledge Handbook of Diplomacy and Statecraft*, edited by B. J. C. McKercher, pp. 441–452. Abingdon: Routledge, 2011.

Inboden, William. "What is Power? And How Much of It Does America Have?." *The American Interest*, Vol. 5, No. 2 (November/December 2009), pp. 15–19 & 22–27.

International Churchill Society. "Quotes Falsely Attributed to Winston Churchill: Jaw-Jaw." Online at: https://www.winstonchurchill.org/resources/quotes/quotes-falsely-attributed (accessed September 9, 2017).

Internet Live Stats. "Total Number of Websites." Online at: http://www.internetlivestats.com/total-number-of-websites/ (accessed August 2, 2018).

Internet Live Stats. "Trends & More (Statistics)." Online at: http://www.internetlivestats.com/ statistics/ (accessed August 2, 2018).

Jarausch, Konrad H. "Intellectual Dissonance: German-American (Mis-)Understandings in the 1990s." In *The German-American Encounter: Conflict and Cooperation between Two Cultures, 1800-2000*, edited by Frank Trommler and Elliott Shore, pp. 219–233. New York, N.Y.: Berghahn Books, 2001.

Joffe, Josef. "The Default Power: The False Prophecy of America's Decline." *Foreign Affairs*, Vol. 88, No. 5 (September/October 2009), pp. 21–35.

Kaarbo, Juliet and James Lee Ray. *Global Politics*. Boston, Mass.: Wadsworth, 2011.

Kagan, Frederick W. "Power and Persuasion" *The Wilson Quarterly*, Vol. 29, No. 3 (Summer 2005), pp. 57–65.

Kagan, Robert. "Not Fade Away." *The New Republic*, January 11, 2012. Online at: http://www. newrepublic.com/article/politics/magazine/99521/america-world-power-declinism (accessed February 10, 2015).

Kagan, Robert. "Power and Weakness." *Policy Review*, No. 113 (June/July 2002), pp. 3–28.

Kaplan, Abraham. *The Conduct of Inquiry: Methodology for Behavioral Sciences*. San Francisco, Cal.: Chandler Publishing Company, 1964.

Kathe, Steffen R. *Kulturpolitik um jeden Preis: Die Geschichte des Goethe-Instituts von 1951 bis 1990*. München: Martin Meidenbauer, 2005.

Keck, Zachary. "The Hard Side of Soft Power." *The Diplomat*, July 24, 2013. Online at: http:// thediplomat.com/2013/07/the-hard-side-of-soft-power/ (accessed June 1, 2016).

Kennedy, Paul. *The Rise and Fall of the Great Powers*. New York, N.Y.: Vintage Books, 1987.
Keohane, Robert O. *After Hegemony: Cooperation and Discord in World Political Economy*. Princeton, N.J.: Princeton University Press, 1984.
Keohane, Robert O. and Joseph S. Nye, Jr. "Transnational Relations and World Politics: An Introduction." *International Organization*, Vol. 25, No. 3 (Summer 1971), pp. 329–349.
Keohane, Robert O. and Joseph S. Nye, Jr. "Power and Interdependence." *Survival*, Vol. 15, No. 4 (1973), pp. 158–165.
Keohane, Robert O. and Joseph S. Nye, Jr. *Power and Independence: World Politics in Transition*. Boston, Mass.: Little Brown and Company, 1977.
Keohane, Robert O. and Joseph S. Nye, Jr. "Power and Interdependence Revisited." *International Organization*, Vol. 41, No. 4 (Autumn 1987), pp. 725–753.
Keohane, Robert O. and Joseph S. Nye, Jr. "Power and Interdependence in the Information Age." *Foreign Affairs*, Vol. 77, No. 5 (September/October 1998), pp. 81–94.
Keohane, Robert O. and Joseph S. Nye, Jr. *Power and Independence: World Politics in Transition*. Boston, Mass.: Longman, 2012.
Kilbane, Mark. "Military Psychological Operations as Public Diplomacy." In *Routledge Handbook of Public Diplomacy*, edited by Nancy Snow and Philip M. Taylor, pp. 187–192. New York, N. Y.: Routledge, 2009.
Kingsbury, Paul, Michael McCall, and John W. Rumble, eds. *The Encyclopedia of Country Music*. New York, N.Y.: Oxford University Press, 2012.
Kivimäki, Timo. "'Reason' and 'Power' in Territorial Disputes: The South China Sea." *Asian Journal of Social Science*, Vol. 30, No. 3 (2002), pp. 525–546.
Kounalakis, Markos and Andras Simonyi. *The Hard Truth about Soft Power, CPD Perspectives on Public Diplomacy*, Paper 5, 2011, Los Angeles, Cal.: Figueroa Press, 2011.
Krige, John. "Technological Leadership and American Soft Power." In *Soft Power and US Foreign Policy: Theoretical, Historical and Contemporary Perspectives*, edited by Inderjeet Parmar and Michael Cox, pp. 121–136. Abingdon: Routledge, 2010.
Kugler, Jacek and William Domke. "Comparing the Strength of Nations." *Comparative Political Studies*, Vol. 19, No. 1 (April 1986), pp. 39–69.
Kühnhardt, Ludger. *Von der ewigen Suche nach Frieden: Immanuel Kants Vision und Europas Wirklichkeit*. Bonn: Bouvier Verlag, 1996.
Kühnhardt, Ludger. "Globality: Concept and Impact." In *The Bonn Handbook of Globality, Volume 1*, edited by Ludger Kühnhardt and Tilman Mayer, pp. 19–33. Cham: Springer International Publishing, 2019.
Kurlantzick, Joshua. *Charm Offensive: How China's Soft Power is Transforming the World*. New Haven, Conn.: Yale University Press, 2007.
Layne, Christopher. "The Unbearable Lightness of Soft Power." In *Soft Power and US Foreign Policy: Theoretical, Historical and Contemporary Perspectives*, edited by Inderjeet Parmar and Michael Cox, pp. 51–82. Abingdon: Routledge, 2010.
Lebow, Richard Ned. "The Long Peace, the End of the Cold War, and the Failure of Realism." *International Organization*, Vol. 48, No. 2 (Spring 1994), pp. 249–277.
Lebow, Richard Ned. *A Cultural Theory of International Relations*. Cambridge: Cambridge University Press, 2008.
Lebow, Richard Ned and Thomas Risse-Kappen, eds. *International Relations Theory and the End of the Cold War*. New York, N.Y.: Columbia University Press, 1995.
Lee, Geun. "A Theory of Soft Power and Korea's Soft Power Strategy." *The Korean Journal of Defense Analysis*, Vol. 21, No. 2 (June 2009), pp. 205–218.
Legro, Jeffrey W. and Andrew Moravcsik. "Is Anybody Still a Realist?." *International Security*, Vol. 24, No. 2 (Fall 1999), pp. 5–55.
Leonard, Mark. *What Does China Think?* New York: PublicAffairs, 2008.
Levitt, Theodore. "The Globalization of Markets." *Harvard Business Review*, May 1983. Online at: https://hbr.org/1983/05/the-globalization-of-markets (accessed September 28, 2015).
Lewis, C. S. *The Chronicles of Narnia: Book 1, The Magician's Nephew*. New York, N.Y.: HarperTrophy, 1994.

Lock, Edward. "Soft Power and Strategy: Developing a 'Strategic' Concept of Power." In *Soft Power and US Foreign Policy: Theoretical, Historical and Contemporary Perspectives*, edited by Inderjeet Parmar and Michael Cox, pp. 32–50. Abingdon: Routledge, 2010.

Locke, John. "An Essay Concerning Human Understanding." *Great Books of the Western World*, edited by Robert Maynard Hutchins, Volume 35, pp. 83–395. Chicago, Ill.: Encyclopædia Britannica, 1952.

Lukes, Steven. *Power: A Radical View*. Basingstoke: Palgrave Macmillan, 2005.

Lukes, Steven. "Power and the Battle for the Hearts and Minds." *Millennium: Journal of International Studies*, Vol. 33, No. 3 (2005), pp. 477–493.

Lukes, Steven. "Power." In *The Oxford Companion to International Relations*, edited by Joel Krieger, Volume 2, pp. 197–199. Oxford: Oxford University Press, 2014.

Maaß, Kurt-Jürgen. "Vielfältige Umsetzungen – Ziele und Instrumente der Auswärtigen Kulturpolitik." In *Kultur und Außenpolitik: Handbuch für Wissenschaft und Praxis*, edited by Kurt-Jürgen Maaß, pp. 47–54. Baden Baden: Nomos Verlagsgesellschaft, 2015.

Madison, James. "Helvidius Number I." In *The Pacificus-Helvidius Debates of 1793-1794: Toward the Completion of the American Founding, Alexander Hamilton and James Madison*. Edited and with an Introduction by Morton J. Frisch, pp. 55–64. Indianapolis, Ind.: Liberty Fund, 2007.

Mann, James. *Rise of the Vulcans: The History of Bush's War Cabinet*. New York, N.Y.: Viking, 2004.

Mattern, Janice Bially. "Why 'Soft Power' Isn't So Soft: Representational Force and the Sociolinguistic Construction of Attraction in World Politics." *Millennium: Journal of International Studies*, Vol. 33, No. 3 (2005), pp. 583–612.

Mattern, Janice Bially. "Why 'Soft Power' Isn't So Soft: Representational Force and Attraction in World Politics." In *Power in World Politics*, edited by Felix Berenskoetter and M.J. Williams, pp. 98–119. New York, N.Y.: Routledge, 2008.

Mayer, Tilman, Robert Meyer, Lazaros Miliopoulos, H. Peter Ohly, and Erich Weede. "Globalisierung im Fokus von Politik, Wirtschaft, Gesellschaft: Einführende Betrachtungen." In *Globalisierung im Fokus von Politik, Wirtschaft, Gesellschaft: Eine Bestandsaufnahme*, edited by Tilman Mayer, Robert Meyer, Lazaros Miliopoulos, H. Peter Ohly, and Erich Weede, pp. 9–25. Wiesbaden: Verlag für Sozialwissenschaften, 2011.

Mead, Walter Russell. "America's Sticky Power." *Foreign Policy*, No. 141 (March/April 2004), pp. 46–53.

Mead, Walter Russell. *Power, Terror, Peace, and War: America's Grand Strategy in a World at Risk*. New York, N.Y.: Alfred A. Knopf, 2004.

Meagher, Robert E. "A Man Is Defined by His Longings." *The New York Times*, October 12, 1971, p. L43.

Mearsheimer, John J. "Anarchy and the Struggle for Power." In *Essential Readings in World Politics*, edited by Karen Mingst and Jack Snyder, pp. 60–79. New York, N.Y.: W. W. Norton and Company, 2008.

Montesquieu. *Reflections on the Causes of the Rise and Fall of the Roman Empire*. London: Geo. B. Whittaker, 1825.

Moravcsik, Andrew. "Taking Preferences Seriously: A Liberal Theory of International Politics." *International Organization*, Vol. 51, No. 4 (Autumn 1997), pp. 513–533.

Morgenthau, Hans J. *Politics Among Nations: The Struggle for Power and Peace*. New York, N.Y.: McGraw-Hill, 2006.

Morriss, Peter. *Power: A Philosophical Analysis*. Manchester: Manchester University Press, 2002.

Murdoch, Adrian. *Rome's Greatest Defeat: Massacre in the Teutoburg Forest*. Stroud: The History Press, 2008.

Nippel, Wilfried. "The Roman Notion of *Auctoritas*." In *The Concept of Authority: A Multidisciplinary Approach, From Epistemology to the Social Sciences*, edited by Pasquale Pasquino and Pamela Harris, pp. 13–34. Rome: Fondazione Adriano Olivetti, 2007.

Nisbet, Robert. "The Twilight of Authority." *The Public Interest*, Vol. 15 (Spring 1969), pp. 3–9.

Nisbet, Robert. *Twilight of Authority*. New York, N.Y.: Oxford University Press, 1975.

Nossel, Suzanne. "Smart Power." *Foreign Affairs*, Vol. 83, No. 2 (March/April 2004), pp. 131–142.

Nye, Joseph S., Jr. "Neorealism and Neoliberalism." *World Politics*, Vol. 40, No. 2 (January 1988), pp. 235–251.

Nye, Joseph S., Jr. *Bound to Lead: The Changing Nature of American Power.* New York: Basic Books, 1990.

Nye, Joseph S., Jr. "Soft Power." *Foreign Policy*, No. 80 (Autumn 1990), pp. 153–171.

Nye, Joseph S., Jr. "The Power We Must Not Squander." *The New York Times*, January 3, 2000. Online at: http://www.nytimes.com/2000/01/03/opinion/the-power-we-must-not-squander.html (accessed October 10, 2015).

Nye, Joseph S., Jr. "The Decline of America's Soft Power: Why Washington Should Worry." *Foreign Affairs*, Vol. 83, No. 3 (May/June 2004), pp. 16–20.

Nye, Joseph S., Jr. *Soft Power: The Means to Success in World Politics.* New York, N.Y.: PublicAffairs, 2004.

Nye, Joseph S., Jr. "Soft Power and Higher Education." *Forum Futures 2005.* EDUCAUSE, January 1, 2005. Online at: https://net.educause.edu/ir/library/pdf/ffp0502s.pdf (accessed February 19, 2015), pp. 11–14.

Nye, Joseph S., Jr. "Think Again: Soft Power." *Foreign Policy*, February 23, 2006. Online at: http://foreignpolicy.com/2006/02/23/think-again-soft-power/ (accessed February 13, 2015).

Nye, Joseph S., Jr. "Foreword." In *Soft Power Superpowers: Cultural and National Assets of Japan and the United States*, edited by Watanabe Yasushi and David L. McConnell, pp. ix–xiv. Armonk, N.Y.: M.E. Sharpe, 2008.

Nye, Joseph S., Jr. "Notes for a Soft-Power Research Agenda." In *Power in World Politics*, edited by Felix Berenskoetter and M.J. Williams, pp. 162–172. New York, N.Y.: Routledge, 2008.

Nye, Joseph S., Jr. "Get Smart: Combining Hard and Soft Power." *Foreign Affairs*, Vol. 88, No. 4 (July/August 2009), pp. 160–163.

Nye, Joseph S., Jr. "Harvard Professor Joseph Nye on Hard and Soft Power: 'It Is Pointless to Talk to Al-Qaida.'" Interview conducted by Gabor Steingart and Gregor Peter Schmitz, *Der Spiegel*, 34/2009, August 17, 2009. Online at: http://www.spiegel.de/international/world/harvard-professor-joseph-nye-on-hard-and-soft-power-it-is-pointless-to-talk-to-al-qaida-a-643189-2.html (accessed July 17, 2018).

Nye, Joseph S., Jr. "Responding to My Critics and Concluding Thoughts." In *Soft Power and US Foreign Policy: Theoretical, Historical and Contemporary Perspectives*, edited by Inderjeet Parmar and Michael Cox, pp. 215–227. Abingdon: Routledge, 2010.

Nye, Joseph S., Jr. "The Future of American Power: Dominance and Decline in Perspective." *Foreign Affairs*, Vol. 89, No. 6 (November/December 2010), pp. 2–12.

Nye, Joseph S., Jr. *The Future of Power.* New York, N.Y.: PublicAffairs, 2011.

Nye, Joseph S., Jr. "China's Soft Power Strategy." In *Bridging the Trust Divide: Cultural Diplomacy and Fostering Understanding Between China and the West*, edited by Helmut K. Anheier and Bernhard Lorentz, pp. 30–33. Essen: Stiftung Mercator, 2012.

Nye, Joseph S., Jr. "Hard, Soft, and Smart Power." In *The Oxford Handbook of Modern Diplomacy*, edited by Andrew F. Cooper, Jorge Heine, and Ramesh Thakur, pp. 559–574. Oxford: Oxford University Press, 2013.

Nye, Joseph S., Jr. "The Information Revolution and Power." *Current History*, Vol. 133, No. 759 (2014), pp. 19–22.

Nye, Joseph S., Jr. *Is the American Century Over?*. Cambridge: Polity Press, 2015.

Nye, Joseph S., Jr. "Soft Power: The Origins and Political Progress of a Concept." *Palgrave Communications*, Vol. 3 (February 21, 2017). Online at: https://www.nature.com/articles/palcomms20178 (accessed August 14, 2017).

Organski, A. F. K. *World Politics.* New York, N.Y.: Alfred Knopf, 1958.

Oxford Dictionary of English, edited by Angus Stevenson. Oxford: Oxford University Press, 2010.

Paliwoda, Stanley J. and Stephanie Slater. "Globalisation Through the Kaleidoscope." *International Marketing Review*, Vol. 26, No. 4/5 (2009), pp. 373–383.

Patterson, James T. *Restless Giant: The United States from Watergate to Bush v. Gore*. New York, N.Y.: Oxford University Press, 2005.

Patton, George S. *War as I Knew It*. Boston, Mass.: Houghton Mifflin Company, 1995.

Pierson, Paul. "Power and Path Dependence." In *Advances in Comparative-Historical Analysis*, edited by James Mahoney and Kathleen Thelen, pp. 123–146. Cambridge: Cambridge University Press, 2015.

Pratkanis, Anthony. "Public Diplomacy in International Conflicts: A Social Influence Analysis." In *Routledge Handbook of Public Diplomacy*, edited by Nancy Snow and Philip M. Taylor, pp. 111–153. New York, N.Y.: Routledge, 2009.

Reagan, Ronald. "Remarks on the Occasion of 83rd Birthday Gala." Simi Valley, Cal., February 3, 1994. Online at: http://www.americanrhetoric.com/speeches/ronaldreagan83rdbirthday.htm (accessed November 16, 2015).

Riley, Patrick. "The General Will Before Rousseau." In *Jean-Jacques Rousseau: Critical Assessment of Leading Political Philosophers, Volume III: Political Principles and Institutions*, edited by John T. Scott, pp. 135–162. Abingdon: Routledge, 2006.

Robert, Rüdiger. "Globalisierung als Herausforderung für das politische System." In *Bundesrepublik Deutschland: Politisches System und Globalisierung, Eine Einführung*, edited by Rüdiger Robert, pp. 27–47. Münster: Waxmann, 2007.

Robertson, Thomas S. "The Process of Innovation and the Diffusion of Innovation." *Journal of Marketing*, Vol. 31, No. 1 (January 1967), pp. 14–19.

Rödder, Andreas. *21.0: Eine kurze Geschichte der Gegenwart*. München: C. H. Beck, 2015.

Roselle, Laura, Alister Miskimmon, and Ben O'Loughlin. "Strategic Narrative: A New Means to Understand Soft Power." *Media, War & Conflict*, Vol. 7, No. 1 (2014), pp. 70–84.

Rowland, Robert C. and John M. Jones. *Reagan at Westminster: Foreshadowing the End of the Cold War*. College Station, Tex.: Texas A&M University Press, 2010.

Rueschemeyer, Dietrich. "Can One or a Few Cases Yield Theoretical Gains?" In *Comparative Historical Analysis in the Social Sciences*, edited by James Mahoney and Dietrich Rueschemeyer, pp. 305–336. Cambridge: Cambridge University Press, 2003.

Russell, Bertrand. *Power: A New Social Analysis*. London: George Allen and Unwin, 1938.

Schneider, Cynthia P. "Culture Communicates: US Diplomacy at Work." In *The New Public Diplomacy: Soft Power in International Relations*, edited by Jan Melissen, pp. 147–168. Basingstoke: Palgrave Macmillan, 2005.

Schroeder, Paul W. "Historical Reality vs. Neorealist Theory." *International Security*, Vol. 19, No. 1 (Summer 1994), pp. 108–148.

Schwarz, Hans-Peter. "America, Germany, and the Atlantic Community after the Cold War." In *The United States and Germany in the Era of the Cold War, 1945-1990: A Handbook, Volume II: 1968-1990*, edited by Detlef Junker, associated editors Philipp Gassert, Wilfried Mausbach, and David B. Morris, pp. 535–565. Cambridge: Cambridge University Press, 2004.

Scott-Smith, Giles. "Exchange Programs and Public Diplomacy." In *Routledge Handbook of Public Diplomacy*, edited by Nancy Snow and Philip M. Taylor, pp. 50–55. New York, N.Y.: Routledge, 2009.

Scott-Smith, Giles. "Soft Power in an Era of US Decline." In *Soft Power and US Foreign Policy: Theoretical, Historical and Contemporary Perspectives*, edited by Inderjeet Parmar and Michael Cox, pp. 165–181. Abingdon: Routledge, 2010.

Shambaugh, David. *China Goes Global: The Partial Power*. New York: Oxford University Press, 2013.

Singer, J. David and Melvin Small. *The Wages of War, 1816-1965: A Statistical Handbook*. New York, N.Y.: John Wiley, 1972.

Snow, Nancy. "Rethinking Public Diplomacy." In *Routledge Handbook of Public Diplomacy*, edited by Nancy Snow and Philip M. Taylor, pp. 3–11. New York, N.Y.: Routledge, 2009.

Solomon, Ty. "The Affective Underpinnings of Soft Power." *European Journal of International Relations*, Vol. 20, No. 3 (2014), pp. 720–741.

Stoll, Richard J. and Michael D. Ward, eds. *Power in World Politics*. Boulder, Colo.: Lynne Rienner Publishers, 1989.

Su Changhe. "Soft Power." In *The Oxford Handbook of Modern Diplomacy*, edited by Andrew F. Cooper, Jorge Heine, and Ramesh Thakur, pp. 544–558. Oxford: Oxford University Press, 2013.

Süßmilch, Johann Peter. *Die göttliche Ordnung in den Veränderungen des menschlichen Geschlechts, aus der Geburt, dem Tode und der Fortpflanzung desselben erwiesen*. Göttingen: Jürgen Chrom Verlag, 1988.

Taylor, A. J. P. *The Struggle for Mastery in Europe, 1848-1918*. Oxford: Oxford University Press, 1954.

The New York Times Article Archive. Online at: http://www.nytimes.com/ref/membercenter/nytarchive.html (accessed August 2, 2018).

Thussu, Daya. *De-Americanizing Soft Power Discourse?*. CPD Perspectives on Public Diplomacy, *Paper 2, 2014*. Los Angeles, Cal.: Figueroa Press, 2012.

Treverton, Gregory F. *America, Germany, and the Future of Europe*. Princeton, N.J.: Princeton University Press, 1992.

Van Ham, Peter. "Power, Public Diplomacy, and the *Pax Americana*." In *The New Public Diplomacy: Soft Power in International Relations*, edited by Jan Melissen, pp. 47–66. Basingstoke: Palgrave Macmillan, 2005.

Vasilevskyte, Simona. "Discussing Soft Power Theory After Nye: The Case of Geun Lee's Theoretical Approach." *Regional Studies*, No. 7 (2013), pp. 145–157.

Virmani, Arvind. "VIP^2: A Simple Measure of a Nation's (Natural) Global Power." *Indian Council for Research on International Economic Relations*, July 2005. Online at: http://www.icrier.org/pdf/VIPP4.pdf (accessed July 24, 2014).

Walker, Christopher. "The Hijacking of 'Soft Power.'" *Journal of Democracy*, Vol. 27, No. 1 (January 2016), pp. 49–63.

Waltz, Kenneth N. *Man, the State and War: A Theoretical Analysis*. New York, N.Y.: Columbia University Press, 1959.

Waltz, Kenneth N. "Reflections on Theory of International Politics: A Response to My Critics." In *Neorealism and its Critics*, edited by Robert O. Keohane, pp. 322–345. New York, N.Y.: Columbia University Press, 1986.

Waltz, Kenneth N. "Structural Realism after the End of the Cold War." *International Security*, Vol. 25, No. 1 (Summer 2000), pp. 5–41.

Weber, Max. *The Theory of Social and Economic Organization*. Translated by A. M. Henderson and Talcott Parsons, Edited with an Introduction by Talcott Parsons. New York, N.Y. Free Press, 1947.

Wells, Peter S. *The Barbarians Speak: How the Conquered Peoples Shaped Roman Europe*. Princeton, N.J.: Princeton University Press, 1999.

Wells, Peter S. *The Battle That Stopped Rome: Emperor Augustus, Arminius, and the Slaughter of the Legions in the Teutoburg Forest*. New York, N.Y.: Norton & Company, 2003.

Wendt, Alexander. "Anarchy is What States Make of It: The Social Construction of Power Politics." *International Organization*, Vol. 46, No. 2 (Spring 1992), pp. 391–425.

Wendt, Alexander. *Social Theory of International Politics*. Cambridge: Cambridge University Press, 1999.

Whiton, Christian. *Smart Power: Between Diplomacy and War*. Washington, D.C.: Potomac Books, 2013.

Wilson, Ernest J., III. "Hard Power, Soft Power, Smart Power." *The Annals of the American Academy of Political and Social Science,* Vol. 616, Public Diplomacy in a Changing World (March 2008), pp. 110–124.

Wirsching, Andreas. *Der Preis der Freiheit: Geschichte Europas in unserer Zeit*. München: C. H. Beck, 2012.

Wohlforth, William C. "Realism and the End of the Cold War." *International Security*, Vol. 19, No. 3 (Winter 1994/1995), pp. 91–129.

Zaharna, R. S. *The Cultural Awakening in Public Diplomacy, CPD Perspectives on Public Diplomacy, Paper 4, 2012*. Los Angeles, Cal.: Figueroa Press, 2012.

Zahran, Geraldo and Leonardo Ramos. "From Hegemony to Soft Power: Implications of a Conceptual Change." In *Soft Power and US Foreign Policy: Theoretical, Historical and Contemporary Perspectives*, edited by Inderjeet Parmar and Michael Cox, pp. 12–31. Abingdon: Routledge, 2010.

Zakaria, Fareed. "The Future of American Power: How America Can Survive the Rise of the Rest." *Foreign Affairs*, Vol. 87, No. 3 (May/June 2008), pp. 18–43.

Chapter 3
A Taxonomy of Soft Power: Introducing a New Conceptual Paradigm

Having discussed the origins of the concept of soft power, its basic mechanisms, its placement in International Relations theory, as well as (alleged and actual) short-comings, the introduction of a taxonomy of soft power and its associated subunits as put forth in the following chapter shall contribute to a more precise and applicable operationalization of the concept.[1] The next section, therefore, addresses the first research question deduced above and presents a new and comprehensive taxonomy of soft power, thus providing a more tangible and applicable theoretical-conceptual framework.

The wide use and attested murkiness of the concept of soft power discussed above calls for further specification since any term that increasingly becomes all-embracing tends to lose its analytical validity.[2] With regard to soft power, this observation is at least in part accounted for by the fact that Joseph Nye himself gave ample scope for interpretation and over the years has put forth different understandings of his own concept.[3] Peter Baumann and Gisela Cramer have in this regard recently noted, "The very success of the term soft power among the wider public seems to suggest that there is a need for it. Yet, since Nye did not clearly define what soft power is, there is

---

[1]The nucleus of the following section can be found in two papers, entitled "Making the Intangibles Tangible: Soft Power and its Subunits" and "A Taxonomy of Soft Power: Deconstructing the Concept of Soft Power and Introducing Indicators for Empirical Analysis," respectively presented by the author at the International Studies Association West Annual Conferences 2014 and 2017 in Pasadena, California. While the basic structure and certain passages have been adopted in the work in hand, the line of argumentation has been substantially elaborated and supplemented. The author wishes to cordially thank his fellow panelists and particularly discussants Patrick James (2014) and J. Ann Tickner (2017) for their constructive critique and helpful suggestions.

[2]Joseph S. Nye, Jr. and Robert O. Keohane, "Transnational Relations and World Politics: An Introduction," *International Organization*, Vol. 25, No. 3 (Summer 1971), p. 346.

[3]Inderjeet Parmar and Michael Cox, "Introduction," in *Soft Power and US Foreign Policy: Theoretical, Historical and Contemporary Perspectives*, eds. Inderjeet Parmar and Michael Cox (Abingdon: Routledge, 2010), p. 2.

© Springer Nature Switzerland AG 2020
H. W. Ohnesorge, *Soft Power*, Global Power Shift,
https://doi.org/10.1007/978-3-030-29922-4_3

also the need for a more systematic scholarly discussion."[4] Additionally, many works by scholars and commentators on the issue of soft power subsume different aspects and mechanisms under the overarching term. Christopher Layne accordingly quipped that "the term soft power these days is so expansive that it can be said to include just about everything including the kitchen sink (and military power)."[5] Kostas Ifantis on a comparable note argued, "There seems to be a tendency to call anything attractive 'soft power.'"[6] At the same time, while contributing valuable insights into the mechanisms of soft power, previous attempts of concretization remain far from satisfactory with regard to a comprehensive and differentiated understanding of soft power. On the one hand, studies frequently focus on the underlying tools of soft power without considering their respective reception or contexts.[7] On the other hand, many studies mingle different components of the overarching concept. Even Nye himself, according to Geraldo Zahran and Leonardo Ramos, at times

> blurs a complex relation between behaviours, resources and strategy when he adopts the term [. . .] soft power as a synonym for co-operation power and soft power resources. This ends up by making Nye's texts easy to read, but confusing and unclear if one tries to examine the real meaning of his references to soft power.[8]

Artem Patalakh has recently noted in the same vein,

> Similarly to any kind of a purposeful action, a soft power strategy has its sources and instruments (or means) through which it can be achieved. [. . .]
>
> It is noteworthy that in Nye's theory the distinction between the two is somewhat elusive: while there is a clear logical discrimination between sources and instruments, sometimes they coincide, which is deemed to be a weak point of Nye's theory.[9]

Consequently, a highly inclusive yet little applicable understanding of soft power has emerged today that frequently encompasses a wide range of qualitatively

---

[4]Peter Baumann and Gisela Cramer, "Power, Soft or Deep? An Attempt at Constructive Criticism," *Las Torres de Lucca: International Journal of Political Philosophy*, No. 10 (January–June 2017), p. 179.

[5]Christopher Layne, "The Unbearable Lightness of Soft Power," in *Soft Power and US Foreign Policy: Theoretical, Historical and Contemporary Perspectives*, eds. Inderjeet Parmar and Michael Cox (Abingdon: Routledge, 2010), p. 58.

[6]Kostas Ifantis, "Soft Power: Overcoming the Limits of a Concept," in *Routledge Handbook of Diplomacy and Statecraft*, ed. B. J. C. McKercher (Abingdon: Routledge, 2011), p. 445.

[7]Jean-Marc F. Blanchard and Fujia Lu, "Thinking Hard about Soft Power: A Review and Critique of the Literature on China and Soft Power," *Asian Perspective*, Vol. 36, No. 4 (2012), p. 582.

[8]Geraldo Zahran and Leonardo Ramos, "From Hegemony to Soft Power: Implications of a Conceptual Change," in *Soft Power and US Foreign Policy: Theoretical, Historical and Contemporary Perspectives*, eds. Inderjeet Parmar and Michael Cox (Abingdon: Routledge, 2010), pp. 25–26.

[9]Artem Patalakh, "Assessment of Soft Power Strategies: Towards an Aggregative Analytical Model for Country-Focused Case Study Research," *Croatian International Relations Review*, Vol. 22, No. 76 (2016), p. 97.

different components under one single, fashionable term. The concept of soft power, in short, is in dire need of precise operationalization.[10]

In fact, a specification of *any* underlying concept is necessary in order to allow for substantiated empirical analysis.[11] "Theories," wrote Karl Popper in his 1959 classic *The Logic of Scientific Discovery*, "are nets cast to catch what we call 'the world': to rationalize, to explain, and to master it. We endeavour to make the mesh ever finer and finer."[12] The metaphor of the net, applied by the Austrian-British philosopher in what many consider to be his *magnum opus*, certainly is a catchy one. It describes the central objectives of theories while at the same time acknowledging shortcomings and calling for continuous sophistication in order to let no fish slip through. It is in this vein that the introduction of a comprehensive taxonomy shall help to make the study of soft power more feasible and workable by providing, in Popper's terms, a more fine-meshed net to cast out.[13]

To that end, soft power shall subsequently no longer be understood, as has frequently been done, as a somewhat blurred catch-all phrase, but rather be deconstructed into different categories or subunits. Each of these subunits, to be presented and elaborated upon in greater detail in the following, encompasses qualitatively different aspects of soft power. Individually, by drawing on different strands and disciplines of scholarship, they allow for a substantiated operationalization and analysis. Taken together, by presenting a highly synthetic understanding of soft power through the combination of a (neorealist) preference for resource-based understandings with behavioral and relational understandings of power, they are capable to illustrate the workings of the overall concept of soft power.

---

[10]Claudia Auer, Alice Srugies, and Martin Löffelholz, "Schlüsselbegriffe der internationalen Diskussion: Public Diplomacy und Soft Power," in *Kultur und Außenpolitik: Handbuch für Wissenschaft und Praxis*, ed. Kurt-Jürgen Maaß (Baden Baden: Nomos Verlagsgesellschaft, 2015), p. 41.

[11]Arndt Wanka, "Concept Specification in Political Science Research," in *Research Design in Political Science: How to Practice What They Preach*, eds. Thomas Geschwend and Frank Schimmelfennig (Basingstoke: Palgrave Macmillan, 2011), pp. 41–42.

[12]Karl Popper, *The Logic of Scientific Discovery* (London: Hutchinson, 1959), p. 59.

[13]It may be argued that Joseph Nye himself refuses to call soft power a *theory*. Nye thus argued, "Soft power is an analytical concept, not a theory;" Joseph S. Nye, Jr., "Responding to My Critics and Concluding Thoughts," in *Soft Power and US Foreign Policy: Theoretical, Historical and Contemporary Perspectives*, eds. Inderjeet Parmar and Michael Cox (Abingdon: Routledge, 2010), p. 219. In fact, this circumstance is the main reason why in the work in hand the author refers to terms like "concept," "idea," "phenomenon," "notion," etc. with regard to soft power rather than "the theory of soft power." However, Nye's objection seems rather to be aimed particularly against efforts to pigeonhole soft power into the canon of International Relations *theories*—as has been argued above—than against the classification of soft power as a theory per se, allowing for the applicability of Popper's metaphor. Christopher Layne in this regard argued, "Although Nye does not cast soft power as a theory, it needs to be subjected to empirical testing to determine the validity of its claims and the robustness of its causal logic;" Layne, "The Unbearable Lightness of Soft Power," p. 53.

Perhaps the overriding rationale for this deconstruction of soft power into different subunits can best be illustrated by a figurative comparison: When seeking to understand the workings of a complicated technical machine, it may be advisable to first carefully disassemble it and look at the individual components separately in order to comprehend its overall mechanism. In the end, however, it is equally important to (re-)assemble the components in order to get the complete picture right—and the machine working again. Otherwise, all that would remain after deconstruction, in a phrase coined by Quintus Horatius Flaccus, more commonly known as Horace, are the *disiecta membra*,[14] when in fact the aim was to achieve a comprehensive insight into its overall mechanism.

Figure 3.1—can be regarded the very centerpiece in this attempt to deconstruct soft power and present a new and comprehensive conceptual taxonomy. It offers an overview of the four soft power subunits to be subsequently introduced while depicting their contents, distinctions, as well as reciprocal interactions. On the one hand, the figure serves as a guideline and major reference point to elucidate the proposed taxonomy of soft power and its different subunits. By taking established theoretical considerations on soft power as put forth by Joseph Nye and others as starting points, but complementing and substantively elaborating upon them, an integrated and comprehensive understanding of soft power shall thus be presented. On the other hand, the figure also serves as a major point of reference when discussing and presenting a methodological roadmap for empirical analyses of soft power in international relations, as shall subsequently be done. In this sense, Fig. 3.1 constitutes the connecting link between the two research questions addressed by the study at hand.

Before going into detail regarding the four soft power subunits, Fig. 3.1 shall be presented in brief. Horizontally, the figure is divided in what Joseph Nye referred to as the active and the passive approaches to soft power.[15] Thus, on the one hand, an actor may pursue "active efforts to create attraction and soft power."[16] This may be achieved through actively engaging in public diplomacy (which includes, among other elements, cultural and educational exchanges or international broadcasting) or what may be called personal diplomacy (which includes, among others, state visits and public speeches from leading decision-makers). Instruments like these are designed to purposefully disseminate an actor's soft power resources to an international public. On the other hand, while the active form of wielding soft power draws upon the pursuit of deliberately planned programs and measures, the second variety, that is, the passive form of soft power, feeds on attractive pull alone. In such cases, the second subunit (i.e., soft power instruments) is leapfrogged and soft power resources themselves exude attraction, dispensing with the need of deploying

---

[14]Horace famously (and controversially) refers to "disiecti membra poetae;" Horaz, "Sermones/Satiren," in *Sämtliche Werke: Teil II, Satiren und Briefe*, Translated and Edited by Wilhelm Schöne with Hans Färber (München: Ernst Heimeran Verlag, 1960), p. 32 (Hor. Sat. I, 4, 62).

[15]Joseph S. Nye, Jr., *The Future of Power* (New York, N.Y.: PublicAffairs, 2011), p. 94.

[16]Nye, *The Future of Power*, p. 94.

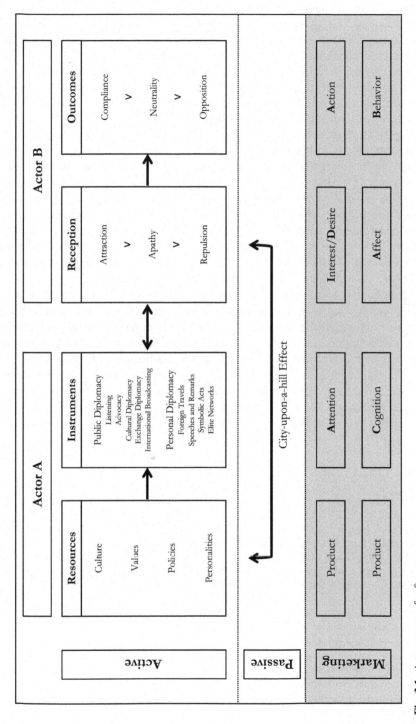

Fig. 3.1 A taxonomy of soft power

specific instruments. Janice Bially Mattern refers to this dimension of soft power as the "passive cultural 'osmosis'" as contrasted to active approaches to wield soft power through instruments such as public diplomacy.[17] Nye himself labels this variety of soft power the "passive city on the hill effect."[18]

When applying a restricted understanding, the passive form of soft power, it may be argued, cannot be regarded as *power* at all. Byung-Chul Han, for example, suggested a strict separation of power and influence, insomuch as influence differs from power with regard to its intentionality.[19] It is in this vein that some observers attach great importance to the factor of intentionality and even argue "that it would not be sensible to include unintended consequences in the definition of power, since it would render the term so broad that every conceivable action could be included in this category."[20] With respect to soft power, this would mean that whereas the application of soft power instruments such as public or personal diplomacy is pursued intentionally (by nation-states, for example), the passive form of soft power lacks intentionality (as it occurs indiscriminately) and therefore does not represent a form of power. Proponents of such a view certainly make a valid point and consequently, difficulties of attribution, intentionality, and causation of power have rightly been objects of fierce debate. However, although contributing to a considerable expansion of the concept of (soft) power, excluding unintended forms of influencing other actors would fall short of reality. Actor A, influencing Actor B not through the application of (intended) programs or instruments but perhaps by acting as a role model or simply by appearing to be attractive in other ways, still exercises power, particularly from the perspective of B. It is in this vein that F. E. Oppenheim—after elaborately weighing up the pros and cons regarding this subject—argued, "Unintended influence and coercion must be covered by an adequate explication of the concept of power."[21] Within this context, the issue of intentionality is frequently depicted by the metaphorical observation "that it does not

---

[17] Janice Bially Mattern, "Why 'Soft Power' Isn't So Soft: Representational Force and the Sociolinguistic Construction of Attraction in World Politics," *Millennium: Journal of International Studies*, Vol. 33, No. 3 (2005), p. 589, fn. 16.

[18] Nye, *The Future of Power*, p. 98. With this denomination, Nye is referencing, of course, the famous biblical trope of a "city on a hill" as referred to by Jesus Christ in the Sermon on the Mount. In the King James Version of the Bible, Matthew 5:14 thus reads, "Ye are the light of the world. A city that is set on a hill cannot be hid." This trope was brought to particular prominence by John Winthrop, governor of the Massachusetts Bay Colony in the mid-seventeenth century; John Winthrop, "A Model of Christian Charity," in *Puritan Political Ideas: 1558-1794*, ed. Edmund S. Morgan (Indianapolis, Ind.: Hackett Publishing Company, 2003), pp. 75–93.

[19] Byung-Chul Han, *Was ist Macht?* (Stuttgart: Reclam, 2005), p. 24 & p. 98.

[20] Diana E. Krause and Eric Kearney, "The Use of Power Bases in Different Contexts: Arguments for a Context-Specific Perspective," in *Power and Influence in Organizations: New Empirical and Theoretical Perspectives*, eds. Chester A. Schriesheim and Linda L. Neider (Greenwich, Conn.: Information Age Publishing, 2006), p. 64.

[21] Felix E. Oppenheim, "'Power' Revisited," *The Journal of Politics*, Vol. 40, No. 3 (August 1978), p. 601.

matter to the grass whether elephants above make love or war"[22]—a metaphor reputedly coined by Tanzanian President Julius Nyerere with respect to the United States of America and the Soviet Union during the Cold War.[23] In line with this memorable metaphor, passive or unintended forms of power—and soft power in particular—have to be included in any empirical analysis. Especially with regard to the newly introduced soft power resource of personalities, the passive form of soft power becomes eminently important, as shall be demonstrated below. In addition, Nye further differentiated between the "indirect" and "direct" wielding of soft power and maintains that the former concerns the creation of favorable opinions among a foreign public, while the latter more specifically relates to the individual leaders or other influential actors within a society.[24] These varieties shall be picked up in the following as well, despite the fact that a clear division between the two is not always feasible in practice.

Vertically, Fig. 3.1 is divided into two major columns representing two actors who participate in the process of wielding soft power, Actor A and Actor B: In a nutshell, Actor A seeks to get Actor B to want the outcomes it wants through the application of soft power. To achieve this goal, Actor A has—following Joseph Nye—three major soft power *resources* (Subunit I) at its disposal: culture, values, and foreign policy. As shall be discussed in more detail below, the work in hand elaborates on these resources in turn and additionally puts forth a fourth and hitherto neglected resource of soft power: personalities.[25] In order to communicate these resources and if possible translate them into desired outcomes, Actor A may resort to such *instruments* (Subunit II) as subsumed here under the overarching terms of public and personal diplomacy. Instruments such as these do not constitute soft power resources in their own right; rather they can be thought of as a transmission belt since they are communicating or transferring resources to the recipient Actor B.

Turning to the second column, the resources (in the passive variety) or the instruments (in the active variety) of Actor A evoke either attraction, apathy, or repulsion (cf. the symbol ∨ drawn from mathematics and logic in the figure above) on part of Actor B. Actor B, in this sense, is on the *reception* (Subunit III) end of the soft power event chain. Following this chain one step further—and depending on whether attraction, apathy, or repulsion was elicited—Actor B acts either in compliance, neutrality, or opposition with respect to Actor A. Ideally, in case attraction was created by the resources or instruments of Actor A, Actor B consequently acts in compliance with Actor A, which thus gets the *outcomes* (Subunit IV) it intended. This sequence of events, presented here in a condensed and simplified manner and to

---

[22]Felix Berenskoetter, "Thinking about Power," in *Power in World Politics*, eds. Felix Berenskoetter and M.J. Williams (New York, N.Y.: Routledge, 2008), p. 13.

[23]François Heisbourg, "American Hegemony? Perceptions of the US Abroad," *Survival*, Vol. 41, No. 4 (Winter 1999/2000), p. 5.

[24]Nye, *The Future of Power*, pp. 94–95.

[25]See below, Sect. 3.1.4.

be substantially elaborated upon below, represents the basic and ideal-typical workings of soft power as understood in the work in hand.

Finally, two models in advertisement or marketing, which at least in some important aspects bear striking resemblance to the mechanisms of soft power, are referred to at the very bottom of the figure. By way of drawing on models and formulas from other disciplines, the concept of soft power can thus be vividly illustrated and elucidated. Marketing, following the American Marketing Association, may be defined as "the activity, set of institutions, and processes for creating, communicating, delivering, and exchanging offerings that have value for customers, clients, partners, and society at large."[26] In simplified terms, it may therefore be understood as the selling of a product offered by one actor (seller) to another actor (consumer) through advertisement efforts designed to highlight the product's advantages and desirability. One influential model in this regard has long been the so-called AIDA formula, whose origins are generally attributed to American advertisement pioneer Elias St. Elmo Lewis (1872–1948). Lewis thus claimed,

> The mission of an advertisement is to attract a reader, so that he will look at the advertisement and start to read it; then to interest him, so that he will continue to read it; then to convince him, so that when he has read it he will believe it. If an advertisement contains these three qualities of success, it is a successful advertisement.[27]

Building on these assumptions of different consecutive steps in advertisement and its psychological underpinnings, as was becoming increasingly popular at the time, others have subsequently elaborated on the different steps in search of a memorable formula. In 1921, C. P. Russell thus wrote,

> [T]he average writer [of a sales letter] cannot do better than to follow the sequence often recommended for advertisement copy: Attention, Interest, Desire, Action. An easy way to remember this formula is to call in the 'law of association,' which is the old reliable among memory aids. It is to be noted that, reading downward, the first letters of these words spell the opera 'Aida.' When you start a letter, then, say 'Aida' to yourself and you won't go far wrong, at least as far as the form of your letter is concerned.[28]

This sequence, itemized the four elements of attention, interest, desire, and action, to a considerable degree corresponds with the mechanism of soft power as depicted above. Still, while the AIDA model can look back on a long history and has become one of the most influential and referenced marketing formulas, it has meanwhile been modified and refined. One example in this regard is the tripartite CAB model, which distinguishes between cognition, affect, and desire.[29]

---

[26]American Marketing Association, "Definition of Marketing," July 2013, online at: https://www.ama.org/AboutAMA/Pages/Definition-of-Marketing.aspx (accessed December 1, 2014).

[27]Elias St. Elmo Lewis, "Advertisement Department: Catch-Line and Argument," *The Book-Keeper*, Vol. 15 (February 1903), p. 124.

[28]C. P. Russell, "How to Write a Sales-Making Letter: An Old Formula That Will Save Much Rewriting by the Unpracticed Correspondent," *Printers' Ink*, June 2, 1921, p. 49.

[29]Carol Pluzinski and William J. Qualls, "Consumer Response to Marketing Stimuli: The Relationship Between Affect, Cognition, and Behavior," in *NA – Advances in Consumer Research,*

Translating those models to the workings of soft power and its subunits, soft power instruments such as public diplomacy may be regarded as measures to draw the recipients' attention toward a particular resource (or in marketing terms: a product), thus creating interest and desire which in turn lead to action. In the marketing world of advertisement this action means buying a product, in terms of wielding soft power in international relations it means acting in compliance with Actor A. As shall be described in more detail below, "buying" public or personal diplomacy efforts in fact constitutes an integral part in the successful wielding of soft power. Admittedly, the references to marketing models, despite their striking applicability, have to be taken with a grain of salt. Still, they offer valuable insights and certain parallels between advertisement and the wielding of soft power have moreover already been recognized by other writers. Christopher Layne, for example, argued that "soft power really reflects the injection of business school ideas about marketing into the American foreign policymaking process. Soft power is a means of marketing the American 'brand.'"[30]

In the final analysis, Fig. 3.1 emphasizes that soft power, although originating from a set of different resources, ought to be understood as a relational form of power in so far as it depends on the "wielder"—Actor A—and the "receiver"—Actor B—alike. It also underlines that the overall notion of soft power can be thought of as encompassing different stages that are—time-wise as well as qualitatively—distinguishable. The existence of different stages in the exercise of soft power can to some extent be already found in literature.[31] Nye, for example, briefly introduced this idea when he presents a simple arrow diagram of how soft power resources can be turned into outcomes.[32] The soft power subunits introduced in the following, however, offer a new level of differentiation with regard to the concept of soft power, thus making it more tangible and applicable. In order to illustrate the notion of soft power as conceived by the proposed taxonomy, each subunit shall be successively elaborated upon in the following by (1) outlining the general rationale behind it, (2) explaining its position and function in the overall concept of soft power, (3) illustrating it empirically by drawing on historical as well as model examples, and finally (4) deducing and discussing respective indicators allowing for precise operationalization and empirical application.

Volume 13, ed. Richard J. Lutz (Provo, Utah: Association for Consumer Research, 1986), pp. 231–234.

[30]Layne, "The Unbearable Lightness of Soft Power," p. 53.

[31]Geun Lee, "A Theory of Soft Power and Korea's Soft Power Strategy," *The Korean Journal of Defense Analysis*, Vol. 21, No. 2 (June 2009), pp. 210–211.

[32]Nye, *The Future of Power*, p. 100.

3.1   Subunit I: Resources

The first subunit encompasses the resources attributed to the wielding of soft power. As has been argued above, resources frequently play an important part in different understandings of power. Instead of tanks, aircraft carriers, natural resources, or other "raw materials" generally attributed to the realm of hard power, the following subchapter discusses the concurrent resources of soft power. From the outset, as we shall see below in more detail, these resources are less tangible than the ones generally attributed to hard power.[33] Still, starting from the works of Joseph Nye but elaborating and complementing them, certain resources of soft power can be identified.

In his early writings on soft power, Nye argued that the "universalism of a country's culture and its ability to establish a set of favorable rules and institutions that govern areas of international activity are critical sources of power."[34] In this understanding, as Nye elaborated, soft power "tends to arise from such resources as cultural and ideological attraction as well as the rules and institutions of international regimes."[35] Specifically, Nye emphasized the role of institutions and regimes and thus identified the "ability of a nation to structure a situation so that other nations develop preferences or define their interest in ways consistent with one's own nation."[36] This assumption is highly reminiscent of Susan Strange's concept of structural power, which, in her own words, "confers the power to decide how things shall be done, the power to shape frameworks within which states relate to each other."[37] Subsequently, however, Nye generally omitted this aspect of soft power deriving from international agreements and institutions (perhaps due to the observed conjunction to Strange's notion of structural power), which therefore shall be considered no further at this point.[38]

---

[33]Su Changhe, "Soft Power," in *The Oxford Handbook of Modern Diplomacy*, eds. Andrew F. Cooper, Jorge Heine, and Ramesh Thakur (Oxford: Oxford University Press, 2013), p. 551.

[34]Joseph S. Nye, Jr., *Bound to Lead: The Changing Nature of American Power* (New York: Basic Books, 1990), p. 33.

[35]Nye, *Bound to Lead*, p. 191.

[36]Nye, *Bound to Lead*, p. 191.

[37]Susan Strange, *States and Markets* (London: Printer, 1994), p. 25. Perhaps the single most obvious moment in history when this form of power took effect was the time during the last years and in the immediate aftermath of World War II when various international institutions and regimes (including the Untied Nations, the International Monetary Fund or the World Bank) were devised and established that greatly benefited (and still benefit) the victorious powers, with the United States of America leading the way; Paul Kennedy, *The Rise and Fall of the Great Powers* (New York, N.Y.: Vintage Books, 1987), pp. 359–360.

[38]For works on structural power, see, for example, Xuewu Gu, "Strukturelle Macht: Eine dritte Machtquelle?," *Österreichische Zeitschrift für Politikwissenschaft*, Vol. 41, No. 3 (2012), pp. 259–276; Xuewu Gu, "Global Power Shift: Soft, Hard and Structural Power," in *Die Gestaltung der Globalität: Annährungen an Begriff, Deutung und Methodik*, eds. Ludger Kühnhardt and Tilman Mayer (Bonn: Zentrum für Europäische Integrationsforschung, Discussion Paper C198, 2010), pp. 53–60; or Jan-Frederik Kremer and Andrej Pustovitovskij, "Towards a New

In his later writings, building on the other sources of soft power put forth in 1990 (i.e., culture, political values, and ideals), Joseph Nye usually refers to a tripartite classification of the central resources of soft power, "The soft power of a country rests primarily on three resources: its culture (in places where it is attractive to others), its political values (when it lives up to them at home and abroad), and its foreign policies (when they are seen as legitimate and having moral authority.)"[39] This triad of soft power resources is widely accepted and shared by most researchers.[40] Craig Hayden, for example, thus concurrently identified "culture, political ideals, and foreign policy legitimacy"[41] as the three constituent resources of soft power. Therefore, these three resources shall in the following be presented and discussed in turn. At the same time, however, they shall be substantially elaborated upon and not least complemented by a forth, hitherto widely neglected resource.

3.1.1   Culture

In line with the enumeration presented above, culture has frequently been regarded "among the key foundations of soft power"[42]—both in academic writing and in political practice. At the same time, however, it has likewise been noted that culture "does not lend itself to clear analytic determinations: Matters of definition, origin, transmission, reception, and long-term impact remain shadowy or plastic."[43] In a 2013 British Council report John Holden hence argued, "'Culture' is a notoriously difficult word to define."[44] Culture, accordingly, "is a word with many shades of

---

Understanding of Structural Power," in *Power in the 21st Century: International Security and International Political Economy in a Changing World*, eds. Enrico Fels, Jan-Frederik Kremer, and Katharina Kronenberg (Berlin: Springer-Verlag, 2012), pp. 59–80. A recent study on structural power combining theoretical spadework with empirical case studies is Andrej Pustovitovskij, *Strukturelle Kraft in Internationalen Beziehungen: Ein Konzept der Macht in internationalen Verhandlungen* (Wiesbaden: Springer VS, 2016).

[39] Joseph S. Nye, Jr., *Soft Power: The Means to Success in World Politics* (New York, N.Y.: PublicAffairs, 2004), p. 11.

[40] Blanchard and Lu, "Thinking Hard about Soft Power," p. 569.

[41] Craig Hayden, *The Rhetoric of Soft Power: Public Diplomacy in Global Contexts* (Lanham, Md.: Lexington Books, 2012), p. 29.

[42] Ifantis, "Soft Power," p. 442.

[43] Michael Ermarth, "Between Blight and Blessing: The Influence of American Popular Culture on the Federal Republic," in *The United States and Germany in the Era of the Cold War, 1945-1990: A Handbook, Volume II: 1968-1990*, ed. Detlef Junker, associated editors Philipp Gassert, Wilfried Mausbach, and David B. Morris (Cambridge: Cambridge University Press, 2004), p. 335.

[44] John Holden, "Influence and Attraction: Culture and the Race for Soft Power in the 21st Century," *British Council* (2013), online at: https://www.britishcouncil.org/sites/default/files/influence-and-attraction-report.pdf (accessed June 7, 2016), p. 8.

meaning"[45] calling for further elaboration. In fact, culture is perhaps as heavily contested and controversial a concept as power in international relations.[46] Consequently, one has to bear in mind that concepts and understandings of culture vary across different countries or civilizations.[47] In another British Council publication, the authors therefore aptly noted, "Culture is a broad concept which means many different things to different people."[48]

While conceptually originating with the Ancient Greeks, the term itself derives from Latin *cultura*, which initially denoted farming, agriculture, or tilling but subsequently broadened to include also "the nurture of minds."[49] Taking a distinctly English perspective, T. S. Eliot tongue-in-cheek pointed out that the term includes

> all the characteristic activities and interests of a people: Derby Day, Henley Regatta, Cowes, the twelfth of August, a cup final, the dog races, the pin table, the dart board, Wensleydale cheese, boiled cabbage cut into sections, beetroot in vinegar, nineteenth-century Gothic churches and the music of Elgar. The reader can make his own list.[50]

Eliot's enumeration hints at the all-embracing nature of culture and his addendum—compelling the reader to compile "his own list"—not least underlines its fundamental subjectivity. Ralph Linton, among the leading figures in U.S. sociology and anthropology in the twentieth century, accordingly defined culture—perhaps more scientifically if less figurative than Eliot—as the "configuration of learned behaviors and results of behavior whose component elements are shared and transmitted by the members of a particular society."[51] In the same vein, Nye himself offered a definition of culture as "the set of values and practices that create meaning for a society," which, as he agrees, "has many manifestations."[52] Recently, others have argued that culture, "as a human-created and

---

[45]Norman John Greville Pounds, *The Culture of the English People: Iron Age to the Industrial Revolution* (Cambridge: Cambridge University Press, 1994), p. 1.

[46]Frederik Engelstad, "Culture and Power," in *The SAGE Handbook of Power*, eds. Stewart R. Clegg and Mark Haugaard (London: SAGE Publications, 2009), p. 210.

[47]Frank Trommler, "Culture as an Arena of Transatlantic Conflict," in *The United States and Germany in the Era of the Cold War, 1945-1990: A Handbook, Volume II: 1968-1990*, ed. Detlef Junker, associated editors Philipp Gassert, Wilfried Mausbach, and David B. Morris (Cambridge: Cambridge University Press, 2004), p. 270.

[48]Kieron Culligan, John Dubber, and Mona Lotten, "As Others See Us: Culture, Attraction and Soft Power," *British Council* (2014), online at: https://www.britishcouncil.org/sites/default/files/as-others-see-us-report.pdf (accessed June 7, 2016), p. 15.

[49]Richard T. Arndt, *The First Resort of Kings: American Cultural Diplomacy in the Twentieth Century* (Washington, D.C.: Potomac Books, 2005), p. xvii.

[50]T. S. Eliot, *Notes towards the Definition of Culture* (New York, N.Y.: Harcourt, Brace and Company, 1949), p. 30.

[51]Ralph Linton, *The Cultural Background of Personalities* (New York, N.Y.: Appleton-Century-Crofts, 1945), p. 32.

[52]Nye, *Soft Power*, p. 11.

human-perpetuated organic phenomenon," is highly dynamic and should therefore rather be regarded as a verb than as a noun.[53]

Further elaborating upon the question of culture, Nye, following a widely accepted convention, distinguishes between high and popular culture.[54] Whereas in this dichotomy high culture encompasses art, literature, and education and is predominantly appealing to elites, popular culture comprises mass entertainment such as popular music or movies.[55] Between these two varieties, popular culture arguable has a particularly broad impact. Consequently, as Kostas Ifantis has pointed out, the element of "American popular culture is central to Nye's thinking."[56] Though the distinction between high and popular culture is well established, a clear-cut separation between the two is much harder to maintain in practice. Jean-Marc F. Blanchard and Fujia Lu, with particular focus on Chinese culture but easily applicable to other examples as well, hence argued that culture "is an amalgam of elements relating to high and popular, old and modern (youth culture, consumer culture), and regional (variations of Chinese cuisine and language are legendary)."[57] Offering further illustrations, Claudia Auer, Alice Srugies, and Martin Löffelholz exemplarily cite Argentinian tango or Mexican cuisine as possible resources of (national) soft power.[58]

The general connection of culture to the realm of politics has, of course, a long tradition. Underlining this connection, Cynthia Weber has even argued, "*Culture is political, and politics is cultural.*"[59] At the same time, it has for long been connected to power. Michael Mandelbaum accordingly squarely asserted, "Culture *is* power. If war is, as the ancient Greek philosopher Heraclitus said, the father of all things, then culture is the mother. People change their ways and adopt new patterns of behavior because of what they observe others doing."[60] In fact, the identification of culture as a resource for (political) power long predates the writings on soft power by Joseph Nye. A. F. K. Organski, for example, pointed out that cultural ties—including a

---

[53]R. S. Zaharna, *The Cultural Awakening in Public Diplomacy, CPD Perspectives on Public Diplomacy, Paper 4, 2012* (Los Angeles, Cal.: Figueroa Press, 2012), p. 31; see Brian V. Street, "Culture is a Verb: Anthropological Aspects of Language and Cultural Process," in *Language and Culture: British Studies in Applied Linguistics*, eds. David Graddol, Linda Thompson, and Mike Bryam, Volume 7 (Clevedon: Multilingual Matters, 1993), pp. 23–43.

[54]Others, however, have argued that such a separation has increasingly become outdated; Richard Pells, "Double Crossings: The Reciprocal Relationship between American and European Culture in the Twentieth Century," in *Americanization and Anti-Americanism: The German Encounter with American Culture after 1945*, ed. Alexander Stephan (New York, N.Y.: Berghahn Books, 2005), p. 192.

[55]Nye, *Soft Power*, p. 11.

[56]Ifantis, "Soft Power," p. 442.

[57]Blanchard and Lu, "Thinking Hard about Soft Power," p. 576.

[58]Auer, Srugies, and Löffelholz, "Schlüsselbegriffe der internationalen Diskussion," p. 40.

[59]Cynthia Weber, *International Relations Theory: A Critical Introduction* (Abingdon: Routledge, 2005), p. 188.

[60]Michael Mandelbaum, *Mission Failure: America and the World in the Post-Cold War Era* (New York, N.Y.: Oxford University Press, 2016), p. 375; Mandelbaum's emphasis.

shared language—between France and Canada may be applied as a tool for wielding power through what today may be called public diplomacy.[61] In fact, "culture's power is very much acknowledged" today—and has been for a long time.[62] Some, therefore, have argued that "[c]ulture looms large as a causal explanation of human behavior, particularly when cultures are in conflict."[63] After the turn of the millennium and the terrorist attacks of 9/11, however, the significance of culture has gained new momentum in literature on international relations and particularly regarding issues of security.[64]

At times, creative artists themselves have explicitly recognized the (political) power inherent in their own creations, as the recourse to one particular episode vividly illustrates: Sicilian-born American film director Frank Capra, born Francesco Rosario Capra in 1897 has identified what he called "film power,"[65] that is, the power a movie may yield and the political ramifications it may have on the country it depicts in its plot or more generally represents as a product of its culture. In his 1971 autobiography, Capra elaborates on "film power" as he recalls the reactions to the first screening of his 1939 movie *Mr. Smith Goes to Washington*, starring James Stewart and Jean Arthur. The movie depicts the "lost cause" of a youthful and idealistic U.S. Senator, Jefferson Smith (played by James Stewart), who uncovers a vast scheme woven by the seemingly omnipotent media mogul and political puppet master Jim Taylor (played by Edward Arnold) and the corrupt senior senator Joseph Paine (played by Claude Rains). With the help of his disillusioned yet resourceful secretary Clarissa Saunders (played by Jean Arthur), Jefferson Smith ultimately succeeds in putting a stop to the scheme against seemingly overwhelming odds. Despite its uplifting ending, the movie depicts U.S. legislators (as well as journalists) and effectively the whole American political system in an intensely negative light. None other than then-U.S. Ambassador to the Court of St. James's Joseph P. Kennedy therefore strongly condemned the movie, citing its shattering effect on America's international image in the early stages of World War II. In a November 17, 1939, letter to Harry Cohn, head of the Columbia Pictures Cooperation that had produced the film, Ambassador Kennedy hence wrote,

> I have a high regard for Mr. Capra … but his fine work makes the indictment of our government all the more damning to foreign audiences … I feel that to show this film in foreign countries will do inestimable harm to American prestige all over the world.

---

[61]A. F. K. Organski, *World Politics* (New York, N.Y.: Alfred Knopf, 1958), p. 97. See below for the role of public diplomacy to wield (soft) power, Sect. 3.2.1.

[62]Zaharna, *The Cultural Awakening in Public Diplomacy*, p. 9.

[63]Kelton Rhoads, "The Culture Variable in the Influence Equation," in *Routledge Handbook of Public Diplomacy*, eds. Nancy Snow and Philip M. Taylor (New York, N.Y.: Routledge, 2009), p. 180.

[64]Zaharna, *The Cultural Awakening in Public Diplomacy*, p. 13 & p. 18.

[65]Frank Capra, *The Name Above the Title: An Autobiography* (New York, N.Y.: The Macmillan Company, 1971), p. 283.

I regret exceedingly that I find it necessary to say these things ... The fact remains, however, that pictures from the United States are the greatest influence on foreign public opinion of the American mode of life. The times are precarious, the future is dark at best. We must be more careful.[66]

Little did Joseph P. Kennedy foresee that the movie, quite contrary to his gloomy predictions, soon was to become a classic in self-deprecatingly depicting American ideals of liberty and democracy. Being nominated for 11 Academy Awards in 1940 but winning only one, today it is frequently ranked among the greatest movies of all times.[67]

Drawing on culture as a resource of power, as illustrated by this example, entails certain advantages. Thus, especially when compared to traditional hard power resources, the amalgam of culture can constitute a rather affordable and effective source of national power.[68] Being regularly distinctly non-governmental in nature but instead shaped by civil society actors such as individuals, universities, companies, or foundations, culture can thus be spread by commerce, exchanges, personal contacts, tourism, visits, etc. while in the age of globalization and information, even the private dimension of spreading culture becomes increasingly important.[69] At the same time, it can be regarded as frequently being detached from the vicissitudes of politics. In fact, the non-governmental nature of culture has long been recognized. In an effort to raise funds for the construction of the National Cultural Center, President John F. Kennedy (for whom the center would eventually be named after his assassination) emphasized the importance of culture in the heyday of the Cold War in 1962,

Behind the storm of daily conflict and crisis, the dramatic confrontations, the tumult of political struggle, the poet, the artist, the musician, continues the quiet work of centuries, building bridges of experience between peoples, reminding man of the universality of his feelings and desires and despairs, and reminding him that the forces that unite are deeper than those that divide. Thus, art and the encouragement of art is political in the most profound sense.[70]

---

[66]Quoted in Capra, *The Name Above the Title*, p. 292.

[67]The film received the 1940 Academy Award for Best Original Story; Capra laconically recalled in his autobiography, "Moral: Don't make the best picture you ever made in the year that someone makes *Gone with the Wind;*" Capra, *The Name Above the Title*, p. 298.

[68]Nye, *Bound to Lead*, p. 193.

[69]Nye, *Soft Power*, p. 13 & p. 17. See also Laura Roselle, Alister Miskimmon, and Ben O'Loughlin, "Strategic Narrative: A New Means to Understand Soft Power," *Media, War & Conflict*, Vol. 7, No. 1 (2014), p. 73.

[70]John F. Kennedy, "Remarks at the Closed-Circuit Television Broadcast on Behalf of the National Cultural Center," Washington D.C., November 29, 1962, in *Public Papers of the Presidents of the United States: John F. Kennedy, 1962, Containing the Public Messages, Speeches, and Statements of the President, January 1 to December 31, 1962* (Washington, D.C.: United States Government Printing Office, 1963), p. 846.

Almost paradoxically, however, art and culture frequently outlive political institutions and present themselves, contrary to hard power resources, as being distinctly apolitical in nature. Kennedy thus continued,

Aeschylus and Plato are remembered today long after the triumphs of imperial Athens are gone. Dante outlived the ambitions of 13th century Florence. Goethe stands serenely above the politics of Germany, and I am certain that after the dust of centuries has passed over our cities, we, too, will be remembered not for victories or defeats in battle or in politics, but for our contribution to the human spirit.[71]

In line with this argument, even the attribution of the Hollywood movie industry, regularly cited as being among the most seminal soft power resources of the United States altogether, to the country as a whole involves certain caveats. Richard Pells elaborated on this issue,

If movies have been the most important source both of art and entertainment in the twentieth century, then Hollywood, for better or worse, became the cultural capital of the modern world. But it was never an exclusively *American* capital. Like past cultural centers— Florence, Paris, Vienna, Berlin—Hollywood has functioned as an international community, built by immigrant entrepreneurs, and drawing on the talents of actors, directors, writers, cinematographers, editors, costume and set designs, from all over the world.[72]

Still, despite the fact that culture as an important resource of soft power rests, particularly in democracies, in no small parts on (an increasingly international) civil society, this does not mean that governments (e.g., through political efforts such as public diplomacy) cannot leverage such resources for their own ends.[73] In fact, with an eye on John F. Kennedy's remarks cited above, it is highly expressive that the respective national cultural institutes of Germany and Italy are named for the very poets Kennedy referred to: Johann Wolfgang von Goethe and Dante Alighieri.

Turning toward empirical cases, in addition to the example of Hollywood movies briefly referred to above, evidence for the importance of culture as a source of (national) soft power is legion and can be found throughout the ages: from Greek and Roman antiquity to the Italian Renaissance and the Age of Enlightenment up to our own times. Once more demonstrating the long track record of soft power in the annals of history, an early example of its potency can be found in Classical Greece, more precisely in Plutarch's *Lysander*, depicting the life of the eponymous Spartan commander. In 404 BC, when Sparta had at last proven victorious against its rival Athens in the Peloponnesian War, the Spartans decreed that the vanquished Athenians razed their port, Piraeus, as well as their famous Long Walls. While the Athenians agreed to these terms of surrender, they failed to meet them in time. At this moment, Plutarch's report sets in,

---

[71]Kennedy, "Remarks at the Closed-Circuit Television Broadcast on Behalf of the National Cultural Center," pp. 846–847.

[72]Pells, "Double Crossings," p. 194; emphasis added.

[73]Ifantis, "Soft Power," p. 443. See below for governmental efforts in the application of soft power instruments, Sect. 3.2.1.

Lysander, accordingly, when he had taken possession of all the ships of the Athenians except twelve, and of their walls, on the sixteenth of the month Munychion, the same on which they conquered the Barbarian in the sea-fight at Salamis, took measures at once to change their form of government. And when the Athenians opposed him bitterly in this, he sent word to the people that he had caught the city violating the terms of its surrender; for its walls were still standing, although the days were past within which they should have been pulled down; he should therefore present their case anew for the decision of the authorities, since they had broken their agreements. And some say that in very truth a proposition to sell the Athenians into slavery was actually made in the assembly of the allies, and that at this time Erianthus the Theban also made a motion that the city be razed to the ground, and the country about it left for sheep to graze. Afterwards, however, when the leaders were gathered at a banquet, and a certain Phocian sang the first chorus in the 'Electra' of Euripides, which begins with

> 'O thou daughter of Agamemnon,
> I am come, Electra, to thy rustic court,'

all were moved to compassion, and felt it to be a cruel deed to abolish and destroy a city which was so famous, and produced such poets.[74]

As the famous episode illustrates, it was the soft power emanating from Euripides' poetry which changed the Spartans' intentions and thus saved Athens, albeit not its Long Walls, from destruction.[75] More than 2000 years later, John Milton could hence poetize in one of his sonnets, explicitly referencing the *power* of poetry as evidenced by the instance,

> [...] and the repeated air
> Of sad Electra's poet had the power
> To save the Athenian walls from ruin bare.[76]

Edith Hamilton, who likewise recounts the events in her celebrated *The Greek Way*, thus fittingly concluded on the matter,

[T]he banqueters, stern soldiers in the great moment of their hard-won triumph, listening to the beautiful, poignant words, forgot victory and vengeance, and declared as one man that the city such a poet had sprung from should never be destroyed. So important were imponderables to the Greeks. Poetry, all the arts, were matters of high seriousness, which it appeared perfectly reasonable that the freedom of a man and a city's life might hang upon.[77]

---

[74]Plutarch, "Lysander," in *Plutarch's Lives*, With an English Translation by Bernadotte Perrin, Eleven Volumes, Volume IV: Alcibiades and Coriolanus/Lysander and Sulla, Loeb Classical Library (Cambridge, Mass: Harvard University Press, 1959), p. 273 (Plut. Lys. 15).

[75]For a critical discussion of the episode, as well as John Milton's treatment of the matter, see Peter Goldstein, "The Walls of Athens and the Power of Poetry: A Note on Milton's Sonnet 8," *Milton Quarterly*, Vol. 24, No. 3 (1990), pp. 105–108 and John Leonard, "Saving the Athenian Walls: The Historical Accuracy of Milton's Sonnet 8," *Milton Quarterly*, Vol. 32, No. 1 (1998), pp. 1–6.

[76]John Milton, "Sonnet VIII," in *Milton's Sonnets*, With Introduction, Notes, Glossary and Indexes by A. W. Verity (Cambridge: Cambridge University Press, 1906), p. 11.

[77]Edith Hamilton, *The Greek Way* (London: W. W. Norton & Company, 1993), p. 80.

More recently, a prominent twentieth century example for the potency of culture as a soft power resource is the influence of American Jazz music on Václav Havel and the Velvet Revolution.[78] U.S. President Bill Clinton thus declared in 2000 that, upon an earlier state visit to the Czech Republic, Václav Havel "took me to the jazz club where he used to gather and plot the Velvet Revolution."[79] In fact, the particular influence of jazz as a specifically *American* musical expression has already been recognized in the interwar period by German writer and journalist Hans Siemsen who wrote, tongue-in-cheek, in 1921, "Had only the Emperor danced jazz—all that happened would never have occurred. But he would have never learned it. To be Emperor of Germany is easier than to dance jazz."[80] Four decades later, during the heights of the Cold War, the political significance and power of jazz music—as well as political and governmental attempts to tap into it—was emphasized once more. The lyrics of the musical *The Real Ambassadors* (1962), written by Iola Brubeck, wife of jazz musician David Warren "Dave" Brubeck, accordingly read,

> The State Department has discovered jazz.
> It teaches folks like nothing ever has.
> Like when they feel that jazzy rhythm,
> They know we're really with 'em.
> That's what we call cultural exchange.
> No commodity is quite so strange
> As this thing we call cultural exchange...[81]

Besides high culture as a central resource of soft power (think Kennedy's tricolon "the poet, the artist, the musician"), popular culture, though its impact may even be less tangible, accordingly crucially underwrote U.S. soft power during the Cold War and indeed significantly contributed to the nation's triumph in this particular struggle, as some have suggested.[82] French philosopher and political advisor to President François Mitterrand, Régis Debray, in this very vein memorably argued in a 1986

---

[78]Cynthia P. Schneider, "Culture Communicates: US Diplomacy at Work," in *The New Public Diplomacy: Soft Power in International Relations*, ed. Jan Melissen (Basingstoke: Palgrave Macmillan, 2005), p. 148.

[79]William J. Clinton, "Remarks at the White House Conference on Culture and Diplomacy," Washington D.C., November 28, 2000, in *Public Papers of the Presidents of the United States: William J. Clinton, 2000-2001, Book III – October 12, 2000 to January 20, 2001* (Washington, D.C.: United States Government Printing Office, 2001), p. 2586. See also Russell L. Riley, *Inside the Clinton White House: An Oral History* (New York, N.Y.: Oxford University Press, 2016), p. 267, fn. 5.

[80]Quoted in Anton Kaes, "Mass Culture and Modernity: Notes Toward a Social History of Early American and German Cinema," in *America and the Germans: An Assessment of a Three-Hundred-Year History, Volume Two: The Relationship in the 20th Century*, eds. Frank Trommler and Joseph McVeigh (Philadelphia, Pa. University of Pennsylvania Press, 1985), p. 325.

[81]Quoted in Schneider, "Culture Communicates," p. 147.

[82]Nye, *Soft Power*, p. 49; Matthew Fraser, "American Pop Culture as Soft Power: Movies and Broadcasting," in *Soft Power Superpowers: Cultural and National Assets of Japan and the United States*, eds. Watanabe Yasushi and David L. McConnell (Armonk, N.Y.: M.E. Sharpe, 2008), p. 173.

interview, "[A]s if power in history is the same as force of arms! What myopia and shortsightedness! There is more power in rock music, videos, blue jeans, fast food, news networks and TV satellites than in the entire Red Army."[83] More recently, Stefan Halper and Jonathan Clarke have elaborated on the same point,

> McDonald's, of course, is not only the symbol of an omnipresent American commercialism. Coca-Cola has been the drink of choice for decades, and teens from Malaysia to Morocco are not complete without their Nike shoes; each is a product targeted to a global 'mass consumer society.' And each has become a symbol overloaded with complex cultural associations demonstrating, among other things, the power and success of American commerce and the appeal of the American way of life. Many feel, for example, when they drink Coke or eat at McDonald's or Burger King, they are participants, if only for a moment, in the American Dream.[84]

These particular soft power resources, however influential, once more underline the fact that soft power (especially in contrast to hard power) is not exclusively in the hand of the government but on the contrary is deeply rooted in civil society.[85] At the same time, while public approval to an actor's policies tends to be somewhat volatile and subject to quick changes due to respective decision-makers in office, recently disclosed scandals or other factors, the cultural attraction that contributes to an actor's soft power tends to be more resilient and less likely subject to short-term changes. Nye thus justly argued—with respect to the United States—that "American culture is often more attractive than U.S. policies."[86]

Regarding empirical analyses examining the influence of culture as a soft power resource, the pervasiveness of an Actor A's culture can be considered an informative indicator. Bearing in mind the relative and contextual nature of soft power, the dissemination of an actor's culture should be examined in particular with regard to the recipient (Actor B). At it, in order to draw a picture as complete as possible, a broad understanding of culture—ranging from popular to high culture—should be adopted.

3.1.2 Values

Despite the overwhelming centrality of culture in literature on soft power, Joseph Nye has noted that "[o]f course, soft power is more than just cultural power."[87]

---

[83]Régis Debray, "The Third World: From Kalashnikovs to God and Computers," *New Perspectives Quarterly*, Vol. 3, No. 1 (Spring 1986), online at: http://www.digitalnpq.org/archive/1986_spring/kalashnikov.html (accessed August 4, 2017).

[84]Stefan Halper and Jonathan Clarke, *America Alone: The Neo-Conservatives and the Global Order* (Cambridge: Cambridge University Press, 2004), p. 259.

[85]Nye, *Soft Power*, pp. 14–15.

[86]Joseph S. Nye, Jr., "The Decline of America's Soft Power: Why Washington Should Worry," *Foreign Affairs*, Vol. 83, No. 3 (May/June 2004), p. 18.

[87]Joseph S. Nye, Jr., "Limits of American Power," *Political Science Quarterly*, Vol. 117, No. 4 (Winter 2002/03), p. 554.

Accordingly, in line with his enumeration of soft power resources presented above, the (political) values an actor advocates or stands for constitute a second major resource of soft power. The influence of values in situations of negotiation and persuasion has a long tradition dating back as far as ancient Greece and the writings of Aristotle.[88] However, as with the resource of culture, the factor of values in foreign policy (and public diplomacy) have seen an increased significance after 9/11.[89] Russell A. Berman has thus recently argued regarding the importance of values in relations between international actors, "It is not unreasonable to assume that estimations of another country are based partly on perceptions of value systems: shared values may support a positive estimation, whereas conflicting values may lead to negative judgments."[90] And Joseph Nye, subsuming the significance of values under his paradigm of soft power, likewise pointed out, "The values a government champions in its behavior at home (for example, democracy), in international institutions (working with others), and in foreign policy (promoting peace and human rights) strongly affect the preferences of others."[91] In his elaboration on the influence of (political) values as a source of soft power, Nye thus distinguished between three levels: domestic values, values championed in inter-state cooperation, and values advocated in one's foreign policy.

First, on a domestic level, a particular political system and the values it espouses can serve as a powerful resource of soft power. On the one hand, a democratic system of government—and its associated values of liberty, equality, justice, or human rights—can exude strong forces of attraction.[92] In fact, democratic political orders have long-since been regarded as harboring formidable attractive powers toward others. Thucydides, in his *Peloponnesian War*, hence has Athenian statesman and *strategos* Pericles declare in his famous Funeral Oration with respect to the democratic system of his home town, "We have a form of government which does not emulate the practice of our neighbours: we are more an example to others than an imitation of them."[93] During the 1950s, to provide a more recent example in this regard, the attractive power of a democratic political system was a crucial component of the so called Magnet Theory ("Magnettheorie"), that is, the belief that a democratic West Germany would irresistibly attract the German Democratic Republic to

---

[88]Zaharna, *The Cultural Awakening in Public Diplomacy*, p. 37.

[89]Zaharna, *The Cultural Awakening in Public Diplomacy*, p. 37.

[90]Russell A. Berman, *Anti-Americanism in Europe: A Cultural Problem* (Stanford, Cal.: Hoover Institution Press, 2008), p. 30.

[91]Nye, *Soft Power*, p. 14.

[92]Nye, *Soft Power*, p. 55. Ludger Kühnhardt, for example, elaborated on the (attractive) power of human rights; Ludger Kühnhardt, *Die Universalität der Menschenrechte: Studie zur ideengeschichtlichen Bestimmung eines politischen Schlüsselbegriffes* (München: Günter Olzog Verlag, 1987), pp. 378–380.

[93]Thucydides, *The Peloponnesian War*, A New Translation by Martin Hammond (New York, N.Y.: Oxford University Press, 2009), p. 91 (Thuc. II, 37).

increased democratization and, ultimately, lead to a peaceful German Reunification.[94] On the other hand, since attraction lies in the eyes of the beholder, authoritarian systems of government and their corresponding values can likewise exude soft power.[95]

Secondly, subscribing to a multilateral approach in dealing with other states rather than consistently pursuing unilateral solo runs can be regarded as an important ingredient of soft power based on values. With particular respect to the United States, but easily transferable, unilateralism has been defined as "an approach to U.S. involvement in the world that minimizes and wherever possible excludes the participation of other governments and organizations."[96] While arguably beneficial in terms of greater freedom of action without the necessity of consulting and coordinating with others, going it alone may yield negative consequences for one's soft power. Already in his 1990 work *Bound to Lead*, Nye has accordingly identified the recourse to multilateralism and the strengthening of international institutions as crucial.[97] More recently, Nye elaborated, "Since the currency of soft power is attraction based on shared values and the justness and duty of others to contribute to policies consistent with those shared values, multilateral consultations are more likely to generate soft power than mere unilateral assertion of values."[98] Other scholars, such as Su Changhe, agree to the importance of a country's "attitude to multilateralism" in the evaluation of its soft power.[99] Su therefore argued that "the more a country complies with international rules and norms, the more reputation and social capital it can create in the international society."[100] Accordingly, the stance of a given actor toward multilateral treaties and organizations should be taken into account. Among these, relations to the United Nations, appropriately called "the preeminent institution of multilateralism"[101] in the world, takes pride of place. Along these lines, Sashi Tharoor elaborated with particular respect to the United States, but again easily generalizable,

> Working within the UN allows the United States to maximize what Joseph Nye calls its 'soft power'—the ability to attract and persuade others to adopt the American agenda—rather than relying purely on the dissuasive or coercive 'hard power' of military force. [...] The

---

[94]Tilman Mayer, *Das Prinzip Nation: Dimensionen der nationalen Frage am Beispiel Deutschlands* (Opladen: Leske & Budrich, 1987), p. 233.

[95]Christopher Walker, "The Hijacking of 'Soft Power,'" *Journal of Democracy*, Vol. 27, No. 1 (January 2016), pp. 49–63.

[96]Richard N. Haass, *The Reluctant Sheriff: The United States After the Cold War* (New York, N.Y.: Council on Foreign Relations, 1997), p. 87.

[97]Nye, *Bound to Lead*, p. 200.

[98]Nye, *Soft Power*, p. 64

[99]Su, "Soft Power," p. 552.

[100]Su, "Soft Power," p. 551.

[101]Shashi Tharoor, "Why America Still Needs the United Nations," *Foreign Affairs*, Vol. 82, No. 5 (September/October 2003), p. 67.

organization's role in legitimizing state action has been both its most cherished function and, in the United States, its most controversial.[102]

Finally, championing values like human rights and democracy in one's foreign policy represents the third variety of soft power deriving from the resource of (political) values—as long as governmental policies are in tune with them.[103] In this regard, Nye emphasized the need of "consistency of practice with values."[104] However, while the potency of values has long been recognized, actually expressing them and enhancing them in international relations may be far more difficult.[105]

Illustrative examples of value-based foreign policy include what has been called the "niche diplomacy" of countries such as Norway or Canada.[106] Both countries, through their commitment to peacekeeping and human rights, have thus been successful in increasing their international influence, as Alan K. Henrikson has pointed out, "Although militarily weak, they are global players. It has been said that each 'punches above its weight' in the world public arena."[107] The two nations, therefore, can draw on their soft power, developed over a considerable period of time, in order to compensate for potential deficits in the dimension of hard power. Another case in point is the normative power of the European Union (EU) that plays an important part of the (global) influence of the Union.[108] Joseph Nye offered a further example of the attractive pull of U.S. values when he argued that in 1989 student protesters in Beijing's Tiananmen Square created a model of the Statue of Liberty while demonstrating for the values she stands for.[109] Besides underlining the attractive pull of (political) values, this episode once again hints at the high contextuality of soft power. For just as certain as models of the Statue of Liberty being carried by Chinese protesters in 1989 attracted some people to the values and ideals these models embody, others arguably were repelled by them. The interplay of attraction and repulsion may therefore effectively result in an annulation of soft power.[110] Additionally, as Nye has argued, merely evoking values like human rights and democracy is not sufficient, rather governments should live up to and bolster

---

[102]Tharoor, "Why America Still Needs the United Nations," p. 68. The issue of legitimacy shall be picked up again and elaborated upon below.

[103]Nye, *Soft Power*, p. 55.

[104]Joseph S. Nye, Jr. "Hard, Soft, and Smart Power," in *The Oxford Handbook of Modern Diplomacy*, eds. Andrew F. Cooper, Jorge Heine, and Ramesh Thakur (Oxford: Oxford University Press, 2013), p. 568.

[105]Zaharna, *The Cultural Awakening in Public Diplomacy*, p. 40.

[106]Alan K. Henrikson, "Niche Diplomacy in the World Public Arena: The Global 'Corners' of Canada and Norway," in *The New Public Diplomacy: Soft Power in International Relations*, ed. Jan Melissen (Basingstoke: Palgrave Macmillan, 2005).

[107]Henrikson, "Niche Diplomacy in the World Public Arena," p. 82.

[108]Anna Michalski, "The EU as a Soft Power: The Force of Persuasion," in *The New Public Diplomacy: Soft Power in International Relations*, ed. Jan Melissen (Basingstoke: Palgrave Macmillan, 2005), p. 127.

[109]Nye, *Soft Power*, p. 51.

[110]Nye, *Soft Power*, pp. 12–13 & p. 55.

them by pursuing a legitimate foreign policy.[111] Finally, as Todd Hall has demonstrated with regard to Japan after the Meiji Restoration in the second half of the nineteenth century, sharing, endorsing, and assuming political values of other countries does not necessarily mean to "want what they want." On the contrary, assuming political values of Western powers (including the notion of ruling over an overseas empire), "put Japan on collision course with the very states it emulated, ending in the massive bloodshed of World War II."[112] The episode once more illustrates that an analysis of whether or not soft power is at work can only be conducted through in-depth case studies, taking into account particular circumstances and characteristics.

Bearing in mind the aspects identified by Joseph Nye and other scholars elaborated above as constituting crucial components of soft power derived from the resource of values, a set of indicators can be deduced to which particular attention should be paid in empirical analyses of the workings of soft power: (1) values represented and espoused by an actor both domestically and internationally, (2) the consistency with which expressed values are adhered to in political practice, and (3) the degree of involvement in multilateral institutions and frameworks as contrasted with the degree of unilateral action.

3.1.3 Policies

The policies championed by a government both at home and abroad constitute the third resource of soft power identified by Joseph Nye.[113] It is in this vein that Kostas Ifantis noted, with particular respect to the United States, that "government policies have a powerful impact on foreign perceptions."[114] In this context, the dimension of *foreign* policies features especially prominently in the respective literature. However, in an age of real-time exchange of news and ideas, the divide between domestic and foreign policy is increasingly blurred and therefore, more than ever before, *domestic* policies should also be taken into consideration.

Regarding the influence of certain policies on an actor's soft power, Nye highlighted the importance of legitimacy of an actor's (foreign) policy.[115] In this regard, an actor may be in a position to increase its soft power if its (foreign) policies are perceived as being legitimate—both in their ends as well as in their means. Regarding the importance of (perceptions of) legitimacy Robert W. Tucker and David C. Hendrickson have elaborated,

---

[111]Nye, *Soft Power*, p. 55.
[112]Todd Hall, "An Unclear Attraction: A Critical Examination of Soft Power as an Analytical Category," *The Chinese Journal of International Politics*, Vol. 3, No. 2 (2010), p. 203.
[113]Nye, *Soft Power*, p. 13.
[114]Ifantis, "Soft Power," p. 446.
[115]Nye, *Soft Power*, p. 11.

Legitimacy arises from the conviction that state action proceeds within the ambit of law, in two senses: first, that action issues from rightful authority, that is, from the political institution authorized to take it; and second, that it does not violate a legal or moral norm. Ultimately, however, legitimacy is rooted in opinion, and thus actions that are unlawful in either of these senses may, in principle, still be deemed legitimate. That is why it is an elusive quality. Despite these vagaries, there can be no doubt that legitimacy is a vital thing to have, and illegitimacy a condition devoutly to be avoided.[116]

Despite its recognized importance, Robert Kagan has aptly noted that "legitimacy is a genuinely elusive and malleable concept."[117] In this context (as also hinted at by Tucker and Hendrickson), it is once more important to bear in mind the highly relational quality of soft power as perceptions of legitimacy may differ widely among recipients. This observation is very much in line with Francis Fukuyama's statement that "it matters not what *we* believe to be legitimate, but rather what *other* people believe is legitimate."[118]

Besides (perceptions of) legitimacy, Nye noted that the soft power deriving from an actor's (foreign) policies rests as much on the substance, that is, the content and goals, as on the tactics and style, that is, the ways and means in which a nation pursues its policies.[119] Kostas Ifantis accordingly opined that "substance and style of foreign policy is also a powerful factor"[120] of an actor's soft power. Therefore, only when rhetoric and deeds, promise and performance, go hand in hand, can soft power be successfully derived from governmental politics. Otherwise, when promise and performance are not in line or even contradict each other, negative repercussions on a nation's soft power are likely to occur. It is in this vein that Matthew Wallin has argued, "Words without action are merely words, and actually further sentiments of disappointment when not followed through with policy commitments."[121] In this regard, one is reminded of the adage "that it is more important to *show*, than to *tell*"[122] as well as the Confucian saying "virtue is not left to stand alone; he who practices it will have neighbours."[123]

---

[116]Robert W. Tucker and David C. Hendrickson, "The Sources of American Legitimacy," *Foreign Affairs*, Vol. 83, No. 6 (November/December 2004), p. 18.

[117]Robert Kagan, "America's Crisis of Legitimacy," *Foreign Affairs*, Vol. 83, No. 2 (March/April 2004), p. 77.

[118]Francis Fukuyama, "The Neoconservative Moment," *The National Interest*, No. 76 (Summer 2004), p. 63; Fukuyama's emphasis.

[119]Nye, *Soft Power*, p. 68.

[120]Ifantis, "Soft Power," p. 443.

[121]Matthew Wallin, "The New Public Diplomacy Imperative: America's Vital Need to Communicate Strategically," *American Security Project White Paper*, online at: https://americansecurityproject.org/ASP%20Reports/Ref%200071%20-%20The%20New%20Public%20Diplomacy%20Imperative.pdf (accessed March 15, 2014).

[122]Peter van Ham, "Power, Public Diplomacy, and the *Pax Americana*," in *The New Public Diplomacy: Soft Power in International Relations*, ed. Jan Melissen (Basingstoke: Palgrave Macmillan, 2005), p. 63.

[123]Quoted in Su, "Soft Power," p. 553.

Furthermore, as Joseph Nye has argued, "[d]omestic or foreign policies that appear to be hypocritical, arrogant, indifferent to the opinion of others, or based on a narrow approach to national interests can undermine soft power."[124] With particular reference to the United States, Harold Hongju Koh has in respect warned in May 2003 that "the perception that the United States applies one standard to the world and another to itself sharply weakens America's claim to lead globally through moral authority. This diminishes U.S. power to persuade through principle, a critical element of American 'soft power.'"[125] In this regard, one is reminded of Ophelia's admonition to her brother Laertes in Shakespeare's *Hamlet*,

> Do not, as some ungracious pastors do,
> Show me the steep and thorny way to heaven,
> Whiles, like a puff'd and reckless libertine,
> Himself the primrose path of dalliance treads,
> And recks not his own rede.[126]

Consequently, the phenomenon of hypocrisy in an actor's rhetoric and policies, or to paraphrase Heinrich Heine, of publicly preaching water while secretly drinking wine,[127] constitutes a crucial indicator to be considered in empirical analyses of an actor's soft power.

Recalling episodes in which foreign policies championed by respective governments led to an increase as well as decrease in U.S. soft power in the past, Nye offered a set of examples: On the one hand, the human rights policies of the Carter administration or the promotion of democracy championed by both the Reagan and the Clinton administrations contributed to U.S. attractiveness. On the other hand, the conduct of wars in Vietnam or Iraq greatly diminished it.[128] Connected with this observation, just as government politics can help create soft power, they can just as easily—and perhaps even more easily—squander soft power capital through rash, hypocritical actions that are guided by self-interest.[129]

In this context, as argued, domestic and foreign policies are highly interdepended in their effects on national soft power. Christopher Hill and Sarah Beadle have accordingly noted, "Soft power begins at home, as reputation and trust are both intimately linked to the nature of domestic achievements."[130] Concerning empirical examples in this regard, consider for instance the negative effect of loose domestic

---

[124]Nye, *Soft Power*, p. 14.

[125]Harold Hongju Koh, "On American Exceptionalism," *Stanford Law Review*, Vol. 55, No. 5 (May 2003), p. 1487.

[126]William Shakespeare, "Hamlet: Prince of Denmark," in *The Complete Works of William Shakespeare*, Edited with a Glossary by W. J. Craig (London: Oxford University Press, 1923), pp. 1011–1012 (Act I, Scene 3).

[127]Heinrich Heine, *Deutschland: Ein Wintermärchen* (Stuttgart: Reclam 2001), p. 10 (I, 29–32).

[128]Nye, *Soft Power*, pp. 13–14.

[129]Nye, *Soft Power*, p. 14.

[130]Christopher Hill and Sarah Beadle, *The Art of Attraction: Soft Power and the UK's Role in the World* (London: The British Academy, 2014), p. 7.

gun control laws with respect to U.S. soft power as perceived from a European perspective, or, to offer another example, racial segregation in the 1950s and 1960s in the United States and its impact on U.S. soft power in Africa.[131] It may be argued that President Kennedy well understood this phenomenon of the interconnectedness of domestic politics and international prestige, particularly at a time when the United States was competing with the Soviet Union in the larger context of the Cold War. Not only did Kennedy originate the Peace Corps in order to, with Hillary Clinton, "show the world a different face of the United States."[132] He also emphasized the need to domestically live up to this very image the Peace Corps was set to represent abroad. In his 1963 State of the Union Address Kennedy thus argued, "We shall be judged more by what we do at home than by what we preach abroad."[133] In this regard, Kennedy realized, as did his predecessor Eisenhower, that the issue of civil rights and racial segregation was not merely a domestic issue alone but also one with vast repercussions on the U.S. standing in the world.[134] Kennedy hence declared on June 11, 1963,

> We preach freedom around the world, and we mean it, and we cherish our freedom here at home; but are we to say to the world, and, much more importantly, for each other, that this is a land of the free except for the Negroes; that we have no second-class citizens except Negroes; that we have no class or caste system, no ghettos, no master race, except with respect to Negroes?[135]

Besides this interconnectedness of domestic and foreign policies, researchers have again stressed the importance of relationality and context dependence regarding this third resource of soft power. Kostas Ifantis hence aptly argued that certain governmental policies may "have both positive and negative effects."[136] This observation holds true not only for two different actors at a selected point in time but also for one actor over the course of time. Concurrently, when empirically researching the soft power of a given actor as well as possible shifts within its soft power toward another actor, it is important to bear in mind that any evaluation of an

---

[131]Nye, *Soft Power*, p. 13.

[132]Hillary Rodham Clinton, "Leading Through Civilian Power," *Foreign Affairs*, Vol. 89, No. 6 (November/December 2010), p. 24.

[133]John F. Kennedy, "Annual Message to the Congress on the State of the Union," Washington, D.C., January 14, 1963, in *Public Papers of the Presidents of the United States: John F. Kennedy, 1963, Containing the Public Messages, Speeches, and Statements of the President, January 1 to November 22, 1963* (Washington, D.C.: United States Government Printing Office, 1964), p. 15.

[134]Joseph S. Nye, Jr., "The Power We Must Not Squander," *The New York Times*, January 3, 2000, online at: http://www.nytimes.com/2000/01/03/opinion/the-power-we-must-not-squander.html (accessed October 10, 2015).

[135]John F. Kennedy, "Radio and Television Report to the American People on Civil Rights," Washington, D.C., June 11, 1963, in *Public Papers of the Presidents of the United States: John F. Kennedy, 1963, Containing the Public Messages, Speeches, and Statements of the President, January 1 to November 22, 1963* (Washington, D.C.: United States Government Printing Office, 1964), p. 469. For a similar line of argumentation, see Erwin D. Canham, *The American Position in the World* (Claremont, Cal.: Claremont Graduate School and University Center, 1965), pp. 22–23.

[136]Ifantis, "Soft Power," p. 446.

actor's soft power derived from its policies should *not* start from the premise of asking whether a certain policy is "right" or "wrong." What is more, an actor's perception of any given policy does not in itself vindicate such a judgment. Rather, any analysis should empirically focus on the nature of respective perceptions of and possible support or opposition to a given policy, rather than normatively assessing them. It is in this sense that Stephen M. Walt has argued, "Disagreement with U.S. foreign policy does not mean the policy is wrong, but it does mean U.S. actions come with a price."[137]

To sum up, governmental policies both at home and abroad, their perceived legitimacy, as well as their respective substance and style constitute a third soft power resource. While *foreign* policies feature particularly prominently in the literature of soft power and admittedly they more often than not have by their very nature a particular impact abroad, *domestic* policies should be included as well. Concerning benchmarks to take into consideration, one may therefore first consider general trends in content and conduct of the respective actor's foreign policy. To that purpose, respective grand strategies or prevalent doctrines—in the case of the United States exemplified for instance by the respective administration's National Security Strategy (NSS) and further fundamental documents or speeches by leading officials—can serve as valuable points of departure. Grand strategy has been defined as "the lynchpin that unites goals and tactics"[138] or "the overall vision of a state's national security goals and a determination of the most appropriate means to achieve these goals."[139] The comprehensive character of the concept "grand strategy" becomes evident when considering Glenn P. Hastedt's elaboration, "Grand strategy differs from military strategy or diplomatic strategy by its scope. Where they are concerned with the effective use of hard power or soft power, grand strategy is concerned with a government-wide approach that brings together all elements of power."[140] Taking into consideration such basic currents in an actor's foreign policy as identified by its grand strategy, however, can only serve as a starting point. Besides the analysis of fundamental goals and tactics of an actor's foreign policy, therefore, particular political programs or decisions should also be considered as further indicators for analyzing the soft power of a given actor—again both on a

---

[137]Stephen M. Walt, "Taming American Power," *Foreign Affairs*, Vol. 84, No. 5 (September/October 2005), p. 109.

[138]Glenn P. Hastedt, *American Foreign Policy: Past, Present, and Future* (Lanham, Md.: Rowman & Littlefield, 2015), p. 11.

[139]Brian Schmidt, "Theories of US Foreign Policy," in *US Foreign Policy*, eds. Michael Cox and Doug Stokes (Oxford: Oxford University Press, 2012), p. 16.

[140]Hastedt, *American Foreign Policy*, p. 11. For (recent) elaborations on the concept of grand strategy as well as empirical studies, see Charles Hill, *Grand Strategies: Literature, Statecraft, and World Order* (New Haven, Conn.: Yale University Press, 2010); Edward N. Luttwak, *The Grand Strategy of the Roman Empire: From the First Century CE to the Third* (Baltimore, Md.: John Hopkins University Press, 2016); Ionut Popescu, *Emergent Strategy and Grand Strategy: How American Presidents Succeed in Foreign Policy* (Baltimore, Md.: John Hopkins University Press, 2017); and, perhaps most importantly, John Lewis Gaddis, *On Grand Strategy* (New York, N.Y.: Penguin Press, 2018).

domestic and an international level. In order to select those policies, one may first consider those that have proven to be of particular importance on a global scale and second—bearing in mind the relation character of soft power—those policies that have in different ways particularly concerned Actor B.

Consequently, a set of indicators can be derived from the above discussion as well as existing literature with respect to soft power based upon the resource of (governmental) policies: (1) major components and goals identified in an actor's grand strategy as well as their perceived legitimacy; (2) the means with which an actor seeks to achieve its stated goals. Thus, the general relation to hard and soft power in an actor's foreign policy shall be considered. At it, the frequency with which an actor seeks to pursue its foreign policy goals by military means, that is, its relation and recourse to the military as a foreign policy instrument, has been identified as a crucial earmark. Su accordingly claimed that a "low frequency in using military force in achieving goals"[141] generally increases an actor's soft power; (3) the importance ascribed to the prevalence of national interest. In this regard, the conduct of foreign policy merely for the sake of enforcing what an actor declares to constitute its vital national interests is likely to decrease national soft power, whereas acting beyond one's own national interests for some global, common good (including standing up for human rights abroad) is likely to increase it. (4) Additionally, the degree to which selected policies are in line with international law should be included in the analysis. Beyond that, acting under the provisions of international law can be regarded as increasing the chances of foreign policies constituting a soft power resource. Connected with this point, (5) the perceived legitimacy and credibility of an actor's policies should be taken into account.[142] If such policies thus enjoy credibility and legitimacy, they can be considered powerful soft power sources. Finally, (6) prevalent domestic policies and issues should be taken into account.

In the light of the aforesaid, the two soft power resources of values and policies are highly interdependent and in practice, it may indeed be hard to distinguish between them in each and every case (e.g., with respect to the indicator of acting out of national interest vs. for common good). The set of indicators introduced above, however, allows for a more tangible analysis of an actor's soft power deriving from these particular resources.

3.1.4   Personalities

With the identification of the three soft power resources discussed so far—culture, values, and policies—Joseph Nye has decisively and lastingly influenced the discourse on and understanding of soft power. However, as shall be discussed in the following, a fourth and hitherto widely neglected soft power resource can be

---

[141]Su, "Soft Power," p. 552.

[142]Both aspects—credibility and legitimacy—shall be elaborated upon below.

identified, capable of generating extensive soft power in its own right: the soft power resource of personalities.[143]

The recognition of the power of individuals to influence the very course of history naturally has a millennia-old tradition in philosophy, historiography, and—more recently—the social sciences.[144] Among the many scholars subscribing to this view, it was Thomas Carlyle who perhaps expressed this notion most pointedly—and controversially. In his collection of six lectures held in London in 1840 and published in 1841 as *On Heroes, Hero-Worship, and the Heroic in History*, the Scottish scholar proclaimed,

> Universal History, the history of what man has accomplished in this world, is at bottom the history of the Great Men who have worked here. They were the leaders of men, these great ones; the modellers, patterns, and in a wider sense creators, of whatsoever the general mass of men contrived to do or to attain; all things that we see standing accomplished in the world are properly the outer material result, the practical realisation and embodiment, of Thoughts that dwelt in the Great Men sent into the world: the soul of the whole world's history, it may justly be considered, were the history of these.[145]

Subsequently, Carlyle's "Great Man Theory" became popular among philosophers and historians and constitutes an influential current in nineteenth-century historism.[146] It found its way into Georg Wilhelm Friedrich Hegel's philosophy of history[147] as well as Jacob Burckhardt's *Weltgeschichtliche Betrachtungen*.[148] Others, such as Carlyle's contemporary Herbert Spencer, however, have voiced fierce criticism.[149] Tolstoy, for example, famously denotes the individual—even generals, rulers, kings, or emperors—as "history's slaves" and history a mere

---

[143]Parts of the following subchapter on the soft power of individuals—in particular with regard to Max Weber's notion of charisma to be elaborated upon below—have been presented by the author as a paper ("A Weberian Reading on Soft Power: Introducing Individual Charisma as a Soft Power Resource") at the International Studies Association Annual Convention 2016 in Atlanta, Georgia, on March 18, 2016. The author wants to express his thanks to panel chair Stephen Burgess and discussant Lauren Moslow as well as fellow panelists and participants for their valuable feedback and constructive suggestions.

[144]Xuewu Gu and Hendrik W. Ohnesorge, "Wer macht Politik? Überlegungen zum Einfluss politischer Persönlichkeiten auf weltpolitische Gestaltung," in *Politische Persönlichkeiten und ihre weltpolitische Gestaltung: Analysen in Vergangenheit und Gegenwart*, eds. Xuewu Gu and Hendrik W. Ohnesorge (Wiesbaden: Springer VS, 2017), pp. 3–5.

[145]Thomas Carlyle, *On Heroes, Hero-Worship, and the Heroic in History: Six Lectures* (London: James Fraser, 1841), pp. 1–2.

[146]Jens Nordalm, "Historismus im 19. Jahrhundert: Zur Fortdauer einer Epoche des geschichtlichen Denkens," in *Historismus im 19. Jahrhundert*, ed. Jens Nordalm (Stuttgart: Reclam, 2006), p. 8.

[147]Georg Wilhelm Friedrich Hegel, *Vorlesungen über die Philosophie der Geschichte* (Stuttgart: Reclam, 1961), pp. 74–78.

[148]Jacob Burckhardt, *Weltgeschichtliche Betrachtungen* (Stuttgart: Alfred Kröner, 1978), pp. 209–248.

[149]James MacGregor Burns, *Transforming Leadership: A New Pursuit of Happiness* (New York, N. Y.: Grove Press, 2003), p. 13.

"unconscious, general, hive life of mankind."[150] Nevertheless, by the early twentieth century, the notion of an individual decisively influencing world history had become a prominent feature in historiography and literature.[151]

A.F.K. Organski, for example, holds in his *World Politics* that clearly "it does make a difference who happens to lead a nation at a particular time," although structures in which the respective leader is set also matter.[152] It is in the same vein that Christopher Clark, in his masterful account of the outbreak of the First World War, argues, "It is a central argument of this book that the events of July 1914 make sense only when we illuminate the journeys travelled by key decision-makers."[153] Personalities, however, may not only influence the decisions of on particular states but also have decisive influence on bilateral relations, as Stephen F. Szabo illustrates with reference to US–German relations, particularly under George W. Bush and Gerhard Schröder.[154] While writings on the issue of the role of individuals abound, the underlying questions of the roles of agency and structure still remain unanswered to a great part.[155]

In political science and International Relations, the research field of personality and politics pays tribute to such views, influenced decisively by the writings of Fred I. Greenstein.[156] Rooted in political psychology, this highly interdisciplinary branch of research focuses, in the words of Margaret Hermann, on "describing the role people play in politics."[157] At it, particular emphasis is frequently put on leading

---

[150]Leo Tolstoy, *War and Peace* (Chicago, Ill.: Encyclopædia Britannica, 1952), p. 343.

[151]Examples in this regard are abundant. See, for instance, Stefan Zweig's *Sternstunden der Menschheit*. In its first edition (1927), Zweig depicts 5 episodes—later to be extended to 14—which share the focus on one individual and its respective influence on the course of history; Stefan Zweig, *Sternstunden der Menschheit: Vierzehn historische Miniaturen* (Frankfurt am Main: Fischer Taschenbuch Verlag, 2010). Another popular representative of this view was Winston Churchill who in his first edition of his *Great Contemporaries* presents 21 biographical essays of influential individuals of his own time; Winston S. Churchill, *Great Contemporaries* (London: Thornton Butterworth, 1937).

[152]Organski, *World Politics*, p. 95.

[153]Christopher Clark, *The Sleepwalkers: How Europe Went to War in 1914* (London: Penguin Books, 2013), p. xxviii.

[154]Stephen F. Szabo, *Parting Ways: The Crisis in German-American Relations* (Washington, D.C.: Brookings Institution Press, 2004), pp. 9–10.

[155]Burns, *Transforming Leadership*, p. 15.

[156]For works by Fred I. Greenstein see, for example, "The Impact of Personality on Politics: An Attempt to Clear Away Underbrush," *The American Political Science Review*, Vol. 61, No. 3 (September 1967), pp. 629–641; *Personality and Politics: Problems of Evidence, Interference, and Conceptualization* (Chicago, Ill.: Markham, 1969); "Can Personality and Politics be Studied Systematically," *Political Psychology*, Vol. 13, No. 1 (March 1992), pp. 105–128; "Personality and Politics," in *Encyclopedia of Government and Politics*, eds. Mary Hawkesworth and Maurice Kogan (New York, N.Y.: Routledge, 2004), pp. 351–369.

[157]Margaret G. Hermann, "Political Psychology as a Perspective in the Study of Politics," in *Political Psychology*, ed. Kristen R. Monroe (Mahwah, N.J.: Erlbaum, 2002), p. 46. See also Paul 't Hart, "Political Psychology," in *Theory and Methods in Political Science*, eds. David Marsh and Gerry Stoker (London: Palgrave Macmillan, 2010), pp. 99–113.

or "visible" individuals (think Carlyle's "Great Men" or Clarke's "key decision-makers") in powerful positions. At times, however, more clandestine *éminences grises*, puppet masters working outside the spotlight, individuals whom Stefan Zweig aptly called "Hintergrundgestalten,"[158] (or "background figures") and their roles should also be taken into account.

With particular respect to soft power, scholars have from time to time also recognized the possibility of individuals wielding attractive power, including Nye himself.[159] Nye has thus argued that "[e]ven individual celebrities are able to use their soft power."[160] This assumption has found its way into studies seeking to measure or rank the soft power of selected actors. Ernst & Young, for example, thus included the soft power of "icons" into their calculation of a soft power index and cite Nelson Mandela as a prominent example.[161] Geun Lee has likewise hinted at the wielding of soft power through individuals,

> Heroes and celebrities can exert soft power in two ways. One is by their role models, and comments on charitable efforts for certain universal values, and the other is by instilling a sense of pride within their own countries. The former can set an international agenda to achieve certain national or international goals, while the latter provokes nationalistic cohesion or wide support for their government. Here, heroes or celebrities can act independently or in cooperation with their governments.[162]

The first way, that of the role model eliciting a certain behavior is well established and has a long tradition in literature. For example, the Xenophontic Cyrus the Great, founder of the Achaemenid Empire in the sixth century BC, drew his powers in large part from his exemplary function, as repeatedly stressed in Xenophon's *Cyropaedia*.[163] Regarding the ability to influence the (national or even global) agenda, Joseph Nye himself specifically included agenda setting in his power

---

[158]Stefan Zweig, *Joseph Fouché: Bildnis eines politischen Menschen* (Frankfurt am Main: Fischer Taschenbuch Verlag, 2012), p. 13.

[159]Nye, *Soft Power*, p. 6. See also Nye's work on leadership; Joseph S. Nye, Jr., "Transformational Leadership and U.S. Grand Strategy," *Foreign Affairs*, Vol. 85, No. 4 (July/August 2006), pp. 139–145 & 147–148; Joseph S. Nye, Jr., "Soft Power, Hard Power and Leadership," *Harvard Kennedy School*, October 27, 2006, online at: http://www.hks.harvard.edu/netgov/files/talks/docs/ 11_06_06_seminar_Nye_HP_SP_Leadership.pdf (accessed April 26, 2015); Joseph S. Nye, Jr. *The Powers to Lead* (Oxford: Oxford University Press, 2008), pp. 61–69; and Joseph S. Nye, Jr., *Presidential Leadership and the Creation of the American Era* (Princeton, N.J.: Princeton University Press, 2013), pp. 12–14.

[160]Nye, "Hard, Soft, and Smart Power," p. 568.

[161]Ernst & Young, "Rapid-Growth Markets Soft Power Index: Spring 2012," 2012, online at: http:// emergingmarkets.ey.com/wp-content/uploads/downloads/2012/05/TBF-606-Emerging-markets-soft-power-index-2012_LR.pdf (accessed October 1, 2015), p. 8.

[162]Lee, "A Theory of Soft Power and Korea's Soft Power Strategy," p. 213.

[163]Xenophon, *Kyrupädie: Die Erziehung des Kyros*, Edited and Translated by Rainer Nickel (München: Artemis & Winkler, 1992), pp. 87–91, pp. 551–553, pp. 555–557 & pp. 561–563 (Xen. Cyrop. 1, 6, 20-25; 8, 1, 12; 8, 1, 21 & 8, 1, 39).

spectrum and assigned it to the soft power side.[164] The idea of agenda setting has thus been included in his earlier works, but later "faded into the background" while others, like John Ikenberry, have elaborated on the term.[165] With regard to individuals putting certain issues on the (domestic as well as global) agenda, numerous historical examples come to mind: Country Music legend Johnny Cash not only sang about (and in) prisons but also championed prison reforms, a subject on which he spoke before the U.S. Congress Subcommittee on National Penitentiaries as well as with President Richard M. Nixon in a July 1972 meeting[166]; Marlon Brando refused to accept the Academy Award for his role in *The Godfather* in 1973 and was represented by actress Sacheen Littlefeather at the awards ceremony in order to draw public attention to the mistreatment of Native Americans[167]; Princess Diana lobbied for demining and The Diana, Princess of Wales Memorial Fund was established and received large sums due to extensive media attention after the princess' tragic death in 1997[168]; artists like Bono, for example, by founding Debt, AIDS, Trade, Africa (DATA) in 2002, have contributed greatly to the advance the global agenda of poverty reduction[169]; movie legend Peter Ustinov or tennis superstar Roger Federer served as Goodwill Ambassadors for the United Nations Children's Fund (UNICEF), drawing attention to the goals and policies of the United Nations and its programs.[170] For his philanthropic work, Roger Federer has in fact been included in the *TIME Magazine* list of the 100 most influential individuals in 2018, with a commendation penned by Bill Gates and his portrait even appearing on one of the covers of the respective issue.[171] Other sports icons have been counted among the most influential figures of the twentieth century due to their power to influence people all around the world as well. Perhaps the most prominent among these was Muhammad Ali, who was ranked by *TIME Magazine* among the 20 most

---

[164]Nye, *Soft Power*, p. 8.

[165]Brantly Womack, "Dancing Alone: A Hard Look at Soft Power," *Japan Focus*, November 16, 2005, online at: http://www.japanfocus.org/site/make_pdf/1975 (accessed February 16, 2015).

[166]David Kyle Johnson and Lance Schmitz, "Johnny Cash, Prison Reform, and Capital Punishment," in *Johnny Cash and Philosophy: The Burning Ring of Truth*, eds. John Huss and David Werther (Chicago and La Salle, Ill.: Open Court, 2008), p. 156.

[167]Bruce E. Johansen, *Encyclopedia of the American Indian Movement* (Santa Barbara, Cal.: ABC-CLIO, 2013), pp. 176–178.

[168]Michael J. Flynn, "Political Minefield," in *Landmines and Human Security: International Politics and War's Hidden Legacy*, eds. Richard A. Matthew, Bryan McDonald, and Kenneth R. Rutherford (Albany, N.Y.: State University of New York Press, 2004), p. 122. See also Zahran and Ramos, "From Hegemony to Soft Power," p. 20.

[169]Ali S. Wyne, "Public Opinion and Power," in *Routledge Handbook of Public Diplomacy*, eds. Nancy Snow and Philip M. Taylor (New York, N.Y.: Routledge, 2009), p. 40.

[170]Geoffrey Allen Pigman, *Contemporary Diplomacy: Representation and Communication in a Globalized World* (Cambridge: Polity Press, 2010), p. 97.

[171]Wilder Davies, "The Story Behind the 2018 TIME 100 Covers," *TIME Magazine*, April 19, 2018, online at: http://time.com/5245018/time-100-2018-covers/ (accessed April 24, 2018).

influential Americans of all times—alongside George Washington, Thomas Jefferson, and Abraham Lincoln.[172] Michael Jordan, who in the words of historian H. W. Brands "by the 1990s was a celebrity with stature that transcended basketball and even sports in general,"[173] can be considered another case in point.

Added to the observable attractive and agenda-setting power of personalities, based neither on physical coercion or economic inducement, it is also true that certain individuals stand for and represent their home country—for better or for worse—particularly of course in the political arena. As one Australian commentator put it, "[I]t helps a country's public image when its head of state is widely liked rather than widely disliked."[174] With respect to the United States, the U.S. President as both the elected head of state and government, thus becomes a symbol of the country at large, its policies as well as its values. In his March 3, 2016, statement on then-candidate Donald J. Trump, 2012 Republican presidential candidate Mitt Romney in this vein proclaimed, "The President of the United States has long been the leader of the free world. The president and yes the nominees of the country's great parties help define America to billions of people. All of them bear the responsibility of being an example for our children and grandchildren."[175] While arguably true for the United States in particular, the same holds true, of course, for other countries' elected officials as well.

Despite the plethora of empirical examples to be found (some of which to be invoked at greater lengths below) and occasional references to be found in literature, conceptualization of the attractive power of individuals and an integration of the individual into the concept of soft power remain far from satisfactory. Yet, as shall be demonstrated in the following, one particular sociological notion offers a highly eligible—yet hitherto widely neglected[176]—conceptual vehicle for the integration of personalities as a fourth resource into the framework of soft power: Max Weber's notion of charisma.

Starting with the philological roots of the term, "charisma" derives from the Greek χάρισμα and can be translated as "gift of grace."[177] The root word χάρισ

---

[172]TIME Staff, "The 20 Most Influential Americans of All Time," *TIME Magazine*, July 24, 2012, online at http://newsfeed.time.com/2012/07/25/the-20-most-influential-americans-of-all-time/ (accessed June 10, 2016).

[173]H. W. Brands, *American Dreams: The United States Since 1945* (New York, N.Y.: The Penguin Press, 2010), p. 300.

[174]Quoted in Joseph S. Nye, Jr., "Good Start, Long Road," *The American Interest*, Vol. 5, No. 3 (Winter 2010), p. 13.

[175]Mitt Romney, "Speech about Donald Trump," Salt Lake City, Utah, March 3, 2016, online at http://time.com/4246596/donald-trump-mitt-romney-utah-speech/ (accessed April 12, 2016).

[176]An example of integrating Weber's notion of (individual) charisma into power in general can be found in P. David Marshall, *Celebrity and Power: Fame in Contemporary Culture* (Minneapolis, Minn.: University of Minnesota Press, 1997), pp. 20–22.

[177]Berit Bliesemann de Guevara and Tatjana Reiber, "Popstars der Macht: Charisma und Politik," in *Charisma und Herrschaft*, eds. Berit Bliesemann de Guevara and Tatjana Reiber (Frankfurt: Campus, 2011), p. 15.

can already be found in Homer's *Iliad* and *Odyssey* and translates into (outward) grace, beauty, or favor.[178] Today, the term is used in an extremely broad sense and has virtually become a catchphrase.[179] The media as well as the public commonly denote a great number of personalities, hailing from such diverse fields of activity as the arts, science, sports, or politics, as having (or lacking) charisma.[180] In academic anthologies dealing with selected charismatic personalities over the centuries, however, considerably fewer cases are commonly selected.[181] This observation can be attributed to the fact that scientific studies usually understand charisma in a much narrower sense of the word as put forth by Max Weber in his *Wirtschaft und Gesellschaft*, first published in 1922.[182] Subsequently, in another interesting parallel to the notion of soft power, the concept of charisma has provoked broad application while at the same time scholars have grappled with an "almost universal difficulty of providing concise theoretical and operational (empirical) definitions of the concept."[183] Today, works on charisma are often highly interdisciplinary and the disciplines of sociology, political science, psychology, and theology, among others, have substantially contributed to the development of the concept.[184]

Initially, Max Weber developed the concept by drawing on two fundamental sources: On the one hand, the notion of Caesarism, which had become an influential current since the mid-nineteenth century, and on the other hand the religious notion of charisma as employed with regard to the organization of early Christian communities.[185] Hence, while Weber cannot be credited with inventing the sociological

---

[178]Christoph R. Hatscher, *Charisma und Res Publica: Max Webers Herrschaftssoziologie und die Römische Republik* (Franz Steiner Verlag: Stuttgart, 2000), p. 39.

[179]Hatscher, *Charisma und Res Publica*, p. 21.

[180]Wilfried Nippel, "Charisma und Herrschaft," in *Virtuosen der Macht: Herrschaft und Charisma von Perikles bis Mao*, ed. Wilfried Nippel (München: C. H. Beck, 2000), p. 7. See also Bliesemann de Guevara and Reiber, "Popstars der Macht," p. 15.

[181]Wilfried Nippel, ed., *Virtuosen der Macht: Herrschaft und Charisma von Perikles bis Mao* (München: C. H. Beck, 2000), for example, includes 15 personalities in a timespan of 25 centuries.

[182]Max Weber, *Wirtschaft und Gesellschaft* (Tübingen, J. C. B. Mohr, 1922). The following paragraph draws on its English translation: Max Weber, *Economy and Society: An Outline of Interpretive Sociology*, eds. Guenther Roth and Claus Wittich (Berkeley, Cal.: University of California Press, 1978). The notion of charisma is set forth in Chapter XIV (pp. 1111–1157) of the work.

[183]Kathryn L. Burke and Merlin B. Brinkerhoff, "Capturing Charisma: Notes on an Elusive Concept," *Journal for the Scientific Study of Religion*, Vol. 20, No. 3 (September 1981), p. 274. See also Arthur Schweitzer, "Theory and Political Charisma," *Comparative Studies in Society and History*, Vol. 16, No. 2 (March 1974), p. 150 and Martin E. Spencer, "What is Charisma?," *The British Journal of Sociology*, Vol. 24, No. 3 (September 1973), pp. 341–342. It may be argued that it is the shared fate of (scientific) concepts to lose their analytical value and robustness once they have gained broad popularity and application.

[184]Jane A. Halpert, "The Dimensionality of Charisma," *Journal of Business and Psychology*, Vol. 4, No. 4 (Summer 1990), p. 399.

[185]Nippel, "Charisma und Herrschaft," p. 8.

concept of charisma,[186] his main achievement was its secularization, since it hitherto had been applied only with respect to the (early) Christian Church, notably in the writings of legal historian and canon lawyer Rudolph Sohm.[187] Weber, though paying tribute to the term's origin in early Christian vocabulary,[188] did not accept Sohm's restrictions with regard to the application of charisma but argued instead, "In principle, these phenomena are universal, even though they are often most evident in the religious realm."[189]

In his writings, Weber contrasted the notion of charisma with other forms of legitimacy such as bureaucracy or patriarchalism[190] and identified three (ideal) types of legitimate authority: First, legal authority, "resting on a belief in the legality of enacted rules and the right of those elevated to authority under such rules to issue commands;" second, traditional authority, "resting on an established belief in the sanctity of immemorial traditions and the legitimacy of those exercising authority under them;" and third, charismatic authority, "resting on devotion to the exceptional sanctity, heroism or exemplary character of an individual person, and of the normative patterns or order revealed or ordained by him."[191] With regard to the third variety, of special relevance in the following, Weber argued that "it is the charismatically qualified leader as such who is obeyed by virtue of personal trust in his revelation, his heroism or his exemplary quality so far as they fall within the scope of the individual's belief in his charisma."[192]

In Weber's understanding, three varieties of charisma can be differentiated: hereditary charisma, office charisma, and pure, individual charisma.[193] The first variety, hereditary charisma, is transferable through belonging to a certain family or bloodline.[194] The affiliation to royal families constitutes a prominent example. It is in this vein that Bertrand Russell noted, "The Norman Conquest produced, in England, a royal family which, after a time, was thought to possess a Devine Right to the throne."[195] In the Middle Ages, however, not only secular rulers enjoyed the attribution of charisma; charisma at times also played a role in the investiture of bishops from selected noble families who were believed to be particularly

---

[186]It may be argued that Weber has played the same role for the dissemination and establishment of the concept of charisma as Joseph Nye did with regard to the concept of soft power.

[187]Guenther Roth, "Introduction," in Max Weber, *Economy and Society: An Outline of Interpretive Sociology*, eds. Guenther Roth and Claus Wittich (Berkeley, Cal.: University of California Press, 1978), p. xcvi. See also Weber, *Economy and Society*, p. 1112 and Schweitzer, "Theory and Political Charisma," pp. 151–152.

[188]Weber, *Economy and Society*, p. 216.

[189]Weber, *Economy and Society*, p. 1112.

[190]Roth, "Introduction," p. xcvi. See also Weber, *Economy and Society*, p. 216, p. 954, & p. 1112.

[191]Weber, *Economy and Society*, p. 215. See also Weber, *Economy and Society*, pp. 241–245.

[192]Weber, *Economy and Society*, p. 216.

[193]Weber, *Economy and Society*, p. 216 & p. 1135.

[194]Weber, *Economy and Society*, p. 1136.

[195]Bertrand Russell, *Power: A New Social Analysis* (London: George Allen and Unwin, 1938), p. 85.

predestinated for holding the mediatorial office between God and Man.[196] Frequently, belonging to a royal line has hence even been connected with possessing healing powers, for example, in the case of the Stuarts in late seventeenth-century England.[197] In fact, this notion has a long tradition and can already be found in Tacitus' *Histories*, where Vespasian, who upon his accession to the Roman imperial throne ended the vicissitudes of civil war in the Year of the Four Emperors (AD 69), is said to have cured the infirmities of two inhabitants of Alexandria, "manifesting," as Tacitus tells us, "the goodwill of Heaven and the special favour of Providence towards him."[198] In literature, the same notion famously found expression in J. R. R. Tolkien's *The Lord of the Rings*, "For it is said in old lore: *The hands of the king are the hands of a healer*. And so the rightful king could ever be known."[199] In our days, the membership to political dynasties (e.g., the Kennedys or the Bushes in the United States or the Nehru-Gandhi family in India) approximates the attribution of hereditary charisma. The same holds true for numerous other countries with highly diverse political systems and cultures all around the world.[200]

The second variety, office charisma, can be defined as "the belief in the specific state of grace of a social institution."[201] In this variety, charisma derives from holding a particular office such as the papacy or—to offer a secular example—the presidency of the United States. In this instance, charisma derives not so much from the individual itself but rather from the particular office one is elected to, especially if it is long-standing or prestigious.

Finally, pure charisma denotes the belief in the extraordinariness of an individual, an idea, or even an object of its own account. While arguably the most common, charisma is not merely awarded to individuals alone, but can also be attributed to certain countries or ideologies. Alexander Vuving has in this sense aptly argued,

> Beauty is the pivotal power currency that makes charismatic leaders. This holds true for both individuals and states. In the 20th century, the United States, the Soviet Union, and the People's Republic of China were arguably the most charismatic countries, each finding resonance among a specific group of states and individuals.[202]

---

[196]Ernst W. Wies, *Otto der Große: Kämpfer und Beter* (Esslingen: Bechtle, 1998), p. 85.

[197]Thomas O'Malley, "Religion and the Newspaper Press, 1660-1685: A Study of the *London Gazette*," in *The Press in English Society from the Seventeenth to Nineteenth Centuries*, eds. Michael Harris and Alan Lee (Rutherford, N.J.: Fairleigh Dickinson University Press, 1986), p. 39.

[198]P. Cornelius Tacitus, *The Histories*, Translated with Introduction and Notes by W. Hamilton Fyfe, Volume II (Oxford: Clarendon Press, 1912), p. 195 (Tac. Hist. IV, 81). See also C. Suetonius Tranquillus, *Die Kaiserviten: De Vita Caesarum/Berühmte Männer: De Viris Illustribus*, Edited and Translated by Hans Martinet (Berlin: Walter de Gruyter, 2014), pp. 841–843 (Suet. Ves. 7).

[199]J. R. R. Tolkien, *The Return of the King: Being the Third Part of the Lord of the Rings* (New York, N.Y.: HarperCollins, 2007) p. 1126; Tolkien's emphasis.

[200]"The Power of Families: Dynasties," April 18, 2015, *The Economist*, p. 7.

[201]Weber, *Economy and Society*, p. 1140.

[202]Alexander L. Vuving, "How Soft Power Works," Paper Presented at the *American Political Science Association*, Toronto, Ontario, September 3, 2009, p. 12.

In this pure variety, "charisma is a gift that inheres in an object or person simply by virtue of natural endowment."[203] It is recognized as something that is not available to everybody but rather it constitutes a "gift" accessible only to a select few.[204] Frequently, it is attributed to warriors or "heroes" who have distinguished themselves in times of danger or war at the peril of their health or even their lives.[205] Others, such as Wolfgang Lipp,[206] have argued that particularly individuals at the margins of society who are discriminated against or stigmatized for one reason or another, are capable to revert stigmatization and turn it into individual charisma.[207] Additionally, personal charisma often takes on religious or messianic traits. The charismatic leader thus is, in the eyes of his followers, "sent from God" and capable of leading his "disciples" from times of distress toward a better tomorrow. Therefore, the leader's "ability to articulate a compelling vision of a bright future is the sine qua non of charisma."[208] The charismatic leader hence has the ability to wield great influence over his followers due to his attractiveness, and hence qualifies as what Georg Wilhelm Friedrich Hegel called a "Seelenführer"—a spiritual leader of man.[209]

However, charisma in all its different manifestations is not an individual quality per se but rather an attribute awarded to an individual (or an object, idea, etc.) by its devotees, thus establishing a relationship.[210] As Arthur Schweitzer noted, only if "the self-confidence of the leader and the devotion of the followers interact and reinforce each other," a charismatic relationship is established.[211] The charisma of an individual leader is therefore crucially dependent on recognition by his disciples or followers.[212] Thomas E. Dow, Jr., elaborated on the importance of the follower and emphasized one's "identification with the charismatic leader, in that the leader, on the basis of his apparent gifts of body and mind, his heroism, is perceived as a model."[213] Additionally, the charismatic relationship is highly contextual and can

---

[203]Weber, *Economy and Society*, p. 400.

[204]Weber, *Economy and Society*, p. 1112.

[205]Bliesemann de Guevara and Reiber, "Popstars der Macht," p. 22.

[206]Wolfgang Lipp, "Charisma – Schuld und Gnade: Soziale Konstruktion, Kulturdynamik, Handlungsdrama," in *Charisma: Theorie – Religion – Politik*, eds. Winfried Gebhardt, Arnold Zingerle, Michael N. Ebertz (Berlin: Walter de Gruyter, 1993), pp. 15–32.

[207]Bliesemann de Guevara and Reiber, "Popstars der Macht," p. 22.

[208]Cynthia G. Emrich, Holly H. Brower, Jack M. Feldman, and Howard Garland, "Images in Words: Presidential Rhetoric, Charisma, and Greatness," *Administrative Science Quarterly*, Vol. 46, No. 3 (September 2001), p. 527.

[209]Hegel, *Vorlesungen über die Philosophie der Geschichte*, p. 76.

[210]Robert J. House, William D. Spangler, and James Woycke, "Personality and Charisma in the U.S. Presidency: A Psychological Theory of Leader Effectiveness," *Administrative Science Quarterly*, Vol. 36, No. 3 (September 1991), p. 366.

[211]Schweitzer, "Theory and Political Charisma," p. 153.

[212]Weber, *Economy and Society*, pp. 1112–1113; Nippel, "Charisma und Herrschaft," p. 9.

[213]Thomas E. Dow, Jr., "An Analysis of Weber's Work on Charisma," *The British Journal of Sociology*, Vol. 29, No. 1 (March 1978), pp. 83–84.

only be understood against the backdrop of the respective time and place in which it is set.[214] Bryan R. Wilson offers an illustrative example in this regard and pointed out, "If a man runs naked down the street proclaiming that he alone can save others from impending doom, and if he immediately wins a following, then he is a charismatic leader: A social relationship has come into being. If he does not win a following, he is simply a lunatic."[215] Regarding the emergence of a charismatic relationship, Weber argued that these are most likely to occur in crises or "moments of distress."[216] It is this observation that later induced M. Rainer Lepsius to coin the term of a (latent or manifest) "charismatic situation."[217] Many writers have in this tradition identified a time "of great radical social change which causes distress and dissatisfaction" as making the rise of a charismatic personality more likely.[218] However, charisma, and particularly pure charisma, itself is also highly unstable, allowing for the bearer to lose his charisma as quickly as he may have gained it.[219] This observation leads to empirical examples illustrating the (soft) power of charisma.

Napoleon Bonaparte, for instance, "swaying the world by the force of his will, legitimized by charismatic magnetism and personal success in military command,"[220] as Henry Kissinger has written, has been considered an exceptionally charismatic person. While eminent tactical abilities and fabled military triumphs undoubtedly contributed to his stellar career, it was the Corsican's charisma and force of personality that paved his road to success in the first place.[221] In fact, Napoleon's coup d'état of 18 Brumaire, which effectively ended the rule of the Directory and thus—in the eyes of most historians—the French Revolution, may be regarded as a paramount example of the soft power of an individual worth elaborating upon: Having only the pay of a general at his disposal (which his wife Josephine had spent rather lavishly in his absence) and no troops at his command, Napoleon lacked hard power resources to enforce or buy his will and thus had to rely solely on

---

[214]Bliesemann de Guevara and Reiber, "Popstars der Macht," pp. 19–20 & pp. 32–38.

[215]Bryan R. Wilson, *The Noble Savages: The Primitive Origins of Charisma and its Contemporary Survival* (Berkeley, Cal.: University of California Press, 1975), p. 5.

[216]Weber, *Economy and Society*, p. 1111. See also Bliesemann de Guevara and Reiber, "Popstars der Macht," pp. 20–23 and Hans-Peter Schwarz, "Charismatische (Ver-)Führer," *Totalitarismus und Demokratie*, Vol. 1, No. 1 (2004), p. 29.

[217]M. Rainer Lepsius, "Das Modell der charismatischen Herrschaft und seine Anwendbarkeit auf den 'Führerstaat' Adolf Hitlers," in *Demokratie in Deutschland: Soziologisch-historische Konstellationsanalysen, Ausgewählte Aufsätze*, ed. M. Rainer Lepsius (Göttingen: Vandenhoeck & Ruprecht, 1993), pp. 100–101.

[218]Douglas F. Barnes, "Charisma and Religious Leadership: An Historical Analysis," *Journal for the Scientific Study of Religion*, Vol. 17, No. 1 (March 1978), p. 4.

[219]Weber, *Economy and Society*, p. 1113. See also Thomas E. Dow, Jr., "The Theory of Charisma," *The Sociological Quarterly*, Vol. 10, No. 3 (Summer 1969), p. 312.

[220]Henry Kissinger, *World Order: Reflections on the Character of Nations and the Course of History* (London: Allen Lane, 2014), p. 45.

[221]Michael Gamper, *Der große Mann. Geschichte eines politischen Phantasmas* (Göttingen: Wallstein Verlag, 2016), pp. 178–180.

his personality to succeed in his quest for power in 1799—which he did brilliantly.[222] He thus successfully drew on what has been called "the history-changing power of his person."[223] Many contemporaries shared the view of Napoleon's extraordinary individual power and attraction: Hegel, upon seeing him riding into Jena in 1806, for instance, famously called Napoleon "Weltseele zu Pferde"[224] (or "world soul on horseback"[225]) and Johann Wolfgang von Goethe, who in October 1808 personally met Napoleon in Erfurt, admired the Corsican immensely and considered him a "Naturgewalt"[226] (or "force of nature"). Others, including Napoleon's fiercest opponents on the battlefield, shared this admiration and subscribed to his personal attraction as well. Arthur Wellesley, first Duke of Wellington, Napoleon's opponent in the Peninsular War and the victor of Waterloo, thus declared, "I would at any time rather have heard that a reinforcement of forty thousand men had joined the French army, than that *he* had arrived to take the command."[227] After Leipzig (1813), and especially after Waterloo (1815), however, *le petit caporal* had lost a great share of his attraction for good.[228] A mere 6 years after his ultimate defeat at the hands of Wellington and Prussian Generalfeldmarschall Gebhard Leberecht von Blücher, Napoleon died an exile on the windswept island of St. Helena in 1821. In this very respect, Weber has aptly pointed out, "When the tide that lifted a charismatically led group out of everyday life flows back into the channels of workaday routines, at least the "pure" form of charismatic domination will wane,"[229] a phenomenon Weber labeled as the "routinization of charisma."[230] However, the charisma of an individual does not necessarily end with their demise. On the contrary, in some instances death, particularly if it is

---

[222]Vincent Cronin, *Napoleon: Eine Biographie* (Hamburg: Classen Verlag, 1973), p. 217.

[223]Michael Vlahos, "Public Diplomacy as Loss of World Authority," in *Routledge Handbook of Public Diplomacy*, eds. Nancy Snow and Philip M. Taylor (New York, N.Y.: Routledge, 2009), p. 32.

[224]Quoted in Jörg Baberowski, *Der Sinn der Geschichte: Geschichtstheorien von Hegel bis Foucault* (München: C. H. Beck, 2005), p. 33.

[225]Quoted in Robert C. Solomon, *In the Spirit of Hegel* (Oxford: Oxford University Press, 1983), p. 36. See also Kissinger, *World Order*, p. 47.

[226]Gerhard Müller, "'…eine wunderbare Aussicht zur Vereinigung deutscher und französischer Vorstellungsarten': Goethe und Weimar im Rheinbund," in *Europa in Weimar: Visionen eines Kontinents*, ed. Hellmut Th. Seemann (Göttingen: Wallstein Verlag, 2008), p. 261. For an excellent study of the relationship and especially the 1808 meeting between the two luminaries of their age, see Gustav Seibt, *Goethe und Napoleon: Eine historische Begegnung* (München: C. H. Beck, 2008).

[227]Quoted in Elizabeth Longford, *Wellington: The Years of the Sword* (New York, N.Y.: Smithmark, 1968), pp. 348–349; emphasis added.

[228]Burns, *Transforming Leadership*, p. 11.

[229]Weber, *Economy and Society*, p. 1121. See also Hegel, *Vorlesungen über die Philosophie der Geschichte*, p. 76.

[230]Weber, *Economy and Society*, pp. 1121–1123. It may be argued that these situations appear particular after a crisis has been overcome. Consider, for example, the voting out of office of Winston Churchill within months after the Allied victory in World War II.

untimely or violent and leading to perceptions of martyrdom, can contribute to the attribution and increase of charisma.[231] (Think, for example, of Mahatma Gandhi, John F. and Robert F. Kennedy, Ernesto "Che" Guevara, Martin Luther King, Olof Palme, or Princess Diana.)

That the three varieties of charisma outlined above (i.e., hereditary, office, and pure charisma) are to be regarded as ideal types which in reality can coexist and reinforce each other, is evidenced, for example, by the case of Pope John Paul II: As pope and successor to Saint Peter he certainly has been attributed office charisma. As an individual, however, he also has been credited with pure, genuine charisma.[232] In the case of John F. Kennedy, to offer another example, the office charisma of the presidency was amalgamated with the hereditary charisma of belonging to an influential political dynasty and not least with his personal, pure charisma grounded in his own personality.[233]

In Weber's understanding of the term, charisma is a non-normative, value-free concept.[234] Charismatic relationships, therefore, are not restricted to come into being for a good or noble cause. Instead, as various studies have indicated, both the democratic leader and the autocratic dictator can be attributed with charisma.[235] Accordingly, especially for his propensity to transcend and burst established structures of checks and balances, the charismatic leader is frequently viewed in a particularly critical light from the perspective of democratic theory.[236]

A further important element in the notion of charisma is the factor of change or transformation. While other forms of authority change behavior "from without," charisma "manifests its revolutionary power from within, from a central *metanoi* [change] of the followers' attitudes."[237] In this understanding, a direct line can be drawn from the difference between hard power resting on "outside" forces of coercion and inducement, and soft power, resting on the "inside" force of attraction. Accordingly, Weber noted that "in a revolutionary and sovereign manner, charismatic domination transforms all values and breaks all traditional and rational norms:

---

[231] Bliesemann de Guevara and Reiber, "Popstars der Macht," pp. 44–47.

[232] See, for example, *House Resolution* 190, "Honoring the Life and Achievements of his Holiness Pope John Paul II and Expressing Profound Sorrow on his Death," 109th Congress, 1st Session, April 6, 2005, *Congressional Record* 151, Pt. 4 (2005), p. 5749. See also Peter Hebblethwaite, *Pope John Paul II and the Church* (Kansas City, Mo.: National Catholic Reporter, 1995), p. 23.

[233] John C. Culver, "Recorded Interview by Vicki Daitch," Boston, Mass., May 12, 2003, *John F. Kennedy Library Oral History Program*, online at: http://www.jfklibrary.org/Asset-Viewer/ Archives/JFKOH-JCC-01.aspx (accessed April 12, 2016), p. 9.

[234] Weber, *Economy and Society*, pp. 1112–1113.

[235] Bliesemann de Guevara and Reiber, "Popstars der Macht," p. 15. See also Schweitzer, "Theory and Political Charisma," p. 150 and Schwarz, "Charismatische (Ver-)Führer," p. 16. Interestingly, observations concerning the non-normative nature of Weber's notion of charisma bear a striking resemblance to similar observations regarding the concept of soft power; see above, Sect. 2.5.3.2

[236] Schwarz, "Charismatische (Ver-)Führer," p. 17.

[237] Weber, *Economy and Society*, pp. 1116–1117; Weber's emphasis.

'It has been written ..., but I say unto you..."[238] With this phrasing, Max Weber relates, of course, to the Sermon on the Mount[239] and with his reference to Jesus Christ thus insinuates an individual who may be considered the quintessential charismatic character in history. A charismatic leader, therefore, develops the ability to "transform the needs, values, preferences, and aspirations" and is able to "motivate followers to make significant personal sacrifices in the interest of some mission and to perform above and beyond the call of duty."[240]

In the final analysis, as has been demonstrated above, the two concepts of soft power and charisma provide interesting points of contact and convergence (e.g., their intangibility and relational character) and even share some basic vocabulary (e.g., attraction and change from within rather than without). Taking these observations as a starting point and integrating charisma into the concept of soft power, personalities can indeed be regarded as constituting a fourth and independent resource of soft power.

After the conceptual discussion of charisma and its integration into the soft power taxonomy, further recourse to empirical evidence shall elucidate the fourth resource of soft power at greater length. In this regard, the present work has already repeatedly alluded to the soft power wielded by individuals, including one fictional character (Tom Sawyer) and one historical figure (Napoleon Bonaparte) in particular. Throughout the ages, countless further examples of individuals yielding considerable soft power can in fact be cited. American military historian Theodore A. Dodge, for example, identified the ability to winning the hearts of their soldiers through "personal magnetism" as one of the shared qualities of those he called the *Great Captains*, including Alexander, Hannibal, and Caesar.[241] A particularly famous and frequently mentioned example of an individual who has exerted personal soft power and through it has changed the very course of history is the case of Prussian King Frederick the Great (1712–1786).[242] It shall therefore be elaborated upon in the following in some detail.

---

[238]Weber, *Economy and Society*, p. 1113.

[239]See Matthew 5: 21–48 in particular.

[240]House, Spangler, and Woycke, "Personality and Charisma in the U.S. Presidency," p. 364. Mindful of these words, Tom Sawyer, as referred to in the introduction of the work in hand, may very well be considered a charismatic leader.

[241]Theodore A. Dodge, *The Great Captains: The Art of War in the Campaigns of Alexander, Hannibal, Caesar, Gustavus Adolphus, Frederick the Great, and Napoleon* (New York, N.Y.: Barnes & Noble, 1995), p. 100.

[242]Nye, *The Future of Power*, pp. 81–82; Joseph S. Nye, Jr., "Notes for a Soft-Power Research Agenda," in *Power in World Politics*, eds. Felix Berenskoetter and M. J. Williams (New York, N. Y.: Routledge, 2008), p. 162.

Young Crown Prince Frederick succeeded his father, Frederick William I, known as the Soldier King, to the throne as Frederick II in 1740.[243] Although inspired by the ideas of Enlightenment[244] and author of *Der Antimachiavell*,[245] published in September 1740, the king did not waste time and in November 1740 declared war on Austria over questions of succession and the status of Silesia. While the Treaty of Berlin ended the conflict in 1742, which was to become known as the First Silesian War, hostilities started anew in 1744. This, the Second Silesian War ended 1 year later with the Treaty of Dresden, stipulating Prussian control over Silesia. However, the matter still was not lastingly resolved and in 1756, the Third Silesian War (also known, among other designations, as the Seven Years' War and—on the North American continent—as the French and Indian War) broke out. While Frederick initially won a number of victories (e.g., at Roßbach and Leuthen[246]), in the course of further events, Prussia stood on the very brink of destruction. After defeats in the Battles of Hochkirch (against Austria) and Kunersdorf (against Russia), coalition troops were about to march on Berlin and Frederick even entertained suicidal thoughts.[247] Discord and indecision among the Austrian and Russian troops, however, eliminated this immediate threat on the Prussian capital and left achieved victories unexploited. This unexpected turn of events caused Frederick II to proclaim the "Miracle of the House of Brandenburg" ("*le miracle de la maison de Brandenbourgh*") in a letter to his brother, Prince Henry—a phrase that was to become characteristic for the entire Seven Years' War.[248] However, trouble was still brewing and over the course of the next years, the Prussian King—outnumbered by a large coalition against him—fought a lost cause.[249]

The decisive turn, in the eyes of many historians, however, did not take place on the battlefields of Silesia but in the chambers of St. Petersburg: the death of Czarina

---

[243]Not until 1772 was Frederick II formally known as King *of* Prussia. From 1701 until said year, the Electors of Brandenburg were styled King *in* Prussia.

[244]For example, with Voltaire one of the most celebrated representatives of Enlightenment was resident guest at Fredrick's Potsdam court at Sanssouci from 1750 to 1753.

[245]Friedrich der Große, "Der Antimachiavell," in *Ausgewählte Schriften*, ed. Ulrike-Christine Sander (Frankfurt am Main: Fischer, 2011), pp. 9–46.

[246]In the Battle of Leuthen (December 5, 1757), Frederick the Great beat numerically superior Austrian troops under Prince Charles Alexander of Lorraine emulating the oblique order famously applied by Epaminondas in the Battle of Leuctra, 371 BC; Dodge, *The Great Captains*, p. 156.

[247]Michael Kotulla, *Deutsche Verfassungsgeschichte: Vom Alten Reich bis Weimar, 1495-1934* (Berlin: Springer, 2008), p. 197; Johannes Kunisch, *Friedrich der Große: Der König und seine Zeit* (München: Deutscher Taschenbuch Verlag, 2009), p. 405.

[248]Kunisch, *Friedrich der Große*, p. 407. Far beyond the eighteenth century, the myth of the "Miracle of the House Brandenburg" surfaced again during the final days of World War II as Adolf Hitler hoped for a break between the allies in the face of Germany's utter defeat, especially after the death of Roosevelt on April 12, 1945; S. M. Plokhy, *Yalta: The Price of Peace* (New York, N.Y.: Viking, 2010), p. 129; Christian Graf von Krockow, *Friedrich der Große: Ein Lebensbild* (Köln: Bastei Lübbe, 2012), pp. 187–188; Kissinger, *World Order*, p. 37.

[249]Kotulla, *Deutsche Verfassungsgeschichte*, p. 198; Johannes Dassow, *Friedrich II. von Preussen und Peter III. von Russland* (Diss. Friedrich-Wilhelms-Universität zu Berlin, 1908), pp. 21–22.

Elizabeth on January 1762 and the succession of her nephew Peter III to the Russian throne. Thereupon a second miracle—even more momentous than the first—came to pass: Peter III withdrew his armies, signed a separate peace with Prussia in May, and 6 weeks later concluded a (admittedly short-lived) treaty of alliance with the former enemy.[250]

In fact, the death of the Romanov Empress, who had harbored a cordial dislike for the Prussian King,[251] has for long been considered—starting with contemporaries including Frederick himself—as a crucial turning point in history.[252] But what had caused this sudden change in fortune? The newly crowned Peter III, born the son of Charles Frederick, Duke of Holstein-Gottorp and his wife Anna, daughter of Peter the Great, had for long been a staunch admirer of the Prussian King.[253] Peter thus considered Frederick to be "one of the greatest heroes the world has ever seen"[254] and had once called him his "Herrn und Meister" ("lord and master").[255] While the new Czar displayed a great affinity for everything Frederick purportedly embodied and stood for, it was the military prowess of the Prussian King that perhaps attracted him the most.[256] The deep interest in and enthusiasm for the king's military exploits are displayed in Peter's sound knowledge of the Prussian military establishment and its recent campaigns and—after his accession to the throne—resulted in reforms of the Russian army based on the model of Frederick's troops—including the style of uniforms.[257] Thus, the newly enthroned czar was intensely drawn to the Prussian king and openly displayed a deep sense of affinity for him. Interestingly, Christian Graf von Krockow not only elaborated upon the much-noticed attraction Peter III felt toward Frederick the Great but also noted that eminent British statesman William

---

[250]Kotulla, *Deutsche Verfassungsgeschichte*, p. 198.

[251]It may be argued that the feeling was reciprocal: When Frederick II heard of the death of his antagonist he rejoiced, "The Messalina of the North is dead. *Morta la Bestia;*" quoted in David Fraser, *Frederick the Great: King of Prussia* (London: The Penguin Press, 2000), p. 457. For other—even less chivalrous—designations see Jürgen Luth, *Der Große: Friedrich II. von Preußen* (München: Siedler, 2011), p. 244 and von Krockow, *Friedrich der Große*, p. 81.

[252]Dassow, *Friedrich II. von Preussen und Peter III. von Russland*, p. 22 & p. 31.

[253]See, for example, Nye, *The Future of Power*, p. 82; Daniel L. Byman and Kenneth M. Pollack, "Let us Now Praise Great Men: Bringing the Statesman Back In," *International Security*, Vol. 25, No. 4 (Spring 2001), p. 107; Kotulla, *Deutsche Verfassungsgeschichte*, p. 198; Fraser, *Frederick the Great*, pp. 457–458; Dassow, *Friedrich II. von Preussen und Peter III. von Russland*, p. 15; and Kissinger, *World Order*, p. 37 & p. 49. While explicitly recognizing the czar's admiration for Frederick, Dassow also hints at the strategic benefits Peter hoped to gain from a close association with the Prussian king; Dassow, *Friedrich II. von Preussen und Peter III. von Russland*, p. 15.

[254]Quoted in Fraser, *Frederick the Great*, p. 457.

[255]Quoted in Dassow, *Friedrich II. von Preussen und Peter III. von Russland*, p. 24.

[256]Dassow, *Friedrich II. von Preussen und Peter III. von Russland*, p. 17. This observation once again illustrates the high interconnectedness of hard and soft power as well as the soft power potential which can at times be drawn from hard power resources; see above, Sect. 2.5.2.1.

[257]Dassow, *Friedrich II. von Preussen und Peter III. von Russland*, pp. 25–27; von Krockow, *Friedrich der Große*, p. 98.

Pitt likewise doted on the Prussian King "wie ein verliebter Jüngling" ("like a lovestruck youth"), a fact which not least resulted in increased British support for its continental ally.[258] In the final analysis, therefore, some very tangible outcomes resulting from the soft power resource of individuals can indeed be identified in the case of Frederick the Great.[259]

A second historical example to be elaborated upon refers to the power of the papacy. On May 2, 1935, the governments of the French Republic and the Soviet Union signed the Franco-Soviet Treaty of Mutual Assistance in Paris which went into effect on March 27, 1936.[260] In accord with Article 2 of the treaty, the two powers reciprocally promised to "immediately give each other aid and assistance" in case any one of the two signatory powers would be object to "unprovoked attack on the part of a European State." Given its recent rearmament, the treaty, of course, was predominantly directed against Nazi Germany, which increasingly threatened world peace.[261] In the course of consolations and negotiations, French Foreign Minister Pierre Laval had visited Moscow and met with General Secretary of the Communist Party of the Soviet Union Joseph Stalin to discuss further details. The wording of the meeting between the two went down in history through Winston Churchill, who not only led Britain as Prime Minister during World War II, but also became one of its most popular and widely read chroniclers, its antecedents, course, and ramifications.[262] In the first volume of his seminal work on World War II, *The Gathering Storm*, Churchill thus set down that during French-Soviet negotiations Stalin and Soviet Foreign Minister Vyacheslav Molotov were eager to receive information on the strength and readiness of the French Army, including the number of French divisions on the Western Front or the seniority of the military personnel in said divisions. When the topic had been covered satisfactorily, the Roman Catholic Pierre Laval asked the leader of the atheistic Soviet Union, "Can't you do something to encourage religion and the Catholics in Russia? It would help me so much with the Pope." The reason behind this question was Laval's eagerness to gain endorsement for his government's policy of rapprochement toward the Soviet Union from the

---

[258]von Krockow, *Friedrich der Große*, pp. 88–89.

[259]Some observers argue that this very preference for Prussia led to discontentedness and grievances at the court in St. Petersburg and contributed to Peter's swift fall, culminating in his assassination in July 1762; Dassow, *Friedrich II. von Preussen und Peter III. von Russland*, p. 27 & p. 66.

[260]"France-U.S.S.R. Treaty of Mutual Assistance," *The American Journal of International Law*, Vol. 30, No. 4, Supplement: Official Documents (October 1936), pp. 177–180. For further information see William Evans Scott, *Alliance against Hitler: The Origins of the Franco-Soviet Pact* (Durham, N.C.: Duke University Press, 1962).

[261]Jacques Néré, *Foreign Policies of the Great Powers: Volume VII, The Foreign Policy of France from 1914 to 1945* (London: Routledge, 2004), p. 155.

[262]In fact, Churchill's 1953 Nobel Prize for Literature was bestowed, in the words of the Nobel Committee, not only for his "brilliant oratory" but also "for his mastery of historical and biographical descriptions;" Nobel Prize, "The Nobel Prize in Literature 1953: Winston Churchill, Facts," online at: http://www.nobelprize.org/nobel_prizes/literature/laureates/1953/churchill-facts.html (accessed April 28, 2015).

Holy See and Pope Pius XI. Stalin, however, was undiscerning of the pope's significance (at least in this context) and famously retorted, "Oho! The Pope! How many divisions has *he* got?" While Winston Churchill noted that Laval's answer has not been passed on to him, he argued that the Roman Catholic Laval "might certainly have mentioned a number of legions not always visible on parade."[263] In any case, the invisible legions of the pope may not have mattered much to Joseph Stalin at the time; for his successors in the 1980s they certainly took on greater significance.

Thus, more than 40 years after Stalin's famous question, recently elected Pope John Paul II paid a visit to his native Poland—then under Soviet influence—to become the first Pontifex Maximus to visit a Communist-ruled country. The pope, accorded in Poland with a "rapturous reception"[264] delivered a sermon and celebrated Holy Mass on Warsaw's Victory Square on June 2, 1979, attended by hundreds of thousands of Poles. He also spoke before Polish civil authorities about "peace, coexistence, and of the drawing together of the nations in the modern world" which, as he went on, "can be achieved only on the principle of respect for the objective rights of the nation, such as: the right to existence, to freedom, to be a social and political subject, and also to the formation of its own culture and civilization."[265] Upon leaving Poland from Krakow-Balice airport (later named in honor of the pope), John Paul II remarked on June 10, 1979,

> Our times have great need of an act of witness openly expressing the desire to bring nations and regimes closer together, as an indispensable *condition for peace in the world.* Our times demand that we should not lock ourselves into the rigid boundaries of systems, but seek all that is necessary *for the good of man*, who must find everywhere the awareness and certainty of his authentic citizenship. I would have liked to say the awareness and certainty of his *preeminence* in whatever system of relations and powers.[266]

With his emphatic rhetoric and spiritual leadership displayed in his 1979 travel to Poland as well as in the years to follow, Pope John Paul II, in the eyes of historians, played no small part in the fall of Communism and the end of the Cold War, although this notion did not become prevailing opinion until recently and particularly after the pontiff's death in 2005.[267] Lech Walesa, for example, founded the trade union

---

[263]The whole episode, including the quotations, can be found in Winston S. Churchill, *The Second World War: Volume I, The Gathering Storm* (London: Cassell, 1949), p. 121.

[264]John Lewis Gaddis, *George F. Kennan: An American Life* (New York, N.Y.: The Penguin Press, 2011), p. 644.

[265]Pope John Paul II, "Meeting with the Civil Authorities: Address of His Holiness John Paul II," Warsaw, 2 June 1979, *The Holy See, Apostolic Journey to Poland*, online at: http://www.vatican.va/ holy_father/john_paul_ii/speeches/1979/june/documents/hf_jp-ii_spe_19790602_polonia-varsavia-autorita-civili_en.html (accessed June 2, 2014).

[266]Pope John Paul II, "Farewell Ceremony at Balice Airport: Address of His Holiness John Paul II," Balice Airport, 10 June 1979, *The Holy See, Apostolic Journey to Poland*, online at: http://www. vatican.va/holy_father/john_paul_ii/speeches/1979/june/documents/hf_jp-ii_spe_19790610_polo nia-balice-congedo_en.html (accessed June 2, 2014); emphasis in the original.

[267]George Weigel, *The End and the Beginning: Pope John Paul II – The Victory of Freedom, the Last Years, the Legacy* (New York, N.Y.: Image, 2011), pp. 183–184. See also Niall Ferguson,

Solidarity in a Gdansk shipyard "with the pope's picture nearby"[268] little more than a year after the pontiff had visited Poland. John Lewis Gaddis, one of the leading authorities on the Cold War, in this context pointed out, "When John Paul II kissed the ground at the Warsaw airport on June 2, 1979, he began the process by which communism in Poland—and ultimately everywhere else in Europe—would come to an end."[269] Therefore, the pope's visit to Poland and his general influence on the end of the Cold War have demonstrated, again in the words of Gaddis,

> that the *material* forms of power upon which the United States, the Soviet Union, and their allies had lavished so much attention for so long—the nuclear weapons and missiles, the conventional military forces, the intelligence establishments, the military-industrial complexes, the propaganda machines—began to lose their potency. Real power rested, during the final decade of the Cold War, with leaders like John Paul II, whose mastery of *intangibles*—of such qualities as courage, eloquence, imagination, determination, and faith—allowed them to expose disparities between what people believed and the systems under which the Cold War had obliged them to live. The gaps were most glaring in the Marxist-Leninist world: so much so that when fully revealed there was no way to close them other than to dismantle communism itself, and thereby end the Cold War.[270]

At least since the Middle Ages, papal *material* powers had stretched far beyond the confines of the Italian peninsula and during the Renaissance the popes had become, as Bertrand Russell once aptly put it, "merely one of the Italian princes, engaged in the incredibly complicated and unscrupulous game of Italian power politics."[271] Ever since the popes forsook their secular dominions and Vatican City became an independent state, however, no successor to the Chair of Peter has been wielding any noteworthy *material* power, at least in Gaddis' sense of the word.[272] Nevertheless, the popes' *intangibles*, it may be argued, have won many a battle in the past: Not through military or economic coercion, but through spiritual leadership and attraction.[273] Bearing in mind this form of power vested in the papacy, no other than Napoleon Bonaparte replied, when asked by his envoy in Rome, François Cacault, about his intentions toward Pope Pius VII, who had been elected in March 1800, that he was going to treat him as if he commanded 200,000 men.[274]

"Think Again: Power," *Foreign Policy*, No. 134 (January/February 2003), p. 22 and Archie Brown, *The Rise and Fall of Communism* (New York, N.Y.: Ecco, 2009), p. 475.

[268] John Lewis Gaddis, *The Cold War* (London: Penguin Books, 2005), p. 197.

[269] Gaddis, *The Cold War*, p. 193.

[270] Gaddis, *The Cold War*, pp. 195–196; Gaddis' emphasis.

[271] Bertrand Russell, *History of Western Philosophy* (London: Routledge, 2004), p. 6.

[272] Vincent Cronin even argues that the popes' spiritual authority had never been greater than *after* they had been deprived of much of their worldly holdings and material powers by the Italian state in 1870; Cronin, *Napoleon*, p. 289.

[273] A preeminent example for the (spiritual and rhetorical) power of the pope is, of course, the call to the first crusade by Pope Urban II at the Council of Clermont in November 1095; Dana Carleton Munro, "The Speech of Pope Urban II. at Clermont, 1095," *The American Historical Review*, Vol. 11, No. 2 (January 1906), pp. 231–242.

[274] Cronin, *Napoleon*, p. 278.

Today, more than 200 years after Napoleon's dictum and some 80 years after Stalin posed his famous question regarding the papal divisions, it is generally agreed that John Paul II, in lieu of commanding military or economic powers, resorted to the moral and spiritual powers vested in the office of the pontiff. It was, however, not only the office itself but particularly the then-incumbent John Paul II as an individual who played a decisive role in bringing the Cold War to an end, an achievement which arguably contributed to the pope's uncommonly swift canonization in April 2014. Mikhail Gorbachev, Stalin's later successor as General Secretary of the Communist Party of the Soviet Union from 1985 to 1991, is thus known to have remarked in 1992 that "everything that happened in Eastern Europe in these last few years would have been impossible without this pope."[275] Pope John Paul II and his influence on the end of the Cold War, therefore, offers a further excellent example of how individuals can develop and exert soft power—both in its active and passive variety—in their own right.

In this sense, the Pontifex Maximus is rightly regarded as an actor on the international stage whose power cannot be measured by counting the number of divisions he commands or the economic output of the state he heads. In fact, international relations scholars such as classical realist Arnold Wolfers recognized the influence of the Vatican in world politics more than half a century ago.[276] Explicitly referencing Pope John Paul II, who had been "an actor before he became a priest," John Lewis Gaddis even noted, "Few leaders of this era could match him in his ability to use words, gestures, exhortations, rebukes—even jokes—to move the hearts and minds of the millions who saw and heard him."[277] That policy-makers today share this observation is evidenced, for example, by United States Senate Concurrent Resolution 87, which in 2000 attributed to the Holy See, "significant contributions to international peace and human rights" and thus pronounced against its expulsion as Permanent Observer to the United Nations.[278] Today, after the election of Pope Francis in 2013, the position of the pope in international relations is perhaps more exalted than it has been for long. Accordingly, Elizabeth Dias has recently spoken of "The New Roman Empire" ruled by Francis, who has been pursuing a global agenda ranging from climate change to Cuban-U.S. rapprochement.[279] At the same time, *Forbes* has ranked the Argentinian pope number 4 in its 2015 ranking of "The World's Most Powerful People," behind Vladimir Putin,

---

[275] Quoted in Scott Appleby, "Pope John Paul II," *Foreign Policy*, No. 119 (Summer 2000), p. 12.

[276] Arnold Wolfers, *Discord and Collaboration: Essays on International Politics* (Baltimore, Md.: John Hopkins University Press, 1962), p. 23.

[277] Gaddis, *The Cold War*, p. 195.

[278] Senate Concurrent Resolution 87, "Commending the Holy See for Making Significant Contributions to International Peace and Human Rights, and Objecting to Efforts to Expel the Holy See from the United Nations by Removing the Holy See's Permanent Observer Status in the United Nations, and for Other Purposes," 106th Congress, 2nd Session, March 1, 2000, *Congressional Record* 146, Pt. 2 (2000), pp. 1905–1907.

[279] Elizabeth Dias, "The New Roman Empire," *TIME Magazine*, September 28, 2015, pp. 26–31.

Barack Obama, and Angela Merkel, but well ahead of, for example, Chinese President Xi Jinping.[280]

Finally, the presidency of the United States offers yet another expressive example regarding the soft power of individuals. Mitt Romney's assessment already cited above accordingly rings true, "The President of the United States has long been the leader of the free world. The president and yes the nominees of the country's great parties help define America to billions of people. All of them bear the responsibility of being an example for our children and grandchildren."[281] Briefly considering the last two holders of the office, George W. Bush (2001–2009) and Barack Obama (2009–2017), as well as the current incumbent in the White House, Donald J. Trump, actually provides striking evidence in this regard. Polls thus impressively attest to the assessment that it were in particular the personalities (or more precisely, the perception of these personalities), which crucially influenced the image of the United States around the world during their respective terms of office. In fact, drawing on data provided by the Pew Research Center's Global Indicator Database and choosing the three key European U.S. allies United Kingdom, France, and Germany as examples, an expressive picture can be drawn, as depicted in Fig. 3.2.

As figures show, at least with respect to the three countries exemplarily considered here, a correlation between the opinion of the United States as a country (straight lines) and the confidence in the respective president (dotted lines) can clearly be established. A further in-depth examination is, of course, necessary in order to detect coherences. With respect to all three U.S. Presidents, however, the bare figures can in fact be substantiated by a plethora of conforming assessments by different observers. For example, after Barack Obama's election to the White House, commentators soon spoke of an "Obama Effect," describing "the importance of the U.S. President's popularity among foreign publics in shaping the United States' image and its soft power."[282] In her memoirs, none other than Hillary Clinton, Secretary of State during Obama's first term, subscribed to such an effect, "Probably our greatest asset in turning the tide of European public opinion was 'the Obama Effect.' Across the continent many Europeans were incredibly excited about our new President."[283] Obama, as Joseph Nye has noted, in fact "became almost a cult figure in his popularity in much of Europe."[284] In this context, very much in line with the conceptual elaboration presented above, one German observer especially emphasized the major importance Obama's charisma had in this respect.[285] After the most

---

[280]Forbes, "The World's Most Powerful People: 2015 Ranking," online at: http://www.forbes.com/powerful-people/list/#tab:overall (accessed November 30, 2015).

[281]Romney, "Speech about Donald Trump."

[282]Nicolas Isak Dragojlovic, "Priming and the Obama Effect on Public Evaluations of the United States," *Political Psychology*, Vol. 32, No. 6, The Obama Presidency Special Issue (December 2011), p. 990.

[283]Hillary Rodham Clinton, *Hard Choices* (New York, N.Y.: Simon & Schuster, 2014), p. 206.

[284]Nye, *The Future of Power*, p. 163.

[285]Peter Rudolf, *Das 'neue' Amerika: Außenpolitik unter Barack Obama* (Berlin: Suhrkamp, 2010), p. 74 & p. 159.

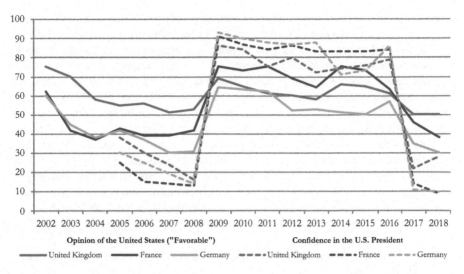

Fig. 3.2 The personality factor for the U.S. image: evidence from the United Kingdom, France, and Germany [Own illustration based on data retrieved from Pew Research Center, "Global Attitudes & Trends: Global Indicators Database," online at: http://www.pewglobal.org/database/ (accessed May 29, 2019)]

recent change in government in Washington, a comparable—yet inverted—the effect has become apparent once more. As Fig. 3.2 shows, a deep plunge can be detected in the image of the United States and more dramatically so with respect to the confidence in the U.S. President among the three countries considered at this point. In line with these figures, one columnist aptly contended in *The New York Times* on October 15, 2017, "Trump is reviled around the globe and America's reputation is going down with its captain."[286] Of course, these findings can only be regarded as cursory evidence. Nevertheless, they offer further—and highly expressive—insight into the soft power of individuals and not least can serve as starting points for further research.

Taken together, the historical episodes referred to above impressively illustrate the observation that personalities can indeed be regarded as constituting an independent and in fact highly consequential soft power resource. In this regard, derived from existing literature as well as the empirical examples discussed, a set of indicators can be deduced allowing for an analysis of what might be called individual soft power brokers: To start with, the (1) character of major (political) representatives—and in particular the political leader, that is, the respective chancellor, premier, and president—shall be considered. In this context, it shall be explored whether leading officials are attributed charisma by respective audiences. Max

[286]Charles M. Blow, "Trump, Chieftain of Spite," *The New York Times*, October 15, 2017, online at: https://www.nytimes.com/2017/10/15/opinion/columnists/trump-spite-obama-legacy.html (accessed October 16, 2017).

Weber's notion of charisma—augmented by subsequent writers—can in this regard serve as the main conceptual vehicle, while, in line with the observations laid out above, the highly contextual as well as relational character of charisma has to be taken into account. Additionally, (2) respective cabinet members as well as (groups of) advisors a leading decision-maker appoints and consults shall be examined. Thus, not only the personality and perception of the leader per se but also his brain trust may prove informative. It is hence a long-standing proverb that a man (or a woman) is known and judged by the company he (or she) keeps. Finally, bearing in mind the relational character of soft power in general, (3) personal relationships between the key representatives of Actors A and B as well as between respective representatives and the general public of Actor B shall be considered. Highlighting the importance of personal and informal relations between top-level representatives in international relations, Felix Philipp Lutz has aptly noted,

> More lies behind international relations than the machinery of ministries and diplomacy, formal structures, and institutions. Foreign policy is also developed and influenced by people who can draw upon personal and informal relationships that enable them to pursue their aims outside their official contracts.[287]

Joseph Nye has in this regard argued that "leaders may be attracted and persuaded by the benignity, competence, or charisma of other leaders" and referring to the soft power wielded by Russian Czar Peter the Great, Prussia's Frederick the Great, and—more recently—U.S. President Barack Obama vis-à-vis other leaders, he himself offers multifarious empirical evidence of this assumption.[288] Interestingly, leading practitioners of international affairs frequently concur to such assessments. Henry Kissinger thus famously admitted during a 1974 background talk with reporters, "As a professor, I tended to think of history as run by impersonal forces. But when you see it in practice, you see the difference personalities make."[289] More recently, Hillary Clinton, Kissinger's later successor as the head of the U.S. State Department, assured her readers, "Relations between nations are based on shared values—but also on personalities. The personal element matters more in international affairs than many would expect, for good or ill."[290] In view of such statements, by academics as well as practitioners in international affairs, the nature of the relationships between respective leaders—with regard to their mutual trust or suspicion, understanding or indifference, appreciation or disregard toward one another—has to be given particular attention.

---

[287]Felix Philipp Lutz, "Transatlantic Networks: Elites in German-American Relations," in *The United States and Germany in the Era of the Cold War, 1945-1990: A Handbook, Volume II: 1968-1990*, ed. Detlef Junker, associated editors Philipp Gassert, Wilfried Mausbach, and David B. Morris (Cambridge: Cambridge University Press, 2004), p. 445.

[288]Nye, *The Future of Power*, p. 94.

[289]Quoted in Walter Isaacson, *Kissinger: A Biography* (New York, N.Y.: Simon & Schuster, 1992), p. 13.

[290]Clinton, *Hard Choices*, p. 207.

3.2 Subunit II: Instruments

Having discussed the resources of soft power (Subunit I), we shall now examine conceivable soft power instruments, which—as depicted in Fig. 3.1—constitute the second soft power subunit. Before discussing the workings of different soft power instruments at greater length, it is imperative to emphasize once more that soft power—at least in part—lies beyond governmental control.[291] Till Geiger thus aptly stated that "governments will never be able to control all aspects of soft power or produce it at will."[292] Joseph Nye likewise noted that "American soft power is generated only in part by what the government does through its policies and public diplomacy."[293]

Particularly with respect to the passive variety of soft power, this assessment certainly rings true: Being decisively shaped by civil society actors within in a state (e.g., corporations, universities, non-governmental organizations), governmental programs or instruments alone are thus insufficient for the successful wielding of soft power—particularly with regard to the soft power resource of values and culture.[294] With reference to the single resource of soft power perhaps most frequently discussed, Michael Mandelbaum hence aptly argued, "Culture is powerful but it is not a form of power in the sense that it can be wielded to achieve a specific goal. [...] Culture operates like the forces of nature: it is mighty but not controllable."[295] Despite such caveats, however, governmental involvement in the cultural output of a given country can frequently be identified: U.S. State Department efforts to spread jazz music during the Cold War, for instance, have already been introduced above.[296] The efforts by the U.S. Department of Defense to have a say in the production of Hollywood movies, leading to the establishment of a Special Assistant for Entertainment Media in the Pentagon as well as the creation of Los Angeles offices for the four service branches (Army, Navy, Air Force, and Marine Corps), can be regarded as another expressive example.[297] Especially with respect to the soft power resource of policies, governmental influence is, of course, obvious.

---

[291]Nye, *Soft Power*, p. 32; Joseph S. Nye, Jr., "The Future of Soft Power in US Foreign Policy," in *Soft Power and US Foreign Policy: Theoretical, Historical and Contemporary Perspectives*, eds. Inderjeet Parmar and Michael Cox (Abingdon: Routledge, 2010), p. 9.

[292]Till Geiger, "*The Power Game*, Soft Power and the International Historian," in *Soft Power and US Foreign Policy: Theoretical, Historical and Contemporary Perspectives*, eds. Inderjeet Parmar and Michael Cox (Abingdon: Routledge, 2010), p. 102.

[293]Joseph S. Nye, Jr., "Responding to My Critics and Concluding Thoughts," in *Soft Power and US Foreign Policy: Theoretical, Historical and Contemporary Perspectives*, eds. Inderjeet Parmar and Michael Cox (Abingdon: Routledge, 2010), p. 223.

[294]Nye, *Soft Power*, p. 17 & p. 32.

[295]Mandelbaum, *Mission Failure*, p. 375.

[296]See above, Sect. 3.1.1.

[297]Tanner Mirrlees, *Hearts and Mines: The US Empire's Culture Industry* (Vancouver: University of British Columbia Press, 2016), pp. 181–188.

Even more so, the active variety of soft power, that is, the deliberate wielding of soft power for the sake of getting desired outcomes, is a distinctly governmental process, indeed. Measures including state-sponsored scholarships (such as the Fulbright Program) or international broadcasting (such as Voice of America), for example, have aptly been identified as powerful tools applied by governments to wield national soft power.[298] In fact, contrary to hard power resources, whose mere existence may lead to desired outcomes (think of the strategy of deterrence during the Cold War) even though they are not actually applied, soft power resources to a far greater degree have to be shared and actively wielded.[299] Policies of deterrence—in 1963 President John F. Kennedy famously spoke of "weapons acquired for the purpose of making sure we never need to use them"[300]—are, therefore, mostly inapplicable to the domain of soft power. Janice Bially Mattern accordingly recognized the pivotal role communication plays in the wielding of soft power—particularly in the information age of the twenty-first century—and thus noted that only if soft power resources are made known to (foreign) audiences, power can be gained from them.[301] Interestingly, it was Donald Trump who on a related note pointed out in *The Art of the Deal*,

> You can have the most wonderful product in the world, but if people don't know about it, it's not going to be worth much. There are singers in the world with voices as good as Frank Sinatra's, but they're singing in their garages because no one has ever heard of them. You need to generate interest, and you need to create excitement.[302]

In this sense (governmental) soft power instruments are in fact of vital importance in the wielding of soft power. While recognizing their centrality, Joseph Nye himself has presented but imprecise enumerations of conceivable instruments in this regard.[303] Moreover, he does not always distinguish clearly between soft power instruments and their underlying resources.[304] The subsequent elaboration on two major sets of soft power instruments—public diplomacy and what may be called personal diplomacy—both encompassing a number of different dimensions in their

---

[298] Joseph S. Nye, Jr., *The Paradox of American Power: Why the World's Only Superpower Can't Go It Alone* (Oxford: Oxford University Press, 2002), p. 73.

[299] Roselle, Miskimmon, and O'Loughlin, "Strategic Narrative," p. 73.

[300] John F. Kennedy, "Commencement Address at American University in Washington," Washington, D.C., June 10, 1963, in *Public Papers of the Presidents of the United States: John F. Kennedy, 1963, Containing the Public Messages, Speeches, and Statements of the President, January 1 to November 22, 1963* (Washington, D.C.: United States Government Printing Office, 1964), p. 460.

[301] Mattern, "Why 'Soft Power' Isn't So Soft," pp. 588–589.

[302] Donald J. Trump with Tony Schwartz, *Trump: The Art of the Deal* (London: Arrow Books, 2016), p. 56.

[303] Nye, "The Future of Soft Power in US Foreign Policy," p. 5.

[304] Nye, "Notes for a Soft-Power Research Agenda," p. 171.

own right and taken together constituting the second soft power subunit, shall provide a remedy to these shortcomings.

3.2.1   Public Diplomacy

The notion of public diplomacy frequently appears within the discourse on soft power and the two concepts seem to be as much as interlocked.[305] Within the context of the soft power taxonomy introduced, public diplomacy—as depicted in Fig. 3.1— is understood as a vital instrument to wield soft power and it shall therefore be presented in greater detail.

From the outset, while interest in public diplomacy has increased greatly over the past years, the concept still remains heavily contested and controversial.[306] Geoffrey Cowan and Nicholas J. Cull accordingly noted that "few fields are as relevant, compelling, or ready for serious study. Few reveal so much neglect and past folly, but few contain so much hope for the future."[307] In fact, regarding a definition of public diplomacy, a "litany of attempts"[308] has been made over time. Among the most influential of these attempts still is the one presented by Edmund A. Gullion, who in the mid-1960s defined public diplomacy as "the means by which governments, private groups and individuals influence the attitudes and opinions of other peoples and governments in such a way as to exercise influence on their foreign policy decisions."[309]

---

[305] See, for example, Auer, Srugies, and Löffelholz, "Schlüsselbegriffe der internationalen Diskussion," p. 39 and Brian Hocking, "Rethinking the 'New' Public Diplomacy," in *The New Public Diplomacy: Soft Power in International Relations*, ed. Jan Melissen (Basingstoke: Palgrave Macmillan, 2005), pp. 28–29.

[306] Bruce Gregory, "Public Diplomacy: The Sunrise of an Academic Field," *The Annals of the American Academy of Political and Social Sciences*, Vol. 616, Public Diplomacy in a Changing World (March 2008), p. 274; van Ham, "Power, Public Diplomacy, and the *Pax Americana*," p. 57; Shaun Riordan, "Dialogue-based Public Diplomacy: A New Foreign Policy Paradigm?," in *The New Public Diplomacy: Soft Power in International Relations*, ed. Jan Melissen (Basingstoke: Palgrave Macmillan, 2005), p. 180.

[307] Geoffrey Cowan and Nicholas J. Cull, "Public Diplomacy in a Changing World," *The Annals of the American Academy of Political and Social Sciences*, Vol. 616, Public Diplomacy in a Changing World (March 2008), p. 8.

[308] John Robert Kelley, "Between 'Take-offs' and 'Crash Landings': Situational Aspects of Public Diplomacy," in *Routledge Handbook of Public Diplomacy*, eds. Nancy Snow and Philip M. Taylor (New York, N.Y.: Routledge, 2009), p. 73.

[309] Quoted in Claudia Auer, *Theorie der Public Diplomacy: Sozialtheoretische Grundlegung einer Form strategischer Kommunikation* (Wiesbaden: Springer VS, 2017), p. 26.

Arguably a reason for the persistent difficulties in providing a precise definition, public diplomacy constitutes a highly interdisciplinary concept.[310] Accordingly, Eytan Gilboa offers an illustration depicting as many as 13 different disciplines that have contributed to public diplomacy.[311] Indeed, there are numerous "bordering" concepts that are frequently even used synonymously or are confused with the concept of public diplomacy, including propaganda, public relations, public affairs, or psychological warfare.[312] Among these concepts, propaganda deserves particular mention.[313] Bertrand Russell has aptly pointed out in his *History of Western Philosophy*, "To achieve a political end, power, of one kind or another, is necessary. [...] It is true that power, often, depends upon opinion, and opinion upon propaganda."[314] In fact, propaganda and public diplomacy have often been conflated. In an October, 2001 op-ed in the *Washington Post*, Richard Holbrooke for example—while arguing for a central organization of a commencing "battle of ideas" in the wake of the nascent "War on Terror"—thus famously argued, "Call it public diplomacy, or public affairs, or psychological warfare, or—if you really want to be blunt—propaganda."[315] Propaganda has in this sense been considered the "negative, pejorative corollary"[316] or even "virtually interchangeable"[317] with public diplomacy. Defined as "the planned dissemination of information, arguments, and appeals designed to influence the beliefs, thoughts, and actions of specific foreign target groups,"[318] propaganda shares certain aspects of public diplomacy, indeed. However, it is also fundamentally different, insofar as public diplomacy has been described as a "two-way-street" as opposed to the highly one-directional mechanisms of propaganda.[319] Accordingly, propaganda is lacking the reciprocal and

---

[310]György Szondi, "Central and Eastern European Public Diplomacy: A Transitional Perspective on National Reputation Management," in *Routledge Handbook of Public Diplomacy*, eds. Nancy Snow and Philip M. Taylor (New York, N.Y.: Routledge, 2009), p. 293.

[311]Eytan Gilboa, "Searching for a Theory of Public Diplomacy," *The ANNALS of the American Academy of Political and Social Sciences*, Vol. 616, Public Diplomacy in a Changing World, No. 1 (March 2008), p. 74.

[312]Gilboa, "Searching for a Theory of Public Diplomacy," p. 56.

[313]Jan Melissen, "The New Public Diplomacy: Between Theory and Practice," in *The New Public Diplomacy: Soft Power in International Relations*, ed. Jan Melissen (Basingstoke: Palgrave Macmillan, 2005), p. 16.

[314]Russell, *History of Western Philosophy*, p. 470.

[315]Richard Holbrooke, "Get the Message Out," *The Washington Post*, October 28, 2001, online at: http://www.washingtonpost.com/wp-dyn/content/article/2010/12/13/AR2010121305410.html (accessed April 26, 2017).

[316]Nancy Snow and Philip M. Taylor, "Preface and Introduction," in *Routledge Handbook of Public Diplomacy*, eds. Nancy Snow and Philip M. Taylor (New York, N.Y.: Routledge, 2009), p. ix.

[317]Melissen, "The New Public Diplomacy," p. 17.

[318]Klaus Knorr, *The Power of Nations: The Political Economy of International Relations* (New York, N.Y.: Basic Books, 1975), p. 6.

[319]Melissen, "The New Public Diplomacy," p. 18. On the characterization of public diplomacy as a "two-way street" see also Joseph S. Nye, Jr., "Public Diplomacy and Soft Power," *The Annals of the American Academy of Political and Social Sciences*, Vol. 616, Public Diplomacy in a Changing World (March 2008), p. 103.

relational aspect—so central to the concept of public diplomacy today.[320] Moreover, a second crucial distinction lies in the content that is transported: Whereas propaganda intends to paint a decidedly one-sided picture (obviously in favor of the sender), public diplomacy is (at least in theory) much more balanced. Joseph Nye, with respect to the United States, accordingly argued that "government broadcasting to other countries that is evenhanded, open and informative helps to enhance American credibility and soft power in a way that propaganda never can."[321] Public diplomacy, therefore, imparts information in a matter-of-fact, unflattering, and authentic way. The approach to public diplomacy championed by Edward R. Murrow, director of the United States Information Agency (USIA) under John F. Kennedy, serves as a prime example in this regard with the famous mission statement, "Tell America's story, warts and all, and the world will admire us for it."[322] The first words broadcast by Voice of America—originally uttered in German—on February 25, 1942, likewise give expression to this approach, "Daily, at this time, we shall speak to you about America and the war. The news may be good or bad. We shall tell you the truth."[323] President Dwight D. Eisenhower, a staunch proponent of the establishment of the USIA in the early stages of the Cold War, equally noted that the new agency's "sole and essential purpose was to let all the world know the truth and only the truth about our policies, plans, actions, and purposes."[324]

While the days of Eisenhower can certainly be regarded as a heyday, the practice of public diplomacy with its central aim to influence foreign publics has, of course, a millennia-old tradition.[325] The very term "public diplomacy" itself, as Nicholas J. Cull has shown, can likewise look back on a long history, dating back to its earliest attested appearance in *The Times* in 1856 and another occurrence in *The New York Times* 15 years later.[326] In its earliest applications, however, the term was rather understood as a counterpart to the long-prevailing practice of secret diplomacy, against which Woodrow Wilson later contrasted what he called "diplomacy

---

[320]Mark Leonard with Catherine Stead and Conrad Smewing, *Public Diplomacy* (London: The Foreign Policy Centre, 2002), pp. 46–50.

[321]Joseph S. Nye, Jr., "Propaganda Isn't the Way: Soft Power," *International Herald Tribune*, January 10, 2003.

[322]Joseph E. Persico, *Edward R. Murrow: An American Original* (New York, N.Y.: McGraw-Hill, 1988), p. 470.

[323]Quoted in Sanford J. Ungar, "Pitch Imperfect: The Trouble at the Voice of America," *Foreign Affairs*, Vol. 84, No. 3 (May/June 2005), p. 8.

[324]Dwight D. Eisenhower, *The White House Years: Waging Peace, 1956-1961* (Garden City, N.Y.: Doubleday, 1965), p. 136.

[325]Nicholas J. Cull, "Public Diplomacy: Taxonomies and Histories," *The Annals of the American Academy of Political and Social Sciences*, Vol. 616, Public Diplomacy in a Changing World (March 2008), p. 31; Cowan and Cull, "Public Diplomacy in a Changing World," p. 6; Zaharna, *The Cultural Awakening in Public Diplomacy*, p. 7.

[326]Nicholas J. Cull, "Public Diplomacy before Gullion: The Evolution of a Phrase," in *Routledge Handbook of Public Diplomacy*, eds. Nancy Snow and Philip M. Taylor (New York, N.Y.: Routledge, 2009), p. 19.

[that] shall proceed always frankly and in the *public* view"[327] in the first of his Fourteen Points.[328] It was, however, especially after World War II that public diplomacy in its more modern understanding rose to particular prominence and became more closely linked to the application of information techniques in the conduct of diplomacy.[329] With technological advancements and global interconnectedness gradually gathering pace, the importance of global public opinion has thus increasingly been recognized at that time. English diplomat Sir Pierson J. Dixon, for example, has accordingly argued with respect to the British position in the Middle East after World War II,

> Thinking over our difficulties in Egypt, it seems to me that the essential difficulty arises from the very obvious fact that we lack power. [...] Power, of course, is not to be measured in terms alone of money and troops: a third ingredient is prestige, or in other words what the rest of the world thinks of us.[330]

However, such notions hardly went unchallenged and many opposed the intensified importance ascribed to world opinion. Former U.S. Secretary of War and High Commissioner for Germany, John J. McCloy, for example, exclaimed during a meeting with President John F. Kennedy, "'World opinion'? I don't believe in world opinion. The only thing that matters is power."[331] More recent skeptics, like Christopher Layne, likewise pointed out that "[i]nternational politics is not a popularity contest."[332]

Despite such sometimes-heard caveats, a long historic tradition recognizing the importance of public opinion—both at home and abroad—as well as attempts to influence it can be established and traced back over centuries or even millennia: Seneca (54 BC–AD 39) wrote in his *Controversiae*, "crede mihi, sacra populi lingua est"[333] and in AD 798, Alcuin, counselor to Charlemagne, refers to the famous dictum "Vox populi, vox Dei."[334] In the sixteenth century, Niccolò Machiavelli treats public opinion not only in his famous *Prince*[335] but also in his *Discourses on the First Ten*

---

[327]Woodrow Wilson, "The Program of Peace: Address to Congress," Washington, D.C., January 8, 1918, in *War Addresses of Woodrow Wilson*, With an Introduction and Notes by Arthur Roy Leonhard (Boston, Mass.: Ginn and Company, 1918), p. 97; emphasis added.

[328]Cull, "Public Diplomacy before Gullion," p. 20.

[329]Cull, "Public Diplomacy before Gullion," pp. 20–21.

[330]Quoted in John Kent, "The Egyptian Base and the Defence of the Middle East, 1945-1954," *The Journal of Imperial and Commonwealth History*, Vol. 21, No. 3 (1993), p. 51.

[331]Quoted in Nye, *Soft Power*, p. 9. See also Nye, "Public Diplomacy and Soft Power," p. 96.

[332]Layne, "The Unbearable Lightness of Soft Power," p. 71.

[333]L. Annaeus Seneca, "Controversiarum: Liber I, 1," in *L. Annaei Seneca Patris: Scripta Quae Manserunt*, ed. Herman J. Müller (Hildesheim: Georg Olms Verlag, 1990), p. 21 (Sen. Con. I, 1, 10). Seneca's dictum translates, "Believe me, holy is the speech of the people."

[334]Jinty Nelson, "Lay Readers of the Bible in the Carolingian Ninth Century," in *Reading the Bible in the Middle Ages*, eds. Jinty Nelson and Damien Kempf (London: Bloomsbury, 2015), p. 47. Translated, the dictum reads, "the voice of the people, is the voice of God."

[335]Niccolò Machiavelli, *Der Fürst* (Frankfurt am Main: Insel Verlag, 2001), pp. 54–58.

Books of Titus Livius[336] as well as in his lesser known *Life of Castruccio Castracani*. In the latter, the titular hero, the Lucan condottiere Castruccio Castracani, rises—in the blink of an eye—from prisoner to prince by the favor of the people alone.[337] Further early references to public opinion can be found, for example, in the works of John Locke, David Hume, and Jean-Jacques Rousseau.[338] William Shakespeare's Henry IV, first king from the House of Lancaster who ascended the throne after his predecessor Richard II had been deposed by parliament, likewise knew that it was "Opinion, that did help me to the crown."[339] It were, however, the great revolutions of the late eighteenth century, which gave particular rise to a steadily increasing importance of public opinion.[340] During the American Revolution, *The Declaration of Independence*, for example, famously evoked "a decent respect to the opinions of mankind" which required the Founding Fathers to "declare the causes which impel them to the separation" from the British Crown. On the other side of the Atlantic, leading politicians of the age recognized the power of public opinion as well, including the two great figures of Continental diplomacy in the nineteenth century, Metternich and Talleyrand.[341] The latter, Talleyrand, thus famously instructed his fellow diplomats, "Faites aimer la France!"[342]

At the same time, besides the growing recognition of its importance, active efforts were undertaken to influence public opinion on one's purposes. In 1814, to offer an early example, Arthur Wellesley, first Duke of Wellington, embarked on the mission to convince the restored Bourbon King Louis XVIII to abolish French slave-trade upon becoming ambassador in Paris. Having to deal with a reluctant monarch, the British field marshal set out "to create a public opinion in France [. . .] by means of books and pamphlets."[343] With the help of Madame de Staël and others, he was at last successful in his endeavor and the king promised to end slave trade within

---

[336]Niccolò Machiavelli, "Discourses on the First Ten Books of Titus Livius," in *The Historical, Political, and Diplomatic Writings of Niccolo Machiavelli*, Translated from the Italian by Christian E. Detmold, Volume II (Boston, Mass.: James R. Osgood and Company, 1882), pp. 406–409.

[337]Niccolò Machiavelli, *Das Leben Castruccio Castracanis aus Lucca* (München: C. H. Beck, 1998), p. 17.

[338]Elisabeth Noelle-Neumann, "Public Opinion and the Classical Tradition: A Re-evaluation," *Public Opinion Quarterly*, Vol. 43, No. 2 (Summer 1979), p. 147.

[339]William Shakespeare, "The First Part of King Henry the Fourth," in *The Complete Works of William Shakespeare*, Edited with a Glossary by W. J. Craig (London: Oxford University Press, 1923), p. 489 (Act III, Scene II).

[340]Paul Sharp identified revolutionary moments or states as particularly predestined for public diplomacy techniques; Paul Sharp, "Revolutionary States, Outlaw Regimes and the Techniques of Public Diplomacy," in *The New Public Diplomacy: Soft Power in International Relations*, ed. Jan Melissen (Basingstoke: Palgrave Macmillan, 2005), pp. 106–123.

[341]Hocking, "Rethinking the 'New' Public Diplomacy," p. 29.

[342]Sebastian Körber, "Imagepflege als Daueraufgabe: Das vielschichtige Deutschlandbild," in *Kultur und Außenpolitik: Handbuch für Wissenschaft und Praxis*, ed. Kurt-Jürgen Maaß (Baden Baden: Nomos Verlagsgesellschaft, 2015), p. 160.

[343]Longford, *Wellington*, p. 371.

5 years.[344] Wellington's great antagonist, Napoleon Bonaparte, however, according to Michael Vlahos, "believed that battle was dominant, and that public diplomacy, like Herald in [Shakespeare's] *Henry V*, was a mere helpmate. Public diplomacy was not seen an equal key to a world-revising strategy—except for the domestic audience, and of course the families of soldiers."[345]

It was Scottish philosopher and political theorist James Mill who around the same time recognized that public opinion not only has a clout in democracies but also "has an influence, and a great influence, upon the most despotical and barbarous governments on the face of the earth."[346] In the years to come, the importance of public opinion seemed to solidify and only a few decades after Mill, Abraham Lincoln could remark in the first Lincoln-Douglas Debate in Ottawa, Illinois, on August 21, 1858, "In this and like communities, public sentiment is everything. With public sentiment, nothing can fail; without it, nothing can succeed."[347] Exactly 100 years after Lincoln and in the wake of steady progress in information and communication technologies, A. F. K. Organski noted,

> Finally, it should be noted that public opinion plays a new role in holding nations to their friends. Modern government and modern warfare both require mass support, and as a result, national governments find it necessary to mobilize popular sentiment behind any important move in international politics.[348]

Over the course of the decades following Organski's assessment, the influence of public opinion has, if anything, seen a further increase in its significance. Giles Scott-Smith thus recently detected "a rise in importance of public opinion for foreign policy formation."[349]

At the same time, with increasing interconnectedness across the world, not only domestic but also international public opinion gained considerable momentum. In

---

[344]This diplomatic success, however, was quickly overtaken by events due to Napoleon's return from Elba and his Hundred Days during which he promptly abolished the practice; Longford, *Wellington*, pp. 370–372 & p. 396.

[345]Vlahos, "Public Diplomacy as Loss of World Authority," p. 35. It is an interesting fact that in one of the more recent adaptations of *Henry V*, Kenneth Branagh's celebrated and award-winning 1989 movie, the role of French herald Mountjoy has experienced considerable enlargement as compared to Shakespeare's original play.

[346]James Mill, "Summary Review of the Conduct and Measures of the Seventh Imperial Parliament," in *Parliamentary History and Review: Containing Reports of the Proceedings of the Two Houses of Parliament during the Session of 1826:–7 Geo. IV, With Critical Remarks on the Principal Measures of the Session* (London: Longman, Rees, Orme, Brown, and Green, 1826), p. 783.

[347]Abraham Lincoln, "First Joint Debate," Ottawa, Ill., August 21, 1858, in *The Works of Abraham Lincoln: Volume III, Speeches and Debates, 1856-1858*, eds. John H. Clifford and Marion M. Miller (New York, N.Y.: C.S. Hammond & Co., 1908), pp. 162–163.

[348]Organski, *World Politics*, p. 315.

[349]Giles Scott-Smith, "Soft Power in an Era of US Decline," in *Soft Power and US Foreign Policy: Theoretical, Historical and Contemporary Perspectives*, eds. Inderjeet Parmar and Michael Cox (Abingdon: Routledge, 2010), p. 167.

light of global demonstrations against an imminent U.S. invasion of Iraq, Patrick E. Tyler, for example, has pointed out in *The New York Times* on February 17, 2003, "[T]here may still be two superpowers on the planet: the United States and world public opinion."[350] In fact, the 2003 Iraq War has frequently been cited as a particularly prominent example in this regard. Joseph Nye hence elaborated on the relation of public opinion, soft power, and political repercussions on this very occasion,

> For example, in regard to Iraq in 2003, Turkish officials were constrained by public and parliamentary opinion and unable to allow the American 4th Infantry Division to cross their country. The Bush administration's lack of soft power hurt its hard power. Similarly, Mexican President Vincente Fox wished to accommodate George W. Bush by supporting a second UN resolution authorizing invasion, but was constrained by public opinion. When being pro-American is a political kiss of death, public opinion has an effect on policy.[351]

More recently still, and with particular reference to the deployment of armed drones, Marcus Schulzke has in the same vein fittingly remarked, "Although international opinion does not affect politicians' electoral prospects to the same extent as domestic opinion, it is an increasingly important consideration."[352]

Along with the growing recognition of the importance of (global) public opinion, scholars have increasingly engaged to empirically trace its effect and detect tangible policy outcomes brought about by foreign attitudes to a nation's foreign policy. The recent study by Benjamin E. Goldsmith and Yusaku Horiuchi on the influence of public opinion on U.S. foreign policy both abroad and at home in this regard concluded,

> Public opinion about US foreign policy indeed appears to matter when countries make decisions on issues of importance to the US. [. . .] Foreign leaders, it seems, do pay attention to the attitudes of their own publics when they weigh decisions—such as whether to send troops into harm's way—which might incur significant public concern or opposition.[353]

Bearing in mind such statements, Ali S. Wyne's assertion that one should "regard world opinion as a critical, but malleable, force that is to be engaged actively"[354] seems well founded, indeed. This assessment on both the importance and malleability of global public opinion brings us back to the concept of public diplomacy as an instrument applied by an actor in international affairs in order to favorably shape opinions abroad.

---

[350]Patrick E. Tyler, "A New Power In the Streets," *The New York Times*, February 17, 2003, online at: http://www.nytimes.com/2003/02/17/world/threats-and-responses-news-analysis-a-new-power-in-the-streets.html (accessed June 13, 2016).

[351]Nye, "Responding to My Critics and Concluding Thoughts," p. 219.

[352]Marcus Schulzke, *The Morality of Drone Warfare and the Politics of Regulation* (London: Palgrave Macmillan, 2017), p. 189.

[353]Benjamin E. Goldsmith and Yusaku Horiuchi, "In Search of Soft Power: Does Foreign Public Opinion Matter for US Foreign Policy?," *World Politics*, Vol. 64, No. 3 (July 2012), pp. 581–582.

[354]Wyne, "Public Opinion and Power," p. 47.

It was, as argued, primarily the Cold War between the United States and the Soviet Union that led to the emergence of modern forms of public diplomacy.[355] Some observers even argue that a struggle with the instruments of public diplomacy commenced yet before the arms race in the realm of hard power took off.[356] At a time when the bipolar system that for decades defined international relations came to an end, Hans N. Tuch provided another influential definition of public diplomacy, stressing its communicative character. In his influential *Communicating with the World*, Tuch defined public diplomacy "as *a government's process of communicating with foreign publics in an attempt to bring about understanding for its nation's ideas and ideals, its institutions and culture, as well as its national goals and current policies.*"[357] More recent additions include definitions by Paul Sharp ("the process by which direct relations are pursued with a country's people to advance the interests and extend the values of those being represented"[358]) or Bruce Gregory ("ways and means by which states, associations of states, and nonstate actors *understand* cultures, attitudes, and behavior; *build and manage* relationships; and *influence* opinions and actions to advance their interests and values"[359]).

These more recent additions express a novel understanding of and approach to the concept in an "attempt to adjust public diplomacy to the conditions of the information age."[360] This development has led to the establishment of what has been called the "new public diplomacy."[361] By "shifting from one-way informational diplomatic objectives to two-way interpretative public exchanges,"[362] the focus now more than ever before lies on the exchange character of public diplomacy. While the old public diplomacy frequently was characterized by "one-way-messaging strategies," the new public diplomacy is characterized by "a more relational approach,"[363] marked by reciprocity rather than one-sidedness. According to R. S. Zaharna, this trend toward greater collaboration will presumably gather further pace for years to

---

[355]Matthew C. Armstrong, "Operationalizing Public Diplomacy," in *Routledge Handbook of Public Diplomacy*, eds. Nancy Snow and Philip M. Taylor (New York, N.Y.: Routledge, 2009), p. 64.

[356]Melissen, "The New Public Diplomacy," p. 4.

[357]Hans N. Tuch, *Communicating with the World: U.S. Public Diplomacy Overseas* (New York, N. Y.: St. Martin's Press, 1990), p. 3; Tuch's emphasis.

[358]Sharp, "Revolutionary States, Outlaw Regimes and the Techniques of Public Diplomacy," p. 106.

[359]Gregory, "Public Diplomacy," p. 276; Gregory's emphasis.

[360]Gilboa, "Searching for a Theory of Public Diplomacy," p. 58.

[361]See, for example, Jan Melissen, ed., *The New Public Diplomacy: Soft Power in International Relations* (Basingstoke: Palgrave Macmillan, 2005) or Jan Melissen, *Wielding Soft Power: The New Public Diplomacy* (The Hague: Netherlands Institute of International Relations Clingendael, 2005). See also Kathy R. Fitzpatrick, *U.S. Public Diplomacy in a Post-9/11 World: From Messaging to Mutuality, CPD Perspectives on Public Diplomacy, Paper 6, 2011* (Los Angeles, Cal.: Figueroa Press, 2011), pp. 6–14.

[362]Nancy Snow, "Rethinking Public Diplomacy," in *Routledge Handbook of Public Diplomacy*, eds. Nancy Snow and Philip M. Taylor (New York, N.Y.: Routledge, 2009), p. 10.

[363]Zaharna, *The Cultural Awakening in Public Diplomacy*, p. 11.

come.[364] Jan Melissen thus noted, "The new public diplomacy moves away from—to put it crudely—peddling information to foreigners and keeping the foreign press at bay, towards *engaging* with foreign audiences."[365] Elsewhere, Melissen likewise argued "that public diplomacy today is increasingly based on listening to 'the other,' that it is about dialogue rather than monologue, and is not just aimed at short-term policy objectives but also at long-term relationship-building."[366] Therefore, while the old variety is strongly connected to the Cold War era (and shared some components of propaganda, indeed), the new model of public diplomacy is taking into account a number of developments that, as already argued above, have lastingly changed the conduct of international relations at large. In recent years, Pierre Pahlavi hence noted, advances in information and communications technologies, trends of globalization and growing interdependence, growing global democratization, and the rise of non-state actors in international relations have created a "global information society"[367]—rendering public diplomacy all the more important today. Nancy Snow, therefore, aptly pointed out, "Global publics will not allow themselves just to be talked to, but are demanding fuller participation in dialogue and feedback through the help of Web 2.0 communication technologies and new media like Second Life, Facebook, YouTube, and MySpace."[368] In fact, social media platforms such as these have increasingly led to new degrees of empowerment and interconnectedness of the global audience hitherto unimaginable. In view of such developments, "public diplomacy is now so central to diplomacy that it is no longer helpful to treat it as a sub-set of diplomatic practice."[369] To put it in a nutshell, public diplomacy has become the new normal.

Besides these developments rendering public diplomacy particularly significant today, a further single event, which contributed to its growing importance—and novel understanding—were the terrorist attacks on the United States on September 11, 2001. The importance of 9/11 for the discourse on and practice of public diplomacy is widely shared by observers and practitioners.[370] In fact, public diplomacy has become a particularly popular term in the context of the "War on Terror"

---

[364]Zaharna, *The Cultural Awakening in Public Diplomacy*, p. 26.

[365]Melissen, "The New Public Diplomacy," p. 13; emphasis added. This new paradigm in public diplomacy went hand in hand with comparable developments in communication theories; Zaharna, *The Cultural Awakening in Public Diplomacy*, p. 48.

[366]Jan Melissen, "Public Diplomacy," in *The Oxford Handbook of Modern Diplomacy*, eds. Andrew F. Cooper, Jorge Heine, and Ramesh Thakur (Oxford: Oxford University Press, 2013), p. 441.

[367]Pierre Pahlavi, "The Use of New Media in the Modern Asymmetric Warfare Environment," in *Handbook of Defence Politics: International and Comparative Perspectives*, eds. Isaiah Wilson III and James J. F. Forest (London: Routledge, 2008), pp. 137.

[368]Snow, "Rethinking Public Diplomacy," p. 8.

[369]Bruce Gregory, "American Public Diplomacy: Enduring Characteristics, Elusive Transformations," *The Hague Journal of Diplomacy*, Vol. 6, Nos. 3-4 (2011), p. 353.

[370]See, for example, Melissen, "The New Public Diplomacy," p. 8 and Hocking, "Rethinking the 'New' Public Diplomacy," p. 28.

and its rise within this particular context has even been compared to the ascent of other buzzwords associated with former conflicts: "camouflage" in World War I, "Blitzkrieg" and "Kamikaze" in World War II, or "containment" and "deterrence" in the Cold War.[371] As a consequence of the terrorist attacks, subsequent years have witnessed, particularly in the United States, "more attention to, discussion of, and concern for the role and goals of public diplomacy than at perhaps any time in our history."[372] One question that in the wake of the attacks was paramount in the minds of the American public as well as leading officials within the George W. Bush administration, therefore was, as George W. Bush himself put it, "Why do they hate us?"[373] In a short period of time, further questions arose, asking how Al Qaeda could have been so successful, not only with respect to the planning and execution of the attacks but also regarding the persuasion of considerable numbers of acolytes in different corners of the world to support their cause. Various observers drew attention to this very point at the time. Diplomatic luminary Richard Holbrooke, for example, asked in *The Washington Post* op-ed already cited above, "How could a mass murderer who publicly praised the terrorists of Sept. 11 be winning the hearts and minds of anyone? How can a man in a cave outcommunicate the world's leading communications society?"[374] As a consequence, in the wake of the terrorist attacks of 9/11, public diplomacy has indeed become "beyond any doubt the hottest item on the US foreign policy establishment."[375] As a result, countless reports by governmental agencies as well as think tanks have been presented[376] and task forces dealing with the issue have been established.[377] However, this development is by no means restricted to the United States alone. Rather, public diplomacy has become "one of the most salient political communication issue in the twenty-first century"[378] on a worldwide scale and regardless of size or regime type of respective countries.[379] The events of September 11, 2001, can consequently be seen as a catalyst for the global rise in significance of public diplomacy that has been fostered by a number of concurrent developments.

---

[371]Cowan and Cull, "Public Diplomacy in a Changing World," p. 6.

[372]Joseph Duffey, "How Globalization Became U.S. Public Diplomacy at the End of the Cold War," in *Routledge Handbook of Public Diplomacy*, eds. Nancy Snow and Philip M. Taylor (New York, N.Y.: Routledge, 2009), p. 332.

[373]George W. Bush, *Decision Points* (New York, N.Y.: Crown Publishers, 2010), p. 192. See also Richard A. Clark, *Against All Enemies: Inside America's War on Terror* (New York, N.Y.: Free Press, 2004), p. 33.

[374]Holbrooke, "Get the Message Out."

[375]Jan Melissen, "Introduction," in *The New Public Diplomacy: Soft Power in International Relations*, ed. Jan Melissen (Basingstoke: Palgrave Macmillan, 2005), p. xix.

[376]Gilboa, "Searching for a Theory of Public Diplomacy," p. 56.

[377]van Ham, "Power, Public Diplomacy, and the *Pax Americana*," p. 56; see also Schneider, "Culture Communicates," p. 148.

[378]Snow and Taylor, "Preface and Introduction," p. ix.

[379]Melissen, "The New Public Diplomacy," p. 8.

In view of these developments referred to above and accelerated by 9/11, Jan Melissen has aptly pointed out that today "diplomacy is operative in a network environment rather than the hierarchical state-centric model of international relations."[380] The understanding of diplomacy and particularly public diplomacy as a network is a topos frequently found in literature.[381] (Others, however, have argued that power relationships with its entwined paths today would more accurately be depicted with a mandala formation.[382]) Once more, the new paradigm for public diplomacy has to be seen in the broader context of changes taking place in international relations. R. S. Zaharna thus aptly argued,

> Networking has become the new model of persuasion in the global communication era. If the Cold War was about information command and control and the Information Age was about bits and bytes, the global communication era is about networks.[383]

Along with these changes comes a "growing agentive capacity of, for example, individuals and nongovernmental organisations."[384] And while many observers also point at potential dangers and challenges of this new configuration, it is widely believed that the advantages of the practice of public diplomacy in such a manner far outweigh its challenges.[385] At the same time, these changes and developments will require different skills and approaches for practitioners in public diplomacy.[386] Taken together, these developments account for a network understanding of public diplomacy today, an understanding depicted in Fig. 3.3.

The model illustration pays tribute to the developments outlined above, particularly the rise of various new, non-state actors such as (clockwise) international organizations (IO), individuals (I), non-governmental organizations (NGO), and multinational enterprises (MNE). Positioned at the core of this multi-actor network

---

[380]Melissen, "The New Public Diplomacy," p. 12.

[381]See for example, Anne-Marie Slaughter, "America's Edge: Power in the Networked Century," *Foreign Affairs*, Vol. 88, No. 1 (January/February 2009), p. 94; Zaharna, *The Cultural Awakening in Public Diplomacy*, p. 45; Hocking, "Rethinking the 'New' Public Diplomacy," p. 29; John Hemery, "Training for Public Diplomacy: An Evolutionary Perspective," in *The New Public Diplomacy: Soft Power in International Relations*, ed. Jan Melissen (Basingstoke: Palgrave Macmillan, 2005), p. 208; Riordan, "Dialogue-based Public Diplomacy," p. 192; and Nye, *The Future of Power*, p. 108.

[382]Rosita Dellios and R. James Ferguson, "Sino-Indian Soft Power in a Regional Context," *Culture Mandala: The Bulletin of the Centre for East-West Cultural and Economic Studies*, Vol. 9, No. 2 (2011), pp. 15–34.

[383]R. S. Zaharna, "The Network Paradigm of Strategic Public Diplomacy," *Foreign Policy in Focus*, ed. John Gershman, September 30, 2005, online at: http://fpif.org/the_network_paradigm_of_strategic_public_diplomacy/ (accessed June 29, 2015).

[384]Wyne, "Public Opinion and Power," p. 47.

[385]Cull, "Public Diplomacy," p. 53.

[386]Naren Chitty, "Australian Public Diplomacy," in *Routledge Handbook of Public Diplomacy*, eds. Nancy Snow and Philip M. Taylor (New York, N.Y.: Routledge, 2009), p. 315; Jorge Heine, "From Club to Network Diplomacy," in *The Oxford Handbook of Modern Diplomacy*, eds. Andrew F. Cooper, Jorge Heine, and Ramesh Thakur (Oxford: Oxford University Press, 2013), p. 62; Melissen, "Public Diplomacy," p. 451.

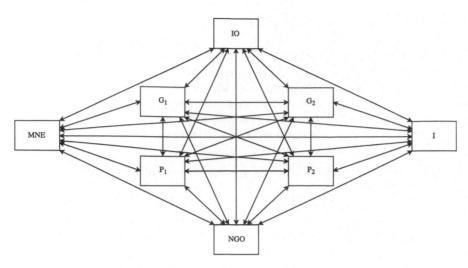

Fig. 3.3 Public diplomacy: a network model (The illustration has been inspired by two—far less sophisticated—graphic representations in Nye, *The Future of Power*, p. 102)

illustrating the workings of public diplomacy today, the state and its official diplomatic representatives continue to play an important role. Of course, traditional forms of diplomacy still matter.[387] The picture, however, is further complicated by the fact that respective governments (G_1 and G_2) are by no means monolithic. Rather, a variety of different administrative units within or below respective national governments increasingly edge toward the stage (including federal states, communities, or cities) However, the international system today is characterized by a "fluidity of evolving power dynamics."[388]

This observation directly leads to the nexus of public diplomacy and power. Nancy Snow has in this regard matter-of-factly stated, "Public diplomacy is inevitably linked to power."[389] In a 2002 report, the U.S. Advisory Commission on Public Diplomacy likewise recognized "its value as a strategic element of power in the information age."[390] Accordingly, the practice of public diplomacy "is closely tied to foreign policy objectives"[391] and hence is non-altruistic, but decidedly interest-

---

[387]Riordan, "Dialogue-based Public Diplomacy," p. 193.

[388]Wyne, "Public Opinion and Power," p. 47.

[389]Snow, "Rethinking Public Diplomacy," p. 3.

[390]United States Advisory Commission on Public Diplomacy, "Building America's Public Diplomacy Through a Reformed Structure and Additional Resources," *A 2002 Report of the U.S. Advisory Commission on Public Diplomacy*, online at: https://www.state.gov/documents/organization/13622.pdf (accessed April 25, 2017), p. 9.

[391]Michael McClellan, "Public Diplomacy in the Context of Traditional Diplomacy," in *Favorita Papers 01/2004: Public Diplomacy*, ed. Gerhard Reiweger (Vienna: Diplomatische Akademie, 2004), p. 24. See also Hocking, "Rethinking the 'New' Public Diplomacy," p. 37.

driven.[392] And—as with soft power—there is nothing normative about the concept. As Anthony Pratkanis has observed, "The typical image of public diplomacy is that it is nice and warm and comforting in contrast to the harsh realities of hardball diplomacy and military action."[393] However, he continued, public diplomacy campaigns can occasionally "be quite competitive, nasty, brutish, and even evil" when geared to "the *promotion* of national interests by informing and *influencing* the *citizens of other nations.*"[394] Correspondingly, Paul Sharp detected "something fundamentally illiberal about regarding human beings in terms of great lumps of humanity that can be nudged and shaped into beliefs, values and patterns of behavior that accord with some conception of our own values and interests."[395] The U.S. State Department likewise leaves no doubt as to the intentions of U.S. public diplomacy,

> The mission of American public diplomacy is to support the achievement of U.S. foreign policy goals and objectives, advance national interests, and enhance national security by informing and influencing foreign publics and by expanding and strengthening the relationship between the people and Government of the United States and citizens of the rest of the world.[396]

Public diplomacy can in this sense indeed be understood as a "political instrument"[397] and more precisely "an essential post-modern tool of statecraft."[398] With particular respect to the soft power discourse, public diplomacy is frequently identified as a paramount tool or transmission belt for the wielding of soft power.[399] Public diplomacy has accordingly alternately be identified as an "instrument through which soft power is projected,"[400] "one of soft power's key instruments,"[401] or "[o]ne of the major ways that governments attempt to wield soft power."[402] And while the overarching concept of soft power may be considered "a mindset," public diplomacy can be thought of as "a tool."[403] The *Wissenschaftlicher Dienst des*

---

[392]Melissen, "The New Public Diplomacy," p. 14.

[393]Anthony Pratkanis, "Public Diplomacy in International Conflicts: A Social Influence Analysis," in *The New Public Diplomacy: Soft Power in International Relations*, ed. Jan Melissen (Basingstoke: Palgrave Macmillan, 2005), p. 111.

[394]Pratkanis, "Public Diplomacy in International Conflicts," pp. 111–112; Pratkanis' emphasis.

[395]Sharp, "Revolutionary States, Outlaw Regimes and the Techniques of Public Diplomacy," p. 120.

[396]United States Department of State, "Under Secretary for Public Diplomacy and Public Affairs," online at: https://www.state.gov/r/ (accessed April 29, 2017).

[397]Gregory, "Public Diplomacy," p. 276.

[398]van Ham, "Power, Public Diplomacy, and the *Pax Americana*," p. 57.

[399]Nye, "Public Diplomacy and Soft Power," p. 95; Nye, *Soft Power*, pp. 107–125; Melissen, *Wielding Soft Power*, p. 3.

[400]Falk Hartig, *Chinese Public Diplomacy: The Rise of the Confucius Institute* (Abingdon: Routledge, 2015), p. 6.

[401]Melissen, "The New Public Diplomacy," p. 4. See also Körber, "Imagepflege als Daueraufgabe," p. 161.

[402]Nye, "Hard, Soft, and Smart Power," p. 569.

[403]Markos Kounalakis and Andras Simonyi, *The Hard Truth about Soft Power, CPD Perspectives on Public Diplomacy, Paper 5, 2011* (Los Angeles, Cal.: Figueroa Press, 2011), p. 36.

Bundestages accordingly lists public diplomacy as an "aktives Mittel" ("active instrument") to wield soft power.[404] Public diplomacy, therefore, "can be the *mechanism* to deploy soft power, but it is not the same thing as soft power, any more than the army and hard power are the same thing."[405] Consequently, public diplomacy is integrated into the introduced soft power taxonomy as one of the premier instruments to wield soft power.

Besides their non-normative nature, both concepts share further characteristics that deserve mention: As does soft power,[406] public diplomacy "works best with a long horizon."[407] Walter Laqueur thus holds that its "perspective is not measured in weeks or months. To be effective it has to be evaluated in longer time frames."[408] However, particularly in Western foreign ministries,[409] quick results are frequently mandated and expected, not least to justify future funding in times of budget cuts or concerns for reelection. However, as Nicholas J. Cull has warned, "[a]ttempts to evaluate cultural diplomacy can seem like a forester running out every morning to see how far his trees have grown overnight."[410] Connected with this observation is the insight that public diplomacy cannot successfully be conducted in times of crisis.[411] According to expression by U.S. radio broadcaster and then-director of the USIA, Edward R. Murrow, made after he had been asked to mitigate the damage done to the U.S. image in the wake of the failed 1961 Bay of Pigs Invasion, has become legendary, "If they want me in on the crash landings, I'd better damn well be in on the take-offs."[412] Despite these objections, public diplomacy tends to be of special importance in times of (foreign policy) crisis.[413] Nye thus observed that France increasingly focused on its cultural attraction after her defeat in the Franco-Prussian War of 1870/1871.[414] To a certain extent this may be attributed to the observation that most often "public diplomacy has historically been an instrument of

---

[404]Huberta von Voss-Wittig, "Soft Power," Wissenschaftlicher Dienst des Deutschen Bundestages, *Aktueller Begriff*, No. 45/06 (November 3, 2006), online at: https://www.bundestag.de/blob/189706/8c40cb75069889f8829a5a0db838da1f/soft_power-data.pdf (accessed September 15, 2015), p. 1.

[405]Nicholas J. Cull, *Public Diplomacy: Lessons from the Past, CPD Perspectives on Public Diplomacy* (Los Angeles, Cal.: Figueroa Press, 2011), p. 15; Cull's emphasis.

[406]See below, Sect. 3.4.

[407]Melissen, "The New Public Diplomacy," p. 15.

[408]Walter Laqueur, "Save Public Diplomacy: Broadcasting America's Message Matters," *Foreign Affairs*, Vol. 73, No. 5 (September/October 1994), p. 22. See also Riordan, "Dialogue-based Public Diplomacy," p. 192.

[409]Riordan, "Dialogue-based Public Diplomacy," p. 192.

[410]Cull, "Public Diplomacy," p. 44.

[411]Armstrong, "Operationalizing Public Diplomacy," p. 69.

[412]Quoted in Kelley, "Between 'Take-offs' and 'Crash Landings,'", p. 72.

[413]Gerhard Reiweger, "Introduction," in *Favorita Papers 01/2004: Public Diplomacy*, ed. Gerhard Reiweger (Vienna: Diplomatische Akademie, 2004), p. 5.

[414]Nye, *Soft Power*, p. 100.

foreign policy to meet wartime needs."[415] With regard to U.S. public diplomacy Bruce Gregory has thus argued,

> The U.S. government's international, cultural, information, and broadcasting organizations were created in cycles linked to war or the threat of war—the Creel Committee in World War I; the State Department's Bureau of Cultural Affairs, the Office of the Coordinator of Inter-American Affairs, the office of War Information, and the Voice of America in World War II; and the U.S. Information Agency (USIA) and Radio Free Europe/Radio Liberty (RFE/RL) in the cold war.[416]

The aforementioned surge in the interest and practice of public diplomacy after 9/11 and in the course of the "War on Terror," may be seen as a further point in case.

After introducing the concept of public diplomacy and exploring its relation to soft power, how can public diplomacy be operationalized in order to offer a framework for substantiated analysis? In fact, in order to allow for empirical research and comparison, such an operationalization is vital. However, this task does not present itself as an easy one, as Eytan Gilboa has noted,

> Despite growing significance of public diplomacy in contemporary international relations, scholars have not yet pursued or even sufficiently promoted systematic theoretical research in this field. They have developed models and tools for analysis in several relevant disciplines but have not proposed a comprehensive and integrated framework.[417]

In literature, different suggestions can be found as to the establishment of such an "integrated framework." In operationalizing and classifying different aspects of public diplomacy, various criteria have been identified, including "level of participation," "degree of coordination," "scope," "time duration," or "policy objective."[418] Accordingly, different scholars have based their frameworks along a time axis, that is, distinguishing respective timeframes in which public diplomacy initiatives operate.[419] Nye, for example, in many of his writings and by drawing on the work of Mark Leonard, Catherine Stead, and Conrad Smewing, distinguishes between "daily communications," "strategic communication," and "lasting relationships."[420] Nye labels these three dimensions as the "three concentric circles or stages of public diplomacy."[421] While the first of these circles may be measured in days or

---

[415]Richard Nelson and Foad Izadi, "Ethics and Social Issues in Public Diplomacy," in *The New Public Diplomacy: Soft Power in International Relations*, ed. Jan Melissen (Basingstoke: Palgrave Macmillan, 2005), p. 334.

[416]Gregory, "Public Diplomacy," p. 279.

[417]Gilboa, "Searching for a Theory of Public Diplomacy," p. 72.

[418]R. S. Zaharna, "Mapping out a Spectrum of Public Diplomacy Initiatives: Information and Relational Communication Frameworks," in *Routledge Handbook of Public Diplomacy*, eds. Nancy Snow and Philip M. Taylor (New York, N.Y.: Routledge, 2009), p. 93.

[419]See, for example, Gilboa, "Searching for a Theory of Public Diplomacy," p. 72; Gregory, "Public Diplomacy," p. 276; and Guy J. Golan, "An Integrated Approach to Public Diplomacy," *American Behavioral Scientists*, Vol. 57, No. 9 (2013), p. 1252.

[420]Nye, "Public Diplomacy and Soft Power," pp. 101–102. See also Nye, *Soft Power*, pp. 107–110 and Nye, "Hard, Soft, and Smart Power," pp. 570–571.

[421]Nye, *The Future of Power*, p. 105.

weeks, the second takes months or years, and the third even decades.[422] By offering various examples of public diplomacy initiatives in each of the three circles, Nye underlines and justifies his classification. However, a clear distinction between the three, due to their concentric and overlapping nature, is hardly possible and thus poses considerable difficulties for empirical application and analysis.

Offering remedy to this issue and consequently allowing for a more substantiated and sophisticated operationalization, Nicholas J. Cull's taxonomy of public diplomacy is drawing rather on contentual or modal than on temporal distinctions.[423] Recognizing that "[p]ublic diplomacy covers an array of different activities,"[424] an operationalization along the lines of distinctive categories seems particularly suitable since it facilitates a differentiated empirical analysis. Cull's proposal, partly congruent to the ones put forth by Ali Fisher[425] or Bruce Gregory[426] but more elaborate and precise, shall therefore serve as the framework for the operationalization of public diplomacy as a premier instrument of soft power. Table 3.1 offers an overview of the five categories in Cull's classification of public diplomacy.

Following Nicholas J. Cull, the five respective components can be defined as "an actor's attempt to manage the international environment..."

With the five categories depicted in Table 3.1 (i.e., listening, advocacy, cultural diplomacy, exchange diplomacy, and international broadcasting), Cull opens a wide spectrum of activities that in the following shall be presented in turn:

1. Listening can be regarded as the quintessential public diplomacy activity, since, in the words of Cull, "it precedes all successful public diplomacy."[427] Nye equally noted that "[c]onsultation and listening are essential in the generation of soft power."[428] Likewise, Ali Fisher argued that "[l]istening is more than just polling, it is demonstrating that views of those overseas are taken seriously and consideration is given to those perspectives."[429] Listening thus crucially includes the study of others' views on any given actor or issue. When done candidly, it may yield considerable (soft power) consequences. This very aspect of listening and taking into consideration others' views of oneself found famous expression in

---

[422]Nye, *The Future of Power*, pp. 105–106.

[423]Cull, "Public Diplomacy," pp. 31–54.

[424]Giles Scott-Smith, "Exchange Programs and Public Diplomacy," in *Routledge Handbook of Public Diplomacy*, eds. Nancy Snow and Philip M. Taylor (New York, N.Y.: Routledge, 2009), p. 50.

[425]Ali Fisher, "Four Seasons in One Day: The Crowded House of Public Diplomacy in the UK," in *Routledge Handbook of Public Diplomacy*, eds. Nancy Snow and Philip M. Taylor (New York, N. Y.: Routledge, 2009), pp. 251–261.

[426]Bruce Gregory offers a quadripartite "unpacking" of public diplomacy, distinguishing between "understanding," "planning," "engagement," and "advocacy;" Gregory, "American Public Diplomacy," pp. 355–361.

[427]Cull, "Public Diplomacy," p. 32.

[428]Nye, "The Future of Soft Power in US Foreign Policy," p. 11.

[429]Fisher, "Four Seasons in One Day," p. 252.

Table 3.1 Five components of public diplomacy according to Nicholas J. Cull

Component	Definition[a]	Examples[b]
Listening	"...by collecting and collating data about public and their opinions overseas and using that data to redirect its policy or its wider public diplomacy approach accordingly."	– Rebranding Switzerland (2000–2007) – U.S. Shared Values Campaign (2001–2002)
Advocacy	"...by undertaking an international communication activity to actively promote a particular policy, idea, or that actor's general interests in the minds of a foreign public."	– NATO Double-Track Policy (1983) – U.S. War in Vietnam (1960s)
Cultural diplomacy	"...through making its cultural resources and achieve-ments known overseas and/or facilitating cultural transmission abroad."	– U.S. Family of Man Exhibit (1955–1963) – Image of the Soviet Union (Cold War Period)
Exchange diplomacy	"...by sending its citizens overseas or reciprocally accepting citizens from overseas for a period of study and/or acculturation."	– Franco-German Exchanges (1945–1988) – Sayyid Qutb (1948)
International broadcasting	"...by using the technologies of radio, television, and the Internet to engage with foreign publics."	– BCC and U.S. Isolation (1939–1941) – British/Free French Broadcasting (World War II)

Own table based on Cull, "Public Diplomacy," pp. 31–54
[a]Cull, "Public Diplomacy," pp. 32–34
[b]The first example in each respective category is referred to by Nicholas J. Cull as a model for a particularly successful public diplomacy initiative, whereas the second example depicts an abortive initiative; Cull, "Public Diplomacy," pp. 37–46

some of the final verses in Robert Burns' 1786 poem *To a Louse* which run, in Michael R. Burch's English translation,

> O would some Power with vision teach us,
> To see ourselves as *others* see us!
> It would from many a blunder free us,
> And foolish notions.[430]

That the importance of this first dimension of public diplomacy is not merely recognized in theory but also in practice is evident, for example, in "Rebranding Switzerland" (2002–2007), a campaign that sought to improve the image of Switzerland by analyzing existing views in select countries.[431] More recently,

---

[430]Robert Burns, "To a Louse," Modern English Translation by Michael R. Burch, online at: http://www.thehypertexts.com/Robert%20Burns%20Translations%20Modern%20English.htm (accessed July 14, 2015); Burch's emphasis.
[431]Cull, "Public Diplomacy," pp. 37–38.

U.S. foreign policy-makers (perhaps also in view of past blunders including the infamous Shared Values Campaign[432]) have also expressed the high importance they attribute to the dimension of listening. Thus, in an address delivered at the Center for Strategic and International Studies Global Security Forum in 2013, then-U.S. Secretary of Defense Chuck Hagel declared,

> In the 21st century, the United States must continue to be a force for, and an important symbol of, humanity, freedom, and progress for all mankind. We must also make a far better effort to understand how the world sees us, and why. We must listen more. We *must* listen more.[433]

2. Turning toward the second category in Cull's taxonomy of public diplomacy, advocacy describes activities centering around the explanation and promotion of particular policies or purposes. It has been noted that this practice in particular can look back on an extraordinarily long history. Cull thus noted, "Ancient examples of advocacy may be found in Herodotus, where envoys from Xerxes of Persia appeal to the people of Argos for their neutrality in the Empire's invasion of Greece in 480 B.C."[434] In more recent times, advocacy can still be identified as playing an important role in achieving foreign policy objectives. Accordingly, Cull attested special importance to advocacy with regard to NATO's 1979 double-track decision, which drew harsh criticism in European populations and opinions on which changed only after the policy had been actively promoted and depicted as vital for securing world peace in the view of Soviet military build-up.[435]

3. Arguably, the third dimension, cultural diplomacy, looms, especially large in the discourse on public diplomacy. Defined as "the act of presenting a cultural good to an audience in an attempt to engage them in the ideas which the producer perceives to be represented by it,"[436] this dimension can be considered the quintessential soft power instrument designed at showcasing cultural resources (Subunit I) to an international audience. In fact, cultural diplomacy is thus frequently even used synonymously for public diplomacy in its entirety. In this sense, it has been regarded as "a prime example of 'soft power.'"[437] Schneider accordingly noted, "It is not difficult to understand the potency of cultural diplomacy. What is more persuasive: a démarche delivered by an Ambassador to a foreign minister urging greater liberalization and emphasis on human rights, or films and music that express individuality and freedom?"[438] While recognized for its potency, it certainly cannot be single-handedly considered a cure for a

---

[432]Cull, "Public Diplomacy," pp. 43–44.

[433]Chuck Hagel, "CSIS Global Security Forum," Washington D.C., November 5, 2013, online at: http://www.defense.gov/Speeches/Speech.aspx?SpeechID=1814 (accessed July 13, 2015); Hagel's emphasis.

[434]Cull, "Public Diplomacy," pp. 32–33.

[435]Cull, "Public Diplomacy," pp. 38–39.

[436]Fisher, "Four Seasons in One Day," p. 253.

[437]Schneider, "Culture Communicates," p. 147.

[438]Schneider, "Culture Communicates," p. 148.

negative reputation of a country due to unpopular politics. Patricia M. Goff accordingly pointed out, "Cultural diplomacy cannot work miracles."[439] However, as one observer has noted matter-of-factly, "as a foreign policy tool, arts diplomacy certainly is far better for the American image – and certainly cheaper – than bombing Baghdad."[440] As we shall see with respect to the outcomes of soft power in general below, cultural diplomacy again works with a lengthy time frame. Goff thus aptly noted that it "plants a seed. As such, it may take root over time."[441] Among others, cultural diplomacy includes such diverse activities as hosting cultural or sports events, conducting exhibitions, or running cultural institutes. Again, examples abound throughout the ages[442]: the Roman practice of instructing the sons of foreign nobles in the Latin language and Roman culture,[443] the work of cultural institutes such as Germany's Goethe Institutes,[444] or the creation and sponsorship of national cultural centers come to mind. To elaborate on the latter, plans for the United States cultural center celebrating the nation's art and displaying it to the (world) public first put forth in the 1930s were intensified in the 1950s and eventually—in September 1958—President Eisenhower signed into law a bill proposing the creation of a National Cultural Center.[445] As a particularly successful example in terms of cultural diplomacy around the same time, Nicholas J. Cull refers to the Family of Man Exhibit, a photographic exhibition developed by the New York Museum of Modern Art in the early 1950s, which showcased more than 500 pictures from photographers originating from 68 countries and depicting everyday scenes of human life from all around the world.[446]

---

[439]Patricia M. Goff, "Cultural Diplomacy," in *The Oxford Handbook of Modern Diplomacy*, eds. Andrew F. Cooper, Jorge Heine, and Ramesh Thakur (Oxford: Oxford University Press, 2013), p. 433.

[440]John Brown, "Arts Diplomacy: The Neglected Aspect of Cultural Diplomacy," in *Routledge Handbook of Public Diplomacy*, eds. Nancy Snow and Philip M. Taylor (New York, N.Y.: Routledge, 2009), p. 59.

[441]Goff, "Cultural Diplomacy," p. 432.

[442]A brief history of cultural diplomacy from early Bronze Age to the Classical Greeks and Romans to the Middle Ages and the Renaissance up to World War I is provided by Richard T. Arndt; Arndt, *The First Resort of Kings*, pp. 1–23.

[443]Cull, "Public Diplomacy," p. 33. See below, Sect. 3.5.

[444]Oliver Zöllner, "German Public Diplomacy: The Dialogue of Cultures," in *Routledge Handbook of Public Diplomacy*, eds. Nancy Snow and Philip M. Taylor (New York, N.Y.: Routledge, 2009), p. 265.

[445]Roger Meersman, "The John F. Kennedy Center for the Performing Arts: From Dream to Reality," *Records of the Columbia Historical Society, Washington, D.C.*, Vol. 50 (1980), pp. 525–540.

[446]Cull, "Public Diplomacy," pp. 39–40.

4. Fourth, exchange diplomacy adds a further dimension to the concept of public diplomacy. It has been described as "the most two-way form of public diplomacy."[447] At the same time, it may be the one with the longest time frame. By sending citizens abroad and hosting foreign citizens in return, mutual understanding between the partners can be nurtured and lasting relationships can be established. Exchanges occur at various levels or participants' ages and include school, student, academic, and professional exchanges. Although these exchanges may be apolitical or private in nature, by creating lasting networks they can entail consequences for international affairs in subsequent years and decades.[448] Comparatively evaluating exchanges over a longer time period, Carol Atkinson hence concluded, "Research has consistently shown that exchange students return home with a more positive view of the country in which they have studied and the people with whom they interacted."[449] It is in this vein that William Inboden included the number of foreign students in a given country as part of his proposed metric to calculate national power.[450] Su Changhe likewise noted that "[e]ducation may be seen as the most effective way to produce and promote soft power."[451] Asked on the significance of exchanges for the wielding of soft power, Joseph Nye elaborated,

> I think the more we have contacts with other peoples, the more you get face-to-face contacts, the more essentially we're able to get an understanding of American values. It's not by broadcast, it's by these contacts. You have 750,000 foreign students at this country every year. That's a great source of soft power for us.[452]

Again, both scholars and policy-makers have recognized the potency of this tool. Then-German Chancellor Helmut Kohl (CDU), for example, underlined the significance of student exchanges and academic cooperation with the United States, declaring, "Das sind langfristige Projekte, aber wenn die Beziehungen, vor allem mit der jungen Generation, langfristig gut installiert werden, werden die nach uns Kommenden die Vorteile davon haben."[453] The special importance the German Chancellor attributed to such exchanges found its expression not least in

---

[447]Scott-Smith, "Exchange Programs and Public Diplomacy," pp. 51–52.

[448]Scott-Smith, "Exchange Programs and Public Diplomacy," pp. 50–51.

[449]Carol Atkinson, "Does Soft Power Matter? A Comparative Analysis of Student Exchange Programs 1980–2006," *Foreign Policy Analysis*, Vol. 6, No. 1 (2010), p. 3.

[450]William Inboden, "What is Power? And How Much of It Does America Have?," *The American Interest*, Vol. 5, No. 2 (November/December 2009), p. 25.

[451]Su, "Soft Power," p. 550.

[452]Quoted in Hayden, *The Rhetoric of Soft Power*, p. 262.

[453]Helmut Kohl, *Berichte zur Lage: 1989-1998, Der Kanzler und Parteivorsitzende im Bundesvorstand der CDU Deutschlands*, ed. Günter Buchstab and Hans-Otto Kleinmann. Forschungen und Quellen zur Zeitgeschichte, Band 64 (Düsseldorf: Droste, 2012), pp. 142–143. See also Helmut Kohl, *Erinnerungen: 1990–1994* (München: Droemer, 2007), p. 523.

the fact that Kohl sent his sons Walter and Peter to Harvard and the Massachusetts Institute of Technology (MIT), respectively.[454]

Various examples of exchange diplomacy, diverging in range and focus, can once more be found in different times and places, dating back even to "intercommunity child-fostering practiced in Nordic and Celtic Europe."[455] More recently, the U.S. Fulbright exchange program,[456] the German Academic Exchange Service (DAAD) and its programs,[457] or (student) exchanges organized by the Japan Foundation[458] come to mind. The Fulbright Program, for example, has developed a considerable reach since its establishment in 1952 and by now can look back on more than 300,000 alumni all around the world, thus shadowing in range other programs including the Rhodes Scholarship, available only to a much smaller circle (including, e.g., Senator J. William Fulbright, for whom the popular U.S. exchange program is named, U.S. President Bill Clinton, and legendary singer-songwriter and actor Kris Kristofferson).[459] Another U.S. program, directed in particular at foreign elites, is the International Visitor Leadership Program (IVLP). Christopher Midura, Acting Director of the Office of Policy, Planning, and Resources for Public Diplomacy and Public Affairs thus testified before the U.S. Senate Committee on Homeland Security and Governmental Affairs in 2008,

> The Fulbright Program remains the unchallenged world leader among academic exchange programs, while the International Visitor Leadership Program brings to the United States each year approximately 4,000 foreign professionals in a wide variety of fields for invaluable exposure to our culture, our society, and our policies. IVLP alumni have included 277 foreign heads of State [sic!].[460]

---

[454]Josef Joffe, "America the Inescapable," *The New York Times*, June 8, 1997, A Special Issue: How the World Sees Us, online at: http://www.nytimes.com/1997/06/08/magazine/america-the-inescapable.html (accessed August 10, 2016).

[455]Cull, "Public Diplomacy," p. 33. See also Arndt, *The First Resort of Kings*, p. 2.

[456]Bill Ivey and Paula Cleggett, "Cultural Diplomacy and the National Interest: In Search of a 21st Century Perspective," *The Curb Center for Art, Enterprise, and Public Policy, Vanderbilt University*, pp. 7–8, online at: http://www.vanderbilt.edu/curbcenter/files/Cultural-Diplomacy-and-the-National-Interest.pdf (accessed July 14, 2015).

[457]Zöllner, "German Public Diplomacy, pp. 265–266.

[458]Tadashi Ogawa, "Origin and Development of Japan's Public Diplomacy," in *Routledge Handbook of Public Diplomacy*, eds. Nancy Snow and Philip M. Taylor (New York, N.Y.: Routledge, 2009), p. 272.

[459]Nancy Snow, "Valuing Exchange of Persons in Public Diplomacy," in *Routledge Handbook of Public Diplomacy*, eds. Nancy Snow and Philip M. Taylor (New York, N.Y.: Routledge, 2009), pp. 234–237. For a study on U.S. Rhodes Scholars, see Thomas J. and Kathleen Schaeper, *Cowboys into Gentlemen: Rhodes Scholars, Oxford, and the Creation of an American Elite* (New York, N.Y.: Berghahn Books, 1998).

[460]United States Senate Committee on Homeland Security and Governmental Affairs, *A Reliance on Smart Power: Reforming the Public Diplomacy Bureaucracy, Hearing Before the Oversight of Government Management, the Federal Workforce, and the District of Columbia Subcommittee*, Washington, D.C., September 23, 2008, 110th Congress, Second Session (Washington, D.C.: United States Government Printing Office, 2009), pp. 4–5.

In fact, the IVLP has repeatedly been ranked "the most valuable tool of U.S. public diplomacy" by U.S. ambassadors.[461] Nicholas J. Cull, offering another positive and influential example, cited in particular the success of the German-Franco exchange programs that include a variety of activities and that have lastingly contributed to rapport and close ties between the two countries that had been at bitter enmity with each other for centuries.[462] Today, virtual exchanges stand alongside these more "classical" forms.[463] A case in point in this regard are Massively Multiplayer Online Role-Playing Games, such as Blizzard Entertainment's *World of Warcraft*, [464] which since its launch in 2004 has been connecting tens of millions of players from all over the world.[465]

The positive effect of exchanges for the conduct of international affairs can frequently be found in literature and is supported by countless empirical examples. At it, exchanges ideally constitute a win-win situation for both participating parties.[466] However, as Giles Scott-Smith has noted, "[i]t is impossible to predict exactly how an exchange experience will influence an individual, and the elements of chance and contingency are unavoidable."[467] Su accordingly noted with respect to students who had taken part in an exchange program to the United States, "There is no implication that these students must take pro-American attitudes when they graduate and return to their homelands."[468] The example of Egyptian writer Sayyid Qutb, who had spent time abroad on a scholarship in Colorado in the late 1940s and—being disgusted by what he had perceived as decadence and profligacy in the United States—returned home to become one of the founders of the Muslim Brotherhood, maybe the most prominent point in case.[469] Still, Su has aptly argued, despite the caveat mentioned above, that returnees from exchange programs in the United States "are really a force which must not be ignored in the process of promoting the U.S. cultures."[470]

---

[461] Sherry Mueller, "The Nexus of U.S. Public Diplomacy and Citizen Diplomacy," in *Routledge Handbook of Public Diplomacy*, eds. Nancy Snow and Philip M. Taylor (New York, N.Y.: Routledge), p. 104.

[462] Cull, "Public Diplomacy," pp. 40–42.

[463] Fisher, "Four Seasons in One Day," p. 253.

[464] Cull, "Public Diplomacy," p. 51.

[465] In early 2014, Blizzard announced that by then over 100 million accounts had been created with players hailing from 244 countries and territories; see Blizzard Entertainment, "World of Warcraft: Azeroth by the Numbers," January 28, 2014, online at: http://us.battle.net//wow/en/blog/12346804 (accessed July 14, 2015).

[466] Cull, "Public Diplomacy," p. 33.

[467] Scott-Smith, "Exchange Programs and Public Diplomacy," p. 52.

[468] Su, "Soft Power," p. 550.

[469] Cull, "Public Diplomacy," pp. 45–46. See also Scott-Smith, "Exchange Programs and Public Diplomacy," p. 52 and Peter L. Bergen, *The Longest War: The Enduring Conflict between America and al-Qaeda* (New York, N.Y.: Free Press, 2011), p. 22. Bergen refers to Qutb as "the Lenin of the jihadist movement;" Bergen, *The Longest War*, p. 349.

[470] Su, "Soft Power," p. 550.

Seeking to identify an indicator for empirical analysis, the number of foreign students in a given country has therefore been suggested.[471]

5. Finally, international broadcasting is identified by Cull as a further specific in his taxonomy of public diplomacy. It can be defined as "a complex combination of state-sponsored news, information and entertainment directed at a population outside the sponsoring state's boundaries."[472] Its roots can be traced back to World War II, when radio and newsreel gradually gained currency. Later, during the Cold War, television became the predominant medium and meanwhile—in the information age of the twenty-first century—online communication and broadcasting have continuously been replacing more traditional media.[473] The powers of information and broadcasting (in its broadest sense) have long been recognized. And while today more sophisticated and swifter instruments are at hand, earlier instruments with a comparable direction of impact can be found: Hohenstaufen Emperor Frederick II (r. 1220–1250), widely known for his learning and broad scientific interests, has thus spread circulars on his activities to other courts.[474] However, the practice of international broadcasting gathered pace especially through the rapid development in information and communication technology.[475] In the early twentieth century, many nation-states including Germany, the United Kingdom, and the United States thus initiated early efforts of radio broadcasting and subsequently—with technological advancement—intensified their activities.[476] An example of particular influence (and success) in this regard, is the British Broadcasting Corporation (BBC). In fact, in the view of Niall Ferguson, "it was the advent of wireless radio—and specifically the creation of the British Broadcasting Cooperation—that really ushered in the age of soft power in Nye's sense of the term."[477]

Taken together, Nicholas J. Cull's taxonomy and its five distinct categories offer a sensible operationalization of the highly interdisciplinary and broad concept of

---

[471]Ingrid d'Hooghe, *The Limits of China's Soft Power in Europe: Beijing's Public Diplomacy Puzzle* (The Hague: Netherlands Institute of International Relations Clingendael, 2010), p. 12.

[472]Monroe E. Price, Susan Haas, and Drew Margolin, "New Technologies and International Broadcasting: Reflections on Adaptations and Transformations," *The Annals of the American Academy of Political and Social Science*, Vol. 616, Public Diplomacy in a Changing World (2008), pp. 152–153.

[473]Lee Claire Seungeun, "China's International Broadcasting as a Soft Power Ma(r)ker: Its Market Formation and Audience Making," *ERCCT Online Paper Series*, EOPS No. 0027, November 2013, online at: http://www.ercct.uni-tuebingen.de/Files/ERCCT%20Online%20Paper%20Series/Young %20Scholar%20Workshop%202013/EOPS27,%20Lee%20Claire%20Seungeun,%20China's% 20International%20Broadcasting%20as%20a%20Soft%20Power%20Ma(r)ker%20Its%20Market %20Formation%20and%20Audience%20Making.pdf (accessed July 14, 2014), pp. 5–6.

[474]Cull, "Public Diplomacy," p. 34.

[475]See above for the influence of information and communication technologies on the conduct of international relations in general and (public) diplomacy in particular, Sects. 1.2 and 3.2.1.

[476]Nye, *Soft Power*, pp. 100–105.

[477]Niall Ferguson, *Colossus: The Price of America's Empire* (New York, N.Y.: Penguin Press, 2004), p. 20.

public diplomacy. In practice, to be sure, the different components are frequently housed in one government department and are conducted interconnectedly, ideally complementing and enhancing one another. Ben M. Cherrington, the first head of the newly created Division of Cultural Relations within the U.S. State Department, hence argued as early as 1939 in a list that in a way anticipated Cull's very taxonomy of public diplomacy,

> The new Division of Cultural Relations will direct the official international activities of the Department of State with respect to cultural relations. It will seek above all to coordinate the wide diversity of activities which are being carried out throughout the country. These activities will embrace the exchange of professors, teachers, and students; cooperation in the field of music, art, literature, and other intellectual activities; encouragement of the distribution of libraries of representative works of the United States and suitable translations of such works into other languages as well as from foreign languages to English; collaboration in the preparation for and participation by this government in international expositions, especially in the field of art; cooperation of this government in international radio broadcasts; and, in general, the dissemination abroad of the representative intellectual and cultural works of the United States.[478]

Consequently, taking a closer look at respective programs in the realm of public diplomacy provides resilient indicators when seeking to empirically examine an actor's soft power. More precisely, when assessing the instrument of public diplomacy, understood as a tool to wield soft power in international relations, empirical research thus should focus on the (1) the overall organization of an actor's public diplomacy apparatus, (2) personnel selected, both in respective positions of leadership as well as with respect to the overall size of staff, and (3) resources allotted and available to an actor's efforts in public diplomacy. Till Geiger has accordingly argued, "In contrast to more tangible forms of power, soft power is intangible and to some degree defies measurement except by proxies such as expenditure on public diplomacy."[479] Besides these "proxies," (4) particular programs or initiatives across the five respective categories identified by Nicholas J. Cull as well as an assessment as to their success or failure (especially with respect to Actor B) should be taken into account.

3.2.2 Personal Diplomacy

Corresponding with the soft power resource of personalities introduced above, personal diplomacy can be considered a second major set of instruments for the wielding of soft power.[480] Recognizing the growing importance of select individuals

---

[478]Ben M. Cherrington, "The Division of Cultural Relations," *Foreign Affairs*, Vol. 3, No. 1 (January 1939), pp. 136–137.

[479]Geiger, *"The Power Game*, Soft Power and the International Historian," pp. 86–87.

[480]The designation, i.e., *personal* diplomacy, is not to be understood as a reverse of *public* diplomacy (i.e., understood as *secret* diplomacy), but rather it emphasizes the particular importance of individuals and personal contact and exchange.

on the international stage and their power to set the agenda or promote certain causes, Andrew F. Cooper has coined the term "celebrity diplomacy."[481] As evidenced, for example, by the selection of Bono as well as Bill and Melinda Gates as *TIME Magazine's* Persons of the Year in 2005, the influence of celebrities as influential actors in diplomacy has in recent years been increasingly acknowledged.[482] Regarding celebrities' power, Cooper has noted, "Celebrities have the power to frame issues in a manner that attracts visibility and new channels of communication at the mass as well as the elite levels."[483] In today's world, argued Douglas Kellner, this variety of diplomacy "is growing in scope and perhaps significance."[484] Though involving a number of concerns as to actual influence, (democratic) representation, and other issues connected with "celebrity diplomacy," various examples come to mind in which individuals, due to their enhanced (international) status, have actively sought to shape the agenda or support a certain cause—both in the indirect form of reaching out to the public and in the direct form of appealing to political leaders. A recent example of the latter variety can be found in the visit of George Clooney and his wife Amal Alamuddin to German Chancellor Angela Merkel in early 2016 in order to discuss refugee issues.[485] As already argued above with respect to the soft power resource of personalities, attribution of what Cooper calls "celebrity diplomats"[486] to a certain country is frequently hardly possible when understanding the term in the narrow sense. However, lines at times are blurred between "celebrity diplomats" and "diplomat celebrities," that is, especially former statesmen or diplomats who include such influential individuals as U.S. Presidents Herbert Hoover, Jimmy Carter, or Bill Clinton, who after their tenure in the White House utilized their status in international relations to champion certain causes.[487] In the case of Jimmy Carter, for example, it has in fact frequently been argued that his decade-long work as ex-president—making him the longest-serving former U.S. President as of this writing—may very well have been more consequential than his 4 years in the Oval Office.[488] Another example in this

---

[481] Andrew F. Cooper, *Celebrity Diplomacy* (Boulder, Colo.: Paradigm Publishers, 2008).

[482] Cooper, *Celebrity Diplomacy*, p. 1. See also Alan Cowell, "Power of Celebrity at Work in Davos," *International Herald Tribune*, January 29-30, 2005, p. 1 & p. 4 and Lena Partzsch, *Die neue Macht von Individuen in der globalen Politik. Wandel durch Prominente, Philanthropen und Social Entrepreneurs* (Baden-Baden: Nomos, 2014).

[483] Cooper, *Celebrity Diplomacy*, p. 7.

[484] Douglas Kellner, "Celebrity Diplomacy, Spectacle and Barack Obama," *Celebrity Studies*, Vol. 1, No. 1 (March 2010), p. 121.

[485] Julie Vitkovskaya, "Merkel Meets Amal Clooney and Her Husband to Discuss Refugees," *The Washington Post*, February 12, 2016, online at: https://www.washingtonpost.com/news/world views/wp/2016/02/12/germanys-merkel-meets-amal-clooney-and-her-husband-to-discuss-refu gees/ (accessed June 14, 2016).

[486] Cooper, *Celebrity Diplomacy*, p. 4.

[487] Cooper, *Celebrity Diplomacy*, p. 5.

[488] John Dillon, "The Record-Setting Ex-Presidency of Jimmy Carter," *The Atlantic*, September 9, 2012, online at: http://www.theatlantic.com/politics/archive/2012/09/the-record-setting-ex-

regard (and combining many of the components of personal diplomacy to be elaborated upon in the following) is Winston Churchill's influence on European integration in the immediate post-war years, during which the former (and future) British Prime Minister did *not* officially represent the United Kingdom as its head of government, but nonetheless wielded considerable power. Marco Duranti elaborated on this issue in a recent study,

> He [Churchill] brought to the European unity movements a unique combination of attributes: the star power to hold the attention of the media, the rhetorical skills to generate public enthusiasm, and the diplomatic skills to build consensus, not to mention his considerable charisma and charm. [...]
>
> By no means could Churchill have achieved results of his own. Even so, it is hard to imagine that, without the catalyzing effect of his leadership provided, European integration would have attracted sufficient numbers of figures with the political muscle necessary to sway enough government officials and parliamentarians to the cause.[489]

The issue of attribution, of course, becomes more clear-cut with a second variety of personal diplomacy that shall be at the very center of this subunit: the influence of incumbent decision-makers on the soft power of their respective home country or entity they represent.

In the phrasing of Nicholas J. Cull (and partly borrowing his words), personal diplomacy can succinctly be defined as an actor's attempt to manage the international environment by visiting foreign decision-makers as well as public and engaging actively with them through means of joint appearances, speechmaking, or symbolic acts. As such, it is actively pursued, for example, by representatives of a nation-state or an international organization and is directed, at least in part, explicitly at the publics of other nations.[490] As indicated by the definition, different aspects of personal diplomacy, though interdependent at times, can be distinguished.

1. The instrument of foreign travels of political decision-makers and diplomats in general has long since been an important component in the conduct of international relations. However, foreign travels by heads of state or government saw particular increase in the late nineteenth and early twentieth century. Thus, the first foreign leader to visit the United States was Hawaiian King Kalakaua in 1874,[491] and the first foreign travel of a U.S. President took place on November

---

presidency-of-jimmy-carter/262143/ (accessed June 14, 2016). See also John Dumbrell, *The Carter Presidency: A Re-Evaluation* (Manchester: Manchester University Press, 1995), p. 16.

[489]Marco Duranti, *The Conservative Human Rights Revolution: European Identify, Transnational Politics, and the Origins of the European Convention* (New York, N.Y.: Oxford University Press, 2017), p. 97.

[490]Of course, foreign travels as well as other aspects of personal diplomacy may also reverberate onto domestic audiences back home.

[491]U.S. Department of State, "Visits by Foreign Leaders in 1874," *Office of the Historian*, online at: https://history.state.gov/departmenthistory/visits/1874 (accessed July 14, 2015).

1906 when Theodore Roosevelt visited Panama.[492] Over the course of the twentieth century, foreign travel had become a regular for heads of state as well as foreign ministers, and addressing foreign public through speeches grew to an important ingredient in diplomacy, not least due to decreasing costs in transportation and travel as well as growing capacities in (global) media coverage. As a consequence, foreign travels and state visits have become an integral part in the conduct of international relations today. Former British Secretary of State for Foreign and Commonwealth Affairs, Peter Lord Carrington, for example, has accordingly argued in his memoirs, "I believe that these days a Foreign Secretary must travel."[493] With respect to travels by U.S. Presidents, Jeffrey E. Cohen has found that foreign travels have not only increased sixfold since the 1950s but also developed qualitatively since

now presidents also routinely appear in public when visiting other nations. For instance, presidents now commonly hold joint press conferences and public announcements with the leader of the foreign nation, give interviews with foreign journalists, visit locations of local symbolic importance, and directly address the local citizenry.[494]

Besides this recent recognition of the increasing importance of travels among decision-makers, state visits, in this particular case by taking the example of the German Federal President, have in fact already been identified as an instrument of soft power.[495] At the same time, the duration of a foreign visit, as well as places visited by a national representative are regularly highly symbolic and hence closely monitored by both domestic and foreign observers. For example, when Bill Clinton visited the People's Republic of China for 9 days in 1998 without paying a visit to Japan, wary Japanese observers detected signs of a weakening bilateral relationship with Washington.[496]

That this variety of soft power instruments is not restricted to representatives of nation-states was exemplified by then-U.N. Secretary General Dag Hammarskjöld who practiced extensively what has become known as "travel diplomacy."[497] Other popular episodes highlighting its importance are manifold and include, for example,

---

[492]U.S. Department of State, "Presidential and Secretaries Travels Abroad: Presidents, Theodore Roosevelt," *Office of the Historian*, online at: https://history.state.gov/departmenthistory/travels/president/roosevelt-theodore (accessed July 14, 2015).

[493]Peter Lord Carrington, *Reflecting on Things Past: The Memoirs of Peter Lord Carrington* (New York, N.Y.: Harper & Row, 1988), p. 327.

[494]Jeffrey E. Cohen, "Presidential Attention Focusing in the Global Arena: The Impact of International Travel on Foreign Publics," *Presidential Studies Quarterly*, Vol. 46, No. 1 (March 2016), pp. 30–31.

[495]Lars C. Colschen, *Deutsche Außenpolitik* (Paderborn: Wilhelm Fink, 2010), pp. 70–71.

[496]John F. Mearsheimer, "The Future of the American Pacifier," *Foreign Affairs*, Vol. 80, No. 2 (September/October 2001), p. 50.

[497]Peter Wallensteen, "Dag Hammarskjöld's Diplomacy: Lessons Learned," in *Peace Diplomacy, Global Justice and International Agency: Rethinking Human Security and Ethics in the Spirit of Dag Hammarskjöld*, eds. Carsten Stahn and Henning Melber (Cambridge: Cambridge University Press, 2014), p. 381.

Henry Kissinger's famous "shuttle diplomacy" in the Middle East,[498] Konrad Adenauer's visit to France (including Paris and Reims) in July and Charles de Gaulle's return visit to the Federal Republic of Germany (including Bonn and Ludwigsburg) in September 1962, which included public addresses, state dinners, and receptions. With his public appearances and addresses—frequently delivered in German—de Gaulle hence won the hearts and minds of the German public through personal diplomacy.[499] His parting remarks delivered from the Bonn Rathaus on September 5, 1962, explicitly referencing French "hearts and minds," meanwhile rank among the classic tropes of German-French friendship,

> Wenn ich Sie so um mich herum versammelt sehe, wenn ich Ihre Kundgebungen höre, empfinde ich noch stärker als zuvor die Würdigung und das Vertrauen, das ich für Ihr großes Volk, jawohl—für das große deutsche Volk hege. Sie können versichert sein, dass in Frankreich, wo man beobachtet und verfolgt, was jetzt in Bonn geschieht, eine Welle der Freundschaft in den Geistern und den Herzen aufsteigt und um sich greift. Es lebe Bonn! Es lebe Deutschland! Es lebe die deutsch-französische Freundschaft.[500]

These reciprocal visits by Adenauer and de Gaulle not only had immense symbolic meaning but also brought about tangible political outcomes as they contributed to the tightening of relations between Bonn and Paris in general and anticipated the Élysée Treaty of 1963 in particular.[501] A further point in case is John F. Kennedy's extended trip through Europe in the summer of 1963, which took him to the Federal Republic of Germany, West Berlin, Ireland, the United Kingdom, Italy, and Vatican City. It has been argued that particularly his trip to the Federal Republic "was undertaken in direct response to de Gaulle's challenge to the United States in January of that year in form of vetoing Britain's membership of the EEC and of concluding the Franco-German treaty."[502] In this sense, personal diplomacy can indeed be regarded as a crucial instrument in furthering national interests. Today, Kennedy's address at Berlin's Rudolph-Wilde-Platz[503] looms large for U.S.-German

---

[498] Amos Perlmutter, "Crisis Management: Kissinger's Middle East Negotiations (October 1973-June 1974)," *International Studies Quarterly*, Vol. 19, No. 3 (September 1975), pp. 316–343.

[499] Armin Fuhrer and Norman Haß, *Eine Freundschaft für Europa: Der lange Weg zum Élysée-Vertrag* (München: Olzog Verlag, 2013), p. 282.

[500] Charles de Gaulle, "Ansprache von General de Gaulle an die Bevölkerung auf dem Marktplatz in Bonn am 5. September 1962," *Informationsblätter der Französischen Botschaft Bonn-Bad Godesberg: Heft Nr. 264*, 15. September 1962, p. 12.

[501] William R. Nester, *De Gaulle's Legacy: The Art of Power in France's Fifth Republic* (New York, N.Y.: Palgrave Macmillan, 2014), pp. 55–56.

[502] Geir Lundestad, *The United States and Western Europe since 1945: From "Empire" by Invitation to Transatlantic Drift* (Oxford: Oxford University Press, 2003), p. 111.

[503] John F. Kennedy, "Remarks in the Rudolph Wilde Platz, Berlin," West Berlin, June 26, 1963, in *Public Papers of the Presidents of the United States: John F. Kennedy, 1963, Containing the Public Messages, Speeches, and Statements of the President, January 1 to November 22, 1963* (Washington, D.C.: United States Government Printing Office, 1964), pp. 524–525. The square in front of the Rathaus Schöneberg on which Kennedy delivered his remarks on June 26, 1963, has been renamed to its present designation, John-F.-Kennedy-Platz, 8 days after the president's assassination in November 1963.

relations—which had been strained after the building of the Berlin Wall in 1961—and crucially contributed to the cementation of "German Atlanticism."[504] Further famous and consequential examples include Anwar al-Sadat's 1977 trip to Jerusalem during which the Egyptian President "[spoke] directly to the people of Israel and over the heads of Israel's leaders to help mobilize efforts for a change in the direction of peace negotiations,"[505] which ultimately bore fruits with the signing of the Camp David Accords in September 1978.[506] Many further examples, right up to the more recent travel of Barack Obama to Havana in March 2016 may be added to the list.[507]

2. Frequently, foreign visits are not only directed at visiting and conferring with foreign decision-makers on a personal basis but are also regularly accompanied by speeches and public statements, as the examples referred to above have already illustrated. Delivering speeches, making (prepared or spontaneous) remarks, or appearing at (joint) press conferences can therefore be regarded as a further important ingredient of personal diplomacy. Besides these more traditional varieties of speechmaking, social media services including Facebook and Twitter provide further platforms for (political) individuals to address foreign and domestic audiences alike by means of personal diplomacy.

In fact, rhetoric, defined by Aristotle "as the faculty of observing in any given case the available means of persuasion,"[508] has long been considered a powerful tool to "win the hearts and minds" of others and not least convince them of a certain action. Thus, the ancient Greeks were firm believers in the power of the spoken word in the age of the polis and even knew a distinct goddess for (rhetorical) persuasion and seduction, Peitho.[509] In Homer's *Iliad*, among the eldest and arguably most influential works of Western literature, the figure of Nestor of Gerenia provides a famous archetype of this power of oratory. Throughout Homer's epic poem, Nestor, King of Pylos, is thus depicted as a powerful orator, whose eloquence is capable even to assuage the quarreling Agamemnon and Achilles in the work's opening book. In Alexander Pope's classical, early eighteenth-century rendering,

---

[504]Jeffrey Vanke, "Consensus for Integration: Public Opinion and European Integration in the Federal Republic, 1945-1966," in Die Bundesrepublik Deutschland und die europäische Einigung 1949-2000: Politische Akteure, gesellschaftliche Kräfte und internationale Erfahrungen, eds. Mareike König und Matthias Schulz (Stuttgart: Franz Steiner Verlag, 2004), p. 338.

[505]Pratkanis, "Public Diplomacy in International Conflicts," p. 113.

[506]William B. Quandt, *Camp David: Peacemaking and Politics* (Washington, D.C.: The Brooking Institutions, 1986).

[507]Damien Cave, "With Obama Visit to Cuba, Old Battle Lines Fade," *The New York Times*, March 26, 2016, online at: http://www.nytimes.com/2016/03/27/world/americas/with-obama-visit-to-cuba-old-battle-lines-fade.html (accessed June 14, 2016).

[508]Aristotle, *The Art of Rhetoric* (London: Harper Press, 2012), p. 8 (Aristot. Rh. I, 2).

[509]Jean-Pierre Vernant, *Die Entstehung des griechischen Denkens* (Frankfurt am Main: Suhrkamp, 1982), p. 44. For the genealogy and role of Peitho, see Hesiod, *Theogonie/Werke und Tage*, Edited and Translated by Albert von Schirnding, With an Introduction and a Register by Ernst Günther Schmidt (München: Artemis & Winkler, 1991), pp. 31–33 & p. 89 (Hes. Th. 337-366 & Hes. WD 69-75).

> To calm their passions with the words of age,
> Slow from his seat arose the Pylian sage,
> Experience'd Nestor, in persuasion skill'd,
> Words sweet as honey from his lips distill'd.[510]

A few centuries later, during the classical period of ancient Greece, Plato extensively discussed the potency of oratory in his Socratic dialogue *Gorgias*, depicting it as an eminently powerful tool of persuasion and manipulation.[511] In Roman times, influential writers who have addressed rhetoric and its powers include, among others, Cicero (e.g., *De Inventione*, *De Oratore*, *Orator*, and *Partitiones Oratoriae*), Quintilian (*Institutio Oratoria*), as well as Tacitus. The latter, to elaborate on just one example in greater detail, thus famously wrote in his *Dialogus de Oratoribus*, one of the author's shorter works upon the precise dating of which much ink has been spilled,

> If practical advantage is to be the rule of all we think and all we do, can there be any safer line to take than the practice of an art which gives you an ever ready weapon with which to protect your friends, to succour those to whom you are a stranger, to bring deliverance to persons in jeopardy, and even to strike fear and terror into the hearts of malignant foes— while you yourself have no anxiety, entrenched as you are behind a rampart of inalienable authority and power? While things are going well with you, it is in the refuge it affords to others, and in the protection it gives them, that its efficacy and usefulness are most in evidence; but when danger hurtles round your own head, then surely no sword or buckler in the press of arms gives stouter support than does eloquence to him who is imperilled by a prosecution; for it is a sure defence and a weapon of attack withal, that enables you with equal ease to act on the defensive or to advance to the assault, whether in the law courts, or in the senate house, or in the Emperor's cabinet council.[512]

Likewise, Tacitus' contemporary Plutarch repeatedly stressed the potency of eloquence in his *Parallel Lives*.[513] In late antiquity, Sextus Aurelius Victor, presumably born in the Roman province Africa around AD 320, reaffirmed his pre-

---

[510]Homer, *The Iliad*, Translated by Alexander Pope (London: W. Suttaby and C. Corral, 1806), p. 38 (Hom. Il. I, 246-284)

[511]Platon, "Gorgias," in *Werke in acht Bänden: Zweiter Band*, Edited by Gunther Eigler, Redacted by Heinz Hofmann, Translated by Friedrich Schleiermacher (Darmstadt: Wissenschaftliche Buchgesellschaft, 2011), pp. 296–503; esp. pp. 297–301 & pp. 325–333 (Plat. Gorg.).

[512]P. Cornelius Tacitus, *Agricola/Germania/Dialogus*, Translated by M. Hutton and W. Peterson, Revised by R. M. Ogilvie, E. H. Warmington, and M. Winterbottom, Loeb Classical Library 35 (Cambridge, Mass.: Harvard University Press, 1970), p. 241 (Tac. Dial. 5).

[513]Plutarch, *Fünf Doppelbiographien: 1. Teil, Alexandros und Caesar, Aristeides und Marcus Cato, Perikles und Fabius Maximus*, Translated by Konrat Ziegler and Walter Wuhrmann, Selected by Manfred Fuhrmann, With an Introduction and Notes by Konrat Ziegler (Zürich: Artemis & Winkler, 1994), pp. 497–499 & p. 553 (Plut. Comp. Aristid. Cat. 29 (2) & Plut. Per. 15); Plutarch, *Fünf Doppelbiographien: 2. Teil, Gaius Marcius und Alkibiades, Demosthenes und Cicero, Anhang*, Translated by Konrat Ziegler and Walter Wuhrmann, Selected by Manfred Fuhrmann, With an Introduction and Notes by Konrat Ziegler (Zürich: Artemis & Winkler, 1994), p. 801, p. 901, pp. 927–928, & p. 985 (Plut. Alc. 10; Plut. Dem. 5; & 18; Plut. Cic. 12 & 13).

decessors' verdicts in his *Liber de Caesaribus*.[514] In early modern times, it was Thomas Hobbes who famously argued in his *Leviathan*, "Eloquence is power; because it is seeming Prudence."[515] And none other than Winston Churchill, to provide a final and more recent example, confided to his friend and political mentor Bourke Cockran in a letter, "I know that there are few more fascinating experiences than to watch a great mass of people under the wand of the magician. There is no gift—so rare or so precious as the gift of oratory—so difficult to define or impossible to acquire."[516]

Besides tying rhetoric to power, it has also been frequently discussed with respect to charisma, which often goes hand in hand with supreme rhetorical skill. Max Weber has accordingly spoken of the "charisma of rhetoric."[517] As already noted above, "[t]he ability to articulate a compelling vision of a bright future is the sine qua non of charisma,"[518] which most notably occurs through speeches. Pericles, one of the few historical characters explicitly attributed with charisma by Weber, for example, drew his powers in large part through his persuasive rhetoric which has been brought unto us through the works of Thucydides and others.[519] Another, more recent example in this regard already referred to above is that of Winston Churchill and his influence on European integration, which was crucially founded on his charisma as well as his oratory, especially his famous "United States of Europe" speech delivered in Zurich on September 19, 1946, which by his own admission decisively influenced U.S. Secretary of State George Marshall to instigate the European Recovery Program.[520]

As a component of personal diplomacy, speeches are usually directed at the local population of the state visited and can serve as more general expressions of solidarity and support with another country. Beyond that, speeches to foreign audiences may also serve the purpose of presenting and advocating a particular policy in order to achieve support for it. (Think, e.g., Helmut Schmidt's pivotal address advocating the dual-track decision before the International Institute for Strategic Studies in 1977.) Respective heads of state and/or government and high-ranking officials play a crucial role in this regard. With respect to the U.S. presidency, former president Theodore Roosevelt famously coined the term of the "bully pulpit," metaphorically

---

[514]S. Aurelius Victor, *Die Römischen Kaiser: Liber de Caesaribus*, Edited, Translated, and Annotated by Kirsten Groß-Albenhausen and Manfred Fuhrmann (Zürich/Düsseldorf: Artemis & Winkler, 1997), pp. 141–143 (Aur. Vict. De Caes. 42, 1-5).

[515]Thomas Hobbes, *Leviathan*, With an Essay by the Late W. G. Pogson Smith (Oxford: Clarendon Press, 1909), p. 67.

[516]Quoted in Martin Gilbert, *Churchill and America* (New York, N.Y.: Free Press, 2005), p. 26.

[517]Weber, *Economy and Society*, p. 1129

[518]Emrich, Brower, Feldman, and Garland, "Images in Words," p. 527.

[519]Peter Spahn, "Perikles: Charisma und Demokratie," in *Virtuosen der Macht: Herrschaft und Charisma von Perikles bis Mao*, ed. Wilfried Nippel (C. H. Beck: München, 2000), p. 23 & p. 37.

[520]Gilbert, *Churchill and America*, p. 26 & pp. 380–381.

describing the prominent position of the president to set and influence the agenda through acts of speechmaking.[521] The U.S. President—as well as other heads of state and government around the world—accordingly is in a position to advocate certain policies to domestic and foreign public alike. It is in this vein that Martha Joynt Kumar argued, "The heart of the advocacy operation is the president himself and the speeches and remarks he regularly gives."[522] Joseph Nye likewise identified an individual's capability to convey a policy vision as well as their ability to communicate among the qualities required to exercise soft power.[523] With particular regard to the United States, for example, scholarship has thus demonstrated "the considerable role presidential rhetoric plays in constructing, shaping, and reinforcing America's image at home and abroad."[524] All in all, rhetoric has been a topic of extensive writing since antiquity and, not least in the wake of recent developments in information and communication technologies, speechmaking plays a prominent part in wielding soft power through personal diplomacy today.

3. Frequently, foreign travels by decision-makers exceed state visits as well as speechmaking and include also symbolic acts, that is, actions that epitomize a certain policy or program and/or attract broad transnational or even global attention. Such acts may—be they planned or spontaneous—often become emblematic for the relation of states or peoples and include wreath-laying ceremonies, the visiting of memorial sites, public displays of cordial friendships between representatives of states, amicable gestures, and comparable acts. Again, various historical examples come to mind: Willy Brandt's Warsaw Genuflection in 1970, Helmut Kohl's and François Mitterrand's joint visit of the Verdun battlefield in 1984, or again more recent, the historic handshake between Barack Obama and Raul Castro as well as the hug between the U.S. President and 79-year old survivor of the atomic bombing of Hiroshima Shigeaki Mori in May 2016.[525] As with speechmaking, these acts by state representatives exceed the

---

[521]Michael Patrick Cullinane, "A (Near) Great President: Theodore Roosevelt as the First Modern President," in *Perspectives on Presidential Leadership: An International View of the White House*, eds. Michael Patrick Cullinane and Clare Frances Elliott (New York, N.Y.: Routledge, 2014), pp. 80–81.

[522]Martha Joynt Kumar, "Managing the News," in *The Polarized Presidency of George W. Bush*, eds. George C. Edwards III and Desmond S. King (Oxford: Oxford University Press, 2007), p. 362.

[523]Nye, "Transformational Leadership and U.S. Grand Strategy," pp. 143–144.

[524]Rico Neuman and Kevin Coe, "The Rhetoric in the Modern Presidency: A Quantitative Analysis," in *The Rhetoric of American Exceptionalism: Critical Essays*, eds. Jason A. Edwards and David Weiss (Jefferson, N.C.: McFarland, 2011), p. 13.

[525]On the four abovementioned episodes see, for example, Michael Wolffsohn and Thomas Brechenmacher, *Denkmalsturz? Brandts Kniefall* (München: Olzog, 2005); Christoph Schneider, *Der Warschauer Kniefall: Ritual, Ereignis und Erzählung* (Konstanz: UVK-Verlag 2006); Lars Rosumek, *Die Kanzler und die Medien: Acht Porträts von Adenauer bis Merkel* (Frankfurt am Main: Campus Verlag, 2007), p. 173; Karen DeYoung and Nick Miroff, "Obama, Castro to Talk on Sidelines of Summit," *The Washington Post*, April 10, 2015, online at: https://www.washingtonpost.com/world/obama-raul-castro-speak-by-phone-before-heading-to-panama-summit/2015/04/10/2da5c2f6-de22-11e4-b6d7-b9bc8acf16f7_story.html (accessed June 14, 2016); and Jonathan Soble, "Hiroshima Survivor Cries, and Obama Gives Him a Hug," *The New York Times*,

communication of specific political programs or intentions toward their foreign counterparts. Particularly with growing media coverage in the twentieth and twenty-first centuries, symbolic acts, which can look back on a century-old tradition, can be disseminated more broadly and rapidly than ever before and have thus continuously been gaining in importance.

4. Finally, the establishment and cultivation of elite networks can be considered a fourth variety of personal diplomacy and consequently an instrument of wielding soft power. With respect to the influence of such networks on an actor's soft power, Joseph Nye has argued that "[e]lite relations and networks often play an important role."[526] By focusing specifically upon (present day or future) decision-makers, this variety can be attributed to the direct form of wielding soft power, leapfrogging the general public and instead operating directly between elites. Elites, defined as "groups of individuals whose hold on power, positions, and potential resources provide them with opportunities for influence that enable them to play a decisive role in shaping policy, economics, and culture,"[527] thus have rightly been recognized as being of paramount influence in bilateral relations. With respect to the importance of elites in the wielding of soft power, Su Changhe accordingly acknowledged that "[t]he production of soft power is also highly related to opinion leaders."[528] Felix Philipp Lutz likewise recognized the broad variety of contexts in which elites may wield influence in bilateral relations, including political parties, foundations, think tanks, commissions, and chambers of commerce.[529]

Concerning empirical examples of elite networks actively promoted in order to lastingly improve relations, Inderjeet Parmar has elaborated upon the role of Henry Kissinger's Harvard Seminar as well as the Salzburg Seminar on American Studies for transatlantic relations during the Cold War.[530] In his study, Parmar argued that recognizing "European envy and resentment of American power and wealth, as well as ignorance or misunderstanding of the new superpower's society, culture and politics," the originators of said programs focused on

cultural or public diplomacy specifically targeted at European elites to persuade them that the USA was a force for good in the world, defending freedom and fighting tyranny; that its culture was deep and not shallow, that its material wealth was not alone the obsession of its culture, that it had an abiding and serious interest in abstract problems and ideas—in art,

May 27, 2016, online at: http://www.nytimes.com/2016/05/28/world/asia/hiroshima-obama-visit-shigeaki-mori.html (accessed June 14, 2016).

[526]Nye, *The Future of Power*, p. 94.

[527]Lutz, "Transatlantic Networks," p. 445.

[528]Su, "Soft Power," p. 549.

[529]Lutz, "Transatlantic Networks," p. 446.

[530]Inderjeet Parmar, "Challenging Elite Anti-Americanism in the Cold War: American Foundations, Kissinger's Harvard Seminar and the Salzburg Seminar in American Studies," in *Soft Power and US Foreign Policy: Theoretical, Historical and Contemporary Perspectives*, eds. Inderjeet Parmar and Michael Cox (Abingdon: Routledge, 2010), pp. 108–120.

music, and philosophy. In short, the aim was to show that US power was not the naked expression of a dangerously shallow society, a volatile political system prone to witch-hunts led by demagogues or a hollow political elite. They wanted to promote the image of a national leadership that was cultured, sophisticated, educated, serious, rational, sober, reflective and thoughtful. It was a leadership that could be trusted to use its power wisely in the interest of the world system, not purely in its own narrow national interest.[531]

The Harvard Seminar counts among its alumni "such leaders as Japan's Yasuhiro Nakasone (1953), France's Giscard d'Estaing (1954), and Malaysia's Mahathir Mohammed (1968)."[532] Consequently, both seminars "created enduring nuclei of scholars and other opinion-formers, networked with American institutions and faculty, and with each other, functioning effectively long after the short Seminars were over."[533] A further example in this regard, operating in German-American relations, is constituted by the Atlantik-Brücke. Established in 1952, the informal network has proven highly influential in fostering German-American relations, albeit its operating principles and hence also its successes (or failures) are quite difficult to assess.[534] Besides the relations between individual decision-makers and the general public as well as among decision-makers themselves, already referred to above, the existence, actions, and effectiveness of such networks ought to be taken into account when assessing the significance of soft power in any given relationship.

In sum, the addition of personal diplomacy as a second set of soft power instruments besides public diplomacy adds a further perspective that—as history has shown—has been a potent force indeed and consequently deserves particular attention when empirically assessing instruments of soft power. While its signifi-cance is widely shared among decision-makers, the tangible effects of foreign travels are frequently hard to measure. Accused of having traveled too much during his time as Secretary of the British Foreign and Commonwealth Office (1979–1982), Peter Lord Carrington hence argued,

> If anybody thinks I travelled too much, some journeys unnecessary, I doubt if he has been Foreign Secretary. I believe that I travelled, on the whole, to good effect: but good effect which could seldom be measured and will never be exactly recorded. Mood, impression and personal influence can be neither quantified nor proved.[535]

Despite these intricacies, not incomparable to the corresponding soft power resource of personalities, certain indicators can be deduced in order to provide an operationalization making the instrument of personal diplomacy more accessible for empirical analyses. Research should thus take into account (1) the number of times decision-makers and representatives of Actor A traveled abroad, particularly to meet with elites and the public of Actor B, as well as the duration and quality of these

---

[531]Parmar, "Challenging Elite Anti-Americanism in the Cold War," p. 109.

[532]Parmar, "Challenging Elite Anti-Americanism in the Cold War," p. 114.

[533]Parmar, "Challenging Elite Anti-Americanism in the Cold War," p. 116.

[534]Ludger Kühnhardt, *Atlantik-Brücke: Fünfzig Jahre deutsch-amerikanische Partnerschaft* (Berlin: Propyläen, 2002), pp. 347–348.

[535]Carrington, *Reflecting on Things Past*, p. 328.

stays, (2) influential speeches delivered or remarks made during those visits, as well as (3) symbolic acts performed abroad or together with recipient decision-makers. Finally, (4) the existence and influence of elite networks on bilateral relations between respective actors under consideration should be included.

Taken together, the two sets of soft power instruments of public diplomacy (including the subcategories of listening, advocacy, cultural diplomacy, exchange diplomacy, and international broadcasting) as well as personal diplomacy (including the components of foreign travels, speechmaking, symbolic acts, and elite networks), offer resilient criteria for an empirical analysis of the wielding of soft power. However, these aspects alone tell us little about the other side of the soft power relationship as well as the ultimate success or failure of its wielding, something to which we shall turn in the following at greater length.

3.3 Subunit III: Reception

Having elaborated on the first two soft power subunits (i.e., resources and instruments), we shall now turn to the second major column of Fig. 3.1. Hence, the third soft power subunit shall be introduced: the subunit of reception. In the following, therefore, Actor B's perception of Actor A's soft power resources or instruments shall occupy center stage.

As argued above, soft power, as one of its key instruments public diplomacy, is best understood as a two-way street.[536] Thus, particularly when compared to the wielding of hard power, soft power is marked by considerable reciprocity between actors involved since both the agent and the target of soft power projection play a crucial role in its creation and ultimate success or failure.[537] Joseph Nye in this regard noted that "soft power is a relationship of attraction that depends on the eyes of the beholders."[538] Therefore, employing soft power tends to be less unilateral than the recourse to hard power measures and positive reception, consequently, is highly significant for the creation of desired outcomes through soft power.[539] For this reason, any successful wielding of soft power has to take into account the respective characteristics of the target group.[540] Soft power, as has been argued above in more detail, hence is a particularly relational form of power that depends heavily on the

---

[536]Armstrong, "Operationalizing Public Diplomacy," p. 68; hence the two-way arrow in the illustration above.

[537]Nye, *The Future of Power*, p. 92. See also Nye, "Notes for a Soft-Power Research Agenda," p. 169.

[538]Nye, "The Future of Soft Power in US Foreign Policy," p. 4. In his earlier writings, however, Nye may not have been as explicit regarding a *relational* understanding of soft power; Lock, "Soft Power and Strategy," pp. 34–37.

[539]Nye, "The Decline of America's Soft Power," p. 20; Nye, "Notes for a Soft-Power Research Agenda," p. 169.

[540]Auer, Srugies, and Löffelholz, "Schlüsselbegriffe der internationalen Diskussion," p. 41.

respective target and context.[541] William P. Kiehl, with respect to public diplomacy, hence argued that "it is all about *context* and *relationships*."[542] With particular respect to soft power, Artem Patalakh has likewise aptly noted "that taking into account the distinctive features of the recipient is indispensable in case studies of the applicant's soft power strategy."[543]

The centrality of perception in international relations is not only frequently emphasized by scholars but shared by practitioners and political decision-makers as well. The U.S. State Department accordingly noted,

> In an age of instant global communication, public perceptions of U.S. policies and values have a significant impact on the conduct of American foreign policy. International relations are no longer defined primarily by policies and ideologies, but by perceptions of culture, traditions, values, and beliefs.[544]

Reception, in this sense, has rightly been called "[t]he other side of the communication coin"[545] or in fact its "starting point."[546] Matthew C. Armstrong has even asserted, "In the 21st century, perceptions matter more than facts."[547]

Before outlining the mechanism and significance of the third soft power subunit, however, it is important to bear in mind that success or failure in the wielding of soft power not only is in the eyes of the beholder but may also be the subject of misperceptions. It is in this vein that Julius Heisbourg has opined, "The beholders' own cultural traits will inevitably colour their perceptions."[548] Ali S. Wyne likewise argued, "Perceptions are based not only on information, but also on falsehoods, distortions, your own biases, and herd behavior. Perceptual power is the most important form of power."[549] Todd Hall, to offer a further example, in the same way noted that it may not always be the case that "the message being sent is the same as that being received."[550] In sum, as Peter van Ham aptly put in a nutshell, "It's not what you *say*, but what others *hear*, that is important!"[551]

Despite these intricacies, or rather because of them, what is called the subunit of reception within the proposed taxonomy of soft power is of particular importance.

---

[541]Blanchard and Lu, "Thinking Hard about Soft Power," p. 571.

[542]William P. Kiehl, "The Case for Localized Public Diplomacy," in *Routledge Handbook of Public Diplomacy*, eds. Nancy Snow and Philip M. Taylor (New York, N.Y.: Routledge, 2009), p. 213.

[543]Patalakh, "Assessment of Soft Power Strategies," p. 89.

[544]U.S. Department of State, "FY 2008 Budget in Brief," *Bureau of Budget Management*, February 5, 2007, online at: http://www.state.gov/s/d/rm/rls/bib/2008/html/79739.htm (accessed September 30, 2015).

[545]Zaharna, *The Cultural Awakening in Public Diplomacy*, p. 35.

[546]Melissen, "The New Public Diplomacy," p. 7.

[547]Armstrong, "Operationalizing Public Diplomacy," p. 63.

[548]Heisbourg, "American Hegemony," p. 7.

[549]Wyne, "Public Opinion and Power," p. 47.

[550]Hall, "An Unclear Attraction," p. 200.

[551]van Ham, "Power, Public Diplomacy, and the *Pax Americana*," p. 61; van Ham's emphasis.

Within this subunit, as depicted in Fig. 3.1, three ideal typical varieties regarding the perception on part of Actor B are conceivable: attraction, apathy, or repulsion.

1. A certain soft power instrument applied by Actor A in order to wield soft power may thus be favorably perceived by Actor B, resulting in attraction. (In case of the city-upon a-hill effect, i.e., in the passive form of soft power, resources themselves may create attraction.) As already argued above, the notion of attraction has become central in the soft power discourse.[552] Attraction on part of the "target" has accordingly been described as "the quintessential soft power feature"[553] and Craig Hayden even noted that "attraction is clearly the archetypical soft power behavior."[554] Consequently, it deserves particular attention within the third soft power subunit.

The centrality of attraction within the soft power discourse is not least reflected by its repeated occurrence in the very definition of soft power. As already mentioned, Joseph Nye defined soft power as "the ability to get what you want through *attraction* rather than coercion or payments"[555] and he goes on, "If I am persuaded to go along with your purpose, without any explicit threat or exchange taking place—in short, if my behavior is determined by an observable but intangible *attraction*—soft power is at work."[556] Hence, creating attraction is highly significant for the achievement of desired outcomes through soft power.[557] As a consequence, the role of attraction in the context of soft power has been compared to the paramount influence of Adam Smith's "invisible hand" ruling the market.[558] However, despite its attested centrality in the context of soft power, literature on the topic of attraction in world politics is rather few and far between and research still proves deficient.[559] The concept of attraction, though vital, thus still remains contested today. Joseph Nye himself noted in this regard,

> Attraction is more complex than it first appears. It can refer to drawing attention—whether positive or negative—as well as creating alluring or positive magnetic effects. Like magnetism or gravitational pull, attention may be welcome or unwelcome, depending on the context.[560]

---

[552]Edward Lock, "Soft Power and Strategy: Developing a 'Strategic' Concept of Power," in *Soft Power and US Foreign Policy: Theoretical, Historical and Contemporary Perspectives*, eds. Inderjeet Parmar and Michael Cox (Abingdon: Routledge, 2010), p. 38.

[553]Ty Solomon, "The Affective Underpinnings of Soft Power," *European Journal of International Relations*, Vol. 20, No. 3 (2014), p. 736.

[554]Hayden, *The Rhetoric of Soft Power*, p. 29.

[555]Nye, *Soft Power*, p. x; emphasis added.

[556]Nye, *Soft Power*, p. 7; emphasis added.

[557]Nye, "The Decline of America's Soft Power," p. 20.

[558]Nye, *Soft Power*, p. 7.

[559]Mattern, "Why 'Soft Power' Isn't So Soft," pp. 585 & p. 591.

[560]Nye, *The Future of Power*, pp. 91–92.

Having established the important role as well as the complexity of attraction, Nye asks, "What generates positive attraction?"[561] Referencing the work of Alexander Vuving, he identifies "three clusters of qualities of the agent and action that are central to attraction: benignity, competence, and beauty (charisma)," and he elaborates that whereas *benignity* is a mode of relating to others and results in being perceived as exuding "sympathy, trust, credibility, and acquiescence," displaying *competence* in doing things results in "admiration, respect, and emulation," and, finally, *charisma* "is an aspect of an agent's relation to ideals, values, and vision, and it tends to produce inspiration and adherence."[562]

Additionally, Nye emphasized the central role of credibility for the creation of attraction in world politics and hence noted that political entities compete in their quest for credibility today more than ever before.[563] Other scholars agree to the centrality of credibility for the creation of soft power and attraction.[564] Just as credibility is central for deterrence through hard power, as Giles Scott-Smith has aptly argued, credibility is likewise important for the wielding of soft power and public diplomacy.[565] Nicholas J. Cull likewise asserted that "the effectiveness of each form of public diplomacy hinges on credibility"[566] and Philip M. Taylor even claimed that credibility "is the single most important word in the lexicon of successful influence activities."[567] Robert H. Gass and John S. Seiter, likewise recognizing its importance for successful public diplomacy, identified three dimensions of credibility: expertise, trustworthiness, and goodwill.[568] In this understanding, expertise requires that an actor "must be seen as knowledgeable about the issue at hand, competent in dealing with the issue, and capable of making the best decision on that issue."[569] Trustworthiness assumes that two actors in world politics trust each other

---

[561]Nye, *The Future of Power*, p. 92.

[562]Nye, *The Future of Power*, p. 92; with reference to Vuving, "How Soft Power Works."

[563]Nye, "Public Diplomacy and Soft Power," p. 100. See also Nye, "Responding to My Critics and Concluding Thoughts," p. 223 and Nye, "Hard, Soft, and Smart Power," p. 570.

[564]See, for example, Camelia Elena Ratiu, *EU Soft Power at Its Best: Zur Leistungsfähigkeit der Europäischen Union als Demokratieförderer in Transformationsstaaten, Eine vergleichende Analyse der EU-Demokratieförderungspolitik in Slowenien, Kroatien und Serbien* (Hamburg: Verlag Dr. Kovac, 2011), p. 81. For a recent study on the significance of credibility in international affairs, see Sergey Smolnikov, *Great Power Conduct and Credibility in World Politics* (Cham: Palgrave Macmillan 2018).

[565]Scott-Smith, "Soft Power in an Era of US Decline," p. 165 & p. 167.

[566]Cull, "Public Diplomacy," p. 34.

[567]Philip M. Taylor, "Public Diplomacy and the Information War on Terror," in *Soft Power and US Foreign Policy: Theoretical, Historical and Contemporary Perspectives*, eds. Inderjeet Parmar and Michael Cox (Abingdon: Routledge, 2010), p. 162.

[568]Robert H. Gass and John S. Seiter, "Credibility and Public Diplomacy," in *Routledge Handbook of Public Diplomacy*, eds. Nancy Snow and Philip M. Taylor (New York, N.Y.: Routledge, 2009), pp. 158–160.

[569]Gass and Seiter, "Credibility and Public Diplomacy," p. 158.

when interacting or negotiating. Trust, therefore, "is vital for actors on the world stage."[570] This dimension, as underlined by the empirical evidence supplied by Gass and Seiter, is highly dependent on the individuals representing respective actors in world politics. Hence, this dimension of credibility corresponds with the soft power resource of personalities introduced above and not least with the soft power instrument of personal diplomacy. However, as Gass and Seiter have argued, at times a nation may actually benefit of its leader being not trusted abroad since Kim Jong Il's or Mahmoud Ahmadinejad's assertive statements and martial rhetoric may have actually furthered their course.[571] The same may be said about President Richard Nixon's "Madman Theory," devised in order to make his North Vietnamese counterparts think he would stop at nothing—including using nuclear weapons—to defeat communism and end the Vietnam War.[572] Finally, Gass and Seiter identified goodwill as a third dimension of credibility, understood as "convey[ing] respect for others and a genuine interest in their well-being"—exemplified for instance by the aid provided by the United States to Indonesia after the 2004 tsunami.[573] Rather than acting out of self-interest or in a hypocritical way, governments therefore may foster their credibility by acting (or at least by being *perceived* as acting) out of motives of goodwill toward others. Nye himself has identified this nexus when he noted, "Domestic or foreign policies that appear to be hypocritical, arrogant, indifferent to the opinion of others, or based on a narrow approach to national interests can undermine soft power."[574]

However, as Gass and Seiter have aptly asserted, the creation of credibility is far from stable but rather subject to changes over time. They therefore hold that, "[l]ike a bull or a bear market, credibility comes and goes. Popular leaders cannot rest on their laurels."[575] Furthermore, Gass and Seiter asserted that credibility is not only volatile but also highly contextual and relational and "embodies a cultural component as

---

[570]Gass and Seiter, "Credibility and Public Diplomacy," p. 158.

[571]Gass and Seiter, "Credibility and Public Diplomacy," p. 159.

[572]H. R. Haldeman with Joseph DiMona, *The Ends of Power* (New York, N.Y.: Times Books, 1978), p. 98; Robert Dallek, *Nixon and Kissinger: Partners in Power* (London: Allen Lane, 2007), pp. 106–109.

[573]Gass and Seiter, "Credibility and Public Diplomacy," p. 159. In doing so, it may be argued, Washington followed in Beijing's footsteps, which had gained much political goodwill in Indonesia during the Asian Financial Crisis of 1998/1999 when it provided economic assistance to Jakarta and refrained from devaluating the yuan. This not only helped Indonesia stabilizing its ailing economy, but also contributed to a change of perceptions of China within Indonesia's political elite and subsequently fostered closer cooperation between both countries in several areas; Enrico Fels, "Dancing with the Dragon: Indonesia and Its Relations to a Rising China", in *Indonesia's Search for Democracy: Political, Economic, and Social Developments*, eds. Matthias Heise and Kathrin Rucktäschel (Baden-Baden: Nomos, 2013), p. 177 & p. 179.

[574]Nye, *Soft Power*, p. 14.

[575]Gass and Seiter, "Credibility and Public Diplomacy," p. 156.

well."[576] It is in this vein of contextuality that an initiative designed to increase one's soft power abroad may "fail, or worse, backfire [...] if it simply fails to resonate with a foreign public in the same way the planners hoped that it would."[577] Scholars such as Seong-Hun Yun and Jeong-Nam Kim have hence explicitly highlighted what they call the "relational perspective" of soft power.[578] Consequently, wielding soft power may at times not only fail to create attraction but instead may result on the contrary.[579] This observation leads to the other extreme in the soft power subunit of reception, that is, repulsion.

2. Repulsion, as opposed to the attributes of attraction mentioned above (i.e., benignity, competence, and beauty/charisma), occurs "[w]hen an actor or action is perceived as malign, manipulative, incompetent, or ugly."[580] Regarding this phenomenon, various examples come to mind. A prominent case in point in this regard may be the hosting of sport mega events, particularly the Olympic Games, considered "the ultimate sport mega-event."[581] In fact, such events are frequently counted among the most popular soft power instruments.[582] Their hosting has been described as a nation's "arrival on the world stage, and [it] bestows on the host the world's full attention for many days."[583] Interestingly, recent years have seen a dramatic increase in the hosting of such sport events (including Olympic Summer and Winter Games or FIFA World Cups) by the emerging BRICS states.[584] However, host countries of such events are under what might be called "close surveillance" for the time of the hosting, putting the country into the very spotlight of global media. Along with increased public and media attention toward the host country, coverage may at times even be particularly critical and grievances within the country may be highlighted to a global audience more intensively than usual. Hence, a country's soft power instrument may ultimately

---

[576]Gass and Seiter, "Credibility and Public Diplomacy," p. 157.

[577]Zaharna, *The Cultural Awakening in Public Diplomacy*, p. 20.

[578]Seong-Hun Yun and Jeong-Nam Kim, "Soft Power: From Ethnic Attraction to National Attraction in Sociological Globalism," *International Journal of Cultural Relations*, Vol. 32, No. 6 (November 2008), p. 567.

[579]Nye, *The Future of Power*, p. 92.

[580]Nye, *The Future of Power*, p. 92.

[581]David Black and Byron Peacock, "Sport and Diplomacy," in *The Oxford Handbook of Modern Diplomacy*, eds. Andrew F. Cooper, Jorge Heine, and Ramesh Thakur (Oxford: Oxford University Press, 2013), p. 716.

[582]See, for example, Blanchard and Lu, "Thinking Hard about Soft Power," p. 576 and Jonathan Grix and Donna Lee, "Soft Power, Sports Mega-Events and Emerging States: The Lure of the Politics of Attraction," *Global Society*, Vol. 27, No. 4 (2013), pp. 521–536.

[583]Håvard Mokleiv Nygård and Scott Gates, "Soft Power at Home and Abroad: Sport Diplomacy, Politics and Peace-Building," *International Area Studies Review*, Vol. 16, No. 3, (September 2013), p. 238.

[584]Framing mega sport events as including FIFA World Cups, Olympic Summer and Olympic Winter Games (i.e., arguably those sport events with the largest international audience and scope), six out of nine events under consideration have been hosted by BRICS states between 2008 and 2018.

fail to succeed and may even rebound in what might be called a boomerang effect.[585] Su accordingly pointed out, "When applied improperly, the soft use of power may stir antagonistic feelings in other countries, with severe backlash."[586] In reference to the world of physics, soft power may in these instances be considered a repulsive—rather than an attractive—force.

As argued, the reception of soft power resources or instruments as "beautiful" vs. "ugly" is highly depended, among other things, upon context and culture. In fact, the influence of respective cultures on both sides of the soft power equation has been observed by a number of scholars, including R. S. Zaharna.[587] Likewise, Nye asserted that "[w]hat produces attraction for one target may produce revulsion for another."[588] Eytan Gilboa similarly noted, "Soft power may be relevant to one society but exactly the opposite to another. American values, for example, may be appreciated in Australia and Canada but totally rejected in Iran or Saudi Arabia."[589] In the very same vein, Nye emphasized that "a given cultural artifact, such as a Hollywood movie that portrays liberated women acting independently, may produce positive attraction in Rio but revulsion in Riyadh."[590] Or, as Kostas Ifantis put it, "Cultural features may be attractive in Asia but repulsive in the Middle East."[591] Richard Pells offered a vivid empirical example in this regard when he argued that the popular U.S. television series *Dallas*, which ran from 1978 to 1991, has been received and interpreted differently across the globe due to "distinctive cultural assumptions and expectations of views in disparate parts of the world."[592]

Concurrently, different resources or instruments of soft power may at times evoke different—even contrary—receptions not only with respect to two different target countries but also within a single country. As Naren Chitty has observed, "A country's policies may be detested in a second country while its cultural exports may be found to be delectable."[593]

Finally, further complicating the matter, even one resource (e.g., culture) or instrument (e.g., cultural diplomacy) may by itself elicit different reactions in a given country at a given time. Recognizing this very conundrum, Edward D. Canham stated in his 1965 *The American Position in the World*, "The vulgarity

---

[585]Recent studies have elaborated upon the success of sport mega events in this regard. See, for example, Martin Müller, "After Sochi 2014: Costs and Impacts of Russia's Olympic Games," *Eurasian Geography and Economics*, Vol. 55, No. 6 (2014), pp. 628–655.

[586]Su, "Soft Power," p. 554.

[587]Zaharna, *The Cultural Awakening in Public Diplomacy*, p. 11.

[588]Nye, *The Future of Power*, p. 92.

[589]Gilboa, "Searching for a Theory of Public Diplomacy," p. 62.

[590]Nye, *The Future of Power*, pp. 92–93, see also Nye, *Soft Power*, pp. 12–13 & p. 52.

[591]Ifantis, "Soft Power," p. 445.

[592]Pells, "Double Crossings," p. 199.

[593]Naren Chitty, "Soft Power, Civic Virtue and World Politics (Section Overview)," in *The Routledge Handbook of Soft Power*, eds. Naren Chitty, Li Ji, Gary D. Rawnsley, and Craig Hayden (Abingdon: Routledge, 2017), p. 25.

of our mass culture is a very remarkable force in the world. I cannot quite decide whether it does us more good or more harm in the world."[594] And while he admitted that certain "aspects of our exported mass culture are strictly revolting," he nonetheless noted,

> On the other hand, our popular music has penetrated deep into the Soviet Union and helps awaken youth there to the vigor and gratification of free self-expression. A very evocative scene took place at a recent May Day parade in Red Square. While the might of Soviet missiles was paraded past Lenin's tomb, and the official bands played, a little private combo of Soviet strummers and tooters set itself up in a corner and beat out 'When the Saints Come Marching In.'[595]

Additionally, even within a given country, receptions between the general public and political elites may deviate considerably. As Artem Patalakh has noted, "[I]n certain cases, the applicant's strategy can be shipwrecked if it manages to attract only a recipient's elite but not its public."[596] Taken together, these intricacies once more impressively underline the importance of context and the need for in-depth empirical studies in order to examine the workings of soft power.

Having established the importance of context for success or failure in the creation of positive reception, Nye noted that the resource of culture as an ingredient of soft power is more likely to achieve positive reception and, in the end, desired outcomes, in cases in which the agent's and the target's culture "are somewhat similar rather than widely dissimilar."[597] Angus Taverner equally noted that "it seems to be particularly difficult to persuade audiences from widely divergent cultural backgrounds to develop a consistency of view."[598] Others, however, disagree with this assumption and rather invoke what has been called "The Myth of the Other."[599] In this view, it is the very difference of another culture that makes it attractive in the eyes of the beholder. Gary D. Rawnsley supports this view when he argued, "I disagree [with Nye's assessment] since the exotic 'other' has proven tremendously alluring to dissimilar cultures, and China's successful use of the cultural approach to public diplomacy has brought that nation and its history to the attention of the West."[600] Since both views may have their merits, only in-depth case studies can promise to yield resilient results allowing for an assessment of the (positive or negative) reception of certain soft power resources or instruments in a given context.

---

[594]Canham, *The American Position in the World*, p. 24.

[595]Canham, *The American Position in the World*, pp. 25–26.

[596]Patalakh, "Assessment of Soft Power Strategies," p. 94.

[597]Nye, *Soft Power*, pp. 15–16.

[598]Angus Taverner, "The Military Use of Soft Power," in *Soft Power and US Foreign Policy: Theoretical, Historical and Contemporary Perspectives*, eds. Inderjeet Parmar and Michael Cox (Abingdon: Routledge, 2010), p. 145.

[599]Longxi Zhang, "The Myth of the Other: China in the Eyes of the West," *Critical Inquiry*, Vol. 15, No. 1 (Autumn 1988), pp. 108–131.

[600]Gary D. Rawnsley, "China Talks Back: Public Diplomacy and Soft Power for the Chinese Century," in *Routledge Handbook of Public Diplomacy*, eds. Nancy Snow and Philip M. Taylor (New York, N.Y.: Routledge, 2009), p. 289.

In any case, this dissent yet again offers proof of the need for detailed empirical studies.

Additionally, the wielding of soft power may also result in repulsion through a (perceived) dominance of a given culture over another. Concepts such as "artistic hegemony" or "cultural imperialism"—themselves both condemned and hailed[601]— have expressed this insight.[602] Addressing this very reproach of U.S. cultural imperialism in an increasingly globalized world, then-Secretary of State Madeleine Albright told her audience at a 2000 White House conference, "There are some who describe our country as hegemonic, equate globalization with Americanization, and say unkind things about our hamburgers."[603] While Albright arguably sought to humorously dismiss such charges, a degree of opposition toward global U.S. cultural influence can certainly be detected in different places all around the world. In this regard, what might be called the paradox of power plays an important role. Ali S. Wyne hence pointed out, "There is certainly some truth to the contention that resentment of a country's foreign policy scales with its power: As the world's most powerful country, the United States is thus bound to inspire great opposition."[604] This observation, it may be added, applies for the realms of hard and soft powers alike.

3. Besides attraction and repulsion, created by soft power resources or instruments, a third ideal-type reception is conceivable as depicted in Fig. 3.1: apathy. Apathy may be considered a middle case between attraction and repulsion. Joseph Nye not incomparably noted that soft power resources may create attraction, revulsion, or—"indifference."[605] However, while recognizing the possibility of a "third way," Nye does not elaborate upon it any further. In fact, apathy, in the understanding of the study at hand, may in itself be caused in two different ways. On the one hand, it is possible that a given soft power resource or instrument may be perceived both positively and negatively at the same time. In this sense, attraction and repulsion may balance each other in a given society, among decision-makers, or over a certain period of time with possible advantages or disadvantages thus nullified.[606] In terms of physics, centrifugal and attractional forces may cancel each other, leaving an object in a comparatively stable orbit. On the other hand, it is also possible that a soft power resource or instrument attributed to Actor A (this holds true for all soft power resources) may not be

---

[601] Daniel Rothkopf, "In Praise of Cultural Imperialism," *Foreign Policy*, No. 107 (Summer 1997), pp. 38–53.

[602] Gilboa, "Searching for a Theory of Public Diplomacy," p. 62. See Josef Joffe, "The Perils of Soft Power," *The New York Times*, May 14, 2006, online at: http://www.nytimes.com/2006/05/14/magazine/14wwln_lede.html (June 2, 2016).

[603] Quoted in Matthew Fraser, *Weapons of Mass Distraction: Soft Power and American Empire* (New York, N.Y.: St. Martin's Press, 2003), pp. 18–19.

[604] Wyne, "Public Opinion and Power," p. 41.

[605] Nye, *The Future of Power*, p. 92.

[606] Geiger, "*The Power Game*, Soft Power and the International Historian," p. 87.

perceived at all on part of Actor B. Due to the relational and contextual character of soft power, this constellation does not disqualify the resource itself but rather results in apathy on the side of Actor B. The same applies to a given soft power instrument (say an international broadcasting program) devised by Actor A which—for example, for technical reasons, due to censorship, or even coincidentally—simply never reaches Actor B as intended. Again, this neither results in attraction or repulsion, but rather Actor B remains in a state of ignorance toward a given soft power instrument. It may be argued that in such instances, even though the first two subunits can be identified, soft power resources and/or the instruments do not exceed the sphere of Actor A (i.e., the first column depicted in Fig. 3.1), their existence notwithstanding.[607]

Given these different and intricate contingencies, it is the task of the researcher to analyze respective perceptions on part of Actor B in each and every case, as a quick view to empirical evidence illustrates. The establishment of the meanwhile more than 500 Confucius Institutes around the world may serve as a vivid example in this regard. Evocative of comparable institutions like the Alliance Française or the German Goethe Institutes or the Chinese cultural institutes can themselves be classified as soft power instruments. Predominantly located at university or college campuses all around the globe, these institutes teach, among other things, locals in Chinese language and culture.[608] In many cases, the institutes, offering a first-hand perspective on Chinese culture and language, are perceived positively as polls and surveys have demonstrated. However, regarding the reception of these institutes the picture is highly diverging as individual case studies on the subject have also demonstrated.[609] A report by the American Association of University Professors (AAUP), for example, indicates that instead of the intended creation or facilitation of attraction toward China by establishing Confucius Institutes on U.S. university and college campuses, the opposite has occasionally been evoked in practice. The AAUP report from June 2014 thus concluded,

> Confucius Institutes function as an arm of the Chinese state and are allowed to ignore academic freedom. Their academic activities are under the supervision of Hanban, a Chinese state agency which is chaired by a member of the Politburo and the vice-premier of the People's Republic of China. Most agreements establishing Confucius Institutes feature nondisclosure clauses and unacceptable concessions to the political aims and practices of the government of China. Specifically, North American universities permit Confucius

---

[607] In a sense, this observation is highly reminiscent of one of the most fundamental questions in existential philosophy. It shall be picked up again with respect to the soft power subunit of outcomes; see Sect. 3.4.

[608] Joshua Kurlantzick, *Charm Offensive: How China's Soft Power is Transforming the World* (New Haven, Conn.: Yale University Press, 2007), p. 68.

[609] See, for example, Rui Yang, "Soft Power and Higher Education: An Examination of China's Confucius Institutes," *Globalisation, Societies and Education*, Vol. 8, No. 2 (2007), pp. 235–245. See also Xuewu Gu, *Die Große Mauer in den Köpfen: China, der Westen und die Suche nach Verständigung* (Hamburg: Edition Körber-Stiftung, 2014), pp. 69–71.

Institutes to advance a state agenda in the recruitment and control of academic staff, in the choice of curriculum, and in the restriction of debate.[610]

This brief example demonstrates the importance of taking into consideration the respective circumstances when assessing the perception of soft power resources and instruments in different contexts. Empirical analyses whether a given soft power instrument evokes attraction (on the one end of the spectrum) or repulsion (on the other end) or apathy (as a middle case) must therefore be conducted on a case-to-case basis while crucially taking into account respective circumstances and starting points.

Concerning indicators to be drawn upon in empirical studies, research may be performed, for example, by the conduction or consultation of surveys or opinion polls. Although drawbacks have also been mentioned in literature, as shall be argued, opinion polls have been identified "as prime indicators" when assessing the success or failures of specific public diplomacy programs.[611] Ingrid d'Hooghe accordingly commented, "There are a number of measurement instruments to indicate the success of a country's soft power, of which the opinion poll is regarded as the most useful."[612] Joseph Nye agreed to this assessment when he argued, "Whether a particular asset is an attractive soft power resource can be measured through polls or focus groups."[613] Consequently, opinion polls and surveys are among the most popular and frequently referenced sources for researching the effectiveness of an actor's soft power.[614] Survey providers and opinion research centers frequently called upon in this regard include the Pew Research Center (particularly its "Global Attitudes & Trends"[615]), the Program on International Policy Attitudes (PIPA), or Gallup. Besides, more specific surveys on particular issues as well as single polls can be taken into account, depending on the respective empirical case(s). In this context, a recurrent nature of polls with consistent methodology proves to be particularly important when trying to detect possible shifts in the soft power of any actor toward another.

However, scholars have also identified considerable difficulties with regard to opinion polls. Christopher Layne, for example, has hence claimed that "public attitudes are notoriously transient"[616] and William Inboden cautioned against the "vicissitudes of opinion polling."[617] Echoing further weaknesses, Jean-Marc

---

[610]American Association of University Professors, "On Partnerships with Foreign Governments: The Case of Confucius Institutes," Prepared by the Association's Committee A on Academic Freedom and Tenure, June 2014, online at: http://www.aaup.org/file/Confucius_Institutes_0.pdf (accessed November 11, 2014).

[611]Zaharna, *The Cultural Awakening in Public Diplomacy*, pp. 50–51.

[612]d'Hooghe, *The Limits of China's Soft Power in Europe*, p. 12.

[613]Nye, "Public Diplomacy and Soft Power," p. 95.

[614]Blanchard and Lu, "Thinking Hard about Soft Power," p. 576.

[615]Pew Research Center, "Global Attitudes & Trends: Global Indicators Database."

[616]Layne, "The Unbearable Lightness of Soft Power," p. 56.

[617]Inboden, "What is Power?," p. 25.

F. Blanchard and Fujia Lu noted that "polls are also crude devices."[618] Nye himself—though recognizing them as "a good first approximation"—accordingly cautioned,

> [O]ne must be careful not to read too much into opinion polls. They are an essential but imperfect measure of soft-power resources because answers may vary depending on the way that questions are formulated, and unless the same questions are asked consistently over some period, they represent snapshots rather than a continuous picture.[619]

Other scholars and practitioners in the field of public opinion research agree with this assessment. Ronald D. Asmus accordingly asserted that "[t]he public can hold views that are at times inconsistent or even contradictory"[620] and François Heisbourg, with respect to the perceptions of the United States abroad, likewise maintained that these may at times be "contrasted and indeed contradictory."[621] Additionally, as Ingrid d'Hooghe pointed out, recent statements by national decision-makers regarding a certain country are likely to influence public sentiment and thus the results of opinion polls.[622] Bearing in mind these caveats, public opinion polls can nevertheless be regarded "as a barometer of public sentiments."[623]

Since the aim of any researcher should be, with Nye, to draw "a continuous picture," however, further instruments besides opinion polls should be included to determine Actor B's reception of another actor's soft power resources or instruments, since a sole reliance on surveys would fall short.[624] D'Hooghe thus asserts that "there are certain limitations to the use of opinion polls as an instrument to measure perceptions"—including the selection and formulation of questions as well as the timing or date of the interview.[625] Discussing ways to examine the attraction created by (Chinese) soft power efforts, Jean-Marc F. Blanchard and Fujia Lu have accordingly noted,

> Techniques for gauging such attraction include examining the public and private statements of key decisionmakers, reviewing government or program documents, interviewing targets, examining how China justifies its actions (e.g., with reference to a particular international law or norm), and content analysis.[626]

With their enumeration, Blanchard and Lu have introduced a number of further ways to assess respective soft power receptions. Accordingly, empirical analyses concerning the success or failure of soft power in a certain context should also

---

[618]Blanchard and Lu, "Thinking Hard about Soft Power," p. 576.

[619]Nye, *Soft Power*, p. 18. See also Nye, "Responding to My Critics and Concluding Thoughts," p. 218.

[620]Ronald D. Asmus, *German Strategy and Opinion After the Wall, 1990-1993* (Santa Monica, Cal.: RAND, 1994), p. 3.

[621]Heisbourg, "American Hegemony," p. 5.

[622]Ingrid d'Hooghe, *China's Public Diplomacy* (Leiden: Brill Nijhoff, 2015), p. 349.

[623]Asmus, *German Strategy and Opinion After the Wall*, p. 3.

[624]Gilboa, "Searching for a Theory of Public Diplomacy," p. 56.

[625]d'Hooghe, *The Limits of China's Soft Power in Europe*, p. 12.

[626]Blanchard and Lu, "Thinking Hard about Soft Power," p. 576.

include the statement of (governmental) officials, leading politicians, as well as further influential voices of opinion leaders. Bearing in mind the distinction elaborated upon above, it may be argued that opinion polls are valuable instruments in order to detect the *indirect* form of soft power, that is, soft power wielded with respect to the general public. Recognizing also the *direct* form, however, perceptions by (governmental and societal) elites are no less important and should accordingly be taken into account as well. Artem Patalakh has in this regard aptly noted that "to assess the success of an applicant's soft power strategy, its reception by both the recipient's elite and population must be taken into account."[627] In fact, elite perception prove of particular importance not least since the chains of effect in wielding soft power in this way are frequently considerably shorter. Consequently, statements of governmental and/or societal elites should be considered by way of analyzing (public) statements, speeches, or documents. Additionally, memoirs or autobiographical writings may prove of particular interest in this regard.

Furthermore, and partly overlapping, content or media analysis has repeatedly been identified as yet another suitable method to determine an actor's reception.[628] Bearing in mind that the reception of a certain country's soft power efforts is not always readily substantiated via opinion polls, it may thus prove incisive to consider general trends and influential voices in the media. In this regard, the 2011 study by Lucas Pettersson, examining (changing) images of the United States and their respective political leaders within the German media over a selected period of time (i.e., from the early 1980s to the first Obama administration), offers both a vivid example and a valuable starting point for media analysis.[629] Pettersson thus conducted "qualitative textual analysis of editorials, commentaries and articles of an analytical character during four different time periods."[630] Building on such analyses, and taking into consideration leading newspapers of the respective recipient country in particular, such media analyses constitute another indicator promising tangible results in the subunit of reception.

In the final analysis, (1) public opinion polls, if possible those conducted on a recurrent basis, (2) contemporary statements and subsequent memoirs of political representatives and/or (societal) elites, and finally (3) media or content analyses should be taken into account as indicators for the subunit of reception in empirical investigations of the workings of soft power in international relations. Taken together, these indicators qualify as meaningful measuring sticks allowing for a more tangible assessment of Actor B's perception. However, the soft power subunit

---

[627]Patalakh, "Assessment of Soft Power Strategies," p. 93.

[628]See, for example, Blanchard and Lu, "Thinking Hard about Soft Power," p. 576; d'Hooghe, *The Limits of China's Soft Power in Europe*, p. 12; and Li Ji, "Measuring Soft Power (Section Overview)," in *The Routledge Handbook of Soft Power*, eds. Naren Chitty, Li Ji, Gary D. Rawnsley, and Craig Hayden (Abingdon: Routledge, 2017), p. 80.

[629]Lucas Pettersson, "Changing Images of the USA in German Media Discourse During Four American Presidencies," *International Journal of Cultural Studies*, Vol. 14, No. 1 (2011), pp. 35–51.

[630]Pettersson, "Changing Images," p. 37.

of reception vividly illustrates that power—and particularly soft power—is highly relational and crucially depends on respective contexts. These observations, once more, call for meticulous in-depth case studies in order to examine the success or failure of soft power—especially when trying to detect whether soft power resources and instruments have led not only to a positive reception but also to desired outcomes. In line with the soft power taxonomy introduced, we shall now turn to this very issue in the following section.

3.4 Subunit IV: Outcomes

Concordant with the above observations, Benjamin E. Goldsmith and Yusaku Horiuchi have argued that the respective perception on the part of Actor B constitutes an integral part in the soft power equation and accordingly the two authors have noted "that in international relations soft power manifests itself in views held by country B's mass public about country A's *foreign policy*."[631] In the understanding of the work in hand, however, the element of Actor B's reception, that is, the opinion held by a given actor toward another, while undoubtedly crucial in the wielding of soft power, shall be regarded as merely one factor in the equation—and not its ultimate result.[632] Besides the previous subunits presented and elaborated upon—resources, instruments, and reception—the fourth subunit to be discussed in the following has therefore likewise to be taken into consideration.

It is in this vein that Christopher Layne—in terms of the connection between Subunit III and IV—noted that "there must be a demonstrated causal connection between public opinion and state policy."[633] The establishment of "causal connections," of course, is a problem frequently encountered in the social sciences: in most cases, in fact, more explanations than just *one* are conceivable to explain any event in world history.[634] Likewise, Jack A. Goldstone has pointed out that "the same outcome is often produced by varied and different combinations and levels of causes, so that a single set of necessary and sufficient conditions for specific outcomes does not exist."[635]

---

[631]Goldsmith and Horiuchi, "In Search of Soft Power," p. 556; Goldsmith's and Horiuchi's emphasis.

[632]Additionally, it may be argued, the focus on the soft power resource of foreign policy—as proposed by Goldsmith and Horiuchi—falls short and leaves out the crucial resources of culture, values, and personalities, which have been elaborated upon above.

[633]Layne, "The Unbearable Lightness of Soft Power," p. 56.

[634]Andreas Dür, "Discriminating Among Rival Explanations: Some Tools for Small-n Researchers," in *Research Design in Political Science: How to Practice What They Preach*, eds. Thomas Geschwend and Frank Schimmelfennig (Basingstoke: Palgrave Macmillan, 2011), p. 183.

[635]Jack A. Goldstone, "Comparative Historical Analysis and Knowledge Accumulation in the Study of Revolutions," in *Comparative Historical Analysis in the Social Sciences*, eds. James Mahoney and Dietrich Rueschemeyer (Cambridge: Cambridge University Press, 2003), p. 44.

Despite these intricacies, any comprehensive taxonomy of the mechanisms of soft power requires the inclusion of this fourth subunit to a special degree. Bearing in mind Robert Dahl's previously cited definition of power ("A has power over B to the extent that A can get B to do something that B would not otherwise do"[636]), the subunit of outcomes in fact gains center stage in the process of wielding soft power in as much as the *changing* of behavior ("something that B *would not otherwise do*") is of particular importance in this understanding of power, as has been recognized by many scholars.[637] Since soft power is understood as, in Nye's words, "simply a form of power—one way of getting desired outcomes,"[638] this observation applies to soft power no less than it does to hard power. Soft power, therefore, reposes on an actor's capability of *changing* the preferences of other actors,[639] and as a consequence acting in accord with one's own values, policies, or goals.

With these observations in mind, Benjamin E. Goldsmith and Yusaku Horiuchi have asked the straightforward question, "Does 'soft power' matter in international relations?"[640] and subsequently they aptly asserted, "Without some effect on international outcomes, the term soft *power* would, of course, be a misnomer."[641] Hence, it is not enough to conclude any analysis of whether an actor has successfully wielded soft power at the reception stage (i.e., Subunit III), for example, by revealing positive perceptions or sentiments through recourse to opinion polls or other indicators. Rather, it is particularly important to also take the final step along the soft power road and include the fourth subunit, or—in other words—the empirically identifiable behavior of an actor attributable to the exercise of soft power. Joseph Nye has thus rightly emphasized that ultimately "it is outcomes, not resources, that we care about."[642] It is in this vein that Li Ji has aptly observed, "Soft power resources need to be communicated to reach or be accessed by a target population, and they need to be converted into effective power capabilities to achieve desired outcomes."[643]

---

[636]Robert A. Dahl, "The Concept of Power," *Behavioral Science*, Vol. 2, No. 3 (1957), pp. 202–203.

[637]Leslie H. Gelb, *Power Rules: How Common Sense Can Rescue American Foreign Policy* (New York, N.Y.: HarperCollins, 2009), p. 32. See also Ernest J. Wilson III, "Hard Power, Soft Power, Smart Power," *The Annals of the American Academy of Political and Social Sciences*, Vol. 616, Public Diplomacy in a Changing World (March 2008), p. 114 and Galit Ailon, "What B Would Otherwise Do: A Critique of Conceptualizations of 'Power' in Organizational Theory," *Organization*, Vol. 13, No. 6 (2006), p. 772.

[638]Joseph S. Nye, Jr., "Foreword," in *Soft Power Superpowers: Cultural and National Assets of Japan and the United States*, eds. Watanabe Yasushi and David L. McConnell (Armonk, N.Y.: M.E. Sharpe, 2008), p. xiii.

[639]Nye, *Soft Power*, p. 5.

[640]Goldsmith and Horiuchi, "In Search of Soft Power," p. 555.

[641]Goldsmith and Horiuchi, "In Search of Soft Power," p. 560; Goldsmith's and Horiuchi's emphasis.

[642]Nye, "Hard, Soft, and Smart Power," p. 561.

[643]Ji, "Measuring Soft Power (Section Overview)," p. 86.

With regard to public diplomacy, identified above as an instrument to wield soft power, comparable observations have been made by different scholars. Ali Fisher thus noted that "PD is not merely about selling policy, it is about achieving specific objectives, it is about changing behavior rather than just perceptions."[644] In April 23, 2007, address on public diplomacy then-Undersecretary in the British Foreign and Commonwealth Office Lord Triesman accordingly argued with regard to public diplomacy in the United Kingdom,

> The logic of public diplomacy in the past went something like this: if foreigners have a warm feeling about Britain, they are more likely to feel similarly about our role in the world. So the effort pandered to the traditional comfortable view of the UK: red London buses and post boxes, black cabs, shortbread, scotch [sic!] whisky, cream teas, Shakespeare.[645]

However, Lord Triesman went on, today this was no longer what he intended or envisioned for the "new" public diplomacy of the United Kingdom. Rather, he emphasized,

> [W]e are determined to find new ways of measuring whether we are having the impact we intend. I do not believe it is necessary for the UK to get credit for its role in raising consciousness or nudging a foreign government towards a new policy. I want to see the change take place. I don't mind if there are no bouquets. [...] What matters is getting the right *results*.[646]

Scholars frequently subscribe to this particular practitioner's assessment. Gary D. Rawnsley, for instance, has noted with regard to Chinese public diplomacy,

> What is important to address is not the novelty of the approach but its effect. In other words, we need to examine how these public diplomacy resources might contribute to realizing China's foreign policy objectives, and the PRC is starting to demonstrate a more mature and nuanced understanding of how public diplomacy may connect in a profitable way with China's international ambitions.[647]

Joseph Nye himself addressed the reproach of soft power being merely a popularity contest by arguing that its wielding "is not just a matter of ephemeral popularity; it is a means of obtaining *outcomes* the United States wants."[648] Goldsmith and Horiuchi, in their study cited above, hence sought to carve out "identifiable foreign policy choices that can be tied empirically to mass-level perceptions."[649]

In sum, scholars as well as practitioners frequently agree on the importance of observable results when examining the soft power of a given actor. However, this final aspect—subsumed here under the fourth subunit of outcomes—is not only crucial but perhaps also hardest to identify empirically. Arguably, most observers

---

[644]Fisher, "Four Seasons in One Day," p. 255.

[645]David Triesman, The Lord Triesman, "Public Diplomacy: Steps to the Future," London School of Economics, April 23, 2007, online at: http://www.lse.ac.uk/publicEvents/pdf/20070423_LordTriesman.pdf (accessed August 25, 2015).

[646]Triesman, "Public Diplomacy;" emphasis added.

[647]Rawnsley, "China Talks Back," p. 286.

[648]Nye, "The Decline of America's Soft Power," p. 17; emphasis added.

[649]Goldsmith and Horiuchi, "In Search of Soft Power," p. 556.

would agree that soft power, at least to a certain extent, actually matters in international relations. Even authors critical toward the potential of soft power such as Eliot A. Cohen have thus acknowledged, "The magnetism of the United States has real political consequences."[650] Others have likewise recognized that "what soft power can accomplish is significant, varied, and even surprising."[651] To empirically trace such accomplishments brought about by attractive soft power, however, proves to be far more difficult, albeit it does not necessarily need to be a lost cause.

Briefly summarizing Fig. 3.1, and hence the introduced taxonomy of soft power, up to this point, Actor A's soft power resources (i.e., Subunit I), transmitted by its soft power instruments (Subunit II) may result in a reception (Subunit III) of either attraction, apathy, or repulsion on the part of Actor B. (In the passive variety of soft power the respective reception occurs through the inherent appeal of the resources alone while the second subunit is leapfrogged.) In the final step, to be elaborated upon in the following, this process leads—in parallel with the three varieties of reception—to three conceivable varieties of outcomes, that is, compliance, inaction, or opposition. In the following, we shall at first discuss the three conceivable ideal types of outcomes in more detail before turning to difficulties in detecting and distinguishing them. Finally, empirical examples as well as indicators eligible to serve as points of reference for empirical analyses shall be offered.

1. Beginning with the first outcome variety, that is, compliance, this path may be considered the ideal or desirable mode of action from the perspective of Actor A. Hence, he would have successfully wielded soft power in the sense that Actor B would have changed his behavior in accord with the wishes of Actor A. To paraphrase Nye's very definition of soft power, Actor A would thus have gotten the outcomes he wanted from Actor B by ways of having successfully wielded soft power.

2. In cases in which the wielding of soft power fails, that is, instances in which Actor B is either apathetic or even repulsed by Actor A's resources or instruments, Actor A is unable to get the outcomes he wants. In this case, Actor B may even oppose Actor A, who would thus have failed to effectively convert his soft power resources into desired outcomes. As has been argued above, soft power resources and instruments may not only fail to succeed but at times may even prove counterproductive—something that has been called the boomerang effect of soft power.[652] In this sense, opposition can be regarded—diametrically opposed to compliance—as a worst-case scenario in which abortive attempts to wield soft power, far from bringing about desired outcomes, have actually caused *negative* results.

3. Finally, a further outcome is conceptually conceivable: inaction. While in the other two outcome varieties (i.e., compliance and opposition) Actor B acts either

---

[650]Eliot A. Cohen, *The Big Stick: The Limits of Soft Power and the Necessity of Military Force* (New York, N.Y.: Basic Books, 2016), p. 16.

[651]Ifantis, "Soft Power," p. 443.

[652]See above, Sect. 3.3.

in accord or in opposition to Actor A as a consequence of its wielding of soft power, inaction qualifies as a third distinct variety of outcomes. Of course, inaction in the sense of staying neutral on a given question or in a certain dispute may at times also be considered an expression of compliance as well as opposition. For example, the decision of staying out of the American Civil War by the British may at first sight be regarded as inaction. However, there is sound historical evidence to rather characterize this decision as compliance with regard to the urges of the North (the United States) to *not* join the war alongside the South (the Confederate States of America)—a decision that some scholars not least attribute to the North's soft power, which has overridden evident British strategic and economic interests.[653] The abstention from a specific vote or the willingness to refrain from using one's veto power in a deliberative body offers further cases in point. In this sense, it may at times be a desired outcome on the part of Actor A that Actor B does not act at all and Actor B's behavior thus ought to be characterized as compliance. Therefore, in the understanding of the proposed taxonomy, inaction is meant to describe a state in which a certain Actor B does not *change* his (initially intended) behavior and the soft power resources or instruments wielded by Actor A thus fail to take any effect (for better or worse). Hence, Actor A's intention to wield soft power may well have been detected on the part of Actor B, though no effect is discernable. In parallel with the variety of apathy in the subunit of reception, any holistic picture of the mechanism of soft power would be incomplete without including this possible outcome of (undesired) inaction.[654]

However, albeit the depicted process of different varieties of outcomes through soft power may be convincingly illustrated on a theoretical-conceptual level, it is far more difficult to trace and prove it in practice.[655] Consider, for example, the following model case: The People's Republic of China, in accord with the plans laid out by then-President Hu Jintao in a 2007 speech, seeks to globally "enhance culture as part of [Chinese] soft power."[656] In order to translate or communicate the

---

[653]Nye, *The Future of Power*, p. 82; Nye, "Hard, Soft, and Smart Power," p. 566; John M. Owen, "How Liberalism Produces Democratic Peace," in *International Security*, Vol. 19, No. 2 (Fall 1994), pp. 110–114 & pp. 120–121.

[654]This assessment holds true despite conceivable objections based on (Dahlian) understandings of power emphasizing the existence of power only in cases in which actual *changes* in behavior are verifiable.

[655]Hall, "An Unclear Attraction," p. 200. This observation not least finds its expression in the fact that frequently few, if any, indicators are included in soft power indices with respect to actual outcomes; see below.

[656]Hu Jintao, "Hold High the Great Banner of Socialism with Chinese Characteristics and Strive for New Victories in Building a Moderately Prosperous Society in all," Report to the Seventeenth National Congress of the Communist Party of China, October 15, 2007, online at: http://www. china.org.cn/english/congress/229611.htm (accessed November 11, 2014).

soft power resource of culture (Subunit I), China opens a Confucius Institute in an African city, say Nairobi.[657] Within the soft power taxonomy put forth in this study, such a cultural institute qualifies as a soft power instrument (Subunit II). In the institute's first year of operation a given number of students—for the sake of simplicity let us say 1000—attend different classes on Chinese language and culture offered by the Confucius Institute. A subsequent survey conducted among those who attended courses in order to figure out their reception (Subunit III) reveals that of those 1000 students polled, 800 students state that they have a positive image of China and are attracted by Chinese culture. Does this mean that China has success-fully wielded soft power? Unfortunately, it is not quite as simple as that.

The first question that arises from this model example is whether or not the attendance of classes in the Nairobi Confucius Institutes had any impact on the 800 students who stated that they hold a positive image of China—as well as on the 200 who held either negative or neutral views. In other words—since power implies *changing* behaviors in others—did the attendance of courses *change* the students' reception of China? Or are those polled just stating views predating their participa-tion in respective classes which hence have remained unaltered? As Joseph Nye reminded us, "The effectiveness of public diplomacy is measured in minds *changed*."[658] It may in fact even be argued that those attending already had held positive views on China, thus being attracted to taking classes at the Confucius Institutes in the first place, whereas those more critical of China may refuse to take part in its cultural programs whatsoever. In fact, this phenomenon may be considered one of the most fundamental points of criticism toward cultural institutes and pro-grams: that only those attend or take part in such programs who already have a positive image—or at least an open mind—to begin with. Giles Scott-Smith, in this regard optimistically commented, by drawing on postwar programs in Germany, that "critics will rarely be swayed, but doubters may become believers and supporters will feel empowered."[659] In any case, regarding the example of the Nairobian Confucius Institute, the first difficulty could quite easily be worked out by conducting pre-post comparisons among students *prior to* as well as *after* having attended classes, thus allowing for an examination whether and to what extent attitudes have actually changed.

The second question, however, is much harder to address: How can we assess whether or not the high level of attested attraction among African attendees of classes at the Nairobi Confucius Institute results in desired outcomes, that is, out-comes presumably intended by Chinese officials who initiated the Confucius Insti-tute (Subunit IV)? Even assuming that the number of students who are attracted to

---

[657]In fact, the Confucius Institute at the University of Nairobi which opened on December 19, 2005, was the first Chinese cultural institute created in Africa; University of Nairobi Confucius Institute, "Background," online at: http://confucius.uonbi.ac.ke/sites/default/files/chss/arts/linguistics/confu cius/BACK%20GROUND.pdf (accessed August 25, 2015).
[658]Nye, *The Future of Power*, p. 107; emphasis added.
[659]Scott-Smith, "Exchange Programs and Public Diplomacy," p. 55.

China after having attended the Confucius Institute has risen, do those Kenyan students (not to speak of Kenya as a state) now—to paraphrase Nye—want what China wants (e.g., support its policies regarding maritime and territorial disputes in the South China Sea, share Chinese views on free trade, human rights, global economic architecture, or any other conceivable issue)? This dilemma perhaps most acutely opens the entire concept of soft power to attack. To wit, positive impressions or attraction do not necessarily translate into desired outcomes or foreign policy objectives.[660] It is in this vein that Christopher Layne noted, "Even if one accepts that soft power exists and can affect a state's foreign policy, it is hard to trace the relationship between soft power and policy outcomes."[661] Likewise, John Brown, with reference to the success or failure of U.S. cultural diplomacy after 9/11, pointedly asked, "How many terrorists will automatically embrace American values after reading *Moby Dick* or listening to Negro spirituals?"[662]

This observation becomes particularly glaring in contrast to hard or command power instruments and the outcomes such instruments can bring about: Invading a country and physically destroying a nuclear reactor, for example, directly results—if successful—in the desired outcomes, which is bringing to a halt a nation's nuclear program. Trying to use soft power to influence the minds of said state's officials and thus attracting them to *want* to end their nuclear program is far more difficult to achieve, if possible at all.[663] (Intriguingly, however, this very approach features prominently in Joseph Nye's novel *The Power Game*.[664]) It is in the same sense that Matthew Fraser argued with reference to the effectiveness of a nation's arsenal of soft power resources, "True, weapons of mass distraction cannot triumph over weapons of mass destruction. But they can temper the pernicious values and beliefs that build them."[665] Nye himself does not turn a blind eye on this observation either. In fact, he argued that "[s]oft power is not the solution to all problems."[666] However, while he agreed that "[s]oft power alone rarely solves hard problems" he also maintained that it "can create an enabling rather than a disabling environment for policy."[667]

The creation of "an enabling environment" indicates the long-term character of soft power and Nye explicitly conceded that soft power instruments "sometimes take

---

[660]Blanchard and Lu, "Thinking Hard about Soft Power," p. 577.

[661]Layne, "The Unbearable Lightness of Soft Power," p. 55.

[662]Brown, "Arts Diplomacy," p. 58.

[663]It is in this vein that Joseph Nye argued that soft power alone will not "be sufficient to stop the Iranian nuclear program;" Joseph S. Nye, Jr., "Think Again: Soft Power," *Foreign Policy*, February 23, 2006, online at: http://foreignpolicy.com/2006/02/23/think-again-soft-power/ (accessed February 13, 2015).

[664]Joseph S. Nye, Jr., *The Power Game: A Washington Novel* (New York, N.Y.: PublicAffairs, 2004).

[665]Fraser, *Weapons of Mass Distraction*, p. 260.

[666]Nye, *The Future of Power*, p. xiii. See also Zahran and Ramos, "From Hegemony to Soft Power," p. 25.

[667]Nye, "Good Start, Long Road," p. 13.

years to produce desired outcomes."[668] Accordingly, Angus Taverner opined that soft power frequently is "difficult to apply in a precise and timely manner to achieve a set of desired outcomes."[669] Though perhaps particularly difficult to trace and prove empirically, it has been argued that long-term transformations tend to be more effective than short-term changes.[670] Christopher Hill and Sarah Beadle accordingly concluded—with respect to British soft power—that "the assets that really matter are the deeper, slow-moving qualities of a society and not the surface glitter of a successful Olympics or a royal wedding."[671] In the case of the nuclear program referred to above, for example, such a wide timeframe may not be available and soft power may thus prove to be unsuitable to get the desired outcomes.

Applying these observations to the model example of the Confucius Institute in Nairobi introduced above, the point being made becomes even clearer. It has been noted that the assumption of a positive (cultural) impression of a given country leading "automatically" to the support of that country's foreign policy has been extremely oversimplifying.[672] This may be the case. First, however, it may be argued that the very changing or improving the views on China held by the Kenyan students was in fact the only intended outcome of this particular Chinese soft power initiative. In this case, soft power would indeed have been wielded successfully. Second, and more consequential still, the *probability* of achieving desired political outcomes in places where a country's (cultural) attraction has been enhanced is—if anything— potentially increasing. Arguably, the causal chain between visiting a Confucius Institute and supporting Chinese foreign policy is considerably longer than it may regularly be the case with respect to hard power measures, especially when considering the difference between the (usually) private capacities in which those students attend classes and the governmental sphere in which foreign policy decision are generally made. Christopher Layne thus rightly noted that it "is a long way, however, from establishing that soft power's impact upon public opinion in a target state will actually affect that state's foreign policy."[673] Nevertheless, at least—but not exclusively—in democratic governments, chains of legitimacy *do* exist and public support for the politics pursued by any government *does* play a role—an assessment shared in particular by neoliberal scholars in International Relations theory.[674] In fact, as has been argued above, the role of public opinion and domestic support is likely to further increase in the future with the advance of social media and further possibilities of (political) participation. Additionally, the very observation that China as well as countless further nations around the world, be they democratic or not, have in

---

[668]Nye, *Soft Power*, p. 99.

[669]Taverner, "The Military Use of Soft Power," p. 145.

[670]Lee, "A Theory of Soft Power and Korea's Soft Power Strategy," p. 211.

[671]Hill and Beadle, *The Art of Attraction*, p. 7.

[672]Hall, "An Unclear Attraction," p. 201.

[673]Layne, "The Unbearable Lightness of Soft Power," p. 55.

[674]Andrew Moravcsik, "Taking Preferences Seriously: A Liberal Theory of International Politics," *International Organization*, Vol. 51, No. 4 (Autumn 1997), p. 545.

recent years stepped up their soft power efforts, in itself indicates the ever-increasing importance nation-states ascribe to this particular form of power and emphasizes the positive outcomes they expect to draw from them.

With respect to our model example, the attainment of such outcomes may indeed be a protracted process. However, it may be argued that on a societal level, Kenyan public opinion toward China is likely to improve as an increasing number of Kenyan attend the institute and consequently the likelihood of public support for Chinese policies is potentially rising. Additionally, in some cases at least, students who have visited the Confucius Institute may in future years very well find themselves in positions—in the media, social, business, or political sphere—to actively influence or even decide upon their country's foreign policy and in doing so, they may resort to their knowledge about and attraction to China. In this model case, with reference to both public and elite opinion, the indirect and direct way of wielding soft power coincide.

Actually, concerning the latter aspect, the examples of leading political decision-makers such as Anwar al-Sadat, Helmut Schmidt, or Margaret Thatcher, who all had taken part in U.S. exchange programs before holding the most influential government offices in their respective home countries (i.e., Egypt, Germany, and the United Kingdom), provide expressive empirical evidence.[675] With particular regard to U.S. exchange programs, such as the Fulbright Program (already referred to above as a prime example of soft power instruments), and their significance for German-American relations, Jim Cooney and Guido Goldman have for instance noted that some former participants subsequently "assumed key positions in Germany."[676] In the very same vein, Karl-Heinz Füssl argued that "German exchangees returning from the United States had considerable influence on West German society."[677] Concerning results of the overall exchange program, Giles Scott-Smith drew comparable conclusions, "Since 1946 the Fulbright Program has been very successful in developing such an affinity with the United States, firstly via the means of academic exchange itself, and secondly by encouraging the establishment of American Studies in universities around the world."[678] In view of such assessments concerning tangible soft power outcomes, former U.S. Secretary of State Colin Powell certainly had a point when he argued in 2001 that foreign students who had spent time in the U.S. "return home with an increased understanding and often a lasting affection for

---

[675]Nye, *Soft Power*, p. 109.

[676]Jim Cooney and Guido Goldman, "Preface I," in *The United States and German-American Relations Through German Eyes*, eds. Cord Jakobeit, Ute Sacksofsky, and Peter Welzel (New York, N.Y.: Nova Science Publishers, 1996), p. vii.

[677]Karl-Heinz Füssl, "Between Elitism and Education Reform: German-American Exchange Programs, 1945-1970," in *The United States and Germany in the Era of the Cold War, 1945-1990: A Handbook, Volume I: 1945-1968*, ed. Detlef Junker, associated editors Philipp Gassert, Wilfried Mausbach, and David B. Morris (Cambridge: Cambridge University Press, 2004), p. 414.

[678]Scott-Smith, "Exchange Programs and Public Diplomacy," p. 55.

the United States. I can think of no more valuable asset to our country than the friendship of future world leaders who have been educated here."[679]

In view of these conceptual-theoretical reflections and considering also the wide array of historical examples, concrete soft power outcomes can be established. In line with the previously discussed subunits, certain indicators can likewise be identified in order to facilitate a more tangible analysis of such outcomes brought about by the wielding of soft power. Benjamin E. Goldsmith and Yusaku Horiuchi, in this regard, put forth "three distinct outcome variables"[680] in their study to illustrate the significance of soft power,

(1) the commitment of troops to the US-led war in Iraq, (2) compliance with US wishes regarding a waiver exempting its nationals from jurisdiction of the International Criminal Court (ICC), and (3) annual voting patterns in the UN General Assembly (UNGA) on issues highlighted as important by the US in that year.[681]

Despite their strong fixation on the United States (as argued above a regular feature in literature on soft power) and a specific point in time, certain indicators can be deduced from this enumeration, allowing for detection of tangible outcomes in any empirical analysis of the workings of soft power in international relations. To begin with, (1) compliance records in international organizations and forums should be consulted. As evidenced by the work of Stephen Lukes, for instance, scholars have agreed that voting behavior and what Lukes called other "actual choice situations" can instructively be considered in order to detect the preferences of an actor.[682] It is in the same vein that Su Changhe noted that the "compliance record in international institutions" of an actor can be regarded as a meaningful indicator for evaluating its soft power.[683] Of particular relevance in this context are (2) an actor's voting patterns within the United Nations General Assembly. With respect to the United States, for example, the U.S. Department of State has compiled and archived annual congressional reports on voting practices of member states in the U.N. General Assembly as well as the Security Council for several decades.[684] Thus, in order to establish an adverse shift in an actor's soft power toward another, a drop in U.N. voting compliance during a given period can be considered persuasive evidence. Furthermore, in line with the outcome variables put forth by Goldsmith and Horiuchi but far exceeding the narrow example of troop commitments in the context of the Iraq War, (3) compliance in foreign policy decisions, especially those

---

[679]Colin L. Powell, "Statement on International Education Week 2001," Washington D.C., August 7, 2001, online at: http://2001-2009.state.gov/secretary/former/powell/remarks/2001/4462.htm (accessed January 11, 2016).

[680]Goldsmith and Horiuchi, "In Search of Soft Power," p. 557.

[681]Goldsmith and Horiuchi, "In Search of Soft Power," p. 561.

[682]Steven Lukes, "Power and the Battle for the Hearts and Minds," *Millennium: Journal of International Studies*, Vol. 33, No. 3 (2005), p. 482.

[683]Su, "Soft Power," p. 552.

[684]United States Department of State, "Congressional Reports," *Bureau of International Organization Affairs*, online at: http://www.state.gov/p/io/rls/rpt/index.htm (accessed June 15, 2016).

involving the commitment of troops abroad but also including other—perhaps less consequential—decision, can be considered a further evocative and comprehensive indicator. Finally, (4) the number and character of (bilateral or multilateral) treaties concluded or joined may yield instructive results.

Conclusively, in view of the intricate nature of soft power as well as the long timeframe in which it frequently takes effect, brief reflections on two—interconnected—approaches are suggestive when seeking to detect causal relationships between the three previous subunits and tangible soft power outcomes by way of drawing on the indicators deduced: First, scholars may endeavor on deliberations of probability. The concepts of probability and chance have been a constant companion to human interactions virtually from the first and can also look back on a long tradition in the social sciences.[685] While much work has been done on the integration of probability theory and social science,[686] in the present context, as shall be demonstrated in the methodological chapter of the work in hand in greater detail, quantitative calculations do not present themselves as particularly useful when seeking to work out the mechanisms and effects of soft power. However, when seeking to assess whether or not certain detectable outcomes were brought about by the wielding of soft power (rather than by other forces), an interpretative weighing of evidence can be instructive in order to determine which forces were most probably responsible for respective outcomes in a given context. While other factors or forces (including threats or payments) may conceivably have played a contributing role for the occurrence of a certain outcome, scholars might thus determine the overriding influence of soft power.

Secondly, and connected with the first approach, scholars may also draw upon the method of elimination. Practiced for long in diverse scientific branches (including mathematics or medicine), the often arduous and protracted method found its way into the social sciences as well. In 1943, Mapheus Smith concisely captured its essence and advantages, "The net result of the method of elimination thus is demonstration of which is the most adequate interpretation. Such a conclusion is inescapable, because all other possibilities of interpretation have been demonstrated to be less adequate."[687] In fact, by following this approach of sequentially excluding different options, other possible interpretations may not only be identified as having been less adequate but may even be entirely eliminated until just one possible explanation remains. For our particular case, by empirically establishing that no other varieties of power—including (military) coercion or (economic)

---

[685]Daniel Courgeau, *Probability and Social Science: Methodological Relationships between the Two Approaches* (Dordrecht: Springer, 2012), pp. xiii–xxi.

[686]See, for example, Samuel Goldberg, *Probability in Social Science: Seven Expository Units Illustrating the Use of Probability Methods and Models, with Exercises, and Bibliographies to Guide Further Reading in the Social Science and Mathematics Literatures* (Boston, Mass.: Birkhäuser, 1982) and Götz Rohwer and Ulrich Pötter, *Wahrscheinlichkeit: Begriff und Rhetorik in der Sozialwissenschaft* (Weinheim: Juventa Verlag, 2002).

[687]Mapheus Smith, "The Method of Elimination in Scientific Study," *Philosophy of Science*, Vol. 10, No. 4 (October 1943), p. 252.

inducements—have been at play at any given instance in which changed behavior has been detected, such changes can then with good reason be attributed to the workings of soft power. Actually, this very line of thinking can be found in Joseph Nye's statement during his 2009 interview with *Der Spiegel* on the soft power exerted by Osama bin Laden already cited above, "Sure, he has a lot of soft power. He proved this when he brought down the Twin Towers. Bin Laden did not hold a gun to the heads of the people who flew the planes. He did not pay them either. They did it because they were attracted by his convictions."[688]

Of course, seeking probabilistic explanations or pursuing a method of elimination may in itself likewise prove intricate. However, as shall be demonstrated below in the methodological chapter of the work in hand, such approaches (including the inference to the best explanation, IBE) can look back on a long and illustrious tradition in the (social) sciences and provide meaningful practices for the study of soft power in international relations.[689]

In the final analysis, among the four subunits, the subunit of outcomes proves particularly intricate on a conceptual level and resilient empirical evidence may arguably likewise be hardest to come by. Of course, all indicators deduced for this subunit do not a priori assume a monocausal connection between the wielding of soft power and detectable changes in respective categories. Nevertheless, a causality between the wielding of soft power and concrete (foreign policy) outcomes can a posteriori be established—both deductively and inductively—when bearing in mind the conceptual reflections laid out above as well as the wide array of historical examples. Consequently, by applying suitable methodological instruments and approaches, tangible outcomes of the wielding of soft power can in fact be empirically substantiated through in-depth analyses.[690] In fact, scholars may in such a way even be able to venture a prognosis regarding the occurrence of some future outcome by means of wielding soft power. Ultimately, however, one has to bear in mind, as Joseph Nye has aptly asserted, that whether or not the wielding of soft power "produces desired policy outcomes has to be judged in each particular case."[691]

---

[688] Joseph S. Nye, Jr., "Harvard Professor Joseph Nye on Hard and Soft Power: 'It Is Pointless to Talk to Al-Qaida,'" Interview conducted by Gabor Steingart and Gregor Peter Schmitz, *Der Spiegel*, 34/2009, August 17, 2009, online at: http://www.spiegel.de/international/world/harvard-professor-joseph-nye-on-hard-and-soft-power-it-is-pointless-to-talk-to-al-qaida-a-643189-2.html (accessed July 17, 2018).

[689] See below, Sect. 4.1.

[690] For resilient methodological approaches to the study of soft power see below, Chap. 4.

[691] Nye, "Public Diplomacy and Soft Power," p. 95.

3.5 Excursus: The Soft Power of the Roman Empire

Before providing an interim conclusion on the taxonomy of soft power introduced and developed above, a historical excursus shall rejoin the different subunits and offer an illustration of their interaction in a holistic manner. For that purpose, a set of historical examples of the wielding of soft power shall be presented in the following.

Arguably, our notion of the Roman Empire is inextricably linked to the image of the legionary marching in step on the empire's vast stretches of military roads. (Some of which having marked out the ways for our modern European network of roads and some of which, such as the famous Appian Way, originally stretching from Rome to Brundisium, modern-day Brindisi, are actually still walkable today.) However, not only Rome's legionaries but also its civil administrators, builders, and teachers following and complementing the army's conquests crucially contributed to the far-reaching and long-lasting success of the empire. Therefore, the wielding of soft power, it may be argued, was as important as the legionaries' *gladius* for the century-long dominance of Rome in the Mediterranean and larger European world. Eliot A. Cohen has on that very score aptly observed, with respect to both the Roman and the British Empire, "The might of Rome and Britain depended on ideas as much as on power and resources: imperial power resided in science, literature, and education."[692]

Concerning the Roman Empire, stretching from the hills of northern Britannia to the sands of Mesopotamia at its apogee in the early second century, one highly informative example in this regard can be found in the classic historical work *Agricola*.[693] The *Agricola*, actually titled *De vita et moribus Iulii Agricolae*,[694] was written in c. AD 98 (i.e., roughly two decades after the events recounted in it had taken place) and with it, its author, the Roman politician and historian P. Cornelius Tacitus (c. AD 56—after 117), presented a (at least partly panegyric) biography of his father-in-law.[695] Consisting of 46 chapters, the *Agricola* constitutes

---

[692]Eliot A. Cohen, "History and the Hyperpower," *Foreign Affairs*, Vol. 83, No. 4 (July/August 2004), p. 54.

[693]This particular historic example of the workings of soft power, along the lines of the proposed taxonomy, draws in part on a paper entitled "Do as the Romans Do: Education and Language as a Source of Soft Power in Tacitus' *Agricola*" presented by the author at the International Studies Association West Annual Conference 2014 in Pasadena, California, on September 27, 2014. The author wishes to express his gratitude to his fellow panelists and particularly to chair Alison R. Holmes and discussant Douglas John Becker.

[694]The title literally translates *On the Life and Character of Julius Agricola*.

[695]R. M. Ogilvie, "Introduction to the *Agricola*," in P. Cornelius Tacitus, *Agricola/Germania/Dialogus*, Translated by M. Hutton and W. Peterson, Revised by R. M. Ogilvie, E. H. Warmington, and M. Winterbottom, Loeb Classical Library 35 (Cambridge, Mass.: Harvard University Press, 1970), pp. 18–20; W. S. Hanson, "Tacitus' 'Agricola': An Archaeological and Historical Study," in *Rise and Decline of the Roman World, Part II: Participate, Volume 33.3*, ed. Wolfgang Haase (Berlin: Walter de Gruyter, 1989), p. 1742. For more detailed discussions of the work's literary genre and purpose, see also R. M. Ogilvie and Ian Richmond, *Cornelii Taciti: De Vita Agricolae* (Oxford: Clarendon Press, 1967), pp. 11–20 and Andreas Mehl, *Römische Geschichtsschreibung:*

an exceptionally valuable source for the study of Roman Britain in the first century AD, although scholars have rightly cautioned against all deeds and speeches reported in it to be taken all too literally.[696] Still, as R. M. Ogilvie has noted,

> Within the limitations of a literary tradition which preferred brilliance of writing to fullness of information and despite the tastes of a sophisticated audience which expected epigrams and would have been offended by a recital of names of unheard-of people and places, Tacitus gives a factual, accurate and balanced account. Recent archeological discoveries have confirmed it in many particulars.[697]

As shall be demonstrated in the following, the *Agricola*—supplemented by further writings on Roman history both classical and more recent—moreover offers an excellent case in point for the mechanisms of soft power and an examination of its workings along the lines of the proposed taxonomy of soft power. To that end, the work itself as well as its background shall first be introduced in brief.

In the *Agricola*, Tacitus tells about the life and deeds of Roman general Gnaeus Julius Agricola—born in AD 40 at Forum Julii (modern-day Fréjus on the French Mediterranean coast) who in the late first century became governor of the province of Britannia, an office which he held for a longer period of time than any other known provincial governor in Roman history.[698] Describing Britain at the time when Agricola arrived on the island to take up his governorship, Andrew Robert Burn laconically comments, "So this was Britain: dank, primitive and untamed." And he goes on that besides a few Roman forts and market towns "there was not a sign of civilization."[699] This, of course, is highly exaggerating. Native Celtic tribes on the island undoubtedly possessed a rich and ancient cultural heritage. Nor did the indigenous culture altogether vanish after Britain had become part of the Roman Empire, rather the different cultures merged in a process of acculturation, which started even before the actual Roman conquest under Emperor Claudius commenced in AD 43.[700] However, civilization in the *Roman* understanding of the term seems to have been wanting and in fact seems to have begun to thrive particularly in the years under Agricola. R. M. Ogilvie and Ian Richmond thus note, "It is from his [Agricola's] time that the clearest beginnings are seen in Britain in development of orderly, civilized life, the growth of towns, and the diffusion among higher provincial society of the Roman language and ideas."[701]

While the greater part of the *Agricola* itself is dedicated to the governor's military exploits, the chapter dealing explicitly with those measures to be elaborated upon in

---

Grundlagen und Entwicklungen, Eine Einführung (Stuttgart: Verlag W. Kohlhammer, 2001), p. 119.

[696]Hanson, "Agricola," p. 1778.

[697]Ogilvie, "Introduction to the *Agricola*," pp. 16–17.

[698]Ogilvie and Richmond, *De Vita Agricolae*, p. 5; Ogilvie, "Introduction to the *Agricola*," pp. 3–9.

[699]Andrew Robert Burn, *Agricola and Roman Britain* (London: English Universities Press, 1953), p. 28.

[700]Pounds, *The Culture of the English People*, pp. 34–36.

[701]Ogilvie and Richmond, *De Vita Agricolae*, p. 4.

the following ranks among the most popular and frequently quoted passages not only of the work itself but among all existent writings on Roman Britain.[702] In the work's 21st chapter, Tacitus thus explicitly dwells on particular measures taken by Agricola,

> The winter which followed was spent in the prosecution of sound measures. In order that a population scattered and uncivilised, and proportionately ready for war, might be habituated by comfort to peace and quiet, he would exhort individuals, assist communities, to erect temples, market-places, houses: he praised the energetic, rebuked the indolent, and the rivalry for his compliments took the place of coercion. Moreover he began to train the sons of the chieftains in a liberal education, and to give a preference to the native talents of the Briton as against the trained abilities of the Gaul. As a result, the nation which used to reject the Latin language began to aspire to rhetoric: further, the wearing of our dress became a distinction, and the toga came into fashion.[703]

In this passage, Tacitus describes the steps, known today as romanization, initiated by Agricola in the winter of AD 79 in great detail. They include "sound measures" such as the building of "temples, market-places, houses." Additionally, Agricola took different measures designed to spread Roman education and language in Britain and "began to train the sons of the chieftains in a liberal education." To this purpose, he employed schoolmasters and established schools in the province of Britannia. In this regard, R. M. Ogilvie and Ian Richmond have argued that among the teachers employed by Agricola for that purpose probably was Demetrius of Tarsus. Frequently, he is identified with Demetrius Scribonius ("Demetrius the Scribe") of whom Plutarch reports that he later returned home from his post in Britain to his native Tarsus in modern-day Turkey, while two dedications of his are today on display in the city of York (founded by the Romans as Eboracum), where Demetrius is believed to have taught.[704] Tarsus, then under Roman influence, had become Hellenized in previous centuries and was considered one of the centers of Greek civilization, being famous for its schools and philosophers.[705] The Greek world, with Athens, Alexandria, and further places like Rhodes or Tarsus as epicenters, was regarded as the cradle of civilization in Roman eyes, as we know from many classical writers including M. Tullius Cicero and Cornelius Nepos.[706] For any

---

[702]Martin Millett, *The Romanization of Britain: An Essay in Archeological Interpretation* (Cambridge: Cambridge University Press, 1992), p. 69; Hanson, "Agricola," p. 1744.

[703]Tacitus, *Agricola/Germania/Dialogus*, p. 67 (Tac. Agr. 21).

[704]Ogilvie, "Introduction to the *Agricola*," p. 10; Ogilvie and Richmond, *De Vita Agricolae*, p. 224. See also Hanson, "Agricola," p. 1777 and W. S. Hanson, *Agricola and the Conquest of the North* (London: B. T. Batsford, 1987), pp. 73–74. Depictions (and German translations) of the two bronze plaques can be found in Kai Brodersen, *Das römische Britannien: Spuren seiner Geschichte* (Darmstadt: Primus-Verlag, 1998), p. 138.

[705]David Ulansey, *The Origins of the Mithraic Mysteries: Cosmology and Salvation in the Ancient World* (New York: Oxford University Press, 1989), p. 68. Today, of course, Tarsus is most famous for being the birthplace of Paul the Apostle.

[706]M. Tullius Cicero, *De Oratore*, With an Introduction and Notes by Augustus S. Wilkins, Liber I (Oxford: Clarendon Press, 1895), pp. 87–89. (Cic. De Orat. I, 4); Cornelius Nepos, *De Viris Illustribus: Biographien berühmter Männer*, Translated and Edited by Peter Krafft und Felicitas Olef-Krafft (Stuttgart: Reclam, 1993), p. 275 (Nep. Att. III, 1).

Romans, it was in fact the pinnacle of his education to study in Greece under its famous teachers.[707] Consequently, the fact that Agricola employed a Greek schoolmaster hints at the great importance the governor of Roman Britain ascribed to education programs in his province.

Besides employing foreign teachers and promoting schooling in Britain, Agricola may have promoted another measure as well. W. S. Hanson thus holds that some individuals—presumably the sons of local kings or aristocrats—may even have been educated in Rome "to be brought up in the Roman way," a custom Hanson compares to the practice of educating native aristocracy in English schools and universities during the heights of the British Empire.[708] In fact, this approach—a recourse to what today may be called exchange diplomacy—seems to have been common practice as well. Roman historian C. Suetonius Tranquillus (c. AD 69–after 122), more commonly known as Suetonius, for instance, provides a further example of the practice to educate the sons of leading men in his life of Augustus and even records that the first Roman emperor had the children of foreign princes (including Agrippa, grandson of Herod the Great) educated alongside his own.[709]

Admittedly, it may be argued that the course of action pursued by Agricola presents an individual case offering anecdotal evidence at best. However, there is sound evidence, including the instances already referred to, that it was rather common practice for Roman officials to flank military conquest with soft power measures of romanization. In view of comparable examples to be found in literature, later observers thus justly emphasized the spread as well as the importance of such measures throughout the empire. In his magisterial *The History of the Decline and Fall of the Roman Empire* Edward Gibbon, for example, recognized the common Roman recourse to what we might today call measures of soft power, especially with respect to the Latin language,

> So sensible were the Romans of the influence of language over national manners, that it was their most serious care to extend, with the progress of their arms, the use of the Latin tongue. [...] Education and study insensibly inspired the natives of those countries with the sentiments of the Romans; and Italy gave fashions, as well as laws, to her Latin provincials.[710]

In view of such observations, Renaissance scholar Lorenzo Valla certainly had a point when he argued that the Latin tongue "had more power than all the legions combined."[711]

---

[707]Theodor Mommsen, *Römische Geschichte, Dritter Band: Von Sullas Tode bis zur Schlacht von Thapsus* (Berlin: Weidmannsche Buchhandlung, 1861), p. 559.

[708]Hanson, *Agricola and the Conquest of the North*, p. 82.

[709]Suetonius, *Die Kaiserviten: De Vita Caesarum/Berühmte Männer: De Viris Illustribus*, pp. 229–231 (Suet. Aug. 48).

[710]Edward Gibbon, *The Decline and Fall of the Roman Empire, Volume I* (New York, N.Y.: Alfred A. Knopf, 1993), p. 44.

[711]Vincent Cronin, *The Flowering of the Renaissance* (London: Pimlico, 1992), p. 59.

Regarding intentions behind the measures started in the winter of AD 79 in Britannia, Hanson fittingly asserts that romanization "was not a question of altruism" but instead "had its roots in pure pragmatism"[712] and was "simply a matter of effective government."[713] In fact, this practice can be regarded as a crucial component in Roman pacification efforts in provinces throughout the entire empire. Elsewhere, in his *Histories*, Tacitus hence lets Roman general and provincial administrator Quintus Petillius Cerialis praise the benefits of romanization to the Treviri and Lingones tribes.[714] Actually, the mission of pacifying conquered peoples—combined with the unequivocal mandate to crush those resisting—found expression in Virgil's famous instruction vindicating Roman dominion at large,

> Tu regere imperio populos, Romane, memento;
> Hae tibi erunt artes; pacisque inponere morem,
> Pacere subiectis, et debellare superbos.[715]

This observation corresponds perfectly with the non-normative nature of soft power as put forth by Joseph Nye and elaborated upon above. In fact, Tacitus himself does not conceal Agricola's non-altruistic but rather interest-driven motives when he argues that through means of romanization the local inhabitants "might be habituated by comfort to peace and quiet." And after listing the policies put forth by Agricola cited above he acknowledges, "[L]ittle by little the Britons went astray into alluring vices: to the promenade, the bath, the well-appointed dinner table. The simple natives gave the name of 'culture' to this factor of their slavery."[716] A comparable passage on that score can also be found in Gaius Julius Caesar's *Commentarii de Bello Gallico*, in which the Roman general and politician identified the proximity of the Gauls to the amenities of the Roman province as a vital factor contributing to their defeat, whereas the Germans, living further away from Roman rule, had retained their fortitude and freedom.[717]

Summing up the measures undertaken by Agricola in Britannia while switching into twenty-first century parlance and referencing the soft power taxonomy introduced above, the Roman governor, by employing a "visiting professor" from one of the most distinguished centers of Greek learning and by promoting the Roman

---

[712]Hanson, *Agricola and the Conquest of the North*, pp. 73–74. See also Hanson, "Agricola," p. 1775.

[713]Hanson, *Agricola and the Conquest of the North*, p. 82.

[714]Tacitus, *The Histories*, pp. 186–188 (Tac. Hist. IV, 73-74). The author wishes to express his cordial thanks to Dr. Tom van de Loo for suggesting the passage in Tacitus' *Histories*.

[715]Virgil (P. Vergilius Maro), *The Aeneid*, With a Translation by Charles J. Billson, Volume I (London: Edward Arnold, 1906), p. 304 (Verg. Aen. VI, 851-853). Virgil's immortal call translates, "You, Roman, remember to rule the peoples with authority;/These shall be your arts; establish peace based on customs,/Pacify the conquered, and vanquish the haughty;" author's translation.

[716]Tacitus, *Agricola/Germania/Dialogus*, p. 67 (Tac. Agr. 21). It is an interesting fact that a statue of Agricola erected in Victorian times now overlooks the Great Bath, part of the Roman bath houses and one of the most famous remnants of Roman Britain in picturesque Bath, Somerset.

[717]C. Iulius Caesar, *Der Gallische Krieg: De Bello Gallico*, Edited by Otto Schönberger (München: Artemis Verlag, 1990), p. 289 (Caes. Gal. VI, 24).

practice of "studying abroad," applied measures clearly attributable to the arsenal of soft power instruments (Subunit II). As Tacitus notes, these measures of romanization were intended to spread Roman culture (Subunit I) throughout the Roman Empire and were—as was later the case for the British Empire as well—first and foremost directed at the ruling classes, or, with Tacitus, "the sons of the local chieftains."[718] Thus, only a small number of high-ranking and selected individuals enjoyed Roman education.[719] In this context, the fact that romanization was not directed toward the general populace but foremost rather toward a small elite can easily be explained by the circumstance that the Romans did not pursue some altruistic, broadly conceived education program but rather self-servingly sought to influence those who in the future can be expected to reach positions in which they might decide on matters of war and peace. They chiefly resorted, in short, to the direct form of wielding soft power.

Turning to the reception of the measures taken (Subunit III), Tacitus emphasizes the generally positive response to romanization measures and accordingly argues that the Britons who "used to reject the Latin language began to aspire to rhetoric" while "the toga came into fashion."[720] Accordingly, W. S. Hanson has in this regard noted that for the Romans and the local aristocracy "the attractions of romanisation and education were mutual" since the Romans were able to secure peace and economic profitability of the province, while the native ruling elites were able to remain in positions of power within their respective societies.[721] However, other sources reveal that romanization efforts at times also caused ridicule by restive natives and in some cases even proved decidedly ineffective—pointing at the high context dependence of wielding soft power and the possibility of backfiring. A particular prominent case in point in this regard is the example of Cheruscan prince Arminius (whose native Germanic name remains unknown). Arminius had been brought to Rome as a hostage in his youth, received his (military) education in the capital, granted Roman citizenship, and returned to his native Germany as the commander of a Roman auxiliary detachment only to turn against Rome and annihilate three of its legions in the Battle of the Teutoburg Forest in AD 9.[722] It may therefore be argued that the soft power measures of romanization not always bore fruit or brought about the intended outcomes. Interestingly, however, L. Cassius Dio, in his *Roman History*, explicitly referred to the harsh measures taken by P. Quinctilius Varus upon assuming the office of provincial governor in Germania as the true cause for the insurrection under Arminius.[723] (Not

---

[718]Tacitus, *Agricola/Germania/Dialogus*, p. 67 (Tac. Agr. 21).

[719]Ogilvie and Richmond, *De Vita Agricolae*, p. 224.

[720]Tacitus, *Agricola/Germania/Dialogus*, p. 67 (Tac. Agr. 21).

[721]Hanson, *Agricola and the Conquest of the North*, p. 82.

[722]Peter S. Wells, *The Battle That Stopped Rome: Emperor Augustus, Arminius, and the Slaughter of the Legions in the Teutoburg Forest* (New York, N.Y.: Norton & Company, 2003).

[723]L. Cassius Dio, "Die Schlacht im Teutoburger Wald," in *Die Germania des Tacitus und die wichtigsten antiken Schriftsteller über Deutschland*, Edited by Herbert Ronge (München: Ernst

incomparably, Tacitus reports on the causes of Boudica's Rebellion in AD 60/61 in his *Annales*.[724]) Consequently, on closer examination, the instance of Arminius offers yet another token for the potency of Roman soft power—since the very absence of soft power measures, it may be argued, contributed to what was to become a major *dies ater* in the long annals of Roman history.

Not least against this backdrop, questions regarding the ultimate success or failure of the measures of romanization have ultimately to be addressed. Can tangible outcomes (Subunit IV) in fact be attributed to the wielding of Roman soft power in Britannia? In general, Agricola is considered, both by Tacitus and modern commentators, to have been an exceptionally successful governor of Roman Britain. In fact, Ronald Mellor holds Agricola to have been "one of the most successful generals of the Flavian era"[725] and Tacitus himself tells us that at the end of his governorship Agricola "handed over a peaceful and safe province to his successor."[726] Andrew R. Burn agrees to this assessment and points out that when campaigning in the North, Agricola "was never called back to deal with rebellion in his rear."[727] Particularly in contrast to the policies of previous governors of Roman Britain such as Paulinus, Cerialis, or Frontinus (on most of whom Tacitus reports quite critically), Agricola took a different course.[728] In his strategy, as Tacitus tells us, soft power featured prominently indeed,

> Agricola was aware of the temper of the provincials, and took to heart the lesson which the experience of others suggested, that little was accomplished by force if injustice followed. He decided therefore to eliminate the causes of war. He began with himself and his own people: he put in order his own house, a task not less difficult for most governors than the government of a province.[729]

With his combat of injustices and corruption within the Roman ranks, Agricola thus led by example, as argued above a crucial component of soft power. And while also applying, of course, hard power against the Britons, Agricola, again with Tacitus, "paraded before them the attractions of peace."[730] In total, Agricola can therefore be regarded as an exceedingly successful Roman provincial governor who, in the words of Ogilvie and Richmond, "fought with success and administered with efficiency."[731] In fact, R. M. Ogilvie concluded that Agricola "personified the

---

Heimeran Verlag, 1944), pp. 96–99 (Cass. Dio LVI, 18). For the abortive romanization efforts in Germany between the rivers Rhine and Elbe, see also Ralf-Peter Märtin, *Die Varusschlacht: Rom und die Germanen* (Frankfurt am Main: S. Fischer Verlag, 2008), pp. 171–177.

[724]P. Cornelius Tacitus, *Annalen: Annales*, Edited by Erich Heller, With an Introduction by Manfred Fuhrmann (München: Artemis & Winkler, 1992), pp. 662–665 (Tac. Ann. XIV, 29-31).

[725]Ronald Mellor, *Tacitus* (New York, N.Y.: Routledge, 1993), p. 10.

[726]Tacitus, *Agricola/Germania/Dialogus*, p. 101 (Tac. Agr. 40).

[727]Burn, *Agricola and Roman Britain*, p. 92.

[728]Burn, *Agricola and Roman Britain*, p. 91.

[729]Tacitus, *Agricola/Germania/Dialogus*, p. 63 (Tac. Agr. 19).

[730]Tacitus, *Agricola/Germania/Dialogus*, p. 67 (Tac. Agr. 20).

[731]Ogilvie and Richmond, *De Vita Agricolae*, p. 4.

qualities necessary for the successful working of the Roman empire"[732]—an assessment that can be attributed to no small part to the soft power measures of romanization taken by him.

In the final analysis, the episode therefore offers an excellent example of how soft power can help bring about intended outcomes. Leaving the province Britannia and looking at the bigger picture, Rome—through military conquest and the subsequent spread of its culture—had for many peoples become master and role model at the same time.[733] A. R. Burn hence argued that "with the spread of Latin swiftly demolishing the language-barrier, the Roman empire was indeed a 'melting-pot' of peoples only to be matched by the United States."[734] W. S. Hanson likewise noted, "The process of romanisation was [. . .] as crucial to Rome's success as the strength and morale of her army."[735] In short, the potency of soft power has hence long been recognized and can be found in the practice of international affairs even millennia ago. At the same time, as the brief deliberations on the soft power of the Roman Empire have illustrated, the taxonomy of soft power presented above is capable indeed to capture its mechanisms when applied to an empirical example.

3.6 Interim Conclusion II: Deconstructing Soft Power

In a sense, the soft power taxonomy introduced, elaborated, and empirically substantiated above can be considered the very linchpin of the study at hand since it serves as a connecting device between both research questions put forth at the beginning of this study.

On the one hand, and addressing the first research question (Q_1), the deconstruction of soft power into four subunits presents a major elaboration of a hitherto immensely vague concept. The introduced set of four soft power subunits (i.e., resources, instruments, reception, and outcomes) as well as their elaboration and classification into the overall concept of soft power offers useful remedy in this regard by dissecting the concept of soft power into qualitatively different and conceptually tangible units of analysis. At it, while also including resources as the "raw materials" of (soft) power, the taxonomy pays tribute to the highly relational and contextual nature of power in general and soft power in particular that has time and again been discussed and illustrated above. On the other hand, the taxonomy can also serve as a guideline for the empirical analysis of soft power in international relations. At it, it allows for empiric, comparative application along the lines of the

---

[732]Ogilvie, "Introduction to the *Agricola*," p. 21.

[733]Alexander Rubel, "Vorwort," in *Imperium und Romanisierung: Neue Forschungsansätze aus Ost und West zu Ausübung, Transformation und Akzeptanz von Herrschaft im Römischen Reich*, ed. Alexander Rubel (Konstanz: Hartung-Gorre Verlag, 2013), p. 9.

[734]Burn, *Agricola and Roman Britain*, p. 118.

[735]Hanson, *Agricola and the Conquest of the North*, p. 73.

Table 3.2 The four soft power subunits and their respective indicators

Subunit	Component	Indicator(s)
I Resources	(1) Culture	(1) Pervasiveness of (high and popular) culture
	(2) Values	(1) Values represented (2) Consistency of values with political action (3) Commitment to multilateralism
	(3) Policies	(1) Grand strategy (2) Relation to hard and soft power (3) Primacy of national interest vs. common good (4) Adherence to international law (5) Credibility and legitimacy (6) Prevalent domestic policies and issues
	(4) Personalities	(1) Character and charisma of decision-makers (2) Team of cabinet members and advisors (3) Relationships between decision-makers
II Instruments	(1) Public Diplomacy	(1) Overall organizational structure (2) Personnel (leading positions and staff) (3) Budget (4) Particular programs and initiatives
	(2) Personal Diplomacy	(1) Number, duration, and quality of foreign travels (2) Speeches and public remarks (3) Symbolic acts (4) Influential networks
III Reception	Attraction V Apathy V Repulsion	(1) Public opinion polls (2) Contemporary statements and subsequent reminiscences of decision-makers and elites (3) Media and content analysis
IV Outcomes	Compliance V Neutrality V Opposition	(1) Compliance record in international organizations (2) Voting patterns in U.N. General Assembly (3) Compliance in foreign policy decisions (4) Number and character of treaties concluded/joined

four subunits and their respective indicators. All four subunits considered, a total of 28 indicators have thus been deduced and discussed, as conclusively depicted in Table 3.2.

In 2013, Joseph Nye has pointed out, "Contrary to the views of some sceptics, soft power has often had very real effects in history, including on the movement of armies."[736] Benjamin E. Goldsmith and Yusaku Horiuchi, when condensing the results of their research, equally asserted, "In sum, this study suggests not only that soft power offers appealing rhetoric for leaders or a catchy phrase for pundits but also that it has real ramifications for international relations."[737] Bearing in mind the wide array of historical examples referred to above, ranging over different times and

---

[736]Nye, "Hard, Soft, and Smart Power," p. 566.
[737]Goldsmith and Horiuchi, "In Search of Soft Power," pp. 582–583.

places, such statements prove to be well-founded, indeed. In view of the often long and intricate workings of soft power, however, only meticulously designed empirical research will provide truly substantiated results. By providing a comprehensive roadmap, and hence addressing the second research question (Q_2) of the work in hand, the following chapter shall discuss methodological issues and provide resilient approaches for the empirical study of soft power in international relations.

References

Ailon, Galit. "What B Would Otherwise Do: A Critique of Conceptualizations of 'Power' in Organizational Theory." *Organization*, Vol. 13, No. 6 (2006), pp. 771–800.

American Association of University Professors. "On Partnerships with Foreign Governments: The Case of Confucius Institutes." Prepared by the Association's Committee A on Academic Freedom and Tenure. June 2014. Online at: http://www.aaup.org/file/Confucius_Institutes_0. pdf (accessed November 11, 2014).

American Marketing Association. "Definition of Marketing." July 2013. Online at: https://www. ama.org/AboutAMA/Pages/Definition-of-Marketing.aspx (accessed December 1, 2014).

Appleby, Scott. "Pope John Paul II." *Foreign Policy*, No. 119 (Summer 2000), pp. 12–25.

Aristotle. *The Art of Rhetoric*. London: Harper Press, 2012 (Aristot. Rh.).

Armstrong, Matthew C. "Operationalizing Public Diplomacy." In *Routledge Handbook of Public Diplomacy*, edited by Nancy Snow and Philip M. Taylor, pp. 63–71. New York, N.Y.: Routledge, 2009.

Arndt, Richard T. *The First Resort of Kings: American Cultural Diplomacy in the Twentieth Century*. Washington, D.C.: Potomac Books, 2005.

Asmus, Ronald D. *German Strategy and Opinion After the Wall, 1990-1993*. Santa Monica, Cal.: RAND, 1994.

Atkinson, Carol. "Does Soft Power Matter? A Comparative Analysis of Student Exchange Programs 1980-2006." *Foreign Policy Analysis*, Vol. 6, No. 1 (2010), pp. 1–22.

Auer, Claudia. *Theorie der Public Diplomacy: Sozialtheoretische Grundlegung einer Form strategischer Kommunikation*. Wiesbaden: Springer VS, 2017.

Auer, Claudia, Alice Srugies, and Martin Löffelholz. "Schlüsselbegriffe der internationalen Diskussion: Public Diplomacy und Soft Power." In *Kultur und Außenpolitik: Handbuch für Wissenschaft und Praxis*, edited by Kurt-Jürgen Maaß, pp. 39–54. Baden Baden: Nomos Verlagsgesellschaft, 2015.

Aurelius Victor, S. *Die Römischen Kaiser: Liber de Caesaribus*. Edited, Translated, and Annotated by Kirsten Groß-Albenhausen and Manfred Fuhrmann. Zürich/Düsseldorf: Artemis & Winkler, 1997 (Aur. Vict. De Caes.).

Baberowski, Jörg. *Der Sinn der Geschichte: Geschichtstheorien von Hegel bis Foucault*. München: C. H. Beck, 2005.

Barnes, Douglas F. "Charisma and Religious Leadership: An Historical Analysis." *Journal for the Scientific Study of Religion*, Vol. 17, No. 1 (March 1978), pp. 1–18.

Baumann, Peter and Gisela Cramer. "Power, Soft or Deep? An Attempt at Constructive Criticism." *Las Torres de Lucca: International Journal of Political Philosophy*, No. 10 (January-June 2017), pp. 177–214.

Berenskoetter, Felix. "Thinking about Power." In *Power in World Politics*, edited by Felix Berenskoetter and M.J. Williams, pp. 1–22. New York, N.Y.: Routledge, 2008.

Bergen, Peter L. *The Longest War: The Enduring Conflict between America and al-Qaeda*. New York, N.Y.: Free Press, 2011.

Berman, Russell A. *Anti-Americanism in Europe: A Cultural Problem*. Stanford, Cal.: Hoover Institution Press, 2008.

Black, David and Byron Peacock. "Sport and Diplomacy." In *The Oxford Handbook of Modern Diplomacy*, edited by Andrew F. Cooper, Jorge Heine, and Ramesh Thakur, pp. 708–725. Oxford: Oxford University Press, 2013.

Blanchard Jean-Marc F. and Fujia Lu. "Thinking Hard about Soft Power: A Review and Critique of the Literature on China and Soft Power." *Asian Perspective* Vol. 36, No. 4 (2012), pp. 565–589.

Bliesemann de Guevara, Berit and Tatjana Reiber. "Popstars der Macht: Charisma und Politik." In *Charisma und Herrschaft*, edited by Berit Bliesemann de Guevara and Tatjana Reiber, pp. 15–52. Frankfurt am Main: Campus, 2011.

Blizzard Entertainment. "World of Warcraft: Azeroth by the Numbers." January 28, 2014. Online at: http://us.battle.net//wow/en/blog/12346804 (accessed July 14, 2015).

Blow, Charles M. "Trump, Chieftain of Spite." *The New York Times*, October 15, 2017. Online at: https://www.nytimes.com/2017/10/15/opinion/columnists/trump-spite-obama-legacy.html (accessed October 16, 2017).

Brands, H. W. *American Dreams: The United States Since 1945*. New York, N.Y.: The Penguin Press, 2010.

Brodersen, Kai. *Das römische Britannien: Spuren seiner Geschichte*. Darmstadt: Primus-Verlag, 1998.

Brown, Archie. *The Rise and Fall of Communism*. New York, N.Y.: Ecco, 2009.

Brown, John. "Arts Diplomacy: The Neglected Aspect of Cultural Diplomacy." In *Routledge Handbook of Public Diplomacy*, edited by Nancy Snow and Philip M. Taylor, pp. 57–59. New York, N.Y.: Routledge, 2009.

Burckhardt, Jacob. *Weltgeschichtliche Betrachtungen*. Stuttgart: Alfred Kröner, 1978.

Burke, Kathryn L. and Merlin B. Brinkerhoff. "Capturing Charisma: Notes on an Elusive Concept." *Journal for the Scientific Study of Religion*, Vol. 20, No. 3 (September 1981), pp. 274–284.

Burn, Andrew Robert. *Agricola and Roman Britain*. London: English Universities Press, 1953.

Burns, James MacGregor. *Transforming Leadership: A New Pursuit of Happiness*. New York, N.Y.: Grove Press, 2003.

Burns, Robert. "To a Louse." Modern English Translation by Michael R. Burch. Online at: http://www.thehypertexts.com/Robert%20Burns%20Translations%20Modern%20English.htm (accessed July 14, 2015).

Bush, George W. *Decision Points*. New York, N.Y.: Crown Publishers, 2010.

Byman, Daniel L. and Kenneth M. Pollack. "Let us Now Praise Great Men: Bringing the Statesman Back In." *International Security*, Vol. 25, No. 4 (Spring 2001), pp. 107–146.

Caesar, C. Iulius. *Der Gallische Krieg: De Bello Gallico*. Edited by Otto Schönberger. München: Artemis Verlag, 1990 (Caes. Gal.)

Canham, Erwin D. *The American Position in the World*. Claremont, Cal.: Claremont Graduate School and University Center, 1965.

Capra, Frank. *The Name Above the Title: An Autobiography*. New York, N.Y.: The Macmillan Company, 1971.

Carlyle, Thomas. *On Heroes, Hero-Worship, and the Heroic in History: Six Lectures*. London: James Fraser, 1841.

Carrington, Peter, Lord. *Reflecting on Things Past: The Memoirs of Peter Lord Carrington*. New York, N.Y.: Harper & Row, 1988.

Cassius Dio, L. "Die Schlacht im Teutoburger Wald." In *Die Germania des Tacitus und die wichtigsten antiken Schriftsteller über Deutschland*, Edited by Herbert Ronge, pp. 96–103. München: Ernst Heimeran Verlag, 1944 (Cass. Dio).

Cave, Damien. "With Obama Visit to Cuba, Old Battle Lines Fade." *The New York Times*, March 26, 2016. Online at: http://www.nytimes.com/2016/03/27/world/americas/with-obama-visit-to-cuba-old-battle-lines-fade.html (accessed June 14, 2016).

Cherrington, Ben M. "The Division of Cultural Relations." *Foreign Affairs*, Vol. 3, No. 1 (January 1939), pp. 136–138.

Chitty, Naren. "Australian Public Diplomacy." In *Routledge Handbook of Public Diplomacy*, edited by Nancy Snow and Philip M. Taylor, pp. 314–322. New York, N.Y.: Routledge, 2009.

Chitty, Naren. "Soft Power, Civic Virtue and World Politics (Section Overview)." In *The Routledge Handbook of Soft Power*, edited by Naren Chitty, Li Ji, Gary D. Rawnsley, and Craig Hayden, pp. 9–36. Abingdon: Routledge, 2017.

Churchill, Winston S. *Great Contemporaries*. London: Thornton Butterworth, 1937.

Churchill, Winston S. *The Second World War: Volume I, The Gathering Storm*. London: Cassell, 1949.

Cicero, M. Tullius. *De Oratore*. With an Introduction and Notes by Augustus S. Wilkins, Liber I. Oxford: Clarendon Press, 1895 (Cic. De Orat.).

Clark, Christopher. *The Sleepwalkers: How Europe Went to War in 1914*. London: Penguin, 2013.

Clarke, Richard A. *Against All Enemies: Inside America's War on Terror*. New York, N.Y.: Free Press, 2004.

Clinton, Hillary Rodham. "Leading Through Civilian Power: Redefining American Diplomacy and Development." *Foreign Affairs*, Vol. 89, No. 6 (November /December 2010), pp. 13–24.

Clinton, Hillary Rodham. *Hard Choices*. New York, N.Y.: Simon & Schuster, 2014.

Clinton, William J. "Remarks at the White House Conference on Culture and Diplomacy." Washington, D.C., November 28, 2000. In *Public Papers of the Presidents of the United States: William J. Clinton, 2000-2001, Book III – October 12, 2000 to January 20, 2001*, pp. 2585–2589. Washington, D.C.: United States Government Printing Office, 2001.

Cohen, Eliot A. "History and the Hyperpower." *Foreign Affairs*, Vol. 83, No. 4 (July/August 2004), pp. 49–63.

Cohen, Eliot A. *The Big Stick: The Limits of Soft Power and the Necessity of Military Force*. New York, N.Y.: Basic Books, 2016.

Cohen, Jeffery E. "Presidential Attention Focusing in the Global Arena: The Impact of International Travel on Foreign Publics." *Presidential Studies Quarterly*, Vol. 46, No. 1 (March 2016), pp. 30–47.

Colschen, Lars C. *Deutsche Außenpolitik*. Paderborn: Wilhelm Fink, 2010.

Cooney, Jim and Guido Goldman. "Preface I." In *The United States and German-American Relations Through German Eyes*, edited by Cord Jakobeit, Ute Sacksofsky, and Peter Welzel, pp. vii-ix. New York, N.Y.: Nova Science Publishers, 1996.

Cooper, Andrew F. *Celebrity Diplomacy*. Boulder, Colo.: Paradigm Publishers, 2008.

Courgeau, Daniel. *Probability and Social Science: Methodological Relationships between the Two Approaches*. Dordrecht: Springer, 2012.

Cowan, Geoffrey and Nicholas J. Cull. "Public Diplomacy in a Changing World." *The Annals of the American Academy of Political and Social Sciences*, Vol. 616, Public Diplomacy in a Changing World (March 2008), pp. 6–8.

Cowell, Alan. "Power of Celebrity at Work in Davos." *International Herald Tribune*, January 29-30, 2005, p. 1 & p. 4.

Cronin, Vincent. *Napoleon: Eine Biographie*. Hamburg: Classen Verlag, 1973.

Cronin, Vincent. *The Flowering of the Renaissance*. London: Pimlico, 1992.

Cull, Nicholas J. "Public Diplomacy: Taxonomies and Histories." *The Annals of the American Academy of Political and Social Sciences*, Vol. 616, Public Diplomacy in a Changing World (March 2008), pp. 31–54.

Cull, Nicholas J. "Public Diplomacy before Gullion: The Evolution of a Phrase." In *Routledge Handbook of Public Diplomacy*, edited by Nancy Snow and Philip M. Taylor, pp. 19–23. New York, N.Y.: Routledge, 2009.

Cull, Nicholas J. *Public Diplomacy: Lessons from the Past, CPD Perspectives on Public Diplomacy*. Los Angeles, Cal.: Figueroa Press, 2011.

Culligan, Kieron, John Dubber, and Mona Lotten. "As Others See Us: Culture, Attraction and Soft Power." *British Council* (2014). Online at: https://www.britishcouncil.org/sites/default/files/as-others-see-us-report.pdf (accessed June 7, 2016).

Cullinane, Michael Patrick. "A (Near) Great President: Theodore Roosevelt as the First Modern President." In *Perspectives on Presidential Leadership: An International View of the White House*, edited by Michael Patrick Cullinane and Clare Frances Elliott, pp. 73–90. New York, N. Y.: Routledge, 2014.

Culver, John C. "Recorded Interview by Vicki Daitch." Boston, Mass., May 12, 2003. *John F. Kennedy Library Oral History Program.* Online at: http://www.jfklibrary.org/Asset-Viewer/Archives/JFKOH-JCC-01.aspx (accessed April 12, 2016).

D'Hooghe, Ingrid. *The Limits of China's Soft Power in Europe: Beijing's Public Diplomacy Puzzle.* The Hague: Netherlands Institute of International Relations Clingendael, 2010.

D'Hooghe, Ingrid. *China's Public Diplomacy*. Leiden: Brill Nijhoff, 2015.

Dahl, Robert A. "The Concept of Power." *Behavioral Science*, Vol. 2, No. 3 (1957), pp. 201–215.

Dallek, Robert. *Nixon and Kissinger: Partners in Power*. London: Allen Lane, 2007.

Dassow, Joahnnes. *Friedrich II. von Preussen und Peter III. von Russland*. Dissertation, Friedrich-Wilhelms-Universität zu Berlin, 1908.

Davies, Wilder. "The Story Behind the 2018 TIME 100 Covers." *TIME Magazine*, April 19, 2018. Online at: http://time.com/5245018/time-100-2018-covers/ (accessed April 24, 2018).

De Gaulle, Charles. "Ansprache von General de Gaulle an die Bevölkerung auf dem Marktplatz in Bonn am 5. September 1962." *Informationsblätter der Französischen Botschaft Bonn-Bad Godesberg*, No. 264, 15. September 1962, p. 12.

Debray, Régis. "The Third World: From Kalashnikovs to God and Computers." *New Perspectives Quarterly*, Vol. 3, No. 1 (Spring 1986). Online at: http://www.digitalnpq.org/archive/1986_spring/kalashnikov.html (accessed August 4, 2017).

Dellios, Rosita and R. James Ferguson. "Sino-Indian Soft Power in a Regional Context." *Culture Mandala: The Bulletin of the Centre for East-West Cultural and Economic Studies*, Vol. 9, No. 2 (2011), pp. 15–34.

DeYoung, Karen and Nick Miroff. "Obama, Castro to Talk on Sidelines of Summit." *The Washington Post*, April 10, 2015. Online at: https://www.washingtonpost.com/world/obama-raul-castro-speak-by-phone-before-heading-to-panama-summit/2015/04/10/2da5c2f6-de22-11e4-b6d7-b9bc8acf16f7_story.html (accessed June 14, 2016).

Dias, Elizabeth. "The New Roman Empire." *TIME Magazine*, September 28, 2015, pp. 26–31.

Dillon, John. "The Record-Setting Ex-Presidency of Jimmy Carter." *The Atlantic*, September 9, 2012. Online at: http://www.theatlantic.com/politics/archive/2012/09/the-record-setting-ex-presidency-of-jimmy-carter/262143/ (accessed June 14, 2016).

Dodge, Theodore A. *The Great Captains: The Art of War in the Campaigns of Alexander, Hannibal, Caesar, Gustavus Adolphus, Frederick the Great, and Napoleon*. New York, N.Y.: Barnes & Nobles, 1995.

Dow, Thomas E., Jr. "The Theory of Charisma." *The Sociological Quarterly*, Vol. 10, No. 3 (Summer 1969), pp. 306–318.

Dow, Thomas E., Jr. "An Analysis of Weber's Work on Charisma." *The British Journal of Sociology*, Vol. 29, No. 1 (March 1978), pp. 83–93.

Dragojlovic, Nicolas Isak. "Priming and the Obama Effect on Public Evaluations of the United States." *Political Psychology*, Vol. 32, No. 6, The Obama Presidency Special Issue (December 2011), pp. 989–1006.

Duffey, Joseph. "How Globalization Became U.S. Public Diplomacy at the End of the Cold War." In *Routledge Handbook of Public Diplomacy*, edited by Nancy Snow and Philip M. Taylor, pp. 325–334. New York, N.Y.: Routledge, 2009.

Dumbrell, John. *The Carter Presidency: A Re-Evaluation*. Manchester: Manchester University Press, 1995.

Dür, Andreas. "Discriminating Among Rival Explanations: Some Tools for Small-n Researchers." In *Research Design in Political Science: How to Practice What They Preach*, edited by Thomas Geschwend and Frank Schimmelfennig, pp. 183–200. Basingstoke: Palgrave Macmillan, 2011.

Duranti, Marco. *The Conservative Human Rights Revolution: European Identify, Transnational Politics, and the Origins of the European Convention*. New York, N.Y.: Oxford University Press, 2017.

Eisenhower, Dwight D. *The White House Years: Waging Peace, 1956-1961*. Garden City, N.Y.: Doubleday, 1965.

Eliot, T. S. *Notes towards the Definition of Culture*. New York, N.Y.: Harcourt, Brace and Company, 1949.

Emrich, Cynthia G., Holly H. Brower, Jack M. Feldman, and Howard Garland. "Images in Words: Presidential Rhetoric, Charisma, and Greatness." *Administrative Science Quarterly*, Vol. 46, No. 3 (September 2001), pp. 527–558.

Engelstad, Frederik. "Culture and Power." in In *The SAGE Handbook of Power*, edited by Stewart R. Clegg and Mark Haugaard, pp. 210–238. London: SAGE Publications, 2009.

Ermarth, Michael. "Between Blight and Blessing: The Influence of American Popular Culture on the Federal Republic." In *The United States and Germany in the Era of the Cold War, 1945-1990: A Handbook, Volume II: 1968-1990*, edited by Detlef Junker, associated editors Philipp Gassert, Wilfried Mausbach, and David B. Morris, pp. 334–340. Cambridge: Cambridge University Press, 2004.

Ernst & Young. "Rapid-Growth Markets Soft Power Index: Spring 2012." 2012. Online at: http://emergingmarkets.ey.com/wp-content/uploads/downloads/2012/05/TBF-606-Emerging-markets-soft-power-index-2012_LR.pdf (accessed October 1, 2015).

Ferguson, Niall. "Think Again: Power." *Foreign Policy*, No. 134 (January/February 2003), pp. 18–22 & 24.

Ferguson, Niall. *Colossus: The Price of America's Empire*. New York, N.Y.: Penguin Press, 2004.

Fisher, Ali. "Four Seasons in One Day: The Crowded House of Public Diplomacy in the UK." In *Routledge Handbook of Public Diplomacy*, edited by Nancy Snow and Philip M. Taylor, pp. 251–261. New York, N.Y.: Routledge, 2009.

Fitzpatrick, Kathy R. *U.S. Public Diplomacy in a Post-9/11 World: From Messaging to Mutuality, CPD Perspectives on Public Diplomacy, Paper 6, 2011*. Los Angeles, Cal.: Figueroa Press, 2011.

Flynn, Michael J. "Political Minefield." In *Landmines and Human Security: International Politics and War's Hidden Legacy*, edited by Richard A. Matthew, Bryan McDonald, and Kenneth R. Rutherford, pp. 117–124. Albany, N.Y.: State University of New York Press, 2004.

Forbes. "The World's Most Powerful People: 2015 Ranking." Online at: http://www.forbes.com/powerful-people/list/#tab:overall (accessed November 30, 2015).

"France-U.S.S.R. Treaty of Mutual Assistance." *The American Journal of International Law*, Vol. 30, No. 4, Supplement: Official Documents (October 1936), pp. 177–180.

Fraser, Matthew. *Weapons of Mass Distraction: Soft Power and American Empire*. New York, N.Y.: St. Martin's Press, 2003.

Fraser, Matthew. "American Pop Culture as Soft Power: Movies and Broadcasting." In *Soft Power Superpowers: Cultural and National Assets of Japan and the United States*, edited by Watanabe Yasushi and David L. McConnell, pp. 172–187. Armonk, N.Y.: M.E. Sharpe, 2008.

Friedrich der Große. "Der Antimachiavell." In *Ausgewählte Schriften*, edited by Ulrike-Christine Sander, pp. 9–46. Frankfurt am Main: Fischer, 2011.

Fuhrer, Armin and Norman Haß. *Eine Freundschaft für Europa: Der lange Weg zum Élysée-Vertrag*. München: Olzog Verlag, 2013.

Fukuyama, Francis. "The Neoconservative Moment." *The National Interest*, No. 76 (Summer 2004), pp. 57–68.

Füssl, Karl-Heinz. "Between Elitism and Education Reform: German-American Exchange Programs, 1945-1970." In *The United States and Germany in the Era of the Cold War, 1945-1990: A Handbook, Volume I: 1945-1968*, edited by Detlef Junker, associated editors Philipp Gassert, Wilfried Mausbach, and David B. Morris, pp. 409–416. Cambridge: Cambridge University Press, 2004.

Gaddis, John Lewis. *The Cold War*. London: Penguin Books, 2005

Gaddis, John Lewis. *George F. Kennan: An American Life*. New York, N.Y.: The Penguin Press, 2011.

Gaddis, John Lewis. *On Grand Strategy*. New York, N.Y.: Penguin Press, 2018.

Gamper, Michael. *Der große Mann. Geschichte eines politischen Phantasmas*. Göttingen: Wallstein Verlag, 2016.

Gass, Robert H. and John S. Seiter. "Credibility and Public Diplomacy." In *Routledge Handbook of Public Diplomacy*, edited by Nancy Snow and Philip M. Taylor, pp. 154–165. New York, N.Y.: Routledge, 2009.

Geiger, Till. *"The Power Game*, Soft Power and the International Historian." In *Soft Power and US Foreign Policy: Theoretical, Historical and Contemporary Perspectives*, edited by Inderjeet Parmar and Michael Cox, pp. 83–107. Abingdon: Routledge, 2010.

Gelb, Leslie H. *Power Rules: How Common Sense Can Rescue American Foreign Policy*. New York, N.Y.: HarperCollins, 2009.

Gibbon, Edward. *The Decline and Fall of the Roman Empire, Volume I*. New York, N.Y.: Alfred A. Knopf, 1993.

Gilbert, Martin. *Churchill and America*. New York, N.Y.: Free Press, 2005.

Gilboa, Eytan. "Searching for a Theory of Public Diplomacy." *The Annals of the American Academy of Political and Social Science*, Vol. 616, Public Diplomacy in a Changing World (March 2008), pp. 55–77.

Goff, Patricia M. "Cultural Diplomacy." In *The Oxford Handbook of Modern Diplomacy*, edited by Andrew F. Cooper, Jorge Heine, and Ramesh Thakur, pp. 419–435. Oxford: Oxford University Press, 2013.

Golan, Guy J. "An Integrated Approach to Public Diplomacy." *American Behavioral Scientists*, Vol. 57, No. 9 (2013), pp. 1251–1255.

Goldberg, Samuel. *Probability in Social Science: Seven Expository Units Illustrating the Use of Probability Methods and Models, with Exercises, and Bibliographies to Guide Further Reading in the Social Science and Mathematics Literatures*. Boston, Mass.: Brinkhäuser, 1982.

Goldsmith, Benjamin E. and Yusaku Horiuchi. "In Search of Soft Power: Does Foreign Public Opinion Matter for US Foreign Policy?." *World Politics*, Vol. 64, No. 3 (July 2012), pp. 555–585.

Goldstein, Peter. "The Walls of Athens and the Power of Poetry: A Note on Milton's Sonnet 8." *Milton Quarterly*, Vol. 24, No. 3 (1990), pp. 105–108.

Goldstone, Jack A. "Comparative Historical Analysis and Knowledge Accumulation in the Study of Revolutions." In *Comparative Historical Analysis in the Social Sciences*, edited by James Mahoney and Dietrich Rueschemeyer, pp. 41–90. Cambridge: Cambridge University Press, 2003.

Greenstein, Fred I. "The Impact of Personality on Politics: An Attempt to Clear Away Underbrush." *The American Political Science Review*, Vol. 61, No. 3 (September 1967), pp. 629–641.

Greenstein, Fred I. *Personality and Politics: Problems of Evidence, Interference, and Conceptualization*. Chicago, Ill.: Markham, 1969.

Greenstein, Fred I. "Can Personality and Politics be Studied Systematically." *Political Psychology*, Vol. 13, No. 1 (March 1992), pp. 105–128.

Greenstein, Fred I. "Personality and Politics." In *Encyclopedia of Government and Politics*, edited by Mary Hawkesworth and Maurice Kogan, pp. 351–369. New York, N.Y.: Routledge, 2004.

Gregory, Bruce. "Public Diplomacy: Sunrise of an Academic Field." *The Annals of the American Academy of Political and Social Sciences*, Vol. 616, Public Diplomacy in a Changing World (March 2008), pp. 274–290.

Gregory, Bruce. "American Public Diplomacy: Enduring Characteristics, Elusive Transformations." *The Hague Journal of Diplomacy*, Vol. 6, Nos. 3-4 (2011), pp. 351–372.

Grix, Jonathan and Donna Lee. "Soft Power, Sports Mega-Events and Emerging States: The Lure of the Politics of Attraction." *Global Society*, Vol. 27, No. 4 (2013), pp. 521–536.

Gu, Xuewu. "Global Power Shift: Soft, Hard and Structural Power." In *Die Gestaltung der Globalität: Annährungen an Begriff, Deutung und Methodik*, edited by Ludger Kühnhardt and Tilman Mayer, pp. 53–60. Bonn: Zentrum für Europäische Integrationsforschung, Discussion Paper C198, 2010.

Gu, Xuewu. "Strukturelle Macht: Eine dritte Machtquelle?" *Österreichische Zeitschrift für Politikwissenschaft*, Vol. 41, No. 3 (2012), pp. 259–276.

Gu, Xuewu. *Die Große Mauer in den Köpfen: China, der Westen und die Suche nach Verständigung*. Hamburg: Edition Körber-Stiftung, 2014.

Gu, Xuewu and Hendrik W. Ohnesorge. "Wer macht Politik? Überlegungen zum Einfluss politischer Persönlichkeiten auf weltpolitische Gestaltung." In *Politische Persönlichkeiten und ihre weltpolitische Gestaltung: Analysen in Vergangenheit und Gegenwart*, edited by Xuewu Gu and Hendrik W. Ohnesorge, pp. 3–14. Wiesbaden: Springer VS, 2017.

Haass, Richard N. *The Reluctant Sheriff: The United States After the Cold War*. New York, N.Y.: Council on Foreign Relations, 1997.

Hagel, Chuck. "Secretary of Defense Speech: CSIS Global Security Forum." Washington D.C., November 5, 2013. Online at: http://www.defense.gov/Speeches/Speech.aspx?SpeechID=1814 (accessed July 13, 2015).

Haldeman, H. R., with Joseph DiMona. *The Ends of Power*. New York, N.Y.: Times Books, 1978.

Hall, Todd. "An Unclear Attraction: A Critical Examination of Soft Power as an Analytical Category." *The Chinese Journal of International Politics*, Vol. 3, No. 2 (2010), pp. 189–211.

Halper, Stefan and Jonathan Clarke. *America Alone: The Neo-Conservatives and the Global Order*. Cambridge: Cambridge University Press, 2004.

Halpert, Jane A. "The Dimensionality of Charisma." *Journal of Business and Psychology*, Vol. 4, No. 4 (Summer 1990), pp. 399–410.

Hamilton, Edith. *The Greek Way*. London: W. W. Norton & Company, 1993.

Han, Byung-Chul. *Was ist Macht?* Stuttgart: Reclam, 2005.

Hanson, W. S. *Agricola and the Conquest of the North*. London: B. T. Batsford, 1987.

Hanson, W. S. "Tacitus' 'Agricola': An Archaeological and Historical Study." In *Rise and Decline of the Roman World, Part II: Participate, Volume 33.3*, edited by Wolfgang Haase, pp. 1741–1784. Berlin: Walter de Gruyter, 1989.

Hartig, Falk. *Chinese Public Diplomacy: The Rise of the Confucius Institute*. Abingdon: Routledge, 2015.

Hastedt, Glenn P. *American Foreign Policy: Past, Present, and Future*. Lanham, Md.: Rowman & Littlefield, 2015.

Hatscher, Christoph R. *Charisma und Res Publica: Max Webers Herrschaftssoziologie und die Römische Republik*. Stuttgart: Franz Steiner Verlag, 2000.

Hayden, Craig. *The Rhetoric of Soft Power: Public Diplomacy in Global Contexts*. Lanham, Md.: Lexington Books, 2012.

Hebblethwaite, Peter. *Pope John Paul II and the Church*. Kansas City, Mo.: National Catholic Reporter, 1995.

Hegel, Georg Friedrich Wilhelm. *Vorlesungen über die Philosophie der Geschichte*. Stuttgart: Reclam, 1961.

Heine, Heinrich. *Deutschland: Ein Wintermärchen*. Stuttgart: Reclam 2001.

Heine, Jorge. "From Club Diplomacy to Network Diplomacy." In *The Oxford Handbook of Modern Diplomacy*, edited by Andrew F. Cooper, Jorge Heine, and Ramesh Thakur, pp. 54–69. Oxford: Oxford University Press, 2013.

Heisbourg, François. "American Hegemony? Perceptions of the US Abroad." *Survival*, Vol. 41, No. 4 (Winter 1999/2000), pp. 5–19.

Hemery, John. "Training for Public Diplomacy: An Evolutionary Perspective." In *The New Public Diplomacy: Soft Power in International Relations*, edited by Jan Melissen, pp. 196–209. Basingstoke: Palgrave Macmillan, 2005.

Henrikson, Alan K. "Niche Diplomacy in the World Public Arena: The Global 'Corners' of Canada and Norway." In *The New Public Diplomacy: Soft Power in International Relations*, edited by Jan Melissen, pp. 67–87. Basingstoke: Palgrave Macmillan, 2005.

Hermann, Margaret G. "Political Psychology as a Perspective in the Study of Politics." In *Political Psychology*, edited by Kristen R. Monroe, pp. 43–60. Mahwah, N.J.: Erlbaum, 2002.

Hesiod. *Theogonie/Werke und Tage*. Edited and Translated by Albert von Schirnding, With an Introduction and a Register by Ernst Günther Schmidt. München: Artemis & Winkler, 1991 (Hes. Th. & Hes. WD).

Hill, Charles. *Grand Strategies: Literature, Statecraft, and World Order*. New Haven, Conn.: Yale University Press, 2010.

Hill, Christopher and Sarah Beadle. *The Art of Attraction: Soft Power and the UK's Role in the World*. London: The British Academy, 2014.

Hobbes, Thomas. *Leviathan*. With an Essay by the Late W. G. Pogson Smith. Oxford: Clarendon Press, 1909.

Hocking, Brian. "Rethinking the 'New' Public Diplomacy." In *The New Public Diplomacy: Soft Power in International Relations*, edited by Jan Melissen, pp. 28–43. Basingstoke: Palgrave Macmillan, 2005.

Holbrooke, Richard. "Get the Message Out." *The Washington Post*, October 28, 2001. Online at: http://www.washingtonpost.com/wp-dyn/content/article/2010/12/13/AR2010121305410.html (accessed April 26, 2017).

Holden, John. "Influence and Attraction: Culture and the Race for Soft Power in the 21st Century." *British Council* (2013). Online at: https://www.britishcouncil.org/sites/default/files/influence-and-attraction-report.pdf (accessed June 7, 2016).

Homer. *The Iliad*. Translated by Alexander Pope. London: W. Suttaby and C. Corral, 1806 (Hom. Il.)

Horaz (Q. Horatius Flaccus). "Sermones/Satiren." In *Sämtliche Werke: Teil II, Satiren und Briefe*. Translated and Edited by Wilhelm Schöne with Hans Färber, pp. 6–133. München: Ernst Heimeran Verlag, 1960 (Hor. Sat.).

House Resolution 190. "Honoring the Life and Achievements of his Holiness Pope John Paul II and Expressing Profound Sorrow on his Death." 109th Congress, 1st Session, April 6, 2005. *Congressional Record*, Vol. 151, Pt. 4 (2005), pp. 5736–5757.

House, Robert J., William D. Spangler, and James Woycke. "Personality and Charisma in the U.S. Presidency: A Psychological Theory of Leader Effectiveness." *Administrative Science Quarterly*, Vol. 36, No. 3 (September 1991), pp. 364–396.

Hu Jintao. "Hold High the Great Banner of Socialism with Chinese Characteristics and Strive for New Victories in Building a Moderately Prosperous Society in all." Report to the Seventeenth National Congress of the Communist Party of China, October 15, 2007. Online at: http://www.china.org.cn/english/congress/229611.htm (accessed November 11, 2014).

Ifantis, Kostas. "Soft Power: Overcoming the Limits of a Concept." In *Routledge Handbook of Diplomacy and Statecraft*, edited by B. J. C. McKercher, pp. 441–452. Abingdon: Routledge, 2011.

Inboden, William. "What is Power? And How Much of It Does America Have?." *The American Interest*, Vol. 5, No. 2 (November/December 2009), pp. 15–19 & 22–27.

Isaacson, Walter. *Kissinger: A Biography*. New York, N.Y.: Simon & Schuster, 1992.

Ivey, Bill and Paula Cleggett. "Cultural Diplomacy and the National Interest: In Search of a 21st Century Perspective." *The Curb Center for Art, Enterprise, and Public Policy, Vanderbilt University*. Online at: http://www.vanderbilt.edu/curbcenter/files/Cultural-Diplomacy-and-the-National-Interest.pdf (accessed July 14, 2015).

Ji, Li. "Measuring Soft Power (Section Overview)." In *The Routledge Handbook of Soft Power*, edited by Naren Chitty, Li Ji, Gary D. Rawnsley, and Craig Hayden, pp. 75–92. Abingdon: Routledge, 2017.

Joffe, Josef. "America the Inescapable." *The New York Times*, June 8, 1997, A Special Issue: How the World Sees Us. Online at: http://www.nytimes.com/1997/06/08/magazine/america-the-inescapable.html (accessed August 10, 2016).

Joffe, Josef. "The Perils of Soft Power." *The New York Times*, May 14, 2006. Online at: http://www.nytimes.com/2006/05/14/magazine/14wwln_lede.html (accessed June 2, 2016).

Johansen, Bruce E. *Encyclopedia of the American Indian Movement*. Santa Barbara, Cal.: ABC-CLIO, 2013.

Johnson, David Kyle and Lance Schmitz. "Johnny Cash, Prison Reform, and Capital Punishment." In *Johnny Cash and Philosophy: The Burning Ring of Truth*, edited by John Huss and David Werther, pp. 153–168. Chicago and La Salle, Ill.: Open Court, 2008.

Kaes, Anton. "Mass Culture and Modernity: Notes Toward a Social History of Early American and German Cinema." In *America and the Germans: An Assessment of a Three-Hundred-Year History, Volume Two: The Relationship in the 20th Century*, edited by Frank Trommler and Joseph McVeigh, pp. 317–331. Philadelphia, Pa.: University of Pennsylvania Press, 1985.

Kagan, Robert. "America's Crisis of Legitimacy." *Foreign Affairs*, Vol. 83, No. 2 (March/April 2004), pp. 65–87.

Kelley, John Robert. "Between 'Take-offs' and 'Crash Landings': Situational Aspects of Public Diplomacy." In *Routledge Handbook of Public Diplomacy*, edited by Nancy Snow and Philip M. Taylor, pp. 72–85. New York, N.Y.: Routledge, 2009.

Kellner, Douglas. "Celebrity Diplomacy, Spectacle and Barack Obama." *Celebrity Studies*, Vol. 1, No. 1 (March 2010), pp. 121–123.

Kennedy, John F. "Remarks at the Closed-Circuit Television Broadcast on Behalf of the National Cultural Center." Washington D.C., November 29, 1962. In *Public Papers of the Presidents of the United States: John F. Kennedy, 1962, Containing the Public Messages, Speeches, and Statements of the President, January 1 to December 31, 1962*, pp. 846–847. Washington, D.C.: United States Government Printing Office, 1963.

Kennedy, John F. "Annual Message to the Congress on the State of the Union." Washington, D.C., January 14, 1963. In *Public Papers of the Presidents of the United States: John F. Kennedy, 1963, Containing the Public Messages, Speeches, and Statements of the President, January 1 to November 22, 1963*, pp. 11–19. Washington, D.C.: United States Government Printing Office, 1964.

Kennedy, John F. "Commencement Address at American University in Washington." Washington, D.C., June 10, 1963. In *Public Papers of the Presidents of the United States: John F. Kennedy, 1963, Containing the Public Messages, Speeches, and Statements of the President, January 1 to November 22, 1963*, pp. 459–464. Washington, D.C.: United States Government Printing Office, 1964.

Kennedy, John F. "Radio and Television Report to the American People on Civil Rights." Washington, D.C., June 11, 1963. In *Public Papers of the Presidents of the United States: John F. Kennedy, 1963, Containing the Public Messages, Speeches, and Statements of the President, January 1 to November 22, 1963*, pp. 468–471. Washington, D.C.: United States Government Printing Office, 1964.

Kennedy, John F. "Remarks in the Rudolph Wilde Platz, Berlin." West Berlin, June 26, 1963. In *Public Papers of the Presidents of the United States: John F. Kennedy, 1963, Containing the Public Messages, Speeches, and Statements of the President, January 1 to November 22, 1963*, pp. 524–525. Washington, D.C.: United States Government Printing Office, 1964.

Kennedy, Paul. *The Rise and Fall of the Great Powers*. New York, N.Y.: Vintage Books, 1987.

Kent, John. "The Egyptian Base and the Defence of the Middle East, 1945-1954." *The Journal of Imperial and Commonwealth History*, Vol. 21, No. 3 (1993), pp. 45–65.

Keohane, Robert O. and Joseph S. Nye, Jr. "Transnational Relations and World Politics: An Introduction." *International Organization*, Vol. 25, No. 3 (Summer 1971), pp. 329–349.

Kiehl, William P. "The Case for Localized Public Diplomacy." In *Routledge Handbook of Public Diplomacy*, edited by Nancy Snow and Philip M. Taylor, pp. 212–224. New York, N.Y.: Routledge, 2009.

Kissinger, Henry. *World Order: Reflections on the Character of Nations and the Course of History*. London: Allen Lane, 2014.

Knorr, Klaus. *The Power of Nations: The Political Economy of International Relations*. New York, N.Y.: Basic Books, 1975.

Koh, Harold Hongju. "On American Exceptionalism." *Stanford Law Review*, Vol. 55, No. 5 (May 2003), pp. 1479–1527.

Kohl, Helmut. *Erinnerungen: 1990-1994*. München: Droemer, 2007.

Kohl, Helmut. *Berichte zur Lage: 1989-1998, Der Kanzler und Parteivorsitzende im Bundesvorstand der CDU Deutschlands*, edited by Günter Buchstab and Hans-Otto Kleinmann. Forschungen und Quellen zur Zeitgeschichte, Band 64. Düsseldorf: Droste, 2012.

Körber, Sebastian. "Imagepflege als Daueraufgabe: Das vielschichtige Deutschlandbild." In *Kultur und Außenpolitik: Handbuch für Wissenschaft und Praxis*, edited by Kurt-Jürgen Maaß, pp. 160–168. Baden Baden: Nomos Verlagsgesellschaft, 2015.

Kotulla, Michael. *Deutsche Verfassungsgeschichte: Vom Alten Reich bis Weimar, 1495-1934*. Berlin: Springer, 2008.

Kounalakis, Markos and Andras Simonyi. *The Hard Truth about Soft Power, CPD Perspectives on Public Diplomacy*, Paper 5, 2011, Los Angeles, Cal.: Figueroa Press, 2011.

Krause, Diana E. and Eric Kearney. "The Use of Power Bases in Different Contexts: Arguments for a Context-Specific Perspective." In *Power and Influence in Organizations: New Empirical and Theoretical Perspectives*, edited by Chester A. Schriesheim and Linda L. Neider, pp. 59–86. Greenwich, Conn.: Information Age Publishing, 2006.

Kremer, Jan-Frederik and Andrej Pustovitovskij. "Towards a New Understanding of Structural Power." In *Power in the 21st Century: International Security and International Political Economy in a Changing World*, edited by Enrico Fels, Jan-Frederik Kremer, and Katharina Kronenberg, pp. 59–80. Berlin: Springer-Verlag, 2012.

Krockow, Christian Graf von. *Friedrich der Große: Ein Lebensbild*. Köln: Bastei Lübbe, 2012.

Kühnhardt, Ludger. *Die Universalität der Menschenrechte: Studie zur ideengeschichtlichen Bestimmung eines politischen Schlüsselbegriffes*. München: Günter Olzog Verlag, 1987.

Kühnhardt, Ludger. *Atlantik-Brücke: Fünfzig Jahre deutsch-amerikanische Partnerschaft*. Berlin: Propyläen, 2002.

Kumar, Matha Joynt. "Managing the News: The Bush Communications Operation." In *The Polarized Presidency of George W. Bush*, edited by George C. Edwards III and Desmond S. King, pp. 351–383. Oxford: Oxford University Press, 2007.

Kunisch, Johannes. *Friedrich der Große: Der König und seine Zeit*. München: Deutscher Taschenbuch Verlag, 2009.

Kurlantzick, Joshua. *Charm Offensive: How China's Soft Power is Transforming the World*. New Haven, Conn.: Yale University Press, 2007.

Laqueur, Walter. "Save Public Diplomacy: Broadcasting America's Message Matters." *Foreign Affairs*, Vol. 73, No. 5 (September/October 1994), pp. 19–24.

Layne, Christopher. "The Unbearable Lightness of Soft Power." In *Soft Power and US Foreign Policy: Theoretical, Historical and Contemporary Perspectives*, edited by Inderjeet Parmar and Michael Cox, pp. 51–82. Abingdon: Routledge, 2010.

Lee, Geun. "A Theory of Soft Power and Korea's Soft Power Strategy." *The Korean Journal of Defense Analysis*, Vol. 21, No. 2 (June 2009), pp. 205–218.

Leonard, John. "Saving the Athenian Walls: The Historical Accuracy of Milton's Sonnet 8." *Milton Quarterly*, Vol. 32, No. 1 (1998), pp. 1–6.

Lepsius, M. Rainer. "Das Modell der charismatischen Herrschaft und seine Anwendbarkeit auf den 'Führerstaat' Adolf Hitlers." In *Demokratie in Deutschland: Soziologisch-historische Konstellationsanalysen, Ausgewählte Aufsätze*, edited by M. Rainer Lepsius, pp. 95–118. Göttingen: Vandenhoeck & Ruprecht, 1993.

Lewis, Elias St. Elmo. "Advertisement Department: Catch-Line and Argument." *The Book-Keeper*, Vol. 15 (February 1903), pp. 124–128.

Lincoln, Abraham. "First Joint Debate." Ottawa, Ill., August 21, 1858. In *The Works of Abraham Lincoln: Volume III, Speeches and Debates, 1856-1858*, edited by John H. Clifford and Marion M. Miller, pp. 128–173. New York, N.Y.: C.S. Hammond & Co., 1908.

Linton, Ralph. *The Cultural Background of Personalities*. New York, N.Y.: Appleton-Century-Crofts, 1945.

Lipp, Wolfgang. "Charisma – Schuld und Gnade: Soziale Konstruktion, Kulturdynamik, Handlungsdrama." In *Charisma: Theorie – Religion – Politik*, edited by Winfried Gebhardt, Arnold Zingerle, Michael N. Ebertz, pp. 15–32. Berlin: Walter de Gruyter, 1993.

Lock, Edward. "Soft Power and Strategy: Developing a 'Strategic' Concept of Power." In *Soft Power and US Foreign Policy: Theoretical, Historical and Contemporary Perspectives*, edited by Inderjeet Parmar and Michael Cox, pp. 32–50. Abingdon: Routledge, 2010.

Longford, Elizabeth. *Wellington: The Years of the Sword*. New York, N.Y.: Smithmark, 1968.

Lukes, Steven. "Power and the Battle for the Hearts and Minds." *Millennium: Journal of International Studies*, Vol. 33, No. 3 (2005), pp. 477–493.

Lundestad, Geir. *The United States and Western Europe since 1945: From "Empire" by Invitation to Transatlantic Drift*. Oxford: Oxford University Press, 2003.

Luth, Jürgen. *Der Große: Friedrich II. von Preußen*. München: Siedler, 2011.

Luttwak, Edward N. *The Grand Strategy of the Roman Empire: From the First Century CE to the Third*. Baltimore, Md.: John Hopkins University Press, 2016.

Lutz, Felix Philipp. "Transatlantic Networks: Elites in German-American Relations." In *The United States and Germany in the Era of the Cold War, 1945-1990: A Handbook, Volume II: 1968-1990*, edited by Detlef Junker, associated editors Philipp Gassert, Wilfried Mausbach, and David B. Morris, pp. 445–451. Cambridge: Cambridge University Press, 2004.

Machiavelli, Niccolò. "Discourses on the First Ten Books of Titus Livius." In *The Historical, Political, and Diplomatic Writings of Niccolo Machiavelli*. Translated from the Italian by Christian E. Detmold, Volume II, pp. 89–431. Boston, Mass.: James R. Osgood and Company, 1882.

Machiavelli, Niccolò. *Das Leben Castruccio Castracanis aus Lucca*. München: C. H. Beck, 1998.

Machiavelli, Niccolò. *Der Fürst*. Frankfurt am Main: Insel Verlag, 2001.

Mandelbaum, Michael. *Mission Failure: America and the World in the Post-Cold War Era*. New York, N.Y.: Oxford University Press, 2016.

Marshall, P. David. *Celebrity and Power: Fame in Contemporary Culture*. Minneapolis, Minn.: University of Minnesota Press, 1997.

Märtin, Ralf-Peter. *Die Varusschlacht: Rom und die Germanen*. Frankfurt am Main: S. Fischer Verlag, 2008.

Mattern, Janice Bially. "Why 'Soft Power' Isn't So Soft: Representational Force and the Sociolinguistic Construction of Attraction in World Politics." *Millennium: Journal of International Studies*, Vol. 33, No. 3 (2005), pp. 583–612.

Mayer, Tilman. *Das Prinzip Nation: Dimensionen der nationalen Frage am Beispiel Deutschlands*. Opladen: Leske & Budrich, 1987.

McClellan, Michael. "Public Diplomacy in the Context of Traditional Diplomacy." In *Favorita Papers 01/2004: Public Diplomacy*, edited by Gerhard Reiweger, pp. 23–32. Vienna: Diplomatische Akademie, 2004.

Mearsheimer, John F. "The Future of the American Pacifier." *Foreign Affairs*, Vol. 80, No. 2 (September/October 2001), pp. 46–61.

Meersman, Roger. "The John F. Kennedy Center for the Performing Arts: From Dream to Reality." *Records of the Columbia Historical Society, Washington, D.C.*, Vol. 50 (1980), pp. 525–588.

Mehl, Andreas. *Römische Geschichtsschreibung: Grundlagen und Entwicklungen, Eine Einführung*. Stuttgart: Verlag W. Kohlhammer, 2001.

Melissen, Jan. "Introduction." In *The New Public Diplomacy: Soft Power in International Relations*, edited by Jan Melissen, pp. xix–xxiv. Basingstoke: Palgrave Macmillan, 2005.

Melissen, Jan. "The New Public Diplomacy: Between Theory and Practice." In *The New Public Diplomacy: Soft Power in International Relations*, edited by Jan Melissen, pp. 3–27. Basingstoke: Palgrave Macmillan, 2005.

Melissen, Jan, ed. *The New Public Diplomacy: Soft Power in International Relations*. Basingstoke: Palgrave Macmillan, 2005.

Melissen, Jan. *Wielding Soft Power: The New Public Diplomacy*. The Hague: Netherlands Institute of International Relations Clingendael, 2005.

Melissen, Jan. "Public Diplomacy." In *The Oxford Handbook of Modern Diplomacy*, edited by Andrew F. Cooper, Jorge Heine, and Ramesh Thakur, pp. 436–452. Oxford: Oxford University Press, 2013.

Mellor, Ronald. *Tacitus*. New York, N.Y.: Routledge, 1993.

Michalski, Anna. "The EU as a Soft Power: The Force of Persuasion." In *The New Public Diplomacy: Soft Power in International Relations*, edited by Jan Melissen, pp. 124–144. Basingstoke: Palgrave Macmillan, 2005.

Mill, James. "Summary Review of the Conduct and Measures of the Seventh Imperial Parliament." In *Parliamentary History and Review: Containing Reports of the Proceedings of the Two Houses of Parliament during the Session of 1826:–7 Geo. IV., With Critical Remarks on the Principal Measures of the Session*, pp. 772–802. London: Longman, Rees, Orme, Brown, and Green, 1826.

Millett, Martin. *The Romanization of Britain: An Essay in Archeological Interpretation*. Cambridge: Cambridge University Press, 1992.

Milton, John. "Sonnet VIII." In *Milton's Sonnets*. With Introduction, Notes, Glossary and Indexes by A. W. Verity, p. 11. Cambridge: Cambridge University Press, 1906.

Mirrlees, Tanner. *Hearts and Mines: The US Empire's Culture Industry*. Vancouver: University of British Columbia Press, 2016.

Mommsen, Theodor. *Römische Geschichte, Dritter Band: Von Sullas Tode bis zur Schlacht von Thapsus*. Berlin: Weidmannsche Buchhandlung, 1861.

Moravcsik, Andrew. "Taking Preferences Seriously: A Liberal Theory of International Politics." *International Organization*, Vol. 51, No. 4 (Autumn 1997), pp. 513–533.

Mueller, Sherry. "The Nexus of U.S. Public Diplomacy and Citizen Diplomacy." In *Routledge Handbook of Public Diplomacy*, edited by Nancy Snow and Philip M. Taylor, pp. 101–107. New York, N.Y.: Routledge, 2009.

Müller, Gerhard. "'…eine wunderbare Aussicht zur Vereinigung deutscher und französischer Vorstellungsarten:' Goethe und Weimar im Rheinbund." In *Europa in Weimar: Visionen eines Kontinents*, edited by Hellmut Th. Seemann, pp. 256–278. Göttingen: Wallstein Verlag, 2008.

Müller, Martin. "After Sochi 2014: Costs and Impacts of Russia's Olympic Games." *Eurasian Geography and Economics*, Vol. 55, No. 6 (2014), pp. 628–655.

Munro, Dana Carleton. "The Speech of Pope Urban II. at Clermont, 1095." *The American Historical Review*, Vol. 11, No. 2 (January 1906), pp. 231–242.

Nelson, Jinty. "Lay Readers of the Bible in the Carolingian Ninth Century." In *Reading the Bible in the Middle Ages*, edited by Jinty Nelson and Damien Kempf, pp. 43–55. London: Bloomsbury, 2015.

Nelson, Richard and Foad Izadi. "Ethics and Social Issues in Public Diplomacy." In *Routledge Handbook of Public Diplomacy*, edited by Nancy Snow and Philip M. Taylor, pp. 334–351. New York, N.Y.: Routledge, 2009.

Nepos, Cornelius. *De Viris Illustribus: Biographien berühmter Männer*. Translated and Edited by Peter Krafft and Felicitas Olef-Krafft. Stuttgart: Reclam, 1993 (here: Nep. Att.).

Néré, Jacques. *Foreign Policies of the Great Powers: Volume VII, The Foreign Policy of France from 1914 to 1945*. London: Routledge, 2004.

Nester, William R. *De Gaulle's Legacy: The Art of Power in France's Fifth Republic*. New York, N.Y.: Palgrave Macmillan, 2014.

Neuman, Rico and Kevin Coe. "The Rhetoric in the Modern Presidency: A Quantitative Analysis." In *The Rhetoric of American Exceptionalism: Critical Essays*, edited by Jason A. Edwards and David Weiss, pp. 11–30. Jefferson, N.C.: McFarland, 2011.

Nippel, Wilfried. "Charisma und Herrschaft." In *Virtuosen der Macht: Herrschaft und Charisma von Perikles bis Mao*, edited by Wilfried Nippel, pp. 7–22. München: C. H. Beck, 2000.

Nippel, Wilfried, ed. *Virtuosen Der Macht: Herrschaft Und Charisma Von Perikles Bis Mao*. München: C. H. Beck, 2000.

Nobel Prize. "The Nobel Prize in Literature 1953: Winston Churchill, Facts." Online at: http://www.nobelprize.org/nobel_prizes/literature/laureates/1953/churchill-facts.html (accessed April 28, 2015).

Noelle-Neumann, Elisabeth. "Public Opinion and the Classical Tradition: A Re-evaluation." *Public Opinion Quarterly*, Vol. 43, No. 2 (Summer 1979), pp. 143–156.

Nordalm, Jens. "Historismus im 19. Jahrhundert: Zur Fortdauer einer Epoche des geschichtlichen Denkens." In *Historismus im 19. Jahrhundert*. Edited by Jens Nordalm, pp. 7–46. Stuttgart: Reclam, 2006.

Nye, Joseph S., Jr. *Bound to Lead: The Changing Nature of American Power*. New York: Basic Books, 1990.

Nye, Joseph S., Jr. "The Power We Must Not Squander." *The New York Times*, January 3, 2000. Online at: http://www.nytimes.com/2000/01/03/opinion/the-power-we-must-not-squander.html (accessed October 10, 2015).

Nye, Joseph S., Jr. *The Paradox of American Power: Why the World's Only Superpower Can't Go It Alone*. Oxford: Oxford University Press, 2002.

Nye, Joseph S., Jr. "Limits of American Power." *Political Science Quarterly*, Vol. 117, No. 4 (Winter 2002/03), pp. 545–559.

Nye, Joseph S., Jr. "Propaganda Isn't the Way: Soft Power." *International Herald Tribune*, January 10, 2003.

Nye, Joseph S., Jr. "The Decline of America's Soft Power: Why Washington Should Worry." *Foreign Affairs*, Vol. 83, No. 3 (May/June 2004), pp. 16–20.

Nye, Joseph S., Jr. *The Power Game: A Washington Novel*. New York, N.Y.: PublicAffairs, 2004.

Nye, Joseph S., Jr. *Soft Power: The Means to Success in World Politics*. New York, N.Y.: PublicAffairs, 2004.

Nye, Joseph S., Jr. "Soft Power, Hard Power and Leadership." *Harvard Kennedy School*, October 27, 2006. Online at: http://www.hks.harvard.edu/netgov/files/talks/docs/11_06_06_seminar_Nye_HP_SP_Leadership.pdf (accessed April 26, 2015).

Nye, Joseph S., Jr. "Think Again: Soft Power." *Foreign Policy*, February 23, 2006. Online at: http://foreignpolicy.com/2006/02/23/think-again-soft-power/ (accessed February 13, 2015).

Nye, Joseph S., Jr. "Transformational Leadership and U.S. Grand Strategy." *Foreign Affairs*, Vol. 85, No. 4 (July/August 2006), pp. 139–145 & pp. 147–148.

Nye, Joseph S., Jr. "Foreword." In *Soft Power Superpowers: Cultural and National Assets of Japan and the United States*, edited by Watanabe Yasushi and David L. McConnell, pp. ix–xiv. Armonk, N.Y.: M.E. Sharpe, 2008.

Nye, Joseph S., Jr. "Notes for a Soft-Power Research Agenda." In *Power in World Politics*, edited by Felix Berenskoetter and M.J. Williams, pp. 162–172. New York, N.Y.: Routledge, 2008.

Nye, Joseph S., Jr. *The Powers to Lead*. Oxford: Oxford University Press, 2008.

Nye, Joseph S., Jr. "Public Diplomacy and Soft Power." *The Annals of the American Academy of Political and Social Science*, Vol. 616, Public Diplomacy in a Changing World (March 2008), pp. 94–109.

Nye, Joseph S., Jr. "Harvard Professor Joseph Nye on Hard and Soft Power: 'It Is Pointless to Talk to Al-Qaida.'" Interview conducted by Gabor Steingart and Gregor Peter Schmitz, *Der Spiegel*, 34/2009, August 17, 2009. Online at: http://www.spiegel.de/international/world/harvard-professor-joseph-nye-on-hard-and-soft-power-it-is-pointless-to-talk-to-al-qaida-a-643189-2.html (accessed July 17, 2018).

Nye, Joseph S., Jr. "The Future of Soft Power in US Foreign Policy." In *Soft Power and US Foreign Policy: Theoretical, Historical and Contemporary Perspectives*, edited by Inderjeet Parmar and Michael Cox, pp. 4–11. Abingdon: Routledge, 2010.

Nye, Joseph S., Jr. "Good Start, Long Road." *The American Interest*, Vol. 5, No. 3 (Winter 2010), pp. 13–14.

Nye, Joseph S., Jr. "Responding to My Critics and Concluding Thoughts." In *Soft Power and US Foreign Policy: Theoretical, Historical and Contemporary Perspectives*, edited by Inderjeet Parmar and Michael Cox, pp. 215–227. Abingdon: Routledge, 2010.

Nye, Joseph S., Jr. *The Future of Power*. New York, N.Y.: PublicAffairs, 2011.

Nye, Joseph S., Jr. "Hard, Soft, and Smart Power." In *The Oxford Handbook of Modern Diplomacy*, edited by Andrew F. Cooper, Jorge Heine, and Ramesh Thakur, pp. 559–574. Oxford: Oxford University Press, 2013.

Nye, Joseph S., Jr. *Presidential Leadership and the Creation of the American Era*. Princeton, N.J.: Princeton University Press, 2013.

Nygård, Håvard Mokleiv and Scott Gates. "Soft Power at Home and Abroad: Sport Diplomacy, Politics and Peace-Building." *International Area Studies Review*, Vol. 16, No. 3, (September 2013), pp. 235–243.

O'Malley, Thomas. "Religion and the Newspaper Press, 1660-1685: A Study of the *London Gazette*." In *The Press in English Society from the Seventeenth to Nineteenth Centuries*, edited by Michael Harris and Alan Lee, pp. 25–46. Rutherford, N.J.: Fairleigh Dickinson University Press, 1986.

Ogawa, Tadashi. "Origin and Development of Japan's Public Diplomacy." In *Routledge Handbook of Public Diplomacy*, edited by Nancy Snow and Philip M. Taylor, pp. 270–280. New York, N. Y.: Routledge, 2009.

Ogilvie, R. M. "Introduction to the *Agricola*." In P. Cornelius Tacitus, *Agricola / Germania / Dialogus*. Translated by M. Hutton and W. Peterson, Revised by R. M. Ogilvie, E. H. Warmington, and M. Winterbottom, Loeb Classical Library 35, pp. 3–24. Cambridge, Mass.: Harvard University Press, 1970.

Ogilvie, R. M. and Ian Richmond. *Cornelii Taciti: De Vita Agricolae*. Oxford: Clarendon Press, 1967.

Ohnesorge, Hendrik W. "Making the Intangibles Tangible: Soft Power and its Subunits." Paper Presented at the International Studies Association West Annual Conference 2014, Emerging Scholars Forum, Pasadena, California, September 26, 2014.

Ohnesorge, Hendrik W. "Do as the Romans Do: Education and Language as a Source of Soft Power in Tacitus' Agricola." Paper Presented at the International Studies Association West Annual Conference 2014, Pasadena, California, September 27, 2014.

Ohnesorge, Hendrik W. "A Weberian Reading on Soft Power: Introducing Individual Charisma as a Soft Power Resource." Paper Presented at the International Studies Association Annual Conference 2016, Atlanta, Georgia, March 18, 2016.

Ohnesorge, Hendrik W. "A Taxonomy of Soft Power: Deconstructing the Concept of Soft Power and Introducing Indicators for Empirical Analysis." Paper Presented at the International Studies Association West Annual Conference 2017, Emerging Scholars Forum, Pasadena, California, September 22, 2017.

Oppenheim, Felix E. "'Power' Revisited." *The Journal of Politics*, Vol. 40, No. 3 (August 1978), pp. 589–608.

Organski, A. F. K. *World Politics*. New York, N.Y.: Alfred Knopf, 1958.

Owen, John M. "How Liberalism Produces Democratic Peace." *International Security*, Vol. 19, No. 2 (Fall 1994), pp. 87–125.

Pahlavi, Pierre. "The Use of New Media in the Modern Asymmetric Warfare Environment." In *Handbook of Defence Politics: International and Comparative Perspectives*, edited by Isaiah Wilson III and James J. F. Forest, pp. 137–151. London: Routledge, 2008.

Parmar, Inderjeet. "Challenging Elite Anti-Americanism in the Cold War: American Foundations, Kissinger's Harvard Seminar and the Salzburg Seminar in American Studies." In *Soft Power and US Foreign Policy: Theoretical, Historical and Contemporary Perspectives*, edited by Inderjeet Parmar and Michael Cox, pp. 108–120. Abingdon: Routledge, 2010.

Parmar, Inderjeet and Michael Cox. "Introduction." In *Soft Power and US Foreign Policy: Theoretical, Historical and Contemporary Perspectives*, edited by Inderjeet Parmar and Michael Cox, pp. 1–3. Abingdon: Routledge, 2010.

Partzsch, Lena. *Die neue Macht von Individuen in der globalen Politik. Wandel durch Prominente, Philanthropen und Social Entrepreneurs*. Baden-Baden: Nomos, 2014.

Patalakh, Artem. "Assessment of Soft Power Strategies: Towards an Aggregative Analytical Model for Country-Focused Case Study Research." *Croatian International Relations Review*, Vol. 22, No. 76 (2016), pp. 85–112.

Pells, Richard. "Double Crossings: The Reciprocal Relationship between American and European Culture in the Twentieth Century." In *Americanization and Anti-Americanism: The German Encounter with American Culture after 1945*, edited by Alexander Stephan, pp. 189–201. New York, N.Y.: Berghahn Books, 2005.

Perlmutter, Amos. "Crisis Management: Kissinger's Middle East Negotiations (October 1973-June 1974)." *International Studies Quarterly*, Vol. 19, No. 3 (September 1975), pp. 316–343.

Persico, Joseph E. *Edward R. Murrow: An American Original*. New York, N.Y.: McGraw-Hill, 1988.

Pettersson, Lucas. "Changing Images of the USA in German Media Discourse During Four American Presidencies." *International Journal of Cultural Studies*, Vol. 14, No. 1 (2011), pp. 35–51.

Pew Research Center. "Global Attitudes & Trends: Global Indicators Database." Online at: http://www.pewglobal.org/database/ (accessed May 29, 2019).

Pigman, Geoffrey Allen. *Contemporary Diplomacy: Representation and Communication in a Globalized World*. Cambridge: Polity Press, 2010.

Platon. "Gorgias." In *Werke in acht Bänden: Zweiter Band*. Edited by Gunther Eigler, Redacted by Heinz Hofmann, Translated by Friedrich Schleiermacher, pp. 296–503. Darmstadt: Wissenschaftliche Buchgesellschaft, 2011 (Plat. Gorg.).

Plokhy, S. M. *Yalta: The Price of Peace*. New York, N.Y.: Viking, 2010.

Plutarch. "Lysander." In *Plutarch's Lives*. With an English Translation by Bernadotte Perrin, Eleven Volumes, Volume IV: Alcibiades and Coriolanus/Lysander and Sulla, Loeb Classical Library, pp. 233–321. Cambridge, Mass: Harvard University Press, 1959 (Plut. Lys.).

Plutarch. *Fünf Doppelbiographien: 1. Teil, Alexandros und Caesar, Aristeides und Marcus Cato, Perikles und Fabius Maximus*. Translated by Konrat Ziegler and Walter Wuhrmann, Selected by Manfred Fuhrmann, With an Introduction and Notes by Konrat Ziegler. Zürich: Artemis & Winkler 1994 (here: Plut. Comp. Aristid. Cat. & Plut. Per.).

Plutarch. *Fünf Doppelbiographien: 2. Teil, Gaius Marcius und Alkibiades, Demosthenes und Cicero, Anhang*. Translated by Konrat Ziegler and Walter Wuhrmann, Selected by Manfred Fuhrmann, With an Introduction and Notes by Konrat Ziegler. Zürich: Artemis & Winkler 1994. (here: Plut. Alc.; Plut. Dem.; & Plut. Cic.).

Pluzinski, Carol and William J. Qualls. "Consumer Response to Marketing Stimuli: The Relationship Between Affect, Cognition, and Behavior." In *NA – Advances in Consumer Research, Volume 13*, edited by Richard J. Lutz, pp. 231–234. Provo, Utah: Association for Consumer Research, 1986.

Pope John Paul II. "Meeting with the Civil Authorities: Address of His Holiness John Paul II." Warsaw, 2 June 1979. *The Holy See, Apostolic Journey to Poland*. Online at: http://www.vatican.va/holy_father/john_paul_ii/speeches/1979/june/documents/hf_jp-ii_spe_19790602_polonia-varsavia-autorita-civili_en.html (accessed June 2, 2014).

Pope John Paul II. "Farewell Ceremony at Balice Airport: Address of His Holiness John Paul II." 10 June 1979. *The Holy See, Apostolic Pilgrimage to Poland*. Online at: http://www.vatican.va/holy_father/john_paul_ii/speeches/1979/june/documents/hf_jp-ii_spe_19790610_polonia-balice-congedo_en.html (accessed June 2, 2014).

Popescu, Ionut. *Emergent Strategy and Grand Strategy: How American Presidents Succeed in Foreign Policy*. Baltimore, Md.: John Hopkins University Press, 2017.

Popper, Karl. *The Logic of Scientific Discovery*. London: Hutchinson, 1959.

Pounds, Norman John Greville. *The Culture of the English People: Iron Age to the Industrial Revolution*. Cambridge: Cambridge University Press, 1994.

Powell, Colin L. "Statement on International Education Week 2001." Washington, D.C. August 7, 2001. Online at: http://2001-2009.state.gov/secretary/former/powell/remarks/2001/4462.htm (accessed January 11, 2016).

"The Power of Families: Dynasties." April 18, 2015. *The Economist*, p. 7.

Pratkanis, Anthony. "Public Diplomacy in International Conflicts: A Social Influence Analysis." In *Routledge Handbook of Public Diplomacy*, edited by Nancy Snow and Philip M. Taylor, pp. 111–153. New York, N.Y.: Routledge, 2009.

Price, Monroe E., Susan Haas, and Drew Margolin. "New Technologies and International Broadcasting: Reflections on Adaptations and Transformations." *The Annals of the American Academy of Political and Social Science*, Vol. 616, Public Diplomacy in a Changing World (March 2008), pp. 150–172.

Pustovitovskij, Andrej. *Strukturelle Kraft in Internationalen Beziehungen: Ein Konzept der Macht in internationalen Verhandlungen*. Wiesbaden: Springer VS, 2016.

Quandt, William B. *Camp David: Peacemaking and Politics*. Washington, D.C.: The Brooking Institutions, 1986.

Ratiu, Camelia Elena. *EU Soft Power at Its Best: Zur Leistungsfähigkeit der Europäischen Union als Demokratieförderer in Transformationsstaaten, Eine vergleichende Analyse der EU-Demokratieförderungspolitik in Slowenien, Kroatien und Serbien*. Hamburg: Verlag Dr. Kovac, 2011.

Rawnsley, Gary D. "China Talks Back: Public Diplomacy and Soft Power for the Chinese Century." In *Routledge Handbook of Public Diplomacy*, edited by Nancy Snow and Philip M. Taylor, pp. 282–291. New York, N.Y.: Routledge, 2009.

Reiweger, Gerhard. "Introduction." In *Favorita Papers 01/2004: Public Diplomacy*, edited by Gerhard Reiweger, pp. 5–7. Vienna: Diplomatische Akademie, 2004.

Rhoads, Kelton. "The Culture Variable in the Influence Equation." In *Routledge Handbook of Public Diplomacy*, edited by Nancy Snow and Philip M. Taylor, pp. 166–186. New York, N.Y.: Routledge, 2009.

Riley, Russell L. *Inside the Clinton White House: An Oral History*. New York, N.Y.: Oxford University Press, 2016.

Riordan, Shaun. "Dialogue-based Public Diplomacy: A New Foreign Policy Paradigm?." In *The New Public Diplomacy: Soft Power in International Relations*, edited by Jan Melissen, pp. 180–195. Basingstoke: Palgrave Macmillan, 2005.

Rohwer, Götz and Ulrich Pötter. *Wahrscheinlichkeit: Begriff und Rhetorik in der Sozialwissenschaft*. Weinheim and München: Juventa Verlag, 2002.

Romney, Mitt. "Speech about Donald Trump." Salt Lake City, Utah, March 3, 2016. Online at http://time.com/4246596/donald-trump-mitt-romney-utah-speech/ (accessed April 12, 2016).

Roselle, Laura, Alister Miskimmon, and Ben O'Loughlin. "Strategic Narrative: A New Means to Understand Soft Power." *Media, War & Conflict*, Vol. 7, No. 1 (2014), pp. 70–84.

Rosumek, Lars. *Die Kanzler und die Medien: Acht Porträts von Adenauer bis Merkel*. Frankfurt am Main: Campus Verlag, 2007.

Roth, Guenther. "Introduction." In Max Weber, *Economy and Society: An Outline of Interpretive Sociology*, edited by Guenther Roth and Claus Wittich, pp. xxxiii–cx. Berkeley: University of California Press, 1978.

Rothkopf, Daniel. "In Praise of Cultural Imperialism." *Foreign Policy*, No. 107 (Summer 1997), pp. 38–53.

Rubel, Alexander. "Vorwort." In *Imperium und Romanisierung: Neue Forschungsansätze aus Ost und West zu Ausübung, Transformation und Akzeptanz von Herrschaft im Römischen Reich*, edited by Alexander Rubel, pp. 7–10. Konstanz: Hartung-Gorre Verlag, 2013.

Rudolf, Peter. *Das 'neue' Amerika: Außenpolitik unter Barack Obama*. Berlin: Suhrkamp, 2010.

Russell, Bertrand. *Power: A New Social Analysis*. London: George Allen and Unwin, 1938.

Russell, Bertrand. *History of Western Philosophy*. London: Routledge, 2004.

Russell, C. P. "How to Write a Sales-Making Letter: An Old Formula That Will Save Much Rewriting by the Unpracticed Correspondent." *Printers' Ink*, June 2, 1921, pp. 49–52.

Schaeper, Thomas J. and Kathleen. *Cowboys into Gentlemen: Rhodes Scholars, Oxford, and the Creation of an American Elite*. New York, N.Y.: Berghahn Books, 1998.

Schmidt, Brian. "Theories of US Foreign Policy." In *US Foreign Policy*, edited by Michael Cox and Doug Stokes, pp. 5–20. Oxford: Oxford University Press, 2012.

Schneider, Christoph. *Der Warschauer Kniefall: Ritual, Ereignis und Erzählung*. Konstanz: UVK-Verlag, 2006.

Schneider, Cynthia P. "Culture Communicates: US Diplomacy at Work." In *The New Public Diplomacy: Soft Power in International Relations*, edited by Jan Melissen, pp. 147–168. Basingstoke: Palgrave Macmillan, 2005.

Schulzke, Marcus. *The Morality of Drone Warfare and the Politics of Regulation*. London: Palgrave Macmillan, 2017.

Schwarz, Hans-Peter. "Charismatische (Ver-)Führer." *Totalitarismus und Demokratie*, Vol. 1, No. 1 (2004), pp. 15–33.

Schweitzer, Arthur. "Theory and Political Charisma." *Comparative Studies in Society and History*, Vol. 16, No. 2 (March 1974), pp. 150–181.

Scott-Smith, Giles. "Exchange Programs and Public Diplomacy." In *Routledge Handbook of Public Diplomacy*, edited by Nancy Snow and Philip M. Taylor, pp. 50–55. New York, N.Y.: Routledge, 2009.

Scott-Smith, Giles. "Soft Power in an Era of US Decline." In *Soft Power and US Foreign Policy: Theoretical, Historical and Contemporary Perspectives*, edited by Inderjeet Parmar and Michael Cox, pp. 165–181. Abingdon: Routledge, 2010.

Scott, William Evans. *Alliance against Hitler: The Origins of the Franco-Soviet Pact*. Durham, N. C.: Duke University Press, 1962.

Seibt, Gustav. *Goethe und Napoleon: Eine historische Begegnung*. München: C. H. Beck, 2008.

Senate Concurrent Resolution 87. "Commending the Holy See for Making Significant Contributions to International Peace and Human Rights, and Objecting to Efforts to Expel the Holy See from the United Nations by Removing the Holy See's Permanent Observer Status in the United Nations, and for Other Purposes." 106th Congress, 2nd Session, March 1, 2000. *Congressional Record* Vol. 146, Pt. 2 (2000), pp. 1905–1907.

Seneca, L. Annaeus. "Controversiarum: Liber I, 1." In *L. Annaei Seneca Patris: Scripta Quae Manserunt*, edited by Herman J. Müller, pp. 15-29. Hildesheim: Georg Olms Verlag, 1990 (Sen. Con).

Seungeun, Lee Claire. "China's International Broadcasting as a Soft Power Ma(r)ker: Its Market Formation and Audience Making." *ERCCT Online Paper Series*, EOPS No. 0027, November 2013. Online at: http://www.ercct.uni-tuebingen.de/Files/ERCCT%20Online%20Paper% 20Series/Young%20Scholar%20Workshop%202013/EOPS27,%20Lee%20Claire% 20Seungeun,%20China's%20International%20Broadcasting%20as%20a%20Soft%20Power% 20Ma(r)ker%20Its%20Market%20Formation%20and%20Audience%20Making.pdf (accessed July 14, 2014).

Shakespeare, William. "Hamlet: Prince of Denmark." In *The Complete Works of William Shakespeare*. Edited with a Glossary by W. J. Craig, pp. 1006–1049. London: Oxford University Press, 1923.

Shakespeare, William. "The First Part of King Henry the Fourth." In *The Complete Works of William Shakespeare*. Edited with a Glossary by W. J. Craig, pp. 470–503. London: Oxford University Press, 1923.

Sharp, Paul. "Revolutionary States, Outlaw Regimes and the Techniques of Public Diplomacy." In *The New Public Diplomacy: Soft Power in International Relations*, edited by Jan Melissen, pp. 106–123. Basingstoke: Palgrave Macmillan, 2005.

Slaughter, Anne-Marie. "America's Edge: Power in the Networked Century." *Foreign Affairs*, Vol. 88, No. 1 (January/February 2009), pp. 94–113.

Smith, Mapheus. "The Method of Elimination in Scientific Study." *Philosophy of Science*, Vol. 10, No. 4 (October 1943), pp. 250–254.

Smolnikov, Sergey. *Great Power Conduct and Credibility in World Politics*. Cham: Palgrave Macmillan 2018.

Snow, Nancy. "Rethinking Public Diplomacy." In *Routledge Handbook of Public Diplomacy*, edited by Nancy Snow and Philip M. Taylor, pp. 3–11. New York, N.Y.: Routledge, 2009.

Snow, Nancy. "Valuing Exchange of Persons in Public Diplomacy." In *Routledge Handbook of Public Diplomacy*, edited by Nancy Snow and Philip M. Taylor, pp. 233–247. New York, N.Y.: Routledge, 2009.

Snow, Nancy and Philip M. Taylor. "Preface and Introduction." In *Routledge Handbook of Public Diplomacy*, edited by Nancy Snow and Philip M. Taylor, pp. ix-xi. New York, N.Y.: Routledge, 2009.

Soble, Jonathan. "Hiroshima Survivor Cries, and Obama Gives Him a Hug." *The New York Times*, May 27, 2016. Online at: http://www.nytimes.com/2016/05/28/world/asia/hiroshima-obama-visit-shigeaki-mori.html (accessed June 14, 2016).

Solomon, Robert C. *In the Spirit of Hegel*. Oxford: Oxford University Press, 1983.

Solomon, Ty. "The Affective Underpinnings of Soft Power." *European Journal of International Relations*, Vol. 20, No. 3 (2014), pp. 720–741.

Spahn, Peter. "Perikles: Charisma und Demokratie." In *Virtuosen der Macht: Herrschaft und Charisma von Perikles bis Mao*, edited by Wilfried Nippel, pp. 23–38. München: C. H. Beck, 2000.

Spencer, Martin E. "What is Charisma?." *The British Journal of Sociology*, Vol. 24, No. 3 (September 1973), pp. 341–354.

Strange, Susan. *States and Markets*. London: Printer, 1994.

Street, Brian V. "Culture is a Verb: Anthropological Aspects of Language and Cultural Process." In *Language and Culture: British Studies in Applied Linguistics*, edited by David Graddol, Linda Thompson, and Mike Bryam, Volume 7, pp. 23–43. Clevedon: Multilingual Matters, 1993.

Su Changhe. "Soft Power." In *The Oxford Handbook of Modern Diplomacy*, edited by Andrew F. Cooper, Jorge Heine, and Ramesh Thakur, pp. 544–558. Oxford: Oxford University Press, 2013.

Suetonius Tranquillus, C. *Die Kaiserviten: De Vita Caesarum/Berühmte Männer: De Viris Illustribus*. Edited and Translated by Hans Martinet. Berlin: Walter de Gruyter, 2014 (here: Suet. Aug. & Suet. Ves.).

Szabo, Stephen F. *Parting Ways: The Crisis in German-American Relations*. Washington, D.C.: Brookings Institution Press, 2004.

Szondi, György. "Central and Eastern European Public Diplomacy: A Transitional Perspective on National Reputation Management." In *Routledge Handbook of Public Diplomacy*, edited by Nancy Snow and Philip M. Taylor, pp. 292–313. New York, N.Y.: Routledge, 2009.

't Hart, Paul. "Political Psychology." In *Theory and Methods in Political Science*, edited by David Marsh and Gerry Stoker, pp. 99–113. London: Palgrave Macmillan, 2010.

Tacitus, P. Cornelius. *The Histories*. Translated with Introduction and Notes by W. Hamilton Fyfe, Volume II. Oxford: Clarendon Press, 1912 (Tac. Hist.).

Tacitus, P. Cornelius. *Agricola/Germania/Dialogus*. Translated by M. Hutton and W. Peterson, Revised by R. M. Ogilvie, E. H. Warmington, and M. Winterbottom, Loeb Classical Library 35. Cambridge, Mass.: Harvard University Press, 1970 (Tac. Agr./Tac. Ger./Tac. Dial.).

Tacitus, P. Cornelius. *Annalen: Annales*. Edited by Erich Heller, With an Introduction by Manfred Fuhrmann. München: Artemis & Winkler, 1992 (Tac. Ann.).

Taverner, Angus. "The Military Use of Soft Power: Information Campaigns, The Challenge of Application, their Audiences and Effects." In *Soft Power and US Foreign Policy: Theoretical, Historical and Contemporary Perspectives*, edited by Inderjeet Parmar and Michael Cox, pp. 137–151. Abingdon: Routledge, 2010.

Taylor, Philip M. "Public Diplomacy and the Information War on Terror." In *Soft Power and US Foreign Policy: Theoretical, Historical and Contemporary Perspectives*, edited by Inderjeet Parmar and Michael Cox, pp. 152–164. Abingdon: Routledge, 2010.

Tharoor, Shashi. "Why America Still Needs the United Nations." *Foreign Affairs*, Vol. 82, No. 5 (September/October 2003), pp. 67–80.

Thucydides. *The Peloponnesian War*. A New Translation by Martin Hammond. New York, N.Y.: Oxford University Press, 2009 (Thuc.).

TIME Staff. "The 20 Most Influential Americans of All Time." *TIME Magazine*, July 24, 2012. Online at http://newsfeed.time.com/2012/07/25/the-20-most-influential-americans-of-all-time/ (accessed June 10, 2016).

Tolkien, J. R. R. *The Return of the King: Being the Third Part of the Lord of the Rings*. New York, N.Y.: HarperCollins, 2007.

Tolstoy, Leo. *War and Peace*. Chicago, Ill.: Encyclopædia Britannica, 1952.

Triesman, David, The Lord Triesman. "Public Diplomacy: Steps to the Future." London School of Economics, April 23, 2007. Online at: http://www.lse.ac.uk/publicEvents/pdf/20070423_LordTriesman.pdf (accessed August 25, 2015).

Trommler, Frank. "Culture as an Arena of Transatlantic Conflict." In *The United States and Germany in the Era of the Cold War, 1945-1990: A Handbook, Volume II: 1968-1990*, edited by Detlef Junker, associated editors Philipp Gassert, Wilfried Mausbach, and David B. Morris, pp. 257–273. Cambridge: Cambridge University Press, 2004.

Trump, Donald J., with Tony Schwartz. *Trump: The Art of the Deal*. London: Arrow Books, 2016.

Tuch, Hans N. *Communicating with the World: U.S. Public Diplomacy Overseas*. New York, N.Y.: St. Martin's Press, 1990.

Tucker, Robert W. and David C. Hendrickson. "The Sources of American Legitimacy." *Foreign Affairs*, Vol. 83, No. 6 (November/December 2004), pp. 18–32.

Tyler, Patrick E. "A New Power in the Streets." *The New York Times*, February 17, 2003. Online at: http://www.nytimes.com/2003/02/17/world/threats-and-responses-news-analysis-a-new-power-in-the-streets.html (accessed June 13, 2016).

Ulansey, David. *The Origins of the Mithraic Mysteries: Cosmology and Salvation in the Ancient World*. New York: Oxford University Press, 1989.

Ungar, Sanford J. "Pitch Imperfect: The Trouble at the Voice of America." *Foreign Affairs*, Vol. 84, No. 3 (May/June 2005), pp. 7–13.

United States Advisory Commission on Public Diplomacy. "Building America's Public Diplomacy Through a Reformed Structure and Additional Resources." *A 2002 Report of the U.S. Advisory Commission on Public Diplomacy*. Online at: https://www.state.gov/documents/organization/13622.pdf (accessed April 25, 2017).

United States Department of State. "Congressional Reports." *Bureau of International Organization Affairs*. Online at: http://www.state.gov/p/io/rls/rpt/index.htm (accessed June 15, 2016).

United States Department of State. "FY 2008 Budget in Brief." *Bureau of Budget Management*, February 5, 2007. Online at: http://www.state.gov/s/d/rm/rls/bib/2008/html/79739.htm (accessed September 30, 2015).

United States Department of State. "Presidential and Secretaries Travels Abroad: Presidents, Theodore Roosevelt." *Office of the Historian*. Online at: https://history.state.gov/departmenthistory/travels/president/roosevelt-theodore (accessed July 14, 2015).

United States Department of State. "Under Secretary for Public Diplomacy and Public Affairs." Online at: https://www.state.gov/r/ (accessed April 29, 2017).

United States Department of State. "Visits by Foreign Leaders in 1874." *Office of the Historian*. Online at: https://history.state.gov/departmenthistory/visits/1874 (accessed July 14, 2015).

United States Senate Committee on Homeland Security and Governmental Affairs. *A Reliance on Smart Power: Reforming the Public Diplomacy Bureaucracy, Hearing Before the Oversight of Government Management, the Federal Workforce, and the District of Columbia Subcommittee*. Washington, D.C., September 23, 2008, 110th Congress, Second Session, Washington, D.C.: United States Government Printing Office, 2009.

University of Nairobi Confucius Institute. "Background." Online at: http://confucius.uonbi.ac.ke/sites/default/files/chss/arts/linguistics/confucius/BACK%20GROUND.pdf (accessed August 25, 2015).

Van Ham, Peter. "Power, Public Diplomacy, and the *Pax Americana*." In *The New Public Diplomacy: Soft Power in International Relations*, edited by Jan Melissen, pp. 47–66. Basingstoke: Palgrave Macmillan, 2005.

Vanke, Jeffrey. "Consensus for Integration: Public Opinion and European Integration in the Federal Republic, 1945-1966." In *Die Bundesrepublik Deutschland und die europäische Einigung 1949-2000: Politische Akteure, gesellschaftliche Kräfte und internationale Erfahrungen*, edited by Mareike König und Matthias Schulz, pp. 327–340. Stuttgart: Franz Steiner Verlag, 2004.

Vernant, Jean-Pierre. *Die Entstehung des griechischen Denkens*. Frankfurt am Main: Suhrkamp, 1982.

Virgil (P. Vergilius Maro). *The Aeneid*. With a Translation by Charles J. Billson, Volume I. London: Edward Arnold, 1906 (Verg. Aen.).

Vitkovskaya, Julie. "Merkel Meets Amal Clooney and Her Husband to Discuss Refugees." *The Washington Post*, February 12, 2016. Online at: https://www.washingtonpost.com/news/world views/wp/2016/02/12/germanys-merkel-meets-amal-clooney-and-her-husband-to-discuss-refu gees/ (accessed June 14, 2016).

Vlahos, Michael. "Public Diplomacy as Loss of World Authority." In *Routledge Handbook of Public Diplomacy*, edited by Nancy Snow and Philip M. Taylor, pp. 24–38. New York, N.Y.: Routledge, 2009.

Voss-Wittig, Huberta von. "Soft Power." Wissenschaftlicher Dienst des Deutschen Bundestages, *Aktueller Begriff*, No. 45/06, November 3, 2006. Online at: https://www.bundestag.de/blob/ 189706/8c40cb75069889f8829a5a0db838da1f/soft_power-data.pdf (accessed September 15, 2015).

Vuving, Alexander L. "How Soft Power Works." Paper Presented at the *American Political Science Association Annual Meeting*, Toronto, Ontario, September 3, 2009.

Walker, Christopher. "The Hijacking of 'Soft Power.'" *Journal of Democracy*, Vol. 27, No. 1 (January 2016), pp. 49–63.

Wallensteen, Peter. "Dag Hammarskjöld's Diplomacy: Lessons Learned." In *Peace Diplomacy, Global Justice and International Agency: Rethinking Human Security and Ethics in the Spirit of Dag Hammarskjöld*, edited by Carsten Stahn and Henning Melber, pp. 364–386. Cambridge: Cambridge University Press, 2014.

Wallin, Matthew. "The New Public Diplomacy Imperative: America's Vital Need to Communicate Strategically." *American Security Project White Paper*. Online at: https:// americansecurityproject.org/ASP%20Reports/Ref%200071%20-%20The%20New%20Public %20Diplomacy%20Imperative.pdf (accessed March 15, 2014).

Walt, Stephen M. "Taming American Power." *Foreign Affairs*, Vol. 84, No. 5 (September/October 2005), pp. 105–120.

Wanka, Arndt. "Concept Specification in Political Science Research." In *Research Design in Political Science: How to Practice What They Preach*, edited by Thomas Geschwend and Frank Schimmelfennig, pp. 41–61. Basingstoke: Palgrave Macmillan, 2011.

Weber, Cynthia. *International Relations Theory: A Critical Introduction*. Abingdon: Routledge, 2005.

Weber, Max. *Wirtschaft und Gesellschaft*. Tübingen, J. C. B. Mohr, 1922.

Weber, Max. *Economy and Society: An Outline of Interpretive Sociology*. Edited by Guenther Roth and Claus Wittich. Berkeley, Cal.: University of California Press, 1978.

Weigel, George. *The End and the Beginning: Pope John Paul II – The Victory of Freedom, the Last Years, the Legacy*. New York, N.Y.: Image, 2011.

Wells, Peter S. *The Battle That Stopped Rome: Emperor Augustus, Arminius, and the Slaughter of the Legions in the Teutoburg Forest*. New York, N.Y.: Norton & Company, 2003.

Wies, Ernst W. *Otto der Große: Kämpfer und Beter*. Esslingen: Bechtle, 1998.

Wilson, Bryan R. *The Noble Savages: The Primitive Origins of Charisma and its Contemporary Survival*. Berkeley, Cal.: University of California Press, 1975.

Wilson, Ernest J., III. "Hard Power, Soft Power, Smart Power." *The Annals of the American Academy of Political and Social Science,* Vol. 616, Public Diplomacy in a Changing World (March 2008), pp. 110–124.

Wilson, Woodrow. "The Program of Peace: Message to Congress." Washington, D.C., January 8, 1918. In *War Addresses of Woodrow Wilson.* With an Introduction and Notes by Arthur Roy Leonhard, pp. 92–101. Boston, Mass.: Ginn and Company, 1918.

Winthrop, John. "A Model of Christian Charity." In *Puritan Political Ideas: 1558-1794,* edited by Edmund S. Morgan, pp. 75–93. Indianapolis, Ind.: Hackett Publishing Company, 2003.

Wolfers, Arnold. *Discord and Collaboration: Essays on International Politics.* Baltimore, Md.: John Hopkins University Press, 1962.

Wolffsohn, Michael and Thomas Brechenmacher. *Denkmalsturz? Brandts Kniefall.* München: Olzog, 2005.

Womack, Brantly. "Dancing Alone: A Hard Look at Soft Power." *Japan Focus,* November 16, 2005. Online at: http://www.japanfocus.org/site/make_pdf/1975 (accessed February 16, 2015).

Wyne, Ali S. "Public Opinion and Power." In *Routledge Handbook of Public Diplomacy,* edited by Nancy Snow and Philip M. Taylor, pp. 39–49. New York, N.Y.: Routledge, 2009.

Xenophon. *Kyrupädie: Die Erziehung des Kyros.* Edited and Translated by Rainer Nickel. München: Artemis & Winkler, 1992 (Xen. Cyrop.).

Yang, Rui. "Soft Power and Higher Education: An Examination of China's Confucius Institutes." *Globalisation, Societies and Education* Vol. 8, No. 2 (2010), pp. 235–245.

Yun, Seong-Hun and Jeong-Nam Kim. "Soft Power: From Ethnic Attraction to National Attraction in Sociological Globalism." *International Journal of Cultural Relations,* Vol. 32, No. 6 (November 2008), pp. 565–577.

Zaharna, R. S. "The Network Paradigm of Strategic Public Diplomacy." *Foreign Policy in Focus,* edited by John Gershman, September 30, 2005. Online at: http://fpif.org/the_network_para digm_of_strategic_public_diplomacy/ (accessed June 29, 2015).

Zaharna, R. S. "Mapping out a Spectrum of Public Diplomacy Initiatives: Information and Relational Communication Frameworks." In *Routledge Handbook of Public Diplomacy,* edited by Nancy Snow and Philip M. Taylor, pp. 86–100. New York, N.Y.: Routledge, 2009.

Zaharna, R. S. *The Cultural Awakening in Public Diplomacy, CPD Perspectives on Public Diplomacy, Paper 4, 2012.* Los Angeles, Cal.: Figueroa Press, 2012.

Zahran, Geraldo and Leonardo Ramos. "From Hegemony to Soft Power: Implications of a Conceptual Change." In *Soft Power and US Foreign Policy: Theoretical, Historical and Contemporary Perspectives,* edited by Inderjeet Parmar and Michael Cox, pp. 12–31. Abingdon: Routledge, 2010.

Zhang, Longxi. "The Myth of the Other: China in the Eyes of the West." *Critical Inquiry,* Vol. 15, No. 1 (Autumn 1988), pp. 108–131.

Zöllner, Oliver. "German Public Diplomacy: The Dialogue of Cultures." In *Routledge Handbook of Public Diplomacy,* edited by Nancy Snow and Philip M. Taylor, pp. 262–269. New York, N.Y.: Routledge, 2009.

Zweig, Stefan. *Sternstunden der Menschheit: Vierzehn historische Miniaturen.* Frankfurt am Main: Fischer Taschenbuch Verlag, 2010.

Zweig, Stefan. *Joseph Fouché: Bildnis eines politischen Menschen.* Frankfurt am Main: Fischer, 2012.

Chapter 4
A Methodological Roadmap for the Study of Soft Power

After having developed the theoretical-conceptual framework of soft power with the newly introduced taxonomy and its four subunits, the subsequent chapter addresses the second research question posed above (Q_2). Accordingly, issues regarding a suitable research design for the empirical study of soft power in international relations shall be discussed in the following.

"Research design" has been described as "the logical sequence that connects the empirical data to a study's initial research questions and, ultimately, to its conclusions."[1] More detailed, Charles C. Ragin defined it as

> a plan for collecting and analyzing evidence that will make it possible for the investigator to answer whatever questions he or she has posed. The design of an investigation touches almost all aspects of the research, from the minute details of data collection to the selection of the techniques of data analysis.[2]

The formulation of a research design, that is, the "logical structure of the inquiry,"[3] is contingent upon, among other things, the particular aim and research question of the study, the theoretical framework, methodological approaches, as well as available resources.[4] In an instructive comparison, David A. de Vaus has therefore likened the task of elaborating a substantiated research design to the process of building a house: Before gathering up the raw materials to be used or devising a timeframe, any builder has to be clear on what kind of edifice he/she is planning to erect. Multistory office buildings thus require different materials or approaches than

---

[1]Robert K. Yin, *Case Study Research: Design and Methods* (Los Angeles, Cal.: SAGE Publications, 2014), p. 28.

[2]Charles C. Ragin, *Constructing Social Research: The Unity and Diversity of Method* (Thousand Oaks, Cal.: Pine Forge Press, 1994), p. 191.

[3]David A. de Vaus, *Research Design in Social Research* (London: SAGE Publications, 2001), p. 9.

[4]Uwe Flick, "Design und Prozess qualitativer Forschung," in *Qualitative Forschung: Ein Handbuch*, eds. Uwe Flick, Ernst von Kardorff, and Ines Steinke (Reinbek bei Hamburg: Rowohlt Taschenbuch Verlag, 2012), p. 253.

© Springer Nature Switzerland AG 2020
H. W. Ohnesorge, *Soft Power*, Global Power Shift,
https://doi.org/10.1007/978-3-030-29922-4_4

do industrial plants or single-family houses. Equally so, any scientist has to devise a plan or structure before collecting data or analyzing them.[5] "The function of a research design," de Vaus concluded, "is to ensure that the evidence obtained enables us to answer the initial question as unambiguously as possible."[6]

Consequently, the formulation of an elaborated research design is indispensable for any substantiated scientific research from the outset—regardless of the scientific area.[7] However, bearing in mind the many challenges any researcher is confronted with in particular when examining the workings of soft power in international relations, this task becomes exceptionally important. Jean-Marc F. Blanchard and Fujia Lu accordingly noted that researchers in the field of soft power "have to address a slew of methodological issues"[8] in order to reach resilient results. This "slew of methodological issues" shall be addressed on the following pages. To that end, some fundamentals in methodology shall be examined before discussing the two different approaches of quantitative and qualitative research as well as their respective advantages and disadvantages for the study of soft power in international relations. Within this context, the method of comparative-historical analysis shall be presented as being particularly suitable. Furthermore, appropriate timeframes, possible actors of analysis, as well as types of data to be examined in empirical studies of soft power shall be reflected upon. By drawing on established research methodologies—and by adapting and combining them innovatively—a tailor-made methodological roadmap for the empirical study of soft power in international relations shall thus be presented.

4.1 Fundamentals in Methodology

In line with this course of action, some basics in methodology have to be discussed at first. A methodology has been defined as

---

[5]de Vaus, *Research Design in Social Research*, pp. 8–9. Comparisons of literature to works of architecture have, of course, a long history and date back as far as Horace, who in the first century BC famously wrote in his *Odes*, "Exegi monumentum aere perennius/ Regalique situ pyramidum altius,/ Quod non imber edax, non aquilo imoptens/ Possit diruere aut innumerabilis/ Annorum series et fuga temporum;" Horaz, "Carmina/Oden," in *Sämtliche Werke: Teil I, Opden und Eopden*, edited by Hans Färber after Kayser, Nordenflycht, and Burger (München: Ernst Heimeran Verlag, 1960, p. 176 (Hor. Carm. III, 30). A. Hamilton Bryce provides an English translation, "A monument I have reared more durable than brass, and loftier than the princely structure of the pyramids, which neither biting rain can overthrow, nor fierce north wind nor lapse of countless years and flight of time;" Horace, *The Odes of Horace: Books III and IV, with the Carmen Seculare and the Epodes*, Translated by A. Hamilton Bryce (London: George Bell and Sons, 1909), p. 72.

[6]de Vaus, *Research Design in Social Research*, p. 9.

[7]Bob Hancké, "The Challenge of Research Design," in *Theory and Methods in Political Science*, eds. David Marsh and Gerry Stoker (Basingstoke: Palgrave Macmillan, 2010), pp. 235–236.

[8]Jean-Marc F. Blanchard and Fujia Lu, "Thinking Hard about Soft Power: A Review and Critique of the Literature on China and Soft Power," *Asian Perspective*, Vol. 36, No. 4 (2012), p. 575.

a body of practices, procedures, and rules used by researchers to offer insight into the workings of the world. They are central to the scientific enterprise, as they allow researchers to gather empiric and measurable evidence and to analyze the evidence in an effort to expand knowledge.[9]

Today, a huge variety of methods exists in political science, providing different tools to understand the complex world around us.[10] Any researcher, therefore, has to select from a plethora of different research approaches.[11] At it, the selection of the overall methodological approach essentially depends on two factors: the respective ontology and epistemology championed by the researcher as well as the particular research question to be addressed.[12]

Accordingly, not least one's own ontological and epistemological positions "shape the approach to theory and the methods which the social scientist uses."[13] Ontology, derived from and composed of Greek ὄντως (ontos) and λόγος (logos), literally translates into "the study of being" or "the science of that what is." It therefore "deals with the things that we think exist in the world."[14] Ontological questions hence ask how the "reality" around us is configured.[15] Paul Furlong and David Marsh accordingly concluded, "The key ontological question is: What is the form and nature of reality and, consequently, what is there that can be known about it?"[16] On a metaphysical level such questions include, as argued by Xuewu Gu, "Is there a God?" or "Is the sky blue?"[17] On a more concrete, political science-related level, ontology "concerns what can be studied, what can be compared, and what constitutes the political" and therefore "concerns the countries, events, actors,

---

[9]Matthew Lange, *Comparative-Historical Methods* (Los Angeles, Cal.: SAGE Publications, 2013), p. 3.

[10]Gerry Stoker, "Introduction to Part 2," in *Theory and Methods in Political Science*, eds. David Marsh and Gerry Stoker (Basingstoke: Palgrave Macmillan, 2010), p. 181.

[11]John W. Creswell, *Research Design: Qualitative, Quantitative, and Mixed Methods Approaches* (Thousand Oaks, Cal.: SAGE Publications, 2003), p. 3.

[12]While those questions are decisive and shall therefore be considered in the following, the subsequent paragraphs are considered to provide merely an outline of select approaches, rather than a comprehensive discussion of some of the most fundamental (and contested) questions in the philosophy of science. Frequently, further literature is referenced allowing for a deepened engagement with respective issues.

[13]Paul Furlong and David Marsh, "A Skin Not a Sweater: Ontology and Epistemology in Political Science," in *Theory and Methods in Political Science*, eds. David Marsh and Gerry Stoker (Basingstoke: Palgrave Macmillan, 2010), p. 184.

[14]Janet M. Box-Steffensmeier, Henry E. Brady, and David Collier, "Political Science Methodology," in *The Oxford Handbook of Political Methodology*, eds. Janet M. Box-Steffensmeier, Henry E. Brady, and David Collier (Oxford: Oxford University Press, 2011), p. 5. See also Mark Bevir, "Meta-Methodology: Clearing the Underbrush," in *The Oxford Handbook of Political Methodology*, eds. Janet M. Box-Steffensmeier, Henry E. Brady, and David Collier (Oxford: Oxford University Press, 2011), p. 60.

[15]Xuewu Gu, *Theorien der Internationalen Beziehungen: Einführung* (Berlin: Walter de Gruyter, 2018), p. 15.

[16]Furlong and Marsh, "A Skin Not a Sweater," p. 185.

[17]Gu, *Theorien der Internationalen Beziehungen*, p. 15.

institutions, and processes among other things that are observable and in need of explanation."[18]

In International Relations, proponents of different theoretical schools of thought take different ontological positions of how the international system of states is characterized. Neorealists, for example, emphasize the inherently and invariably anarchic shape of interstate relations. Others, however, reject such views and stress the interaction and interdependence of various actors in the international sphere while considering change and progress possible.[19] While the study at hand considers international relations to be an interaction of various (groups of) actors (including nation-states, subnational entities, non-governmental organizations, international organizations, and even individuals) in an interdepended world, the more important issue at this point concerns differences in the ontological positions distinguishable in the philosophy of science since they crucially affect research approaches. Furlong and Marsh in this regard differentiate between what has been called foundationalism (while other synonymous terms exist, including objectivism and realism) and anti-foundationalism (a term which again is frequently used interchangeably with con-structivism and relativism).[20]

From the perspective of foundationalism, "the world is viewed as composed of discrete objects which possess properties that are independent of the observer/ researcher."[21] In their classic *Metaphors We Live By*, George Lakoff and Mark Johnson noted that advocates of this perspective, labeled "objectivists" by the authors, stipulate "that there is such a thing as *objective* (absolute and unconditional) *truth*."[22] Those holding this view "claim that there is a world out there"[23] that is independent of the construction or perception of the observer.

As opposed to this view, anti-foundationalism posits that the reality is socially constructed. Furlong and Marsh accordingly hold that "anti-foundationalists argue that there is not a real world out there independent of our knowledge of it."[24] However, they caution that this claim "is a limited one. We are not claiming that such researchers do not acknowledge that there are tables/mountains/institutions and so on. Rather, they contend that this 'reality' has no social role/causal power independent of the agent's/group's/society's understanding of it."[25] We shall return to this distinction at greater length in a moment.

---

[18]Todd Landman, *Issues and Methods in Comparative Politics: An Introduction* (Abingdon: Routledge, 2008), p. 17.

[19]Gu, *Theorien der Internationalen Beziehungen*, p. 15.

[20]Furlong and Marsh, "A Skin Not a Sweater," pp. 189–190.

[21]Furlong and Marsh, "A Skin Not a Sweater," p. 190.

[22]George Lakoff and Mark Johnson, *Metaphors We Live By* (Chicago, Ill.: University of Chicago Press, 1980), p. 159; Lakoff's and Johnson's emphasis.

[23]Bevir, "Meta-Methodology," p. 60.

[24]Furlong and Marsh, "A Skin Not a Sweater," p. 191.

[25]Furlong and Marsh, "A Skin Not a Sweater," p. 191.

Table 4.1 Three varieties in epistemology

	Positivism	Realism	Interpretivism
Basic ontology	Foundationalist	Foundationalist	Anti-foundationalist
Central research approach	Causal inferences	Causal inferences	Interpretation
Scope of explanatory Potential	All social structures and phenomena of the "real" world are observable	"Deep" social structures and phenomena may be hidden from observation	No social structures and phenomena are observable independent of our interpretation and construction
Objective, value-free research possible?	Yes	No	No

Own table based on Furlong and Marsh, "A Skin Not a Sweater," pp. 191–206

While ontology, recalling the definition referenced above, "deals with the things that we think exist in the work, [...] epistemology [deals] with how we come to know about those things."[26] The term "epistemology" itself derives from Greek ἐπιστήμη (episteme) and λόγος (logos) and can hence be translated into "the study of knowledge" or "the science of understanding." Epistemology, as a philosophical branch, therefore, deals with questions of *if* and *how* reliable knowledge of the world around us (however, it may be constituted) can be generated.[27] Again, there are different positions regarding epistemology that frequently are classified into the two varieties of scientism (positivism) and hermeneutics (or interpretivism).[28] Furlong and Marsh, albeit recognizing this established dichotomy between scientism and hermeneutics, offer a more elaborate schematic and propose a trichotomy in epistemological positions by differentiating between positivism, realism, and interpretivism, the core positions of which are depicted in Table 4.1.

To start with the far right column, interpretivism follows an anti-foundationalist ontology and holds "that the world is socially or discursively constructed."[29] Consequently, "[i]f our world is deeply socially constructed [...] there is little 'real world' for political science to study."[30] Therefore, while a range of varieties exists within this epistemological approach itself, proponents of this view in general hold that the world and its structures "cannot be understood independently of our interpretation of them" and as a consequence methods derived from the *natural*

---

[26]Box-Steffensmeier, Brady, and Collier, "Political Science Methodology," p. 5.

[27]Gu, *Theorien der Internationalen Beziehungen*, pp. 15-16. See also Lange, *Comparative-Historical Methods*, p. 4.

[28]Furlong and Marsh, "A Skin Not a Sweater," p. 191; Gu, *Theorien der Internationalen Beziehungen*, pp. 15–16.

[29]Furlong and Marsh, "A Skin Not a Sweater," p. 199.

[30]Craig Parsons, "Constructivism and Interpretative Theory," in *Theory and Methods in Political Science*, eds. David Marsh and Gerry Stoker (Basingstoke: Palgrave Macmillan, 2010), p. 80.

sciences are not applicable to the *social* sciences.[31] Accordingly, social science can in this view at best aim at understanding (*verstehen*) rather than explaining (*erklären*) the socially constructed world around us.[32] Such postmodern views have received growing attention in recent decades.[33] However, in contrast to positivist approaches, in the discipline of International Relations they still, according to Furlong and Marsh, "are seen as minority dissidents."[34]

Turning to the far left column in Table 4.1, positivism starts from a foundationalist ontology and argues that in the social sciences causal inferences can be made, unbiased and based on empirical observation of the entire "world out there" including all of its structures and substructures.[35] Richard Ned Lebow accordingly argued that positivism "assumes that reality has an objective existence that is outside and independent of language and conceptual categories used to describe and analyze it."[36] Along these lines, this view is influenced by the natural sciences (particularly by epistemological positions tracing back to David Hume that are based on visual observation and empirical evidence) in the sense that it allows to detect causes and offer explanations for them.[37] Consequently, positivism and interpretivism, it may be argued, occupy the two extremes on the epistemological spectrum.

Finally, realists (cf. the middle column in Table 4.1), while sharing the basic foundationalist ontology of positivism and agreeing on the possibility of drawing causal inferences, posit that there are some "deep" social structures and certain social phenomena that cannot be grasped by empirical observation alone.[38] Thus, "to a realist there is often a dichotomy between reality and appearance" and proponents of this view, as Furlong and Marsh go on, "do not accept that what appears to be so, or perhaps more significantly, what actors say is so, is necessarily so."[39] In this view, Martin Hollis and Steve Smith aptly argue that even though one may "see structures in the social world and yet cannot prove, in a Positivist [sic!] sense, their existence,"

---

[31]Furlong and Marsh, "A Skin Not a Sweater," p. 199; Gu, *Theorien der Internationalen Beziehungen*, pp. 15–16. On socially constructed knowledge claims see also Creswell, *Research Design*, pp. 8–9.

[32]Richard Ned Lebow, "Social Science and History: Ranchers versus Farmers?," in *Bridges and Boundaries: Historians, Political Scientists, and the Study of International Relations*, eds. Colin Elman and Miriam Fendius Elman (Cambridge, Mass.: MIT Press, 2001), p. 134.

[33]Lange, *Comparative-Historical Methods*, pp. 4–5.

[34]Colin Elman and Miriam Fendius Elman, "Negotiating International History and Politics," in *Bridges and Boundaries: Historians, Political Scientists, and the Study of International Politics*, eds. Colin Elman and Miriam Fendius Elman (Cambridge, Mass.: The MIT Press, 2001), p. 4.

[35]Furlong and Marsh, "A Skin Not a Sweater," pp. 193–194. See also Lange, *Comparative-Historical Methods*, p. 5.

[36]Lebow, "Social Science and History," p. 134.

[37]Furlong and Marsh, "A Skin Not a Sweater," p. 191; Gu, *Theorien der Internationalen Beziehungen*, pp. 15–16.

[38]Furlong and Marsh, "A Skin Not a Sweater," p. 204.

[39]Furlong and Marsh, "A Skin Not a Sweater," p. 204.

one may "get the best explanations by inferring their existence."[40] Hollis and Smith refer to this approach as the "inference to the best explanation."[41] This inference to the best explanation (IBE) as a core element in realist epistemology has, of course, a long tradition. Accordingly, IBE has been coined by Gilbert H. Harman in 1965 who, in order to illustrate its meaning, argued,

> 'The inference to the best explanation' corresponds approximately to what others have called 'abduction,' 'the method of hypothesis,' 'hypothetic inference,' 'the method of elimination,' 'eliminative induction,' and 'theoretical inference.' [. . .] In making this inference one infers, from the fact that a certain hypothesis would explain the evidence, to the truth of that hypothesis. In general, there will be several hypotheses which might explain the evidence, so one must be able to reject all such alternative hypotheses before one is warranted in making the inference. Thus one infers, from the premise that a given hypothesis would provide a 'better' explanation for the evidence than would any other hypothesis, to the conclusion that the given hypothesis is true.[42]

Others have subsequently elaborated on IBE,[43] and Peter Lipton has provided a number of examples to underline its mechanism as well as prevalence in the sciences: From Charles Darwin's theory of natural selection to astronomers' theories of receding galaxies, IBE hence has for long played a prominent part in scientific reasoning. A further illustrative example elaborated upon by Lipton is the reasoning by the literary figure of Sherlock Holmes with respect to his nemesis, Professor James Moriarty, known as the Napoleon of Crime,

> Detectives infer that it was Moriarty who committed the crime, because this hypothesis would best explain the fingerprints, blood stains, and other forensic evidence. Sherlock Holmes to the contrary, this is not a matter of deduction. The evidence will not entail that Moriarty is to blame, since it always remains possible that someone else was the perpetrator. Nevertheless, Holmes is right to make his inference, since Moriarty's guilt would provide a better explanation on the evidence than would anyone else's.[44]

To quote the legendary Consulting Detective residing in London's 221B Baker Street (whose fictional nature has not kept him from having been referred to in the most diverse branches of science), "It is an old maxim of mine that when you have excluded the impossible, whatever remains, however, improbable, must be the truth."[45]

---

[40]Martin Hollis and Steven Smith, *Explaining and Understanding International Relations* (Oxford: Clarendon Press, 1990), p. 207.

[41]Hollis and Smith, *Explaining and Understanding International Relations*, p. 207.

[42]Gilbert H. Harman, "The Inference to the Best Explanation," *Philosophical Review*, Vol. 74 (January 1964), pp. 88–89.

[43]See, for example, Peter Lipton, *Inference to the Best Explanation* (London: Routledge, 2004) and Yemima Ben-Menahem, "The Inference to the Best Explanation," *Erkenntnis*, Vol. 33, No. 3 (November 1990), pp. 319–344.

[44]Peter Lipton, "Causation and Explanation," in *The Oxford Handbook of Causation*, eds. Helen Beebee, Christopher Hitchcock, Peter Menzies (Oxford: Oxford University Press, 2009), pp. 628–629.

[45]Arthur Conan Doyle, "The Beryl Coronet," p. 632. Modified expressions to the same effect appear, frequently almost verbatim, elsewhere in the Holmesian canon, including in 1 of its 4 novels

Table 4.2 The interplay of ontology, epistemology, and methodology

Ontology	Foundationalism		Anti-foundationalism
Epistemology	Positivism	Realism	Interpretivism
Methodology	Quantitative privileged	Quantitative and qualitative	Qualitative privileged

Own table based on diagram in Furlong and Marsh, "A Skin Not a Sweater," p. 186

   From the perspective of the author, the realist epistemology best captures possibilities as well as limitations in seeking to gain comprehensive knowledge of the world we live in and unveil its phenomena and structures. At the same time, and to be elaborated in the following, it is eminently suited for the study of soft power in international relations. By combining the best of both worlds, as Furlong and Marsh have thus fittingly noted, modern realist epistemology "attempts to acknowledge much of the interpretative critique, while retaining a commitment to causal explanation and, specifically, the causal powers of observable structures."[46]

   The epistemological perspective of the respective researcher (as well as his or her ontology) decisively influences the availability of methods in order to address one's research questions.[47] Furlong and Marsh accordingly argued that following a realist epistemology (just like following any other epistemology) has crucial methodological implications.[48] This interplay between ontology, epistemology, and methodology can be visualized in the Table 4.2.

   As depicted in Table 4.2, when subscribing to a foundational ontology and realist epistemology, as is being done by the present study, quantitative and qualitative methods are equally at the researcher's disposal to address his or her research questions.[49] In order to make a well-founded choice for the empirical study of soft power in international relations in this regard, we shall now take a closer look at these two approaches.

---

and 2 of its 56 short stories: *The Sign of the Four*, p. 122; "The Bruce-Partington Plans", p. 1161; and "The Blanched Soldier," p. 1268. All page references apply to Arthur Conan Doyle, *Sherlock Holmes: The Complete Stories* (Ware: Wordsworth Editions Limited, 2007).

[46]Furlong and Marsh, "A Skin Not a Sweater," p. 205.

[47]Gu, *Theorien der Internationalen Beziehungen*, pp. 14–15.

[48]Furlong and Marsh, "A Skin Not a Sweater," p. 205.

[49]Furlong and Marsh, "A Skin Not a Sweater," p. 205.

4.2   A Tale of Two Approaches: Quantitative and Qualitative Methods

In a time of "passionate debates about method and approach" and "adversarial or perhaps even openly hostile gestures among competing research paradigms,"[50] discussions between proponents of quantitative and qualitative research methods have become charged with emotion. Gary King, Robert O. Keohane, and Sidney Verba accordingly argued that the different approaches "sometimes seem to be at war" with each other[51] and Philip A. Schrodt has concurrently noted that "while this debate is not in any sense about religion, its dynamics are best understood as though it were about religion."[52] James Mahoney and Gary Goertz, while also recalling the frequent references to religion, including Schrodt's, "prefer to think of the two traditions as alternative cultures."[53]

Constituting one of these two "alternative cultures," quantitative research, on the one hand, can be defined as "a basic strategy of social research that usually involves analysis of patterns of covariation across a large number of cases. This approach focuses on variables and relationships among variables in an effort to identify general patters of covariation."[54] Carrie Williams presented another definition and noted that quantitative research "involves the collection of data so that information can be quantified and subjected to statistical treatment" while it "also involves data collection that is typically numeric and the researcher tends to use mathematical models as the methodology of data analysis."[55] As evident from these exemplary definitions, quantitative research commonly involves a large number of cases and "uses numbers and statistical methods"[56] in order to draw inferences. Accordingly, by including many cases (i.e., conducting large-N research) and applying methods of calculation, researchers seek to obtain statistically significant results across cases.[57] In this regard, some scholars espouse the view "that if a causal mechanism holds for

---

[50]James Mahoney and Dietrich Rueschemeyer, "Comparative Historical Analysis: Achievements and Agendas," in *Comparative Historical Analysis in the Social Sciences*, eds. James Mahoney and Dietrich Rueschemeyer (Cambridge: Cambridge University Press, 2003), pp. 15 & 24.

[51]Gary King, Robert O. Keohane, and Sidney Verba, *Designing Social Inquiry: Scientific Inference in Qualitative Research* (Princeton, N.J.: Princeton University Press, 1994), p. 3.

[52]Philip A. Schrodt, "Beyond the Linear Frequentist Orthodoxy," *Political Analysis*, Vol. 14, No. 3 (2006), pp. 335.

[53]James Mahoney and Gary Goertz, "A Tale of Two Cultures: Contrasting Quantitative and Qualitative Research," *Political Analysis*, Vol. 14, No. 3 (2006), p. 227.

[54]Ragin, *Constructing Social Research*, p. 190.

[55]Carrie Williams, "Research Methods," *Journal of Business & Economic Research*, Vol. 5, No. 3 (March 2007), p. 66.

[56]King, Keohane, and Verba, *Designing Social Inquiry*, p. 3.

[57]Jonathan Hopkin, "The Comparative Method," in *Theory and Methods in Political Science*, eds. David Marsh and Gerry Stoker (Basingstoke: Palgrave Macmillan, 2010), pp. 294–300.

five instead of two cases, it is more valid."[58] Consequently, quantitative research even has been attributed the capacity for "probabilistic prediction, tending to abstract particular phenomena from their contexts."[59] In the wake of the behavioral revolution in the social sciences, quantitative methods grew immensely popular in the 1960s.[60]

Qualitative research, on the other hand, can be defined as "a basic strategy of social research that usually involves in-depth examination of a relatively small number of cases. Cases are examined intensively with techniques designed to facilitate the clarification of theoretical concepts and empirical categories."[61] Keohane, King, and Verba have hence argued that qualitative research

> covers a wide range of approaches, but by definition, none of these approaches relies on numerical measurements. Such work has tended to focus on one or a small number of cases, to use intensive interviews or depth analysis of historical materials, to be discursive in method, and to be concerned with a rounded or comprehensive account of some event or unit. Even though they have a small number of cases, qualitative researchers generally unearth enormous amounts of information from their studies. Sometimes this kind of work in the social sciences is linked with area or case studies where the focus is on a particular event, decision, institution, location, issue, or piece of legislation.[62]

Accordingly, a major difference between the two approaches lies in the quantity of selected cases to be considered for analysis: while quantitative research usually draws on a large number of cases (large-N), qualitative research usually examines fewer or even single cases (small-N) in more detail. In fact, this very distinction is regarded as one of the basic dichotomies in designing research in the social sciences.[63]

Concerning the significance of qualitative research in the social sciences, David Collier and Colin Elman have noted, "Qualitative methods in political science have undergone a remarkable transformation" and recently "this branch of methodology has been experiencing a resurge."[64] Ariadne Vromen likewise argued that while "there has been a renewed focus on the use of qualitative methods in political

---

[58]Hancké, "The Challenge of Research Design," p. 240. See also King, Keohane, and Verba, *Designing Social Inquiry*, p. 24.

[59]Hopkin, "The Comparative Method," p. 301.

[60]Charles H. Franklin, "Quantitative Methodology," in *The Oxford Handbook of Political Methodology*, eds. Janet M. Box-Steffensmeier, Henry E. Brady, and David Collier, (Oxford: Oxford University Press, 2011), p. 797.

[61]Ragin, *Constructing Social Research*, p. 190.

[62]King, Keohane, and Verba, *Designing Social Inquiry*, p. 4.

[63]Thomas Geschwend and Frank Schimmelfennig, "Introduction: Designing Research in Political Science – A Dialogue between Theory and Data," in *Research Design in Political Science: How to Practice What They Preach*, eds. Thomas Geschwend and Frank Schimmelfennig (Basingstoke: Palgrave Macmillan, 2011), p. 10. James Mahoney and Gary Goertz provide a tabular overview of differences regarding ten identified criteria (including approaches to explanations, scope, generalization, case selection, etc.); Mahoney and Goertz, "A Tale of Two Cultures," p. 229.

[64]David Collier and Colin Elman, "Qualitative and Multimethod Research: Organizations, Publications, and Reflections on Integration," in *The Oxford Handbook of Political Methodology*, eds.

science," in comparison to quantitative methods they may still remain marginalized, although the discipline of international relations constitutes a prominent exception.[65] In any event, while some predict qualitative methods a bright future, others hold it to be ephemeral.[66] Hence, some critics consider the qualitative approach to be inferior in comparison to the statistical methods applied in quantitative studies. Jonathan Hopkin, addressing this very reproach, however, argued that "there is no *a priori* reason to regard case-oriented, qualitative-comparative research as methodologically 'soft', and indeed this approach can provide a far more rigorous and sophisticated response to some types of research questions."[67] Despite these positive appraisals, challenges and methodological questions facing qualitative research remain[68]—and shall be addressed below.

In spite of the oft-quoted dichotomy between the "alternative cultures" and their substantial differences—or perhaps precisely because of these differences—recent years have seen an impressive increase in mixed-methods approaches seeking to combine the best of both worlds.[69] John W. Creswell accordingly noted, "Mixed methods research has come of age" and "is useful to capture the best of both quantitative and qualitative approaches."[70] King, Keohane, and Verba likewise argued,

---

Janet M. Box-Steffensmeier, Henry E. Brady, and David Collier (Oxford: Oxford University Press, 2011), pp. 779.

[65] Ariadne Vromen, "Debating Methods: Rediscovering Qualitative Approaches," *In Theory and Methods in Political Science*, eds. David Marsh and Gerry Stoker (Basingstoke: Palgrave Macmillan, 2010), pp. 252 & 265.

[66] Hubert Knoblauch, "Zukunft und Perspektiven qualitativer Forschung," in *Qualitative Forschung: Ein Handbuch*, eds. Uwe Flick, Ernst von Kardorff, and Ines Steinke (Reinbek bei Hamburg: Rowohlt Taschenbuch Verlag, 2012), pp. 623–624.

[67] Hopkin, "The Comparative Method," p. 300.

[68] Christian Lüders, "Herausforderungen qualitativer Forschung," in *Qualitative Forschung: Ein Handbuch*, eds. Uwe Flick, Ernst von Kardorff, and Ines Steinke (Reinbek bei Hamburg: Rowohlt Taschenbuch Verlag, 2012), pp. 632–633.

[69] Hopkin, "The Comparative Method," p. 306. For further information on integrating both research methods see, for example, James D. Fearon and David D. Laitin, "Integrating Qualitative and Quantitative Methods," in *The Oxford Handbook of Political Methodology*, eds. Janet M. Box-Steffensmeier, Henry E. Brady, and David Collier (Oxford: Oxford University Press, 2011), pp. 756–776; Udo Kelle and Christian Erzberger, "Qualitative und quantitative Methoden: Kein Gegensatz," in *Qualitative Forschung: Ein Handbuch*, eds. Uwe Flick, Ernst von Kardorff, and Ines Steinke (Reinbek bei Hamburg: Rowohlt Taschenbuch Verlag, 2012), pp. 299–309; Norbert Groeben and Ruth Rustemeyer, "On the Integration of Quantitative and Qualitative Methodological Paradigms (Bases on the Example of Content Analysis)," in *Trends and Perspectives in Empirical Social Research*, eds. Ingwer Borg and Peter Ph. Mohler (Berlin: Walter de Gruyter, 1994), pp. 308–326; and Collier and Elman, "Qualitative and Multimethod Research, pp. 779–795.

[70] Creswell, *Research Design*, pp. 4 & 22. See also R. Burke Johnson and Anthony J. Onwuegbuzie, "Mixed Method Research: A Research Paradigm Whose Time Has Come," *Educational Researcher*, Vol. 33, No. 7 (October 2004), pp. 14–26.

[D]ifferences between the quantitative and qualitative traditions are only stylistic and are methodologically and substantively unimportant. All good research can be understood—and is indeed best understood—to derive from the same underlying logic of inference. Both quantitative and qualitative research can be systematic and scientific. [. . .]

Most research does not fit clearly into one category or the other. The best often combines features of each. In the same research project, some data may be collected that is amenable to statistical analysis, while other equally significant information is not.[71]

Despite these rather conciliatory notes, there are certain puzzles that do not lend themselves to both approaches in equal measure but rather suggest either one or the other. Hence, besides the questions of ontology and epistemology addressed above, it is also—and no less crucially—a matter of the topic of inquiry itself, which affects methodological approaches applied by the researcher. John W. Creswell in this sense noted succinctly, "Certain types of social research problems call for specific approaches."[72] Since the research problem to be addressed is—ideally—at the discretion of the respective researcher, it is likewise for him or her to decide which approach to pursue. However, as Xuewu Gu has rightly noted, despite this methodological freedom of choice, any selection requires sound justification.[73] On that score, taking into account the conceptual requirements involving the empirical study of soft power in international relations, various reasons justify and indeed dictate a qualitative approach.

First, and perhaps most decisively, when bearing in mind the relational character of soft power and the particular context dependence of its success or failure, any quantitative large-N analysis applying statistical methods is bound to fall short. By contrast, qualitative studies are eminently suited since they "look at the phenomena within their contexts."[74] Ariadne Vromen accordingly underlined the "centrality of meaning, context and history"[75] in qualitative research. "*Qualitative* researchers," concluded Anselm L. Strauss, "tend to lay considerable emphasis on situational and often structural contexts."[76] Consequently, qualitative research does *not* constitute what has been called "mindless fact gathering."[77] Rather, qualitative methods with their in-depth analysis and the awareness of the importance of context are particularly suited for explaining historical developments and processes.[78] Charles C. Ragin has thus argued,

Because they conduct in-depth investigations of individual cases, case-oriented researchers are able to identify complex patterns of conjunctural causation. While researchers interested

---

[71]King, Keohane, and Verba, *Designing Social Inquiry*, pp. 4–5.

[72]Creswell, *Research Design*, p. 21.

[73]Gu, *Theorien der Internationale Beziehungen*, pp. 16–17.

[74]Hopkin, "The Comparative Method," p. 301.

[75]Vromen, "Debating Methods," p. 255.

[76]Anselm L. Strauss, *Qualitative Analysis for Social Scientists* (Cambridge: Cambridge University Press, 1987), p. 2; Strauss' emphasis.

[77]de Vaus, *Research Design in Social Research*, p. 2.

[78]Vromen, "Debating Methods," p. 249.

only in testing general theories might find this level of detail uninteresting, in-depth study offers important insight into the diversity and complexity of social life, which, in turn, offers rich material for theoretical development and refinement.[79]

It is in this vein that due to its particularly detailed and step-by-step mode of analysis, James Mahoney and Gary Goertz—as well as others—have compared qualitative research to detective work.[80] They accordingly argued,

> Qualitative researchers are in some ways analogous to criminal detectives: they solve puzzles and explain particular outcomes by drawing on detailed fact gathering, experience working with similar cases, and knowledge of general causal principles. From the standpoint of this 'detective' method, not all pieces of evidence count equally for building an explanation. Rather, certain observations may be 'smoking guns' that contribute substantially to a qualitative researcher's view that a theory is valid.[81]

As underlined by this comparison, qualitative research is particularly eligible for in-depth examinations of few or even a single case.[82] Focusing on a small number of cases and analyzing them qualitatively hence "prefers depth to breath."[83] Accordingly, by seeking an in-depth understanding of few or even one case "the qualitative researcher tries to convey the full picture and this is often referred to as 'thick' description."[84] These advantages, agreed upon by a plethora of scholars, render qualitative approaches eminently suitable for the study of soft power, indeed.

Second, and connected with the first advantages, an analysis of the workings of the soft power of one actor toward another—as has likewise repeatedly been stressed in the conceptual-theoretical chapter of this work—requires an in-depth analysis over an extended period of time. Rather than presenting a mere snapshot, qualitative research conducted in this manner thus paints a more detailed picture and not least allows for the detection of possible soft power shifts in a given relationship and over the course of time. Although various attempts to quantify soft power through indices and other instruments have been presented, qualitative approaches offer the most suitable approach in this regard.

---

[79]Charles C. Ragin, "Turning the Tables: How Case-Oriented Research Challenges Variable-Oriented Research," *Comparative Social Research*, Vol. 16 (1997), p. 37.

[80]In applying this metaphor, Mahoney and Goertz reference other scholars who have made similar comparisons including Jack A. Goldstone, "Methodological Issues in Comparative Macrosociology," *Comparative Social Research*, Vol. 16 (1997), pp. 107–120; Stephen Van Evera, *Guide to Methods for Students of Political Science* (Ithaca. N.Y.: Cornell University Press, 1997); Timothy J. McKeown, "Case Studies and the Statistical Worldview: Review of King, Keohane, and Verba's *Designing Social Inquiry: Scientific Inference in Qualitative Research*," *International Organization*, Vol. 53, No. 1 (Winter 1999), pp. 161–190; and Alexander L. George and Andrew Bennett, *Case Studies and Theory Development in the Social Sciences* (Cambridge, Mass.: MIT Press, 2005), p. 90.

[81]Mahoney and Goertz, "A Tale of Two Cultures," p. 241.

[82]King, Keohane, and Verba, *Designing Social Inquiry*, p. 4.

[83]Geschwend and Schimmelfennig, "Introduction," p. 11.

[84]Vromen, "Debating Methods," p. 257.

Third, the respective indicators within the four subunits introduced in the theoretical-conceptual framework (cf. Table 3.2) do not lend themselves to quantitative measurement in all cases. Admittedly, opinion polls, for example, maybe utilized in quantitative analyses as well and the recourse to them and comparable statistics has in fact frequently been considered a way of quantitatively measuring soft power. However, as has been argued above, an exclusive focus on such metrics would fall decidedly short in praxis. Therefore, public opinion polls are merely one way of assessing an actor's reception (Subunit III) of another's soft power sources (Subunit I) and/or instruments (Subunit II). Only by putting them into perspective and supplementing them with further indicators, including content analysis, substantiated results about soft power outcomes (Subunit IV) in international relations can be reached. These observations hold true all the more with regard to the other subunits and their respective components, for example, the soft power resources of culture, policies, values, and personalities or the soft power instrument of personal diplomacy.

Finally, qualitative research is particularly suited for clarifying and elaborating theoretical concepts. Any thorough empirical application of the introduced taxonomy of soft power thus vindicates qualitative methods in order to submit the proposed taxonomy to a rigorous field test and thus assess its resilience in practice. Charles Ragin, as already cited above, has thus stated that "to facilitate the clarification of theoretical concepts and empirical categories"[85] is a central objective of qualitative research and cases are therefore selected accordingly. In the same vein, Mahoney and Goertz have asserted, "It is common in qualitative analysis for scholars to spend much time and energy developing clear and precise definitions for concepts that are central to their research."[86] Hence, through the in-depth knowledge gained through qualitative case studies, theories, and concepts may subsequently be elaborated and adjusted.[87] In light of these observations, qualitative research proves particularly suitable once more.

All things considered, a qualitative approach of focusing on a few cases and allowing for in-depth analyses is eminently suited to the study of soft power in international relations. Despite its obvious advantages, however, this course of action runs the risk of yielding results merely relevant to the respective cases.[88] Consequently, the focus on a few select cases frequently is at the expense of generalizability.[89] James D. Fearon and David D. Laitin accordingly noted that qualitative single case studies are inadequate for allowing generalizations "[a]

---

[85]Ragin, *Constructing Social Research*, p. 190.

[86]Mahoney and Goertz, "A Tale of Two Cultures," p. 244.

[87]Charles C. Ragin and Lisa M. Amoroso, *Constructing Social Research: The Unity and Diversity of Method* (Thousand Oaks, Cal.: Pine Forge Press, 2011), p. 115.

[88]Hopkin, "The Comparative Method," p. 300. See also Mahoney and Rueschemeyer, "Comparative Historical Analysis," pp. 17–18.

[89]Vromen, "Debating Methods," p. 255.

lmost by definition."[90] However, although generalizations may not be excluded per se,[91] an outcome-centric qualitative research design focusing on few cases does not have the intention of allowing for comprehensive generalization.[92] As Ariadne Vromen aptly argued, "Generalizability over many cases is rarely a goal of qualitative analysis."[93] Rather, it is directed to offer "explanation of outcomes in individual cases."[94] In fact, due to the high context dependence and eminently relational character of soft power, generalizations may quickly run into difficulties in the first place by the very nature of soft power itself. However, while taking into account the intricacies of soft power, such generalizations may at least to a certain degree be possible by (1) retrospectively accumulating and evaluating a set of several qualitative studies or (2) by a priori designing qualitative analyses in a comparative manner.

In fact, as Craig Hayden has noted (referencing works by both James Pamment and Jing Sun), "Comparative research, in particular, can offer insights that demonstrate the utility of soft power as a theory of practice as much as a theory of influence in international affairs."[95] Likewise, scholars of public diplomacy, understood as a fundamental soft power instrument within the context of the soft power taxonomy presented, have in particular called for comparative analysis since "it demonstrates both similarities and differences among actors and programs."[96] Pursuing a qualitative-comparative approach to the study of soft power in international relations, therefore, proves particularly promising since it allows not only for the identification of differences and similarities between different actors, thus offering the possibility to recognize patterns, but also the detection of changes and developments in a given relationship, for example, the existence of possible (soft) power shifts. This aspect, as well as different options for comparative research designs, shall be picked up again below in greater detail.

---

[90]Fearon and Laitin, "Integrating Qualitative and Quantitative Methods," p. 756. See also de Vaus, *Research Design in Social Research*, p. 237.

[91]Hopkin, "The Comparative Method," p. 303;

[92]Andreas Dür, "Discriminating Among Rival Explanations: Some Tools for Small-n Researchers," in *Research Design in Political Science: How to Practice What They Preach*, eds. Thomas Geschwend and Frank Schimmelfennig (Basingstoke: Palgrave Macmillan, 2011), pp. 183–184.

[93]Vromen, "Debating Methods," p. 255. See also James Mahoney and P. Larkin Terrie, "Comparative-Historical Analysis in Contemporary Political Science," in *The Oxford Handbook of Political Methodology*, eds. Janet M. Box-Steffensmeier, Henry E. Brady, and David Collier (Oxford: Oxford University Press, 2011), p. 746; Nathaniel Beck, "Is Causal-Process Observation an Oxymoron?," *Political Analysis*, Vol. 14, No. 3 (2006), pp. 347–352; W. Phillips Shively, "Case Selection: Insights from Rethinking Social Inquiry," *Political Analysis*, Vol. 14, No. 3 (2006), pp. 344–347; and Fearon and Laitin, "Integrating Qualitative and Quantitative Methods," p. 773.

[94]Mahoney and Goertz, "A Tale of Two Cultures," p. 230.

[95]Craig Hayden, "Scope, Mechanism, and Outcome: Arguing Soft Power in the Context of Public Diplomacy," *Journal of International Relations and Development*, Vol. 20, No. 2 (2017), p. 349.

[96]Eytan Gilboa, "Searching for a Theory of Public Diplomacy," *The ANNALS of the American Academy of Political and Social Sciences*, Vol. 616, Public Diplomacy in a Changing World, No. 1 (March 2008), p. 70.

In the final analysis, pursuing a qualitative approach with its possibilities of "'thick' description"[97] of few select or even a single case by far offers the most eligible approach to examining the often elusive workings of soft power in international relations. In view of the relationality and context dependence of soft power, elaborated upon above at greater length, a qualitative approach is, in fact, virtually indispensable. Still, having decided upon such an approach, there are various techniques which might be applied *within* a qualitative research framework.[98] Before turning to these techniques in more detail, selected attempts to quantify soft power through different indices shall briefly be recounted.

4.2.1   Attempts to Quantify Soft Power

At one point, Joseph Nye has compared the mechanisms of soft power to the "invisible hand" in the works of Adam Smith, as it also constitutes a strong yet highly intangible force.[99] Today, Adam Smith, the Scottish economist and philosopher of the Enlightenment Era, is best remembered, of course, for his *An Inquiry into the Nature and Causes of the Wealth of Nations*, published in 1776, the same year Thomas Jefferson drafted the *Declaration of Independence*. Though having in the aftermath becomes *the* central metaphor connected with the *Wealth of Nations*, Smith himself only once—and in fact marginally—refers to this metaphor in his extensive work.[100] Still, comparing Smith's "invisible hand" to the workings of soft power fits remarkably well. For, as elaborated upon above, soft power has been a constant and powerful force in international relations for ages, albeit often eluding concrete measurement and exact examination. Paraphrasing William Cowper's famous hymn "God Moves in a Mysterious Way" written in 1773, one might thus indeed argue that soft power "moves in a mysterious way its wonders to perform."

The fundamental question to be addressed in the following, therefore, is how to best grasp and measure this highly intangible, even mysterious form of power. From the outset, scholars generally agree upon the high elusiveness of soft power: Ingrid d'Hooghe argued, "There is no satisfactory way to measure a country's soft

---

[97]Vromen, "Debating Methods," p. 257.

[98]Vromen, "Debating Methods," p. 258.

[99]Joseph S. Nye, Jr., *Soft Power: The Means to Success in World Politics* (New York, N.Y.: PublicAffairs, 2004), p. 7.

[100]Adam Smith, *An Inquiry into the Nature and the Causes of the Wealth of Nations*, Edited, with an Introduction, Notes, Marginal Summary and an Enlarged Index by Edwin Cannan, Volume 1 (Methuen & Co.: London, 1904), p. 421. As Emma Rothschild has shown, Smith referred to the metaphor of the "invisible hand" (which can already be found in Ovid's *Metamorphoses* or Shakespeare's *Macbeth*) in two further works, his *History of Astronomy* (published in 1795) and *The Theory of Moral Sentiments* (first published in 1759); Emma Rothschild, "Adam Smith and the Invisible Hand," *The American Economic Review*, Vol. 84, No. 2 (May 1994), pp. 319–320.

power;"[101] Su Changhe pointed out that "measurement of soft power is difficult. [...] [I]t seems that nobody could tell us *how much* soft power a country possesses in international relations;"[102] Till Geiger asserted, "In contrast to more tangible forms of power, soft power is intangible and to some degree defies measurement except by proxies such as expenditure on public diplomacy;"[103] and in his study on Russian soft power, Jaroslaw Ćwiek-Karpowicz observed, "The influence of soft power is very difficult to measure. It is associated with intangible resources such as culture or ideology, as well as the ability to use them skillfully in order to gain allies through attraction rather than coercion or payments."[104]

Despite these generally agreed-upon intricacies, various attempts have been made to quantify soft power and hence compare or rank different actors regarding their respective soft power. Among such indices are studies that focus on selected regions (such as Christopher B. Whitney's and David Shambaugh's "Soft Power in Asia: Results of a 2008 Multinational Survey of Public Opinion"published by The Chicago Council on Global Affairs in partnership with the East Asia Institute[105]) or groups of states (such as Ernst & Young's "Rapid-Growth Markets Soft Power Index: Spring 2012.)"[106] Other indices, for example, Jonathan McClory's "The New Persuaders,"meanwhile published in three editions by the Institute for Government for the years 2010–2012,[107] or the "Nations Brands Index," developed by Simon

---

[101]Ingrid d'Hooghe, *The Limits of China's Soft Power in Europe: Beijing's Public Diplomacy Puzzle* (The Hague: Netherlands Institute of International Relations Clingendael, 2010), p. 12.

[102]Su Changhe, "Soft Power," in *The Oxford Handbook of Modern Diplomacy*, eds. Andrew F. Cooper, Jorge Heine, and Ramesh Thakur (Oxford: Oxford University Press, 2013), p. 551; Su's emphasis.

[103]Till Geiger, "The Power Game, Soft Power and the International Historian," in *Soft Power and US Foreign Policy: Theoretical, Historical and Contemporary Perspectives*, eds. Inderjeet Parmar and Michael Cox (Abingdon: Routledge, 2010), pp. 86–87.

[104]Jaroslaw Ćwiek-Karpowicz, "Limits to Russian Soft Power in the Post-Soviet Area," in *Economization versus Power Ambitions: Rethinking Russia's Policy towards Post-Soviet States*, ed. Stefan Meister (Baden-Baden: Nomos, 2013), p. 47.

[105]Christopher B. Whitney and David Shambaugh, "Soft Power in Asia: Results of a 2008 Multinational Survey of Public Opinion," *The Chicago Council on Global Affairs* in partnership with the *East Asia Institute*, Chicago, Ill., 2009, online at: http://www.brookings.edu/~/media/Events/2008/6/17%20east%20asia/0617_east_asia_report.pdf (accessed October 1, 2015).

[106]Ernst & Young, "Rapid-Growth Markets Soft Power Index: Spring 2012," 2012, online at: http://emergingmarkets.ey.com/wp-content/uploads/downloads/2012/05/TBF-606-Emerging-markets-soft-power-index-2012_LR.pdf (accessed October 1, 2015).

[107]Jonathan McClory, "The New Persuaders: An International Ranking of Soft Power," *Institute for Government*, London, December 7, 2010, online at: http://www.instituteforgovernment.org.uk/sites/default/files/publications/The%20new%20persuaders_0.pdf (accessed October 1, 2015); Jonathan McClory, "The New Persuaders II: A 2011 Global Ranking of Soft Power," *Institute for Government*, London, December 1, 2011, online at: http://www.instituteforgovernment.org.uk/sites/default/files/publications/The%20New%20PersuadersII_0.pdf (accessed October 1, 2015); Jonathan McClory, "The New Persuaders III: A 2012 Global Ranking of Soft Power," *Institute for Government*, London, September 6, 2013, online at: http://www.instituteforgovernment.org.uk/

Anholt and the Gesellschaft für Konsumforschung and launched in 2005,[108] assess 40 and 50 nation-states, respectively. A more recent addition in this regard is "The Soft Power 30: A Global Ranking on Soft Power." The index, authored by Jonathan McClory, has meanwhile been published by communication consultancy Portland (alongside varying partners) in three editions in the years 2015,[109] 2016,[110] and 2017.[111] Drawing on Nye's three soft power resources, the 2016 edition incorporated "over 75 metrics across six sub-indices of objective data and seven categories of new international polling data"[112] and hence presents a particularly sophisticated attempt to quantify soft power. In fact, Joseph Nye accordingly has called the index "the clearest picture to date of global soft power."[113]

Despite their often sophisticated calculation methods, attempts to *quantify* soft power through such indices and the ranking of countries according to their metrics— particularly on a global scale—can only offer a starting point for a further in-depth examination. Since power, and soft power, in particular, is best understood as a relationship and highly dependent on respective contexts and circumstances, further, *qualitative* research thus is indispensable. Bearing in mind such considerations on the nature of soft power, scholars are often justly critical of existing soft power indices. Jean-Marc F. Blanchard and Fuija Lu, for example, noted that "one must not aggregate blindly, as the amalgamation of diverse but poor-quality indexes may create more problems than it solves."[114] As with other forms of power, measurement of soft power hence frequently falls prey to what has been called "vehicle fallacy,"[115] that is, equating soft power behavior with its underlying resources.[116] And, as Blanchard and Lu went on, understandings of soft power as being the

---

sites/default/files/publications/The%20new%20persuaders%20III_0.pdf   (accessed   October 1, 2015).

[108]Simon Anholt, "Anholt Nation Brands Index: How Does the World See America?," *Journal of Advertising Research*, Vol. 45, No. 3 (September 2005), pp. 296–304.

[109]Jonathan McClory, "The Soft Power 30: A Global Ranking of Soft Power," *Portland*, London, 2015, online at: http://www.comres.co.uk/wp-content/uploads/2015/07/Report_Final-published. pdf (accessed August 16, 2016).

[110]Jonathan McClory, "The Soft Power 30: A Global Ranking of Soft Power, 2016," *Portland*, London, 2016, online at: http://softpower30.portland-communications.com/wp-content/themes/ softpower/pdfs/the_soft_power_30.pdf (accessed August 16, 2016).

[111]Jonathan McClory, "The Soft Power 30: A Global Ranking of Soft Power, 2017," *Portland*, London, 2017, online at: http://softpower30.com/wp-content/uploads/2017/07/The-Soft-Power-30- Report-2017-Web-1.pdf (accessed July 30, 2017).

[112]McClory, "The Soft Power 30, 2016," p. 7.

[113]Quoted in McClory, "The Soft Power 30, 2016," p. 5.

[114]Blanchard and Lu, "Thinking Hard about Soft Power," p. 570.

[115]Peter Morriss, *Power: A Philosophical Analysis* (Manchester: Manchester University Press, 2002), p. 18. See above, Sect. 2.2.

[116]Joseph S. Nye, Jr., "Responding to My Critics and Concluding Thoughts," in *Soft Power and US Foreign Policy: Theoretical, Historical and Contemporary Perspectives*, eds. Inderjeet Parmar and Michael Cox (Abingdon: Routledge, 2010), p. 219. See also Edward Lock, "Soft Power and Strategy: Developing a 'Strategic' Concept of Power," in *Soft Power and US Foreign Policy:*

same as the underlying tools or instruments are equally oversimplifying and in fact faulty.[117] With Laura Roselle, Alister Miskimmon, and Ben O'Loughlin,

> The same capabilities-centric mindset soon took hold even in the midst of communication revolution ushered in by the emergence of the internet: counting of nuclear arsenals and conventional weapons has been replaced with counting Twitter or Facebook followers and State Department language streams.[118]

In the final analysis, while contributing valuable starting points to the discussion and analysis of soft power in international relations (e.g., some of the indicators developed above can also be found in different soft power indices), indices measuring soft power can merely serve as a point of departure when seeking to assess the soft power of any actor since they can provide a rather crude sketch, at best. Consequently, when examining the workings of soft power in international relations, especially when seeking to carve out the significance of one particular actor's soft power toward another and all the more yet when trying to detect possible shifts within this relationship over a given period of time, further methods have to be applied. A method decidedly suitable in this regard shall be presented in the following.

4.2.2 Comparative-Historical Analysis: A Silver Bullet?

The method of comparative-historical analysis (CHA) grew out of interdisciplinary approaches and—as the name suggests—draws substantively on techniques of historiography. Historiography has been "defined as the writing of history based on a selective, critical reading of sources that synthesizes particular bits of information into a narrative description or analysis of a subject."[119] Frequently identified as constituting one of the most fundamental differences between historians and political scientists, however, is what has been called the nomothetic and ideographic divide, the terms having been brought to prominence by German philosopher Wilhelm Windelband as a distinction between natural and cultural sciences in the late nineteenth century and later elaborated upon by his student Heinrich Rickert.[120] Deriving its designation from the Greek νόμος (nomos), translating to "law" or

---

Theoretical, Historical and Contemporary Perspectives, eds. Inderjeet Parmar and Michael Cox (Abingdon: Routledge, 2010), pp. 45–46.

[117]Blanchard and Lu, "Thinking Hard about Soft Power," p. 582.

[118]Laura Roselle, Alister Miskimmon, and Ben O'Loughlin, "Strategic Narrative: A New Means to Understand Soft Power," Media, War & Conflict, Vol. 7, No. 1 (2014), p. 71.

[119]Cameron G. Thies, "A Pragmatic Guide to Qualitative Historical Analysis in the Study of International Relations," International Studies Perspectives, Vol. 3, No. 4 (2002), p. 351.

[120]Jack S. Levy, "Explaining Events and Developing Theories: History, Political Science, and the Analysis of International Relations," in Bridges and Boundaries: Historians, Political Scientists, and the Study of International Relations, eds. Colin Elman and Miriam Fendius Elman (Cambridge, Mass.: MIT Press, 2001), p. 45. See also de Vaus, Research Design in Social Research, p. 233.

"statue," nomothetic explanations "pursue insight that is generalizable and can be applied to multiple cases."[121] Matthew Lange accordingly argued that "[a]t an extreme, nomothetic explanations pursue law-like generalization that apply to the universe of cases."[122] Ideographic explanations, on the other hand, deriving from the Greek ἴδιος (idios), translating to "distinct" or "specific,"

> explore either what happened in a particular case or what the characteristics of a particular case were through in-depth analysis of the case. Authors pursuing this type of analysis commonly believe that extreme social complexity caused by free will and multicausality prevents researchers from discoveries that can be extended across a large set of cases.[123]

While the former is generally attributed to be the core interest of political scientists, the latter is frequently pursued by historians. With Jack S. Levy, the

> primary goal of historians is to describe, understand, and interpret individual events or temporally and spatially bounded series of events, whereas the primary goal of political scientists is to generalize about the relationship between variables and, to the extent possible, construct law-like propositions about social behavior.[124]

It is in the same vein that Joseph Nye noted three decades ago that "history is the study of events that have happened only once, political science is the effort to generalize about them."[125] Robert Jervis, however, while also recognizing differences between historians and political scientists in this regard, argued that those alleged—and often repeated—distinctions should not be exaggerated.[126] Actually, the postulated distinction can be considered as oversimplifying and assertions to that effect frequently are little more than mere "caricatures."[127]

In fact, diverse overlaps can be identified between the two disciplines, especially with respect to the related areas of international or diplomatic history and international relations. For, as Colin Elman and Miriam Fendius Elman pointed out, "political scientists who study international relations share international historians' focus on particular, important events, and feel uncomfortable generating universally

---

[121]Lange, *Comparative-Historical Methods*, p. 7.

[122]Lange, *Comparative-Historical Methods*, p. 7.

[123]Lange, *Comparative-Historical Methods*, p. 11.

[124]Levy, "Explaining Events and Developing Theories," p. 41; see Jack S. Levy, "Too Important to Leave to the Other: History and Political Science in the Study of International Relations," *International Security*, Vol. 22, No. 1 (Summer 1997), pp. 22–33.

[125]Joseph S. Nye, Jr., "Old Wars and Future Wars: Causation and Prevention," *Journal of Interdisciplinary History*, Vol. 18, No. 4 (Spring 1988), p. 581. See also Paul W. Schroeder, "International History: Why Historians Do it Differently than Political Scientists," in *Bridges and Boundaries: Historians, Political Scientists, and the Study of International Relations*, eds. Colin Elman and Miriam Fendius Elman (Cambridge, Mass.: MIT Press, 2001), pp. 406–407.

[126]Robert Jervis, "International History and International Politics: Why Are They Studied Differently," in *Bridges and Boundaries: Historians, Political Scientists, and the Study of International Relations*, eds. Colin Elman and Miriam Fendius Elman (Cambridge, Mass.: MIT Press, 2001), p. 389.

[127]Nye, "Old Wars and Future Wars," p. 581.

applicable law-like generalizations."[128] Others have recognized that due to the complexity of the social world, law-like generalizations are hardly possible,[129] a conceivable exception being what has become known as Democratic Peace Theory—and even its propositions are heavily contested.[130] All in all, shared interests and subjects offer valuable starting points for "cross-fertilization" between the two disciplines of historiography and political science.[131] After all, as Stephen Haber, David M. Kennedy, and Stephen D. Krasner have fittingly argued,

> Historians who study diplomatic history and political scientists who study international politics, despite some genuine differences, have always been engaged in a similar enterprise. Both have always been committed to a positivist methodology in which claims have had to be supported by empirical data. [...]
>
> What is most notable about diplomatic history and international relations theory are not their differences, but their similarities with regard to subject matter and, in the end, commitment to objective evidence.[132]

It is in this vein that Richard Ned Lebow compared the differences and similarities between the two branches to the differences between "ranchers" and "farmers," both frequently claiming the fruitful plains and spacious skies of the Old West, albeit with different purposes in mind: the former to raise cattle, the latter to grow crops.[133] Accordingly, while boundaries concerning substance as well as style remain,[134] there are also a great number of resilient bridges between the disciplines, allowing for reciprocal exchange and enrichment. Besides having "a common heritage," as Stephen Pelz rightly argued, "historians and political scientists can learn a great deal from each other."[135]

This learning from each other includes technical as well as methodological aspects of research and has intensified considerably since the end of the Cold War.[136] The application of historical methods in the political sciences has

---

[128]Elman and Elman, "Negotiating International History and Politics," p. 16.

[129]Lange, *Comparative-Historical Methods*, p. 2.

[130]Levy, "Explaining Events and Developing Theories," p. 82. For democratic peace theory (and its critics) see, for example, Bruce Russett, *Grasping the Democratic Peace: Principles for a Post-Cold War World* (Princeton, N.J.: Princeton University Press, 1994) and Sebastian Rosato, "The Flawed Logic of Democratic Peace Theory," *American Political Science Review*, Vol. 97, No. 4 (November 2003), pp. 585–602.

[131]Elman and Elman, "Negotiating International History and Politics," pp. 1 & 28.

[132]Stephen Haber, David M. Kennedy, and Stephen D. Krasner, "Brothers under the Skin: Diplomatic History and International Relations," *International Security*, Vol. 22, No. 1 (Summer 1997), p. 34.

[133]Lebow, "Social Science and History," p. 111.

[134]Elman and Elman, "Negotiating International History and Politics," pp. 11–27.

[135]Stephen Pelz, "Toward a New Diplomatic History: Two and a Half Cheers for International Relations Methods," in *Bridges and Boundaries: Historians, Political Scientists, and the Study of International Relations*, eds. Colin Elman and Miriam Fendius Elman (Cambridge, Mass.: MIT Press, 2001), p. 110.

[136]Elman and Elman, "Negotiating International History and Politics," pp. 32–33.

accordingly gained momentum as the inclusion of historical case studies in political science research indicates.[137] Particularly with regard to the application of a case study methodology, as stated by Andrew Bennett and Alexander L. George, "researchers in history and political science have more in common with one another than they do with some schools of thought within their own disciplines."[138] Hence the notion that historical methods may be applied within the social sciences is widely shared.[139] One particularly suitable, frequently applied, and highly interdisciplinary approach in this regard—drawing upon, it may be argued, the best of both worlds— is what has been called comparative-historical analysis.

The approach has broadly been defined as including "any and all studies that juxtapose historical patterns across cases."[140] While case studies in general frequently occupy an ontological middle ground between ideographic and nomothetic approaches,[141] CHA is particularly capable of bridging the divide through a combination of different methods and procedures.[142] In the words of Matthew Lange, CHA thus "helps limit the Scylla of overly general explanations in the absence of knowledge about actual causal processes and the Charybdis of getting lost in the details of a single case and overlooking commonalities across cases."[143] Lange hence noted,

> Comparative-historical methods combine comparative and within-case methods, and therefore have affinities with both comparative/nomothetic methods and within-case/ideographic methods. Similar to statistical and experimental methods, comparative-historical methods employ comparison as a means of gaining insight into causal determinants. Similar to ethnographic and historical methods, comparative historical methods explore the characteristics and causes of particular phenomena.[144]

In this understanding, the "C" (for "comparative") in "CHA" represents the nomothetic direction of impact, whereas the "H" (for "historic") represents the ideographic direction of the analysis.

According to James Mahoney and Dietrich Rueschemeyer, among the most respected authorities who wrote prolifically on the subject, CHA "is defined by a concern with causal analysis, an emphasis on processes over time, and the use of

---

[137]Levy, "Explaining Events and Developing Theories," p. 76.

[138]Andrew Bennett and Alexander L. George, "Case Studies and Process Tracing in History and Political Science: Similar Strokes for Different Foci," in *Bridges and Boundaries: Historians, Political Scientists, and the Study of International Relations*, eds. Colin Elman and Miriam Fendius Elman (Cambridge, Mass.: MIT Press, 2001), p. 137.

[139]King, Keohane, and Verba, *Designing Social Inquiry*, pp. 4–5.

[140]Mahoney and Rueschemeyer, "Comparative Historical Analysis," p. 10. For an elaboration on the decisive features of CHA as identified by Mahoney and Rueschemeyer, see pp. 11–14.

[141]John Gerring, "What Is a Case Study and What Is It Good for?," *American Political Science Review*, Vol. 98, No. 2 (May 2004), pp. 351–352.

[142]Lange, *Comparative-Historical Methods*, pp. 7 & 176.

[143]Lange, *Comparative-Historical Methods*, p. 182.

[144]Lange, *Comparative-Historical Methods*, pp. 13–14.

systematic and contextualized comparison."[145] With its defining characteristics (i.e., causal analysis, focus on processes, systematic comparison,[146] and also taking into account respective contexts[147]), the approach fits in perfectly with the requirements imposed by the study of soft power in international relations: It allows, through a combination of various methods, for comparisons, causal inferences regarding the mechanisms and ramifications of soft power, as well as the detection of possible soft power shifts in the relations of two (or more) actors by tracking processes over time and providing historical in-depth analysis of different cases.

Before presenting the decisive elements of the research approach in greater detail, a brief glance in the rearview mirror shall provide furthers insights into the tradition and workings of CHA. Since the childhood days of the social sciences, comparative-historical methods have been applied and scholars using its methodology include some of the most classical and influential names in the field, including Adam Smith, Alexis de Tocqueville, and Max Weber as well as "modern classics" such as Charles Tilly, Immanuel Wallerstein, and Theda Skocpol.[148] Kathleen Thelen and James Mahoney thus accredited the approach with "a long and distinguished pedigree in political science" and claimed that it "has stood the test of time."[149] According to Wolfgang Streeck, who provided an examination of the roots and developments of CHA, the "[r]ise of comparative-historical analysis as an academic-scholarly pursuit—as an empirical-analytical macro sociology free of historical determinism and teleology—began with the reception of Max Weber in the United States in the course of the 1930s and 1940s."[150] Despite the long and illustrious list of proponents as well as their century-old tradition, comparative-historical methods hence saw a particular resurgence after World War II and over the last decades have become subject to a

---

[145]Mahoney and Rueschemeyer, "Comparative Historical Analysis," p. 6.

[146]Mahoney and Rueschemeyer, "Comparative Historical Analysis," pp. 10 & 14. See also Mahoney and Terrie, "Comparative-Historical Analysis in Contemporary Political Science," p. 739.

[147]Kathleen Thelen and James Mahoney, "Comparative-Historical Analysis in Contemporary Political Science," in *Advances in Comparative-Historical Analysis*, eds. James Mahoney and Kathleen Thelen (Cambridge: Cambridge University Press, 2015), p. 7.

[148]Lange, *Comparative-Historical Methods*, pp. 1–2, 23 & 175. For an extend overview of the history of comparative-historical analysis, including prominent proponents and their works, see Lange, *Comparative-Historical Methods*, pp. 22–39. See also Mahoney and Rueschemeyer, "Comparative Historical Analysis," p. 3; Theda Skocpol, "Doubly Engaged Social Science: The Promise of Comparative Historical Analysis," in *Comparative Historical Analysis in the Social Sciences*, eds. James Mahoney and Dietrich Rueschemeyer (Cambridge: Cambridge University Press, 2003), p. 410; and Mahoney and Terrie, "Comparative-Historical Analysis in Contemporary Political Science," p. 737.

[149]Thelen and Mahoney, "Comparative-Historical Analysis in Contemporary Political Science," p. 3.

[150]Wolfgang Streeck, "Epilogue: Comparative-Historical Analysis, Past, Present, Future," in *Advances in Comparative-Historical Analysis*, eds. James Mahoney and Kathleen Thelen (Cambridge: Cambridge University Press, 2015), p. 276.

great number of scientific symposia, edited volumes, and monographs.[151] Accordingly, the approach "came of age over the past quarter of a century"[152] and, with Mahoney and Rueschemeyer, it "has reasserted itself at the center of today's social sciences."[153] Following Theda Skocpol, today it even constitutes "one of the most fruitful research approaches in modern social science."[154]

At it, CHA is characterized by a high degree of multidisciplinarity, encompassing various methods and research techniques.[155] Lange accordingly identified a "hodgepodge of methods"[156] available to CHA which "does not define itself primarily in terms of a single metatheory, a specific method, or a particular type of data. Scholars in this camp are typically quite pragmatic, even opportunistic, in these respects."[157] Theda Skocpol likewise argued that scholars pursuing CHA "remain resolutely committed to methodological and theoretical eclecticism as the best way for social science to proceed toward genuinely cumulative 'substantive enlightenment.'"[158] In fact, in virtue of methodological variety and possible combinations of different methods, CHA is "splendidly open to synergy and innovation."[159] However, despite the recognized multidisciplinarity and methodological eclecticism, statistical and experimental methods are seldom used and regularly not even feasible within CHA, whereas scholars frequently focus on a small number of cases and apply qualitative methods.[160]

Not least due to this great elasticity, CHA has been applied by scholars from various scientific disciplines including—in roughly ascending order regarding frequency of use—anthropologists, economists, historians, sociologists, and political

---

[151]Thelen and Mahoney provide an overview of recent examples of award-winning books applying CHA; Thelen and Mahoney, "Comparative-Historical Analysis in Contemporary Political Science," pp. 28–31.

[152]Skocpol, "Doubly Engaged Social Science," p. 413.

[153]Mahoney and Rueschemeyer, "Comparative Historical Analysis," p. 3.

[154]Skocpol, "Doubly Engaged Social Science," p. 424.

[155]Pavel Osinsky and Jari Eloranta, "Comparative Historical Analysis: Some Insights from Political Transitions of the First Half of the Twentieth Century," online at: http://www2.warwick.ac.uk/fac/soc/economics/events/seminars-workshops-conferences/conferences/conf/eloranta.pdf (accessed September 22, 2015), p. 2. This observation accounts for the fact that today "comparative historical *analysis*" rather than the previously used "comparative-historical *sociology*" has become the prevalent designation; Lange, *Comparative-Historical Methods*, p. 2.

[156]Lange, *Comparative-Historical Methods*, p. 7.

[157]Thelen and Mahoney, "Comparative-Historical Analysis in Contemporary Political Science," p. 19.

[158]Skocpol, "Doubly Engaged Social Science," p. 411.

[159]Skocpol, "Doubly Engaged Social Science," p. 419. See also Lange, *Comparative-Historical Methods*, p. 181.

[160]Lange, *Comparative-Historical Methods*, pp. 14–15. See also Mahoney and Rueschemeyer, "Comparative Historical Analysis," p. 6.

Table 4.3 The defining characteristics of comparative-historical analysis

No.	Characteristics	Components
1	Underlying epistemology	– Insight in social phenomena possible – Adherence to social-scientific methods
2	Units of analysis	– "Big questions" – Frequently macro-level analysis – Allowing for the influence of individuals
3	Comparative methods	– Multiple cases allowing for comparison – Frequently small-N, in-depth analysis – Different comparative methods
4	Within-Case methods	– Causal narrative – Process tracing – Pattern matching

Own table based on Lange, *Comparative-Historical Methods*, pp. 3–6

scientists.[161] Since CHA constitutes a "multidisciplinary endeavor,"[162] researchers applying this method deal with a huge variety of issues including revolutions, economic and institutional development, as well as various further topics.[163]

In the final analysis, despite constituting a particularly demanding approach through the application of different methods[164] and requiring a highly developed and in-depth knowledge of the cases under consideration, CHA meanwhile (or rather, once more) ranks among the foremost approaches in the social sciences.[165] While questions as to the exact definition of the methods of CHA persist and its boundaries are rather fuzzy,[166] Matthew Lang has identified four defining characteristics of CHA. These characteristics, depicted in Table 4.3, shall successively be elaborated upon in greater detail in the following.[167]

1. To start with the first characteristic (i.e., "Underlying Epistemology"), researchers engaged in CHA generally subscribe to the belief that social scientific insight into the "world out there" is possible, that is, they adhere to a positivist or—in the understanding of Paul David Marsh referred to above—realist epistemological stance. Accordingly, proponents of CHA argue that "social scientists can gain knowledge about social relations by using social scientific methods" and consequently postmodern epistemological views are incommensurate with CHA and its

---

[161]Lange, *Comparative-Historical Methods*, pp. 34–37. See also Edwin Amenta, "Comparative and Historical Research in Comparative and Historical Perspective," in *Comparative Historical Analysis in the Social Sciences*, eds. James Mahoney and Dietrich Rueschemeyer (Cambridge: Cambridge University Press, 2003), p. 91.

[162]Osinsky and Eloranta, "Comparative Historical Analysis," p. 2.

[163]Mahoney and Rueschemeyer, "Comparative Historical Analysis," p. 4. Mahoney and Rueschemeyer also present a number of (prominent) works applying CHA.

[164]Lange, *Comparative-Historical Methods*, p. 182.

[165]Mahoney and Rueschemeyer, "Comparative Historical Analysis," p. 5.

[166]Lange, *Comparative-Historical Methods*, pp. 1 & 6.

[167]Lange, *Comparative-Historical Methods*, p. 3.

methodologies.[168] The epistemological perspective underlying the work in hand corresponds perfectly with this characteristic of CHA.

2. The second characteristic depicted in Table 4.3 (i.e., "Units of Analysis") indicates that most CHA-based research shares the similarity on focusing on "aggregate cases," that is, nation states, large social movements, empires, etc.[169] CHA, thus, tends to ask what has been called "big questions"[170] or "first-order questions," to apply a term coined by James Rule.[171] Accordingly, CHA frequently addresses "questions about large-scale outcomes that are regarded as substantively and normatively important by both specialists and nonspecialists."[172] This feature is famously captured in the title of Charles Tilly's *Big Structures, Large Processes, Huge Comparisons.*[173] The generally observed "macroscopic orientation," however, does not exclude meso- and micro-level analysis, allowing researchers to "[zoom] in to inspect specific crucial episodes or patterns at closer range."[174] Additionally, as Lange argued, the preference for large-scale processes in the tradition of CHA does by no means "prevent comparative-historical researchers from recognizing the causal importance of individuals."[175] Max Weber, for example, also "paid considerable attention to individuals."[176] This point, bearing in mind the fourth soft power subunit introduced above in particular, constitutes a further reason why CHA is especially suitable for the empirical study of soft power in international relations.

3. While the first two characteristics hint at two fundamental aspects of CHA, the remaining two address more concrete methodological questions. The third characteristic (i.e., "Comparative Methods") thus puts the "C" in CHA and indicates the key position of comparative methods.[177] CHA, by its very name, thus requires the reference to multiple cases allowing for cross-case comparison. Sometimes these include "several cases, anywhere between thirty and several hundreds—or

---

[168]Lange, *Comparative-Historical Methods*, p. 5.

[169]Thelen and Mahoney, "Comparative-Historical Analysis in Contemporary Political Science," p. 5. See also Lange, *Comparative-Historical Methods*, p. 5.

[170]Amenta, "Comparative and Historical Research in Comparative and Historical Perspective," p. 105.

[171]Skocpol, "Doubly Engaged Social Science," p. 409. See James B. Rule, *Theory and Progress in Social Science* (Cambridge, Cambridge University Press, 1997), pp. 45–47.

[172]Mahoney and Rueschemeyer, "Comparative Historical Analysis," p. 7. See also Lange, *Comparative-Historical Methods*, p. 33.

[173]Charles Tilly, *Big Structures, Large Processes, Huge Comparisons* (New York, N.Y.: Russell Sage Foundation, 1984).

[174]Thelen and Mahoney, "Comparative-Historical Analysis in Contemporary Political Science," pp. 5–6.

[175]Lange, *Comparative-Historical Methods*, p. 5.

[176]Lange, *Comparative-Historical Methods*, p. 5. It may arguably be more than mere coincidence that Weber, among the last century's most influential and prolific sociological, political, or historical scholars, also decisively shaped the concept of charisma; see above, Sect. 3.1.4.

[177]Lange, *Comparative-Historical Methods*, p. 4.

even thousands."[178] Far more frequent in CHA, however, is a focus on a small number of cases.[179] Thus, recourse to small-N comparisons—typically considering anything between two and ten cases[180]—"is viewed by some as the only real comparative method within the comparative historical toolkit."[181] CHA, frequently focusing on limited cases, therefore, allows for looking at longer time periods in much more detail than large-N frameworks would permit.[182] Lange, thus, noted that any *"increase* in the number of cases commonly causes a *decrease* in the depth of the within-case analysis."[183] It is in the same vein that Mahoney and Rueschemeyer hold that focusing on fewer cases qualitatively "makes possible a dialogue between theory and evidence of an intensity that is rare in quantitative social research."[184] Once more, these observations constitute a decisive advantage of CHA about the study of soft power in international relations, which—as has been extensively argued above—requires in-depth analysis over an extended period of time.

However, this leaning toward a comparatively small number of cases to be analyzed in great detail also entails one of the most fundamental points of criticism already briefly addressed above: the problem of generalization and (theoretical) relevance. Dietrich Rueschemeyer accordingly admitted, "The crux of skepticism about comparative historical analysis is the 'small-N problem'—the combination of many factors assumed to be causally relevant with evidence from only a small number of comparable cases."[185] It is in the very same vein that Lange noted, "Although small-N comparison are able to offer explanations that apply to a larger set of cases, they are ill-suited to offering extremely nomothetic explanations because the limited number of cases severely limits generalizability of their findings."[186] Along with the frequently missing generalizability goes the accusation that any in-depth research of a few cases may constitute "insuperable obstacles for learning anything that is theoretically relevant."[187] However, recourse to and

---

[178]Lange, *Comparative-Historical Methods*, pp. 86–87.

[179]Lange, *Comparative-Historical Methods*, pp. 14 & 178. See also David Collier, "Comparative Historical Analysis: Where Do We Stand?," *Newsletter of the APSA Organized Section in Comparative Politics*, Vol. 9, No. 2 (Summer 1998), p. 2 and Jack A. Goldstone, "Comparative Historical Analysis and Knowledge Accumulation in the Study of Revolutions," in *Comparative Historical Analysis in the Social Sciences*, eds. James Mahoney and Dietrich Rueschemeyer (Cambridge: Cambridge University Press, 2003), p. 46.

[180]Lange, *Comparative-Historical Methods*, p. 87.

[181]Lange, *Comparative-Historical Methods*, p. 95.

[182]Osinsky and Eloranta, "Comparative Historical Analysis," p. 21.

[183]Lange, *Comparative-Historical Methods*, p. 149; emphasis added.

[184]Mahoney and Rueschemeyer, "Comparative Historical Analysis," p. 13.

[185]Dietrich Rueschemeyer, "Can One or a Few Cases Yield Theoretical Gains?," in *Comparative Historical Analysis in the Social Sciences*, eds. James Mahoney and Dietrich Rueschemeyer (Cambridge: Cambridge University Press, 2003), p. 305.

[186]Lange, *Comparative-Historical Methods*, p. 113.

[187]Rueschemeyer, "Can One or a Few Cases Yield Theoretical Gains?," p. 305.

analysis of only a few cases (or even a single case) does not aim at generalizations in the first place but rather at a deepened or new understanding of the case(s) in question.[188] Nevertheless, as Rueschemeyer has convincingly demonstrated, the alleged absence of generalizability in CHA does not necessarily need to be the case.[189] For, as argued above, it is particularly the comparative nature—even if research is restricted to a relatively small number of cases—that allows for generalizing the results.[190]

Besides being able to contribute to knowledge accumulation and offering novel explanations, comparative-historical analysis furthermore "also produces conceptual innovations of broad applicability."[191] In this sense, CHA is particularly suited to provide for a first field test of the proposed taxonomy of soft power and its respective subunits. This being said, different types of small-N comparisons are available in CHA, which among others include statistical comparisons, Boolean comparison, or Millian comparison.[192] The most common type of comparison applied in CHA, however, arguably is the method of narrative comparison, which does not entail comparing numerical variables but rather offers comparison through means of narrative.[193]

Bearing in mind that CHA is, as quoted, "splendidly open to synergy and innovation,"[194] its comparative characteristic can arguably best be complemented by drawing on what has been called the method of "structured, focused comparison." The establishment of benchmarks and categories of comparison is, of course, decisive for any comparative analysis. Eytan Gilboa, who emphasized the particular advantages of comparative case studies for research in public diplomacy, for example, noted that category selection is of particular importance in this area of research. And while he argued that different categories are conceivable, the selection of which "should be done according to specific research goals and methodologies" and by selecting certain categories and comparing them across cases, "[c]omparative research on public diplomacy should follow what Alexander George (1979) called 'structured focused comparison.'"[195] This method of structured, focused comparison

---

[188]Goldstone, "Comparative Historical Analysis and Knowledge Accumulation in the Study of Revolutions," p. 51.

[189]Rueschemeyer, "Can One or a Few Cases Yield Theoretical Gains?," pp. 307–324 & 332.

[190]Lange, *Comparative-Historical Methods*, p. 176.

[191]Thelen and Mahoney, "Comparative-Historical Analysis in Contemporary Political Science," p. 14.

[192]For an overview over these modes of comparison, which at this point shall not be elaborated upon in greater detail, see Lange, *Comparative-Historical Methods*, p. 118.

[193]Lange, *Comparative-Historical Methods*, p. 96.

[194]Skocpol, "Doubly Engaged Social Science," p. 419. See also Lange, *Comparative-Historical Methods*, p. 181.

[195]Gilboa, "Searching for a Theory of Public Diplomacy," pp. 70 & 72.

was introduced, as Gilboa indicated, by Alexander L. George in 1979.[196] In subsequent writings, George elaborated upon the method and concisely defined it and its central components,

> The method is 'structured' in that the researcher writes general questions that reflect the research objective and that these questions are asked of each case under study to guide and standardize data collection, thereby making systematic comparison and cumulation of the findings on the case possible. The method is 'focused' in that it deals only with certain aspect of the historical case examined.[197]

Structured, focused comparison hence, with Jack Levy, constitutes a method "in which each case is structured by a single set of questions and focused on those aspects of each case that the theory defines as relevant."[198] Or, to once more evoke Karl Popper's metaphor of the net referred to above, structured, focused comparison allows the researcher to decide which part of the loot to look at in more detail and which part to cast overboard again once the net has been heaved on deck. David de Vaus has in this regard aptly remarked, "A case study deals with the *whole* case but this cannot possibly mean that the case study consists of *everything* about the case."[199] Instead, as Gary Goertz and James Mahoney have argued with respect to case study research, "Many different observations at different points in time will be considered. The analyst will normally identify historical junctures when key events directed the case toward certain outcomes and not others."[200]

Consequently, "key events" and relevant information should be preferentially considered in the empirical analysis of soft power in international relations. However, it has in this regard been argued that the selection of events or variables to be included in the analysis "is both a fundamental and a tricky decision in any research design."[201] From the start, the selection of variables should not take place arbitrarily but should rather happen theory guided, deriving from existing literature and supplemented by the introduction of hitherto neglected variables.[202] Alexander L. George and Andrew Bennett hence accordingly remind us, "The important device

---

[196]Alexander L. George, "Case Studies and Theory Development: The Method of Structured, Focused Comparison," in *Diplomacy: New Approaches in History, Theory, and Policy*, ed. Paul Gordon Lauren (New York, N.Y.: Free Press, 1979), pp. 43–68.

[197]George and Bennett, *Case Studies and Theory Development in the Social Sciences*, p. 67. See also Alexander L. George and Timothy J. McKeown, "Case Studies and Theories of Organizational Decision-Making," *Advances in Information Processing in Organizations*, Vol. 2 (1995), pp. 41–43.

[198]Levy, "Explaining Events and Developing Theories," p. 76.

[199]de Vaus, *Research Design in Social Research*, pp. 224–225; de Vaus' emphasis.

[200]Gary Goertz and James Mahoney, *A Tale of Two Cultures: Qualitative and Quantitative Research in the Social Sciences* (Princeton, N.J.: Princeton University Press, 2012), p. 89.

[201]Ulrich Sieberer, "Selecting Independent Variables: Competing Recommendations for Factor-Centric and Outcome-Centric Research Designs," in *Research Design in Political Science: How to Practice What They Preach*, eds. Thomas Geschwend and Frank Schimmelfennig (Basingstoke: Palgrave Macmillan, 2011), p. 163.

[202]Sieberer, "Selecting Independent Variables," p. 165.

of formulating a set of standardized, general questions to ask of each case will be of value only if those questions are grounded in—and adequately reflect—the theoretical perspective and research objectives of the study."[203]

In this very sense, the deconstruction of soft power into four subunits as well as their respective components and deduced indicators offer substantiated criteria to make any comparative-historical analysis of the workings of soft power in international relations both structured (by applying the same framework in each of the cases) and focused (by concentrating on the mechanisms and components identified as being crucial). In sum, the comparative element of CHA with its focus on a small number of cases and the application of the narrative comparison, complemented by the tool of structured, focused comparison, presents itself eminently suited for any empirical study of soft power in international relations.

4. The fourth characteristic (i.e., "Within-Case Methods"), finally, emphasizes the "H"—or the "historical"—in CHA.[204] Accordingly, in CHA, "the investigator situates the study within the relevant contexts, takes a sophisticated approach to historiography, thinks seriously about issues of process, timing, and historical trajectories, and gains a deep understanding of the cases."[205] Besides the comparative element, the application of within-case methods can be considered the second *conditio sine qua non* of comparative-historical analysis, offering particular insight into the mechanisms of the respective cases.[206] While an important element in case studies in general,[207] within-case methods in CHA are considered the "primary source of causal inference."[208] With regard to CHA, Lange identified three different varieties of within-case methods: pattern matching, process tracing, and causal narrative.[209] (These methods, however, may in practice not always be as clearly distinguishable as they are in theory, not least since different understandings of the respective varieties can be found in the literature.[210] In the following, the work in hand follows Lang's highly elaborate understandings and definitions while putting special emphasis on the respective methods identified as particularly suitable for empirical analysis of soft power in international

---

[203] George and Bennett, *Case Studies and Theory Development in the Social Sciences*, p. 71.

[204] Lange, *Comparative-Historical Methods*, p. 4.

[205] Amenta, "Comparative and Historical Research in Comparative and Historical Perspective," p. 94.

[206] Lange, *Comparative-Historical Methods*, p. 176.

[207] George and McKeown, "Case Studies and Theories of Organizational Decision-Making," p. 23.

[208] Lange, *Comparative-Historical Methods*, p. 40.

[209] Lange, *Comparative-Historical Methods*, pp. 4 & 43.

[210] Lange, *Comparative-Historical Methods*, p. 48. It should be noted that others propose different varieties of within-case methods; Goldstone, "Comparative Historical Analysis and Knowledge Accumulation in the Study of Revolutions," p. 44. The triad of "pattern matching," "process tracing," and "causal narrative," however, is widely shared; see, for example, James Mahoney, "Strategies of Causal Assessment in Comparative Historical Analysis," in *Comparative Historical Analysis in the Social Sciences*, eds. James Mahoney and Dietrich Rueschemeyer (Cambridge: Cambridge University Press, 2003), pp. 360–367.

relations.) Between them, the three varieties constitute what Lange labeled secondary methods, that is, "techniques for gathering, analyzing, and synthesizing diverse evidence in order to gain insight into the research question."[211] Such secondary methods

> resemble detective work, as the researcher is forced to collect and sift through evidence in an effort to make sense of the case. As with a good detective, the researcher must not only gather clues that offer insight into who committed the 'crime', but also use impressive analytic skills to assemble the evidence and draw as much insight from it as possible.[212]

The first among the secondary within-case methods mentioned, that is, pattern matching, constitutes a tool for theory testing in comparative-historical analysis.[213] Lange elaborated,

> As its name suggests, pattern matching is a technique used to explore whether or not the pattern of a case matches the pattern predicted by a theory. As such, it involves using a case study to test a pre-established theory by checking to see if the case follows the predictions of the theory.[214]

James Mahoney, following Donald T. Campbell, accordingly asserted that pattern matching "provides a powerful tool for theory falsification in small-N research."[215] Despite its usefulness in this particular respect, its application is, of course, highly dependent on the research objective.[216] With respect to the intended provision of a roadmap for the empirical study of soft power in international relations, therefore, this first method proves impractical.

A second secondary within-case method identified above is process tracing. It describes

> the attempt to trace empirically the temporal and possibly causal sequences of events within a case that intervene between independent variables and observed outcomes. [...]

> It can identify paths to an outcome, point out variables that were left out in the initial comparison of cases, check for spuriousness, and permit causal inference on the basis of a few cases or even a single case.[217]

Accordingly, it presents a particularly focused type of within-case methods, which seeks to illuminate causal connections between two phenomena or events.[218] Jack A. Goldstone, hence noted that it "consists of analyzing a case into a sequence

---

[211]Lange, *Comparative-Historical Methods*, p. 55.

[212]Lange, *Comparative-Historical Methods*, p. 42. For a further reference to detective work, see also p. 15.

[213]Lange, *Comparative-Historical Methods*, p. 4.

[214]Lange, *Comparative-Historical Methods*, p. 53.

[215]Mahoney, "Strategies of Causal Assessment in Comparative Historical Analysis," p. 361.

[216]Lange, *Comparative-Historical Methods*, p. 169.

[217]Bennett and George, "Case Studies and Process Tracing in History and Political Science," p. 144.

[218]Lange, *Comparative-Historical Methods*, p. 4; see also p. 48.

(or several concatenating sequences) of events and showing how those events are plausibly linked given the interests and stations faced by groups or individual actors."[219] While it may also be applied to theory testing and development,[220] compared to other methods it is "disadvantaged because it provides a less holistic analysis and can only be employed when there is a pre-established relationship— either statistical or sequential."[221] For these reasons, the second secondary within-case method proves likewise impractical with respect to the objective of the work in hand, which is to provide a roadmap for the empirical analysis of the mechanisms of soft power in international relations.

Finally, causal narrative, as the third secondary within-case method, provides a remedy to this observed shortcoming and takes a more holistic perspective.[222] In the words of Matthew Lange, it "describes processes and explores causal determinants. Narrative analysis usually takes the form of a detective-style analysis which seeks to highlight causal impact of particular factors within particular cases."[223] With its designation drawn from William H. Sewell, Jr.,[224] causal narrative "has superior ability to provide insight into causal determinants."[225] By relying on the method of historical narrative,[226] it "explores the causes of a particular social phenomenon through a narrative analysis, that is a narrative that explores what caused something."[227] Narrative, in this understanding, has been defined by Lawrence Stone as "the organization of material in a chronologically sequential order, and the focusing

---

[219]Goldstone, "Comparative Historical Analysis and Knowledge Accumulation in the Study of Revolutions," p. 47.

[220]Bennett and George, "Case Studies and Process Tracing in History and Political Science," p. 148.

[221]Lange, *Comparative-Historical Methods*, p. 51. For further literature on the highly influential method see, for example, David Collier, "Understanding Process Tracing," *PS: Political Science and Politics*, Vol. 44, No. 4 (October 2011), pp. 823–830; Andrew Bennett, "Process Tracing: A Bayesian Perspective," in *The Oxford Handbook of Political Methodology*, eds. Janet M. Box-Steffensmeier, Henry E. Brady, and David Collier (Oxford: Oxford University Press, 2011), pp. 702–721; David Waldner, "Process Tracing and Causal Mechanisms," in *The Oxford Handbook of Philosophy of Social Science*, ed. Harold Kincaid (Oxford: Oxford University Press, 2012), pp. 65–84; Bernhard Kittel and David Kuehn, "Introduction: Reassessing the Methodology of Process Tracing," *European Political Science*, Vol. 12, No. 1 (2013), pp. 1–9; Pascal Vennesson and Ina Wiesner, "Process Tracing in Case Studies," in *Routledge Handbook of Research Methods in Military Studies*, eds. Joseph Soeters, Patricia M. Shields, and Sebastiaan Rietjens (London: Routledge, 2014), pp. 92–103; and Andrew Bennett and Jeffrey Checkel, eds., *Process Tracing: From Metaphor to Analytic Tool* (Cambridge: Cambridge University Press, 2015).

[222]Lange, *Comparative-Historical Methods*, p. 51.

[223]Lange, *Comparative-Historical Methods*, p. 4.

[224]Mahoney, "Strategies of Causal Assessment in Comparative Historical Analysis," p. 365; see William H. Sewell, Jr., "Three Temporalities: Toward an Eventful Sociology," in *The Historic Turn in the Human Sciences*, ed. Terrence J. McDonald (Ann Arbor: University of Michigan Press, 1996).

[225]Lange, *Comparative-Historical Methods*, p. 117.

[226]Mahoney, "Strategies of Causal Assessment in Comparative Historical Analysis," p. 365.

[227]Lange, *Comparative-Historical Methods*, p. 43.

of the content into a single coherent story, albeit with subplots."[228] Lange himself defined it as "a sequential account—or story—of an event or series of events which organizes material chronologically to provide an overview of either what happened or the characteristics of some social phenomenon."[229]

The telling of "stories" in graceful and captivating prose has, of course, been the hallmark of great history throughout the ages and can be found in the works of such luminaries of the craft as the classics Thucydides and Tacitus as well as more modern additions such as Gibbon and Macaulay.[230] A recent example can be found in *Battle Cry of Freedom: The Civil War Era*, James M. McPherson's Pulitzer Prize-winning account on the causes, antecedents, and course of the American Civil War, part of the multi-volume series *Oxford History of the United States*. In the preface, the author accordingly argues,

> I have tried to integrate the political and military events of this era with important social and economic developments to form a seamless web synthesizing up-to-date scholarship with my own research and interpretations. Except for Chapter 1, which traces the contours of American society and economy in the middle decades of the nineteenth century, I have chosen a narrative framework to tell my story and point its moral. This choice proceeds not only from the overall design of the *Oxford History* but also from my own convictions about how best to write the history of these years of successive crises, rapid changes, dramatic events, and dynamic transformations. A topical or thematic approach could not do justice to this dynamism, this complex relationship of cause and effect, this intensity of experience, especially during the four years of war when development in several spheres occurred almost simultaneously and impinged on each other so powerfully and immediately as to give participants the sense of living a lifetime a year.[231]

Causal narrative, as a widely applied within-case method in comparative-historical analysis, likewise draws on such historical narratives,[232] while putting particular emphasis on causal relationships. Accordingly, causal narrative constitutes "an excellent method for analyzing complex processes and concepts, as it allows detail and a more holistic analysis that considers multiple factors as well as their interaction and sequencing."[233] Consequently, the causal narrative presents an eminently suited secondary method for the study at hand, which seeks to provide an approach "to tell the story" of the workings of soft power in international relations.

While the abovementioned secondary methods provide techniques of analysis, primary methods are applied in order to collect data to be analyzed subsequently. Matthew Lange in this regard identified a number of primary within-case methods that—in the course of the research process—precede secondary methods, although

---

[228]Lawrence Stone, *The Past and the Present Revisited* (London: Routledge, 1987), p. 74.

[229]Lange, *Comparative-Historical Methods*, p. 44.

[230]Stone, *The Past and the Present Revisited*, p. 74.

[231]James M. McPherson, *Battle Cry of Freedom: The Civil War Era* (New York, N.Y.: Oxford University Press, 1988), p. ix.

[232]Mahoney, "Strategies of Causal Assessment in Comparative Historical Analysis," p. 365.

[233]Lange, *Comparative-Historical Methods*, p. 45.

in practice they may not always be separable.[234] Among primary methods (e.g., internal comparison, network analysis, Geographic Information System[235]), historical methods are most frequently applied and aim toward describing (rather than explaining) particular phenomena.[236]

In the final analysis, qualitative methods are particularly eligible for a substantiated empirical analysis of soft power in international relations. Among them, comparative-historical analysis is eminently capable, by including the best of both worlds, to bridge the divide between historiography and political science and—with its utterly suitable secondary methods—allows for an in-depth analysis of a select number of cases while at the same time rendering comparisons possible in order to identify developments over time. In this way, the comparative-historical analysis offers a silver bullet indeed for the delicate task of empirically studying the workings of soft power. An important aspect of this endeavor, the factor of time, that is, the selection of suitable periods of analysis, shall now be considered in greater detail.

4.3 Periods of Analysis

Scholars frequently stress the importance of time and sequence in social science research.[237] Robert K. Yin accordingly emphasized the significance of "specific time boundaries to define the estimated beginning and ending of a case."[238] Especially for researchers applying comparative-historical analysis, this factor is vitally important. Matthew Lange hence argued that "researchers must also consider the most appropriate temporal boundaries because cases commonly persist over extended periods of time."[239] It is in the same vein that James Mahoney and Dietrich Rueschemeyer pointed out that CHA frequently focuses on examinations "within delimited historical contexts."[240] While the selection of a specific timeframe is, of course, particularly influenced by one's research question,[241] it is once more vital to state one's reasons for selecting one particular time period over others. For an empirical analysis of soft power in international relations, reflection on the importance of a suitable timeframe is especially important.

---

[234]Lange, *Comparative-Historical Methods*, pp. 55–57.

[235]Lange, *Comparative-Historical Methods*, pp. 58–67.

[236]Lange, *Comparative-Historical Methods*, p. 56.

[237]See, for example, Hancké, "The Challenge of Research Design," pp. 240–242; de Vaus, *Research Design in Social Research*, p. 227; Mahoney and Rueschemeyer, "Comparative Historical Analysis," p. 7; and Thelen and Mahoney, "Comparative-Historical Analysis in Contemporary Political Science," p. 22.

[238]Yin, *Case Study Research*, p. 33.

[239]Lange, *Comparative-Historical Methods*, p. 41.

[240]Mahoney and Rueschemeyer, "Comparative Historical Analysis," p. 13.

[241]Lange, *Comparative-Historical Methods*, pp. 41–42.

From the outset, as has already been argued above in greater detail, soft power usually takes a considerable amount of time to exert its influence. What is more, the *detection* of this influence on the part of the researcher may take even longer. Consequently, it is appropriate to take into account a lengthy period of time when seeking to analyze soft power in international relations. At the same time, a longer-range timeframe is likewise needed for any substantiated comparative-historical analysis from a methodological viewpoint. Matthew Lange has in this regard aptly argued that in CHA "both the cause and outcomes can take considerable time to occur" and therefore "a synchronic snapshot of the present" does not suffice when trying to gain in-depth insight.[242] Frequently, time periods subject to CHA may even be calculated in decades, as the work of Deborah Yashar, for example, illustrates.[243] Still, having established the need for an extended timeframe spanning several years or even decades (rather than examining one particular point in time), at which point in time should such an analysis set in?

An appropriate pointer in this regard is the identification of what has been called "watershed moments." The metaphorical term—meanwhile much and arguably over-used—has been defined as "something that fundamentally changes the direction of things, just as a physical watershed marks the point where river waters divide, draining toward the Mississippi River, say, on one side and toward the Atlantic Ocean on the other."[244] Frequently, such "watershed moments" change the way in which we view the world and even divide our very calendar in a "before" and an "after." Often they can be identified to the day, sometimes even to the hour; sometimes contemporaries in the midst of events recognize that they are present at a decisive turning point in world history; sometimes it is for the quill of the historian of later days to assign such significance from a safe distance. Frequently, such "watershed" dates are connected to a specific nation-state, as Jay Winik, for example, has noted in his classic *April 1865: The Month That Saved America*,

> For historians, it is axiomatic that there are dates on which history turns, and that themselves become packed with meaning. For the English, it is 1066, the bittersweet year of the Norman Conquest and the beginning of the most widely spoken language across the globe today. For the French, there is the powerful symbol of 1789, marking the dawn of liberty and equality, and, just as accurately, the stunning transition between the old order and modern French society. For Americans, one magic number is, of course, 1492, the year marking the discovery of America, which is to say its Europeanization, or 1776, the American Declaration of Independence. But April 1865 is another such pivotal date.[245]

---

[242]Lange, *Comparative-Historical Methods*, p. 144.

[243]Thelen and Mahoney, "Comparative-Historical Analysis in Contemporary Political Science," p. 22; see Deborah Yashar, *Contesting Citizenship in Latin America: The Rise of Indigenous Movements and the Postliberal Challenge* (New York, N.Y.: Cambridge University Press, 2005).

[244]Richard W. Bulliet, "9/11: Landmark or Watershed," *Ten Years after September 11: A Social Science Research Council Essay Forum*, online at: http://essays.ssrc.org/10yearsafter911/911-landmark-or-watershed/ (accessed September 24, 2015).

[245]Jay Winik, *April 1865: The Month That Saved America* (New York, N.Y.: Harper Perennial, 2006), pp. xii-xiii.

In other instances, major turning points in history have affected much more than merely a single nation-state or even a region of the world, but rather have brought with them ramifications on a global scale. Among such turning points in world history are the births or revelations of founders of religions such as Jesus Christ or Muhammad. A sure indicator as to its significance, the traditional birthdate of Jesus, for example, was even set to mark the beginning of the Christian Era in time reckoning itself after the sixth-century monk Dionysius Exiguus introduced a new calendar, which gradually superseded previous ways (including the traditional Roman *ab urbe condita*).[246] Other, more secular world events with vast ramifications include the disintegration of empires, such as the Fall of the Western Roman Empire in 476 and of its eastern counterpart a millennium later in 1453, two dates which frequently are considered to mark the beginning and the end of the Middle Ages in European history, respectively.[247] Another event which—quite literally— marked the beginning of a new calendar and which constitutes a pivotal historical turning point is the French Revolution.[248] The revolution—though rather a series of events from the opening of the *États généraux* in Versailles in May 1789 to the Storming of the Bastille some 10 weeks later to the execution of Louis XVI and Marie-Antoinette in 1793 to the Reign of Terror in the years 1793 and 1794 to Napoleon's *coup d'état* in 1799—shook the very foundations of European political landscape and is generally considered to have marked the end of the *Ancien Régime* and the start of political modernity.[249]

Exactly 200 years after the Storming of the Bastille, another *Ancien Régime* came to its end, less violently and gruesomely perhaps in its demise, yet constituting a further great turning point in world history and international relations nonetheless: the collapse of the Soviet Union and the end of the Cold War. The precise end date of the Cold War (and in some respect also its start[250]) may still be a matter of dispute and different events are in the contention. Was it the fall of the Berlin Wall in November 1989, German Reunification on October 1990, or the formal dissolution of the Soviet Union in December 1991, which finally ended the East-West

---

[246]Ralph W. Mathisen, *People, Personal Expression, and Social Relations in Late Antiquity, Volume II: Selected Latin Texts from Gaul and Western Europe* (Ann Arbor, Mich.: University of Michigan Press, 2003), p. 15. See also Andreas Hinz, *Zeit als Bildungsaufgabe in theologischer Perspektive* (Münster: LIT, 2003), pp. 67–70.

[247]Randall Lesaffer, *European Legal History: A Cultural and Political Perspective*, Translated by Jan Arriens (Cambridge: Cambridge University Press, 2009), p. 11.

[248]In fact, in the course of the French Revolution, a *calendrier républicain français* had been introduced and subsequently used for a decade; Matthew Shaw, *Time and the French Revolution: The Republican Calendar, 1789-Year XIV* (Woodbridge: Boydell & Brewer, 2011).

[249]See, for example, Ferenc Fehér, ed., *The French Revolution and the Birth of Modernity* (Berkeley, Cal.: University of California Press, 1990); Eli Sagan, *Citizens and Cannibals: The French Revolution, the Struggle for Modernity, and the Origins of Ideological Terror* (Lanham: Rowman & Littlefield, 2001); and Noah Schusterman, *The French Revolution: Faith, Desire, and Politics* (London: Routledge, 2014).

[250]John Lewis Gaddis, *The Cold War* (London: Penguin Books, 2005), p. 27.

confrontation?[251] Addressing such difficulties in setting a precise date, contemporaries have argued that the end of the Cold War, not unlike the French Revolution, "was not an isolated event,"[252] but rather a series of consecutive events spanning several years. Lothar Rühl accordingly noted that a specific date marking the end of the Cold War cannot be set.[253] Perhaps Richard N. Haass, with reference to the end of World War II in Europe and Asia, made this point most vividly when he argued, "It is possible to date V-E or V-J Day with precision, but V-CW Day is elusive."[254]

What is generally agreed upon, however, is that the termination of the East-West conflict, despite observed difficulties in precisely dating it, heralded a new age in international politics. In fact, it has explicitly been counted among the world's crucial "watershed events."[255] Practitioners as well as observers—both contemporary and present-day—frequently outdo each other in the application of drastic metaphors and historic comparisons in this regard: Henry Kissinger observed "a "momentous change;"[256] Christoph Bertram detected a "historical earthquake;"[257] Hans-Peter Schwarz identified a "weltpolitischen Umbruch 1989–1991" (or "geopolitical breaking point")[258] and elsewhere spoke of "the defining year of 1990" during which "deep-reaching changes took place in power relations in Europe and in the broader Atlantic realm;"[259] Andreas Wirsching speaks of the "Zäsur von 1989" (or "caesura of 1989")[260]; and Andreas Rödder recently likewise noted that the end of the decade-long conflict brought about a new order in world politics, a

---

[251]Other dates have been suggested as well; see, for example, John Mueller, "When did the Cold War End?," Paper Prepared for Delivery at the 2002 Annual Meeting of the *American Political Science Association*, Boston, Mass., August 29–September 1, 2002.

[252]Christoph Bertram, "US-German Relations in a World at Sea," *Daedalus*, Vol. 121, No. 4 (Fall 1992), p. 120.

[253]Lothar Rühl, "Das Ende des Kalten Krieges," in *Neue Dimensionen internationaler Sicherheitspolitik*, eds. Reinhard Meier-Walser and Alexander Wolf (München: Hanns-Seidel-Stiftung, 2011), p. 21.

[254]Richard N. Haass, *The Reluctant Sheriff: The United States After the Cold War* (New York, N. Y.: Council on Foreign Relations, 1997), p. 21.

[255]Linda B. Miller, "The Clinton Years: Reinventing US Foreign Policy?," *International Affairs*, Vol. 70, No. 4 (October 1994), p. 622.

[256]Henry Kissinger, *Diplomacy* (New York, N.Y.: Simon & Schuster, 1994), p. 762.

[257]Bertram, "US-German Relations in a World at Sea," p. 127. The same metaphor of an earthquake is applied in Steven Muller, "Introduction: America and Germany, A New Chapter Opens," in *From Occupation to Cooperation: The United States and United Germany in a Changing World Order*, eds. Steven Muller and Gebhard Schweigler (New York, N.Y.: W. W. Norton & Company, 1992), pp. 15–16.

[258]Hans-Peter Schwarz, *Republik ohne Kompaß: Anmerkungen zur deutschen Außenpolitik* (Berlin: Ullstein, 2005), p. 11.

[259]Hans-Peter Schwarz, "America, Germany, and the Atlantic Community after the Cold War," in *The United States and Germany in the Era of the Cold War, 1945-1990: A Handbook, Volume II: 1968-1990*, ed. Detlef Junker, associated editors Philipp Gassert, Wilfried Mausbach, and David B. Morris (Cambridge: Cambridge University Press, 2004), p. 535.

[260]Andreas Wirsching, *Der Preis der Freiheit: Geschichte Europas in unserer Zeit* (München: C. H. Beck, 2012), p. 12.

situation which he compared to earlier major turning points in European history, including 1648, 1815, and 1945.[261] Consequently, observers frequently speak of a post-Cold War international system[262] or—less regularly—a "post-Wall world,"[263] and labeled the commencing age as the post-Cold War Era.[264] However, not only later historians and political scientists hold this view, but political decision-makers of the day shared such assessments. For example, long-time US governmental official Paul H. Nitze spoke of a "new world" that was emerging after the end of the Cold War[265] and Colin Powell likewise emphasized the geopolitical importance of November 9, 1989.[266] It is in the same vein that US President George Herbert Walker Bush repeatedly spoke of the dawning of a "new world order"[267] and it was, finally, Mikhail Gorbachev who upon resigning as President of the Soviet Union, declared on December 25, 1991, "We're now living in a new world."[268]

A more recent event, which in fact has been collated with this particular turning point, occurred on September 11, 2001, with the terrorist attacks on the United States of America in Washington, D.C. and New York City. Besides the end of the Cold War, the significance and impact of these attacks have frequently been compared to other crucial dates in American and world history, including, most prominently, Pearl Harbor.[269] Many observers, therefore, agree that September 11 constitutes a

---

[261] Andreas Rödder, *21.0: Eine kurze Geschichte der Gegenwart* (München: C. H. Beck, 2015), p. 339.

[262] Ewan Harrison, *The Post-Cold War System: Strategies, Institutions, and Reflexivity* (London: Routledge, 2004).

[263] Gebhard Schweigler, "Conclusion: Problems and Prospects for Partners in Leadership," in *From Occupation to Cooperation: The United States and United Germany in a Changing World Order*, eds. Steven Muller and Gebhard Schweigler (New York, N.Y.: W. W. Norton & Company, 1992), pp. 227, 243, & 249.

[264] Michael A. McFaul and James M. Goldgeier, "A Tale of Two Worlds: Core and Periphery in the Post-Cold War Era," *International Organization*, Vol. 46, No. 2 (Spring 1992), pp. 467–491. According to Michael Mandelbaum, the post-Cold War order came to an end with the 2014 Russian invasion in Ukraine; Michael Mandelbaum, *Mission Failure: America and the World in the Post-Cold War Era* (New York, N.Y.: Oxford University Press, 2016), pp. 311–366.

[265] Paul H. Nitze, "Visions of Leadership: The United States," in *From Occupation to Cooperation: The United States and United Germany in a Changing World Order*, eds. Steven Muller and Gebhard Schweigler (New York, N.Y.: W. W. Norton & Company, 1992), pp. 27 & 46.

[266] Colin L. Powell, "A Strategy of Partnerships," *Foreign Affairs*, Vol. 83, No. 1 (January/February 2004), p. 28.

[267] See, for example, George H. W. Bush, "Remarks at the Fundraising Dinner for Gubernatorial Candidate Pete Wilson in San Francisco, California," San Francisco, Cal., February 28, 1990, in *Public Papers of the Presidents of the United States: George Bush, 1990, Book I – January 1 to June 30, 1990* (Washington, D.C.: United States Government Printing Office, 1991), p. 289.

[268] Mikhail S. Gorbachev, "End of the Soviet Union: Text of Gorbachev's Farewell Address," *The New York Times*, December 26, 1991, online at: http://www.nytimes.com/1991/12/26/world/end-of-the-soviet-union-text-of-gorbachev-s-farewell-address.html (accessed September 28, 2015).

[269] John Lewis Gaddis compared the psychological impact of the events not only to December 7, 1941, but also to November 22, 1963, the day President John F. Kennedy was assassinated in

major turning point in American history[270] and qualifies as yet another watershed moment, which fundamentally altered the world in an instant.[271] Especially, the foreign policy of the United States of America took a decisive turn in the wake of the attacks, the ramifications of which can still strongly be felt around the world.

In the final analysis, when looking for a timeframe, and especially a specific starting point, for an empirical study of soft power in international relations, watershed moments provide eminently suited springboards. Among the most recent of such events, the end of the Cold War arguably takes pride of place, not only because international relations at large saw a profound recalibration but also because it likewise heralded the acceleration of globalization, a surge in democratization, as well as a thrust in information and communication technologies. As already argued above, these trends not least account for the growing importance of soft power in international relations itself.[272] Finally, the selection of the end of the Cold War as a starting point (e.g., over the also highly incisive events of 9/11), eminently meets the requirements of an extended timeframe for a substantiated analysis of soft power.

4.4 Actors and Cases of Analysis

Any qualitative empirical study of soft power in international relations that pursues the method of comparative-historical analysis and thus focuses on a small number of cases, by and large, qualifies as a case study. However, this observation in a way poses more questions than it answers. It has thus been argued that a straightforward definition of "case study" as a methodological tool is not easily done with a few words and attempts in this direction are often over-simplifying.[273] John Gerring accordingly argued that "the term 'case study' is a definitional morass."[274] Despite these alleged difficulties in definition, Peter Swanborn has presented one particularly elaborate definitional attempt of case studies as

---

Dallas, Texas; John Lewis Gaddis, *Surprise, Security, and the American Experience* (Cambridge, Mass.: Harvard University Press, 2004), p. 2.

[270]Walter LaFeber, "The Rise and Fall of Colin Powell and the Powell Doctrine," *Political Science Quarterly*, Vol. 124, No. 1 (Spring 2009), p. 84.

[271]See, for example, John Dumbrell, "The Neoconservative Roots of the War in Iraq," in *Intelligence and National Security Policymaking on Iraq: British and American Perspectives*, eds. James P. Pfiffner and Mark Pythian (Manchester: Manchester University Press, 2008), p. 29 and Charles Krauthammer, "The Neoconservative Convergence," *Commentary*, Vol. 120, No. 1 (July/August 2005), p. 26.

[272]Additionally, the very concept of soft power was introduced at this particular point in time. However, as we have seen, the concept itself can look back on a long and illustrious tradition and the workings of soft power can be detected throughout the ages.

[273]Yin, *Case Study Research*, p. 24.

[274]Gerring, "What Is a Case Study and What Is It Good for?," pp. 341–342.

the study of a *social phenomenon*:

- carried out within the boundaries of one social system (the case), or within the boundaries of a few social systems (the cases), such as people, organisations, groups, individuals, local communities, or nation states, in which the phenomenon to be studied enrols
- in the case's natural context
- by monitoring the phenomenon during a certain period, or alternatively, by collecting information afterwards with respect to the development of the phenomenon during a certain period
- in which the researcher focuses on process-tracing: the description and explanation of social processes that unfold between persons participating in the process, people with their values, expectations, opinions, perceptions, resources, controversies, decisions, mutual relations and behaviour, or the description and explanation of processes within and between social institutions
- where the researcher, guided by an initially broad research question, explores the data and only after some time formulates more precise research questions, keeping an open eye to unexpected aspect of the process by abstaining from pre-arranged procedures and operationalisations
- using several data sources, the main ones being (in this order) available documents, interviews with informants and (participatory) observation
- in which (optionally), in the final stage of an applied research case study project, the investigator invites the studied persons and stakeholders to a debate on their subjective perspectives, to confront them with preliminary research conclusions, in order not only to attain a more solid base for the final research report, but sometimes also to clear up misunderstandings, ameliorate internal social relations and point everyone in the same direction.[275]

Multi-worded definitional attempts like these already hint at the fact that the case study ranks among the most challenging methodological approaches in the social sciences.[276] Alexander L. George and Andrew Bennett, presenting a more pointed definition, hence argued that the case study approach encompasses "the detailed examination of an aspect of a historical episode to develop or test historical explanations that may be generalizable to other events."[277] While arguing that definitions are frequently flawed, John Gerring defined it as *"an intensive study of a single unit for the purpose of understanding a larger class of (similar) units."*[278] Accordingly, Gerring elsewhere noted, *"Case* connotes a spatially delimited phenomenon (a unit) observed at a single point in time or over some period of time."[279]

With respect to the present endeavor, that is, an analysis of the wielding of the soft power of one select actor (Actor A) toward another (Actor B), it may be argued that such a study more precisely qualifies as a *single* case study. Indeed, methodological approaches focusing on single case can look back on a long tradition and "have in

---

[275]Peter G. Swanborn, *Case Study Research: What, Why and How?* (London: SAGE Publications, 2010), p. 13; Swanborn's emphasis.

[276]Yin, *Case Study Research*, p. 3.

[277]George and Bennett, *Case Studies and Theory Development in the Social Sciences*, p. 5.

[278]Gerring, "What Is a Case Study and What Is It Good for?," p. 341; Gerring's emphasis.

[279]John Gerring, *Case Study Research: Principles and Practices* (New York, N.Y.: Cambridge University Press, 2007), p. 19; Gerring's emphasis.

some sense been around as long as recorded history."[280] Frequently such single case studies contribute immensely to knowledge creation regarding a particular event, epoch, or phenomenon, and at times even to theory development.

Thucydides, writing in the fifth century BC, can be regarded as an early and prominent example in this regard. In his *Peloponnesian War*, Thucydides presents an account of the eponymous war between the Peloponnesian League, led by Greek city-state Sparta, and the Delian League, led by its long-standing rival Athens. Thucydides dwells extensively on the antecedents of the war, during the early stages of which he himself had fought as an Athenian *strategos* until he was dismissed and exiled after his failure to protect Amphipolis against the Spartans under Brasidas.[281] By studying existing sources thoroughly and critically, he may indeed be considered, as Jean Bodin argued in the sixteenth century, "the true father of history," despite the fact that this distinction had for long been conferred upon his Greek predecessor Herodotus.[282] In any case, the Athenian *strategos* and historiographer Thucydides identified Sparta's perception of threat nurtured by the Athenian military buildup as decisive for the outbreak of war, which lasted for decades and ended in a victory for the Peloponnesian League.[283] Thucydides' study, to use the words of Alexander L. George and Andrew Bennett cited above, therefore, not only offers a "detailed examination of an aspect of a historical episode" but also provides "historical explanations that may be generalizable to other events."[284] The logic of increased armament by one party being perceived as a threat or challenge for the existing power structure by a second party, causing it to likewise seek armament itself, as described by Thucydides in the *Peloponnesian War*, has thus later been identified as constituting a generalizable phenomenon in international relations. John H. Herz, coining the term "security dilemma," which can be dated back to the strive between Sparta and Athens, accordingly noted,

> Groups or individuals living in such a constellation [of an anarchic society] must be, and usually are, concerned about their security from being attacked, subjected, dominated, or annihilated by other groups and individuals. Striving to attain security from such attack, they are driven to acquire more and more power in order to escape the impact of the power of

---

[280]George and Bennett, *Case Studies and Theory Development in the Social Sciences*, p. 5.

[281]Wolfgang Schadewaldt, *Die Anfänge der Geschichtsschreibung bei den Griechen: Herodot, Thukydides* (Frankfurt am Main: Suhrkamp, 1982), pp. 306–307.

[282]This tradition harks back to Cicero; M. Tullius Cicero, *Über die Gesetze: De Legibus/Stoische Paradoxien: Paradoxa Stoicum*, Edited, Translated, and Annotated by Rainer Nickel (München: Artemis & Winkler, 1994), p. 11 (Cic. Leg. I, 5); Hegel, for example, likewise considers Herodotus the father of history; Georg Wilhelm Friedrich Hegel, *Vorlesungen über die Philosophie der Geschichte* (Stuttgart: Reclam, 1961), p. 41. For two recent studies on the perception of Thucydides through the centuries, see Katherine Harloe and Neville Morley, eds. *Thucydides and the Modern World: Reception, Reinterpretation and Influence from Renaissance to the Present* (Cambridge: Cambridge University Press, 2012) and Klaus Meister, *Thukydides als Vorbild der Historiker: Von der Antike bis zur Gegenwart* (Paderborn: Ferdinand Schöningh, 2013).

[283]Thucydides, *The Peloponnesian War*, A New Translation by Martin Hammond (New York, N. Y.: Oxford University Press, 2009), p. 13 (Thuc. I, 23).

[284]George and Bennett, *Case Studies and Theory Development in the Social Sciences*, p. 5.

others. This, in turn, renders the others more insecure and compels them to prepare for the worst. Since none can ever feel entirely secure in such a world of competing units, power competition ensues, and the vicious circle of security and power accumulation is on.[285]

Today, some more recent single case studies are among the most famous and referenced literature in political science and international relations.[286] Robert K. Yin, for example, lists Graham Allison's *Essence of Decision: Explaining the Cuban Missile Crisis*[287] or William F. Whyte's *Street Corner Society: The Social Structure of an Italian Slum*[288] as popular examples.[289]

Despite its long tradition and valuable contributions to the canon of international history, political science and international relations literature, case studies have alternatingly been in and out of favor in the social sciences over the last decades.[290] Thus, while the case study had been considered a popular method attended to by many political scientists after World War II, the methodological approach of focusing on individual cases more and more fell into disgrace.[291] Accordingly, David A. de Vaus argued that "[f]or many years the case study has been the ugly duckling of research design."[292] Today, the case study remains highly controversial and while many critics point toward the methodological "softness" of the case study, it constitutes a frequently attended approach that "survives in a curious methodological limbo."[293] In the final analysis, the case study can be regarded as an approach with an especially long tradition and while methodological pitfalls persist and have to be addressed, it remains an instrument firmly fixed in the stock-in-trade of political science. After all, the selection of the case study approach, more than anything else, depends on the respective research question and the desire for an in-depth analysis of a selected phenomenon[294]—an approach that has been identified as eminently suited for the empirical study of soft power in international relations.

Considering the study of soft power as wielded by one actor toward another as a *single* case study, however, would fall short. In fact, comparative-historical analysis,

---

[285] John H. Herz, "Idealist Internationalism and the Security Dilemma," *World Politics*, Vol. 2, No. 2 (January 1950), p. 157. See also Gaddis, *The Cold War*, p. 27.

[286] Yin, *Case Study Research*, pp. 7–8. See also Rueschemeyer, "Can One or a Few Cases Yield Theoretical Gains?," p. 307 and Gerring, "What Is a Case Study and What Is It Good for?," p. 341.

[287] Graham Allison, *Essence of Decision: Explaining the Cuban Missile Crisis* (Boston, Mass.: Little Brown, 1971).

[288] William F. Whyte, *Street Corner Society: The Social Structure of an Italian Slum* (Chicago, Ill.: The University of Chicago Press, 1943).

[289] Yin, *Case Study Research*, pp. 7–8. Further famous case studies are mentioned, for example, in Rueschemeyer, "Can One or a Few Cases Yield Theoretical Gains?," pp. 307–310 as well as in Gerring, "What Is a Case Study and What Is It Good for?," p. 341.

[290] George and Bennett, *Case Studies and Theory Development in the Social Sciences*, p. 5.

[291] George and Bennett, *Case Studies and Theory Development in the Social Sciences*, p. 68.

[292] de Vaus, *Research Design in Social Research*, p. 219.

[293] Gerring, "What Is a Case Study and What Is It Good for?," p. 341.

[294] Yin, *Case Study Research*, p. 4; Robert K. Yin, *Applications of Case Study Research* (Los Angeles, Cal.: SAGE Publications, 2012), pp. 4–5.

a methodological approach especially promising as discussed above, in itself actually requires—for the sake of comparability as a central and indeed mandatory component in CHA—at least *two* cases. What is more, as argued above, particularly with respect to the study of soft power in international relations, comparative studies have been identified as being, especially advantageous since they allow for the identification of similarities and distinctions between actors and trends or developments across time. Not least against this backdrop, perhaps even more so than *single* case studies, *comparative* case studies can be considered "very common methodologies in the social sciences and are very useful tools for knowledge creation and advancement."[295]

Having identified a qualitative research design and the application of comparative-historical analysis as eminently suited for the empirical study of soft power in international relations, a further and no less substantial question arises: the equally crucial and difficult question of case selection.

Of course, case selection is highly dependent on the respective research question asked.[296] At the same time, as Gary King, Robert O. Keohane, and Sidney Verba have noted, case selection is among the most crucial issues to be addressed in any research, "No issue is so ubiquitous early in the design phase of a research project as the question: which cases (or more precisely, which observations) should we select for study?"[297] It is in the same vein that Dirk Leuffen asserted that, particularly in small-N research, "the importance of case selection can hardly be overstated."[298] Especially for comparative-historical researchers, as Matthew Lange has noted, while principally any case can be selected, "case-selection is an important element of research."[299] At the same time, in the eyes of many scholars, the selection of cases for research is frequently "considered a particularly delicate and demanding step"[300] and ever and anon even presents "a formidable problem."[301] In particular, while cases are usually selected randomly in large-N research,[302] researchers engaged in

---

[295]Gilboa, "Searching for a Theory of Public Diplomacy," p. 56.

[296]Dirk Leuffen, "Case Selection and Selection Bias in Small-n Research," in *Research Design in Political Science: How to Practice What They Preach*, eds. Thomas Geschwend and Frank Schimmelfennig (Basingstoke: Palgrave Macmillan, 2011), p. 158. See also Lange, *Comparative-Historical Methods*, pp. 41–42 and Hancké, "The Challenge of Research Design," p. 240.

[297]King, Keohane, and Verba, *Designing Social Inquiry*, p. 128. See also Hans Merkens, "Auswahlverfahren, Sampling, Fallkonstruktion," in *Qualitative Forschung: Ein Handbuch*, eds. Uwe Flick, Ernst von Kardorff, and Ines Steinke (Reinbek bei Hamburg: Rowohlt Taschenbuch Verlag, 2012), p. 287.

[298]Leuffen, "Case Selection and Selection Bias in Small-n Research," p. 158.

[299]Lange, *Comparative-Historical Methods*, p. 148.

[300]Leuffen, "Case Selection and Selection Bias in Small-n Research," p. 145.

[301]John Gerring, "Case Selection for Case-Study Analysis: Qualitative and Quantitative Techniques," in *The Oxford Handbook of Political Methodology*, eds. Janet M. Box-Steffensmeier, Henry E. Brady, and David Collier (Oxford: Oxford University Press, 2011), p. 645.

[302]Mahoney and Goertz, "A Tale of Two Cultures," pp. 229 & 239; Gerring, "Case Selection for Case-Study Analysis," p. 645; King, Keohane, and Verba, *Designing Social Inquiry*, p. 124; Leuffen, "Case Selection and Selection Bias in Small-n Research," p. 145.

small-N studies have a number of techniques at their disposal to select their cases non-randomly.[303] However, in qualitative research, "cases are generally selected intentionally"[304] and "purposefully."[305] Anything but truly random case selection, though, opens the door for selection bias and cherry picking.[306] For these reasons, sound and substantiated rationales are necessary and any case selection, particularly in small-N research, has to be justified.[307]

In fact, with respect to the work in hand, the question of selecting units of analysis presents itself twofold, since both the actors (Actor A and Actor B) and the cases for comparison have to be selected. In the following, rationales for selection on both counts shall be presented.

4.4.1   Actors: Selecting Agent(s) and Theater(s)

For reasons outlined above, any substantiated empirical study of soft power requires an in-depth analysis of respective actors involved as well as their reciprocal relationship. With Joseph Nye, "Power is a relational concept, and it makes little sense to describe a relationship without specifying both parties and the context of the relationship."[308] Accordingly, the specification of (at least) two parties involved in the process of wielding soft power is necessary to begin with.

In this sense, and in reference to proposed taxonomy of soft power (cf. Fig. 3.1), any researcher has to select (at least) one actor wielding soft power. This actor (Actor A) can, thus, be considered the *agent* of soft power and its selection is, of course, the crucial starting point for any empirical analysis. While we will presently turn to the range of conceivable actors in detail, a second actor, being at the receiving end of the soft power equation, has to be selected as well (Actor B).

Actor B, in this view, maybe considered the *theater* in which or toward which Actor A (and possibly further actors) is wielding soft power. The term "theater of war" found its way into the vocabulary of military theory and political science through Carl von Clausewitz' *On War*,

---

[303]Gerring, "Case Selection for Case-Study Analysis," p. 645. Gerring offers a tabular overview of some of these techniques on pp. 647–648.

[304]Leuffen, "Case Selection and Selection Bias in Small-n Research," p. 147.

[305]Benoît Rihoux, "Case-Oriented Configurational Research: Qualitative Comparative Analysis (QCA), and Related Techniques," in *The Oxford Handbook of Political Methodology*, eds. Janet M. Box-Steffensmeier, Henry E. Brady, and David Collier (Oxford: Oxford University Press, 2011), p. 723.

[306]Lange, *Comparative-Historical Methods*, pp. 158–160; Janina Thiem, "Dealing Effectively with Selection Bias in Large-n Research," in *Research Design in Political Science: How to Practice What They Preach*, eds. Thomas Geschwend and Frank Schimmelfennig (Basingstoke: Palgrave Macmillan, 2011), p. 130.

[307]Hancké, "The Challenge of Research Design," p. 240.

[308]Nye, "Responding to My Critics and Concluding Thoughts," p. 220.

This term denotes properly such a portion of the space over which War prevails as has its boundaries protected and thus possesses a kind of independence. This protection may consist in fortresses, or important natural obstacles presented by the country, or even in its being separated by a considerable distance from the rest of the space embraced in the operations.— Such a portion is not a mere piece of the whole, but a small whole complete in itself; and consequently it is more or less in such a condition that changes which take place at other points in the area over which military operations are simultaneously in progress have only indirect and no direct influence upon it.[309]

Thus, defined by the Prussian major general and war theorist, the term has subsequently gained currency in practice as well as historiography. In World War II, for example, US operations were commonly divided into a Mediterranean, a Pacific, and a European *Theater*.[310] Bearing in mind von Clausewitz' original definition and the origin of the term, the term has, of course, a notably military complexion. However, it may very well be applied to the exercise of power as well and by no means is restricted to the wielding of war in its traditional, hard power sense. In fact, literature on soft power and public diplomacy quite frequently employs decidedly bellicose vocabulary: the "*battle* for the hearts and minds," for example, has become a fixed trope within the canon of soft power literature.[311] In this sense, speaking of a theater in which soft power is wielded by a particular actor seems utterly appropriate, indeed.

At the same time, it also proves necessary from both a methodological and conceptual perspective. On the one hand, it accounts for Matthew Lange's call for "spatial boundaries"[312] in comparative-historical analysis in general, allowing for a more focused in-depth analysis. On the other hand, it pays tribute to the abovementioned relational and contextual character of soft power. Soft power, as we have seen, is no soliloquy, but rather a dialogue that requires counterparts. Taking into account these observations, besides the selection of an agent wielding soft power, choosing a theater therefore becomes eminently important as well.

Regarding the selection of possible cases on both counts, the taxonomy of soft power presented above is characterized by a high degree of flexibility and elasticity. Therefore, it is applicable—*mutatis mutandis*—to virtually every actor in

---

[309]Carl von Clausewitz, *On War*, Translated by Colonel J. J. Graham. New and Revised Edition with Introduction and Notes by Colonel F. N. Maude, Volume 2 (London: Kegan Paul, Trench, Trubner & Co., 1918), p. 2.

[310]See, for example, Peter R. Mansoor, "US Grand Strategy in the Second World War," in *Successful Strategies: Triumphing in War and Peace from Antiquity to Present*, eds. Williamson Murray and Richard Hart Sinnreich (Cambridge: Cambridge University Press, 2014), p. 346.

[311]See, for example, Steven Lukes, "Power and the Battle for the Hearts and Minds," *Millennium: Journal of International Studies*, Vol. 33, No. 3 (2005), pp. 477–493; Gilboa, "Searching for a Theory of Public Diplomacy," p. 55; Jan Melissen, "The New Public Diplomacy: Between Theory and Practice," in *The New Public Diplomacy: Soft Power in International Relations*, ed. Jan Melissen (Basingstoke: Palgrave Macmillan, 2005), p. 4; and Alexander T. J. Lennon, ed., *The Battle for Hearts and Minds: Using Soft Power to Undermine Terrorist Networks* (Cambridge, Mass.: MIT Press, 2003); emphasis added.

[312]Lange, *Comparative-Historical Methods*, p. 41.

international relations. Such actors may include, among others, nation-states, subnational actors, international organizations, (international) non-governmental organizations, or networks, as well as further non-state actors. While arguably the most common line of inquiry is an analysis of soft power as wielded by one nation-state toward another (the same holds true for CHA in general[313]), the taxonomy of soft power thus also provides the possibility to analyze the soft power relationship between states and non-state actors or even among non-state actors themselves. Consequently, the soft power wielded by international organizations, by transnational networks, or non-governmental organizations, among other conceivable actor types, can likewise be analyzed by means of the soft power taxonomy. The same holds true on the reception end of the soft power equation. This flexibility, while also highly advantageous from a conceptual point of view, renders the universe of potential cases particularly vast.

While the selection of potential cases for analysis along the lines of the soft power taxonomy is thus virtually unrestricted and at the discretion at the respective researcher, a number of different techniques for case selection are available and can be consulted. John Gerring, for example, provided and elaborated upon a comprehensive set of different selection techniques.[314] While not all conceivable techniques for case selection need to be discussed at this point, one particularly promising methodology in small-N research is choosing what has been called "substantively important cases," signifying that a case is "of special normative interest because of a past or current major role in domestic or international politics."[315] James Mahoney and Dietrich Rueschemeyer likewise argued that "most comparative historical work aims for explanations of *important* outcomes."[316] Besides the importance of the case on an empirical level, "theoretical prominence"[317] may serve as another reason for choosing a particular case over another. Harry Eckstein, for example, called such instances "crucial cases" for theory building and testing.[318] With reference to the weight of important cases when testing or applying a theory, Jack A. Goldstone has thus remarked, exemplarily referring to the explanatory power of Marxist theory with regard to the French Revolution,

---

[313]Osinsky and Eloranta, "Comparative Historical Analysis," p. 1; Mahoney and Rueschemeyer, "Comparative Historical Analysis," p. 14.

[314]Gerring, "Case Selection for Case-Study Analysis," pp. 645–684; esp. 647–648. See also Jason Seawright and John Gerring, "Case Selection Techniques in Case Study Research: A Menu of Qualitative and Quantitative Options," *Political Research Quarterly*, Vol. 61, No. 2 (June 2008), pp. 294–308; esp. 297–298.

[315]Mahoney and Goertz, "A Tale of Two Cultures," p. 242.

[316]Mahoney and Rueschemeyer, "Comparative Historical Analysis," p. 13; emphasis added.

[317]Gerring, "Case Selection for Case-Study Analysis," p. 679.

[318]Lange, *Comparative-Historical Methods*, p. 152. See Harry Eckstein, "Case Selection and Theory in Political Science," in *Handbook of Political Science, Volume 7. Political Science: Scope and Theory*, eds. Fred Greenstein and Nelson Polsby (Reading, Mass.: Addison-Wesley, 1975).

It might still be that the Marxist view held in other cases, but finding that it did not hold in one of the historically most important revolutions (that is, a revolution in one of the largest, most influential, and most imitated states of its day and a frequent example for Marxist theories) would certainly shake one's faith in the value of the theory [i.e., Marxist assumptions on the causes of revolutions].[319]

Furthermore, more practical reasons can guide the selection of possible cases, as well. Various scholars have recognized that such pragmatic or logistical reasons—including the availability of data and the language in which such data is available—are by no means negligible.[320] Researchers, thus, have to select also their objects of analysis—at least in part—based on considerations concerning the availability of and access to data suitable to address respective research questions posed.[321] Matthew Lange accordingly pointed out, "When selecting cases, researchers must therefore consider whether appropriate data is available" and though involving the danger of bias, he argued that selecting cases on such bases constitutes a "practical reality."[322] Furthermore, the language in which data are available is important.[323] This point concerns primary as well as secondary data and becomes particularly important regarding the conduct or existence of surveys or interviews. Language skills of the respective researcher are, of course, the second side of the same coin.[324] Finally, and not to be scoffed at, objects of analysis can—and frequently are—at least supplementary, also be selected on the basis of the respective researcher's individual interests. In fact, when conducting lengthy and tedious empirical research, as is required by the study of soft power in international relations, this aspect acquires particular significance.

4.4.2 Cases: Selecting Objects of Comparison

Besides the initial selection of both an agent (Actor A) and a theater (Actor B) interacting in the wielding of soft power, as outlined above, individual cases for comparison have to be selected as a next step. For a start, as James Mahoney and Dietrich Rueschemeyer have noted, in comparative-historical analysis in general "[t]he 'cases' chosen for comparison vary a great deal."[325]

With particular respect to the empirical analysis of soft power in international relations, two fundamental modes of selecting such cases for comparison are

---

[319]Goldstone, "Comparative Historical Analysis and Knowledge Accumulation in the Study of Revolutions," pp. 45-46.

[320]Gerring, "Case Selection for Case-Study Analysis," p. 679; Lange, *Comparative-Historical Methods*, p. 151. The selection of data sources will be discussed below; see Sect. 4.5.

[321]Gerring, "Case Selection for Case-Study Analysis," p. 679.

[322]Lange, *Comparative-Historical Methods*, p. 151.

[323]Gerring, "Case Selection for Case-Study Analysis," p. 679.

[324]Lange, *Comparative-Historical Methods*, p. 151.

[325]Mahoney and Rueschemeyer, "Comparative Historical Analysis," p. 14.

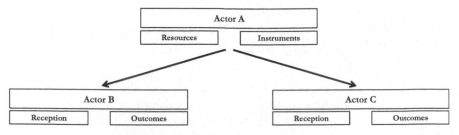

Fig. 4.1 Case selection, option 1: one agent, two theaters

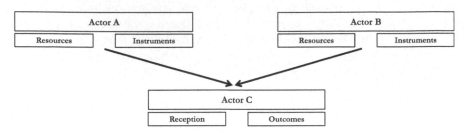

Fig. 4.2 Case selection, option 2: two agents, one theater

conceivable: First, the addition of (at least) one actor on either end of the soft power equation provides an obvious possibility. An analysis of one actor or agent wielding soft power (Actor A) toward two recipients or theaters (Actor B and Actor C) or vice versa (i.e., two agents, one theater) at a given time thus offers a plausible mode of comparison. Second, an analysis of one agent (Actor A) wielding soft power toward one theater (Actor B) can be made comparative in character by partitioning the actors along temporal lines. By subdividing the analysis of two consistent actors into different time periods, cases for comparison can thus be created as well. Both varieties shall be presented and discussed in the following conceptually and by way of arbitrarily chosen model examples.[326]

4.4.2.1 Actor-Related Comparisons

The first mode of comparison introduced above follows an actor-related approach: By adding (at least) one further actor besides Actor A and Actor B, any study of soft power easily becomes comparative in nature. In this regard, two subsidiary varieties are conceivable, as depicted in Figs. 4.1 and 4.2 to be elaborated upon in turn in the following.

---

[326]Although, as has been argued above, the taxonomy of soft power does not dictate such an approach and a variety of different actor types may be selected, empirical examples in the following refer to nation states for the sake of simplicity.

On the one hand, as depicted in Fig. 4.1, one might thus look at one agent wielding soft power (Actor A) toward two recipients (Actors B and C). By adding a second theater, one might thus detect differences and similarities as well as recurrent patterns or points of departure, which might prove highly expressive for any substantive analysis of the workings as well as the success or failures of soft power in international relations as wielded by one select actor. Of course, further actors could be added as well (Actor D, Actor E, etc.). However, any extension in this regard should be done cautiously, because it tends to decrease the in-depth nature of empirical analysis dictated by the requirements of soft power. Nevertheless, comparative studies in this manner have frequently been advocated and, as has recently been demonstrated by Artem Patalakh, the addition of further actors wielding soft power (or "competitors" in Patalakh's terms), promises, especially meaningful results.[327] By way of example, one might thus examine the soft power wielded by China (Actor A) toward Germany (Actor B) and France (Actor C). For the selection of respective actors, selection techniques referred to above may be drawn upon.

On the other hand, one might also expand the agent side of the soft power equation: By adding another wielder of soft power, a comparative study can thus likewise be conducted, as depicted in Fig. 4.2. Again, the drawbacks brought about by too broad a study (especially decrease of depth and difficulties arising from context dependence) have to be observed and weighed against possible advantages. Looking at the soft power wielded by China (Actor A) and the United States (Actor B) toward Germany (Actor C), for example, thus likewise promises meaningful results.

4.4.2.2 Temporal Comparisons

While this first mode of comparison operates, as argued, on an actor-related basis (i.e., adding at least one further actor on either the agent or theater side but retaining a single period of analysis applied to all agents/theaters), another form of comparison is conceivable as well. Edwin Amenta, thus noted, while two or more nation-states may most frequently be selected as cases for empirical analysis, "also one-country studies that situate empirical questions in a comparative context or make significant macrolevel comparisons in causal argumentation" are conceivable as cases of comparison.[328] Concerning CHA, in particular, James Mahoney and Dietrich Rueschemeyer likewise hold that "studies that focus on a single geographic unit

---

[327] Artem Patalakh, "Assessment of Soft Power Strategies: Towards an Aggregative Analytical Model for Country-Focused Case Study Research," *Croatian International Relations Review*, Vol. 22, No. 76 (2016), pp. 100–103.

[328] Amenta, "Comparative and Historical Research in Comparative and Historical Perspective," p. 93.

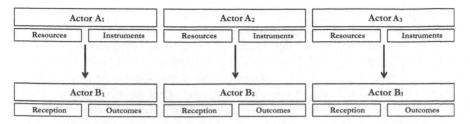

Fig. 4.3 Case selection, option 3: one agent, one theater, across time

may treat *periods of time as cases* and engage in systematic comparison in this fashion."[329]

This very mode of comparison is depicted in Fig. 4.3: By subdividing two consistent actors (Actor A as an agent; Actor B as theater) in a temporal manner, different cases of analysis can thus be created.

In fact, such an approach of regarding, in the words of Mahoney and Rueschemeyer, different "periods of time as cases" seems particularly promising for the in-depth nature crucially required for an analysis of soft power in international relations, especially so when seeking to detect possible shifts and changes of soft power in a given relationship. At the same time, such a suggested division of the past into different temporal episodes—which in turn may be treated as comparative cases—has a long tradition. Jeffrey Haydu accordingly noted,

> Sociologists and historians routinely divide the past into temporal chunks, although they often argue about the dates and characteristics that most usefully set one period off from another. These periods can be viewed as separate cases, and comparing them has much in common with comparing social institutions (such as welfare states or religions) or processes (such as revolutions or professionalization) that occur in different places.[330]

Matthew Lange likewise stressed that the primary within-case method of internal comparison in CHA "involves either comparing the subcomponents of a whole with one another or *comparing the whole with itself at different periods of time*."[331] Such an approach would, with Lange, "help the researcher to analyze how the case transformed and to highlight potential causes of change,"[332] an approach increasingly gaining currency in CHA.[333] It is in the same vein that Tulia G. Falleti and James Mahoney assert that time sequences "are often the central units of analysis and the main components of comparison. Comparative-historical work, including work

---

[329]Mahoney and Rueschemeyer, "Comparative Historical Analysis," p. 15; emphasis added.

[330]Jeffrey Haydu, "Making Use of the Past: Time Periods as Cases to Compare and as Sequences of Problem Solving," *American Journal of Sociology*, Vol. 104, No. 2 (September 1998), p. 340.

[331]Lange, *Comparative-Historical Methods*, p. 58; emphasis added.

[332]Lange, *Comparative-Historical Methods*, p. 58.

[333]Lange, *Comparative-Historical Methods*, p. 8.

focused on a single national unit, is comparative in part because different sequences of events are systematically juxtaposed."[334]

John Gerring further elaborated upon this point with a memorable scenario: a hypothetical case study on the French Revolution. Can the French Revolution be regarded as the single case in this regard? Would only the addition of the American Revolution, for example, constitute a second case and hence make the study comparative in nature? Not so, argued Gerring. Rather the French Revolution should be regarded as a "unit" of analysis and by looking at this "unit" over time, different cases might be conceived. For example, considering France on the eve, in the midst, and in the aftermath of the revolution would "create multiple cases out of that individual unit."[335] In fact, as Gerring argued, "A single unit observed at a single point in time without the addition of within-unit cases offers no evidence whatsoever of a causal proposition."[336] Considering different points in time and thus dividing the "unit" into different cases, by contrast, allows for comparisons across time rather than providing a mere snapshot and thus grants high levels of comparability. In particular, when trying to identify possible shifts and changes within a certain "unit," this periodization proves especially expedient.

Applying this observation to the study of soft power in international relations, the relationship between Actor A and Actor B can, with John Gerring's terminology, be considered as the "unit" of analysis, or, applying another term, the meta-case, whereas the relationships at A_1/B_1, A_2/B_2, and A_3/B_3 (etc.) constitute respective cases. This, however, still leaves open the question concerning any meaningful periodization of the unit/meta-case into different cases and to be looked at comparatively.

For a start, it is important to recall that "[n]o periodization scheme is innocent"[337] and the implementation of temporal structures heavily depends on one's own research question.[338] Still, different rationales for such a separation are conceivable, including the separation alongside major turning points in a given relationship between Actor A and Actor B. In this regard, the significance of "watershed events" has already been elaborated upon above and such events might well provide a division scheme in their own right. However, in view of the high-context dependence and further requirements for the study of soft power, an especially promising

---

[334]Tulia G. Falleti and James Mahoney, "The Comparative Sequential Method," in *Advances in Comparative-Historical Analysis*, eds. James Mahoney and Kathleen Thelen (Cambridge: Cambridge University Press, 2015), p. 235.

[335]Gerring, "What Is a Case Study and What Is It Good for?," p. 343.

[336]Gerring, "What Is a Case Study and What Is It Good for?," p. 344.

[337]Ira Katznelson, "Periodization and Preferences: Reflections on Purposive Action in Comparative Historical Social Science," in *Comparative Historical Analysis in the Social Sciences*, eds. James Mahoney and Dietrich Rueschemeyer (Cambridge: Cambridge University Press, 2003), p. 289.

[338]Paul Pierson, "Big, Slow-Moving, and . . . Invisible: Macrosocial Processes in the Study of Comparative Politics," in *Comparative Historical Analysis in the Social Sciences*, eds. James Mahoney and Dietrich Rueschemeyer (Cambridge: Cambridge University Press, 2003), p. 179.

approach to separate the unit of analysis into different cases is a division based on changes of government or heads of state.

First, dividing or even naming larger historical episodes along the lines of the respective heads of state or government has, of course, a long tradition across different epochs and political systems. Thus, different times in history have been designated by the defining personality of their age: the Augustan Age (30 BC to AD 14),[339] the Elizabethan Era (1558–1603),[340] or the Wilhelmine Period (1888/ 1890–1914/1918)[341] are striking examples. During the times of the Roman Republic, the years themselves were named after respective consuls holding this, the highest office in the *cursus honorum*, while subsequently counting the years beginning with the ascension to the throne of respective rulers became a frequent practice in Visigoths kingdoms and the Byzantine Empire alike.[342] In the United States , to turn to a more recent example, time reckoning itself along the tenures of individual presidents is, of course, not customary.[343] Denominating certain periods of time after the respective president in office, however, is a familiar practice in the United States as well: the Roosevelt Era,[344] the Kennedy Era,[345] or the Reagan Era[346] are just a few prominent twentieth century examples. While offering convenient historical demarcations, this practice not least illustrates the importance of the respective president for US politics and—in retrospect—history. Bob Woodward, arguably

---

[339]See, for example, Henry Thompson Rowell, *Rome in the Augustan Age* (Norman, Okla.: University of Oklahoma Press, 1962). For a classical reference to this designation, see C. Suetonius Tranquillus, *Die Kaiserviten: De Vita Caesarum/Berühmte Männer: De Viris Illustribus*, Edited and Translated by Hans Martinet (Berlin: Walter de Gruyter, 2014), p. 315 (Suet. Aug. 100).

[340]See, for example, Curtis C. Breight, *Surveillance, Militarism and Drama in the Elizabethan Era* (Basingstoke: Palgrave Macmillan, 1996).

[341]See, for example, Ruth Glatzer, ed., *Das Wilhelminische Berlin: Panorama einer Metropole, 1890-1918* (Berlin: Siedler, 1997).

[342]Mathisen, *People, Personal Expression, and Social Relations in Late Antiquity, Volume II*, pp. 14–15.

[343]However, not incomparable to the Roman *ab urbe condita* or the French Revolutionary Calendar, U.S. presidential proclamations frequently refer to the independence of the United States as a starting date for time reckoning. In proclaiming "Flag Day and National Flag Week" on June 11, 1977, Jimmy Carter hence (to just offer one example of this practice) declared, "In witness whereof, I have hereunto set my hand this eleventh day of June in the year of our Lord nineteen hundred seventy-seven, and *of the Independence of the United States of America the two hundred and first;*" Jimmy Carter, "Flag Day and National Flag Week, 1977," Proclamation 4508, June 11, 1977, in *Public Papers of the Presidents of the United States: Jimmy Carter, 1977, Book I – January 20 to June 24, 1977* (Washington, D.C.: United States Government Printing Office, 1977), p. 1098; emphasis added.

[344]See, for example, Richard Polenberg, *The Era of Franklin D. Roosevelt, 1933-1945: A Brief History with Documents* (New York, N.Y.: Bedford/St. Martin's, 2000).

[345]See, for example, Asa McKercher, *Camelot and Canada: Canadian-American Relations in the Kennedy Era* (New York, N.Y.: Oxford University Press, 2016).

[346]See, for example, Doug Rossinow, *The Reagan Era: A History of the 1980s* (New York, N.Y.: Columbia University Press, 2015).

one of the most avid observers of the US presidency over the course of the last decades, in this sense identified presidential elections as "defining moments that go way beyond legislative programs or the role of government."[347]

In literature, therefore, various studies can be found operating along these very lines. For instance, a recent study explicitly applying comparative-historical analysis and considering administrations as cases of comparison is James Petras' study on US–Venezuelan relations.[348] Lucas Pettersson, to offer a further example, has analyzed respective administrations of four different US presidents—Ronald Reagan, Bill Clinton, George W. Bush, and Barack Obama—with regard to changing images of the United States in German media discourse, spanning a total of 28 years from 1981 to 2009.[349] A comparative study that draws explicitly on three such cases (viz., the Clinton, Bush, and Obama administrations) can also be found in Bastiaan van Apeldoorn's and Naná de Graaff's comparative analysis of US elite networks and grand strategy after the Cold War.[350] Accordingly, selecting presidential administrations as cases of comparison is well founded in scholarly tradition. The same holds true, of course, for the heads of state and/or the government of other countries.

Second, the segmentation of the meta-case into comparative cases in such a manner pays tribute to the influence of individuals, which, as has been argued above, shall be considered as an important component of both the first and second subunit. Additionally, such an individual influence is also frequently recognized in and covered by comparative-historical analysis in general.[351] However, any distinction along such lines does not suggest that the soft power of any actor depends *solely* on the administration in power or even the respective head of state. Such assumptions would, in fact, run contrary to the theoretical assumptions outlined above, according to which soft power also includes a crucial non-governmental, societal, or cultural component.[352] However, as has been illustrated above, perceptions of a certain actor can indeed be attributed to a considerable extent to the perception of the individual(s) representing it.

Third, since soft power instruments—as identified in the second soft power subunit—are frequently conceived, financed, and implemented by governmental

---

[347]Bob Woodward, *The Choice* (New York, N.Y.: Simon & Schuster, 1996), p. 11.

[348]James Petras, "US-Venezuela Relations: A Case Study of Imperialism and Anti-Imperialism," *Voltaire Network*, October 22, 2013, online at: http://www.voltairenet.org/article180663.html#nb1 (accessed September 30, 2015).

[349]Lucas Pettersson, "Changing Images of the USA in German Media Discourse During Four American Presidencies," *International Journal of Cultural Studies*, Vol. 14, No. 1 (2011), pp. 35–51.

[350]Bastiaan van Apeldoorn and Naná de Graaff, "Corporate Elite Networks and US Post-Cold War Grand Strategy from Clinton to Obama," *European Journal of International Relations*, Vol. 20, No. 1 (2012), pp. 29–55; Bastiaan van Apeldoorn and Naná de Graaff. *American Grand Strategy and Corporate Elite Networks: The Open Door Since the End of the Cold War* (London: Routledge, 2016).

[351]Lange, *Comparative-Historical Methods*, pp. 5–6.

[352]See above, Sect. 3.1.1.

agencies and actors, a distinction along these lines seems sensible as well, as new administrations frequently come into office with (or are even elicited because of) notably different worldviews and priorities. Thus, respective changes in US administrations, for example, have brought about fundamental changes in (foreign as well as domestic) policy orientations and practices in the past, for example, the shifts in policy orientations from Jimmy Carter to Ronald Reagan in 1981 or Bill Clinton to George W. Bush in early 2001. With particular regard to the latter, Ernst-Otto Czempiel hence argued that such variations—with overall global conditions and the United States position of power unaltered at the time of the change in government—are in fact to be attributable to changes in political elites.[353] The same holds true for other countries as well, of course. Not least against this backdrop of changing personnel coupled with extensive executive powers, observers have thus spoken of an "elective dictatorship" (as coined by Lord Hailsham in 1976) with respect to the United Kingdom and its premiership.[354] Of course, this observation applies in particular to cases in which the new chief executive belongs to another party than his or her predecessor did. Especially in such cases, of course, the change does not only manifest itself in the individuals at the helm but also in their respective teams of advisers coming in or their particular management styles pursued.[355]

In the final analysis, selecting cases for comparative analysis along temporal lines (with different schemes for periodization available), allows for an in-depth analysis and comparison between different points in time, making it possible to carve out developments as well as changes while at the same time paying tribute to the relational and contextual nature of soft power.

4.5   Data Sources

Having discussed suitable schemes for periodization and case selection, which data should be included in any substantiated study of the mechanisms of soft power? This question, to be finally addressed in the following, is likewise highly important. "[D]ata," Matthew Lange hence justly argued, "are the most central component of the scientific enterprise," and cautioned that "the quality of an analysis is only as good as

---

[353]Ernst-Otto Czempiel, *Weltpolitik im Umbruch: Die Pax Americana, der Terrorismus und die Zukunft der internationalen Beziehungen* (München: C. H. Beck, 2002), p. 97.

[354]Duncan Watts, *British Government and Politics: A Comparative Guide* (Edinburgh: Edinburgh University Press, 2012), pp. 115 & 154.

[355]Margret G. Hermann and Thomas Preston, "Presidents, Advisers, and Foreign Policy: The Effect of Leadership Style on Executive Arrangements," *Political Psychology*, Vol. 15, No. 1, Special Issue: Political Psychology and the Work of Alexander L. George (March 1994), pp. 75–96; David Mitchell, "Does Context Matter: Advisory Systems and the Management of the Foreign Policy Decision-Making Process," *Presidential Studies Quarterly*, Vol. 40, No. 4 (December 2010), pp. 631–659.

its data."[356] Data, in this sense, have been defined as "recorded empirical observations on the *CASES* under study."[357] Recognizing the centrality of data in any empirical examination, questions concerning conceivable data sources to draw upon in an empirical study of soft power in international relations have to be addressed.

Concerning the collection of data for the empirical study of soft power, we may once more invoke Karl Popper's metaphor of the net repeatedly referenced above.[358] In line with this imagery, researchers on soft power should cast out their net into the ocean of empirical evidence and see what can be reeled in. For a start, considering the interdisciplinarity and wide range of the concept of soft power, any researcher might, in fact, be interested in everything the vast ocean has to offer. However, to stay in picture, a portion of the loot may have to be thrown back into the sea as any haul may include unwanted or unneeded items. For this task, the theoretical-conceptual framework as depicted in Fig. 3.1, combined with the indicators deduced and summarized in Table 3.2, can yet again serve as a guideline.

In general, any study of soft power in international relations has to draw on a broad a spectrum of sources. It is in this vein that Michael S. Lewis-Beck has argued, "Social scientists gather data from a wide variety of sources, including experiments, surveys, public records, historical documents, statistical yearbooks, and direct field observation."[359] At it, primary and secondary materials should both be taken into account. In fact, comparative-historical analysis, with its in-depth approach to a select and limited number of cases, frequently draws on both primary and secondary sources.[360] Primary sources, on the one hand, include "documentary records or materials that have survived from a particular historical era; that are contemporary or nearly contemporary with the period being studied."[361] Ariadne Vromen defined primary sources as

> original documents produced by political actors ranging from executive, parliamentary or judicial arms of governments, policy-making agencies or non-governmental organizations. Primary sources can also be archival materials such as photos, diaries, meeting notes and memoirs. Strictly speaking, primary sources are generally considered to be documents that reflect a position of an actor and do not have analysis in them.[362]

---

[356]Lange, *Comparative-Historical Methods*, pp. 140 & 143.

[357]Michael S. Lewis-Beck, "Data," in *The SAGE Encyclopedia of Social Science Research Methods: Volume 1*, eds. Michael S. Lewis-Beck, Alan Bryman and Tim Futing Liao (Thousand Oaks, Cal.: SAGE Publications, 2004), p. 234; Lewis-Beck's emphasis.

[358]See above, Chap. 3 and Sect. 4.2.2.

[359]Lewis-Beck, "Data," p. 234.

[360]Lange, *Comparative-Historical Methods*, p. 141.

[361]Quoted in James M. Shiveley and Phillip J. VanFossen, *Using Internet Primary Sources to Teach Critical Thinking Skills in Government, Economics, and Contemporary World Issues* (Westport, Conn.: Greenwood Press, 2000), p. 17.

[362]Vromen, "Debating Methods," pp. 261–262.

Bearing in mind the huge diversity of material potentially under consideration,[363] Matthew Lange accordingly listed "newspapers and other sources of print media, government documents, ledgers and account books, diaries and personal memoirs, and letters of correspondence" as primary sources, some of which might today be accessed electronically.[364] Besides drawing on such data, (elite) interviews (e.g., with personally involved decision-makers) or oral histories offer another valuable source of information.[365]

At this point, it is important to stress that qualitative research methods, as identified as suitable or in fact mandatory for the empirical study of soft power in international relations, do by no means preclude the reference to statistics and numbers.[366] In fact, extensive recourse to quantitative data, that is, "numbers that have intrinsic meaning,"[367] has a long tradition in comparative-historical analysis as well and quantitative data and opinion polls, in particular, can also be consulted. Jack A. Goldstone accordingly noted pertaining to his study of revolutions already referenced above,

> This CHA is certainly not made without quantitative analysis or large amounts of statistical data. In fact, I used hundreds of statistical and historical observations regarding prices, wages, rents, population, the fate of families, declarations of support or conflict by leading actors, and sequences of events to demonstrate that in England, France, Turkey, and China from 1500 to 1700 those periods during which population mounted were marked by rising prices, increasing state debts and fiscal difficulties, repeated conflicts over taxes, heightened elite mobility, falling real wages, and growing political tensions.[368]

Secondary sources, on the other hand, are particularly important in comparative-historical analysis. They include monographs, analyses, interpretations, etc. and "are usually empirical sources that interpret and form conclusions based on data from other sources."[369] Concerning different disciplinary preferences, Jack S. Levy has argued that "[h]istorians have traditionally insisted on the central importance of primary sources, while political scientists have been more willing to rely on secondary sources based on the work of historians."[370] The reliance on secondary sources has frequently evoked criticism,[371] for as Matthew Lange has aptly argued, "just like a game of 'telephone', the original message can be altered by each subsequent interpretation of the data, marking the final message starkly different

---

[363] Strauss, *Qualitative Analysis for Social Scientists*, p. 1. For a discussion of different sources, see also Yin, *Case Study Research*, pp. 103–130 and Yin, *Applications of Case Study Research*, pp. 10–13.

[364] Lange, *Comparative-Historical Methods*, p. 141.

[365] Vromen, "Debating Methods," pp. 258–259; Lange, *Comparative-Historical Methods*, p. 142.

[366] Mahoney and Goertz, "A Tale of Two Cultures," p. 245.

[367] Lewis-Beck, "Data," p. 234.

[368] Goldstone, "Comparative Historical Analysis and Knowledge Accumulation in the Study of Revolutions," p. 49.

[369] Lange, *Comparative-Historical Methods*, p. 142.

[370] Levy, "Explaining Events and Developing Theories," p. 59.

[371] Collier, "Comparative Historical Analysis," p. 4.

from the original."[372] Therefore, not least in order to best navigate the shoals of bias, alongside a critical reading of secondary sources, a particular focus should be put on primary data.[373] In practice, however, the distinction between the two varieties of sources may not always be as clear-cut as it presents itself in theory and transcripts and analyses, for example, can sometimes be found in one work.[374]

For any empirical study of soft power, especially if its selected period of analysis extends into the present, journalistic works in the form of newspaper articles or published monographs deserve special attention. Famously called "the first rough draft of history," a phrase popularized by Philip L. Graham,[375] former publisher and co-owner of *The Washington Post*, journalist materials can become especially valuable on two accounts: On the one hand, in cases of a particularly great topicality of the analysis, some episodes may not yet have been treated extensively in journal articles, let alone in substantive monographs. Additionally, primary sources, frequently subject to lengthy periods of non-disclosure, may not (yet) be available at all. On the other hand, especially with respect to the reception side of the soft power equation (i.e., subunit III), journalistic accounts are highly expressive and in fact mandatory.

In sum, and in line with the different indicators developed above, various primary and secondary sources come into consideration. These include, to provide a mere selection of the diverse pool of material conceivable, governmental documents, reports, and budgets; published articles, speeches, and statements by decision-makers on both sides of the soft power equation; surveys and interviews; and not least the body of (secondary) literature on relations between respective actors in general and their soft power dimension in particular. In the final analysis, therefore, casting out the net in the vast ocean of evidence and taking into account materials as eclectic and extensive as possible ultimately offers the most promising approach to empirically trace the workings of soft power in international relations and reach resilient results. To once more quote Sherlock Holmes, the 221B Baker Street consulting detective, "Each fact is suggestive in itself. Together they have a cumulative force."[376]

---

[372]Lange, *Comparative-Historical Methods*, p. 145.

[373]Lange, *Comparative-Historical Methods*, p. 172.

[374]Lange, *Comparative-Historical Methods*, pp. 142–143. For example, the published collection of transcripts of tapes recorded in the White House during the Cuban Missile Crisis not only includes transcriptions of said tapes but also interpretations and analyses by the editors; Ernest R. May and Philip D. Zelikow, eds., *The Kennedy Tapes: Inside the White House During the Cuban Missile Crisis* (New York, N.Y.: W. W. Norton & Co, 2002).

[375]Jack Shafer, "Who Said It First: Journalism Is the 'First Rough Draft of History,'" *Slate*, August 30, 2010, online at: http://www.slate.com/articles/news_and_politics/press_box/2010/08/who_said_it_first.html (accessed September 2, 2017).

[376]Arthur Conan Doyle, "The Bruce-Partington Plans," p. 1155. A similar statement can be found in Arthur Conan Doyle, "The Devil's Foot," p. 1209. Again, pages refer to Arthur Conan Doyle, *Sherlock Holmes: The Complete Stories* (Ware: Wordsworth Editions Limited, 2007).

4.6 Interim Conclusion III: Roads Less Traveled

Bearing in mind, the plethora of intricacies confronting the researcher when seeking to unveil the mechanisms of soft power in international relations, sound methodological approaches are indispensable. The compressive methodological roadmap for the study of soft power spread out above—with its different components including the method of comparative-historical analysis in combination with that of structured, focused comparison, with its discussion of conceivable schemes for selecting meaningful periods of analysis as well as actors and cases for comparison, and with its debate of data sources to draw upon—provides such an approach. While not to be thought of as a methodological straightjacket, the roadmap presented charters a promising way toward the study of soft power, which all too often has hitherto eluded robustness, by eclectically and innovatively combining a variety of established research methodologies that have been identified as eminently eligible.

As argued above, many scholars—both critics and advocates of the concept of soft power—have not unjustly warned against the methodological pitfalls in empirical examinations of the mechanisms and actual impact of soft power in international relations. While such pitfalls undoubtedly exist, they should not discourage researchers from empirically tracing its mechanism and ramifications. Quite the contrary: The intricate nature of the study of soft power arguably appeals stronger to the researcher's inquisitiveness than do other endeavors that may appear simpler to pursue. In fact, just because a road is long and winding, this does not mean one should not strive to follow it. If anything, a road with many bends and windings, junctions and detours, and even the occasional pothole or dead end may ultimately be all the more attractive to set out on and reaching one's goal in such a manner may eventually be all the sweeter. After all, to paraphrase Robert Frost, taking roads less traveled by is what makes all the difference.[377]

References

Allison, Graham. *Essence of Decision: Explaining the Cuban Missile Crisis*. Boston, Mass.: Little Brown, 1971.

Amenta, Edwin. "Comparative and Historical Research in Comparative and Historical Perspective." In *Comparative Historical Analysis in the Social Sciences*, edited by James Mahoney and Dietrich Rueschemeyer, pp. 91–130. Cambridge: Cambridge University Press, 2003.

Anholt, Simon. "Anholt Nation Brands Index: How Does the World See America?." *Journal of Advertising Research*, Vol. 45, No. 3 (September 2005), pp. 296–304.

Beck, Nathaniel. "Is Causal-Process Observation an Oxymoron?" *Political Analysis*, Vol. 14, No. 3 (2006), pp. 347–352.

Ben-Menahem, Yemima. "The Inference to the Best Explanation." *Erkenntnis*, Vol. 33, No. 3 (November 1990), pp. 319–344.

---

[377]Robert Frost, "The Road Not Taken," in *The Road Not Taken and Other Poems* (New York, N. Y.: Dover Publications, 1993), p. 1.

Bennett, Andrew and Alexander L. George. "Case Studies and Process Tracing in History and Political Science: Similar Strokes for Different Foci." In *Bridges and Boundaries: Historians, Political Scientists, and the Study of International Relations*, edited by Colin Elman and Miriam Fendius Elman, pp. 137–166. Cambridge, Mass.: MIT Press, 2001.

Bennett, Andrew and Jeffrey Checkel, eds. *Process Tracing: From Metaphor to Analytic Tool.* Cambridge: Cambridge University Press, 2015.

Bennett, Andrew. "Process Tracing: A Bayesian Perspective." In *The Oxford Handbook of Political Methodology*, edited by Janet M. Box-Steffensmeier, Henry E. Brady, and David Collier, pp. 702–721. Oxford: Oxford University Press, 2011.

Bertram, Christoph. "US-German Relations in a World at Sea." *Daedalus*, Vol. 121, No. 4 (Fall 1992), pp. 119–128.

Bevir, Mark. "Meta-Methodology: Clearing the Underbrush." In *The Oxford Handbook of Political Methodology*, edited by Janet M. Box-Steffensmeier, Henry E. Brady, and David Collier, pp. 48–70. Oxford: Oxford University Press, 2011.

Blanchard Jean-Marc F. and Fujia Lu. "Thinking Hard about Soft Power: A Review and Critique of the Literature on China and Soft Power." *Asian Perspective* Vol. 36, No. 4 (2012), pp. 565–589.

Box-Steffensmeier, Janet M., Henry E. Brady, and David Collier. "Political Science Methodology." In *The Oxford Handbook of Political Methodology*, edited by Janet M. Box-Steffensmeier, Henry E. Brady, and David Collier, pp. 3–31. Oxford: Oxford University Press, 2011.

Breight, Curtis C. *Surveillance, Militarism and Drama in the Elizabethan Era.* Basingstoke: Palgrave Macmillan, 1996.

Bulliet, Richard W. "9/11: Landmark or Watershed." *Ten Years after September 11: A Social Science Research Council Essay Forum.* Online at: http://essays.ssrc.org/10yearsafter911/911-landmark-or-watershed/ (accessed September 24, 2015).

Bush, George H. W. "Remarks at the Fundraising Dinner for Gubernatorial Candidate Pete Wilson in San Francisco, California." San Francisco, Cal., February 28, 1990. In *Public Papers of the Presidents of the United States: George Bush, 1990, Book I – January 1 to June 30, 1990*, pp. 288–291. Washington, D.C.: United States Government Printing Office, 1991.

Carter, Jimmy. "Flag Day and National Flag Week, 1977." Proclamation 4508, June 11, 1977. In *Public Papers of the Presidents of the United States: Jimmy Carter, 1977, Book I – January 20 to June 24, 1977*, pp. 1097–1098. Washington, D.C.: United States Government Printing Office, 1977.

Cicero, M. Tullius. *Über die Gesetze: De Legibus/Stoische Paradoxien: Paradoxa Stoicum.* Edited, Translated, and Annotated by Rainer Nickel. München: Artemis & Winkler, 1994 (Cic. Leg./Cic. Parad.).

Clausewitz, Carl von. *On War.* Translated by Colonel J. J. Graham. New and Revised Edition with Introduction and Notes by Colonel F. N. Maude, Volume 2. London: Kegan Paul, Trench, Trubner & Co., 1918.

Collier, David. "Comparative Historical Analysis: Where Do We Stand?." *Newsletter of the APSA Organized Section in Comparative Politics*, Vol. 9, No. 2 (Summer 1998), pp. 1–2 & 4–5.

Collier, David. "Understanding Process Tracing." *PS: Political Science and Politics*, Vol. 44, No. 4 (October 2011), pp. 823–830.

Collier, David and Colin Elman. "Qualitative and Multimethod Research: Organizations, Publications, and Reflections on Integration." In *The Oxford Handbook of Political Methodology*, edited by Janet M. Box-Steffensmeier, Henry E. Brady, and David Collier, pp. 779–795. Oxford: Oxford University Press, 2011.

Creswell, John W. *Research Design: Qualitative, Quantitative, and Mixed Methods Approaches.* Thousand Oaks, Cal.: SAGE Publications, 2003.

Ćwiek-Karpowicz, Jaroslaw. "Limits to Russian Soft Power in the Post-Soviet Area." In *Economization versus Power Ambitions: Rethinking Russia's Policy towards Post-Soviet States*, edited by Stefan Meister, pp. 47–58. Baden-Baden: Nomos, 2013.

Czempiel, Ernst-Otto. *Weltpolitik im Umbruch: Die Pax Americana, der Terrorismus und die Zukunft der internationalen Beziehungen.* München: C. H. Beck, 2002.

D'Hooghe, Ingrid. *The Limits of China's Soft Power in Europe: Beijing's Public Diplomacy Puzzle*. The Hague: Netherlands Institute of International Relations Clingendael, 2010.

de Vaus, David. *Research Design in Social Research*. London: SAGE Publications, 2001.

Doyle, Arthur Conan. *Sherlock Holmes: The Complete Stories*. Ware: Wordsworth Editions Limited, 2007.

Dumbrell, John. "The Neoconservative Roots of the War in Iraq." In *Intelligence and National Security Policymaking on Iraq: British and American Perspectives*, edited by James P. Pfiffner and Mark Pythian, pp. 19–39. Manchester: Manchester University Press, 2008.

Dür, Andreas. "Discriminating Among Rival Explanations: Some Tools for Small-n Researchers." In *Research Design in Political Science: How to Practice What They Preach*, edited by Thomas Geschwend and Frank Schimmelfennig, pp. 183–200. Basingstoke: Palgrave Macmillan, 2011.

Eckstein, Harry. "Case Selection and Theory in Political Science." In *Handbook of Political Science, Volume 7. Political Science: Scope and Theory*, edited by Fred Greenstein and Nelson Polsby, pp. 94–137. Reading, Mass.: Addison-Wesley, 1975.

Elman, Colin and Miriam Fendius Elman. "Negotiating International History and Politics." In *Bridges and Boundaries: Historians, Political Scientists, and the Study of International Relations*, edited by Colin Elman and Miriam Fendius Elman, pp. 1–36. Cambridge, Mass.: MIT Press, 2001.

Ernst & Young. "Rapid-Growth Markets Soft Power Index: Spring 2012." 2012. Online at: http://emergingmarkets.ey.com/wp-content/uploads/downloads/2012/05/TBF-606-Emerging-markets-soft-power-index-2012_LR.pdf (accessed October 1, 2015).

Falleti, Tulia G. and James Mahoney. "The Comparative Sequential Method." In *Advances in Comparative-Historical Analysis*, edited by James Mahoney and Kathleen Thelen, pp. 211–239. Cambridge: Cambridge University Press, 2015.

Fearon, James D. and David D. Laitin. "Integrating Qualitative and Quantitative Methods." In *The Oxford Handbook of Political Methodology*, edited by Janet M. Box-Steffensmeier, Henry E. Brady, and David Collier, pp. 756–776. Oxford: Oxford University Press, 2011.

Fehér, Ferenc, ed. *The French Revolution and the Birth of Modernity*. Berkeley, Cal.: University of California Press, 1990.

Flick, Uwe. "Design und Prozess qualitativer Forschung." In *Qualitative Forschung: Ein Handbuch*, edited by Uwe Flick, Ernst von Kardorff, and Ines Steinke, pp. 252–265. Reinbek bei Hamburg: Rowohlt Taschenbuch Verlag, 2012.

Franklin, Charles H. "Quantitative Methodology." In *The Oxford Handbook of Political Methodology*, edited by Janet M. Box-Steffensmeier, Henry E. Brady, and David Collier, pp. 796–813. Oxford: Oxford University Press, 2011.

Frost, Robert. "The Road Not Taken." In *The Road Not Taken and Other Poems* (New York, N.Y.: Dover Publications, 1993), p. 1.

Furlong, Paul and David Marsh. "A Skin Not a Sweater: Ontology and Epistemology in Political Science." In *Theory and Methods in Political Science*, edited by David Marsh and Gerry Stoker, pp. 184–211. Basingstoke: Palgrave Macmillan, 2010.

Gaddis, John Lewis. *Surprise, Security, and the American Experience*. Cambridge, Mass.: Harvard University Press, 2004.

Gaddis, John Lewis. *The Cold War*. London: Penguin Books, 2005.

Geiger, Till. "*The Power Game*, Soft Power and the International Historian." In *Soft Power and US Foreign Policy: Theoretical, Historical and Contemporary Perspectives*, edited by Inderjeet Parmar and Michael Cox, pp. 83–107. Abingdon: Routledge, 2010.

George, Alexander L. "Case Studies and Theory Development: The Method of Structured, Focused Comparison." In *Diplomacy: New Approaches in History, Theory, and Policy*, edited by Paul Gordon Lauren, pp. 43–68. New York, N.Y.: Free Press, 1979.

George, Alexander L. and Andrew Bennett. *Case Studies and Theory Development in the Social Sciences*. Cambridge, Mass.: MIT Press, 2005.

George, Alexander L. and Timothy J. McKeown. "Case Studies and Theories of Organizational Decision-Making." *Advances in Information Processing in Organizations*, Vol. 2 (1995), pp. 21–58.

Gerring, John. "What Is a Case Study and What Is It Good for?" *American Political Science Review*, Vol. 98, No. 2 (May 2004), pp. 341–354.

Gerring, John. "Case Selection for Case-Study Analysis: Qualitative and Quantitative Techniques." In *The Oxford Handbook of Political Methodology*, edited by Janet M. Box-Steffensmeier, Henry E. Brady, and David Collier, pp. 645–684. Oxford: Oxford University Press, 2011.

Gerring, John. *Case Study Research: Principles and Practices*. New York, N.Y.: Cambridge University Press, 2007.

Geschwend, Thomas and Frank Schimmelfennig. "Introduction: Designing Research in Political Science – A Dialogue between Theory and Data." In *Research Design in Political Science: How to Practice What They Preach*, edited by Thomas Geschwend and Frank Schimmelfennig, pp. 1–18. Basingstoke: Palgrave Macmillan, 2011.

Gilboa, Eytan. "Searching for a Theory of Public Diplomacy." *The Annals of the American Academy of Political and Social Science*, Vol. 616, Public Diplomacy in a Changing World (March 2008), pp. 55–77.

Glatzer, Ruth, ed. *Das Wilhelminische Berlin: Panorama einer Metropole, 1890–1918*. Berlin: Siedler, 1997.

Goldstone, Jack A. "Methodological Issues in Comparative Macrosociology." *Comparative Social Research*, Vol. 16 (1997), pp. 107–120.

Goldstone, Jack A. "Comparative Historical Analysis and Knowledge Accumulation in the Study of Revolutions." In *Comparative Historical Analysis in the Social Sciences*, edited by James Mahoney and Dietrich Rueschemeyer, pp. 41–90. Cambridge: Cambridge University Press, 2003.

Gorbachev, Mikhail S. "End of the Soviet Union: Text of Gorbachev's Farewell Address." *The New York Times*, December 26, 1991. Online at: http://www.nytimes.com/1991/12/26/world/end-of-the-soviet-union-text-of-gorbachev-s-farewell-address.html (accessed September 28, 2015).

Groeben, Norbert and Ruth Rustemeyer. "On the Integration of Quantitative and Qualitative Methodological Paradigms (Bases on the Example of Content Analysis)." In *Trends and Perspectives in Empirical Social Research*, edited by Ingwer Borg and Peter Ph. Mohler, pp. 308–326. Berlin: Walter de Gruyter, 1994.

Gu, Xuewu. *Theorien der Internationalen Beziehungen: Einführung*. Berlin: Walter de Gruyter 2018.

Haass, Richard N. *The Reluctant Sheriff: The United States After the Cold War*. New York, N.Y.: Council on Foreign Relations, 1997.

Haber, Stephen, David M. Kennedy, and Stephen D. Krasner. "Brothers under the Skin: Diplomatic History and International Relations." *International Security*, Vol. 22, No. 1 (Summer 1997), pp. 34–43.

Hancké, Bob. "The Challenge of Research Design." In *Theory and Methods in Political Science*, edited by David Marsh and Gerry Stoker, pp. 232–248. Basingstoke: Palgrave Macmillan, 2010.

Harloe, Katherine and Neville Morley, eds. *Thucydides and the Modern World: Reception, Reinterpretation and Influence from Renaissance to the Present*. Cambridge: Cambridge University Press, 2012.

Harman, Gilbert H. "The Inference to the Best Explanation." *Philosophical Review*, Vol. 74 (January 1964), pp. 88–95.

Harrison, Ewan. *The Post-Cold War System: Strategies, Institutions, and Reflexivity*. London: Routledge, 2004.

Hayden, Craig. "Scope, Mechanism, and Outcome: Arguing Soft Power in the Context of Public Diplomacy." *Journal of International Relations and Development*, Vol. 20, No. 2 (2017), pp. 331–357.

Haydu, Jeffrey. "Making Use of the Past: Time Periods as Cases to Compare and as Sequences of Problem Solving." *American Journal of Sociology*, Vol. 104, No. 2 (September 1998), pp. 339–371.

Hegel, Georg Friedrich Wilhelm. *Vorlesungen über die Philosophie der Geschichte*. Stuttgart: Reclam, 1961.

Hermann, Margret G. and Thomas Preston. "Presidents, Advisers, and Foreign Policy: The Effect of Leadership Style on Executive Arrangements." *Political Psychology*, Vol. 15, No. 1, Special Issue: Political Psychology and the Work of Alexander L. George (March 1994), pp. 75–96.

Herz, John H. "Idealist Internationalism and the Security Dilemma." *World Politics*, Vol. 2, No. 2 (January 1950), pp. 157–180.

Hinz, Andreas. *Zeit als Bildungsaufgabe in theologischer Perspektive*. Münster: LIT, 2003.

Hollis, Martin and Steven Smith. *Explaining and Understanding International Relations*. Oxford: Clarendon Press, 1990.

Hopkin, Jonathan. "The Comparative Method." In *Theory and Methods in Political Science*, edited by David Marsh and Gerry Stoker, pp. 285–307. Basingstoke: Palgrave Macmillan, 2010.

Horace (Q. Horatius Flaccus). *The Odes of Horace: Books III and IV, with the Carmen Seculare and the Epodes*. Translated by A. Hamilton Bryce. London: George Bell and Sons, 1909.

Horaz (Q. Horatius Flaccus). "Carmina/Oden." In *Sämtliche Werke: Teil I, Oden und Epoden*. Edited by Hans Färber after Kayser, Nordenflycht, and Burger, pp. 6–219. München: Ernst Heimeran Verlag, 1960 (Hor. Carm.).

Jervis, Robert. "International History and International Politics: Why Are They Studied Differently." In *Bridges and Boundaries: Historians, Political Scientists, and the Study of International Relations*, edited by Colin Elman and Miriam Fendius Elman, pp. 387–402. Cambridge, Mass.: MIT Press, 2001.

Johnson, R. Burke and Anthony J. Onwuegbuzie. "Mixed Method Research: A Research Paradigm Whose Time Has Come." *Educational Researcher*, Vol. 33, No. 7 (October 2004), pp. 14–26.

Katznelson, Ira. "Periodization and Preferences: Reflections on Purposive Action in Comparative Historical Social Science." In *Comparative Historical Analysis in the Social Sciences*, edited by James Mahoney and Dietrich Rueschemeyer, pp. 270–301. Cambridge: Cambridge University Press, 2003.

Kelle, Udo and Christian Erzberger. "Qualitative und quantitative Methoden: Kein Gegensatz." In *Qualitative Forschung: Ein Handbuch*, edited by Uwe Flick, Ernst von Kardorff, and Ines Steinke, pp. 299–309. Reinbek bei Hamburg: Rowohlt Taschenbuch Verlag, 2012.

King, Gary, Robert O. Keohane, and Sidney Verba. *Designing Social Inquiry: Scientific Inference in Qualitative Research*. Princeton, N.J.: Princeton University Press, 1994.

Kissinger, Henry. *Diplomacy*. New York, N.Y.: Simon & Schuster, 1994.

Kittel, Bernhard and David Kuehn. "Introduction: Reassessing the Methodology of Process Tracing." *European Political Science*, Vol. 12, No. 1 (2013), pp. 1–9.

Knobloch, Hubert. "Zukunft und Perspektiven qualitativer Forschung." In *Qualitative Forschung: Ein Handbuch*, edited by Uwe Flick, Ernst von Kardorff, and Ines Steinke, pp. 623–632. Reinbek bei Hamburg: Rowohlt Taschenbuch Verlag, 2012.

Krauthammer, Charles. "The Neoconservative Convergence." *Commentary*, Vol. 120, No. 1 (July/August 2005), pp. 21–26.

LaFeber, Walter. "The Rise and Fall of Colin Powell and the Powell Doctrine." *Political Science Quarterly*, Vol. 124, No. 1 (Spring 2009), pp. 71–93.

Lakoff, George and Mark Johnson. *Metaphors We Live By*. Chicago, Ill.: University of Chicago Press, 1980.

Landman, Todd. *Issues and Methods in Comparative Politics: An Introduction*. Abingdon: Routledge, 2008.

Lange, Matthew. *Comparative-Historical Methods*. Los Angeles, Cal.: SAGE Publications, 2013.

Lebow, Richard Ned. "Social Science and History: Ranchers versus Farmers?." In *Bridges and Boundaries: Historians, Political Scientists, and the Study of International Relations*, edited by Colin Elman and Miriam Fendius Elman, pp. 112–135. Cambridge, Mass.: MIT Press, 2001.

Lennon, Alexander T. J., ed. *The Battle for Hearts and Minds: Using Soft Power to Undermine Terrorist Networks*. Cambridge, Mass.: MIT Press, 2003.

Lesaffer, Randall. *European Legal History: A Cultural and Political Perspective*. Translated by Jan Arriens. Cambridge: Cambridge University Press, 2009.

Leuffen, Dirk. "Case Selection and Selection Bias in Small-n Research." In *Research Design in Political Science: How to Practice What They Preach*, edited by Thomas Geschwend and Frank Schimmelfennig, pp. 145–161. Basingstoke: Palgrave Macmillan, 2011.

Levy, Jack S. "Too Important to Leave to the Other: History and Political Science in the Study of International Relations." *International Security*, Vol. 22, No. 1 (Summer 1997), pp. 22–33.

Levy, Jack S. "Explaining Events and Developing Theories: History, Political Science, and the Analysis of International Relations." In *Bridges and Boundaries: Historians, Political Scientists, and the Study of International Relations*, edited by Colin Elman and Miriam Fendius Elman, pp. 39–83. Cambridge, Mass.: MIT Press, 2001.

Lewis-Beck, Michael S. "Data." In *The SAGE Encyclopedia of Social Science Research Methods: Volume 1*, edited by Michael S. Lewis-Beck, Alan Bryman and Tim Futing Liao, p. 234. Thousand Oaks, Cal.: SAGE Publications, 2004.

Lipton, Peter. *Inference to the Best Explanation*. London: Routledge, 2004.

Lipton, Peter. "Causation and Explanation." In *The Oxford Handbook of Causation*, edited by Helen Beebee, Christopher Hitchcock, Peter Menzies, pp. 619–631. Oxford: Oxford University Press, 2009.

Lock, Edward. "Soft Power and Strategy: Developing a 'Strategic' Concept of Power." In *Soft Power and US Foreign Policy: Theoretical, Historical and Contemporary Perspectives*, edited by Inderjeet Parmar and Michael Cox, pp. 32–50. Abingdon: Routledge, 2010.

Lüders, Christian. "Herausforderungen qualitativer Forschung." In *Qualitative Forschung: Ein Handbuch*, edited by Uwe Flick, Ernst von Kardorff, and Ines Steinke, pp. 632–642. Reinbek bei Hamburg: Rowohlt Taschenbuch Verlag, 2012.

Lukes, Steven. "Power and the Battle for the Hearts and Minds." *Millennium: Journal of International Studies*, Vol. 33, No. 3 (2005), pp. 477–493.

Mahoney, James. "Strategies of Causal Assessment in Comparative Historical Analysis." In *Comparative Historical Analysis in the Social Sciences*, edited by James Mahoney and Dietrich Rueschemeyer, pp. 337–372. Cambridge: Cambridge University Press, 2003.

Mahoney, James and Gary Goertz. "A Tale of Two Cultures: Contrasting Quantitative and Qualitative Research." *Political Analysis*, Vol. 14, No. 3 (2006), pp. 227–249.

Mahoney, James and Gary Goertz. *A Tale of Two Cultures: Qualitative and Quantitative Research in the Social Sciences*. Princeton, N.J.: Princeton University Press, 2012.

Mahoney, James and Dietrich Rueschemeyer. "Comparative Historical Analysis: Achievements and Agendas." In *Comparative Historical Analysis in the Social Sciences*, edited by James Mahoney and Dietrich Rueschemeyer, pp. 3–38. Cambridge: Cambridge University Press, 2003.

Mahoney, James and P. Larkin Terrie. "Comparative-Historical Analysis in Contemporary Political Science." In *The Oxford Handbook of Political Methodology*, edited by Janet M. Box-Steffensmeier, Henry E. Brady, and David Collier, pp. 737–755. Oxford: Oxford University Press, 2011.

Mandelbaum, Michael. *Mission Failure: America and the World in the Post-Cold War Era*. New York, N.Y.: Oxford University Press, 2016.

Mansoor, Peter R. "US Grand Strategy in the Second World War." In *Successful Strategies: Triumphing in War and Peace from Antiquity to Present*, edited by Williamson Murray and Richard Hart Sinnreich, pp. 314–352. Cambridge: Cambridge University Press, 2014.

Mathisen, Ralph W. *People, Personal Expression, and Social Relations in Late Antiquity, Volume II: Selected Latin Texts from Gaul and Western Europe*. Ann Arbor, Mich.: University of Michigan Press, 2003.

May, Ernest R. and Philip D. Zelikow, eds. *The Kennedy Tapes: Inside the White House During the Cuban Missile Crisis*. New York, N.Y.: W. W. Norton & Co, 2002.

McClory, Jonathan. "The New Persuaders: An International Ranking of Soft Power." *Institute for Government*, London, December 7, 2010. Online at: http://www.instituteforgovernment.org.uk/sites/default/files/publications/The%20new%20persuaders_0.pdf (accessed October 1, 2015).

McClory, Jonathan. "The New Persuaders II: A 2011 Global Ranking of Soft Power." *Institute for Government*, London, December 1, 2011. Online at: http://www.instituteforgovernment.org.uk/sites/default/files/publications/The%20New%20PersuadersII_0.pdf (accessed October 1, 2015).

McClory, Jonathan. "The New Persuaders III: A 2012 Global Ranking of Soft Power." *Institute for Government*, London, September 6, 2013. Online at: http://www.instituteforgovernment.org.uk/sites/default/files/publications/The%20new%20persuaders%20III_0.pdf   (accessed   October 1, 2015).

McClory, Jonathan. "The Soft Power 30: A Global Ranking of Soft Power." *Portland*, London, 2015.   Online   at: http://www.comres.co.uk/wp-content/uploads/2015/07/Report_Final-published.pdf (accessed August 16, 2016).

McClory, Jonathan. "The Soft Power 30: A Global Ranking of Soft Power, 2016." *Portland*, London,   2016.   Online   at: http://softpower30.portland-communications.com/wp-content/themes/softpower/pdfs/the_soft_power_30.pdf (accessed August 16, 2016).

McClory, Jonathan. "The Soft Power 30: A Global Ranking of Soft Power, 2017." *Portland*, London, 2017. Online at: http://softpower30.com/wp-content/uploads/2017/07/The-Soft-Power-30-Report-2017-Web-1.pdf (accessed July 30, 2017).

McFaul, Michael A. and James M. Goldgeier. "A Tale of Two Worlds: Core and Periphery in the Post-Cold War Era." *International Organization*, Vol. 46, No. 2 (Spring 1992), pp. 467–491.

McKeown, Timothy J. "Case Studies and the Statistical Worldview: Review of King, Keohane, and Verba's *Designing Social Inquiry: Scientific Inference in Qualitative Research*." *International Organization*, Vol. 53, No. 1 (Winter 1999), pp. 161–190.

McKercher, Asa. *Camelot and Canada: Canadian-American Relations in the Kennedy Era.* New York, N.Y.: Oxford University Press, 2016.

McPherson, James M. *Battle Cry of Freedom: The Civil War Era.* New York, N.Y.: Oxford University Press, 1988.

Meister, Klaus. *Thukydides als Vorbild der Historiker: Von der Antike bis zur Gegenwart.* Paderborn: Ferdinand Schöningh, 2013.

Melissen, Jan. "The New Public Diplomacy: Between Theory and Practice." In *The New Public Diplomacy: Soft Power in International Relations*, edited by Jan Melissen, pp. 3–27. Basingstoke: Palgrave Macmillan, 2005.

Merkens, Hans. "Auswahlverfahren, Sampling, Fallkonstruktion." In *Qualitative Forschung: Ein Handbuch*, edited by Uwe Flick, Ernst von Kardorff, and Ines Steinke, pp. 286–299. Reinbek bei Hamburg: Rowohlt Taschenbuch Verlag, 2012.

Miller, Linda B. "The Clinton Years: Reinventing US Foreign Policy?." *International Affairs*, Vol. 70, No. 4 (October 1994), pp. 621–634.

Mitchell, David. "Does Context Matter: Advisory Systems and the Management of the Foreign Policy Decision-Making Process." *Presidential Studies Quarterly*, Vol. 40, No. 4 (December 2010), pp. 631–659.

Morriss, Peter. *Power: A Philosophical Analysis.* Manchester: Manchester University Press, 2002.

Mueller, John. "When did the Cold War End?." Paper Prepared for Delivery at the 2002 Annual Meeting of the *American Political Science Association*, Boston, Mass., August 29–September 1, 2002.

Muller, Steven. "Introduction: America and Germany, A New Chapter Opens." In *From Occupation to Cooperation: The United States and United Germany in a Changing World Order*, edited by Steven Muller and Gebhard Schweigler, pp. 14–26. New York, N.Y.: W. W. Norton & Company, 1992.

Nitze, Paul H. "Visions of Leadership: The United States." In *From Occupation to Cooperation: The United States and United Germany in a Changing World Order*, edited by Steven Muller and Gebhard Schweigler, pp. 27–47. New York, N.Y.: W. W. Norton & Company, 1992.

Nye, Joseph S., Jr. "Old Wars and Future Wars: Causation and Prevention." *Journal of Interdisciplinary History*, Vol. 18, No. 4 (Spring 1988), pp. 581–590.

Nye, Joseph S., Jr. *Soft Power: The Means to Success in World Politics*. New York, N.Y.: PublicAffairs, 2004.

Nye, Joseph S., Jr. "Responding to My Critics and Concluding Thoughts." In *Soft Power and US Foreign Policy: Theoretical, Historical and Contemporary Perspectives*, edited by Inderjeet Parmar and Michael Cox, pp. 215–227. Abingdon: Routledge, 2010.

Osinsky, Pavel and Jari Elonranta. "Comparative Historical Analysis: Some Insights from Political Transitions of the First Half of the Twentieth Century." Online at: http://www2.warwick.ac.uk/ fac/soc/economics/events/seminars-workshops-conferences/conferences/conf/eloranta.pdf (accessed September 22, 2015).

Parsons, Craig. "Constructivism and Interpretative Theory." In *Theory and Methods in Political Science*, edited by David Marsh and Gerry Stoker, pp. 80–98. Basingstoke: Palgrave Macmillan, 2010.

Patalakh, Artem. "Assessment of Soft Power Strategies: Towards an Aggregative Analytical Model for Country-Focused Case Study Research." *Croatian International Relations Review*, Vol. 22, No. 76 (2016), pp. 85–112.

Pelz, Stephen. "Toward a New Diplomatic History: Two and a Half Cheers for International Relations Methods." In *Bridges and Boundaries: Historians, Political Scientists, and the Study of International Relations*, edited by Colin Elman and Miriam Fendius Elman, pp. 85–110. Cambridge, Mass.: MIT Press, 2001.

Petras, James. "US-Venezuela Relations: A Case Study of Imperialism and Anti-Imperialism." *Voltaire Network*, October 22, 2013. Online at: http://www.voltairenet.org/article180663. html#nb1 (accessed September 30, 2015).

Pettersson, Lucas. "Changing Images of the USA in German Media Discourse During Four American Presidencies." *International Journal of Cultural Studies*, Vol. 14, No. 1 (2011), pp. 35–51.

Pierson, Paul. "Big, Slow-Moving, and … Invisible: Macrosocial Processes in the Study of Comparative Politics." In *Comparative Historical Analysis in the Social Sciences*, edited by James Mahoney and Dietrich Rueschemeyer, pp. 177–207. Cambridge: Cambridge University Press, 2003.

Polenberg, Richard. *The Era of Franklin D. Roosevelt, 1933–1945: A Brief History with Documents*. New York, N.Y.: Bedford/St. Martin's, 2000.

Powell, Colin L. "A Strategy of Partnerships." *Foreign Affairs*, Vol. 83, No. 1 (January/February 2004), pp. 22–34.

Ragin, Charles C. *Constructing Social Research: The Unity and Diversity of Method*. Thousand Oaks, Cal.: Pine Forge Press, 1994.

Ragin, Charles C. "Turning the Tables: How Case-Oriented Research Challenges Variable-Oriented Research. *Comparative Social Research*, Vol. 16 (1997), pp. 27–42.

Ragin, Charles C. and Lisa M. Amoroso. *Constructing Social Research: The Unity and Diversity of Method*. Thousand Oaks, Cal.: Pine Forge Press, 2011.

Rihoux, Benoît. "Case-Oriented Configurational Research: Qualitative Comparative Analysis (QCA), and Related Techniques." In *The Oxford Handbook of Political Methodology*, edited by Janet M. Box-Steffensmeier, Henry E. Brady, and David Collier, pp. 722–736. Oxford: Oxford University Press, 2011.

Rödder, Andreas. *21.0: Eine kurze Geschichte der Gegenwart*. München: C. H. Beck, 2015.

Rosato, Sebastian. "The Flawed Logic of Democratic Peace Theory." *American Political Science Review*, Vol. 97, No. 4 (November 2003), pp. 585–602.

Roselle, Laura, Alister Miskimmon, and Ben O'Loughlin. "Strategic Narrative: A New Means to Understand Soft Power." *Media, War & Conflict*, Vol. 7, No. 1 (2014), pp. 70–84.

Rossinow, Doug. *The Reagan Era: A History of the 1980s*. New York, N.Y.: Columbia University Press, 2015.

Rothschild, Emma. "Adam Smith and the Invisible Hand." *The American Economic Review*, Vol. 84, No. 2 (May 1994), pp. 319–322.

Rowell, Henry Thompson. *Rome in the Augustan Age*. Norman, Okla.: University of Oklahoma Press, 1962.

Rueschemeyer, Dietrich. "Can One or a Few Cases Yield Theoretical Gains?" In *Comparative Historical Analysis in the Social Sciences*, edited by James Mahoney and Dietrich Rueschemeyer, pp. 305–336. Cambridge: Cambridge University Press, 2003.

Rühl, Lothar. "Das Ende des Kalten Krieges." In *Neue Dimensionen internationaler Sicherheitspolitik*, edited by Reinhard Meier-Walser and Alexander Wolf, pp. 21–33. München: Hanns-Seidel-Stiftung, 2011.

Rule, James B. *Theory and Progress in Social Science*. Cambridge, Cambridge University Press, 1997.

Russett, Bruce. *Grasping the Democratic Peace: Principles for a Post-Cold War World*. Princeton, N.J.: Princeton University Press, 1994.

Sagan, Eli. *Citizens and Cannibals: The French Revolution, the Struggle for Modernity, and the Origins of Ideological Terror*. Lanham, Md.: Rowman & Littlefield, 2001.

Schadewaldt, Wolfgang. *Die Anfänge der Geschichtsschreibung bei den Griechen: Herodot, Thukydides*. Frankfurt am Main: Suhrkamp, 1982.

Schrodt, Philip A. "Beyond the Linear Frequentist Orthodoxy." *Political Analysis*, Vol. 14, No. 3 (2006), pp. 335–339.

Schroeder, Paul W. "International History: Why Historians Do it Differently than Political Scientists." In *Bridges and Boundaries: Historians, Political Scientists, and the Study of International Relations*, edited by Colin Elman and Miriam Fendius Elman, pp. 403–416. Cambridge, Mass.: MIT Press, 2001.

Schusterman, Noah. *The French Revolution: Faith, Desire, and Politics*. London: Routledge, 2014.

Schwarz, Hans-Peter. "America, Germany, and the Atlantic Community after the Cold War." In *The United States and Germany in the Era of the Cold War, 1945-1990: A Handbook, Volume II: 1968-1990*, edited by Detlef Junker, associated editors Philipp Gassert, Wilfried Mausbach, and David B. Morris, pp. 535–565. Cambridge: Cambridge University Press, 2004.

Schwarz, Hans-Peter. *Republik ohne Kompaß: Anmerkungen zur deutschen Außenpolitik*. Berlin: Ullstein, 2005.

Schweigler, Gebhard. "Conclusion: Problems and Prospects for Partners in Leadership." In *From Occupation to Cooperation: The United States and United Germany in a Changing World Order*, edited by Steven Muller and Gebhard Schweigler, pp. 224–249. New York, N.Y.: W. W. Norton & Company, 1992.

Seawright, Jason and John Gerring. "Case Selection Techniques in Case Study Research: A Menu of Qualitative and Quantitative Options." *Political Research Quarterly*, Vol. 61, No. 2 (June 2008), pp. 294–308.

Sewell, William H., Jr. "Three Temporalities: Toward an Eventful Sociology." in *The Historic Turn in the Human Sciences*, edited by Terrence J. McDonald, pp. 245–280. Ann Arbor: University of Michigan Press, 1996.

Shafer, Jack. "Who Said It First: Journalism Is the 'First Rough Draft of History.'" *Slate*, August 30, 2010. Online at: http://www.slate.com/articles/news_and_politics/press_box/2010/08/who_said_it_first.html (accessed September 2, 2017).

Shaw, Matthew. *Time and the French Revolution: The Republican Calendar, 1789-Year XIV*. Woodbridge: Boydell & Brewer, 2011.

Shiveley, James M. and Phillip J. VanFossen. *Using Internet Primary Sources to Teach Critical Thinking Skills in Government, Economics, and Contemporary World Issues*. Westport, Conn.: Greenwood Press, 2000.

Shively, W. Phillips. "Case Selection: Insights from *Rethinking Social Inquiry*." *Political Analysis*, Vol. 14, No. 3 (2006), pp. 344–347.

Sieberer, Ulrich. "Selecting Independent Variables: Competing Recommendations for Factor-Centric and Outcome-Centric Research Designs." In *Research Design in Political Science:*

How to Practice What They Preach, edited by Thomas Geschwend and Frank Schimmelfennig, pp. 163–182. Basingstoke: Palgrave Macmillan, 2011.

Skocpol, Theda. "Doubly Engaged Social Science: The Promise of Comparative Historical Analysis." In *Comparative Historical Analysis in the Social Sciences*, edited by James Mahoney and Dietrich Rueschemeyer, pp. 407–428. Cambridge: Cambridge University Press, 2003.

Smith, Adam. *An Inquiry into the Nature and the Causes of the Wealth of Nations*. Edited, with an Introduction, Notes, Marginal Summary and an Enlarged Index by Edwin Cannan, Volume 1. Methuen & Co.: London, 1904.

Stoker, Gerry. "Introduction to Part 2." In *Theory and Methods in Political Science*, edited by David Marsh and Gerry Stoker, pp. 181–183. Basingstoke: Palgrave Macmillan, 2010.

Stone, Lawrence. *The Past and the Present Revisited*. London: Routledge, 1987.

Strauss, Anselm L. *Qualitative Analysis for Social Scientists*. Cambridge: Cambridge University Press, 1987.

Streeck, Wolfgang. "Epilogue: Comparative-Historical Analysis, Past, Present, Future." In *Advances in Comparative-Historical Analysis*, edited by James Mahoney and Kathleen Thelen, pp. 264–288. Cambridge: Cambridge University Press, 2015.

Su Changhe. "Soft Power." In *The Oxford Handbook of Modern Diplomacy*, edited by Andrew F. Cooper, Jorge Heine, and Ramesh Thakur, pp. 544–558. Oxford: Oxford University Press, 2013.

Suetonius Tranquillus, C. *Die Kaiserviten: De Vita Caesarum/Berühmte Männer: De Viris Illustribus*. Edited and Translated by Hans Martinet. Berlin: Walter de Gruyter, 2014 (here: Suet. Aug. & Suet. Ves.).

Swanborn, Peter G. *Case Study Research: What, Why and How?*. London: SAGE Publications, 2010.

Thelen, Kathleen and James Mahoney. "Comparative-Historical Analysis in Contemporary Political Science." In *Advances in Comparative-Historical Analysis*, edited by James Mahoney and Kathleen Thelen, pp. 3–36. Cambridge: Cambridge University Press, 2015.

Thiem, Janina. "Dealing Effectively with Selection Bias in Large-n Research." In *Research Design in Political Science: How to Practice What They Preach*, edited by Thomas Geschwend and Frank Schimmelfennig, pp. 127–144. Basingstoke: Palgrave Macmillan, 2011.

Thies, Cameron G. "A Pragmatic Guide to Qualitative Historical Analysis in the Study of International Relations." *International Studies Perspectives*, Vol. 3, No. 4 (2002), pp. 351–372.

Thucydides. *The Peloponnesian War*. A New Translation by Martin Hammond. New York, N.Y.: Oxford University Press, 2009 (Thuc.).

Tilly, Charles. *Big Structures, Large Processes, Huge Comparisons*. New York, N.Y.: Russell Sage Foundation, 1984.

Van Apeldoorn, Bastiaan and Naná de Graaff. "Corporate Elite Networks and US Post-Cold War Grand Strategy from Clinton to Obama." *European Journal of International Relations*, Vol. 20, No. 1 (2012), pp. 29–55.

Van Apeldoorn, Bastiaan and Naná de Graaff. *American Grand Strategy and Corporate Elite Networks: The Open Door Since the End of the Cold War*. London: Routledge, 2016.

Van Evera, Stephen. *Guide to Methods for Students of Political Science*. Ithaca. N.Y.: Cornell University Press, 1997.

Vennesson, Pascal and Ina Wiesner. "Process Tracing in Case Studies." In *Routledge Handbook of Research Methods in Military Studies*, edited by Joseph Soeters, Patricia M. Shields, and Sebastiaan Rietjens, pp. 92–103. London: Routledge, 2014.

Vromen, Ariadne. "Debating Methods: Rediscovering Qualitative Approaches." In *Theory and Methods in Political Science*, edited by David Marsh and Gerry Stoker, pp. 249–266. Basingstoke: Palgrave Macmillan, 2010.

Waldner, David. "Process Tracing and Causal Mechanisms." In *The Oxford Handbook of Philosophy of Social Science*, edited by Harold Kincaid, pp. 65–84. Oxford: Oxford University Press, 2012.

Watts, Duncan. *British Government and Politics: A Comparative Guide*. Edinburgh: Edinburgh University Press, 2012.

Whitney, Christopher B. and David Shambaugh. "Soft Power in Asia: Results of a 2008 Multinational Survey of Public Opinion." *The Chicago Council on Global Affairs* in partnership with the *East Asia Institute*. Chicago, Ill., 2009. Online at: http://www.brookings.edu/~/media/Events/2008/6/17%20east%20asia/0617_east_asia_report.pdf (accessed October 1, 2015).

Whyte, William F. *Street Corner Society: The Social Structure of an Italian Slum*. Chicago, Ill.: The University of Chicago Press, 1943.

Williams, Carrie. "Research Methods." *Journal of Business & Economic Research*, Vol. 5, No. 3 (March 2007), pp. 65–72.

Winik, Jay. *April 1865: The Month That Saved America*. New York, N.Y.: Harper Perennial, 2006.

Wirsching, Andreas. *Der Preis der Freiheit: Geschichte Europas in unserer Zeit*. München: C. H. Beck, 2012.

Woodward, Bob. *The Choice*. New York, N.Y.: Simon & Schuster, 1996.

Yashar, Deborah. *Contesting Citizenship in Latin America: The Rise of Indigenous Movements and the Postliberal Challenge*. New York, N.Y.: Cambridge University Press, 2005.

Yin, Robert K. *Applications of Case Study Research*. Los Angeles, Cal.: SAGE Publications, 2012.

Yin, Robert K. *Case Study Research: Design and Methods*. Los Angeles, Cal.: SAGE Publications, 2014.

Chapter 5
Conclusions and Outlook

The work in hand set out to provide a theoretical-conceptual refinement of soft power and subsequently sought to offer methodological approaches to the empirical analysis of its workings in international relations. In the following, the resilience of the conceptual framework itself, that is, the taxonomy of soft power presented, as well as the methodological roadmap spread out shall be critically discussed. Finally, the study risks a cautious glimpse into the future by pondering the significance of soft power in international relations in the time to come. In this context, prospective research questions for future studies are identified.

5.1 Lessons Learned: Evaluating Taxonomy and Roadmap

In line with the first research question posed at the outset of this study, the introduction of a comprehensive taxonomy of soft power provided a theoretical-conceptual differentiation and operationalization of the concept of soft power. As graphically depicted in the work's pivotal illustration (Fig. 3.1), the often diffuse and little differentiated concept of soft power has been analytically divided into four different subunits: soft power resources, instruments, reception, and outcomes. With this course of action, the work addressed major deficiencies which hitherto have plagued the concept as has been recognized by a plethora of both proponents and critics. Additionally, with the introduction of a comprehensive methodological roadmap for the empirical study of soft power in international relations, the second research question has been addressed. By providing an instrument case, well-stacked with different tools identified as particularly suitable for the study of soft power, the empirical analysis of the workings of soft power as well as the detection of possible soft power shifts were made more readily accessible.

Of course, any truly substantive evaluation regarding both the applicability of the taxonomy and the resilience of the roadmap requires detailed empirical field tests. In fact, such a field test of both taxonomy and roadmap presented would be a promising

© Springer Nature Switzerland AG 2020
H. W. Ohnesorge, *Soft Power*, Global Power Shift,
https://doi.org/10.1007/978-3-030-29922-4_5

starting point for future research on the phenomenon of soft power. Still, not least in view of the frequent recourse to empirical examples in the process of developing the taxonomy, some expressive observations can already be made at this point:

First, the division of the concept of soft power into four distinct subunits has proven to be a valuable endeavor since it facilitates a more structured and precise understanding of an often diffuse concept. Only by conceiving the highly interdisciplinary concept as being composed of qualitatively different components and by recognizing their respective interactions can a truly comprehensive picture of the overall mechanisms of soft power be drawn.

Second, the taxonomy of soft power allows to draw inferences regarding both the diverging significance and the distinctive timeframes of different soft power resources and instruments. The resource of culture as well as the instrument of cultural diplomacy (both of which frequently feature prominently in the existing literature on soft power), thus, arguably require the most extensive time scale among the different resources and instruments identified in order to take their full effect. At the same time, and connected with this observation, the resource of culture lies outside governmental control to a far greater degree than do other resources. Consequently, when trying to detect possible shifts in the soft power of a given actor toward another, this particular resource will presumably prove to be more constant whereas other soft power resources and instruments are likely to display greater volatility.

Third, the introduction of a fourth independent resource of soft power (i.e., personalities) and a second corresponding major set of instruments (i.e., personal diplomacy) previously widely neglected in literature is likely to prove especially expedient. In fact, as has been demonstrated with recourse to different empirical examples, these elements in particular, which may jointly be referred to as the personality factor in soft power, have presented themselves as highly influential. At the same time, they are likely to be subject to the greatest fluctuations among the different resources and instruments. In the years to come, the personality factor in the wielding of soft power can nonetheless be expected to take on even greater significance in the wake of various larger trends observable in the conduct of international relations today, including the increasing diversification of actors on the international stage and further advances in information and communication technologies.

Fourth, and connected with these larger trends in international relations, while in existing literature particular emphasis is frequently put—both conceptually and empirically—on *foreign* policies as a decisive resource of an actor's soft power, *domestic* policies should be included more prominently. Not least contingent upon today's global, real-time information flows as well as the political requirements in an interdependent world, borders between both policy dimensions are becoming increasingly blurred. At the same time, soft power ramifications of domestic policies are more efficacious today since such policies are more easily accessible to foreign populations, whereas in the past their impact was limited by the confines of the respective state to a much greater degree. Concurrently, domestic policies are also more easily observable and evaluable for researchers seeking to detect their repercussions on an actor's soft power today. The proposed taxonomy, therefore, aptly refers to *policies*, without qualification as to their foreign or domestic nature, as a crucial soft power resource.

Fifth, despite the analytical advantages of deconstruction, it is important to reassemble the different subunits of the proposed soft power taxonomy (as well as their respective subcategories) at the end of each and every empirical analysis. Otherwise, once more applying Horace's expression, all that would remain are the *disiecta membra* of an entity which only in its entirety captures and represents the intricate workings of soft power at large.

Sixth, the taxonomy of soft power renders itself conspicuous due to its high degree of applicability and flexibility. While in itself presenting a comprehensive grasp of soft power, the taxonomy is not to be understood as a conceptual straight-jacket since it allows for adaptations that might be necessary under respective circumstances. At the same time, it facilitates the analysis of a huge variety of different actor types playing a part in international relations today. While arguably analyses might most commonly still focus on the soft power wielded by one nation-state toward another, the soft power taxonomy may likewise be applied—*mutatis mutandis*—to other actors on both sides of the soft power equation, including subnational entities, international organizations, or transnational networks.

Seventh, now also with an eye on the methodological roadmap spread out in the present work, the identification of a total of 28 indicators deduced to be highly meaningful for the workings of soft power across the four different subunits (cf. Table 3.2), allows for a tangible, structured, and comparative analysis. When seeking to detect differences or similarities as well as developments or shifts in the soft power of a given actor toward another, such a comparative approach is in fact indispensable. At it, qualitative methods alone, while also allowing for the inclusion of quantitative data, meet the conceptual requirements of soft power posed by its relational nature, and a high degree of context dependence. The methodological approach of comparative-historical analysis, coupled with that of structured, focused comparison, meets these requirements particularly well.

Eighth, different resilient schemes for rendering the analysis of soft power comparable can be identified. On the one hand, actor-related comparisons are conceivable, that is, the addition of (at least) one further actor on either the agent or theater side within the soft power relationship. On the other hand, and arguably more promising still since paying closer attention to the relational character and context dependence of soft power, temporal comparisons can be undertaken by dividing the agent and/or theater side of the soft power equation into different temporal cases of comparison.

Lastly, the taxonomy allows for a substantiated classification of empirical evidence. When trying to empirically detect the workings of soft power in international relations, any researcher is confronted with a wealth of different data and material to draw upon. With a final recourse to Karl Popper's net metaphor, the haul is often not only extensive but also highly diverse. The taxonomy of soft power, combined with the method of structured, focused comparison, facilitates a meaningful selection, and classification of the material to be considered.

Bearing in mind these observations and findings, the proposed taxonomy of soft power not only provides a substantive refinement of the concept of soft power itself but in combination with the methodological roadmap spread out also offers an eminently suited and resilient approach to the empirical analysis of its intricate workings in international relations. While by no means claiming to constitute the be-all and end-all in the matter of soft power, the present work, therefore, lays claim to at least having provided a major advancement, both conceptually and methodologically, for the understanding and study of the often obscure yet powerful forces of attraction in world politics, to reference Sir Isaac Newton's words eponymous for the work in hand.

5.2 Looking Ahead: Toward an Age of Soft Power?

In fact, it may with good reason be argued that a more sophisticated understanding, as well as more substantiated analyses of soft power, will become all the more important in the years to come. While always a highly potent force in the long annals of human interactions, soft power has considerably gained in relevance and importance over the past decades. Certainly, soft power does not now—nor will at some future stage—by itself present a magical cure for all ailments of the world. Rather, as it has always done, hard power will remain of great, even vital importance in international affairs. The trends of globalization, democratization, and power dispersion and not least advances in information and communication technologies, however, have contributed to an ever increasing significance of soft power, indeed.

While predictions in political science in general and the future of power, in particular, are always to be taken with a grain of salt (yet another parallel between the phenomenon of power and the weather), the importance of soft power is likely to grow further still for years to come. Besides the trends identified, the limitations of hard power alone, both in its military and its economic face, for dealing with some of the major challenges of the twenty-first century—nuclear proliferation, violent extremism, or climate change most prominently among them—substantiate this assessment.

The fact that various international actors all over the world have in the recent past sought to both actively draw upon as well as vigorously increase their respective soft power constitutes further—and indeed highly expressive—evidence regarding the attested rise in the importance of soft power. An ever growing library of works testifies to these developments: whether with respect to the European Union,[1] the

---

[1] For example, Jean-Yves Haine, "The EU's Soft Power: Not Hard Enough?," *Georgetown Journal of International Affairs*, Vol. 5, No. 1 (2004), pp. 69–77; Mai'a K. Davis Cross and Jan Melissen, eds., *European Public Diplomacy: Soft Power at Work* (New York, N.Y.: Palgrave Macmillan, 2013).

People's Republic of China,[2] the Russian Federation,[3] the United Kingdom,[4] Germany,[5] or myriads of other international actors, soft power has actually become a major ingredient in (national) power strategies today. As these examples illustrate, the strife for soft power transcends cultures, political systems, and world regions and has, in fact, become a global phenomenon. Consequently, a worldwide competition for soft power, what might be called a softpower arms race, is already taking place and will likely persist and even gather in pace in the near future. In fact, the very mechanism identified by Thucydides some 2400 years ago with respect to the struggle between Athens and Sparta holds true no less in the realm of soft power today: efforts by one actor to increase its attractive power result in other nations following suit.

At the same time, as in other varieties of power, an increase in the soft power of one actor does not necessarily result in the decrease of the soft power of another. As Joseph Nye has rightly pointed out, "The development of soft power need not be a zero sum game. All countries can gain from finding each other attractive."[6] While soft power, as has been demonstrated above, is distinctly non-normative in nature since it can be wielded just as selfishly and manipulatively as can any other form of power, increased precedence of the instruments of attraction in world politics over the tools of coercion would certainly be a change for the better.

---

[2]For example, Ingrid d'Hooghe, "Public Diplomacy in the People's Republic of China," in *The New Public Diplomacy: Soft Power in International Relations*, ed., Jan Melissen (Basingstoke: Palgrave Macmillan, 2005), pp. 88–105; Joshua Kurlantzick, *Charm Offensive: How China's Soft Power is Transforming the World* (New Haven, Conn.: Yale University Press, 2007); Mingjiang Li, ed., *Soft Power: China's Emerging Strategy in International Politics* (Lanham, Md.: Lexington Books, 2009); Gary D. Rawnsley, "China Talks Back: Public Diplomacy and Soft Power for the Chinese Century," in *Routledge Handbook of Public Diplomacy*, eds. Nancy Snow and Philip M. Taylor (New York, N.Y.: Routledge, 2009), pp. 282–291; Ingrid d'Hooghe, *The Limits of China's Soft Power in Europe: Beijing's Public Diplomacy Puzzle* (The Hague: Netherlands Institute of International Relations Clingendael, 2010); Hongyi Lai and Yiyi Lu, eds. *China's Soft Power and International Relations* (Abingdon: Routledge, 2012); Ingrid d'Hooghe, *China's Public Diplomacy* (Leiden: Brill Nijhoff, 2015); Falk Hartig, *Chinese Public Diplomacy: The Rise of the Confucius Institute* (Abingdon: Routledge, 2015); Paola Voci and Luo Hui, eds., *Screening China's Soft Power* (Abingdon: Routledge, 2017).

[3]For example, Andrei P. Tsygankov, "If Not by Tanks, Then by Banks? The Role of Soft Power in Putin's Foreign Policy," *Europe-Asia Studies*, Vol. 58, No. 7 (November 2006), pp. 1079–1099; James Sherr, *Hard Diplomacy and Soft Coercion: Russia's Influence Abroad* (London: Chatham House, 2013); Marcel H. Van Herpen, *Putin's Propaganda Machine: Soft Power and Russian Foreign Policy* (Lanham, Md.: Rowman & Littlefield, 2016).

[4]For example, James Pamment, *British Public Diplomacy and Soft Power: Diplomatic Influence and the Digital Revolution* (Cham: Palgrave Macmillan, 2016).

[5]For example, Jonathan Grix and Barrie Houlihan, "Sports Mega-Events as Part of a Nation's Soft Power Strategy: The Cases of Germany (2006) and the UK (2012)," *The British Journal of Politics and International Relations*, Vol. 16, No. 4 (2014), pp. 572–596; Kurt-Jürgen Maaß, ed., *Kultur und Außenpolitik: Handbuch für Wissenschaft und Praxis* (Baden Baden: Nomos Verlagsgesellschaft, 2015).

[6]Joseph S. Nye, Jr., *Is the American Century Over?* (Cambridge: Polity Press, 2015), p. 62.

In the final analysis, the developments outlined above not only make increased political efforts to wield soft power predictable, but also make intensified academic examinations of their success or failure necessary. In view of the monumental challenges facing the world today—challenges which have aptly been called "problems without passports"[7] by the late General Secretary of the United Nations Kofi Annan shortly after the turn of the millennium, which require concerted action of different actors on the international stage, and which frequently elude the instruments of hard power—such predictions seem well founded, indeed. Without a doubt, the forces of attraction in international politics will be vital in a world beset with such challenges. Addressing them adequately, however, is a task no less daunting and wearisome than the whitewashing of 30 yards of board fence appeared to Tom Sawyer on that hot Missouri day.

References

Annan, Kofi. "Problems without Passports." *Foreign Policy*, No. 132 (September/October 2002), pp. 30–31.

Cross, Mai'a K. Davis and Jan Melissen, eds. *European Public Diplomacy: Soft Power at Work*. New York, N.Y.: Palgrave Macmillan, 2013.

D'Hooghe, Ingrid. "Public Diplomacy in the People's Republic of China." In *The New Public Diplomacy: Soft Power in International Relations*, edited by Jan Melissen, pp. 88–105. Basingstoke: Palgrave Macmillan, 2005.

D'Hooghe, Ingrid. *The Limits of China's Soft Power in Europe: Beijing's Public Diplomacy Puzzle*. The Hague: Netherlands Institute of International Relations Clingendael, 2010.

D'Hooghe, Ingrid. *China's Public Diplomacy*. Leiden: Brill Nijhoff, 2015.

Grix, Jonathan and Barrie Houlihan. "Sports Mega-Events as Part of a Nation's Soft Power Strategy: The Cases of Germany (2006) and the UK (2012)." *The British Journal of Politics and International Relations*, Vol. 16, No. 4 (2014), pp. 572–596.

Haine, Jean-Yves. "The EU's Soft Power: Not Hard Enough?." *Georgetown Journal of International Affairs*, Vol. 5, No. 1 (2004), pp. 69–77.

Hartig, Falk. *Chinese Public Diplomacy: The Rise of the Confucius Institute*. Abingdon: Routledge, 2015.

Kurlantzick, Joshua. *Charm Offensive: How China's Soft Power is Transforming the World*. New Haven, Conn.: Yale University Press, 2007.

Lai, Hongyi and Yiyi Lu, eds. *China's Soft Power and International Relations*. Abingdon: Routledge, 2012.

Li, Mingjiang, ed. *Soft Power: China's Emerging Strategy in International Politics*. Lanham, Md.: Lexington Books, 2009.

Maaß, Kurt-Jürgen, ed. *Kultur und Außenpolitik: Handbuch für Wissenschaft und Praxis*. Baden Baden: Nomos Verlagsgesellschaft, 2015.

Nye, Joseph S., Jr. *Is the American Century Over?*. Cambridge: Polity Press, 2015.

Pamment, James. *British Public Diplomacy and Soft Power: Diplomatic Influence and the Digital Revolution*. Cham: Palgrave Macmillan, 2016.

---

[7]Kofi Annan, "Problems without Passports," *Foreign Policy*, No. 132 (September/October 2002), pp. 30–31.

Rawnsley, Gary D. "China Talks Back: Public Diplomacy and Soft Power for the Chinese Century." In *Routledge Handbook of Public Diplomacy*, edited by Nancy Snow and Philip M. Taylor, pp. 282–291. New York, N.Y.: Routledge, 2009.

Sherr, James. *Hard Diplomacy and Soft Coercion: Russia's Influence Abroad*. London: Chatham House, 2013.

Tsygankov, Andrei P. "If Not by Tanks, Then by Banks? The Role of Soft Power in Putin's Foreign Policy." *Europe-Asia Studies*, Vol. 58, No. 7 (November 2006), pp. 1079–1099.

Van Herpen, Marcel H. *Putin's Propaganda Machine: Soft Power and Russian Foreign Policy*. Lanham, Md.: Rowman & Littlefield, 2016.

Voci, Paola and Luo Hui, eds. *Screening China's Soft Power*. Abingdon: Routledge, 2017.

Index

© Springer Nature Switzerland AG 2020
H. W. Ohnesorge, *Soft Power*, Global Power Shift,
https://doi.org/10.1007/978-3-030-29922-4

Printed by Printforce, United Kingdom